ARSENAL STADIUM
HISTORY

hamlyn

ARSENAL STADIUM
HISTORY

The official illustrated history of Highbury Stadium.
93 years of innovation, passion and pride.

Brian Glanville

Additional text: Matthew Brown, Alex Murphy and Ivan Ponting
Statistics: Fred Ollier

First published in Great Britain in 2006 by
Hamlyn, a division of Octopus Publishing Group Ltd
2–4 Heron Quays, London E14 4JP

ISBN-13: 978-0-600-61217-9
ISBN-10: 0-600-61217-1

A CIP catalogue record for this book is available from the British Library

Printed and bound in Italy

10 9 8 7 6 5 4 3 2 1

Contents

Foreword by Peter Hill-Wood

For decades there have been boardroom discussions about whether there was a need to leave our wonderful Highbury home. The ground holds a special place in the hearts and minds of every supporter. Everyone has their own very special memories of Highbury. Mine stretch back to when I first came with my grandfather Sir Samuel Hill-Wood in 1948. Many games had to start earlier to ensure there was enough daylight as we had no floodlights. In fact, I remember the early floodlit games in the 1950s vividly; there were over 60,000 here for a game against Glasgow Rangers in 1951 and night time fixtures here always had a special feel to them.

There have been too many great memories for me to list in my time at the Club. I suppose another night time match, beating Anderlecht to win the European Fairs Cup in 1970, stands out. It was such a special atmosphere and a special achievement as we hadn't won a trophy since 1953. More recently, I think I speak for all Arsenal fans when I say that watching the football that Arsène Wenger's teams have produced here at Highbury has been a true privilege, and to see us make history on the final day of season 2003/04 here, becoming the only team to go unbeaten in the modern era, is a Highbury memory we must all treasure.

My family's association with the Club and the Arsenal Stadium at Highbury dates back 80 years. I loved to talk to my father and grandfather about the great teams of the 1930s who played at Highbury, under the guidance of Herbert Chapman and then George Allison. It's only natural that those ties to the Club make me a little nostalgic for Highbury days past. Certainly in the pages of this book you'll find much that reawakens special memories and emotions. But the new era represented by Emirates Stadium was inevitable. It will allow us to maximise our opportunities in the football market place. And we have managed to find somewhere so close that on match days the travelling routine can be the same and I think that's important for the soul of the football club. Emirates Stadium represents a

marvellous opportunity for us to progress. From the great innovator himself, Herbert Chapman, this Club has always shown that it is willing to embrace new ways of thinking and I believe this bold move will certainly be looked back upon as a major step forward in the Club's progress. When I watch the teams run out at Emirates Stadium for the first time my thoughts will be with my father and grandfather and I'm convinced they would be very proud of what we've done as a Club, moving into the 21st century with a brave decision, made for the right reasons.

The final game at Highbury was a moving occasion and a wonderful spectacle. It showed how much fans feel for the Club and its traditions and values. In the 60 years of watching football at Highbury I had always sat in the same seat, so I should feel a slight loss at leaving, but actually I don't. I really believe it's one of the most important moves that Arsenal could take and I look forward to an exciting new chapter in the story of this wonderful Club.

We can look back with fondness and pride on our first north London home. The Arsenal Stadium History is a fascinating account of the Club and its ground, which will provide a precious reminder of the superb football that Highbury has hosted from its earliest pre-World War I days to the glorious footballing triumphs of recent memory. It is a fitting tribute to a very special place.

Highbury remembered

The historic Arsenal Stadium, nestling among the residential streets of Islington, from its foundation in 1913 until the gates closed after the final match on 7 May 2006, provided a unique backdrop to the footballing memories of generations of supporters and players.

CHAPTER

1

The stadium of Arsenal Football Club at Highbury, hemmed in by streets of Victorian terraced housing, provided a superb stage for the footballing triumphs of the Club and for the memories of generations of fans, from the kick-off of its first match in 1913 until the final whistle blew after the last game on 7 May 2006. There was always something special about Highbury. You only had to turn down Avenell Road on a matchday and glimpse the East Stand rising elegantly from the street to know you were approaching an extraordinary venue. Highbury stood out from a hundred other grounds because it was always more than just a football stadium – it was designed to symbolise Arsenal's dedicated pursuit of values, such as tradition, quality and style, that have endured to this day. Highbury was, above all, a citadel of excellence as much as a sporting arena.

An architectural jewel

The architects and engineers who played their part in crafting the ground down the years pulled off a remarkable feat. Most football grounds are prosaic constructions – jumbled, asymmetrical amalgams of concrete and steel. Highbury, by contrast, was blessed with the kind of clean lines and smart design that might have graced an ocean-going liner or a modernist art gallery.

To step over the threshold into the art-deco-style East Stand vestibule – the fabled Marble Halls – was to step back into an older and better world. The reception areas of football clubs are usually brutal, utilitarian spaces. Not at Highbury. The public space was designed to take the breath away.

Extra care was lavished on designing the polished terrazzo (marble) floor inlaid with the Club's cannon crest, the moulded ceilings and, most famous of all, the Epstein bust of Herbert Chapman, carefully scrutinising every visitor to his domain. These expensive and stylish details spoke volumes about Highbury – and Arsenal.

A leap of faith

The construction of the Arsenal Stadium at Highbury was an impressive and bold act of faith by Sir Henry Norris, the Club's great pioneer. When he took the decision to shift the Club from its heartland south of the river and move it across the Thames, it was a calculated gamble. He reasoned that a location in north London, served with better transport links, would enable the Club to tap into a much greater reservoir of support than they had enjoyed before. Highbury went up very much on the 'build it and they will come principle'. If history had turned out only slightly differently, the Club could have been ignored by its new public, Highbury would have stood empty, and the name would now be little more than a footnote in the annals of the game. But, of course, Norris was gloriously vindicated, as Highbury turned out to be a magnet for the football lovers of north London, and legions of new supporters poured into the ground.

The supreme stadium architect

In 1913, when Arsenal crossed the river, many football grounds were rough-and-ready arenas. They were typically little more than banks of cinders with rough terraces, perhaps with the addition of a rudimentary corrugated iron stand. What grew up on the acres Arsenal bought from the Ecclesiastical Commissioners for £20,000 would become nothing less than a work of art.

The man Norris brought in to build his stadium was the vastly experienced Archibald Leitch. Leitch had built up a reputation as the foremost stadium architect of his time. He had overseen the construction of most of the great British stadiums of the early 1900s. Everton, Tottenham Hotspur, Chelsea and Glasgow Rangers all benefited from his skills. The façade of the main stand at Ibrox and the pavilion at Craven Cottage still bear testament to his extraordinary ability. He had also overseen the relocation of Manchester

Glory awaits

The Arsenal Stadium pictured in 1927, a time when the the Club was still waiting to win its first FA Cup and its first Championship. In the foreground are the terraces of the North Bank and on the far side of the pitch to the east is the original grandstand designed by Archibald Leitch. The south stand, later to be known as the Clock End, is backed by trees.

United and Millwall making him an ideal candidate for the more ambitious translocation of Norris's Woolwich Arsenal.

The movement of Woolwich Arsenal was beset with difficulties. The land sold to the Club by the London College of Divinity had been a green oasis of tennis courts and cricket pitches. The residents now faced a fortnightly invasion by thousands of football supporters. Antagonism was also whipped up by the established neighbouring London clubs, who felt that Arsenal were muscling in on their patch – the grounds of Tottenham Hotspur and Clapton Orient were within five miles. The borough's officers circulated a petition pleading with the Ecclesiastical Commissioners not to lease its land to Arsenal. Undeterred by the demands of the council, a 20-year lease was purchased by the Club, with the one small concession that Arsenal were not to play games on key religious holidays. Nowadays, Arsenal Football Club enjoys an excellent relationship with Islington Council, without whose support, the hugely complex Emirates Stadium project would never have become a reality. It was of enormous importance and pride to the council that Arsenal relocated to its new home within the borough.

Originally Leitch had designed three terraces and one grandstand. It was clear that Norris's ambitions for the Club were grand, but speed was also a priority and the stadium was largely unfinished by the time Arsenal and Leicester Fosse took to the field in 1913. Leitch's original East Stand, in particular, was beset with problems and the huge

boundary wall on the West Terrace had to be completely rebuilt due to its unstable condition. Leitch was continually bombarded by threats by the London County Council over planning and safety concerns, but his persuasive powers were immense and the job was eventually completed.

But this was not the summit of the Club's long-term ambitions for Highbury. Under Herbert Chapman the team had performed wonders on the pitch, and Chapman ensured that everything the team did both off and on the field helped to put Arsenal Football Club 'on the map'. There was no bigger, or more literal, statement of this intent than the renaming of Gillespie Road Tube station. The idea had first occurred to Chapman as a visiting manager to Highbury in 1913. It took hard lobbying, but on 5 November 1932 it became Arsenal (Highbury Hill) and eventually just Arsenal. It is still the only time a station on the London Underground has ever changed its name. It was the Club's desire to have a suitable venue to match their on-field ambitions that drove the board to make Highbury a fitting arena at the cutting edge of football. And, true to the spirit of the Chapman era, they were innovative in their approach.

Art deco and the West and East stands

Where Leitch was a supreme technician, the Club turned to two men with more artistic flair, but no previous experience in sports stadiums, to develop the ground. In 1932 architects Claude Waterlow Ferrier and William Binnie completed the

landmark art-deco style West Stand. 'Art deco' was a modernist design style that originated in Paris at a 1925 exhibition entitled 'Exposition Internationale des Arts Decoratifs et Industriels Modernes'. This style was popular in the late 1920s and 1930s for the design of restaurants and theatres. To build a football stand in that styling was a bold move, one that was followed four years later by the construction of the even more magnificent East Stand.

Standing 80 feet high and 315 feet long the East Stand was a testament to the courage and foresight of the board. It cost the Club a then record £130,000. The imposing edifice on Avenell Road had its grand entrance into the famous Marble Halls crowned by the cannon logo. All that Chapman had achieved before his death in 1934 had been aimed at raising the Club to a standing above that of others in the League – the heated floors in the changing rooms, the under-soil heating, comfortable seating and the renaming of the Tube station. It was these statements of intent that the East Stand would represent. It was an emblem of the Club's commitment to professionalism and modern thinking. In the 1930s to come to Highbury was to feel you were entering an institution of pedigree and style.

The iconic 'AFC' 1930s crest that was introduced by the Club during the redevelopment of the East Stand epitomised Chapman's vision and innovation. The crest was incorporated into the fabric of the Stadium, where it featured on the impressive iron and glass gated East Stand entrance as well as on the East Stand façade itself. It also symbolized the ambition, desire and unity of the Club. Along with all the footballing innovations Chapman introduced to Arsenal and the world of football, one could also say that he showed early foresight in creating a logo that became synonymous with a footballing 'brand'. To have the Club's badge woven into the structure of the ground was the signal that this legacy would last and be recognised for generations.

The Emirates Stadium mirrors the ambition of the 1930s. It shows Arsenal's willingness to embrace the future once more, with the stunning architectural features and state-of-the-art facilities. 'Tradition with vision' is the Club motto for the Emirates Stadium project and it was equally applicable to the development of the East Stand.

Highbury through the decades

Highbury survived through the difficult years of World War I, when in the absence of regular competitive football the Club's coffers were drained. But the Club persisted, and by the 1930s Highbury was among the most popular grounds in the country. The record attendance was set in March 1935, when a vast throng numbering 73,295 watched a match against Sunderland. In the immediate post-World War II years Highbury often hosted attendances of around 62,000.

In the last decade of Highbury's history the ground's capacity was reduced to around 38,500 as a result of the need to become all-seater. But most games were soon sold out, and demand for tickets overwhelmingly outstripped their availability. It was this stark economic fact that made the move to Emirates Stadium inevitable.

One man who lived through many changes at Highbury, and was instrumental in seeing many of them through, was Arsenal's current chairman Peter Hill-Wood. His family have been among Highbury's most dedicated custodians since the very early days, when his grandfather, Sir Samuel Hill-Wood, succeeded Henry Norris as chairman. The continued presence of the Hill-Woods in Highbury's august boardroom has done much to give Arsenal their stability and sense of tradition. Peter Hill-Wood knew when it was time for romance to bend the knee to realism.

Celebrating the Premiership

The pitch at Highbury becomes a scene of celebration as the Premiership trophy is presented in May 2004. Through the corner between the North Bank (left) and the East Stand (right), the rows of Victorian terraced houses that were there before the stadium was built can be glimpsed.

'You've got to accept that things change and not always for the better,' Hill-Wood said in the final weeks before Arsenal left Highbury. 'People ask me about leaving Highbury and moving to the new stadium. We made a decision a few years ago that we wouldn't leave here. Then we decided ten years later that we couldn't stay. We can't compete with the major clubs here in the UK and in Europe with a gate of 38,000. We took a calculated risk in my view to move and we were extremely fortunate to buy the land 500 metres from where we were and build a magnificent stadium, and I am thrilled.'

The home of football

Highbury was more than just a pair of pretty buildings. It was the venue for some of football's most significant moments. The game against Sheffield United in January 1927 was the subject of the first live radio football commentary. The crowds of the 1930s witnessed some exceptional games from Drake, Bastin, James, *et al* including an 8–0 thrashing of Middlesbrough – thanks to four goals from Ted Drake – that guaranteed the Gunners their fourth League title in five years in April 1935.

In 1958 Highbury was the last English ground Manchester United's Busby Babes played on, and it was a thrilling encounter that ended in a 5–4 win for the visitors. Arsenal's first European silverware, the Fairs Cup, was won in dramatic fashion on the Highbury turf thanks to a 3–0 victory over Anderlecht in 1970.

With the arrival of Arsène Wenger came further remarkable matches and triumphs such as the end of season 4–0 victory over Everton that sealed the title in 1998 with Adams scoring that final goal in front of the North Bank; two 7–0 demolitions of Everton and Middlesbrough respectively in 2004 and 2005; a 3–1 win over Aston Villa in October 2004 that saw the Gunners log a record 49 games unbeaten in the League; the humbling of both Juventus and Real Madrid in 2006; and, of course, no one who was there will ever forget the final game, a 4–2 victory over Wigan Athletic to bow out in the style with which they set out in 1913.

The home of entertainment

But it was not only Arsenal matches that thrilled the crowds. Highbury hosted internationals – England versus Italy in Great Britain versus Holland during the 1948 Olympics; and a 6–0 thrashing of Switzerland by England in the same year. Highbury also saw the filming of *The Arsenal Stadium Mystery*, which featured a match against Brentford in May 1939, and witnessed the Boxers versus Jockeys matches in the 1950s. It also played host to the boxing heavyweight title fight between Henry Cooper and Cassius Clay in 1966 and even staged three cricket matches in 1949, 1952 and 1955.

The players remember

Highbury not only captured the imagination of those that came to watch; those who worked there – be it on the pitch or in the back rooms – also recognised it as a special place.

One man who was both fan and employee was Charlie George, the north London boy who grew up watching the Gunners at Highbury, went on to become a Double winner, and remains one of the Club's most popular players of all time. He said: 'I was going to Highbury from when I was about six or seven. I used to stand on the North Bank with the big crush barriers. When a goal was scored, when there were big crowds, the people used to surge forward and you'd end up 15 or 20 feet from where you had been. If you were a youngster they'd pass you over their heads down to the red ash, and then they'd pass you back to where you were standing. I was a local lad, and Arsenal was my team. It's always good to play at your local stadium, especially if that's the team you support.'

From the air
An aerial view of the stadium shows its unique location in the midst of the terraced housing in the Highbury area of Islington. Since the Club's arrival in this part of north London, Arsenal has always drawn on strong local support and has, in its turn, given much back to the community.

Herbert Chapman inspires
Herbert Chapman, manager from 1925 until 1934, was an individual whose impact on the Club was fundamental in moulding the Club's ethos and public profile. The bronze bust of Chapman by Jacob Epstein dominated the Marble Halls in the East Stand.

George loved Highbury because it was in his blood, but generations of footballers from other parts of Britain, and from all over the world, have been won over by the unique atmosphere of the place. Dennis Bergkamp, high up on many supporters' lists of the best Arsenal players ever to grace Highbury, joined from Internazionale in 1995. He left the gaudy magnificence of the monumental San Siro in Milan, took one look at Highbury and knew he was home. 'For me, Highbury was typically English,' he said. 'When I came into Highbury for the first time when I signed, I came on to the pitch. I saw an English stadium, typically close to the pitch. It wasn't what we knew in Europe – a small stadium, quite an old stadium, of course, and a fantastic pitch. That was probably my first impression. Highbury always had a fantastic atmosphere, because everyone was so close to the pitch, and the fans were really a part of the game, so to speak. And luckily enough most of the time we had a full stadium, which creates a good atmosphere. At Highbury you had the combination of a fantastic pitch and the really great atmosphere of the stadium, which for me as a foreigner, was always a marvellous experience.'

Another famous overseas player seduced by his Highbury experience was the incomparable Thierry Henry. The effect the ground had on the Frenchman bordered on the mystical, so powerful were his emotions when he walked into the ground. Even when Highbury was empty, Henry felt a spiritual attachment to his surroundings. In the days before Arsenal left the ground for the last time Henry said: 'There's something about the whole stadium when you're there, something happens to me. I hear moments of games, something that happens in my mind. It just happens when I leave the car park to go to the dressing room past the Clock End, and you turn right in front of the benches. When I walk, it's just strange, I feel like I remember some games that I played, some stuff that I did. Some good moments, some bad moments. It's difficult to describe. You have no-one in the stadium but I can still hear some stuff in my head. I know it's not the most modern stadium ever, but there's something you can't describe, you need to play. It's always something special about Highbury.'

Wenger's Highbury

Like Henry, Arsène Wenger was captivated by the ambience of Highbury from the first moment he sampled it. The energy that crackled around the ground on a matchday entranced him, and his first visit to the ground launched a love affair that lasted until Highbury's last afternoon – that magnificent game against Wigan on 7 May 2006. Wenger has a vivid recollection of the day he first set foot inside the ground. 'I was manager of Monaco at the time and I had been in Turkey two days earlier watching our next opponents in the European Cup. I had to fly back on New Year's Day but I knew that in England they played football at that time of year so I decided to fly back from Ankara to France via London to watch a game. As soon as I got into Highbury I immediately thought that football in England was great. There was a fantastic atmosphere at Highbury and I just wondered, 'Is everywhere like this? Even at that time I thought it would be great to be part of English football one day.' Wenger's love of the ground deepened after he took over as manager and added several glorious episodes to the rich lore of Highbury. He was full of emotion the day before the last-ever match at Highbury, against Wigan Athletic. 'Highbury is something special for me and will remain forever something special.'

Memories from the boardroom

Millions of people down the decades have found that a childhood brush with Highbury could lead to a lifetime's obsession. Ken Friar, a man who more than anyone else could fairly be said to be 'Mr Arsenal', began his long and happy association with the place way back in 1946 – thanks to a miskicked football.

Friar, a Club director and it's longest serving member of staff, was playing football in Avenell Road one day in 1946, and emerged from under a car where he had booted the ball. He was confronted by the then Arsenal manager George Allison, who sternly asked Friar to report to him at Highbury

the following day. Friar found himself employed as a messenger and general helper. From this modest start he rose steadily through the ranks and became managing director in 1983. Through it all, Friar's affinity with Highbury grew stronger, and the place was like a second home to him.

'You still get that feeling as you walk though the front door, that electric feeling. You still get the tingle, especially on match day. I liken it to a circus coming to town. The television wagons come on Friday afternoon, and then slowly but surely the whole circus builds up. You've got the caterers arriving, the programmes, everything you require to run a stadium. On the morning of the match all the different kinds of staff come in, the programme sellers are loading up their trolleys, the turnstile men have arrived, the ground opens up and off you go. And then afterwards it reverses in a similar direction.' Friar's fellow director, David Dein, was also enthralled by Highbury and his early memories reflect this. He remembers, aged 11, standing on the North Bank with his uncle and being caught up in the fervour of the crowd. 'It was just a mass of colour, noise and spectacle. I call it live theatre without a script. Certainly, I was hooked immediately after my first game and became an avid fan, going to home and away games. Coming into the Marble Halls, I still feel very privileged because one is custodian of a heritage.'

From the terraces

Players, managers and directors all fell under Highbury's spell, but it is the thousands of men and women who clicked through the Highbury turnstiles week after week, season after season, that gives Highbury the notion of legacy and often leads to people referencing the spirituality of the place.

Recalling his visit to Highbury – a 1–1 draw with Blackburn Rovers in March 1959 – Robert Berry describes the thrill of his first impressions of a Highbury match day: 'That tingle of expectation as you alight from the train and walk uphill through the tunnel of the underground station to emerge in daylight with the sound and smell that can only be found at the Arsenal. Lots of people milling about, street sellers with red and white scarves, rosettes, badges, hot dogs and onions, the hum of people talking, shouting and waving. I bought my first programme and we made our way along to the North Bank entrance and with it my first look inside a real proper football stadium. The lush green grass, the panorama of faces, the magnificent building with the banks of floodlights along the roof ... This was it. I was there, straining to see my team play for the first time ... All I can recall is the atmosphere, the feeling that everyone around us was willing the Arsenal on. Even the police were Arsenal supporters...'

It wasn't just inside the ground either, it seemed the whole area pulsed to the atmosphere of the stadium on match day, as Alan Tufnell recalls: 'In those faraway days of 70,000 crowds (mostly standing) you could judge by the noise just what was going on, even if you were locked out! ... I well remember being a bit late for one particular kick-off and quite easily being able to hear the noise as far away as Finsbury Park, causing my steps to get faster and faster!'

The legacy of Highbury

It was an unshakeable commitment to the survival of Arsenal Club that provided the impetus for Henry Norris to make the move north from Plumstead to Highbury in 1913. It was Herbert Chapman's vision for what the Club could achieve in terms of honours that was the engine for the redevelopment of Highbury during his tenure as manager. It was also Chapman's desire that the majestic Highbury of the 1930s would leave visiting players and fans in dumbstruck awe and would instill within all those connected with Arsenal a sense of unparalleled pride. Within the bricks and mortar of Highbury, a set of values and traditions were fostered that have been nurtured over the years to make Arsenal the globally recognised and respected football club that it is today. Highbury has amply fulfilled all these aspirations, both for the players and managers of the Club and, perhaps more importantly, for the legions of loyal supporters, who over its 93 years of history populated the terraces of the North Bank, Clock End and the East and West Stands, encouraging the team with their cheering, celebrating their goals with their applause, and delighting in their heroes with their chanting.

In the following chapters, the full story of the Arsenal Stadium at Highbury is described, from the Club's earliest, pre-Highbury beginnings to the last, emotion-filled matchday at the old stadium. The story is one of vision and ambition – traditions that are certain to be transferred to Emirates Stadium as Arsenal Football Club enters a bright new era.

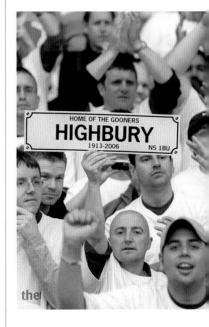

Emotional farewell
Fans salute the team and the stadium at the end of the last match played at Highbury – the League game against Wigan Athletic on 7 May 2006.

WOOLWICH ARSENAL F.C. PLAYERS and OFFICIALS. 1906-7.

From Dial Square to Highbury

The football club we now know as Arsenal emerged as an amateur works team in the industrial outskirts of 19th-century London. Built on the enthusiasm of a group of munitions workers, the Club soon needed to make the transition from makeshift pitches to a fully equipped stadium.

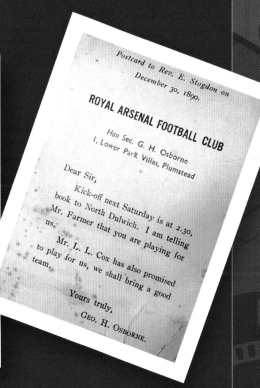

Postcard to Rev. E. Stogdon on
December 30, 1890.

ROYAL ARSENAL FOOTBALL CLUB

Hon Sec. G. H. Osborne
1, Lower Park Villas, Plumstead

Dear Sir,

Kick-off next Saturday is at 2.30, book to North Dulwich. I am telling Mr. Farmer that you are playing for us.

Mr. L. L. Cox has also promised to play for us, we shall bring a good team.

Yours truly,
GEO. H. OSBORNE.

The origins of the team we now know as Arsenal Football Club lie in the 1880s, a period when the British Empire was at its height and Britain was the 'engine room' of the world. It was also a period when football was already flourishing, primarily in northern England and Scotland and, by this time, increasingly in the south.

Football before Arsenal

When the Football Association was founded in 1863, football was the virtual monopoly of a relatively small number of 'gentlemen'; amateur players and officials who'd played the game – or their own particular version of it – at public schools and universities. But by the time Arsenal was founded by workers at a munitions factory in southeast London a couple of decades later, the game's social make-up had been utterly transformed.

The game's first rules, known as the 'Cambridge Rules', were drawn up in October 1863 by Oxbridge graduates and old public schoolboys from Shrewsbury, Eton, Harrow, Rugby,

Woolwich roots

The London suburb of Woolwich in which Arsenal was founded in 1886. The Gunners began life as Dial Square in 1886, became Royal Arsenal very soon afterwards and then became Woolwich Arsenal. The name 'Woolwich' was dropped in 1914 when the club moved north to Highbury.

Marlborough and Westminster, and it was representatives of clubs who drew their inspiration, directly or indirectly, from public school and university football who established the game's first governing body a few days later at the Freemason's Arms in London's Lincoln's Inn Fields. Similarly, it was former public schoolboys who ran the regional football associations that mushroomed across the counties of Britain in the years that followed. This core of enthusiasts established many of the football clubs that dominated the early years of the FA Cup after it was introduced in 1871. To all intents and purposes, organised football was an upper middle class game.

But forms of football had always been part of popular sporting tradition, too. Often these games were violent clashes between villages and had little of the order and rules imposed by public school discipline. The two 'traditions' began to come together as former public schoolboys promoted their game with zeal, introducing football in urban industrial settings and establishing teams at workplaces. There was something of a Christian philanthropic drive to much of this, as sport was seen by the Victorian middle class as a way of encouraging good health and building 'character' among the workers in the shipyards, factories and armies upon which the British Empire depended.

Soon teams were emerging everywhere, springing up in workplaces, schools, youth clubs and churches. The FA with its rules, competitions and county structures provided a framework in which to organise and play. Although the FA Cup was won for its first 11 years by southern-based old boys' teams, and the national game was dominated by 'gentlemen of leisure', football rapidly took on a working class character. The Old Etonians' FA Cup victory in 1882 was the last time an amateur side lifted the trophy, while their opponents that year, the northern, working class Blackburn Rovers, represented the future. Indeed, by this time, the North and the Midlands – the heartlands of England's urban, industrial strength – had already become the hotbeds of football's future. The FA Cup went north for the first time in 1883, won by Blackburn Olympic, a team financed by the owner of a local iron foundry, and between that year and 1915 northern clubs won the FA Cup 21 times and clubs from the Midlands achieved 11 victories. The early 1880s also saw Scotland establishing itself as a producer of footballers – a reputation that would last for 100 years – and a succession of skilful Scottish players migrated south, enticed by the increasingly powerful clubs in Lancashire, Yorkshire and the northeast, the prospect of work and, by the mid 1880s, the chance to earn money from what was already 'the people's game'.

The growing crowds also reflected this social change as football quickly became the most popular working class spectator sport, too. By the 1880s games were watched on a weekly basis by hundreds of thousands of working men committed to their local teams. By 1888, the year the Football League was founded, there was little doubt among the

game's elite about its popularity, nor where the heart of that popularity lay. That year 17,000 people watched the FA Cup final in London between West Bromwich Albion and Preston North End, and one FA official wrote: 'No words of ours can adequately describe the present popularity of football with the public – a popularity which, though great in the metropolis – is infinitely greater in the large provincial towns ... It is no rare thing in the north or midlands for 10,000 people to pay to watch an ordinary club match, or for half as many again to assemble for a "cup tie".'

Football at the Royal Arsenal

One bit-part player in this great national drama was David Danskin, a Scotsman from Kirkcaldy and no mean footballer, who, like many of his compatriots, drifted south to work in the massive Woolwich Arsenal, where artillery guns and munitions were made for the defence of the British Empire. In the autumn of 1886, Danskin organised a whip round among 15 of his co-workers at the Dial Square works to buy a football. Five shillings and sixpence (26 pence in today's money) were collected and Danskin himself made up the rest to the required half guinea. And so the first foundation stone of the Club that was to become Arsenal was laid.

These were indeed pioneering days. Initially there was non-consensus over colours. Richard Pearce, a native of Bolton, and one of the leading lights, attired himself in a black and blue hooped shirt and a pair of cut down long trousers.

Originally named Dial Square after the workshop in which its founding members worked, the team's first match was played on 11 December 1886 against a team called Eastern Wanderers. The venue was a patch of wasteland on the Isle of Dogs, across the Thames from the Arsenal in Woolwich. The game was probably more like a kick-about than a formal match, as the Club's first secretary, Elijah 'George' Watkins described: 'Talk about a football pitch, I could not venture to say what shape it was but it was bounded by backyards as to about two-thirds of the area, and the other portion was – I was going to say a ditch – but I think an open sewer would be more appropriate. We could not decide who won the game because when the ball was not in the back gardens, it was in the ditch; and that was full of the loveliest material that could possibly be. Our fellows looked as though they had been clearing out a mud chute when they had done playing.'

Clocking off
Employees pass through the gates of the Woolwich Arsenal munitions works in the 1880s. The Club's first members worked in Dial Square, one of the workshops in this massive complex.

Pioneering days

The Royal Arsenal team line-up of 1890, at a time when the Club's fixture list consisted of friendlies against sides including 93rd Highlanders, St Bartholomew's Hospital and Old Harrovians.

Despite the lack of cross-bars, team colours or pitch markings, the players did, in fact, manage to keep score – it was 6–0 to Dial Square. A couple of weeks later, on Christmas Day, the victorious players met in the Royal Oak pub next to Woolwich Arsenal station to discuss a name for their new team, to decide team colours and, importantly, to find a pitch on which to play.

Red the colour, Royal Arsenal the name

The team colour, red, was agreed probably because several members of the team had previously played for Nottingham Forest before moving to London to work in the Dial Square factory and had retained their red jerseys. A few weeks later the first kit arrived thanks to goalkeeper Fred Beardsley, one of the former Nottingham Forest players. One weekend he travelled back to his former club and returned with a ball and a set of shirts generously donated by the established Midlands club who already played in red.

The name was more difficult. Some favoured Dial Square, especially some of the more prominent players who worked there. Others who worked elsewhere in the massive

Historic emblem

The first-ever Arsenal Club crest, in use about 1888. With its three vertical cannons, it was based on the coat of arms of the Borough of Woolwich.

munitions complex at Woolwich opposed it. The deadlock was broken by R.B. Thompson, an outside left who'd scored the first goal in that 6–0 victory. As a teacher, he was the only member of the team not working in the Arsenal, and also the youngest member. 'Rather timidly I asked, "Who outside Woolwich ever heard of Dial Square?",' Thompson recalled more than 60 years later. 'Followed by: "Who has not heard of the Royal Arsenal?" The name Royal Arsenal was adopted forthwith.'

Initially, the question of where the newly named club should play was relatively simple – the players merely looked for any convenient public land nearby and chose, initially, Plumstead Common. Strangely, for a club later to be renamed Woolwich Arsenal, the team never actually played in Woolwich. The first game played on Plumstead Common was against Erith on 8 January 1887 and another eight games were played there before the end of the season. Although not quite as rough as the Isle of Dogs, the Common wasn't ideal – uneven, hilly, stony and rutted, it was also used by the Royal Horse Artillery as a practice ground. But the team did have goalposts, and kept them in Beardsley's nearby back garden.

Beardsley was one of a number of the early players who had come from the North and Scotland with experience of playing for more established teams. Many of these men had drifted south, attracted by the work available at the munitions factory. Their experience ensured early success as Royal Arsenal ended its first year with only two defeats from 10 games.

Success at the Manor Ground

The team quickly attracted local support, mostly from fellow munitions workers, and for the 1887/88 season moved to the Sportsman Ground, an old pig farm on the edge of Plumstead Marshes with a rather predictable tendency to become

waterlogged. This was how the players found it on the morning of 11 February 1888 when they turned up for a home game against local rivals Millwall. Luckily, farther up Manor Road towards Plumstead station there was a field used as pastureland that remained dry. One of the players, Jack Humble, rushed round to see the owner, a Mr Cavey, and asked permission to use it. He agreed and for the next two years Royal Arsenal played on the Manor Field (later known as the Manor Ground).

It was while based at the Manor Ground that Arsenal had its first significant successes. In 1889 they reached the semi-final of the London Senior Cup, losing 2–0 to Clapton, and the following season they won the Kent Senior Cup and the Kent Junior Cup. Interestingly, 1890 also saw their first ever victory in Islington – the London borough that would become Arsenal's long-term home – in a six-a-side competition held in Islington's Agricultural Hall.

More significantly, they also won the London Charity Cup beating Old Westminsters 3–1 in the final in front of some 10,000 fans at Leyton. In a little over two years the Club had clearly come a long way. Indeed, the team was becoming so popular – regular crowds were 500 to 1,000 strong – that they often had to rope off the pitch and bring in wagons from the nearby barracks for spectators to stand on.

At this stage, the ground didn't have any proper facilities, either for the fans or the players, who changed in the Green Man pub on Plumstead High Street or at the Railway Tavern beside the station. Players also had to carry out ground duties, such as collecting money. By now, however, Royal Arsenal was recognised as London's strongest amateur club. The enthusiasm of their fans can be gauged by the fact that in 1889, when they faced the then powerful Swifts in a qualifying round of the FA Cup, many of the 8,000-strong crowd cleared the pitch of thick snow so the game could go ahead. Unfortunately, the Swifts won 5–1.

After these early successes, Arsenal began to attract support from further afield. Fans from other parts of the capital would ride their 'penny farthing' bicycles through the Blackwall Tunnel to see them play rather than stay north of the river to watch Clapton or Tottenham Hotspur (an early source of rivalry and bitterness).

The Invicta Ground

Inevitably, the team's success and growing popularity soon prompted another move – across Plumstead High Street to the Invicta Ground which already had a stand, terraces and dressing rooms. The wisdom of this decision was shown a few months later, on Easter Monday 1891, when 12,000 fans turned up to see Royal Arsenal take on the Scottish club, Heart of Midlothian.

But Arsenal's stay at the Invicta Ground (Invicta is the motto of the county of Kent) also proved to be brief and by 1893 they were back at the Manor Ground, their home base for the next two decades. This relocation was sparked by a combination of Arsenal's historic decision to turn professional and seek Football League status, and the greed of the Invicta's landlord, George Weaver, whose plan to make a quick profit out of the team's popularity by raising the rent backfired.

Arsenal's successes in 1889 and 1890 not only attracted more supporters – drawing fans from across Plumstead and Woolwich – but drew the gaze of some of the bigger northern clubs. Inevitably, some of Arsenal's better players began to be lured away by the promise of professional football, which was becoming firmly established outside the southeast. No doubt, for many the chance to get out of the factory and make a living from the game was too good to resist.

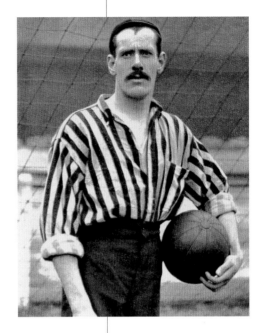

Harry Storer

Goalkeeper for the Club, making 41 League and Cup appearances, Harry Storer was born in Ripley, Derbyshire, in 1870 and joined Arsenal from Loughborough in 1894. He moved to Liverpool in 1895. He is pictured here in the red and light blue striped shirt that was adopted by the Club for the 1894/95 season.

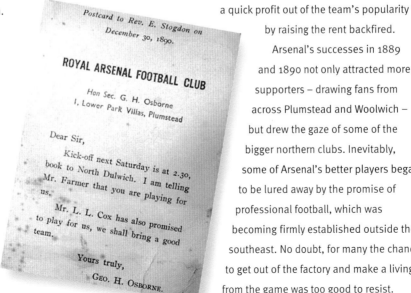

Postcard to Rev. E. Stogdon on December 30, 1890.

ROYAL ARSENAL FOOTBALL CLUB

Hon Sec. G. H. Osborne
I, Lower Park Villas, Plumstead

Dear Sir,

Kick-off next Saturday is at 2.30, book to North Dulwich. I am telling Mr. Farmer that you are playing for us.

Mr. L. L. Cox has also promised to play for us, we shall bring a good team.

Yours truly,
GEO. H. OSBORNE.

Call up notice

Team selection in the early days seems to have been an ad hoc affair. In this letter dated 30 December 1890, Club Secretary George Osborne informs the Rev. E. Stogden that he has been selected to represent Royal Arsenal.

The beginning of professionalism

It was committee member and sometime full back Jack Humble who first proposed that Arsenal itself should turn professional at the Club's 1891 AGM, held in the Windsor Castle Music Hall. Humble was a man from County Durham who'd walked to London to escape poverty aged 18 and become an engine fitter in the Arsenal. When it was suggested that Arsenal become a limited company, he replied: 'The Club (has been) carried on by working men and it is my ambition to see it carried on by them.'

Humble had his way (although Arsenal did become a company two years later) and the Club became the first southern professional side, changing its name in the process to Woolwich Arsenal. This decision effectively ended the Club's association with the London FA whose amateur ethos made it implacably opposed to the 'northern disease' of professionalism. Thus barred from all amateur cup competitions in the south, and with no southern professional league to enter, they initially had to rely on friendlies and games against northerly teams such as Birmingham's Small Heath (later Birmingham City) and Sunderland, games they tended to lose, rather heavily.

Admission to the League

Faced with an inevitable loss of support, Humble and his colleagues first proposed a southern version of the Football League, and when this was scotched by the London FA,

applied to join the League itself. In 1893, the Second Division had been enlarged from a dozen to 15 clubs. Woolwich Arsenal had seemed to have only a remote chance of admission, but when Bootle resigned and relegated Accrington refused to take part in the lower league, Woolwich Arsenal were one of the last three clubs to make up the number, together with Liverpool and Middlesbrough. So it was that in 1893 Woolwich Arsenal became the first southern-based Football League side. Not that its election to the Second Division made it wealthy, and when the Invicta Ground's landlord Mr Weaver sought to exploit the Club's new status by putting up the rent on the ground from £200 to £350 a year, they had no choice but to move.

The obvious solution was to buy the old Manor Ground and, with the help of supporters who worked throughout the summer of 1893, it was prepared for hosting the likes of Liverpool and Newcastle in the 1893/94 season. The road-side field that the players had discovered in 1888 was transformed by the players and supporters who helped to level the ground, build changing rooms, and erect standing terraces out of mounds of earth and wooden planks.

At this point, Woolwich Arsenal did become a limited company, issuing 4,000 £1 shares, many of which were bought by 860 people. These were mostly manual munitions workers who lived nearby, a good indication that although the team had risen rapidly during its first seven years, its support was still based among the working men of the factory

Manchester untied

Arsenal beat Second Division Manchester United 3–2 at their old Bank Street Ground in an FA Cup quarter-final on 10 March 1906. United, like Arsenal, were playing in a ground that was no longer adequate for the crowds that flocked to see the games; the little ground was jammed to the rafters, and dozens found a vantage point on the stand roof.

where it was conceived and founded. Similarly, at least to begin with, Humble's wish to keep Arsenal as a 'working men's team' was met at board level. While the company's first directors included a surgeon and a coffee house proprietor, there was also a builder and six engineers from the Arsenal.

Representative honours

Life in the League wasn't easy for the southern newcomers. Woolwich Arsenal had to contend for years with the relative inaccessibility of its ground, a major factor in their eventual move across the Thames to Highbury in 1913. Only in season 1903/04 did the Club gain promotion to the First Division. In that first season in the Second Divison, Woolwich Arsenal, finishing ninth with 28 points, were totally outshone by fellow newcomers Liverpool, who actually won the League and were accordingly promoted. However, gradually representative honours began to accrue. In April 1895 the Club's goalkeeper Harry Storer was picked to keep goal for the Football League against the Scottish League and on 21 March 1896 the Club had its first full international player when Caesar Llewellyn

Jenkyns, who then wore the Club's transient strip of red and light blue stripes, played for Wales versus Scotland.

In January 1897 a traumatising 4–2 defeat in the FA Cup by their neighbours, non-League Millwall, caused Woolwich Arsenal to appoint their first secretary manager, T.B. Mitchell from Blackburn, who was succeeded by George Elcoat from Stockton. It was Harry Bradshaw, however, who would make a greater impact when he took over the team. One of his most inspired signings was that of the goalkeeper Jimmy Ashcroft form Sheppey United, famed for the power with which he punched the ball, and who would eventually become the Club's first England international.

Into the 20th century

The Boer War (1899–1902) created special difficulties for a club with such close ties with the military. Increased shifts at the Woolwich munitions complex resulted in loss of both players and supporters. During this period crowds slumped to 2,000 average. Only 900 saw the Club's record 12–0 win over Loughborough Town in 1900. However, in February 1903 the Club managed to draw a crowd of around 25,000 for a

first round FA Cup tie against Cup-holders Sheffield United. The sting of the 3–1 defeat must have been mitigated by the record £1,000 takings. In 1904 Woolwich Arsenal eventually achieved promotion to the First Division. This came after the team finished second to Preston North End in the promotion tournament. It was also the year in which Woolwich Arsenal defeated a Parisian team 26–1, the only French goal being scored by a local player named Hodge, who had come on as a substitute. Both Woolwich Arsenal backs had courteously stood aside to let him score, for which they were strongly admonished by the referee.

With a new manager, the Scot Phil Kelso, in charge, the Club reached a milestone by winning a place in the semi-finals of the FA Cup in 1906, getting past the second round for the first time. The opposition was Newcastle United, one of the most successful teams of the era. Arsenal were defeated 2–0 but were back again in the semi-finals the following year, losing to Sheffield Wednesday 3–1. During this period the team drew large crowds at Manor Ground, averaging over 10,000. Interestingly, at this stage the Club was already encouraging the sale of season tickets, more than any other club, providing a bedrock of support.

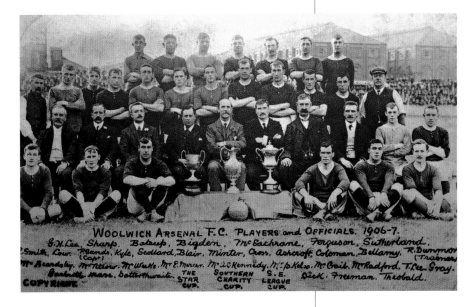

WOOLWICH ARSENAL F.C. PLAYERS and OFFICIALS. 1906-7.

Silverware on show

The Woolwich Arsenal players and officials who reached the FA Cup semi-finals for the second year running in 1906/07. They are seen posing with the season's trophy haul, the Star Cup, the Southern Charity Cup and the South East League Cup.

EARLY HEROES
Andy Ducat 1904/05–1911/12

One of the footballing superstars in the first decade of the 20th century, Andy Ducat was born in Brixton in 1886. Also an accomplished cricketer, he was signed by Woolwich Arsenal from Southend United in January 1905. The quality of his performances for the Gunners ensured that he was a regular first-team choice, playing in 33 League games in 1908/09. He left Woolwich Arsenal for Aston Villa in June 1912. Capped for England six times, while with the Gunners, he won winners medals in the Southern Charity Cup (1905/06), the South Eastern League Championship (1906/07) and The London League Championship (1906/07).

Early stars

Humble recruited star players knowing they would add 1,000 to the gate. The team of this period included Bill Gooing and, famously, Bobby Templeton, the supremely elusive Scottish international left winger. Another regular was Joe Shaw, a right back who would still be on the Arsenal staff in the early 1950s. In 1907 Tim Coleman, a skilful inside right, became the second Arsenal player to be capped for England. His partner at inside left was an Irishman, Tommy Shanks, whose speciality was the penalty kick. Percy Sands, a local schoolmaster, was an amateur centre half who would later turn professional and be skipper when the Club moved to Highbury. Arguably the finest player of all was Andy Ducat, right half and scorer of a hat trick on his debut in 1905.

Financial difficulties

The period 1908–10 saw the Club beset with financial as well as footballing difficulties. In 1908 George Morrell, who had succeeded Phil Kelso as manager in September of that year, had been obliged to transfer no fewer than five of his best players, including their talismanic goalkeeper Jimmy Ashcroft. It was in 1909 that the Club lost one of its brightest stars, a gangling young inside right called Charlie Buchan, who quarrelled with the Club over a mere 11 shillings he demanded as expenses. He walked out to become famous with Sunderland and England, only to return in 1925. Woolwich Arsenal finished 18th in the League in 1909/10.

George Morrell

Manager of the Gunners from 1908–15, Morrell's sad claim to fame remains being the only boss in the Club's history to take them down a division.

Attendances and takings at the Manor Ground dwindled and by 1910 the Club was verging on bankruptcy. At which point Henry Norris appeared on the scene. An entrepreneur and estate agent who had built 2,000 houses in Wimbledon and Fulham, of which he became first Mayor, then Member of Parliament, he was chairman of Second Division Fulham, for whom he had built a fine stadium at Craven Cottage on the bank of the Thames. Attracted by Woolwich Arsenal's First Division status, initially Norris wanted to amalgamate the clubs and play the new team in the First Division. The Football League turned the idea down, so Norris came up with another scheme; the clubs would share the ground at Craven Cottage, but play there on alternate Saturdays. Norris, as in much else, was far ahead of his time, but this idea was rejected too. The other London League clubs would not countenance it. The Football League intervened, unhappy at the prospect of one man controlling two clubs. Faced with what in retrospect can be seen as an historic choice, Norris decided to focus his attention on Woolwich Arsenal, although he remained a director of Fulham until 1914.

Saved from extinction, the Club would not last much longer in the First Division. Season 1912/13 was catastrophic. The sporting legend Andy Ducat had left for Aston Villa in the summer of 1912, and the Club did not have the financial resources to replace him with a player of similar quality. At Christmas, the team was bottom of the First Division with just six points from 18 games. In December 1912, the Club programme bewailed, 'We are still sighing for our first home

victory and the outlook is indeed as black as we have yet witnessed since the existence of the Club.'

Things did not improve when it came to the last League game of the season on 26 April 1912, a home game against Middlesbrough. The match was drawn 1–0 and Woolwich Arsenal finished the season without a home win and a mere 18 points, including just three wins. They were six points below the penultimate team, Notts County. Relegation to the Second Division was inevitable.

The decision to move

In this desperate situation, with the Club having a grand total of £19 in the bank, Norris came up with a radical idea. The Club would have to move. This was necessary to ensure maximum attendances and therefore revenue. Plumstead was notoriously difficult for fans and opposition teams to reach by public transport from the north – it was a long journey into London, then a 40-minute train journey from Cannon Street. Opposition teams sometimes failed to reach the ground on time. Moreover, the ground was right next to engineering works, belching out fumes, and occasional leaks of raw sewage. The *Liverpool Tribune* described Arsenal as the 'team who played at the end of the earth'.

Norris had come to the conclusion that as long as the Club remained in south London, it could not expand its supporter base. The game against Middlesbrough in April had been the team's last appearance at the Manor Ground. And it is here that the story of Arsenal and Highbury begins.

High-kicking Gunners
Woolwich Arsenal in action against Liverpool (in striped shirts) on 2 September 1911. The game was drawn 2–2. The Gunners eventually finished the season in tenth position.

Building Highbury

In Highbury Sir Henry Norris found a location that met all his requirements. His ambition for the Club at last provided Arsenal with a stadium that would soon be among the best in the country, and would provide a fitting home ground for a team that aspired to be the best.

CHAPTER

3

The choice of site for the new stadium was governed by a number of key criteria. The new ground would have to be within London, with a residential population that would provide a sufficient reservoir of support to ensure good attendance figures. It needed to have good transport links and not be too close to another club. Norris's researches led him to consider options as far apart as Battersea and Harringay, but eventually his gaze focused on a patch of land belonging to St John's College of Divinity in the Highbury area of Islington in north London.

Man of vision
Henry Norris, the Father of Highbury. Norris took a struggling south London club, moved it across the river to Islington, and built a ground fit for a big First Division club. Without Norris's vision and ambition, there would have been no Arsenal Football Club as we know it today.

The land, which then consisted of a couple of football pitches, cricket pitches and tennis courts, was in a quiet residential area of terraced housing, but crucially was within a minute's walk of Gillespie Road underground station. Norris would have been quick to appreciate the value of this amenity and the decision was made. After protracted negotiations that required all his business skills, Norris agreed to pay the Ecclesiastical Commissioners £20,000 for a 21-year lease. It was signed by none other than the Archbishop of Canterbury himself, who was, significantly, a close personal friend of Norris. Norris nonetheless had to agree to a clause that specified that no games could be played on Christmas Day or on Good Friday, a restriction that remained in place until 1925.

Norris's contribution

It is difficult to overstate the importance of Henry Norris's role as instigator and financier of Arsenal's historic move north of the Thames to Highbury. There is little doubt that without his ambition, determination and, some would say, callous disregard for the Club's roots and supporters, not to mention his considerable political and personal influence, Woolwich Arsenal would never have left Plumstead for Islington. Who knows, without Norris, Arsenal may well have fallen further into the financial mire and gone the way of so many early Football League clubs, disappearing into the lower levels of the game, or maybe even vanishing altogether.

Norris wasn't about to let that happen, however. He hadn't abandoned Fulham to fail with Arsenal. Whatever it took, this gamble had to work. As it turned out it was just as well the hard-nosed property developer had deep pockets, for by the time the stadium at Highbury was finally finished in 1914, and Arsenal were established in their respectable new north London home, Norris had sunk £125,000 of his own money into the venture and, with war on the horizon, he didn't look likely to recoup his losses any time soon.

The costs to him and the team weren't only financial, however. Such was the level of disapproval – even anger – at Arsenal's proposed move that Norris, allegedly, received death threats during the months of wrangles over the Club's relocation. Whether that's true or not, there was certainly vehement, outspoken opposition on both sides of the water. In less than 30 years, Arsenal had grown from a minor works team, slugging it out on muddy heaths in the bottom right-hand corner of the capital, to a professional Football League club with international players. Their rough and tough location and, all too often, their rough and tough style of play, made them a club that others loved to hate. One Derby County player is reported to have said of the away trip to Woolwich that 'a journey to the molten interior of the earth's core would be more pleasant and comfortable'.

Furious fans

Since the team's founding, the Reds from the Woolwich Arsenal had relied on, even survived off, the support of Woolwich factory workers, munitions makers, soldiers and dockers who embodied the Club's deeply industrial origins. It was these fans, as much as the players or the Club, that made going to play in Plumstead feel like an 'annual trip to hell', as the *Newcastle Echo* once described United's journey to the Manor Ground. Arsenal's crowds of squaddies and

On the left side, vertical text:

WOOLWICH ARSENAL F.C. OFFICIAL PROGRAMME.

Map labels include:

GILLESPIE ROAD / GROUND / Woolwich Arsenal Football Ground / DRAYTON PARK

UNDERGROUND MAP OF LONDON

Interchange Stations

On the right margin, vertical text:

Printed and Published for the Proprietors, The Woolwich Arsenal Football and Athletic Co., Ltd., Avenell Road, Highbury, N.

factory workers were the original 'no one likes us, we don't care' brigade. They had a fierce reputation for hurling 'foul mouthed insults' and 'coarse abuse' at the opposition, as the *Kentish Independent* reported. One match at the Manor Ground was actually abandoned because of the amount of swearing on the terraces, and during another some of the crowd invaded the pitch and beat up the referee.

What must it have meant to these supporters to learn that their team was about to up sticks and shift to a 'posh' part of town? This wasn't just a betrayal of geography, but of culture and class too. After all, these were hardly the natural followers of a man like Norris, a future Tory MP, nor were they people who could aspire to live in the quiet and respectable streets surrounding Highbury Hill. Such was the level of suspicion about their self-made chairman among Arsenal's fans that rumours circulated during the team's final season at the Manor Ground suggesting Norris was deliberately under-investing in the team in order to drive down the crowds and so boost the strength of his arguments for shifting the Club to a more accessible part of town.

Not surprisingly, the supporters' ill feeling often became public. One local fan, a Mr Paul Donaldson, wrote to the *Kentish Gazette* complaining vehemently that: 'Mr Norris has decided that financial gain is more important than protecting our local club. He is making a mistake. You cannot 'franchise' a football club – Woolwich Arsenal must stay near Woolwich.' Another, Mr Walter Bailey, protested in the *Kentish Independent* that: 'The most distant part of London to which they intend moving will effectively prevent those who helped to make the club, and can morally claim it as their birthright, from having anything further to do with it. Is this right?' Another fan accused Norris of gambling 'away the Club's soul.' As so often in football history, however, the voice of the humble supporter was drowned out by the louder arguments of hard financial and business logic.

Local oppositon

Not that Arsenal would be welcomed with open arms north of the river. The *Tottenham Herald*, for example, described Norris as an 'interloper', and printed a cartoon depicting him as a 'Hound of the Baskervilles'. Despite Arsenal's poor form and impending descent to the Second Division, there was clearly some insecurity among the supporters of London's most northerly club, Tottenham Hotspur. The *Herald* also ran editorials begging Spurs fans not to go and support their new north London rivals. Concerns were also voiced by the east London club Clapton Orient, based only four miles east of Highbury in Homerton.

In fact, it's unlikely Norris was banking on the residents of White Hart Lane and Tottenham High Road to fill the Highbury terraces once they were built. Indeed, he had chosen his location carefully, calculating that about 500,000 people lived in the resident-rich catchment areas around Arsenal's

new home, comprising Finsbury, Hackney, Islington and Holborn. Clearly, he hoped to draw some from the City of London and the West End too, only 10 minutes away by underground. He even hoped that other football followers with easy access to transport hubs such as King's Cross – just a few stops down the Piccadilly Line – could be lured to the Football League's newest ground.

Not that the local residents were all that keen. A 'Stop-Arsenal' campaign was launched as soon as news of the move leaked out, and local people set about lobbying borough councillors and officials to prevent this 'vulgar' sport encroaching on their quiet neighbourhood. The minutes of Islington Council from the period record that a Mr Coventon of Highbury Park called on the borough to 'protect the district' from the 'utter ruin' that a football team would bring.

But Norris's tentacles stretched far and wide. The magnate from west London even had contacts in the north London

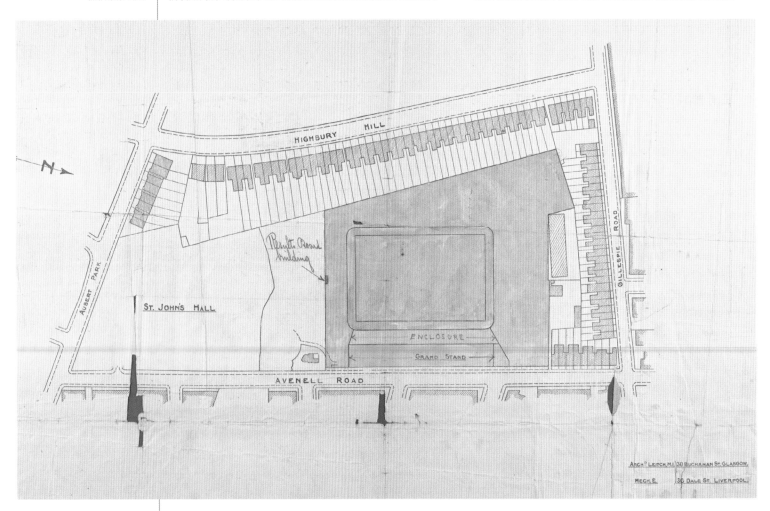

press and ensured that the anti-Arsenal meetings were not reported locally and the protest groups' actions remained unacknowledged. Without the oxygen of publicity, the campaigns simply could not grow. And anyway, what were mere local people against the power-brokers of business? Norris soon had them in his pocket. Cleverly, he persuaded the local business people of Blackstock Road and Finsbury Park that having 30,000 extra customers milling around every other Saturday would be good for profits. They quickly saw his point and have been benefiting ever since.

State-of-the-art design

Norris's connections were also crucial in determining the design and structure of the new ground. In 1904, while he was director of Fulham Football Club, Norris had engaged the services of Archibald Leitch, a Glasgow-based industrial architect who, in 1899, had designed the giant 80,000-capacity Ibrox Park, home of the mighty Glasgow Rangers, and rebuilt it after the infamous Ibrox disaster of 1902. He had also designed stands and terraces for northern clubs south of the border, such as Middlesbrough, Bradford City and Sheffield United, and was fast becoming known as football's engineer.

Norris invited Leitch to draw up plans for modernising Craven Cottage, Fulham's riverside ground in west London. The new ground designed by Leitch opened in September 1905, with a maximum capacity of 20,000 people – an impressive crowd for what was then a Southern League team. Much of the ground Leitch built has survived to this day and parts of it – the famous 'cottage' itself and the Stevenage Road stand – are now Grade II listed buildings.

By 1913, Leitch was a man in demand. He'd shifted his business base from Glasgow to Manchester, having spent the intervening years designing and building football grounds, terraces and stands for many

of England's most famous clubs. He was responsible for Chelsea's Stamford Bridge, Blackburn Rovers' Ewood Park, Everton's Goodison Park and Manchester United's Old Trafford stadium, to name just a few. He was a specialist who pioneered techniques for erecting steel-based stands, wooden stepped terracing, crush barriers and elaborate brick façades, such as the one at Villa Park, home of Aston Villa. In 1908. Leitch designed large parts of Tottenham Hotspur's new ground at White Hart Lane, including the large East Stand, and would work for Spurs a number of times on and off until he died in 1939.

Not that Leitch's relationship with Arsenal's new neighbours would have worried Norris, however. This was business after all. When the FA refused Norris permission to merge his two football concerns, and forced him to choose Arsenal over Fulham, he hired Leitch again.

Three years earlier Leitch had helped Newton Heath's transformation into Manchester United by finding them a new location and building a giant new stadium in west Manchester. He also supervised Millwall's move to the Den, so Norris knew he had some valuable experience of relocating football clubs and siting new stadia. Neither of these two clubs had moved 10 miles and crossed a river, however.

ON THE HIGH ROAD TO RECOVERY.

Dr. Highbury—A very narrow escape indeed. Another twelve months under my colleague here and it would have been all up with you. His treatment would have killed anyone with a less robust constitution. However, I have been called in in time, and with a change of air and plenty of visitors to cheer you up there is no reason why you should not regain all your former vigour.

Dr Highbury prescribes
Early match programmes at Highbury included cartoons of a character called Dr Highbury. Here he is seen providing an effective cure for the ailing Gunner. Dr Plumstead, who has been sacked, is seen in the background.

Early letterhead
Correspondence from Club secretary H.J. Peters dating from 1915, relating to the renewal of the planning licence for the grandstand. The letterhead proudly proclaims the Club's proximity to Gillespie Road underground station.

It's difficult to know how great an influence Leitch had on Norris's decision to choose Highbury but it does seem that he may have been the first person to spot the potential of the six acres attached to St John's College of Divinity. Leitch was working in London a lot at the time, mostly on his plans for Stamford Bridge and White Hart Lane, and had begun looking for a suitable site to build a ground for future FA Cup finals, to replace the distant and dilapidated Crystal Palace. At first, it seems, he hoped the Divinity College site would be suitable for such a stadium. By the beginning of 1913, however, he

had struck a deal with Norris and his co-director William Hall, and dispatched one of his employees, Alfred Kearney, from the Manchester office to oversee Woolwich Arsenal's stadium-building project.

From playing field to stadium

Kearney's account of the trials and tribulations of turning a college playing field into a football stadium, printed in Arsenal's match day programme on 21 December 1963, 50 years after Highbury opened, is fascinating reading, not

least because it reveals that Norris had clearly made up his mind about the Club's new home early in 1913, long before the Football League approved – or did not object to – his proposals. In fact, such was Norris's confidence in the project that not only had he engaged Leitch's company but he'd already hired a team of builders too – Humphreys Ltd, Civil Engineers of Knightsbridge – with whom he'd worked several times on west London housing projects. When Kearney was deposited on Avenell Road at the site of the stadium for the first time he saw 'a forbidding brick wall' running the whole

length of the street, but little else. 'I felt rather like ... "the only one saved from the wreck",' he wrote. However, Kearney soon settled in the area – which he describes as 'a theatrical quarter, being an off-shoot from the Finsbury Park Empire' – and started engineering the ground. Or he would have, if he'd had any plans to work with other than 'a small perspective' which he had put together himself, and those 'just in my head and in my hands'. Each time he drew up a new set of plans Kearney had to speed off to the Engineer's Office of the London County Council to get them approved. 'I had one foot

North Bank in the making
Workmen toil to build the terracing that would become the North Bank at Highbury, on 25 August 1913. Before Arsenal moved in, this quiet, pleasantly wooded corner of Islington was taken up with cricket pitches and tennis courts owned by the Ecclesiastical Commissioners.

in Highbury and one foot in Spring Gardens,' he wrote, 'rushing each drawing I got passed back to the site and fixing up the setting out with the foreman.'

The first stage was to lay out the pitch. This was quite an effort as the southern end of the ground nearest the college (later to be the Clock End) had to be lowered five feet while the opposite end near Gillespie Road (the so-called 'laundry end' and future North Bank) had to be raised by 11 feet. 'Remember there were no bulldozers or mechanical diggers,' wrote Kearney. 'It was all navvies, picks, spades and barrows ... the first job was to take a line across the centre of the pitch dug into the Aubert Park, and have the spoil wheeled to the other end to level out the pitch space. We then started to form the embankment at the other end.'

It's estimated that during 1913 some 200 workmen were employed to level the pitch and build the slopes that would later become Highbury's famous terraces, including the North Bank, initially christened the Laundry End. Much of the material used to construct these banks came from the mud and rubble excavated from the newly constructed Piccadilly underground line, as well as numerous other building sites around the capital. Reading Kearney's description of the dirty and, no doubt, noisy construction process it's no wonder that some local residents were upset by the arrival of this huge building site on their doorsteps. 'Tons of material were required for forming the embankment and news of the "tip" soon went round,' writes Kearney. 'Dozens of people brought us stuff from all over London and the yellow London clay, dropping from the carts, left the streets and roads all around Highbury dyed yellow for many weeks.'

Kearney's words also give us a graphic sense of how different Highbury was in social and economic terms to the streets of Plumstead. 'The hangover of the Victorian era still clung to Highbury, although the city VIPs had more or less left their villas and coaches and horses, etc,' he writes. 'The suburbanites were still feeling superior, however, and a bright boy in Highbury Hill started a petition to get Islington Borough Council to put a stop to this "vulgar project".'

Norris's ability to 'pull strings' behind the scenes saw off that threat, but the project was always short of time and continued to be riddled with problems and set-backs. Kearney wanted to build a retaining wall at the college end but the London County Council (LCC) office wouldn't agree to his plans, palming him off to a local, 'out-of-date' parish council office in Holloway Road that, according to Kearney, 'did not know the difference between a retaining wall and a retaining fee'. As ever, Kearney took his direction from Norris, who simply told him to ignore them and build the thing anyway. Another wall along the line of the back gardens that were attached to houses down Highbury Hill led to further resistance in the form of a solicitor's letter threatening an injunction and claiming it was 'over the building line'. With time starting to run out, Kearney avoided a lengthy legal process by pulling the wall down and rebuilding it six feet closer to the pitch.

The first East Stand

Residents also objected to Leitch's original plans for the grandstand on the east side of the ground backing onto Avenell Road, submitted to the LCC in May 1913. This was a two-tiered structure for 11,000 supporters, not particularly grand but with a brick façade on the road side that would have dominated the houses opposite. In the end, a single-tier grandstand was built with a completely different layout and roof, housing 9,000 supporters. As it was, this took more than a year to finish, during which the LCC constantly badgered Leitch about its incomplete state and warned the Club for allowing the partly finished stand to be used by the public without a council licence. Photographs from Arsenal's first Highbury season show the back and ends of the stand entirely open to the elements apart from some haphazardly slung tarpaulins roped across the gaps.

One of the biggest problems in designing a ground so closely hemmed in by residential streets was deciding where to put the exit gates and access points. Incredibly, for a ground expected to hold up to 60,000 people, initially only three were planned – two on Avenell Road to the east of the ground and one on Gillespie Road to the north. This in itself was a huge problem because Gillespie Road was lined with houses, which backed onto what would become the largest area of terracing. Being close to the road's underground station was one of Highbury's chief plus points so a solution had to be

found, and Kearney describes how the problem was dealt with: 'At the Gillespie Road end we needed an entrance opposite the Tube station, so two houses were bought and pulled down, giving us a good passage and leading to a large area where turnstiles and exit gates could be constructed to feed out up to the "Spion Kop".' Long before the term was used by the fans, many of whom had connections with the military, to describe a stand at Anfield, the name of the location of a famous battle of the Boer War had been used to describe a raised area of the Manor Ground.

Highbury pioneers

The Arsenal team in their first season at Highbury 1913. The dark red 'redcurrant' jerseys were revived for the last season at the stadium, as a reminder of the Club's heritage. Among the players pictured are Joe Shaw (back row, second from left), who was still working for the Club in the mid-1950s.

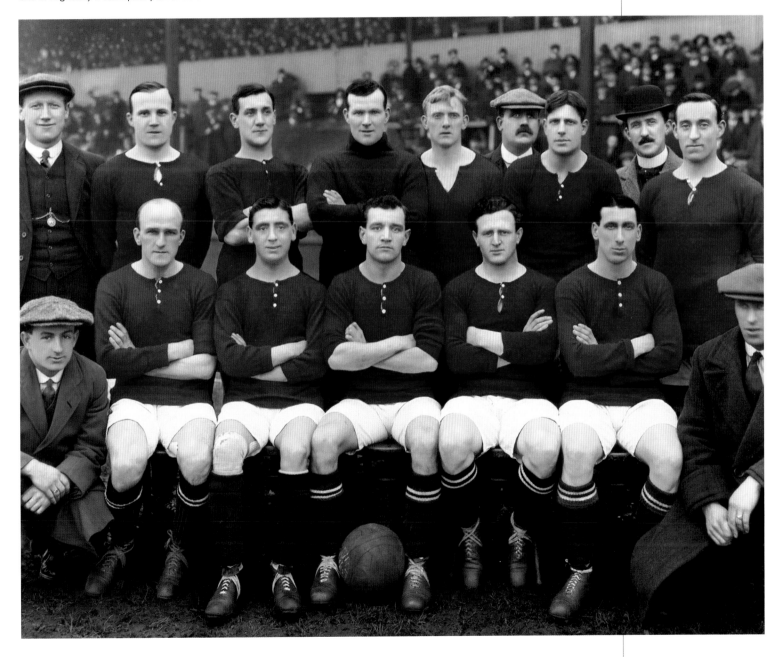

A rough-and-ready opening

Despite numerous 'wobbles' such as these, Kearney and the men from Humphreys just about managed to get the ground ready for the start of the 1913/14 season. But it was a close call. A week before the first match in early September the tireless Kearney was still improvising, using 'hundreds of feet of rough timber and many carpenters' to make rails and passages to guide the spectators in and out through temporary entrances and exits. Turnstiles were delivered but not pay boxes; offices, dressing rooms and bathrooms 'were roughly ready'; baths were in position but 'not connected to supplies and drains'; and army field kitchens were brought in to heat the water.

In short, the building of Arsenal Stadium was a rush job, and somewhat botched together, although Kearney suggests there was a kind of pioneering atmosphere around it all, just as there had been when players and fans worked through the summer to get the Manor Ground into shape back in 1893. 'Even the players and officials of the Club fell in with the spirit and treated it like a picnic, working hard here and there and getting a wonderful kick out of everything they did. They worked like Trojans.'

However, by 11am on the morning of Saturday 6 September 1913, 'D Day' as Kearney describes it, 'things looked grim'. Carts and workmen were still coming and going as people began to gather, so Kearney ordered the gates to be closed while he went off for a somewhat forlorn lunch with the paymaster Norris. When he returned, however, the gates were still open and people were lining up four or five deep in Avenell Road. Clearly, not everyone saw Woolwich Arsenal's arrival in the area as a vulgar intrusion.

Despite much of the ground still resembling a building site – only 30 of the 100 terraces were ready – Arsenal's first game at Highbury went ahead as planned. Arsenal supporters – their numbers no doubt bolstered by the odd curious onlooker – saw their team beat Leicester Fosse 2–1 in a Football League Division Two game, many of them watching from the top of Highbury Hill. The first Highbury goal was scored by Leicester, but centre forward George Jobey, a new signing for the season, soon provided the equaliser becoming the first Gunner to score at Highbury. A further goal for the home team came from Archie Devine from a penalty. The ground's incomplete state was to play a decisive role in one of the best remembered events of that historic day. Goalscorer Jobey injured his ankle in the course of the match and had to be carried from the field by trainer George Hardy. However, the lack of dressing rooms and running water in the ground meant they were forced to take the injured Jobey out of the ground to the nearby players' lodgings for treatment. Not wanting his player to walk, Hardy borrowed a cart from the local milkman, David Lewis, who lived in Gillespie Road, and wheeled Jobey up the hill.

For Kearney, and no doubt for Leitch too (although the Scotsman was curiously absent) far more important than the result that day was the fact that the weather stayed fine and 'the crisis was over'. Kearney stayed at Highbury for four or five more weeks to complete his work, although it took much of the rest of the season before the ground was fully finished. Problems remained too. After a few months, the boundary wall that Kearney had so hastily moved began to buckle and in March 1914 a match had to be postponed while it was hurriedly repaired.

Indeed, for all Leitch's undoubted expertise, Highbury was not one of his greatest achievements. The hurried nature of the job and Arsenal's poor finances ensured that it was never going to compare to the great grounds he was building in Scotland, Yorkshire, the northwest, or even that of Arsenal's fiercest and closest rivals up the Seven Sisters Road. In fact the grandstand remained classified as a temporary structure, requiring its licence to be renewed annually, until it was eventually superseded by the new East Stand. Despite putting so much of his personal fortune into it Norris still didn't have enough money to pay all the contractors. Cash was so scarce that one builder on the grandstand agreed to take a percentage of the gate money, quite a risk for a club

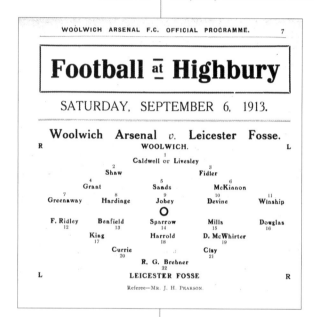

WOOLWICH ARSENAL F.C. OFFICIAL PROGRAMME.   7

Football at Highbury

SATURDAY, SEPTEMBER 6, 1913.

Woolwich Arsenal *v.* Leicester Fosse.

R   WOOLWICH.   L
1
Caldwell or Livesley
2   3
Shaw   Fidler
4   5   6
Grant   Sands   McKinnon
7   8   9   10   11
Greenaway Hardinge Jobey Devine   Winship
O
F. Ridley   Benfield   Sparrow   Mills   Douglas
12   13   14   15   16
King   Harrold   D. McWhirter
17   18   19
Currie   Clay
20   21
R. G. Brebner
22
L   LEICESTER FOSSE   R

Referee—Mr. J. H. Pearson.

now 10 miles from its natural supporters and with no guarantee of success, on or off the field. History doesn't reveal whether the builder's gamble paid off.

Wooing the supporters

The Club was keen to make a new start and begin building up a solid supporter base to provide some much-needed income. As part of its propaganda, Arsenal's staff set about persuading supporters – new and old – that the move north had been necessary, even 'life-saving'. The match programme for that first Highbury game on 6 September included the first appearance of a certain cartoon character called Dr Highbury, who would be a regular figure for several years. Dapper and stylish he's depicted giving his patient, 'the Gunners', a clean bill of health while a rather thin and glum-looking Dr Plumstead looks abandoned in the background.

In the same programme the directors set out their thinking on the Club's rebirth, welcoming fans to 'the most get-at-able' ground in London while regretting that it was not yet 'thoroughly equipped and laid out to its full holding capacity'. 'It can be reached from the City and places adjacent thereto in less time than any other ground, and should, therefore,

prove a great boon to the cosmopolitan enthusiast who finds himself in the City during the "kick off at 2.30pm" season, when every moment saved in travelling is valuable,' they proclaimed. 'We are distinctly hopeful that, with the assistance of the football-loving public of north London, we may soon forget the depressing times we spent at Plumstead, with its poor train service and the lukewarm support received from those in the immediate neighbourhood.'

New fans were welcomed with a leaflet proclaiming 'The banner is still flying', and imploring spectators to 'enrol … as one of our ever-increasing procession of loyal supporters'. 'Let our new ground at Highbury be your favourite football rendezvous,' it said. 'Rest assured you will get good football in return for your patronage.' The directors clearly hoped these new-style supporters would bring a new atmosphere to Arsenal games, both on and off the pitch. 'We want our visiting teams to look forward to a visit to our ground with feelings of pleasure (even though disappointed in the result of the match), and not with fear and trembling as to the possible effects of rough and unsportsmanlike usage.' Going to Highbury would no longer be a 'trip to hell'.

Ongoing improvements

As well as appealing to supporters to continue to attend matches at the new ground, in these early days at Highbury, the directors also pleaded for help from the fans in raising money to improve facilities at the Club's new home, in particular to build more covers over some of the terraces. The Club invited fans to become shareholders and to buy season tickets rather than pay weekly on the gate – thus guaranteeing the Club an income stream. Shares were sold

WOOLWICH ARSENAL F.C. OFFICIAL PROGRAMME.

What " Fosse "-pherine Did!

Dr. Highbury : " Well, my lad, and how do you feel now?'' The Gunner : " Ever so much better, thank you. That tonic you gave me last Saturday did me a world of good, whilst I had quite an army of well-wishers come to see me.'' Dr. Highbury : " Glad to hear it. I am sending you down to Wolverhampton this week, but hope it won't retard your progress."

Magic medicine
In the wake of Woolwich Arsenal's victory over Leicester Fosse, this cartoon in the following week's matchday programme of 1913 celebrates the efficacy of Dr Highbury's treatment.

Hull of a save
Hull City's goalkeeper pushes a shot over the crossbar at Highbury, 20 September 1913. The match ended 0–0 as Jimmy Caldwell was in equally good form on his debut in goal for the Gunners, and a crowd of about 28,000 saw the game.

at £1 each which could be paid for in four monthly instalments. 'You will not miss the small payment and will help to add to the general comfort and efficiency,' said a leaflet. Shareholders could buy season tickets cheaply, guaranteeing them 'a special seat in a special part of the ground'. Normal season tickets cost 21 shillings for men, and 15 shillings for 'Lady's or Boy's tickets', and allowed entrance to all games except Cup ties. 'This is a very low price, especially having regard to the large number of matches to be played,' said an advertisement. Perhaps it was due to the continuing lack of administrative offices at the ground that it was Club Secretary George Morrell's home address in Harringay that appears at the bottom of the flyer.

Although the shareholders' ledger from the period shows that supporters from south London bought shares, it seems the Club's pleas began to work, for Woolwich Arsenal was soon pulling in fans who had probably never set foot in Woolwich. Soon after the ground opened the Club began a public discussion on what it should be called and responses came from people who lived across north London. A Mr W. Dykes from Camden Town suggested the name Avesbury Park, for example, a kind of marriage between Avenell Road and Highbury. And Mr H.W. Cooper from Islington put forward The Fortress, saying: 'We hear of the Canary and his Nest at Norwich, and the Lion in his Den at Millwall, so why not the Gunner in his Fortress?' Arsenal's origins were remembered in another suggestion from 'Iddy': The Gun Park.

Goodbye to Woolwich

By the end of the first season, however, the Club's ties to its southeast London origins were already coming undone. In April 1914 the Club dropped the Woolwich from its name to become simply 'The Arsenal', and the ground became known officially as 'The Arsenal Stadium', but called 'Highbury' by the fans. In time it would become one of the most admired sporting arenas in the country, although it would take a new architect and a lot more money before that happened. In truth, Leitch's slightly rushed 1913 construction never quite fulfilled the Club's ambition – 'that the ground and home of the Pioneers of League Football and professionalism in London shall be second to none in the Kingdom'. That dream wouldn't be realised for another 20 years.

A view to the east

The tarpaulins that were temporarily hung at the back of Leitch's unfinished grandstand can be seen in the backgound, as Huddersfield Town's goalkeeper pulls off a fine save on 14 February 1914. Arsenal lost 1–0 in front of a crowd of 25,000.

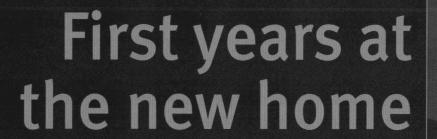

First years at the new home

The years after World War I saw the Gunners evolve from a club that struggled to hold on to its place in the First Division into one that was able to bring some of the largest football crowds in London into its new home at Highbury, and was developing a team and a stadium to match its ambition.

CHAPTER 4

Leslie Knighton
Knighton, from Burton on Trent, took over as manager at Arsenal in 1919 and left in 1925 after repeated clashes with Norris.

A whole new ball game
When Arsenal made the decision to move to Highbury in north London, it was always hoped that the ground would be used for a wide range of activities. That was certainly the case in May 1918, when Highbury staged an Anglo-American baseball match.

Norris's dream of running a large, successful club depended not only on having a decent stadium and a solid supporter base, but on giving the fans consistent First Division football. In 1914 at the end of their first season at Highbury, Woolwich Arsenal finished third in Division Two, missing promotion by one place on goal average. Undoubtedly it was a disappointment. Within months, however, disappointment became disaster as Europe collapsed into war and football, like so many leisure activities, was dwarfed in importance by larger events.

Many players joined the forces. Some, especially those with Woolwich Arsenal connections, returned to munitions work. In a match at Highbury in February 1915 there was a tragic incident involving Bob Benson, an Arsenal and England full back, who was working during the war in the munitions factory. He turned up to watch the game, but agreed to play instead of Ed Liddle, a guest player from West Ham United.

Not having played for nine months, Benson was very unfit and had to leave the pitch and later in the dressing room died of a heart attack.

Crowds declined and although the 1914/15 season went ahead it ended with Arsenal in fifth place and on the way to further financial trouble. After the last game of the season – a 7–0 drubbing of Nottingham Forest at Highbury on 24 April 1915 – the manager George Morrell was sacked to save money. No-one knew at the time, but it was Arsenal's last game in Division Two.

Football matches of various kinds continued at Highbury during the war. Football was played on a regional basis and, although many of its players were fighting in for their country, the Club competed in the London Combination League for the four years of the war, with home matches continuing to be played at Highbury. However, by the end of the war in November 1918, Arsenal were £60,000 in debt. Many thought

its pre-war side was talented enough to climb back up to the top flight. But the team were all five years older. Among the hundreds of thousands of men who died in the trenches were numerous professional footballers, and without them no-one quite knew what the first post-war season, which began in September 1919, would be like. For the fans who frequented Highbury, remarkably, it brought First Division football. Quite how this came about is one of the more extraordinary stories in British football history, or one of its biggest scandals if you happen to be a Tottenham Hotspur fan.

Norris performs magic

At the end of the 1914/15 season Tottenham Hotspur had finished 20th and last in Division One, with Chelsea one place above them. Above Arsenal in Division Two were Derby, Preston North End, Barnsley and Wolverhampton Wanderers, in that order. Before the 1919/20 season it had been decided to extend the Division One to 22 clubs and the normal procedure would have been to re-elect the two bottom clubs in that division and add the top two teams from Division Two. Somehow, between the end of the war and the Football League's AGM in July 1919, Norris persuaded the Football

League that Arsenal should be promoted in place of Spurs. Norris had been knighted in 1917 and became a Tory MP the following year, so his influence would have been considerable and his attentions no doubt flattering to some members of the League. Nevertheless, the shenanigans at the AGM that year stretch the bounds of belief. The League's President, John McKenna, Liverpool's owner and a friend of Norris, ruled that Derby and Preston should be promoted on the nod. He also decided – perhaps on Norris's suggestion – that the members should vote on Chelsea and Spurs separately. Chelsea had finished one point behind Manchester United in 1915 and there had been suggestions that United's last-match victory against Liverpool was rigged. The court cases were inconclusive but there was clearly some sympathy for Chelsea as they too were re-elected .

Then, for no logical reason, McKenna proposed that Arsenal be elected in place of Spurs arguing that they deserved it because they had been league members 15 years longer than Spurs. The fact that Wolves, who had finished fourth, had been members longer than Arsenal wasn't mentioned and a combination of McKenna's influence and Norris' lobbying won the day for the Highbury side. The

Frank Bradshaw

Frank Bradshaw in August 1922, at the start of his last season at Highbury. In the memorable clash with Tottenham Hotspur in 1922, he aroused the ire of the Spurs fans with his tough tackling. Bradshaw, from Sheffield, joined Arsenal from Everton and made his Gunners debut in 1914. In 142 games for the Club the full back scored 14 goals.

Arsenal got 18 votes to Tottenham's eight, with Barnsley (third in Division Two) five and Wolves four. Not surprisingly, feelings of bitterness, were added to the footballing rivalry between the two North London clubs.

North London rivals

To their credit Tottenham's response came on the field. Spurs rocketed back to the top division with record points and win totals in 1920, finished sixth in their first season in the top flight and, in 1921, won the FA Cup. In the early 1920s Spurs were clearly the number one North London side, but the rivalry with Arsenal remained fierce. In 1922, for example, their double derby with Arsenal was inflammable. At this time it was the custom for the home and away encounters in the League to be played consecutively, giving all too little opportunity for any emotions roused by the first game to disappear by the second. In 1922, in the first of these two matches against Tottenham at White Hart Lane, Arsenal, manifestly the underdogs, had the temerity to win. Arsenal at that period could not match Spurs for skill, but they had plenty of resolution and physical force. The tough tackling of the full backs Arthur Hutchins and Frank Bradshaw unsettled both the Tottenham attack and the fans. 'The crowd at once began to howl at the Arsenal players as if they were assassins,' wrote a newspaper. 'Can you wonder that the men from Highbury got a little rattled and out of hand?'

Three Spurs players had to leave the field, hurt, though two were already suffering from previous injuries. Spurs' only goal came when a whistle was blown in the crowd, the Arsenal defence were duped into standing still, and Lindsay, a Spurs forward, ran on to score. Heavy missiles hurled from the crowd struck Hutchins and Billy Blyth, nevertheless the Gunners held on to win 2–1. Spurs, however, had their revenge in the return match, winning 2–0 at Highbury.

Knighton thwarted

Norris's overbearing influence wasn't only apparent in the corridors of football power; he had huge say over the running of The Arsenal Club itself and over the team. In particular, he tended to impose conditions on his managers, most notably after appointing Leslie Knighton in June 1919. Knighton had been a successful manager with Huddersfield and Manchester City, and Norris hoped he would finally bring The Arsenal the success he craved. But he made his new manager's task that much harder by telling him not to sign any players smaller than five feet eight inches, or to spend more than £1,000 on any one transfer. You might think he wanted to build a team of local players, but Norris also instructed Knighton to abandon the Club's scouting system.

Not surprisingly, The Arsenal's results suffered as a result. In their first six years in Division One The Arsenal survived beyond the second round of the FA Cup just once, and finished no higher than ninth in the League. Yet support for the Club remained robust and Norris's gamble of relocation in Highbury appeared to have paid off. In 1919/20 – the first post-War season – Arsenal were attracting an average crowd of over 34,400, which was bettered only by Chelsea and Newcastle. That figure settled down to around the 30,000 mark after the first flush of post-war enthusiasm for football receded, but Arsenal remained one of the country's best-supported clubs.

International reputation

Highbury was quickly earning a reputation as one of the finest football grounds in the country, and by 1920 it was hosting international games, there being no national stadium at that time (Wembley Stadium was not built until 1923). On 15 March 1920 England lost 2–1 to Wales at Highbury, with the Sunderland forward Charlie Buchan – an Arsenal legend of the future – scoring England's goal. Arsenal were also honoured by becoming the first club to host an England game against a foreign team, when on 19 March 1923 England beat Belgium 6–1 at Highbury. Jackie Hegan, the Corinthians outside left, scored twice and there were also goals for the Liverpool inside left Harry Chambers, Sheffield Wednesday outside right David Mercer, Spurs inside right Jimmy Seed and the Bury centre forward Norman Bullock.

else, it was clear that the pills had an effect. The Cup tie was rescheduled for the following Monday, but the fog closed in again and the match was postponed once more. Later in the week, a third, and this time successful attempt was made to play the match; and once more Knighton and his players swallowed the pills. West Ham set the pace, besieging the Arsenal goal. Just before half time, however, Knighton 'noticed

Desperate measures

The Gunners are famous for their record-breaking stay in English football's top division. They remain the only top-flight club never to have been relegated. But in 1924/25, Leslie Knighton's last season as manager, Arsenal finished 20th, cheating relegation by one place. It was in a desperate attempt to address this lack of success on the pitch that in January 1925 Knighton accepted a rather strange offer of help. It came from a Harley Street doctor proffering 'courage pills' to boost the team's chances in its forthcoming third round FA Cup tie against West Ham United.

Ushered into Knighton's presence, the doctor quickly came to the point. He was, he said, a keen fan and felt that on current form, Arsenal had scant chance of survival against West Ham. 'What the boys require,' the doctor said, 'is something in the nature of a courage pill.' He insisted that they did no harm, and left no after-effects.

Knighton eventually agreed to try the 'remedy'. He duly took a box of pills to Upton Park. An hour before the kick off, he and the team swallowed their pills. When kick off approached, Knighton, seeing his team grow restless, felt he 'needed to run, jump, shout.' However, fog had descended on East London and was now so thick that the game couldn't possibly be played, and the referee postponed the match. The trip back to Highbury was an ordeal; of appalling thirst, a bitter taste and a torment of undischarged energy. If nothing

a change.' Arsenal's super-charged players utterly dominated, commanding the field, bombarding the West Ham goal, but somehow the Hammers survived; and it was back to Highbury for the replay. Arsenal's players, who had suffered unpleasant after-effects of the pills, protested furiously against any suggestion that they should take them again. Defiance was absolute. Knighton surrendered. The less hyperactive team was held to a 2–2 draw, but lost the play off at Stamford Bridge 1–0. The experiment with 'medical' assistance was at an end, and since that time the Club has relied on thorough training and high-quality physiotherapy to maximise the team's performance.

Knighton departs

By resisting new signings, Knighton had succeeded in reducing the Club's huge debt year by year, but in when he came to Sir Henry Norris to ask for money to buy a famous inside forward, he saw Norris's 'heavy brows contract.' So Knighton called a Board Meeting (from which Norris was absent) and passionately put his case. He was finally allowed to offer £6,000 for the player. It was ironic that the player in question was Charlie Buchan, the now-celebrated Sunderland inside right, who had left Highbury 16 years previously over an expenses claim. Knighton travelled to Sunderland and talked to the Club's manager, Bob Kyle, for three hours, knowing all too well that Norris had been trying to persuade

the Football League to limit transfer fees to £1,650. He also knew that were he to succeed, Norris would feel defied and humiliated with inevitable consequences for himself. Recklessly, Knighton even raised his offer to £7,000, but the offer was rejected and he returned to London to face Norris. Knighton was sacked.

Bringing in the crowds

Despite Arsenal's poor showing in Division One, Highbury was still drawing some of the biggest crowds in the country. In Knighton's last season in charge, the average crowd was 29,485. That does not sound like a vast throng by later standards, but at the time the Gunners were one of England's best-supported teams. Tottenham's average gate was 28,420, and that season's Champions, Huddersfield Town, averaged fewer than 18,000, and Manchester United could only pull in just over 21,000 at Old Trafford.

A new manager and a new era

1925 must be seen in the watershed of Arsenal's fortunes, the year when they began to emerge from struggle and mediocrity. The driving force of the metamorphosis was, of course, Knighton's successor as manager, Herbert Chapman, who in his nine years at the Club won the FA Cup, twice won the League Championship, and had set the team on the way to winning another.

A Yorkshireman, Chapman had been an inside left of modest abilities, never a regular first team player with Tottenham Hotspur – then a Southern League club. It was almost by chance that he became player-manager of Northampton Town. The job had been offered to the Spurs centre half, Walter Bull, who mentioned in the dressing room that he would not be taking it. Chapman took it instead and his managerial career had begun. Successful with Northampton, he was then appointed manager of Leeds City,

On trial

Gunners centre forward Harry Woods heads the ball during a pre-season trial match between Arsenal's first and second teams at Highbury on 15 August 1925. At this time Highbury was used for most of the team's training.

then in the Second Division. He was forced to leave Leeds because of a financial scandal involving unofficial payments to players, being suspended indefinitely by the FA. However, following an amnesty, in 1919 he became assistant manager, then manager of Huddersfield Town. There, he transformed the Club, which had only reached the First Division in season 1919/20. In 1922 they won the FA Cup, in 1923 they came third in the Division One, and under Chapman's leadership, took the title in the next two seasons.

Significantly perhaps, and in spite of achievements with Huddersfield Town, Chapman himself actually applied for the Arsenal job, responding to Norris's advertisement placed in the Athletic News, stating that 'Only people who will not spend big money on transfer fees need apply.' In taking the great gamble of leaving a club at the height of its prowess for one which had just so nearly been relegated, Chapman was not only utterly sure of his own powers, but convinced that true fame lay in the capital.

Chapman and Whittaker

One of Chapman's first actions was to transform the life of one of his players, Tom Whittaker. On tour with a Football Association party in Australia in the summer of 1925, Whittaker suffered a severe knee injury in a match in Wollongong, ending his playing days. But Chapman's decency, humanity and remarkable insight would come to his rescue. Returning to Highbury, and hobbling his way upstairs to Chapman's office, he found the new manager instantly

likeable and concerned. First, insisted Chapman, the FA must be obliged to pay the £6 wage he had been earning until it was clear he could no longer play football.

Luck was certainly on Whittaker's side. On the voyage home from Australia, he had chanced to meet a woman who told him that the only person who would heal his injury was a famous Liverpudlian surgeon, Sir Robert Jones. Whittaker mentioned Jones to Chapman, who duly passed on the information to the FA, but nothing happened. In the meantime, Whittaker helped Arsenal's experienced, trainer, George Hardy, on an ad hoc basis in the dressing room.

Eventually Chapman arranged for Whittaker to see Sir Robert Jones, who assured him that while he would never again play football, he would regain the use of his right leg. This he did following what turned out to be the first modern operation for cartilage trouble. The Football Association, to Arsenal's fury, agreed to pay Whittaker a mere £350 in compensation. To this they added £100. Soon after that, Chapman summoned Whittaker to his office, said that he wanted to show him something, and took him to the top of the East Stand. After a pause, Chapman pointed to the pitch and said with slow emphasis, 'I am going to make this the greatest club ground in the world, and I am going to make you the greatest trainer in the game. What do you say to that?'

Playing days

Tom Whittaker in 1922 during his playing career, which was cruelly cut short by a serious injury. Whittaker, a wing half, joined the Gunners in 1919 and played 70 matches for the Club, scoring two goals. After he retired as a player in the summer of 1925, he became trainer, assistant manager, then manager of Arsenal in 1947.

So Chapman appointed Whittaker second-team trainer under his friend George Hardy, with whom he was lodging, and sent him to the remarkable Sir Robert Jones for a year's instruction in anatomy, massage, medical gymnastics and electrical therapy. Whittaker modestly recorded that this helped me in the seasons to come, when Arsenal and their players were setting such an infernal rhythm. Yet modesty prevented him from vaunting his own great contribution, the 'magic hands' that cured players who would otherwise have stayed out of action for weeks longer; and this in a time long before the wonders of ultrasound and deep diathermy.

February 1927 was the watershed in Whittaker's career at Highbury. Arsenal were playing Port Vale at home in an FA Cup fourth round replay and finding it hard to break through, when George Hardy was moved to stride to the touchline and shout at one of the forwards to move farther upfield. He had plainly exceeded his brief. Hardy was sacked and Chapman told Whittaker, 'Take over the first team from now.' The fruitful partnership between manager and trainer, which was to be one of the key elements for the future success of the Club was now in place.

Buchan returns

A more spectacular coup for Chapman in 1925 was to succeed where Knighton had failed and bring Charlie Buchan back to Arsenal. Buchan, who had fought in the War, was by then 33 years old, and a member of a famous Sunderland attack. When the parsimony of the then manager George Morrell had lost him to Woolwich Arsenal, Buchan had been snapped up by Northfleet, from where he went to Leyton.

A visionary of the game
Herbert Chapman in 1931, the year he first brought the First Division Championship to Highbury. Chapman bestrode the era like a colossus, transforming not only Arsenal Football Club, but the whole of British football in the process. The game in this country has never known a visionary to equal his stature.

Charlie Buchan 1909/10, 1925/26–1927/28

At his peak before World War I Charlie Buchan was described as the best footballer in England. Born in Plumstead in 1891, he first joined Woolwich Arsenal in 1909 but, after a successful first season, left the Club for Northfleet. He went on to achieve footballing stardom with Sunderland, with whom he won a League Championship medal in 1912/13. After serving with distinction in World War I and a further period with Sunderland, he returned to Arsenal in 1925. Although he won no winners' medals with the Club, his skill and experience, as well as his tactical acumen, helped the Gunners lay the foundations for future success.

Up in Sunderland, Buchan was shocked when one day Chapman walked into his sports shop; first to see him there at all, secondly and chiefly because Chapman informed him that Bob Kyle, the Sunderland manager, had agreed to sell him. Norris may have sent Chapman as his emissary, but he insisted on doing the deal himself. And although it grew clear that he was relaxing the purse strings, he was still determined to strike as hard a bargain as he could. He therefore had to prevail on two fronts; he had to see that an initially most reluctant Buchan was convinced, and he had to knock down Sunderland's price. In the event he succeeded in both endeavours. Sunderland initially demanded £4,000, Kyle insisting that Buchan would score 20 goals a season. Norris shrewdly hoist him with his own petard, offering £2,000 down and £100 for every goal Buchan scored. Eventually Norris, as so often, had his way, and Sunderland had their money. Buchan scored no fewer than 19 League goals and another in the Cup. 'There goes another £100!' the crowd would cheerfully sing, when Buchan scored.

But Buchan himself held out for ten weeks before he ultimately signed. He was perturbed that he would lose the money he made from his successful sports shop. With the maximum wage reduced by the Football League from £9 to £8

after the war, he could hardly afford to move without incentive. Norris later admitted that Buchan had been paid an illegal £125. Chapman always denied any knowledge of these dubious financial arrangements, which later led to an estrangement between him and his Chairman.

The departure of Norris

Chapman and Norris continued to work together at Arsenal until Norris's departure from the Club. Chapman was far more successful than Leslie Knighton had been in getting Sir Henry Norris to loosen the purse strings. Not only was he able to sign Buchan, but also the Scottish international long-kicking keeper Bill Harper, for an even larger fee of £5,000. The footballing results of this new regime would begin to be felt almost immediately.

While the manager would go on to lead his team to famous victories, the career of Arsenal's wily Chairman Sir Henry Norris was coming to an end. He left the Club in the summer of 1927 after a Football Association commission of inquiry found Norris and William Hall, his partner in football from his Fulham days, guilty of irregularities, mainly centring around payments for his car and to his chauffeur from the Club's account. Norris, doubtless fortified by his previous successes in court, sued the FA for libel. This time, however, he had seriously overreached himself and in February 1929 he lost the action. Bizarrely, it emerged in court – and resounded down the years – that he had sold the Club's motor coach, endorsed it in Chapman's name, and paid the money into his wife's account. Norris was later banned from any further involvement in football. This was a sad conclusion to the career of someone who had contributed so massively to the development of the Arsenal Football Club. While he does not seem to have been an engaging figure, the quintessence of the self-made man, arrogant, insensitive and domineering, it should be remembered that it was Norris who took Arsenal across the Thames to Highbury when the Club might otherwise have disappeared, Norris who footed the bill to see that the new stadium was built and Norris, after all, who brought Herbert Chapman to Highbury. Leslie Knighton, himself brusquely treated by Sir Henry, eulogised him in his autobiography. 'Despite everything, I still say he was the best chairman I ever had. He did miles more for football and for

footballers than the public will ever know. If he had not been a rebel against petty authority he would have risen to the greatest position in the game. A financial genius, football was his hobby and delight, even though only a bagatelle compared with some of his business dealings. The game was immensely the poorer for his passing out of it, and it was a tragedy indeed that such a man should have gone under a cloud.' Norris died in 1934.

Sir Henry Norris was replaced in 1927 as Chairman by the less controversial Sir Samuel Hill-Wood, who would establish an enduring dynasty; to this day, a Hill-Wood, Sir Samuel's grandson Peter, holds the position of Chairman, having succeeded his late father Denis. An accomplished cricketer, Sir Samuel had already shown his footballing acumen by turning the little Glossop Football Club from a mere works team into a First Division club. Under his aegis Chapman had free rein and this would famously bear results.

Derby day

Charlie Buchan (left) of Arsenal and Arthur Grimsdell of Tottenham Hotspur shake hands before a match at Highbury on 29 August 1925. This was the first home game of the season that saw a change in the offside law, which transformed British football. The Gunners lost 1–0 in front of a crowd of 53,183. Arsenal finished the season in second place behind Huddersfield Town.

Chapman's Highbury

Arsenal under Herbert Chapman's managership entered what was undoubtedly a golden era. Four decades without winning a major tournament were brought to a close with the FA Cup win of 1930. And the Club's success was reflected in the building of a superb new West Stand for the stadium.

CHAPTER

5

erbert Chapman's arrival at Highbury in 1925 had signalled the start of a new era in Arsenal's history. That year the Club bought the freehold of its Highbury home for £64,000, which freed it from the restrictions on playing games on religious holidays such as Christmas and Easter, and opened the door to further development of the stadium. Norris's previously parsimonious regime had been relaxed, new players were signed – notably Charlie Buchan – and the game itself was changing.

Offside at Highbury

The arrival of Chapman and Buchan at Arsenal coincided with a radical change in the offside law; imposed, as it happens, by the Football Association after a strangely casual trial game at Highbury itself in 1925. In the first half, the existing offside law was used, whereby a player needed three defenders between himself and the opponent's goal-line when the ball was played – effectively two men and the opposing goalkeeper. In the second half, only two defending players were required. Such was the power of the English FA in those remote days that it was able to take such a monumental decision without any intervention by other countries, which simply and keenly fell into line. The result of this trial was to usher in the new offside rule, which in the first few months of its operation in the 1925/26 season resulted in a plethora of goals.

The Third Back Game

Among these high-scoring matches was a 7–0 defeat for Arsenal at Newcastle United. Following this defeat, Charlie Buchan and Chapman worked out a new formation, in which the centre half played in central defence and it was soon adopted on the field of play.

The new formation meant that a roving inside forward was needed. Buchan himself wanted to fill that role, but after extended debate, Chapman decided he was too valuable in his usual attacking role. He then surprised the players by declaring, 'I know

the very man: Andy Neil! He's as slow as a funeral, but he has ball control and can stand with his foot on the ball while making up his mind!' This was Chapman at his most experimental; Neil at the time was in the third team, having previously played for Brighton and Kilmarnock. The stopper centre half, reportedly much against his will, would be the actual centre half, the accomplished Jack Butler, previously the pivot of the half-back line, known as the 'Busy Bees', that also included Alf Baker and Billy Blyth. Blyth too would adopt a new role.

The first team to experience the new Arsenal was West Ham United, who were soundly beaten 4–0 at Upton Park the following Monday. The so-called Third Back Game, also known as the WM formation, was up and away. The Gunners themselves were launched on the most successful season in their history, recovering powerfully from their disastrous start and finishing second in the Championship to Chapman's former club, Huddersfield Town, who thus completed a hat trick of victories. A part of this success could be ascribed to the arrival in February 1926 of Joe Hulme, a lightning-fast winger, signed from Blackburn Rovers for £3,500 and a future Arsenal 'great'.

Gunning for the Cup

Astutely in 1927 Chapman dropped the 'The' from the Club's name, becoming simply Arsenal. His rationale was that they would now come first on the list of League clubs. Up to this point, Arsenal's record in the FA Cup had not been distinguished. Only four times had they gone beyond the last 32 teams. In 1926 Arsenal had reached the last eight, but then lost away to Swansea Town. The following season things went better; the Gunners reached the Wembley final after a demanding passage. First, a 3–2 victory over Sheffield United at Bramall Lane, next a 1–0 success against Port Vale, though only in a replay. In the fifth round at Highbury, Liverpool succumbed to two goals headed from free kicks, and, also at Highbury, Wolverhampton Wanderers were beaten 2–1 by an extraordinary header. It came from Jack Butler, who met a ball from Joe Hulme with his head from a good 25 yards out, and the Gunners were in the semi-final.

This was played at Stamford Bridge, with Arsenal strongly favoured to beat a Southampton side, whose form had belied

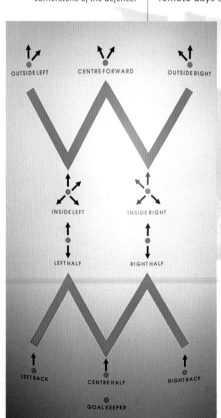

The Third Back game

Also known as the WM formation, Arsenal's tactical masterplan transformed the way the game was played in Britain. The key to the new-look line-up was the addition of an extra man at the back, making the centre half the cornerstone of the defence.

Welsh at Wembley
Arsenal in action against Cardiff City in the FA Cup final at Wembley, 23 April 1927. The Gunners dominated the match but the Welsh team won 1–0 with a goal from Hugh Ferguson in the last quarter of an hour.

its middling position in Division Two. It was a wet and windy day, on which Arsenal were flattered by a 2–1 victory. Goals by Hulme and Charlie Buchan put them 2–0 ahead before Rawlings the Southampton centre forward scored.

A final to forget

Their opponents in the final were Cardiff City, who were aiming to be the first club ever to take the FA Cup out of England. Tom Whittaker, who had been appointed first-team trainer only a couple of months earlier, showed his supreme skills as a healer by getting the right half Alf Baker fit to play. Baker's knee injury was so serious that it seemed a hopeless quest, but Whittaker in his own words worked on it morning, afternoon 'and sometimes far into the night'. Baker promised that if he played, Whittaker would have his Cup final medal. Play he did and was as good as his word, but Whittaker typically refused the gift.

The match turned out to be a mediocre game, played on a slippery pitch and won by one of the most farcical goals ever seen in a Wembley final. The unhappy culprit was the Gunners' Welsh goalkeeper, Dan Lewis, who had recently replaced Bill Harper. Arsenal had had the edge when, after 74 minutes, Cardiff's Scottish centre forward Hugh Ferguson received a throw in from Fred Keenor, Cardiff's famous Welsh international about 25 yards from goal. Ferguson's low shot seemed an easy task for Lewis. But somehow, as if in some horrifying anxiety dream, as Ferguson advanced on him, he lost his grip on the ball, which slid under his left arm. As Lewis turned, he struck the ball with his elbow and it rolled slowly over the line for what was to be the only goal. The Cup had gone to Cardiff.

In the dressing room afterwards, poor Lewis was an inconsolable figure. A team mate tried to console him saying, 'Anyway, though we lost, you've got a medal to show you've been to Wembley.' To which Lewis, head still bowed, miserably replied, 'I haven't. I threw it away in the pitch before we came down the tunnel.'

Other Arsenal players rushed back on to the ground and eventually Bob John found the medal for him. In those Spartan days, there were no such things as Cup final banquets, either for winners or losers. The players' coach took them to Marylebone Station and left them there. It was left to the skipper, Charlie Buchan, to take the players into a nearby pub and buy them a round.

'There were two factors involved,' Tom Whittaker said years later. 'First, the Wembley turf is not played on much and in consequence it polishes the ball. Secondly, Lewis was wearing a new sweater, and it was as shiny as could be.' Three years later, when the Gunners were back at Wembley for the final, with Charlie Preedy in goal, Whittaker made sure to give him a used jersey to wear.

Sound and vision at Highbury

Highbury was the location for two important media firsts. On 22 January 1927 Highbury was the venue for the first radio broadcast of a football match. The game was against Sheffield United and ended in a 1–1 draw. Listeners were able to follow the match with the aid of a grid with numbered squares printed in the Radio Times to represent the pitch.

The commentators referred to the numbers while describing the action. This may be the origin of the phrase, 'back to square one'. Later that year the BBC for the first time broadcast live commentary of the FA Cup final, featuring Arsenal v Cardiff City. The commentator was George Allison, a future Gunners manager. A decade later, Highbury was once again at the forefront of technology, hosting the world's first live television broadcast of a football match on 16 September 1937. The event was a practice game between Arsenal's first team and the reserves.

New season, new stars

1927/28 was something of an anticlimactic season for the Gunners. They came tenth in the League, victims of their defensive inadequacy; they scored 82 goals but conceded

86. But they had a good run in the FA Cup, reaching the semi-finals. It would be the last season for the iconic Charlie Buchan, though his League record, 30 appearances for 16 goals, suggests that he could well have carried on. He had been a colossal influence on Arsenal, their tactics and their prowess from the moment his tall, strong, angular frame arrived at Highbury.

That season saw Jack Lambert make 16 appearances in the attack, as he had the season before. Herbie Roberts, a tall, auburn-haired centre half from Oswestry Town, had just three games, having played twice the season before. Lambert and he had both joined the Gunners in 1926. A Yorkshireman, Lambert had come from Doncaster Rovers, and seemed, though not to Chapman, the ideal bustling, fearless centre forward to exploit Arsenal's breakaway game. Chapman tried in vain to replace him with technically more accomplished centre forwards bought for substantial fees such as Ernie Coleman, Jimmy Dunne and Dave Halliday. Lambert kept coming back and was still working for Arsenal, at their nursery club in Margate, when he was killed in a motor cycle accident in 1940. His record 98 goals in 143 League games were testament enough to his value.

Hapgood at Highbury

In October 1927 the 19-year-old Edris Albert 'Eddie' Hapgood, future left back and captain of Arsenal and England, took the train from Kettering to London to join the Gunners. During the journey he unwisely got embroiled in a gamble and lost all his money. The disconsolate Hapgood was met on the platform by Punch McEwan, Arsenal's irrepressible coach, who laughed at his woes but told him, 'It's all right son, you're with Arsenal now and everything will be taken care of.' Herbert Chapman was reputed to have said that Punch's exuberance 'was worth almost a goal start to Arsenal when the lads were feeling a bit down at half time.'

Remarkably Hapgood had scarcely played football until he was 18 years old. An amateur player, he'd been driving a milk cart for his brother in law's dairy when he was spotted and approached by Bristol Rovers. When they asked him to turn professional, guaranteeing a first team place, he refused, being unwilling to drive a coal cart in summer for one of the directors. Instead, he chose the non-League team Kettering

Town. His transfer fee from Kettering was £1,000, but for Arsenal, this elegant defender would prove priceless. He was a fragile youth at the time and was often knocked out when he headed the ball. Tom Whittaker decided he needed building up, and weaned him from a vegetarian diet on to plentiful steaks. This was somewhat to the dismay of Joe Hulme, who had been sharing digs with Hapgood and eating his share of the meat. Hapgood made just three Division One appearances that season, but 17 the season after, and by season 1929/30 he was solidly established, missing only four Championship games and winning an FA Cup medal.

Chapman goes shopping

Arsenal were unlucky to miss the 1928 FA Cup final, since in the semi-final they had outplayed Blackburn Rovers for much of the match. Their approach, however controversial, was well established by then. Herbert Chapman's dictum was that when his team went on to the field, it did so with one point at 0–0. If in that game the team didn't concede a goal, it would come off the field with that one point. Counter-attack was king. 'We liked the other side to do more of the attacking,' the prolific Cliff Bastin once said.

To replace Charlie Buchan, Chapman enterprisingly brought in the elegant, elusive David Jack. A formidable goal-scorer with a glorious swerve, Jack had left Plymouth Argyle for

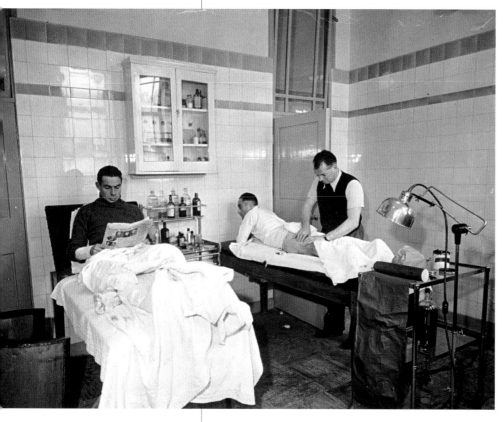

pioneer in the use of massage and electrical stimuli in the treatment of muscle injuries and developed into a world expert in the field of football injuries. With Herbert Chapman's backing he built a treatment room at the ground which became well known as the most advanced infirmary for wounded footballers anywhere. Whittaker filled the facility with the most up-to-date equipment available, including sunlamps, heat lamps and electrical equipment. Whittaker's ability to get players fit quicker than anybody else in the game was a huge advantage for Chapman in an era when first-team squads were far smaller than they are today.

Left-wing partnership

In the 1928/29 season Arsenal finished ninth in the Championship, and reached the sixth round of the FA Cup, where they lost 1–0 away to Aston Villa, Tom Parker unluckily putting the ball through his own goal. In the close season, there were two arrivals of supreme significance, destined to form an illustrious partnership on the left wing; Cliff Bastin and Alex James.

James, the small, sturdy Scottish international inside left, came for another large fee, £9,000 from Preston North End. Chapman wanted him to lurk in midfield and ply the attack with his passes, a role to which James took a few months to adapt. Once he did, however, the transformation was phenomenally effective. Waiting for the clearance or the loose ball, there would be a preliminary flapping of unbuttoned sleeves, a foot would flutter deceptively over the ball, a defender or two would be thrown off balance, then: the pass. It could be to the left wing, where Cliff Bastin lurked – though he didn't hug the touchline, as some have said – a perfectly calibrated ball through the middle, chased by the dreadnought Jack Lambert, or a cross-field pass to the right wing where Joe Hulme could use his speed.

Cliff Bastin, was a quiet, reserved Devonian. A prodigy, who would gain the nickname of Boy Bastin, he was playing Third Division football at inside forward for Exeter City at the age of 15. Extraordinarily composed and mature for a teenager, he had scant interest in playing for Exeter City reserves, preferring to turn out and enjoy himself with local teams such as St Mark's, in the Bible Class League. When he reached the age of 17, Exeter City's directors offered him £4

Healing hands

Tom Whittaker works his magic with Wilf Copping and Norman Sidey in the state-of-the-art treatment room at Highbury, 17 November 1936. Arsenal were years ahead of their time in providing advanced medical equipment at their ground, and led the world in the treatment of football injuries.

Bolton Wanderers, for whom he scored the first FA Cup final goal in the new Wembley Stadium, against West Ham United in 1923 in the so-called 'White Horse Final'. Jack cost the Gunners the then record fee of £10,890. In his first season at Highbury he was leading scorer, with 25 goals in 31 games.

Training and treatment at Highbury

The training regime at Highbury was perhaps the most advanced in the game at that time. This is underlined by an incident early in David Jack's career at Highbury. One day he didn't arrive for training and Tom Whittaker was sent to find out why. There Whittaker found him smoking heavily, his feet on the mantelpiece. 'Oh, I'm all right,' he said, 'but I always had Thursdays off at Bolton!' Such laxity was unknown at Highbury, which in the late 1920s became the most advanced centre for the treatment of sporting injuries in Britain, and perhaps the world.

Until this time, medical care for footballers' ailments was basic by today's standards. But the provision of therapy for players was revolutionised by Arsenal, and by Tom Whittaker, in particular. Whittaker, who had studied anatomy, was a

for first team appearances and £3 in the reserves. He scornfully turned them down, insisting on what was then the maximum of £5 a week; and eventually got it. When he was approached in spring 1929 to join Arsenal, he had reservations, being concerned not to risk losing his accruing benefit money. Nor were Arsenal yet the force they were going to become. Chapman had to use all his powers of persuasion to get Bastin, who was more concerned with playing a tennis match, to agree to the move. Bastin would sign only if his beloved mother were in favour. Her response was 'I've never stood in your way, Cliff. Do just as you please.' Bastin signed.

It was this astonishingly cool temperament, plus of course his huge talent, which would make Bastin such a precocious player. When he reported to Highbury for pre-season training, he was stopped by the commissionaire and asked what he wanted. Somewhat surprised, Bastin answered that he wanted to join the rest of the Arsenal players. Bastin recalled, 'He patted me benevolently on the back and edged me towards the door. "Well, sonny," he said, "you're a bit young at the moment, but never mind! One day you may be good enough to play for Arsenal!"'

Bastin makes his presence felt

Bastin began his Arsenal career in the reserves and was perfectly happy to play for them. But when the first team's form fell away, culminating in a loss at home to Bolton Wanderers in September 1929, Chapman brought Bastin into the first team at inside right, with David Jack moving from there to centre forward. The outside left was Charlie Jones, the Welsh international who had arrived from Nottingham Forest, who would settle down to give his best as a right half.

After some indifferent performances Bastin was dropped from the first team for the last few months of 1929, until Boxing Day, when Chapman picked him for the team against Portsmouth at outside left. Bastin had not played the position since he was nine years old. But subjected to what he called Chapman's 'hypnotic power of convincing', he left Chapman's office convinced he had long been an established left winger. Bastin's admiration for and trust in Chapman was infinite. In the event Arsenal, who had beaten Portsmouth 1–0 at Fratton Park on Christmas Day, then lost at home on Boxing Day, Bastin setting up their only goal.

Campaigning for the Cup

With the New Year came an FA Cup third round tie at Highbury against Chelsea, then in Division Two. Charlie Jones was expected to resume on the left wing, but Bastin kept his place, scoring the Gunners' second goal in the 2–0 victory. Bastin scored again at Highbury in the fourth round of the Cup in a clash with Birmingham City. The result was a 2–2 draw, which meant a replay at Saint Andrew's. This was to be the watershed for Alex James, who got out of a sick bed to flourish at last. Alf Baker's penalty won the game, 1–0.

Now the team was flying. They won 2–0 at Middlesbrough in the fifth round, 3–0 in the sixth at West Ham, and were odds on to beat Hull City, due eventually to be relegated from

Jack's winner at Villa
David Jack scores the winner for Arsenal against Hull City in the FA Cup semi-final replay at Villa Park, 26 March 1930, after the first game at Leeds ended 2–2. The Gunners won the replay 1–0 .

Division Two, in the semi-final at Leeds. In fact, they struggled to get a draw, coming back from 2–0 down at half time, with goals from David Jack and Cliff Bastin.

The replay took place at Villa Park and was an unpleasant affair. 'Some of the Hull players,' as Hapgood remarked, 'tried to play without the ball,' and Childs, their centre half, was eventually sent off (a rarity in those days). Six minutes later, Arsenal scored the winner. Alex James's typical cross-field pass sent Joey Williams down the right flank, and David Jack scored with a right-footed volley.

A glorious return to Wembley

So Arsenal, after a three-year gap, were at Wembley again, and the opposition turned out to be none other than Huddersfield Town, a team full of renowned internationals, and the club Herbert Chapman had so memorably transformed, winners of three successive Championships and of the FA Cup itself in 1922. Arsenal would have to play

without two of their regular defenders. Injury to the unlucky Herbert Roberts meant that the reserve centre-half Bill Seddon took his place.

Unluckier still was Dan Lewis, whose injured knee robbed him of the chance to atone for his disaster in 1927. So the gloriously erratic Charlie Preedy would keep goal. Bought from Wigan, a noted practical joker sometimes the butt of jokes on himself, the Cup Final programme said of him: 'Preedy never hesitates to leave his goal if he thinks the occasion demands.' 'In the event,' Cliff Bastin recalled, 'Charlie's far too daring antics nearly caused heart failure among his colleagues … For there was Charlie, rushing out of his goal at every other moment; either missing the ball completely or making a brilliant save.'

On the way to the ground, a relaxed Alex James had said to Bastin, 'If we get a free kick, Cliff, and it's in my section of the field, I'm going to slip you a very quick pass. I want you to draw the defence, then let me have the ball back, and I'll

crash it into the net.' This met with laughter, but James was serious. After 17 minutes, James was fouled midway inside the opposing half. He snatched up the ball, placed it, shouted, 'Back, Cliff!' gave it to Bastin, who went up the wing, drawing the England right back Roy Goodall towards him. In the penalty box, he saw that Huddersfield's attention was focused on Jack Lambert and David Jack. Bastin passed to James, who, having been nodded permission to take the free kick, ran a few paces then scored. Joe Hulme and Jack Lambert should really have added other goals before half time, but eventually seven minutes from the end, Arsenal scored a characteristic second. A long ball down the middle from Alex James enabled Lambert to shake off a tackle and run on to score. It was a watershed moment in the Club's history – Arsenal's first FA Cup win and their first major trophy. Many more would follow.

Conquering heroes
The victorious Arsenal team are mobbed by thousands of excited fans after beating Huddersfield in the FA Cup final. The Gunners were given a civic reception at Islington Town Hall to celebrate the team's first-ever victory in the competition.

From Cup victory to Championship success

The 1930/31 season saw the Gunners win their first League Championship with a record 66 points and a staggering 127 goals. Of these, no fewer than 38 were scored by Jack Lambert in only 34 games. David Jack got 31, Cliff Bastin, who didn't miss a match, 28. Bill Harper returned from America to play 19 games in goal. At Highbury the fans were treated to a feast of goals from the Gunners, including a 7–1 defeat of Blackpool, with hat-tricks by David Jack and Jimmy Brain, and their biggest ever home victory of 9–1 against Grimsby Town. There were also away successes: notably victory against Chelsea at Stamford Bridge, in which Arsenal came back from 1–0 to score five goals in the last half an hour.

'This Arsenal team,' wrote Bastin, 'was the finest eleven I ever played in. And, without hesitation, I include in that generalisation international teams as well. Never before had

there been such a team put out by any club – and never since have I seen it rivalled.' Yet in the fourth round of the FA Cup, the Gunners went down 2–1 at Chelsea. Arsenal finished that season as Champions with a record-breaking 66 points. They had lost only four games.

A stadium fit for champions

Arsenal's success on the pitch was soon to be reflected in major changes to their stadium. The purchase of the freehold of the 10-acre site in 1925, along with consistently high attendances at Highbury, meant that Arsenal could

press ahead with development, and the serious work began in the summer of 1931. The initial phase of development involved extensions to the terracing at the north and south ends of the ground that added an extra third in area, and to lay the foundations for the planned new West Stand.

The first steps were rather rudimentary, involving the dumping of tons of rubbish on the ground. In an imaginative ploy to increase the height of the banking at the ground, and therefore its capacity, Arsenal asked neighbouring residents to bring their rubbish to the ground, to provide a base for the rebuilding. It is from this period that the legend of the horse entombed for eternity in the North Bank dates.

According to the story, a coalman brought his horse and cart loaded with hard core to Highbury, and prepared to tip it into the hole where the new North Bank would stand. The horse stepped too close to the pit, tumbled in, and died of its injuries. Rather than hauling the carcass of the unfortunate beast out of its makeshift grave, it was simply buried without ceremony under more debris. Decades later works beneath the North Bank failed to uncover the remains of the horse, so

it remains unclear whether this story is based on fact or is just a colourful legend.

While the North Bank received only a basic remodelling, more ambitious plans were laid for the West Stand. To create the design, the Board appointed Claude Waterlow Ferrier, an acclaimed Scottish architect, who had travelled widely in Europe. Working with W.A. Binnie, with whom he formed a partnership in 1927, he had a formidable record, having designed Trafalgar House, the Army and Navy Club in Pall Mall, the National Institute for the Blind and the Western Synagogue off the Edgware Road. Work on the new stand would not begin until the summer of 1932. Meanwhile there was a full season of football to be played.

England v Spain at Highbury

Highbury, even prior to the building of the West Stand, was regarded as one of the nation's premier stadiums, and in December 1931 was called upon to host a return friendly between the national teams of England and Spain. In May 1929, on a boiling hot day in Madrid, Spain had become the

Pain for Spain

Ricardo Zamora saves for Spain at the Clock End during a Spain v England match at Highbury in December 1931. Despite this near miss, England managed to win 7–1.

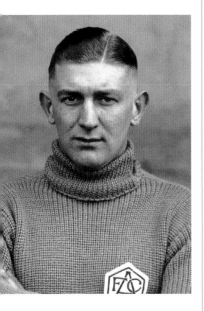

Frank Moss

Frank Moss, Arsenal's goalkeeper 1931–36. The Lancastrian joined the Gunners from Oldham Athletic in November 1931, and played four games for England. He made 143 League appearances for Arsenal.

first foreign team ever to beat England, the result being 4–3. Such was the impassioned interest in the return game that gates were smashed down by fans desperate to get in. England took a fearsome revenge on the Spanish team, winning 7–1 against a team whose renowned goalkeeper, Ricardo Zamora, had one of his few disastrous games.

Strengthened squad

The season of 1931/32 was to be a season of anticlimax, but the establishment of some outstanding players in the first team provided plenty of high points for the supporters at Highbury. At Christmas 1930, George Male, the future England right back and ideal partner for Eddie Hapgood, had made his first team debut at left half, in the 7–1 victory against Blackpool. Male had joined Arsenal from the amateurs, Clapton and gave, according to a reporter, 'an exceedingly promising display'. He became more established in the first team in 1931/32. Another important newcomer was Frank Moss, in goal. Eddie Hapgood thought him one of the best goalkeepers of his time, but his fine career was doomed to be cut sadly short by a constantly dislocated shoulder. A Lancastrian, Moss began with the Leyland Motors works team, where he himself was employed. Preston North End signed him but let him go to Oldham, where he was second choice to the England international, Jack Hacking. In 1931 Chapman signed him and he was instantly successful at Highbury, making 27 League appearances.

February 1932 saw the arrival of a tall teenager from the Hampstead amateur club, the full back Leslie Compton. That first season, he played just four League games and by the time war broke out in 1939 he had still not found a regular first-team place, despite playing a couple of England international trials. His career would blossom much later when he would win two full international caps as a 38-year-old in 1950. A fine cricketer – Middlesex's wicket keeper – as well as a footballer, his career would be overshadowed by his outstanding younger brother, Denis.

A winning winter

Losing all three Christmas games in 1931, the Gunners didn't really get into their stride until the New Year, chasing Everton at the top of the Championship, forging ahead in the FA Cup.

They put 11 goals past non-League Darwen, beat Plymouth Argyle at home, Portsmouth away, and knocked out Huddersfield Town at Leeds Road in the sixth round. Manchester City pressed them hard in the semi-final at Villa Park, and it wasn't until the 89th minute that Arsenal broke away, Bastin sending a long pass to the right flank. Lambert chased it, Felton, the City left back, chose to let the ball run out of play, but Lambert reached it, crossed, and Bastin shot home. Arsenal had once again reached the Cup final.

James misses out

Newcastle United would be the opposition at Wembley. Five days earlier, Chapman, for once in disagreement with Tom Whittaker, decided that neither Alex James nor Joe Hulme would be fit for the final, so neither was among the 14-man squad that went down for seaside training at Brighton. That Wednesday the *Daily Mail* published the team Chapman announced, with the young Pat Beasley at outside right and Bastin and John on the left wing. Then something strange

HIGHBURY HEROES

Alex James 1929/30–1936/37

James was already a famous figure, having previously played for Raith Rovers and Scotland, when Chapman bought him from Preston North End. Playing at inside left, he was one of the glorious Wembley Wizards of 1928, the Scotland forward line of little men that thrashed England 5–1 at Wembley James himself scoring one of the goals. At Arsenal he made 231 League appearances, being on the losing side in only 48 of these. He gained four League Championship medals and two FA Cup winners' medals. After retiring as a player, he returned to the Club to coach the junior teams, until his premature death in 1953.

On the spot
Alex James takes a penalty at Highbury during Arsenal's 2–0 win v Blackpool, 20 February 1932. The Highbury clock can be seen in the background next to the scoreboard over the North Bank, where it was originally sited.

happened; the influential L.V. Manning, of the *Daily Sketch*, actually persuaded James to come to Highbury, bringing Hulme with him, and had the two photographed running round the track, with the provocative headline, 'The two fittest men in football are out of the Cup Final'.

A furious Chapman threatened to sack John Peters the long-serving assistant secretary, for allowing such an intrusion, but he summoned both players to Brighton, announcing that they would try out secretly on the Brighton and Hove Albion ground the following morning. In the event, there were 40 photographers in attendance. First to be rigorously tested by Tom Whittaker and other players was Joe Hulme. Chapman was the last to be satisfied, ordering, 'Give him another tackle, Tom!' until at last he called, 'All right, Joe, you'll do', to the dismay of Pat Beasley; who would have similar disappointment before the 1936 Cup final.

Next, it was Alex James to be put through the ordeal. According to some sources, James seemed fit enough to play till Tom Whittaker at the behest of Chapman put him through one last hard tackle. Whittaker, however, told the tale somewhat differently. He has described how James passed

all the tests he was put through, until Chapman called a halt, and told James he would be playing. Perhaps he would have done had not a photographer, arriving late, pleaded for a picture. A ball was thrown out, Whittaker tackled James yet again, but this time the little Scot collapsed in agony and he was out of the Cup final.

Who would take James' place? In Bastin's view, Chapman made the wrong choices. On the train back to London from Brighton, he told Bastin that he would be playing inside left. This was logical given it had always been Bastin's preferred position. But he hadn't, he recalled, played the position for a long while. He later remembered 'I was even more surprised when I learned that George Male was to be left half and Bob John outside left.' Male having come to Highbury as a right half, while 'Bob was never really happy on the wing'.

The Over the Line final

Arsenal began that final brightly enough, going ahead after 14 minutes with a somewhat fortuitous goal scored by Bob John. Bastin sent Hulme away down the right. McInroy, Newcastle's keeper, and Nelson, their right back, collided in pursuit of the

Arsenal shirt badge
This badge design appeared on the jerseys of the Arsenal team through the 1930s. Shirt badges were yet another of Herbert Chapman's innovations.

ball, which bounced loose and was headed in by Bob John. Newcastle United then equalised with the notorious 'Over The Line' goal. Eddie Hapgood, anticipating the Newcastle outside right, Boyd, who had cut inside, hit a long ball in the direction of Jack Lambert. It never got there. Davison the Newcastle centre half intercepted, and sent another long ball down the right wing. It was chased by the inside right Richardson, who reached it when it seemed clearly to have run over the goal line, crossed it at full pelt, and enabled Allen to head the equaliser past Frank Moss. Bastin said later, 'We all knew quite well it had gone out of play. So, apparently, did everyone, except the referee.'

In the second half Arsenal had several good opportunities. With David Jack now at centre forward, Lambert at inside left, Bastin at inside right, Jack of all people missed an open goal at point blank range. But Allen scored one more goal for Newcastle, which turned out to be the winning goal. Arsenal had finished the season without honours.

The West Stand takes shape

While the end of season 1931/32 turned out to be a disappointment in footballing terms for the Gunners, the close season of 1932 saw the Club beginning work on the magnificent and innovatory West Stand, which would bring Arsenal Stadium to the forefront of the nation's football grounds. Until now this area of Highbury had been an uncovered standing paddock, but this was replaced with one of the most modern and architecturally distinctive stands in the country. Where there had previously been uncovered banking, now there would rise a structure far ahead of its football times, a masterpiece of art deco design.

Speed was of the essence. The structure of the West Stand had to be ready by the start of the following season. This Messrs Wilson Lovatt and Sons, starting just hours after the last match of the season, accomplished in record time; the completed stand was ready a full six weeks ahead of the contract date by Christmas 1932. At £45,000, it was the most expensive football stand in Britain, and was built to seat 4,100 spectators, with standing room for 17,000 more. The subcontractors Messrs Redpath Brown and Co. used over 650

Chapman's crest
This Club crest first appeared in the plans for the new West Stand and may have been designed by the architects Ferrier and Binnie. It has also been suggested that Chapman had a hand in its design. It was subsequently widely used in the fabric of the stadium, including over the door to the Marble Halls in the East Stand.

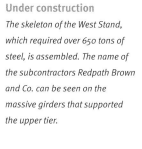

Under construction

The skeleton of the West Stand, which required over 650 tons of steel, is assembled. The name of the subcontractors Redpath Brown and Co. can be seen on the massive girders that supported the upper tier.

tons of steel in the construction of the stand's 'skeleton'. Messrs Samuel Williams and Sons then built the reinforced concrete steppings that form the upper tier.

The finished stand, which stood 70 feet tall and was 315 feet long, incorporated three flats – an innovation that was to prefigure Highbury's future 75 years down the line. The stand even had an electric lift, which whisked spectators from street level to the dizzying altitudes at the top of the stand. Obstruction by the number and size of the supporting columns had been reduced to a minimum. The seats (according to the brochure produced to commemorate the occasion) were of the 'especially designed armchair type', and the roofs had 'the agreeable colouring and enamelled surface of the Vitrelfex steel sheeting', a recent innovation. The pitch also received radical attention. It was entirely remade and a practice field was laid out by the Club's own staff behind the south stand. The Club were fiercely proud of their addition to the north London cityscape, and they were honoured to be able to persuade the Prince of Wales to perform the official opening on 10 December 1932. The commemorative brochure declared, 'In graciously consenting to inaugurate the new buildings of the Arsenal Stadium, His Royal Highness The Prince of Wales has conferred a signal honour, not only upon the Arsenal Football Club, but also upon Association Football as a whole, and his visit, commemorated by this brief record, will ever remain a red-letter day in the annals of the game.' Arsenal celebrated by thrashing Chelsea 4–1.

Famous frontage
The distinctive lettering on the Highbury Hill entrance to the West Stand was at the time the last word in modern design. The entrance would be preserved a part of Highbury's redevelopment.

The opening of the West Stand

On the day the West Stand was opening, Arsenal published a justifiably triumphant illustrated supplement 'A Brief Record' of the Stadium.

'Twenty years ago', it began, 'the area of the ground which is now the Arsenal Stadium formed part of the playing field of St John's College of Divinity and was bordered by lofty trees. In this picture of sylvan calm there was no hint of the pomp and circumstance to come. Few dreamed then of the towering structures, the mighty multitudes, the cheers and groans, the colours and the rattles and all the other appurtenances of professional football which were soon to arrive at Highbury Hill. And twenty years ago few visualised the needy Woolwich Arsenal as being within two decades an outstanding member of the Great Football Association and, under its present name of Arsenal Football Club, celebrating the completion of a magnificent stadium.

'Great indeed has been the change since the club moved its headquarters in 1913. The muddy banks of earth excavated from the Piccadilly Tube up which early enthusiasts had to clamber to view the game, have, like the grove trees which preceded them, disappeared in their turn beneath the spacious concrete terraces which now surround the north, south and west sides of the pitch; and in 1914 was completed the single deck stand for 11,000 spectators upon the eastern side, which also houses the administrative offices of the Club and accommodation for the teams.

'The outbreak of war (1914) precluded further developments at the time, nor was it found possible in

the early post war years to effect any material improvements. In 1925, however, a new epoch commenced. Mr. Herbert Chapman was in this year appointed to the post of manager. Under his brilliant guidance the team entered into such a period of success that additional accommodation became imperative, the increasingly vast crowd who clamoured for admission having frequently to be denied for lack of room. No opportunity was neglected to effect minor improvements and extensions, but still there was not sufficient space to satisfy the demand which never ceased to grow. In consequence in the latter part of the year (1931) a start was made to put into effect a scheme of the comprehensive remodelling of the ground, of which the new West Stand ... is the culminating feature.'

West Stand story

The photographs below tell the story of the building of the stand in 1932, from the drawing produced in May, to the construction of iron skeleton in June and July, and the completion of the stand in November.

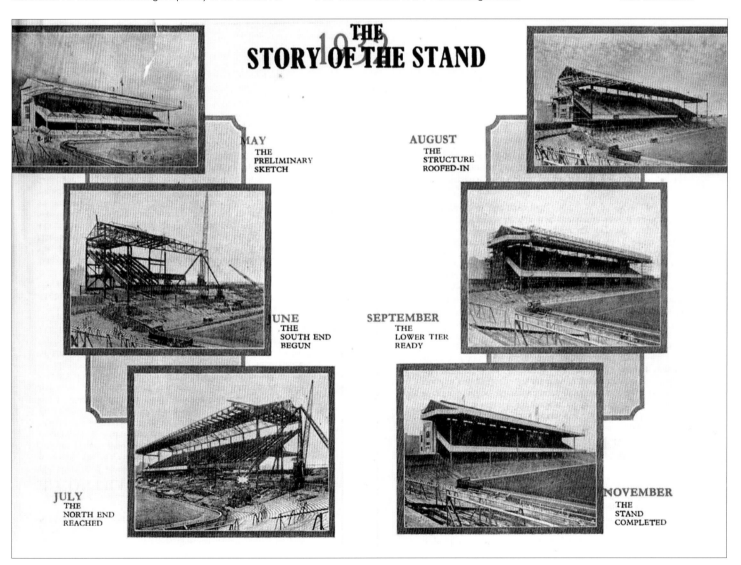

THE STORY OF THE STAND
1932

MAY
THE
PRELIMINARY
SKETCH

AUGUST
THE
STRUCTURE
ROOFED-IN

JUNE
THE
SOUTH END
BEGUN

SEPTEMBER
THE
LOWER TIER
READY

JULY
THE
NORTH END
REACHED

NOVEMBER
THE
STAND
COMPLETED

Chapman the innovator

For Herbert Chapman, innovation both on and off the field was ever the name of the game. The tactical changes he instigated togther with Charlie Buchan have already been described. And there was a constant exchange of ideas with his two great friends Vittorio Pozzo and Hugo Meisl, respectively the inspirational leaders of the Italian and Austrian national teams.

In 1929 Chapman had suggested a 10 yard arc at the edge of the penalty area, guarding against encroachment by players. This was rejected by the FA, only to be adopted in 1937. He was also the first to propose rubber studs on football boots, all weather pitches and roofed stadiums.

In November 1932, on the eve of a London Conference to discuss the possibilities of floodlit football, Arsenal staged such a game successfully at Highbury. The Football Association disapproved of this innovation and it would be 1951 before the footballing establishment would catch up with Chapman's thinking and allow the Club to stage such a game again.

Cliff Bastin 1929/30–1946/47

Plucked out of Division Three, where he was playing for Exeter City, by Herbert Chapman, Cliff Bastin was undoubtedly one of the Arsenal 'greats'. A lethally effective winger, his record of 178 League goals for the Club stood for 50 years before being overtaken by Ian Wright. He finished his footballing career with five Championship medals, two FA Cup winners' medals and 21 England caps. He died in 1991.

The badge, the station and the clock

Chapman also had a keen understanding of the importance of the Club's image, from redesigning the Club badge (see p.66) to improving the stadium and hosting matches against leading foreign teams. He wanted to put Arsenal on the map in a literal sense, by renaming the Gillespie Road underground station near the ground after the club. He thought that if the station were to be called Arsenal, it would increase the Club's status, and also be good for business. At first the officials of the London Electric Railway opposed the plan, suspecting (quite correctly) that Arsenal's motives were commercially inspired. But in the end, in the face of Chapman's determined and

Muscle man

It looks like an instrument of torture, but Alex James is testing a revolutionary piece of training equipment called 'the muscle developer' at Highbury, 6 December 1932. Arsenal led the way for other clubs to follow in groundbreaking new training methods.

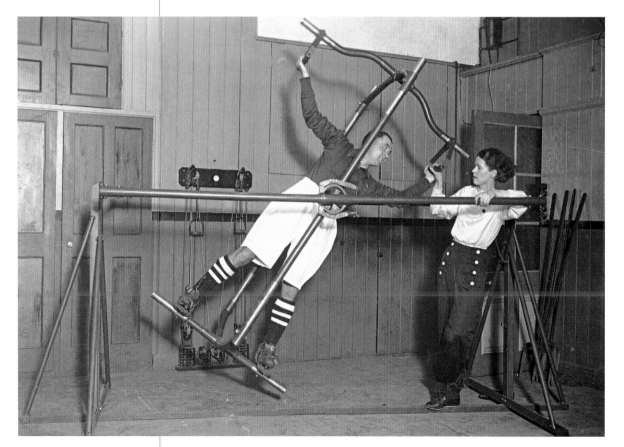

persuasive campaign, they relented. Gillespie Road was renamed Arsenal in November 1932, just a few weeks before the magnificent new West Stand was opened, although in the early 21st century travellers to the station could still spot the name Gillespie Road on the original platform tiles.

In 1928 Chapman also added a famous landmark to the Stadium – a huge 12-foot diameter clock that could be seen from every point in the ground, was placed over the North Bank. Chapman originally wanted the clock to be a 45-minute one, so that the fans could see how much time was left in each half. The FA objected to this, arguing that keeping time was the referee's area of responsibility, and fearing crowd disorder if there was any disagreement with the referee's time-keeping. Chapman compromised and installed a conventional 12-hour clock. It was a useful addition for Arsenal's crowd, and that was enough reason for Chapman. When the North Bank was roofed in 1935, the clock was moved to the south terracing, which subsequently became known as the Clock End.

Team numbers

Another of Chapman's innovations was the introduction of numbers on shirts, which he felt would help the players position themselves more effectively in relationship to each other. This was first done experimentally in August 1928 in an away game against Sheffield Wednesday. The idea was revived for Arsenal's match against Vienna in December 1933 (see below), but it was not until 1939 that the Football League finally accepted the idea.

The first of three

The 1932/33 season started with the fanfare that accompanied the opening of the new West Stand and ended with the celebration of another Championship victory. There had been important team changes. It had been time to replace the admirable Tom Parker who, since his arrival from Southampton, had missed just two games in his initial five full seasons, making 155 consecutive appearances, playing in three FA Cup finals, as captain in two of them. And so it was that Chapman called George Male into his office as a young reserve

wing half, and sent him forth as a future England right back. The 22-year-old Male was at first astonished when Chapman told him he was to fill his new position, but, 'By the time I got out of that office,' he said, 'I wasn't only convinced that I was a full blown right back, I knew without doubt that I was the best right back in the country!'

Alex James in season 1932/33 played 40 of the 42 Championship games, scored just three goals but remained the fulcrum of the attack. Jack Lambert made only a dozen League appearances that season, yet they brought him 14 goals, five of them scored on Christmas Eve 1932 at Highbury against Sheffield United, who were annihilated 9–2. Bastin called it the greatest performance of Lambert's career.

The team were now playing in the red shirts with white sleeves. The story goes that Chapman was inspired by the sight of a woman in the crowd wearing a red sleeveless top over a white shirt and decided to copy that look.

The Gunners regained the Championship in a blaze of goals and glory. Highpoints as the season neared its end included a 5–0 beating of

Clocking on
Builders put a Highbury icon into position on 28 August 1928. The famous clock would soon be slotted into the frame next to the scoreboard above the North Bank.

Ticket for the Reds
A ticket for the match against Portsmouth on 4 November 1933. This seat, an expensive one in the West Stand, cost five shillings.

Aston Villa. The team scored no fewer than 118 goals. An astonishing 33 of those goals went to Cliff Bastin, playing on the left wing, and not missing a game. Ernie Coleman, one of the centre forwards Chapman bought in the hope of replacing Jack Lambert, was the second highest scorer with 24 goals in only 27 games. Coleman had come from Grimsby Town that season for £8,000. By the following season, he was no more than a marginal figure, and went to Middlesbrough in 1934.

Yet that same season Arsenal suffered an astonishing 2–0 away defeat by humble Third Division Walsall in the third round of the FA Cup in January 1933, one of the most sensational results in the history of the competition. With a squad hit by illness and injury, Chapman was forced to use many reserve players. The team, which nevertheless included first-team stalwarts such as Moss, Male, Jack and Bastin, on that day was powerless against the vigorous tackling and the quagmire pitch at Fellows Park.

For once appearing to despise his enemy, Chapman gave chances to a couple of youngsters, Billy Warnes, an amateur outside right, and the ambitious centre forward Charlie Walsh. After Chapman had given the team their pre-match instructions, Walsh assured him that he was raring to go. At which Chapman glanced at him quizzically and said, 'you'd better put your stockings on, or the crowd will laugh at you'. In his anxiety, Walsh had forgotten to change out of his socks and suspenders, The second Walsall goal came when Tommy Black, deputising at left back, gave away a penalty. He was promptly transferred to Plymouth. Bastin felt that Walsall had been bruising opponents.

European visitors

By the 1933/34 season, two new centre forwards had arrived: big, blond Irishman Jimmy Dunne from Sheffield United and Ted Drake, who was to become a legendary figure for the

Numbers game
Arsenal put another Chapman-inspired innovation into effect, wearing numbers on their backs to help the crowd identify the players, 4 December 1933. The Gunners hosted a Vienna XI in a friendly match at Highbury, which the home team won 4–2.

Pre-season training
*Arsenal players led by David Jack
putting in the hard yards in front
of the Clock End at Highbury
before the start of the 1933/34
season on 4 August 1933. The
Gunners finished the campaign as
Champions once again.*

Club. At Highbury on 4 December 1933, Arsenal showed their formidable power by defeating Austria's so-called Wunderteam – playing as Vienna since English clubs were forbidden to play international teams. The Austrians, who had given England a fright at Chelsea a year earlier, though they eventually lost 4–3, had just drawn 2–2 with Scotland in Glasgow, somewhat fortunately. Then they came down to London and on the Saturday watched Arsenal play Liverpool in the League. 'We may lose,' said one of their officials, 'we know that, but after seeing Arsenal play, we know we shall be the better footballers.'

The match was an absorbing contrast between two very different schools of football; the functional and the romantic. Arsenal rose to the occasion, playing their best football for weeks: 35,000 fans on that midweek afternoon saw their Welsh international wing halves, Charlie Jones and Bob John, take a firm hold on Austria's short-passing attackers. With

Arsenal 3–1 up and the minutes ebbing away the Austrians at last got into their stride. Switching positions, gliding past opponents, they dominated the play. Schall, the hard-shooting inside left, made it 3–2, Szesta, the muscular left back, headed a corner kick against the bar: then Arsenal, typically, counter attacked, for Bastin to make it 4–2. It had been a memorable game and the result flattered the Gunners.

'We learned three vital lessons from Arsenal,' said Hugo Meisl, the Austrian supremo. 'One was that we must play a more open game. Our inside forwards were prone to keep the ball too close. Another thing demonstrated to us that our play is not fast enough. We must develop our speed. I also realised that our covering was ineffective. Arsenal's victory has made us feel that club strength in Britain is greater than international strength.' Which may have been true.

Herbert Chapman may have brought in the Third Back Game with all its pragmatism, its devotion to the counter

attack, but he was far too shrewd and broad minded an observer not to lament a more leisurely and artistic era. He wrote: 'It is no longer necessary for a team to play well. They must get the goals, no matter how, and the points. The measure of their skill is, in fact, judged by their position in the League table ... Thirty years ago men went out with the fullest licence to display their arts and crafts. Today, they have to make their contributions to a system. Individuality has to be subordinated to team work ... With us it is a case of goals and points. At times one is persuaded that nothing else matters.'

Chapman's death

The Gunners maintained their ascendancy and retained the Championship in the next two seasons, thus equalling the record set up by Huddersfield Town. But the author of their success did not live to see the team reap the rewards of his visionary leadership. Chapman's sad and premature death, at the age of 55 on 6 January 1934, was surely the consequence of his intense devotion to duty. Always so aware of the needs and welfare of his players, he never spared himself. On Saturday, 30 December, he had taken his team to play Birmingham, a goalless draw. New Year's Day, a Monday, saw him watching Bury play at home to Notts County. On the Tuesday, he was at Hillsbrough to watch Sheffield Wednesday, Arsenal's imminent opponents, play Birmingham. By Wednesday he was suffering from a heavy cold. When Chapman came into the dressing room, complaining of back ache, Tom Whittaker noticed he was looking unwell. 'Relax a while,' he said, 'and then I'll run you back to Brent.' 'I can't, Tom,' was the reply. 'There's a player in a match down at Guildford [where Arsenal's third team were playing] I must see. I'll get back early and go straight to bed.' On Wednesday he went to bed with a high temperature. Pneumonia followed. On Saturday, to the horror and shock of the whole Club, he was dead. 'Chapman had worked himself to a standstill,' wrote Whittaker. 'His resistance had gone and he had nothing left.' He had been to see Chapman at home that Thursday. 'He was tired and weak, but brightened considerably when I told him that I had learned that morning that, for the first time since he had taken over at Highbury, Arsenal were out of debt.' Smiling, Chapman replied, 'That's good news, Tom. Now we can really go places.'

Team tributes

Eddie Hapgood was told the sad news when shaving at home in Finchley. Alice Moss, wife of the goalkeeper, Frank, rushed in, greatly agitated, to tell him. She had seen the newspaper placards. Hapgood was so shocked that for a quarter of an hour he stood dazed, leaving one side of his face lathered. 'Highbury backstage was like a morgue that afternoon and we weren't very keen on the job of playing football.'

Cliff Bastin recalled. 'I could not have felt it more had it been the death of my own father ... In the Arsenal dressing room, nobody had anything to say, yet each of us knew what his companions were thinking. Herbert Chapman had been loved by us all. His fairness, his kind heartedness, his consideration, above all else, for the players under his charge, were qualities which, besides his transcendent genius, ensured a cherished place for him in the memories of all who had come under his magic spell at Highbury.'

At Highbury that afternoon, where the Gunners were at home to Sheffield Wednesday, both teams stood to attention before the game, which was played before a largely silent crowd and drawn, 1–1. The funeral took place four days later before large crowds at St Mary's Church in Hendon. Eddie Hapgood, David Jack, Alex James, Jack Lambert and Joe Hulme were the pall bearers. For several mornings to come, Tom Whittaker heard the clock in his room strike 3am, the time of Chapman's death, though he never heard it chime at any other hour. Bob Wall, who would become secretary of the Club itself, said that for several years to come, he would hear Chapman's steps late in the evening, marching along the upper landing of the stand through the boardroom and cocktail bar, into the Press room and then the stand.

Sad farewell
The North Bank observes a minute's silence for Herbert Chapman before the game against Sheffield Wednesday. The game, which was played out almost in silence, finished 1–1.

The legacy

Although the team's success in the following seasons were perhaps the most fitting memorial, Chapman would be commemorated by an imposing bronze bust by the renowned sculptor Jacob Epstein placed in the soon-to-be-famed marbled entrance hall of the new East Stand, opened in 1936. But who would, who could replace him? The players' choice would have been loyal Joe Shaw, for so many years at the Club as player and official, but Shaw was a shy, self-effacing man, who didn't want the job. Initially he and Whittaker were deputed to run the team, with the help of John Peters.

Allison steps forward

Late in the season, somewhat surprisingly, George Allison was made the new manager. A somewhat controversial choice since Allison, by then 51 years old, had, despite his long connection with the Club, never been a players' man, or any kind of a tactician. Cliff Bastin and Eddie Hapgood never took to him, though they had to acknowledge his skills, as a successful journalist, by then with Hearst Newspapers of America, in projecting and publicising the Club. With his rumbling voice, he was also a popular broadcaster, the first to give radio commentaries on the game, including the 1927 Cup final. Allison once admitted that during a sustained break in one game, when a player was injured, he actually gave a wholly fictitious commentary to fill in the time.

'He was not,' wrote Cliff Bastin years later, 'a successor shaped in the Chapman mould ... With consummate ease, he had the name of Arsenal splashed across the front pages of the British Press, but he lacked Herbert Chapman's gift of getting the best out of his players.' Hapgood wrote: 'He was probably the luckiest football manager of all time. When Mr Allison took over, Arsenal were running on top note, and he kept them there.'

Herbert Chapman is alleged to have told Allison shortly before he died, 'The team's played out, Mr Allison. We must rebuild.' But to Allison's credit until the outbreak of war, Arsenal continued to pile success on success, remaining among the game's most powerful teams. And how could there ever be another Herbert Chapman?

Allison and the war years

George Allison took over a team in dominating form and was able to build on the legacy left by Chapman. The East Stand was magnificently rebuilt and Arsenal went on to win two more First Division titles and the FA Cup before the outbreak of war and the suspension of football at Highbury.

At the start of 1934, in spite of the huge hole left by the loss of Herbert Chapman, and notwithstanding his warnings that the team needed rebuilding, Arsenal was a team in the ascendant. In the immediate aftermath of Chapman's death the traumatised Gunners lost three consecutive games, two of them at home, including a 3–1 defeat in the local derby against Tottenham Hotspur, but the players gradually recovered to win a second successive Championship with 59 points, one more than the previous year, although the total of goals declined steeply from 118 to 75. Of these Cliff Bastin and Ray Bowden (an inside right signed by Chapman in 1933) scored 13 each.

The Club rebuilt

Under George Allison, the footballing management of the team became the responsibility of Joe Shaw, team manager, Tom Whittaker, trainer, and John Peters, secretary. Allison as Club Secretary-Manager was more concerned with the business management of the Club. Under this new regime Arsenal did indeed rebuild as Chapman had recommended, with three major newcomers, making their way into the first team. Ray Bowden replaced David Jack who dropped out at the end of season 1933/34. Jack Crayston, a stylish right half came from Bradford Park Avenue in the 1934 close season. The third addition to the squad was the hugely significant Ted Drake, a battering ram of a centre forward, bought from Southampton in March 1934, who turned out to be the long-sought successor to Jack Lambert. Bowden, who came from Cornwall, had been signed by Plymouth Argyle on his prolific scoring record in local football. He helped them out of the Third Division South, then came to Highbury. A technically gifted player with a swerve not unlike that of his famous predecessor David Jack, his relations with George Allison were not always ideal. Injuries to both ankles tended to take the gloss off his game at Highbury, where his form fluctuated, but at his best he was an outstanding player winning two League medals, one Cup medal and six England caps.

Crayston, who in later years would become assistant manager then manager of Arsenal, had begun his career in League football as a 17-year-old with Barrow. In 1933 he broke both his wrist and his leg, but he recovered well enough for Arsenal to sign him, and he flourished at Highbury. A teetotaller, who was always in bed by 10 o'clock, his skills and ability in the air were complemented by an excellent physique and a formidably long throw in.

Goals galore

Drake was one of a succession of Arsenal footballers who were also accomplished cricketers. In his first full season at Highbury, Drake scored no fewer than 42 goals in 41 games. Hugely powerful, utterly fearless, he cheerfully gave and took knocks and all too often had to be carried off the field on Tom Whittaker's broad shoulders. Perhaps his most remarkable feat came in December 1935 at Villa Park, where he scored all Arsenal's goals in a 7–1 humiliation of Aston Villa. Years later, becoming manager of Chelsea, he would lead them to their first ever Championship in 1955.

Another coup by Arsenal under Allison was the acquisition from Leeds United for £8,000 in 1934 of the rugged left half Wilf Copping. A Yorkshireman from Barnsley, where the local club foolishly turned him down, Copping would say that the first man into a tackle never got hurt, yet his disciplinary record was excellent. Perhaps superstitiously he never shaved before a match. In his first four seasons for the Club he never made fewer than 30 League appearances, and in 1938/39, his final season, he made 26 appearances. He was never more robustly effective than in the match that became famously known as the Battle of Highbury against the recent World Cup victors Italy in November 1934.

Drake in flight
Arsenal's free-scoring centre forward Ted Drake challenges Stoke City goalkeeper Norman Wilkinson at Highbury, March 1937. The match finished goalless, but Arsenal won the title that season by a single point from Wolves.

HIGHBURY HEROES

Ted Drake 1933/35–1938/39

Born in Southampton in 1912, Ted Drake was one of Arsenal's most prolific goal-scorers and one of the most lethal centre forwards in the history of English football.

He signed for the Gunners from Southampton in March 1934 and made an immediate contribution by scoring seven goals in ten games. During his stay at Arsenal he scored 74 goals at Highbury. The highpoint of his career was perhaps the seven goals he scored away against Aston Villa in December 1935. Honours with the Gunners included winners' medals in the League Championship (1934/35, 1937/38) and the FA Cup (1935/36). He was capped for England five times.

The Battle of Highbury

It was the fourth time Highbury had put on an England international. When the England team to meet Italy was announced, five Arsenal players had been chosen: Frank Moss, Wilf Copping, Ray Bowden, Cliff Bastin and Eddie Hapgood. When the first choice right back Tom Cooper withdrew, injured, George Male was called in, the first of his 19 caps. On the Monday, two days before the game, the centre forward, Frank Tilson of Manchester City, dropped out. George Hunt was picked to replace him, but he too cried off, and his replacement was Ted Drake, making seven Arsenal players, a modern record.

Italy's commissario tecnico was Chapman's old friend Vittorio Pozzo, who had based his tactics on those he had studied as an impoverished student, teaching languages across the Midlands, before World War II. No Third Back Game for him. His free-ranging, long-passing centre half was Luisito Monti, nicknamed the Man Who Strolls, though he would not stroll very long at Highbury. In fact he limped off the field after just 90 seconds, when a clash with Ted Drake left him with a broken bone in his foot. Monti claimed that the injury was deliberate, but Drake always denied it.

Drake himself would tell one year afterwards that for the first 20 minutes, England were playing ideal football: 'You couldn't play any better.' Although Italian goalie Ceresoli saved a penalty from the left winger Eric Brook, England went into a 3–0 lead. Brook later atoned, scoring directly from a free kick, after Ceresoli had arrogantly waved away his defensive wall. The longer the game went on, the more violent the frustrated Italians became. In Pozzo's words, they were taking revenge. Hapgood was the victim of Serantoni, the Italian right half, who deliberately smashed an elbow into his face and broke his nose. While Hapgood was being patched up by Tom Whittaker, in the dressing room, Drake scored the third goal for England. Hapgood then jumped up

Derby day
Arsenal fans pack into the North Bank. A vast crowd of 68,828 cram into Highbury to see the north London derby in January 1934. Cliff Bastin scored for the Gunners, but Arsenal lost the match 3–1. Despite that setback Arsenal still won the First Division Championship.

Work begins

Work begins on the demolition of the gabled roof of Archibald Leitch's original grandstand on the east of the stadium in the summer of 1936.

and ran out on to the field again. The second half saw a revitalised Italian team, with Giuseppe Meazza, Italy's graceful, elusive centre forward, scoring twice, and only the gymnastic efforts of Frank Moss in the England goal enabled his team to run out winners at 3–2.

Spurs doubly thrashed

Arsenal duly won their third successive Championship, this time with 58 points, and the satisfaction of a blistering double victory over Spurs: 5–1 at Highbury in front of a crowd of over 70,000 in October 1934; 6–0 at White Hart Lane in March 1935. Other highpoints of the 1934/35 season at Highbury included an 8–0 victory against Leicester City, an 8–1 defeat of Liverpool and an 8–0 win over Middlesbrough, 115 goals in all. That season also saw Highbury attract its highest ever number of spectators. On 9 March 1935, a crowd of 73,295 watched the Gunners draw 0–0 with Sunderland.

Arsenal's command of the Championship was not, however, mirrored by success in the FA Cup. Both in 1933/34 and 1934/35, Arsenal went out of the Cup in the sixth round. In March 1934 they lost 2–1 at home to Aston Villa and a year later they were defeated by the same scoreline away at Sheffield Wednesday. Better things were to come.

The stadium reconstructed

The year after Chapman's death, construction work went on to realise his dream of turning Highbury into the greatest stadium in the country. The extended North Bank was roofed in 1935, and Chapman's giant clock was moved to the opposite end of the ground, which came to be known as the Clock End. Work began on a magnificent new East Stand in 1936. This was sooner than the Club had originally planned, but the old East Stand, which had been built as a temporary structure, was proving too costly to maintain. So although for financial reasons the Club wanted to wait a few years to start the next phase of the Highbury facelift, they decided to press ahead in April 1936. The wreckers moved in at Avenell Road, the old tip-up seats were sold to Ipswich Town, and by the summer of 1936 the old stand had been demolished.

The architect Claude Waterlow Ferrier, who had designed the West Stand had died in 1935, but his partner and

Going down

The stage-by-stage demolition of Archibald Leitch's original grandstand on the east side of the pitch in 1936. A magnificent new edifice would soon arise out of the rubble.

room. Tom Whittaker was provided with state-of-the-art facilities for maintaining players' fitness. Directly above the dressing rooms was a players' gymnasium. It was full of exercise equipment, stationary bikes and weights, and was used every day by Arsenal's players when the Club were still doing all their training at Highbury. When training shifted to London Colney, the gym was converted into a meeting room, then became a laundry, and latterly housed the Club's

Going up

Top: The new East Stand under construction. The stand was built to mirror the art deco lines of the West Stand.
Above: The main entrance to the East Stand was through an imposing portico and wrought iron doors surmounted by the iconic AFC monogram designed in 1932 for the West Stand.

Fitting tribute

The bronze bust of Herbert Chapman by Jacob Epstein takes pride of place in Highbury's Marble Halls. The Club's cannon motif was incorporated into the marble flooring.

erstwhile apprentice William Binnie, who had worked with him on the project, took over. The new structure echoed the art deco styling of the West Stand, lending Highbury a pleasing symmetry, and the stand also incorporated offices, players' facilities and the famous marble entrance hall.

The Marble Halls

Highbury's fabled Marble Halls must rate as among the best-known foyers in Britain. The art deco vestibule was planned to impress visitors with a clear statement about the Club's commitment to enduring quality, and over the ensuing 70 years the Marble Halls, with the niche in which a bronze bust of Herbert Chapman was displayed, became a shrine for generations of Arsenal supporters. Happily, the halls were preserved for posterity when architects came to design Highbury Square, the residential complex due to be built on the site of the Arsenal Stadium. The marbled foyer was included in the plans as a stylish reception area for Highbury's new occupants. The wrought-iron doors at the entrance were emblazoned with the Club's new 'AFC' logo, which were also incorporated into the East Stand façade.

The Marble Halls were the most public of the rooms built into the new East Stand. Just off the entrance area were spacious new dressing rooms, a shower area and the boot

communications department. Highbury's inner sanctum – the boardroom – was near the gym. Few changes were made to its luxurious, Canadian walnut-panelled interior over the next 70 years, and even the furniture stayed the same.

In the new East Stand, the players would enjoy what were in those days luxury facilities. Home and away dressing rooms were spacious, next to a bath room with hot and cold plunges, spray and needle baths, state-of-the-art equipment for minor injuries, a heating system running along a panel beneath the dressing room floors, a treatment room, plus private rooms for trainers. Whatever happened on the pitch, a visit to Highbury was no penance for the visiting teams.

A stadium at a cost

No detail was overlooked in the East Stand blueprints. There was even space set aside for a flag room, where the flags that flew from the stand roof on match days could be kept in pristine condition. At the back of the stand, the design incorporated two commentary boxes. One of these was used by the stadium's public address announcers. The other box was reserved for hospital radio broadcasts. (At that time match commentaries were broadcast direct to local hospitals.) In the mid-1980s both booths were boarded up. The PA announcer moved to another location in the East

East Stand

The famous frontage of the East Stand, opened in 1936, is perhaps the most iconic image of the Arsenal Stadium at Highbury. Later accorded Grade II listed status, the façade was to be preserved as part of the redevelopment of the site.

Bird's-eye view

Highbury seen from the air in 1936, from the west. The expensively re-developed ground, with its superb new East and West Stands, was by now the most magnificent stadium in English club football, and home to the country's greatest team.

Stand, and the increased radio coverage of all Arsenal's home matches meant that dedicated broadcasts for hospitals had become obsolete.

The new stand was built over five floors, with 4,000 seats on each of the two main levels, and a standing area below – but the cost was steep. At £130,000 it came in over £80,000 more than the West Stand had done. Despite the lavish outlay, Arsenal could (and did) congratulate themselves that they now had a ground that was the envy of the Football League and worthy of a club at the height of its powers. With the styling of the stadium, more reminiscent of a grand hotel than the more industrial styling of the stadiums of their London neighbours, such as Spurs and West Ham, Arsenal was making a clear statement that this club was in a league of its own. A testament to the vision of the Club was that this grand stadium design remained largely intact for over half a

century. Arsenal opened the new grandstand in front of a crowd of over 50,000 on 24 October 1936, before the League match against Grimsby Town. Sadly, the result of the game did not match the occasion, ending in a decidedly uncelebratory goalless draw.

A successful Cup campaign

While Arsenal were looking to the future by developing the stadium, they were experiencing unwelcome changes in their performance in the League. Season 1935/36 saw the Gunners slip to sixth position. The players were none too happy when the third round FA Cup draw in January 1936 pitted them against Bristol Rovers of the Third Division South at Eastville. Memories of the humiliation by Walsall in 1933 persisted. Their fears seem justified in a difficult first half when Rovers took the lead, and Bastin hit the post from a penalty. For the

second half, however, Bastin switched places with Bobby Davidson from outside left to inside right and the wheels began to turn. Making light of the muddy pitch, Arsenal scored twice in quick succession through an irresistible Bastin and ran out winners, 5–1. George Allison wrote to Bastin's mother to say how proud she could be of her son, who'd won Arsenal the game. 'A nice if somewhat flamboyant gesture,' recalled Bastin, 'and Mother was touched by it.'

In the fourth round Arsenal were drawn away for the sixth consecutive time. Now, however, the opposition was much stiffer; Liverpool at Anfield. Injured Herbie Roberts gave way to Norman Sidey at centre back; everyone else was an international. W.M. Johnston, the programme editor enthused: 'The Liverpool Cup tie of 1936 will go down in Arsenal history as one of the most glorious performances. Victories, it is true, have been gained with some regularity on the Anfield ground by visiting Arsenal teams, and it is again true that the actual score on this occasion was not an exceptional one. But nevertheless the triumph was complete and outstanding. Liverpool rose to considerable heights, and their performance was probably one of the best efforts they have made in a Cup match. But in spite of this excellence they were well and truly beaten, and eclipsed in every department. The form of our team, severally and collectively, was superb and would probably have accounted for any team in the land. Each player produced his best form and the combination of the team was magnificent. It was most decidedly our best performance of the season, but we may go further and say that we would have to search a long way before we found so convincing a display.'

Ray Bowden scored on 15 minutes, and after a fine solo run down the left flank, crossed for Joe Hulme, 15 minutes from time, to volley the second. The result was

Arsenal on tour
Enthusiastic Arsenal fans at Paddington catch a train west to watch the Gunners take on Bristol Rovers in the FA Cup third round, January 1936. The Gunners won 5–1 and went on to beat Sheffield United 1–0 in the final.

2–0 and Arsenal were through to the fifth round and another away game, this time at Newcastle United, then in Division Two. The result was a 3–3 draw. In the replay the following Wednesday, the Magpies were soundly beaten 3–0 at Highbury, with Bastin scoring twice.

The sixth round at last brought a home tie; a comfortable 4–1 win over Barnsley, with Pat Beasley scoring twice. In the semi-final at Huddersfield, the opposition would be Grimsby Town. Ray Bowden was again at centre forward and it was from his pass that Bastin, just inside the penalty box, shot the only goal of the game. So Arsenal returned to Wembley for the final against Second Division Sheffield United.

Winning at Wembley

It was not one of Arsenal's better days. Bastin indeed thought they had played better in the 1932 final. Switched back to inside right, Bowden was off-colour and Herbie Roberts and Alex James had recently returned after injury. Eddie Hapgood was preoccupied about his mother's health and Frank Moss, whose shoulder was dislocated yet again, was replaced by an initially shaky Alex Wilson. The match remained goalless until the 74th minute, when Cliff Bastin beat his marker on the left wing, crossed, and Ted Drake drove in the winning goal. The FA Cup had returned to Highbury after a wait of six years.

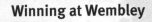

Official programme
A matchday programme from the 1938/39 season. The Gunners finished fifth in Division One in this last full season before the outbreak of war disrupted League football.

Goodbye to James

In season 1936/37 the Gunners took an honourable third place in the Championship. Disappointingly, Arsenal failed to keep the Cup, although they began its defence in a burst of goals: 5–1 at Chesterfield, 5–0 at home to Manchester United, 7–1 away to Burnley where Ted Drake scored four. However, a sixth round 3–1 defeat at West Bromwich Albion ended the Gunners' run.

The sun was beginning to set on the playing career of irreplaceable Alex James, who played his last League game against Bolton in May 1937. And Drake was again the Club's leading goal-scorer with 20 out of the Club's total of 80 goals. The season was notable for the debut of the brilliant teenager Denis Compton, younger brother of Leslie. He was a spectacular outside left with unusual flair, fine control and a devastating left foot; and still greater talents as a batsman for Middlesex and in due course England. A prolific scorer in reserve-team football, he would make 14 League appearances for four goals. His older brother Leslie was also now established as a first-team regular, playing in 15 League games, and at one stage even keeping Arsenal hero Eddie

Hapgood out of the team. At outside right Alf Kirchen now definitively replaced Joe Hulme on the right wing. A player of great power and speed, he could function on either flank. To replace Frank Moss, there was a brave new goalkeeper in George Swindin, a Yorkshireman signed in April 1936 from Bradford City. He would play 19 League games that season and would be first choice keeper until 1954. It was the season in which Bernard Joy took over from Herbie Roberts at centre half. An amateur, he had already won an international cap in May 1936.

Back at the top

Winning their fifth Championship title of the 1930s in season 1937/38, Arsenal confirmed their position as the pre-eminent team of the decade. However, it was a close-run thing; they finished the campaign with a mere 52 points. This was just one point ahead of Wolverhampton Wanderers, who would have taken the title had they not lost 1–0 at Sunderland in their final game, while Arsenal were beating Bolton Wanderers 5–0 at Highbury.

Surprisingly, it was the tiny Eddie Carr who would ensure Arsenal won the Championship. Standing just 5ft 5in, a total physical contrast to the incumbent centre forward Ted Drake, he replaced him, when Drake was injured. Carr played eleven League games and scored a remarkable and decisive seven goals to help clinch the title.

On 23 April 1938 at Championship rivals Preston, Carr was outstanding, heading in a cross from George Male early on, and later adding a second. A week later, Arsenal made hard work of beating Liverpool 1–0 at Highbury, Carr scoring the

goal. So, with Wolves a point ahead, on 7 May Arsenal hosted the vital last game of the season at home. Bolton Wanderers had to be beaten, and beaten they were 5–0. Carr scored twice in the first half, Bastin twice in the second. The other goal was scored by Kirchen. The irony being that despite his fusillade of goals for the Gunners in season 1937/38, his 11 productive games fell short of the 14 required to earn him a medal for the Championship he had done so much to win.

A record signing

In the summer of 1938, George Allison paid a world record £14,000 for Wolves' Welsh international inside left Bryn Jones. The object was to make him the successor to Alex James as master of the Arsenal midfield. His arrival was not universally welcomed. Bastin thought it 'a bad transfer', seeing Jones as 'essentially an attacking player, who was successful at Wolverhampton largely because the rest of the team were playing well'. Bastin dismissed any idea that Jones like James could mature into a constructive role. Eddie Hapgood was equally sceptical. 'I'll always have it that

Television debut
BBC Television make their first tentative steps in televising football, sending a camera crew to film Arsenal training at Highbury, 16 September 1937. George Allison takes the microphone to supply the commentary.

Arsenal should never have paid £14,000 for his transfer.
It was unfair to Jones and the rest of the team ... I am
convinced the responsibility of being the most expensive
player of all time was too much for Bryn ... We had to change
our whole style of play when Bryn stepped in to fill the gap
left by Alex retiring.' Jones began well enough at Arsenal.
On his League debut he scored one of the goals in a 2–0
victory over Portsmouth at Highbury, and two out of two in
the next three games. By the end of the season, however,
he had scored only one more, in 30 appearances.

He struck impressive form,
however, when an Arsenal party full
of young talent went on tour in the
summer of 1939 in Scandinavia.
Arsenal won all of their seven games,
scoring 33 goals against just four.

A golden decade draws
to a close

Season 1938/39 was a low-key affair.
Bastin was plagued by increasing
problems with his hearing, and was
afflicted midway through the season with
duodenal ulcers. A loss of form was

inevitable. He scored only three of the Gunners' 55 League
goals. They finished in fifth position and went out at Stamford
Bridge 2–1 to Chelsea in the third round of the FA Cup, with
Bastin the scorer of their goal. Reg Lewis played 15 games
and scored seven goals, two behind Alf Kirchen, and seven
behind the top scorer, Ted Drake. He was destined to do great
things and score many goals for Arsenal, chiefly as a centre
forward – he got 100 in three wartime seasons. Although he
signed for the Club as an amateur in May 1935, Lewis didn't
turn professional until mid March 1937. Well
balanced, a born opportunist with foot or
head, an elegant ball player, he was unlucky
never to win a full cap nor even to be picked
for the England team in the war.

At the start of that season, Arsenal played
Preston North End at Highbury in the Charity
Shield. It was a gloomy day, visibility was
poor, but at the end of the game, Arsenal
switched on the floodlights, which had
years before been installed in the East
Stand, only to be proscribed by the FA.
They illuminated the ground superbly.
Yet the FA held out against floodlit
football until the 1950s.

The autumn of 1938 saw Highbury stage an important international game, England against the Rest of Europe, somewhat blemished by the fact that the European centre half, the Italian international, Andreolo, spat at the English referee Jimmy Jewell. This insult was swiftly and forcefully avenged with a goal by the England right half, Ken Willingham. England eventually won 3–0.

The following May, it was Andreolo, in Milan, now playing for Italy, who put through the ball for which Silvio Piola, Italy's accomplished centre forward, challenged George Male. As he did so, Piola slipped and flung out a hand, which diverted the ball into the England goal and caught George Male in the eye. The goal scandalously stood, though England later equalised. Male's eye blew up painfully, yet years later he always insisted that Piola hadn't meant it. He probably hadn't.

Fame in film

That last pre-war season was notable for the making of the film *The Arsenal Stadium Mystery*, which is still shown from time to time. Based on a detective novel by Leonard Gribble, it featured most of the Gunners' first team players, with Alf Fields standing in for the school-teaching Bernard Joy. The plot revolved around a match between Arsenal and a fictitious amateur team, the Trojans, at Highbury. Cambridge University players impersonated the Trojans, but the actual match sequences involved shots of a game between Arsenal and Brentford at Highbury on 6 May 1939.

George Allison was unquestionably one of the few real stars of the show, despite the competition from actors Leslie Banks and Esmond Knight. A natural extrovert, and an imposing presence, Allison delivered his lines with fine professionalism. His accent was impeccably upmarket. Allison was even seen at the tactics board, an unfamiliar role for him. Blonde siren Greta Gynt was the femme fatale. Leslie Banks strolls through the film in the role of a detective inspector, wearing a variety of hats and putting a police chorus in tutus through dance routines in preparation for a light-hearted show. In the film, villainous Jack Doyce, the Trojans' inside right, collapses on the field, is carried off, and the match is abandoned. A stentorian radio commentator, E.B.H. Emmett, a thin man with a moustache, orates behind a microphone. Doyce it transpires is dead, poisoned by a

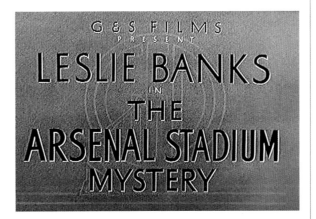

vengeful team mate. Banks puts on his Sherlock Holmes deerstalker to declare the case solved. 'Elementary, my dear Watson,' says Banks, with dire predictability, to his put-upon assistant. But, 'This is the hat I make my arrests in,' he declares, donning a fishing hat. Arsenal's players did their best with what sparse lines they were given, but for today's fans the main interest of this quaint film is in the footage of the stadium and some of its greatest stars at the end of one of the Club's finest decades.

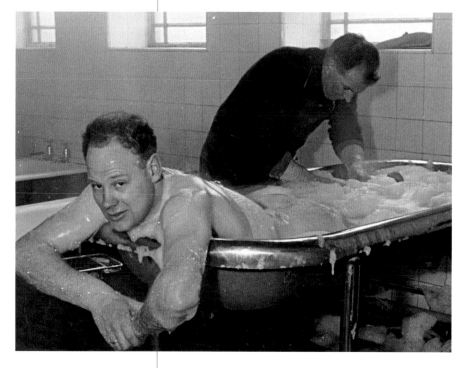

Bath time

George Male soaks away the strains of training at Highbury, 27 April 1940. The full back played 285 League games for the Gunners from 1930–48, without scoring.

War intervenes

Only three League games were played in season 1939/40 before football was suspended for the duration of hostilities. Arsenal began well enough; by distinct contrast with what would happen when these same three fixtures were replayed in 1946. They drew 2–2 at Wolves, beat Blackburn Rovers 1–0 at Highbury, and thrashed Sunderland there 5–2 in the third and final game, four of the goals going to Ted Drake.

Arsenal in exile

Arsenal shared the capital's grim fate as London took a pounding from enemy bombs. Close to prime targets for German bombers, Kings Cross station and the main railway line to the North, the Highbury area suffered numerous direct hits from the Luftwaffe. Local residents took shelter in the underground station or in back-garden shelters.

Damaged by bombing, and with the ground out of action, the Club accepted an offer from their near neighbours and rivals Tottenham Hotspur to share White Hart Lane while the war continued. Footballing hostilities were set aside as Spurs and the Gunners co-habited amicably while they fulfilled their semi-friendly wartime football commitments. This left the Arsenal Stadium free to do its bit for the war effort. Early on in the war it served as a first-aid centre, then as an air raid

patrol headquarters. While he was waiting to join the Air Force, Tom Whittaker was made the Post Warden. A barrage balloon floated over the practice pitch. The changing rooms were on stand-by to be used as a makeshift infirmary in the event of large-scale casualties in the area. Thankfully the need to use the stadium in this way did not arise. As with all public buildings, windows were shuttered to prevent flying glass, including all the glass squares in the East Stand, and an anti-blast wall was constructed in the entrance hall. The ground was adapted to provide sleeping rooms for the use of air raid wardens off duty, equipment stores and facilities for the storage of gas masks. Fire-fighting equipment was also kept in the stadium.

The West Stand was turned into a clearing centre for foreign evacuees, plus an air raid shelter, to be used in the early stages of the war by 1,500 people. Bricked up cubicles were then built to enable families to live together. Subsequently, porcelain sinks, gas-cleansing quarters – fortunately to be redundant – decontamination rooms and accommodation for medical and nursing staff were built. The stadium during the war was truly a centre for the community in the battle on the 'home front'.

The stadium under fire

Though never as badly damaged as Manchester United's Old Trafford, which would not be fit for football till well after the war, Highbury took its share of war wounds. In October 1940, a 1,000-pound bomb fell on the adjacent practice area where a barrage balloon was being flown. A hut in which several RAF personnel were sitting was blown apart. Two of the men were killed, but two miraculously survived, although the force of the explosion was enough to scatter tons of concrete on the terracing of the Clock End.

On 16 April 1941, five incendiary bombs fell through the roof above the North Bank, its roof collapsing in the subsequent intense fire. Further work at the southern end behind the great clock made the practice ground a storage space for bricks and other material to be used to build street shelters. One unfortunate consequence of the incendiary raid was that the goalposts in front of the North Bank were set alight and destroyed. The firm that had supplied them was now engaged in the manufacture of war goods, and George

Allison therefore had to scour London to find replacements, in readiness for the day when Arsenal Stadium would once again be open to football.

Serving their country

Many Arsenal employees left the Club to fight for their country overseas, while others served on the home front. The transient charm of football was placed in perspective while former Highbury heroes were risking their lives on the battle fields. Arsenal supporters feared for one of their favourites when Rome Radio – Mussolini's mouthpiece – claimed that Cliff Bastin had been taken prisoner. But the bulletin was quickly shown to be a piece of black propaganda. Not only had Bastin not been taken prisoner, he had never even left England because his deafness made him unfit for active service overseas. Instead, he spent the war as an air raid precautions officer in London, and served much of his time on top of the stands at Highbury, ready to report on the activities of the Luftwaffe. On his days off, of course, he turned out for Arsenal Football Club.

A scratch team was formed at the ground known as the Arsenal ARPs. Tom Whittaker became its prolific centre forward, Harry Homer, the programme editor, whose great speed was untempered by ball control, was the left winger who, it was jokingly feared, might one day disappear up Highbury Hill. 'Open the gates!' would come the cry when he set off on one of his runs. He too in time would join the Air Force, as would Eddie Hapgood, Ted Drake, Bernard Joy, Jack Crayston, Alf Kirchen, and a couple of new stars, George Marks and Laurie Scott. Others, such as the Compton brothers, George Swindin, Bryn Jones and Reg Lewis went into the Army. Billy Milne, the assistant trainer, succeeded Tom Whittaker as Post Warden at Highbury, when the RAF finally called Whittaker up.

Football for entertainment and fitness

In World War I playing football had been seen as an unnecessary distraction from the war effort, and an unpatriotic act. The attitude to football was different during World War II, when it was seen as a good way of raising morale. It was Government policy to keep leading footballers at home to provide entertainment for an

increasingly bombed and beleaguered civil population. Keeping the game going was therefore classified as useful war work in maintaining morale on the home front. George Allison, for example, was working so hard during the war that he had the referee's room at Highbury converted into a flat so he could spend as much time at the ground as possible.

The Armed Forces benefited from the Arsenal training regime. Many of the players served in the forces as physical training instructors, including such stars as Tommy Lawton and Ted Drake. The work allowed them to play competitive football as well, and some of the players were in such high

Air raid warning
In this notice of the period, supporters watching wartime football are advised to heed air raid warnings. Football continued during the conflict to boost morale, but it was far from business as usual.

AIR RAID SHELTER.

In the event of an Air Raid Warning being given from the Directors' Box, Spectators are requested to take cover in the corridors as indicated.

In their own interest persons are advised not to leave their shelters until the "all clear" has been given.

Will patrons please refrain from changing their positions and going from behind one Goal to the other.

Home front

Many staff members at Highbury became ARP wardens for the duration of the war. Among the volunteers were, from left, Cliff Bastin, Tom Whittaker, George Male and goalkeeper George Marks, pictured here in October 1939.

but quickly established himself, in either full back position, when the war came. He would make 16 wartime appearances for England and win 17 full caps in the post-war years.

It was George Marks' ill fortune that his years of footballing splendour were confined to the war, during which he kept even Frank Swift, who would become a celebrated goalkeeper for England, out of the international side. Joining the Gunners from Salisbury Corinthians, he played only two Division One games in season 1938/39, but he would be a major star of the early 1940s. Marks was strongly built, athletic, with a long kick and a firm command of his own penalty area. Unfortunately, playing at Wembley against Wales in 1943, he incurred an eye injury that would blight the remainder of his career.

demand that they ended up playing more regularly during the course of the war than they had in peacetime.

During the war years club allegiances were loosened. Players were allowed to guest for teams close to the bases where they were stationed. Lawton played twice one Christmas Day – for Everton in the morning then for Tranmere Rovers in the afternoon. Many players counted wartime football among their happiest sporting memories – including Leslie Compton. He was a reserve defender for Arsenal before 1939, but during the war he played as a forward and scored 78 goals in 80 regional league and cup games. He racked up 10 in the 15–2 thrashing of Clapton Orient in 1941.

Newcomers fill the ranks

Laurie Scott, a small, quick, solidly built full back with a notable recovery rate, had transferred to Arsenal in February 1937. He had made no first team appearances before 1939,

Wartime honours

Although the war brought a different perspective to footballing competition, English football clubs did their best to provide their fans with trophies. Arsenal won the Regional League South (A Division) in 1939/40. Season 1940/41 saw the team reach the final of the so-called Football League War Cup, which for two seasons replaced the FA Cup on a national basis. To get to Wembley, Arsenal, on a home and away basis, knocked out Brighton, Watford, West Ham, the holders, then Spurs. Both games against their north London rivals were played at White Hart Lane, Arsenal winning the first of them 2–1 in front of a crowd of 22,000, then the maximum permitted. Bastin scored Arsenal's second goal. George

6

Marks was absent for the return match, and Eddie Hapgood played in goal. The Gunners held out for a 1–1 draw, reaching the semi-final. There they beat Leicester City home and away, Jack Crayston scoring in both games.

Arsenal's opponents in the 1941 final at Wembley were Preston North End. Leslie Compton, then scoring goals galore from the centre forward position, hit the post from a penalty and in Bastin's somewhat surprising words, 'we rather lost heart as a result'. Andy McLaren, the little Scottish inside right, put Preston ahead and with some difficulty. Arsenal managed to equalise, however, through Leslie's younger brother, Denis.

The return match took place at Blackburn, Ted Drake replaced Leslie Compton at centre forward, but all too soon suffered yet another of the knee injuries to which he was prone. For a while he limped along the wing, which could not last long. Arsenal, down to ten men, lost 2–1. Bastin, wearied by being on alternate 24-hour shifts in his wartime duties at Highbury, confessed to being tired, unfit and off form.

Until well into 1943, Arsenal were able to keep the bulk of their gifted team together, and it would arguably have made a strong challenge for honours in any normal season. They won the London League in season 1941/42 and the Football League South in 1942/43.

Lewis scores four

In the Wembley final of that competition in front of a crowd of 75,000 Charlton Athletic, without their talismanic red-haired keeper Sam Bartram, were thrashed 7–1, their only goal of the match coming from a penalty. Bastin kept his place at inside left though it was reported beforehand that either Bryn Jones or the promising young George Curtis, whose names appeared as alternates on the programme, would fill the position. Eddie Hapgood, who defied Tom Whittaker's advice and unwisely played before recovering from an injury, had lost his place by then. Laurie Scott and Leslie Compton were the full backs. George Male was at left half. Reg Lewis scored four for Arsenal, Ted Drake, two, and Denis Compton, one. But Arsenal were brought sharply back to earth when they met the winners of the League North Cup, Blackpool, at Stamford Bridge. In contrast to the Gunners, Blackpool had an array of guest stars, above all the incomparable Stanley

Matthews on the right wing. Reportedly, Arsenal's game plan was to use both Comptons to mark him, but it failed badly. Blackpool won 4–2.

A team depleted

The team now began to suffer from the loss of many of its key players to the services and other types of war work. Military service took Bryn Jones to Italy, George Male to the Middle East, Leslie Compton and Reg Lewis to the Continent with the invading armies, Denis Compton to India. And early in season 1943/44, those two major England internationals Jack Crayston and Alf Kirchen were forced to retire through injury. Kirchen was badly hurt in a match at West Ham and risked being permanently crippled. Fortunately a skilled operation, grafting muscle from his thigh to his knee, enabled him to walk again; and to farm in Norfolk.

Crayston, by this time an RAF officer, gave up football after an ankle injury. He had determined to retire in any case. 'I'd decided to get out of the game,' he told a group of journalists at Stamford Bridge, with typical urbanity, 'before you fellows started using that most worn out of clichés, "a mere shadow of my former self".'

Arsenal filled the gaps as best they could with guest players, notably with the electric Stanley Mortensen, of Blackpool and England, who for a time made up a lively left wing partnership with Billy Wrigglesworth of Manchester United. His future Blackpool partner Stanley Matthews, like Mortensen serving in the RAF, turned out for Arsenal against Millwall early in 1945 and in the notorious game against

On your Marks

George Marks, whose goalkeeping career at Highbury never really started before it was curtailed by war. The Wiltshireman joined Arsenal in 1936, but Marks played just two matches before war broke out, and he was transferred to Blackburn Rovers in 1946.

Dynamo Moscow later that year. The team reached the semi-finals of the League South Cup against Millwall at Stamford Bridge in 1945. However, Mortensen and the guest centre half Fred Hall both missed penalties, and Millwall won 1–0, with a team reinforced by guests, notably the Charlton players, keeper Sam Bartram and inside forward 'Sailor' Brown.

Arsenal meets Moscow

At the start of season 1945/46, although the war was over, wartime football was still the order of the day, and the Arsenal team that met Moscow Dynamo at White Hart Lane in heavy fog in November 1945 was replete with guest players. Dynamo, who had arrived to tour England, were a source of perplexity for British football followers. A confused journalist watched them training at White City, said they were so slow you could almost hear them think and judged that they were no match for our professionals.

Whereupon Dynamo, in front of a gigantic, overflowing crowd at Stamford Bridge, proceeded to play gloriously fast, incisive, imaginative football against Chelsea, even if their equalising goal in a pulsating 3–3 draw was plainly offside. The Russian went on to crush Cardiff City 10–1. One of their pre-tour demands was that they should play Arsenal. George

Allison, who would be fielding yet another makeshift team, was pessimistic about the Gunners' chances. He therefore enlisted no fewer than half a dozen reinforcements, and flew Bernard Joy back from RAF service in Europe. Two players were borrowed from Fulham, the English international left back Joe Bacuzzi, who had actually played against Dynamo for Chelsea, and centre forward Ronnie Rooke, destined to become a prolific goal scorer for the Gunners in ensuing years. Matthews and Mortensen formed a formidable right wing pair. The left wing partnership was between George Drury who'd come from Sheffield Wednesday for £7,000 in 1938, and the Welsh international Horace Cumner, who in 1942 had scored two goals against England.

Fog-bound at White Hart Lane

As the fog closed in on White Hart Lane, it became increasingly clear that the match was unplayable. The Russians, who had stipulated that they would meet only club teams, decided to label the Arsenal team, which included two Welshmen as 'England'.

Latyshev, the referee, decided that the game should go on in spite of the poor visibility, compounding this strange decision with the bizarre strategy of stationing both his

Mighty Moscow

Excited fans queue outside White Hart Lane, where the Gunners played their home matches during the war, to watch Arsenal take on the touring Dynamo Moscow side, 21 May 1945. The Russians won 4–3 in a spectacle marred by thick fog.

linesmen on one touchline, while he himself patrolled the other; thereby rendering it virtually impossible to monitor the game effectively.

'Because of the fog,' wrote Vladimir Sinyavsky, the Russian commentator who had accompanied the squad, 'Dynamo suggested to Allison that the game should be postponed, "since we knew that fog, occurring so frequently in London, would be a help to Arsenal". But Allison refused because people had paid for their seats and bets had been placed.' In truth, Allison appealed during the game to a secretary from the Soviet Embassy to help him abandon the game, but without success. A free kick somewhat mysteriously awarded enabled the Dynamo centre forward Constantin Beskov, later to manage the Soviet national team, to head Dynamo into the lead. In the process, Wyn Griffiths, the Welsh goalkeeper was injured, and the Queens Park Rangers keeper Harry Brown was called from the crowd to substitute him. Two of the goals he subsequently let through seemed offside. Numerous offences seemed to take place in the Dynamo penalty area but none was punished. At one point Dynamo had 12 men on the pitch. At half time, an English interpreter in the Russian dressing room reported that he had heard Yakushin ordering Latychev to abandon the match if Dynamo, then 3–2 down, continued to be behind. Dynamo recovered to win, if that was the word, 4–3. The pity of it was that a match that might have been fascinating was no more than a fiasco, which should never have been started.

Barnes bolsters the team

One major consolation of this period was the emergence of the splendidly versatile young Welsh international Walley Barnes, even though a scintillating beginning was blighted by a severe knee injury in 1945, which threatened his career. Barnes was recommended to the Club by none other than Tom Parker, the former Arsenal captain. He was then playing inside left as an amateur for Southampton. Joining Arsenal in the autumn of 1943, he flourished in a variety of positions, even playing once in goal against Brighton and Hove Albion. As an outside left, he scored for an FA XI against Belgium, on tour. But he seemed most effective as a mobile and resourceful left back. He was back in the League team, after working intensively on his knee, in November 1946 and

Gunners on parade

Squadron Leader Whittaker drills his men on the way to Germany for a football tour in August 1945. Arsenal played a series of matches against service teams to raise morale in Europe.

would stay in the side, switching to right back when Laurie Scott was injured in 1948, and would win many international caps for Wales.

The dashing Dr Kevin O'Flanaghan began playing for Arsenal in the transitional 1945/46 season, when the League South was extended to include teams from the Midlands. A superb all-round athlete, he actually played soccer and rugby for Ireland in consecutive weeks, and he also practised hurling, athletics and Gaelic football. Strong, quick with a forceful right-footed shot, he remained an amateur during his playing career.

The end of wartime football

For Arsenal the war came to an end at the end of season 1945/46, the last season in which they had to play their home games at White Hart Lane. The FA Cup had been revived in 1945/46, although the wartime regime of regional Leagues had continued. For the first and only time, the earlier rounds of the Cup were played on a two-legged basis, decided on goal aggregate. In the first leg of the third round Arsenal met West Ham United at Upton Park and were simply overwhelmed, beaten 6–0. Several changes were made for the second leg at White Hart Lane, and Arsenal did retrieve a little pride by winning 1–0. But they were well and truly out.

The return to Highbury

Arsenal Stadium emerged from the war years battered but ready to play host to the thousands of loyal supporters who enthusiastically returned to Highbury for the 1946/47 season. After a period of rebuilding both stadium and team, the early 1950s were to be another glorious era for the Club.

CHAPTER

7

After the war ended in the summer of 1945, both the team and the stadium were in need of rebuilding. Many of the players who had been the backbone of the team were nearing the end of their playing careers, and the stadium had suffered from bombs and wartime 'adaptations'. However, in the post-war period the enthusiasm for football at Highbury was undimmed. Crowds were huge, despite the fact that there was no cover over the North Bank, after the bombs.

One long-time Arsenal supporter described his introduction to the stadium during this period. 'My father returned home from the war in late 1945 [when he asked] what I would like for my birthday, I had no hesitation in saying that I would like to go to Highbury. The nearest game to my birthday was on 19 October 1946 against Stoke City, who had won six games on the trot. The day came and we travelled up from Gravesend in Kent and arrived at Arsenal tube station. We passed the purveyors of roasted chestnuts, roasted peanuts and souvenir programmes, and reached the North Bank. I remember the imposing East Stand (where I am now a season ticket holder), the slight remaining war damage to the upper tier of the West Stand ... I also remember the turnstiles in each corner of the West Stand lower tier, where one could transfer from the North Bank or Clock End for sixpence ... My father and I had arrived some two and a half hours before kick-off to ensure a place behind a crush barrier and because there was certain to be a good attendance. In the event, the gate was over 60,000.'

In fact, attendances as high as 63,000 were typical during the late 1940s. But Arsenal were burdened with a debt of more than £150,000, incurred principally through the need

Leading the team out
Gunners' captain George Male leads the Arsenal team out on 17 August 1946.

for large-scale ground refurbishment as a result of bomb damage and the fact that the stadium had generated no football income for seven years.

Rescued by 'The Pru'

When hostilities ended, arguably the most popular sporting institution in the land was suffering from many financial headaches, with big clubs as severely affected as the lowliest minnows. At Highbury stands and other fittings were valued at £350,000, but they couldn't be translated into ready cash. It was only when the club managed to transfer its debt from the Prudential insurance company to Barclays Bank that conditions were eased and recovery became possible. In fact, 'The Pru' proved to be a faithful friend to the Gunners, waiving the wartime interest on loans of more than £37,000. The ultimate soundness of the financial revival, with the debt being wiped out within three years, was due in no small measure to the financial acumen of Sir Bracewell Smith, who joined the board in 1938 and became chairman in 1949. A former Lord Mayor of London, he used his vast business knowledge and array of influential contacts to the full. However, it was not until 1954 that the club was able to countenance the rebuilding of the North Bank roof. This was an exact copy of the old structure and was financed by a grant from the War Damages Commission.

Rebuilding on and off the field

Back at last at Highbury for the resumption of League soccer in 1946, the optimism encouraged by Reg Lewis's six goals in the public practice match that raised the curtain proved illusory. The two opening games were a disaster. At Molineux, a vibrant young Wolves side overwhelmed Arsenal 6–1. It was the end of the road for Cliff Bastin, fielded in his old position on the left wing, though his pace had long since gone. When he asked Tom Whittaker what he thought might be wrong, the answer was that 'the ligaments may have tightened up through too much playing'. Bastin was still only 34, but had begun his professional career as a 17-year-old.

The team included wing halves Dave Nelson and George Curtis, who had been reserve forwards before the war. It also saw the First Division debuts of Ian McPherson, a distinguished RAF fighter pilot who had come from Notts

HIGHBURY HEROES
Jimmy Logie 1939/40–1954/55

The 5ft 4in 'Little Scot' was signed in June 1939 from the Lochore Welfare junior club. Within weeks, however, he had joined the Navy and spent the war serving on trawlers. On his return to Highbury after the war, he settled down at inside right with exceptional close control, pace in thought and movement, and the ability to supply his right winger or centre forward with shrewdly timed and struck passes. In the years to come, he would become arguably Arsenal's most influential and irreplaceable player. While with the Gunners, he won two League Championship winners' medals (1947/48, 1952/53) and an FA Cup winners' medal (1949/50). He was capped for Scotland once.

County, Paddy Sloan, an Irish international inside right, from Tranmere Rovers, and Jimmy Logie, destined to become the grand inspiration of the attack.

Leslie Compton took over from a waning Bernard Joy at centre half, and would stay there imposingly for the next six years. The irony being that in all his versatile career to date – accomplished full back, prolific centre forward – Leslie had never played at centre half until in the summer of 1945 the Gunners travelled to Dusseldorf to meet a British Army team. Tom Whittaker asked him if he would 'see what he could do' at centre half for Arsenal. With his strength, his height, his dominance in the air, he would give solidity to an Arsenal defence that desperately needed it. Long before the nickname was applied to Brian Clough, Leslie was christened 'Big Head' at Highbury.

However poor Arsenal's start to the 1946/47 League season, Reg Lewis was irrepressible, scoring 11 goals in the Gunners' first ten matches out of a grand total of 15. A home victory came at long last in October, against Stoke City, who had controversially replaced the incomparable Stanley

Victory and harmony
This version of the Arsenal crest first appeared in the new-style matchday programme of 1949/50. The famous Latin motto, Victoria Concordia Crescit – Victory Grows Out Of Harmony – was devised by the programme editor Harry Homer. For the first time the crest incorporated the coat of arms of the Borough of Islington.

Roofless Gunners
The view from the Clock End to the North Bank, before the start of the season in August 1948. North Bank regulars would have to brave the elements until 1954 when the roof destroyed in the war was rebuilt.

There was another immensely significant signing in 1946 – Ronnie Rooke, a 33-year-old centre forward from Fulham. Surprisingly, the first approach was made by Fulham themselves, since Rooke had been scoring heavily for Fulham since he joined them from Crystal Palace in 1936. Rooke himself was astonished when he was suddenly called out of the bath and told that the Gunners wanted him. The transfer fee was a paltry £1,000 and a couple of Arsenal reserve players, right half David Nelson and the attacker Cyril Grant. Rooke, who had a ferocious left foot, was formidable in the air and was a useful distributor of the ball, took no time at all to show his value.

A marathon against Chelsea

With Paddy Sloan at right half, completing a combative half-back line with Leslie Compton and Joe Mercer, Arsenal quickly climbed away from what had been the very real threat of relegation. In January 1947 their opponents in the third round of the FA Cup were Chelsea, who had eliminated them at the

Snowy business
Arsenal on the defensive during a famous match against Manchester United on 1 February 1947. Play at Highbury went ahead despite a thick blanket of snow covering the pitch, and Arsenal made the better of the conditions to win 6–2.

Matthews with his reserve George Mountford. Bernard Joy, scheduled out of position that day at left back, marked Mountford relentlessly, and Arsenal won 1–0 through a spectacular goal by Dr Kevin O'Flanagan. After a splendid solo run, he let fly with his powerful right foot – an irresistible goal. He would get an equally remarkable goal in a 2–2 draw at Highbury with Bolton Wanderers. On that occasion, O'Flanagan, taking a free kick 30 yards out, wiped the mud off the heavy ball, put it down and smashed it home.

Mercer joins the Gunners

The Bolton Wanderers game was also significant for another reason: Joe Mercer's debut for the Gunners. Tom Whittaker had treated Mercer for an injured knee at Highbury when the England left half was still playing for his original club, Everton. But his relations with them had deteriorated badly. When he and Everton decided to part, Whittaker was advised that Mercer would willingly come to Highbury. Arsenal jumped at it and signed him for a mere £7,000. Though he was obliged to modify the more adventurous game he'd played at wing half for Everton, he was an immense influence and an inspirational captain. If Everton thought they were selling a crock, Mercer would prove them embarrassingly wrong. His career continued to flourish with Arsenal until ended by injury in 1954.

Team talk
Arsenal's manager Tom Whittaker in the home dressing room at Highbury in 1947, talking to Ronnie Rooke (right) and Reg Lewis.

Standing in line

Arsenal fans queue along Avenell Road to watch their side take on Aston Villa at Highbury on 11 September 1948. A crowd of 54,114 saw the Gunners win 3–1. Crowds everywhere rocketed in the post-war era as sports-starved fans lapped up professional football.

same stage in 1939. Three games were eventually necessary to decide the tie. At Stamford Bridge the teams drew 1–1. At the replay at Highbury, Chelsea, with the famous inside-forward trio of Scotland's Tommy Walker and the English internationals Tommy Lawton and Len Goulden, called the tune. Yet it was Arsenal, still kings of the counter-attack, who took the lead in the second half through Ronnie Rooke, now forming such a forceful spearhead with Reg Lewis. A most untypical error by Walley Barnes gave Chelsea the equaliser. Dallying on the ball, he was robbed by the Chelsea right winger, Dickie Spence, who ran on, accurately crossed, and found the unforgiving head of Tommy Lawton. Swindin's gallant goalkeeping had been in vain.

The second replay took place on a Monday at White Hart Lane and Arsenal threw it away. Well on top in the early minutes, with a shot from Jimmy Logie hitting the bar, and a penalty kick by Reg Lewis wide of the left hand post, Arsenal eventually lost 2–0. At the end of a disappointing season, they finished a mere 13th in the League.

Whittaker takes over

The summer of 1947 saw the departure of George Allison after 13 years as the Arsenal manager. Never a players' man, sometimes at odds with his stars, but always an expert publicist, Allison in his long reign had largely kept Arsenal where Herbert Chapman had left them. Had the war not intervened, it's arguable that the team would have continued its progress. After all, a clutch of fine young players had emerged in the late 1930s, even if others, by the end of the war, had grown old together. But 12 years is a long time for any manager to stay in the job, and the demands made on Allison, not least in the topsy-turvy years of the war, must have taken their toll.

Tom Whittaker was a popular successor. He had been a Gunner for nearly 28 years, as a player and as a much-respected trainer and assistant manager (from 1946). He was a father figure to the players, an extraordinary healer whose ministrations had cured not only footballers but tennis stars, jockeys, golfers. He had been put in charge of the England team at the end of season 1945/46; actually the first England manager. Whittaker had also done sterling work in the war, as a squadron leader in the RAF, and was awarded the MBE in 1945 for his war service. Allison in fact bowed out after Arsenal beat Everton at Highbury on 31 May 1947. The directors, led by the Chairman Sir Samuel Hill-Wood, summoned Tom Whittaker to the Board Room and asked him to take on the job.

'I have often asked myself,' Whittaker later wrote, 'did I make a mistake in changing over from trainer to manager? Would I be better employed as a trainer? It's a difficult decision to make, and can only occur to the man who has undertaken both jobs.' It is hard to see how Whittaker could have possibly turned down the job at the club he had served so impressively for so long. Inevitably, he would find that a trainer, however essential to his club, enjoyed an immunity from the full force of criticism endured by any manager. He would eventually find this exposure hard to tolerate.

Seventeen unbeaten

There is no doubt that Whittaker 'hit the ground running', making two important acquisitions in the summer of 1947: Archie Macaulay from Brentford and Don Roper from Southampton. Although neither of the Comptons was yet available owing to their cricketing commitments, the new season could hardly have begun better with a series of six victories, including a double defeat of Charlton Athletic, winning 4–2 at The Valley and 6–0 a week later at Highbury.

Programme for victory

The matchday programme for the League game against Charlton Athletic, which the Gunners were to win emphatically 6–0.

But the most fascinating and dramatic game in the series was that against Manchester United at Highbury on a sunny Saturday afternoon. Under the inspiring aegis of Matt Busby, United deployed a splendidly talented team that pressed the Gunners very hard and probably deserved a draw. In the event they lost 2–1, Ronnie Rooke striking a ferocious left-footed shot from 30 yards out into the top right-hand corner of the United goal to give Arsenal the lead.

In Leslie Compton's absence (he was still wicket-keeping for Middlesex), Alf Fields had stepped into the breach in defence. Dominant in the air, he was solidly effective, but was tragically crippled in the last of the opening six victories by his own goalkeeper. The collision took place at home to Bolton Wanderers. As Fields shaped to clear the ball, George Swindin came tearing out of goal, hurled himself forward, and made disastrous contact with Fields' knee. Fields went off, Arsenal's 10 men still beat Bolton; Alf would never again be a first-team regular, but would become an excellent coach for the Club.

Shock defeat

The Gunners' unbeaten run lasted for 17 games, coming to an end eventually at Derby County where the home team's outside right, Reg Harrison, scored the only goal. But there was a shock to come in the FA Cup in January 1948 – defeat in the third round at Highbury by Second Division Bradford Park Avenue to the accompaniment of triumphant choruses of 'Ilkley Moor Baht Aht' sung by large Yorkshiremen in the West Stand. Billy Elliott, an outside left later to play for England, smashed in the only goal of the game. The Bradford defence held out gallantly, and Arsenal were embarrassingly knocked out. However, honour was restored when Arsenal went to Manchester for the crucial return League game against Manchester United. Old Trafford was still out of commission after wartime bombing, and the match was played at Maine Road, the Manchester City stadium, in front of a record-breaking crowd of over 80,000. The result was an enthralling 1–1 draw, which effectively secured the Championship for the Gunners. The final home game of the season against Grimsby Town saw not only an emphatic 8–0 victory, but also the final appearance of the talismanic George Male, the last remaining player of the Chapman era.

The 1948/49 season saw Arsenal finishing fifth in the League. However, it was notable for the easy 3–0 victory against Tottenham Hotspur in the third round of the FA Cup at Highbury. The key to the match was the irrepressible Jimmy Logie. Spurs' left half and captain, Ronnie Burgess, contributed to Logie's spectacular performance, prey to his old familiar fault of tearing constantly upfield into attack, leaving great space behind him. Ian McPherson, Doug Lishman and Don Roper scored the goals. Lishman had been

On your bike

From left, Arsenal players Don Roper, Reg Lewis, Lionel Smith, Doug Lishman, Denis Compton, Archie Macaulay, Laurie Scott and Alex James try out bikes given to their children by the British Cycle Company, at Highbury on 28 April 1950.

Table football
Arsenal manager Tom Whittaker employs state-of-the-art aids as he talks tactics with his team in the offices in the East Stand.

Swiss mismatch
On 2 December 1948 Highbury hosted an international between England and Switzerland, which the home team won 6–0. England captain Billy Wright of Wolverhamton Wanderers, later to become manager of Arsenal, shakes hands with the Swiss skipper Lauro Amado, watched by referee Karl Van Der Meer of Holland.

signed from Walsall the previous year. A former marine commando, the tall and well built Lishman was already 24 years old by the time he joined Arsenal, plucked out of the obscurity of the Third Division where he seemed to have gone strangely unnoticed.

However, that season the Highbury crowd had been treated to the spectacle of an international friendly between England and Switzerland. Played in December after being delayed by one of London's famously impenetrable 'pea-souper' smogs, a crowd of around 35,000 witnessed a resounding 6–0 victory for the England team.

In September 1949, Arsenal bought a player from Tottenham Hotspur. He was Freddie Cox, an outside right who had been on Spurs' books for 11 years, and was destined to score goals at White Hart Lane of priceless FA Cup importance; though for Arsenal, the eternal rivals, rather than for Spurs. He was a talented but erratic player, fast and, on his day, elusive. As he indeed was in December 1949 when,

1949-50

Badge of honour

The Club logo as it appeared on the Arsenal shirts of the late 1940s and early 1950s.

running riot against Sunderland at Highbury, he created goals for Alex Forbes, Peter Goring and Jimmy Logie in a 5–0 thrashing of the northeasterners.

The Cup regained

Tired perhaps after a summer tour of Brazil, Arsenal began the 1949/50 League season badly, losing four out of the first five games, but recovered their form so that by Christmas the team was in contention for the League leadership. In the event Arsenal would finish a modest sixth, but the FA Cup was to be their consolation prize. Certainly the luck of the draw was very much on the Gunners' side, for they won it without ever having to play a tie outside north London. Narrow wins were the order of the day, even against teams from the lower divisions.

The 1950 semi-final was played at White Hart Lane, Arsenal's wartime home for so many years, and Chelsea were the potentially difficult opposition. In the League, they had won 3–2 at Highbury, but the Gunners had won 2–1 away at Stamford Bridge. The first half was dominated by Chelsea in general and Bentley in particular, who scored two elegant goals. Then in the last minute of the first half, Arsenal gained a corner on the right flank, and Freddie Cox took it with the outside of his right foot. The choice would prove inspired. Caught in a gust of wind, the ball blew into the Chelsea goal, high inside the near post!

In the second half with 15 minutes left, Chelsea still led 2–1. It was now that the Gunners gained another corner, and this time taken by Denis Compton. Up from defence strode his brother Leslie, who had tried and tried again to head home from corners, succeeding just once, in 1947. Small

wonder that Joe Mercer, the captain, should yell at Leslie, 'Get back, get back!' Leslie took no notice of him. He continued his advance, and when the ball came over, jumped to head it fiercely into the net. He then lost his balance, turned a dramatic somersault, and didn't even know that he had scored until his team mates ecstatically congratulated him. Arsenal won the replay at White Hart Lane 1–0 and for the first time since 1936, Arsenal were in the FA Cup Final, their opponents, Liverpool. Both Arsenal goals in a convincing 2–0 victory were expertly taken by Reg Lewis.

Team changes

During the 1950/51 season there were several changes in the regular Arsenal line-up. Lionel Smith, a lanky Yorkshireman who had joined Arsenal in 1939 as a centre back, didn't find a place in the 1950 Cup final team but had made regular appearances that season at left back. Lishman was afflicted by boils in season 1949/50 and broke a leg playing against Stoke at Christmas 1950. By the following season he was fully recovered, scoring hat-tricks in three successive home games, and being called up for the England squad in October 1951, although he never achieved a full England cap. The Stoke game, when he was so badly injured, turned out to be the watershed of Arsenal's season. George Swindin was also hurt that ill-omened day and missed no fewer than 16 games, Cup ties included. Over that Christmas period, Arsenal were leading

the Championship table, but inevitably perhaps the team's form then fell away and the Gunners would finish the season in a disappointing fifth place.

Kelsey arrives at Highbury

But on 24 February 1951, a goalkeeper destined to be famous made his debut at Highbury, albeit an unhappy one. He was Jack Kelsey, a Welsh blacksmith. Kelsey came to Arsenal in September 1949. The omens of Kelsey's arrival could hardly have been gloomier. It wasn't his first visit; he had already played there in a trial match. Recalling his first morning in the new job, 'I don't suppose any young professional could have got off more solidly on the wrong foot.'

When Kelsey arrived at Highbury at 10 o'clock in the morning, the big commissionaire, Len Taylor, at once went to tell Jack Crayston, then the assistant manager, that Kelsey was there. Kelsey sat down in the marble hall to wait. He passed the time as best he could by examining the bust of Herbert Chapman. At three o'clock, when he had been waiting for five hours, Taylor asked him whether he'd had anything to eat, and suggested he go down to a café at the end of the road. But Kelsey was nervous that if he did, Crayston would call him, to find that he wasn't there. Taylor kindly said he would cover for him so Kelsey went down the road, 'to eat one of the most miserable, bolted meals of my life'. It was five o'clock before he was finally called into Crayston's office to sign.

Initially Kelsey trained with the third team, run by George Male, on the Hendon ground at Claremont Road, Cricklewood. There, he said, he learned little of value except from Alex James whom he esteemed as an excellent coach. At Highbury later, he was puzzled by what he called 'the head tennis craze', indulged on a hard-surfaced court adjacent to the East Stand. 'Some of the lads would play from ten to twelve,' Kelsey marvelled.

As for his ill-starred home debut, Kelsey had the misfortune to come up against Hans Jeppson in dynamic form. Jeppson had played forcefully for Sweden in the World Cup in Brazil the previous year. Gordon Hurst put Charlton ahead from the right wing. A second goal came controversially when a Charlton player shouted, 'Leave it!' as Hurst's cross came over. Arthur Shaw, at right half, obediently did, and the same

Boot care at Highbury
Highbury Stadium had a full range of facilities to support the players on the pitch. This included a boot room and a dedicated member of staff to look after this critical element of the players' kit.
Above: Danny Cripps, from Arsenal's back-room staff, carrying out repairs in the boot room at Highbury in the 1950s.
Right: The players' boots carefully hung up in the boot room under the watchful eye of Danny Cripps.

player shot home. Peter Goring made it 2–1, but now Jeppson showed his mastery of Leslie Compton. The Swede easily went past Compton and placed a relatively slow shot past the diving Kelsey and in off the far post. A censorious Tom Whittaker came into the dressing room at half time: 'You're taking this match too lightly! Pull yourselves together!' In vain, as in the second half Jeppson scored twice more to complete his hat-trick.

So Arsenal went down 5–2, to Kelsey's despair. The more so when he discovered that at the nearby Finsbury Park Empire, where the famous act of Old Mother Riley was playing, a scarecrow figure with a 'dead white face' came on to the stage at one point. 'Who are you?' asked Old Mother Riley, played by Arthur Lucan who, when he was told, replied that he thought it might be Arsenal's new goalkeeper. A

mortified Kelsey complained to Tom Whittaker who in turn saw to it that the item came out of the show. Following a 3–1 away defeat by Manchester United, Kelsey made only a couple more League appearances that season and none at all in season 1951/52, when George Swindin didn't miss a game. But his time emphatically would come.

Highbury lights up

It had been a long time coming, but on 19 September 1951, some two decades after the visionary Herbert Chapman had called for a trial of floodlit football, Highbury staged its first major game during the hours of darkness. Back in the 1930s the Football Association had spurned the suggestion, but now Arsenal, who had already tried artificial illumination earlier that year for a light-hearted encounter between Boxers

Heads we win
Members of the team playing 'head tennis' on practice courts behind the Clock End during the 1950s. This was a favourite training activity among the players.

Let there be light

The floodlights go on at Highbury for a match against Glasgow Rangers on 17 October 1951, as Arsenal pioneer evening football.

and Jockeys (see opposite), emerged as pioneers of the future European football explosion, staging an evening friendly against Hapoel of Tel Aviv. The fixture attracted more than 44,000 curious spectators, and they were rewarded with an entertaining if one-sided contest in which the Gunners triumphed, winning 6–1, with Cliff Holton contributing a memorable hat-trick, Reg Lewis netting twice and Arthur Milton completing the scoring.

The rudiments of a lighting system had been installed at Highbury between the wars to allow the players to train in the evenings, but for this public experiment, new 1,500-watt lamps were fitted to the roofs of the West and East stands, and the result was hailed widely as a brilliant spectacle. Extracting the last ounce of drama from the situation, manager Tom Whittaker theatrically waited until shortly before kick-off to give the signal for the lights to be switched

on, the moment being greeted with a massive gasp from the expectant crowd. The future of the game had never been brighter, and many more evening games would follow.

Cricketers, boxers and jockeys

In the post-war years, Highbury hosted a number of light-hearted sporting events. The Club had a unique tradition of cricketing footballers. In 1950/51 Arsenal had an astonishing total of five county cricketers on their books. In August 1949 Arsenal put on a benefit cricket match at Highbury for Denis Compton, pitting an Arsenal XI against an all-star Middlesex team. Following the success of this event, two more such matches were played, in 1952 (for Jack Young) and 1955 (for Leslie Compton). Links with two other sports were cemented in the 1951 footballing contest between Boxers and Jockeys on Highbury's hallowed turf. This event proved such a

Injuries and disappointment

Arsenal might well have done the double in season 1951/52 had it not been for a string of injuries to key players, including Alex Forbes, Arthur Milton, Reg Lewis and Jimmy Logie. Tom Whittaker wrote of 'the utter impossibility' of the League and Cup double. 'I say that under modern handicaps, with 42 League games and at least six cup ties, it just cannot be done. The story of our failure, a story of soccer heroism and cruel luck, is worth re-telling to strengthen any claim that the double is impossible.' Tottenhan Hotspur, of course, would prove him wrong in 1960/61. As it was, the Gunners took an honourable third place in the Championship and were runners up in the FA Cup final.

Ray Daniel, who had made his League debut at the end of season 1948/49, finally became the first choice at centre half. Daniel came to the Gunners after playing as an amateur wing half for Swansea Town. An utter contrast to Leslie Compton, Daniel was mobile and adventurous where Leslie was solid and defensive. He too, alas, was destined to be injured, breaking his wrist at Blackpool a few weeks before the 1952

Sportsman's Aid at Highbury

Rare matchday programmes from the popular Boxers v Jockeys charity games played at Highbury in the 1950s.

success that it became a regular fixture throughout the 1950s.

Suggested originally by international boxing referee Sam Russell as an ingenious fund-raiser for the Sportsman's Aid Society, it featured teams composed of some of the leading pugilists and equestrians of the day. Fans of boxing and racing, as well as football, flocked to witness the comical confrontations between the likes of former British and Empire heavyweight champion Henry Cooper and the tiny Gordon Richards, one of the most revered flat-racers of all time.

Cooper, who in 1966 would return to Highbury to face Cassius Clay (later known as Muhammad Ali) in a bout for the world title, was infectiously enthusiastic about the unorthodox series of entertainments. 'It was a really popular event and we used to get decent-sized crowds, at least 15,000 as I recall. You'd have the likes of myself and (fellow heavyweights) Dick Richardson and Brian London, who were all about 6ft 4in, on the one side, up against the jockeys, who were generally a fair bit smaller! The jockeys used to literally run between our legs, and some of them were right tricky little fellas who could give as good as they got on the physical side, too. In the end my trainer, Jim Wicks, stopped me playing because the games used to play havoc with my leg muscles!' The matches were given added interest by the choice of celebrity referees, including the illustrious footballing cricketers (and Gunners) Denis and Leslie Compton.

Ticket to ride

An original ticket for a Boxers v Jockeys charity football match at Highbury. This game was played under floodlights only six months after Highbury staged its first officially sanctioned floodlit game.

Towering header

Arsenal inside left Doug Lishman rises above Newcastle United captain Joe Harvey in the 1952 FA Cup final at Wembley on 3 May 1952. The Gunners lost the match 1–0 to a George Robledo goal.

FA Cup final. His older brother Bobby, also an Arsenal player, had been tragically killed on a wartime bombing raid while serving in the RAF.

Chelsea was again the opposition in two semi-finals played at White Hart Lane. This time, both games were disappointing. The first was a 1–1 stalemate, but Arsenal won the replay by a comfortable 3–0, the irrepressible Cox scoring two of the goals. After the semi-finals, 8,000 applications for Cup final tickets arrived at Highbury each day. Not to mention good luck charms in the form of dozens of rabbits' feet, herbs, and even a witches' potion.

Defeat at the Hawthorns by West Bromwich Albion had put the Championship out of reach. Manchester United were on level points at the top with Arsenal but had a much superior goal average. Fate had it that Arsenal were due at Old Trafford just one week before the Cup final. Meanwhile after the game at the Hawthorns, Doug Lishman, complaining of pain in his

thigh, was examined by a horrified Whittaker, who suspected severe blood poisoning and packed him off to the Royal Northern Hospital, then Arsenal's first choice for all such emergencies. At Old Trafford, Arsenal's improvised team was crushed 6–1. Arthur Shaw, playing resolutely in the unaccustomed role of centre half, broke his wrist and played no further part in the game.

Honour and glory

The Cup final team included Logie, who was not remotely fit 'with a hole in his thigh big enough to put in a small apple', as Tom Whittaker graphically put it, Daniel and Lishman. The game was effectively won and lost however in the 18th minute. Walley Barnes challenged Jackie Milburn, who tried to backheel the ball. Barnes, trying to evade contact with his knee, caught his studs in the turf and wrenched the ligaments of the knee. Bandaged, he tried gallantly but in

Hibs at Highbury

The programme for the charity match against the Scottish team Hibernian on 22 October 1952. The Gunners gave the visitors a football master class, winning 7–0.

Mist again

Arsenal's home game with Aston Villa falls foul of an old-fashioned London pea-soup fog after just 22 minutes on 2 January 1954. The match was abandoned after 22 minutes.

vain to carry on, and in fact wouldn't play again for another 18 months.

Lishman, however, twice came close to winning it. In only the second minute, he beat the big Newcastle centre half Frank Brennan in the air then, when the ball came down, hooked it fractionally wide of the far post. With 11 minutes left and the game still goalless, Freddie Cox forced a corner, took it himself from the left, and Lishman, surprisingly unmarked, put in a header which beat Ronnie Simpson in goal, but clipped the top of the bar.

Arsenal reorganised as best they could, but with Logie, usually the team's inspiration, struggling the odds were heavily on Newcastle. Ray Daniel, tumbling over Milburn, broke the bone in his already-injured arm, but carried on resiliently, with fine support from Lionel Smith at left back. However, five minutes from time, the talented Chilean international inside right George Robledo headed the ball against the post, and into the net. 'Tom,' said Stan Seymour to Whittaker after the game, 'ours is the Cup, yours is the honour and the glory.'

Arsenal
FOOTBALL CLUB
Season 1952-3

Charity Match   Wednesday, 22nd October, 1952
ARSENAL V. HIBERNIAN
KICK-OFF 7.30 p.m.

6d

Champions again

Changes were made for the 1952/53 season. Joe Wade, a versatile defender who'd made quite an impact in the first post-war season, at last came into his own, playing 40 out of the 42 Championship games at full back. Jack Kelsey established himself as first-choice goalkeeper, making 25 appearances. Ray Daniel would miss only a single League game, but this would be his last season with Arsenal, being transferred to Sunderland after a falling out with Tom Whittaker. The inveterate joker, Arthur Shaw, played 25 games for the Championship team. It was also the season in which Jimmy Logie received his sole cap for Scotland. Logie would probably not have been capped even then had not the Scottish selectors watched him tear the Hibernian defence to pieces in a floodlit friendly at Highbury, where the visitors were annihilated, 7–1.

Arsenal didn't keep their FA Cup challenge going beyond the sixth round, when they succumbed to Blackpool in a thrilling game at Highbury. Stanley Matthews, at his most elusive, made the opening goal for little Ernie Taylor. Arsenal's own little inside forward, Jimmy Logie, equalised. Blackpool's winning goal was at once a triumph and a

disaster for Blackpool's big Scottish international inside left, Alan Brown. Sprinting after a long pass, he was challenged by Kelsey, 'but alas, I did not bargain for Alan's speed. He was there first, by a split second, shot just as I dived, and the ball passed under my body and into the net.' But poor Brown paid heavily for his speed and his bravery. 'His left shin,' recalled Kelsey, 'met my hip at heaven knows how many miles an hour, and it stopped him dead.' The leg was broken and thus it was that Brown, whose goal enabled Blackpool eventually to reach Wembley, played no part in what has come to be known as the 'Matthews Final'.

Kelsey lost his place at Easter, when Arsenal beat Liverpool 5–3 in the League at Highbury, George Swindin coming back for the last seven games. It was a close run thing indeed, with Preston beating Arsenal 2–0 at Deepdale and drawing 1–1 at Highbury, the two teams remaining neck and neck till the very last moment. Preston won their last game 1–0 at Derby through a penalty by Tom Finney, which meant it was imperative for the Gunners to defeat Burnley at Highbury on a Friday evening at the start of May.

Burnley went ahead after eight minutes, but a rampant Alex Forbes equalised, and Arsenal after 26 minutes were 3–1 ahead. Burnley, however, fought back and scored in the second half, but the Gunners, massing in defence, clung on to their lead, and took the title on goal difference.

Mid-table doldrums

The Championship-winning team was growing old together, as indicated by an embarrassing 6–1 defeat in Bruges in a friendly by a dazzling Rapid Vienna. This proved something of a portent, for the team made a disastrous start to the 1953/54 season. Arsenal failed to win the first eight League games. In early September Chelsea won 2–1 at Highbury with embarrassing ease against a much-changed Arsenal side. Then there was a shattering 7–1 defeat at Sunderland. It would be George Swindin's last match. Tom Whittaker vainly sought reinforcements all over England.

The tide turned in mid September with a victory at Chelsea which Tom Whittaker himself judged to be lucky, Doug Lishman scoring twice in a 2–0 win, Arthur Shaw at his best. Two days later, a telephone call out of the blue by Brentford's chairman Frank Davies told Whittaker that Tommy Lawton was

for sale; Brentford were desperate for money. 'I am a lucky young man,' said the 33-year-old Lawton, joining the club against which he had scored those three decisive FA Cup goals in 1947. He'd play nine games that season, but score only once. Rising from an alarming bottom place, Arsenal proceeded to win ten and draw six of the ensuing 18 games. Ultimately, they would take 12th place; just one above where they had finished in the first post-war season. And what's more the Cup had another of its nasty surprises in store.

In the fourth round, after a 5–1 victory against Aston Villa, a home tie against Third Division Norwich City might have seemed a formality. A hard tackle between Norwich's Bobby Brennan and Alex Forbes led to the referee sending both of them off, though Forbes would subsequently be acquitted. The dangerous head of Tommy Johnston, Norwich's Scottish centre forward, beat Kelsey twice, and all Arsenal's late siege could not add to the single untidy goal by Jimmy Logie.

Mercer's farewell

April 1954 saw the team at Highbury against Liverpool in the League. Having lobbied hard for inclusion in the team, the veteran Joe Mercer was stretchered off with a broken leg, yet still with the resilience to wave a smiling farewell to the fans

Stretchered off
Talismanic Gunners skipper Joe Mercer is carried off the Highbury pitch after receiving a careeer-ending injury during Arsenal's 3–0 win against Liverpool on 10 April 1954.

On the brighter side, this was the season in which Peter Goring, who had previously lost form as a centre forward, re-emerged as a highly competent wing half, missing only a single League game. Derek Tapscott, the lively little Welsh opportunist who had made such a dramatic impact when given his chance the previous season, now gained a regular place in the attack. But this was still a team palpably in transition, finishing ninth in the League, and going out to a somewhat freakish goal in the FA Cup to Wolves at Molineux.

New faces of 1955

The following season saw numerous changes. Derek Tapscott confirmed himself as chief bombardier, with 17 goals in 31 matches. Jimmy Bloomfield scored only three, but he was now the acknowledged motivator of the midfield. Ebullient Vic Groves arrived from Orient, a confident, versatile attacker, who as an amateur had had a few League games for Spurs. He and Tapscott would combine profitably.

In the Cup, after being forced to a replay by lowly Bedford Town, they beat Aston Villa 4–1 at Highbury, followed that with victory at Charlton, but went down to Birmingham City at Highbury when, despite a long range goal driven home by Stan Charlton, the muscular full back who had arrived with Groves from Orient, they went down 3–1.

In February Alec Stock arrived at Highbury from Leyton Orient. Whittaker welcomed him, but he was less acceptable to the players. Stock was officially the new assistant manager, despite the fact that Jack Crayston retained that title. Stock travelled with the team to the game at Villa Park, but to their surprise, the players were told they would not be introduced to him until the following Monday. When Monday came, Stock invited the squad to the gym for a 'natter'. This consisted of his telling the team that at the end of the season, 20 of the players would be leaving Highbury. 'We were stunned, all of us,' wrote Kelsey later. 'We were just not used to being spoken to in that way.'

Stock, well known for his capacity to get his teams fit, instituted group rather than individual training, placing an emphasis on sprinting, chasing and turning. He decreed, perhaps unpopularly, there should be no smoking anywhere near the stadium. As it transpired, Stock stayed for barely six weeks. After his departure back to Orient, Arsenal proceeded

Cold War friendly
Arsenal take on Spartak Moscow in a friendly match at Highbury on 9 November 1954. Arsenal lost the match 2–1.

who had admired him for so long. Meanwhile, after an indifferent season, the Gunners finished an undistinguished twelfth in the League.

Season 1954/55 witnessed a home friendly against the other chief Moscow team, Spartak, which was refereed by Nikolai Latychev, the man who had been in charge of the fogged fiasco against Dynamo at White Hart Lane nine years earlier. Once again Latychev gave a crucially wrong decision. Two goals by the clever little Spartak centre forward Simonian had Spartak ahead at 2–1 when Arthur Milton burst into the penalty box from the right wing, only to be brought down from behind by the Russian left back before he could shoot. Latychev did not give the penalty.

At the final whistle when Latychev attempted to shake hands with Jimmy Logie, Jimmy refused. This incurred the anger of the Arsenal chairman, Sir Bracewell Smith. At Christmas when he shook hands with the whole squad, he failed to shake hands with Logie. In February 1955 Jimmy Logie left Highbury for a little-known non-League club in Gravesend and Northfleet.

to win seven of their last nine games, kept a clean sheet in half a dozen of them, and climbed from seventeenth place to a final fifth in the League.

The end of the Whittaker era

Tom Whittaker, the last true embodiment of the Herbert Chapman tradition, died after an operation in University College Hospital on 24 October 1956. Like his mentor Herbert Chapman, Whittaker had died in harness. 'Someone had to drive himself too hard for Arsenal,' he had said. 'Herbert Chapman worked himself to death for the club and if it is to be my fate, I am happy to accept it.' Joe Mercer, Whittaker's first captain, paid him memorable tribute. 'Meeting Tom Whittaker was the best thing that ever happened to me; he was the greatest man I ever met. ...Arsenal was his kingdom, but in every soccer playing country in the world he was acknowledged as a prince of the game. There never has been a greater man in football.' There is no doubt that after Sir Henry Norris and Herbert Chapman, in their deeply different ways, Tom Whittaker was the most important figure in

Babes at Highbury

Manchester United's fabulous Busby Babes made their last home appearance as a team in a match against the Gunners at Highbury on 1 February 1958. Tommy Taylor, right, was one of the players who were tragically killed in the Munich air crash five days after scoring twice in United's 5–4 win.

Arsenal's history. As a trainer, he surpassed the limitations of the role, his great natural gifts as a healer enabling him to cure in record time players who would otherwise have been out of the game for weeks or even months. His achievements as Arsenal manager were outstanding, transforming them as soon as he was appointed from the mediocre team which had flirted with relegation into one which won the League Championship at his first attempt. But by the time he died, Whittaker had been in charge at Highbury for the best part of a decade. In the mid 1950s his team gradually lost its way as

well as many of its star players, and the pressures on Whittaker had become intense. Arsenal in subsequent years were hardly in free fall, but neither would they for a long while be contenders in Cup and League.

Crayston in charge

The natural successor to Whittaker was plainly Jack Crayston, assistant manager, and former star player. He was a popular figure with the players who had come through the reserves. Crayston, to his credit, turned a previously poor season

around, lifting the team to fifth place in the Championship, and embarking on a Cup run which deserved to go further. After knocking out Stoke City, Newport County and Preston North End, the Gunners drew 2–2 at West Bromwich Albion. Albion, however, won the replay at Highbury with a goal that looked well offside.

In December 1957 Arsenal appointed Ron Greenwood as coach. His refreshing and abundant new ideas made training a pleasure. Yet even he could not prevent the debacle of Arsenal's defeat by lowly Northampton Town in the third round of the FA Cup. This was a crushing blow and from that point the writing was probably on the wall for Jack Crayston.

February 1958 saw a memorable home game against Manchester United, memorable in itself for the exhilarating football which produced nine goals, five of them for United, but also, so sadly, for the fact that this was destined to be the last time the dazzling young United side would play together in this country. The following week, after they had played Red Star in the European Cup in Belgrade, their aircraft crashed in the snow at Munich airport, killing and injuring some of the finest players of their era.

During that breathtaking and historic Highbury game it was as if both teams had cast defence to the winds. United roared into a 3–0 half time lead with goals by the powerful prodigy Duncan Edwards, Bobby Charlton and Tommy Taylor. Both Edwards and Taylor were to lose their lives in Munich. But

Arsenal, so recently humiliated at Northampton, rose from the ashes when, a quarter of an hour into the second half and within a mere three minutes, they scored three times to equalise. United's Viollet and Taylor made it 5–3 for United but Arsenal did not give up, reducing the score to 5–4.

Old and new

Crayston resigned in 1958. He was succeeded by another former Arsenal star, the goalkeeper George Swindin. 'They're night and day,' said one player of the combination between the traditionalist George Swindin and the radically inventive Greenwood, but the combination seemed to work. In his first season Swindin achieved an honourable third place in the Championship, but suffered an unlucky exit in the FA Cup replay against Sheffield United in the fifth round. After a 2–2 draw at Highbury when Dennis Evans and Len Julians scored the goals for the Gunners, things would surely have been different had not Jack Kelsey broken an arm in the replay at Sheffield, the Gunners losing 3–0.

The 1959/60 season was less productive; back to a dismal 13th place in the League, a wretched third round exit in the FA Cup at the hands of unfashionable Rotherham United, then enjoying a strong run in the Second Division. The Gunners drew the first game at Rotherham, were held to a 1–1 draw in the replay at Highbury, and finally ignominiously lost 2–0 to the Yorkshire team at Hillsborough.

Long-serving Gunner
Jack Crayston, former player and assistant manager, succeeded Whittaker as manager in 1956, but resigned after two years in the job, shortly after a humiliating FA Cup defeat against Northampton Town.

George the fourth
George Swindin, the fourth of five Georges to have managed Arsenal in the Club's long history, at Highbury on 6 August 1958, at the start of his spell in charge.

The slow road to former glory

For Arsenal the 1960s were a period of reconstruction. Footballing success remained elusive but the Club nevertheless continued to be forward thinking, installing the latest technologies at the stadium and gradually assembling the team that would once again bring trophies to Highbury.

Arsenal were glad to say goodbye to the 1950s. Since winning the FA Cup in 1950 and the League Championship in 1953, Highbury witnessed season after season of under-achievement. John Barnwell, the young Geordie wing half who had been recruited by Whittaker, said: 'It was a period of transition for the club, but for me Highbury is still steeped in happy memories.' Barnwell joined the club as a boy on amateur terms, and before getting anywhere near the first team had to pay his dues on the Highbury groundstaff. 'I have put many pints of my own sweat into that ground,' Barnwell recalls. 'One of our jobs as apprentices was to sweep rubbish down the great terraces, and we'd clean boots and do all the other jobs that needed doing around the ground. But it was a privilege to come to work at Highbury. There was a special atmosphere about it, and the club looked after you. When I was a boy I could have signed for any one of 15 clubs, including Newcastle, Sunderland or Middlesbrough close to my home. But I chose Arsenal, even though it was so far away, because of the spirit of the place, and because I felt my parents trusted that the club would take care of me. And they did.'

Improvements at Highbury

The 1960s was a decade when the ground was in transition as much as the team. Players did much of their training at Highbury in the early 1960s. They were not permitted to scar the sacred playing turf with their studs, so they went through their paces on a shale pitch behind the Clock End. Barnwell relates: 'We got more cuts and injuries training on that surface than we ever did playing in a match. The nearest we got to the actual pitch during the week was running laps around the perimeter.'

While those arrangements might sound rough and ready to modern ears, Arsenal were at the forefront of using modern techniques to get the best out of their players. In the summer of 1960 they even took part in an experiment to fit players with radio receivers allowing coaches to keep in contact during a match. The receiver, weighing 100 grams, was strapped under a player's arm and a wire ran up to an earpiece. Ron Greenwood, then an Arsenal coach, said: 'It could be a useful system if used properly, but something to be used sparingly because in football players must think for themselves.'

Ongoing improvements
In the 1960s various piecemeal improvements were made to the stadium including changes to the turnstiles at the southern end of the ground, as laid out in these plans of 1968.

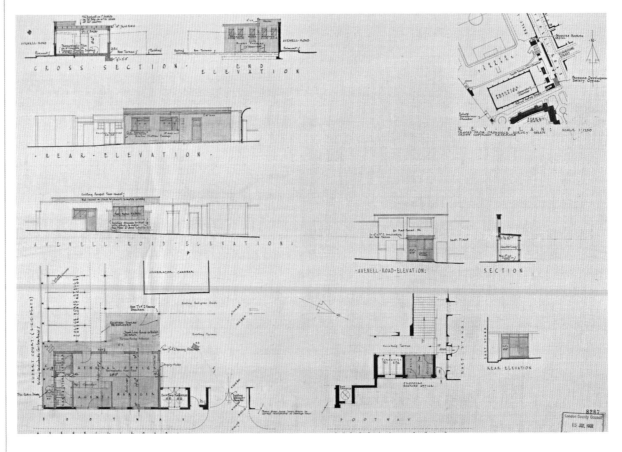

In 1963 the training pitch was roofed over, giving the players some protection from the elements. Ian Cook, curator of the Arsenal Museum, said: 'It looked like it was whacked together in a summer, and it was like an aircraft hangar, with great holes in the sides where the wind would howl through.'

The players certainly needed some protection from the weather in the atrocious winter of 1962–63. Highbury disappeared under a blanket of snow on Boxing Day, and the drifts on the terraces were ten feet deep. After a month, the ice age conditions relented sufficiently to allow the Gunners to play Oxford United at Highbury on 30 January, and the enforced winter break seemed to have done the team good, as they demolished the opposition 5–1.

Heating underfoot

But that chilly experience encouraged Arsenal to fit under-soil heating. A year later they spent £15,000 cutting trenches into the pitch, and laying a network of frost-busting electric coils. The system lasted until 1970, when a new under-soil heating system was installed at a cost of £30,000.

Highbury also saw its first major rebuilding since the 1930s in 1969, when 5,500 seats were installed in the lower West Stand paddock at a cost of £80,000, filling an enclosure where as many as 20,000 standing supporters might have crammed in before.

As Bob Wall, the club secretary, who had worked his way up from office boy in Herbert Chapman's time, presciently put it, 'Eventually, in ten years, you might have everybody sitting down. You can't force

the good old die hard British supporter who wants to stand in the rain, God help him and God bless him, but I think it is the right thing to do.' So in the autumn of 1962, soon after Billy Wright had taken over, Arsenal's architects were working on plans which could increase Highbury's seating to 18,000 by the following season.

Low attendances

The truth is that Highbury could afford to lose some capacity at this time. In the 1959/60 season crowds in the high 40,000s had been common. The visit of Tottenham Hotspur in September 1959 had attracted a gate-topping

Snowed off
Highbury is blanketed in snow, forcing the postponement of a match against Everton on 28 December 1962. The worst winter Britain had seen in decades played havoc with the fixture schedule, prompting Arsenal to lay under-soil heating.

Heating Highbury
Arsenal manager Billy Wright demonstrates Highbury's new under-soil heating system to, from left, Jimmy Magill, Ian Ure, Johnny MacLeod, Alan Skirton, George Eastham and Billy McCullough, 24 April, 1964. Thirty-one miles of heated cable was laid in the pitch to keep frost and snow at bay, allowing the Gunners to play even in the worst winter conditions.

George Eastham

The inside forward whose legal action blew football's iniquitous contract system out of the water, ushering in a fairer deal for professional footballers. Eastham signed for Arsenal in November 1960; he played a total of 207 League games and scored 41 goals for the Gunners before moving to Stoke City.

61,000. It was a different story by the end of the decade. In the 1969/70 season crowds in the 20,000s were more usual. The nadir came in April 1968, when for a home game towards the end of another mediocre campaign – a 3–2 win over Sheffield Wednesday – only 11,262 were present.

Given Arsenal's dwindling fortunes on the pitch, it was perhaps understandable that the stadium was not packed to the rafters for every home match. Watching Arsenal in the 1960s could be something of an ordeal. Lifelong Arsenal supporter Geoffrey Rowley went to his first match as a youngster in the 1930s. The football-watching experience had not changed much 30 years later. He said: 'There was still not much money about, and watching football was a cheap pastime in the 1960s. It was pretty basic. I'd stand on the Clock End, uncovered, and you wouldn't worry too much about bars or cafés or anything like that. But there was a warmth about it that has perhaps left the game. This was before massed singing and chanting was ever heard at games, but you had the roar of the crowd, which was like a language in itself. If for some reason I wasn't at the game, I could stand in our garden near Highbury, and I knew from the roars what was happening. It was a distinct type of roar if Arsenal scored, or they had conceded a goal, and so on.'

Billy Wright

Billy Wright, photographed soon after taking over as Arsenal manager, on 2 May 1962. Wright was an influential centre half and inspirational captain for Wolverhampton Wanderers and England, but he never quite scaled the same heights as a manager.

Facilities for the paying public had hardly improved since the ground opened in 1913. Highbury could be an unpleasant place to be if, for instance, you needed to answer a call of nature. In later years Highbury won awards for the quality of its toilets, but Ian Cook recalls: 'In the 1960s, you were talking about a wall, a trough and an open sewer.'

The nature of the crowds was changing too. In the early 1960s watching football was largely a peaceful affair. Even crowds at Highbury in excess of 60,000 were policed by a sprinkling of bobbies. Segregation of supporters was unheard of. By the end of the decade football crowds had become noisier, more partisan, and violence flickered on the periphery of the game. By the 1970s, gangs of rival football hooligans were turning city centres into warzones on Saturday afternoons. It was all a long way from 1960. Barnwell recalls: 'The crowds were different in the early 1960s. The rivalry between supporters was less intense. People would go to the match to appreciate the game, and they would look forward to seeing the great players on view – even if they were on the other side. You would hear booing, of course. But in general the atmosphere in Highbury and at other grounds was one of enjoyment. It was certainly more enjoyable to be a player in that era, before the game turned into a win-at-all-costs activity.'

There was also a cosier relationship between the players on the pitch and the people who paid their shillings to watch them perform. The football superstar had not yet been born in the early 1960s, and it would be a few more years before players such as Georgie Best and Charlie George found the kind of fame that transcended football. It was easier for supporters to identify with players who weren't vastly richer than themselves. In many cases, the players were worse off than the people who watched them.

Fortunes on the pitch

The start of the 1960s saw Greenwood go to his gleaming future at West Ham United, while Bill Dodgin, Jimmy Bloomfield and Tommy Docherty also left the club. The most significant arrival was that of the blond inside forward George Eastham, after he had won a long battle against his club, Newcastle United, and a historic decision in the High Court from Mr Justice Wilberforce that footballers' contracts were in

Up and away

Arsenal inside right John Radford leaps over Leicester City goalkeeper Gordon Banks in a League game at Highbury on 23 January 1965. The Gunners won 4–3.

restraint of trade. Elegant and balanced, an adept ball player, an economical and inventive user of the ball, Eastham soon became a favourite at Highbury.

1960/61 was a rewarding season for David Herd, scorer of 29 League goals in his 40 matches. Another Ulsterman, Terry Neill, a right half who would turn into an international centre half, and a future manager of the Club had 14 League games and scored one goal. But the Gunners were able to reach only 11th position in the league. And the Club's ambitions in the FA Cup once again proved a mere mirage, the team going out 2–1 in the third round at Sunderland, where David Herd scored the Arsenal goal.

The following season Herd was sold to Manchester United and, conforming with what the Italians call the Immutable Law of the Ex, the tendency of a player to score against his old club, would return to Highbury to score twice when United beat Arsenal in the League. In season 1961/62 however it was Arsenal who twice beat United in the League, by a thumping 5–1 at Highbury, only to lose 1–0 to them at Old Trafford in the fourth round of the Cup. In a season in which the powerfully built Alan Skirton, a winger signed from Bath City, was top scorer with 19 goals, the Gunners could finish only tenth in the Championship and in May 1962 it was announced that the long tradition of Arsenal nurtured managers would be broken at last.

England's hero as manager

The new manager was none other than Billy Wright, a famous captain of England, winner of no fewer than 105 caps. It was plainly a gamble, for Wright had never managed a club; he was, when appointed, England's Under 23 manager. Although the gamble was not a success in terms of trophies,

Baker delivers

Gunners' striker Joe Baker gets his head to the ball against Sheffield United in the League at Highbury, 6 November 1965. The Gunners won 6–2, with Baker, Skirton and Armstrong all scoring twice.

Wright's legacy was to be the young nucleus of the team which was destined to do the double. Wright survived for four years at Highbury, although it became increasingly clear that the burdens of managership were too heavy for one who had always been the quintessential schoolboy's hero.

No fewer than half a dozen of the squad with which Arsenal achieved the Cup and League double of 1970/71 were brought to the club as youngsters by Billy Wright: Pat Rice, Sammy Nelson, Peter Storey, Peter Simpson, Jon Sammels and John Radford. In addition, Bob Wilson, who would become a Scottish international goalkeeper, arrived as an amateur, and Charlie George, that maverick talent, as an apprentice. Significant signings also included the Scottish internationals Ian Ure and Frank McLintock, eventually to flourish as centre backs, and Joe Baker.

It was McLintock, who came from Leicester City as a right half before being so successfully converted to the middle of defence, who said, according to Norman Giller's biography of Billy Wright, that after a humiliating defeat by modest Peterborough United in a fourth round FA Cup tie in 1965, 'This was when Billy should have brought down the iron fist.

HIGHBURY HEROES

Bob Wilson 1963/64–1973/74

Goalkeeping legend Bob Wilson was born in Chesterfield, Derbyshire, and initially trained as a teacher. He started his footballing career with Wolverhampton Wanderers as an amateur, making his League debut in 1963. He soon attracted the attention of of the north London club for whom he would play until he retired from the game a decade later. He signed for Arsenal in the spring of 1964 and became a regular first team player by 1968. His contribution to the defence of the 1970/71 Double-winning team was immense. With the Club he gained winners' medals in the European Fairs Cup (1969/70), League Championship (1970/71). FA Cup (1970/71). He was capped twice for Scotland. He later returned to Highbury as goalkeeping coach.

But it just was not in him. He was simply too kind, too nice.'
The nadir of Wright's period as manager arrived early in May
1966. Inexplicably the Football League had obliged the
Gunners to play at home to Leeds United on the very evening
when Liverpool were due to contest the Final of the European
Cup Winners' Cup in Glasgow. So it was that a mere 4,554
spectators attended the game, and for Billy Wright, the die
was cast, however much Denis Hill-Wood publicly regretted
it. The team, which had taken seventh place in the
Championship in Wright's first season, a respectable
achievement, had by then sunk to 14th.

Highbury turns boxing ring

As the football season closed, Highbury became host to a
memorable sporting event. On 21 May 1966, Arsenal Stadium
staged a world heavyweight title fight between Cassius Clay,
as he then still was, and Henry Cooper, the British champion.
Arsenal director, Ken Friar, who was then Assistant Secretary,
remembers the run up to the fight as 'probably the most
hectic of my life'. Preparations included the complete
renovation and reseeding of the pitch, before it was boarded
over. Hundreds of chairs were brought in for the ringside
seating. Henry Cooper himself remembers his impressions of
the stadium: 'the dressing rooms ... were sheer class. The

facilities were incredible. I'd never seen anything like it ...
if I was a young player and saw those dressing rooms at
Arsenal, that would be enough to make me decide which
club I wanted to play for.'
   In the not quite six rounds the fight lasted, Cooper tried
time and again to exploit his famous left hook but Clay coolly
evaded it, boxing as skilfully as always on the retreat, and
frequently got through Cooper's defence with his insidious
left jabs. At one point, Clay, with glorious swaying motions of
head and body, eluded three of Cooper's left hooks in a row.
Finally, in that sixth round, Cooper staggered away from the
opposite corner to his own, blood pouring down his face from
a cut eye, the fight was stopped and victory was Clay's.

Heavyweights at Highbury
*Muhammad Ali, then known as
Cassius Clay, and Henry Cooper
slug it out in a world heavyweight
title fight at Highbury on 21 May
1966. Clay eventually won after the
fight was halted because of a cut
to Cooper's eye.*

Fight programme
*The souvenir programme for the
contest. The event was watched
by nearly 46,000 spectators
inside the stadium.*

Boarded over
*Preparations get under way
at Highbury for the world
heavyweight title fight between
reigning champion Cassius Clay
and British title holder Henry
Cooper. A boxing ring was
constructed in the centre of the
pitch, which was completely
boarded over.*

Mee and his team

Billy Wright's successor, appointed in the summer of 1966, could scarcely have seemed more of a contrast. Bertie Mee till then had been the club's excellent physiotherapist, a proper heir to Tom Whittaker, though where Whittaker had been a man with famously healing hands, Mee was a product of the age of technical advance; of deep diathermy heat, ultrasound waves and x-ray machines. Though he had briefly played professional football, he was not essentially a 'football man'. But he brought to the job of manager his own virtues of efficiency, authority, and a supreme ability to delegate when necessary.

Frank McLintock, who would be so successfully transformed from a right half to a centre half, albeit against his initial wishes, had no doubt of Bertie Mee's qualities as a manager. 'Bertie had the sense not to interfere. He wasn't too good about football, he didn't know too much about football, but he let David [Sexton] and Don [Howe] get on with it. Bertie's presence was always about. He was a strict little bastard. He kept his distance all the time, he seldom gave us any praise. We didn't need such pats on the back; we just got on with our job.'

Bob Wilson, goalkeeper of the 1970/71 Double-winning team, thought Mee 'was a disciplinarian almost to a fault. At times, he was way over the top. But his skill was in surrounding himself with a brilliant group of coaching assistants, notably Don Howe, and Steve Burtenshaw with the reserve team.' Wilson recalls, too, Bertie Mee's policy that the players must always be smartly attired, in 'the beautiful blue suits from Austin Reed'.

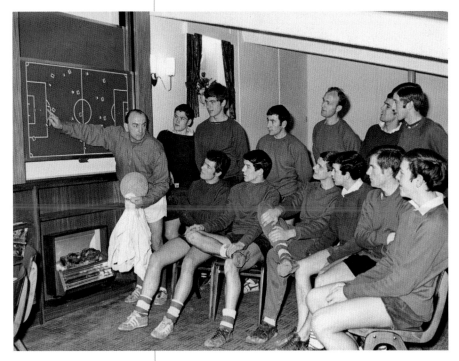

Don Howe recalls the luxurious warmth of the heated dressing room floors, which he had encountered as a visiting player. 'Arsenal was always a superb place to go to play, you learned that over the years. When you got there and walked down the corridor and went into the visitors' dressing room, the floor was warm … and it was lovely to take your shoes off, take your socks off; and you got your feet nice and warm before you went out to play. If you go out there and you've got your feet cold, you've got no feel for the ball.'

He remembers the staff room, used by Bertie: 'If Bertie wanted to talk to an individual player, he would take him into that room. On the walls were pictures of Joe Mercer, Tom Whittaker, the Comptons and all those, with the Cup. This was about 1967; 17 years since Arsenal had won a cup. Everybody saying, we want those bloody old photos down. But Bertie said no; when we win something, we'll take them down and replace them.'

A memorable stadium

Highbury itself made a powerful impact on the players of the period. 'A huge impression,' recalls McLintock, 'strategy, very traditional, everything was so established. The whole stadium just looked solid and dependable. Marble halls, marble staircases. That marble continued into the dressing

Class of '67

The 1966/67 Arsenal team line up at Highbury before playing Chelsea, 4 February 1967. Their all-red shirts were a new design for the season, intended to signal a new start for the team. Back row from left: George Graham, Colin Addison, Frank McLintock, Peter Storey, Peter Simpson, Bob McNab. Front row from left: Gordon Neilson, George Armstrong, Terry Neill, Ian Ure, Jon Sammels. Arsenal won the match 2–1.

Young George

Charlie George during his debut season at Highbury 1969. The striker scored 31 goals in 133 League games for the Gunners before joining Derby County in July 1975.

room, the treatment room, the boot room, and the shower room. It was heated. Instead of standing on cold marble in the winter, you were standing on heated marble, which was quite fantastic as well. They had an x-ray machine in the treatment room, so if there was any doubt about an injury, a fracture, you could go to hospital, immediately.'

Bob Wilson's introduction to Highbury stays vivid in his mind. 'Billy Wright took me on a trip up the stairs, on the landing, into the director's box, and it was the first time I'd seen it, and I thought, wow! He was clever, because the best thing he did was he took me down to the dressing room area

and there's this underfloor heating, under marble. This was amazing. Whether he intentionally did this or not, he took me down the tunnel as if I was playing. I felt as if I was walking not into a football ground but a cathedral. There were stands that were higher than I had ever seen, and the lights strung across the top of the stands. Well, I walked out there and I thought of it as a sort of cathedral.'

The road to recovery

Bertie Mee set about rebuilding. George Eastham and his flair were gone. The burden of construction in midfield now fell

heavily on the competent young East Anglian Jon Sammels though he was perhaps more industrious than inspired. George Graham, an elegant Scottish centre forward nicknamed 'Stroller', came from Chelsea, later to play as supporting cast to the powerful John Radford when he moved – a second Alf Kirchen – from the right wing to centre forward. From Huddersfield Town came the left back Bob McNab.

However, in season 1966/67, the team still looked pedestrian, seventh in the League, beaten by Birmingham in the fifth round of the FA Cup. The following season the team would finish ninth in the Championship. But Arsenal did reach the final of the League Cup in 1967/68, losing 1–0 to Leeds United in a dull game. By 1968/69 it seemed that the new management was working; Arsenal gained their highest League place for years, fourth. But in the FA Cup they yet again succumbed in the fifth round, this time at West Bromwich Albion, while they again reached and lost the final of the League Cup. This time, embarrassingly, it was to Swindon Town of the Third Division. An anticlimax indeed, after Spurs had been defeated 2–1 on aggregate in the semi-finals, Radford scoring in each game.

The darling of the North Bank

The new season (1969/70) saw the debut of Charlie George, the player who literally came straight off the terraces, the darling of the North Bank, to electrify his delighted fans, yet never to fulfil his huge promise. He was, as Frank McLintock, who admired him greatly, said, a player who 'might have been ahead of his time. He had his shirt outside his pants; the sort of thing that modern players do all the time. He captured the supporters' imagination ... [he was] one of their own.'

Expelled from the local Holloway School, a natural rebel, long-haired, defiant, sure of his own great abilities yet so highly strung that, on his own admission, he vomited before every game, George's repertoire was great. Tall and strong, he was a supreme ball player, forceful in the air, as well as a shrewd passer of the ball. In August 1969, George made his League debut at home to Everton. Things would quickly improve. At the Hawthorns George scored the only goal of the game against West Bromwich Albion with a drive from the edge of the penalty box.

European glory

In the domestic cups, Arsenal were frustrated, losing in replays to Blackpool in the FA Cup and Everton in the League Cup. But there was abundant compensation in Europe, where Arsenal in 1970 would take their first trophy.

HIGHBURY HEROES

Charlie George 1969/70–1974/75

Charlie George's natural ability on the ball and his total commitment to the Club made him an instant hero to the fans at Highbury. Islington-born and an Arsenal supporter since childhood, George worked his way up through the Arsenal reserves, making his League debut in August 1969. His career reached its zenith with his astonishing goal that won the FA Cup for the Club in 1971. He eventually left Arsenal in 1975 for Derby County. During his period at Highbury, he gained winners' medals in the European Fairs Cup (1969/70), League Championship and FA Cup (1970/71). He was capped for England once in 1976.

Glittering prize
Bertie Mee poses with the imposing European Fairs Cup at Highbury, 12 May 1970. Arsenal won the trophy by beating the Belgian team Anderlecht in the two-legged final 4–3 on aggregate.

Glentoran of Ulster were their first European Fairs Cup opponents (now known as the UEFA Cup). Arsenal easily won the first leg at home 3–0 but hardly distinguished themselves in the second, losing 1–0. But Arsenal gathered momentum with victories over Sporting Lisbon, Rouen and Dynamo Bacau, the latter thrashed 7–1 at Highbury. The semi-finals brought much harder opposition in Holland in the form of Johan Cruyff's Ajax. In the event, Arsenal were equal to the challenge. At Highbury, in the first leg, George scored twice, chattering away at Cruyff – who nicknamed him 'The Chairman' – throughout the game.

Arsenal scored a famous and resonant home victory against Ajax. who would win the European Cup itself in each of the next three seasons. The margin was 3–0 and even a 1–0 defeat in Amsterdam could not stop the Gunners from

progressing to the two-legged final of the competition against another team from the Low Countries, Belgium's Anderlecht.

Losing the first leg 3–1 in Brussels, Arsenal's chances looked bleak for the return. But they rose splendidly to the occasion, winning 3–0 at Highbury in front of a crowd of 51,612. The goals went to Eddie Kelly, a clever little Scottish midfielder, John Radford, now strongly installed at centre forward, and Jon Sammels. The 17-year trophy drought had been magnificently ended.

Double delight

Arsenal went into the 1970/71 season with justifiable confidence. It would be resplendent, giving the Gunners the Cup and League Double for only the second time that century that a club had achieved this feat, a decade after it had been

Making light of Liverpool
John Toshack of Liverpool challenges at Highbury, 28 November 1970. But Arsenal snuffed out the danger and won the match 2–0 with goals from George Graham and John Radford.

HIGHBURY HEROES

Frank McLintock 1964/65–1972/73

The Gunners' inspirational skipper who led the team back to trophy-winning form in the late 1960s and early 1970s, Glasgow-born McLintock, was signed as a wing half from Leicester City. He played successfully in that position for Arsenal for five years. However, his playing career was launched to a new level by the move in 1969/70 to central defence, a role at which he excelled, becoming an irreplaceable anchor for the team in their quest for the 1971 Double. He was sold to Queens Park Rangers in 1973. His winners' medals included the European Fairs Cup 1969/70, League Championship (1970/71), FA Cup (1970/71). He was capped nine times for Scotland.

achieved by their north London rivals, Tottenham Hotspur. A sweeping 4–0 home win in August against Manchester United featured a powerfully effective new striker, the young inside left Ray Kennedy. With a fierce left foot and his menace in the air, Kennedy would play a telling part in Arsenal's success that season. Peter Storey meanwhile, an uncompromising right back, now became an equally uncompromising right half. John Radford scored a hat-trick that day. Peter Simpson would blend into the defence as left-sided centre back, a player whom Terry Neill admired for his talents, while wondering how much further he might have gone with a less relaxed approach. The team that was to achieve the double was criticised at the time for its supposedly cautious, uninspired nature. There were indeed times when the team could look unadventurous, yet with such players as Charlie George, Eddie Kelly and George Graham, all men of flair, with as lively and consistently dashing a winger as little Geordie Armstrong, it could hardly be written off so readily. Nevertheless the early part of the season was not without its agonising moments, as with the 5–0 defeat at Stoke City on 26 September. But this came only three days after Arsenal had finally beaten Lazio 2–0 at Highbury in the second leg of their European Fairs Cup tie. After the first leg in Rome, which was drawn 2–2, a Lazio player started a brawl by attacking Ray Kennedy during the post-match dinner. Mee got his players away safely.

Early in 1971 Mee told his men they could expect two matches a week for the rest of the season. Goals by Charlie George secured a fifth round FA Cup victory on a heavy pitch against Manchester City at Maine Road, when he scored twice, and a hard won sixth round success against Leicester City at Highbury in a replay, when he headed the only goal before a crowd of 57,443. In March Stoke were beaten 2–0 in a semi-final replay after a 2–2 draw in Sheffield.

Championship climax

So the Gunners' season built up to a last week crescendo in a neck-and-neck finish with Leeds, when, absurdly and unfairly, they were forced to play two crucial games in close

Title clincher
Arsenal celebrate Ray Kennedy's winner at White Hart Lane which secured the Championship on 3 May 1971. The Gunners' 1–0 win against Spurs put them one win away from their first-ever Double as Liverpool waited in the FA Cup final.

succession. On the Monday, away to Spurs at White Hart Lane, the match that would decide the League Championship, followed by the FA Cup final against Liverpool on the Saturday. The north London derby, always so hectically contested, was given added edge by the fact that Spurs were all out to prevent the Gunners equalling their own record, as the only team that century to win the League and Cup double.

And what an astonishing evening that would be! Frank McLintock reckoned that some 40,000 fans were locked out of the ground. Arsenal's team coach inched its way through the thick crowds at a funereal pace. At one point, McLintock looked out to see his wife and Armstrong's out in the road. He had the coach stopped to take them aboard, much to Bertie Mee's displeasure.

Success at Spurs

If Arsenal won the game, they would automatically become the champions. A goalless draw would suffice, but a score-draw would condemn the Gunners to be runners-up. Spurs made it very hard for them. McLintock recalls that Alan Mullery and Alan Gilzean, English and Scottish internationals respectively, were especially committed. 'They were really up for it. They didn't want us to do the Double ... We went out, and I think the players felt in a good mood. We knew we had to win by a goal. We were behind Leeds United all the way, 25 out of the last 26 games; and it was a great game, as well, a spectacle for someone going to watch it.'

The game was settled when Armstrong, out on the left, won the ball away from Joe Kinnear, the Spurs right back, and crossed a ball which Ray Kennedy headed in off the underside of the crossbar. The Championship and the first

part of the Double had gone to Arsenal. And so, five days later, the Gunners travelled across London to Wembley.

'Bill Shankly,' recalled Bob Wilson, of Liverpool's ever volatile manager, 'was trying to do his own psychology bit before the game: "Tell Bob Wilson it's a nightmare pitch for goalkeepers."' Wilson would perhaps have cause to remember as much after the game, even if he and Arsenal would come out on top.

McLintock exhausted

It was not a game that Frank McLintock enjoyed. 'There's a big, big load on your mind,' he recalled, having been four times on the losing side in Wembley finals, 'hoping you perform and don't have another defeat. I was one of the most tired people on the whole field. I'd given everything for 60 games; and six pre-season games. I was jumping against John Toshack, six foot three. Ninety degrees and extra time and a Cup final when I'm going to be beaten again. It was a disaster for me. I managed to do pretty well and keep him quiet, but physically I was spent. I couldn't even crawl up the steps to lift the Cup, I was so desperate. It was an anticlimax, and I would never get the feeling back.'

Ecstasy in extra time

Yet though the game went goalless into extra time, there was no doubt that over the initial 90 minutes, Arsenal were much the better team. John Radford, latterly out of form, simply toyed with Liverpool's bemused central defenders, well supported from midfield by George Graham and Charlie George, with Geordie Armstrong lively on the wing. Ray Clemence, in Liverpool's goal, alone kept them afloat with a catalogue of fine saves. But chances have not only to be made but to be put away. So it was that with George Graham twice coming so close with two fine headers, the game went into extra time; and it was Liverpool who scored.

In just two minutes, Peter Thompson, an ebullient substitute, sent Steve Heighway racing away on the left. As he advanced, Bob Wilson, clearly anticipating a cross came off his line; whereupon Heighway shot between him and the near post. With a gallant save from Brian Hall's volley, Wilson made amends. After 11 minutes of extra time, however, Arsenal were deservedly level. Kennedy and Radford passed

their way forcefully through the thick of the Liverpool defence, Eddie Kelly, on as a lively substitute, struck and Graham appeared to make contact in the process probably confusing Clemence, for the ball eluded him to cross the line.

Six minutes of the second period had gone when George scored his spectacular winner. As George himself remembered it, 'Bob Wilson knocks the ball up field; at the halfway line George Graham heads it on to me. I touch it to John Radford and he runs as I move forward. Raddy sweeps it to me sweet as a nut and from the edge of the box I connect. Bob McNab was first up to me, the captain Frank McLintock shouted at me and the rest is a bit of a blur.'

Those who were there will never forget the sight of George, having struck the winning goal, lying flat on his back, arms outstretched, waiting for his ecstatic team mates to pick him up. The Double was Arsenal's.

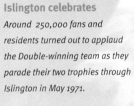

Islington celebrates
Around 250,000 fans and residents turned out to applaud the Double-winning team as they parade their two trophies through Islington in May 1971.

Bringing home the Cup
Gunners' captain Frank McLintock shares the moment with some overjoyed fans as he holds up the FA Cup during the double-winning celebrations around the streets of Islington.

Highbury and the changing face of football

Football clubs in the 1970s and 1980s were in transition. Arsenal embraced the changing times with community schemes and by bringing the stadium into the modern era with the Clock End redevelopment. And the team played their part too, with the glorious finale to the 1988/89 season.

The early 1970s saw football in Britain and Arsenal, in particular, in transition. It was still a raw game, played in front of crowds of largely working-class men. The terraces had only limited areas of seating and facilities for spectators were often basic. Apart from increased seating in the West Stand, Highbury Stadium was largely unchanged since World War II. Yet the experience of watching football at Highbury nevertheless proved magical for a new generation of football supporters, most famously, the novelist Nick Hornby, whose autobiographical account of being an Arsenal supporter through the 1970s and 1980s, *Fever Pitch*, provides an unsurpassed insight into the highs and lows of being a football fan. Hornby describes his first experience of the North Bank in 1972:

'It seemed enormous … a vast expanse of steep grey steps over which had been sprinkled a complex even pattern of metal crush barriers … I loved it there. I loved the different categories of noise; the formal, ritual noise when the players emerged (each player's name called in turn, starting with the favourite, until he responded with a wave); the spontaneous shapeless roar when something exciting was happening on the pitch; the renewed vigour of chanting after a goal or a sustained period of attacking.'

Loss of momentum

In the season after achieving the Double, Arsenal's results were honourable rather than triumphant. They competed strongly both domestically and in Europe, but tended to fall if not at the last then at the penultimate hurdle. A major transfer, in the 1971/72 season, was that of Alan Ball from Everton for the then massive fee of £220,000. A highly mobile, competitive inside forward, Ball was renowned for his role in England's World Cup victory of 1966. His arrival, however, often meant that Charlie George, who preferred a striker's role, would be moved up front, which disrupted the

productive partnership between John Radford and Ray Kennedy.

Having contributed so much to the Double success and seemingly feeling unappreciated, in the summer of 1971 the coach Don Howe unexpectedly left to become manager of his former club, West Bromwich Albion. In his place stepped up the reserves' coach, Steve Burtenshaw, under whom the team made an excellent beginning, thrashing Chelsea 3–0 at Highbury. The only disappointment was the relatively small crowd in the windy, sunlit stadium.

A few weeks later at a sunny Highbury again, a somewhat weakened Leeds United were beaten 2–0. George Graham, splendidly on song, scored a superb first half goal. In early October, Arsenal, still without the injured Charlie George, accumulated a four goal lead at home to Newcastle United, before Malcolm Macdonald replied twice. But in mid-November, with George back in the team the Gunners lost at home to Manchester City, who won there for the first time in eight seasons. A succession of defeats both at home and away ensured that Arsenal would finish the season no higher than fifth in the Championship. Sheffield United accounted for the Gunners in the fourth round of the League Cup, after Newcastle had been routed by an unequivocal 4–0 in the previous round at Highbury.

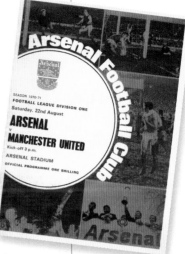

In the FA Cup the Gunners had a better run. Derby were overcome in a three-match series in the fifth round, consisting of 2–2 draw at Derby, a goalless draw at Highbury and a 1–0 win in the decider at Leicester. Charlie George scored both Arsenal's goals in the first tie, as he had in the League. The sixth round brought an uneasy 1–0 win across London at Leyton Orient. That put the Gunners, for the second year running, into the semi-finals against Stoke City, and again it took two games to finish the job. A 1–1 draw at Villa Park was followed by a 2–1 win at Goodison Park.

Domestic and European disappointments

Meanwhile, the Gunners had made a brave bid against Ajax in the European Cup; an Ajax team now far more formidable than when the Gunners had beaten them in the Fairs Cup, competing as holders of the trophy. In Amsterdam, Arsenal were outplayed by these pioneers of Total Football. The final score of 2–1 hardly reflected the reality of the game. In the return at Highbury, Arsenal took the gamble of deploying the gifted little Scottish outside right Peter Marinello, who'd been signed in January 1970 from Hibernian for a fee of £100,000, but hadn't played for the first team for six months. Unfortunately for the Gunners, the only goal of the game was

scored by George Graham. Trying to head the ball back to Bob Wilson, he disastrously headed it past him for an own goal.

Arsenal's opponents in the FA Cup final were Leeds United, who began as favourites. Bob Wilson was expensively absent, after a knee injury sustained in the semi-final; Geoff Barnett took his place. This, the centenary FA Cup final, was blemished by many a foul, and was won by Leeds United 1–0.

Elusive honours

In the 1972/73 season honours were tantalisingly elusive for the Gunners; runners-up to Liverpool in the League and beaten in the FA Cup semi-final by Sunderland. There were two black days in the Championship; a 5–0 defeat by Derby County, away, in November and a 6–1 thrashing at Leeds in the last game of the tournament in May. Highpoints had included a masterly 2–0 victory over Liverpool at Anfield in February, and an FA Cup sixth round victory over Chelsea at Highbury in front of a massive crowd of nearly 63,000.

Among the new faces that season were Jeff Blockley, who came from Coventry to play 20 games at centre half. In the early phase of the season, Peter Marinello made 13 appearances, still seeking to fulfil his promise. Of him, Bertie Mee had said, 'He was subjected to an educational situation

by his colleagues. You can't just tell a player to go out and do it. He's got to acquire the habits over at least a period of six months.' In Marinello's case it was more like two years. Marinello himself said ruefully, 'I didn't think it would take so long,' paying tribute to Steve Burtenshaw's encouragement. Weight-lifting and cross-country running improved his physique. The swerve and the pace remained.

Changing times

At the end of the season, Steve Burtenshaw was replaced as coach by the Liverpudlian Bobby Campbell, who had been coaching Queens Park Rangers. Debatably and perhaps disastrously, the emblematic Frank McLintock left too, allowed to cross London to Queens Park Rangers. Releasing McLintock for a minuscule £25,000, Bob Wilson deemed 'a grievous error'.

The 1973/74 season began with a meaningless home game against Wolverhampton Wanderers, for the fatuous purpose of deciding which of the beaten 1973 semi-finalists should be given third place. Wolves took it 3–1, but Arsenal a week later, at home again, made a promising League start, easily beating Manchester United 3–0, in roasting heat. Charlie George, with his physical advantage over most of his opponents, had a joyful afternoon, a reminder that, on form, he was one of the most talented and original young players in Britain. Ray Kennedy gave Arsenal the lead in the second minute, Radford made it 2–0 in the second half, then who should head elegantly against the Arsenal bar but George Graham, who had transferred to Manchester United. Alan Ball raced through to get Arsenal's third.

A date with City
The matchday programme for the visit of Manchester City on 28 October 1972. The match was a goalless draw.

Having a ball
Alan Ball scores from a penalty in front of the Clock End in an FA Cup quarter-final replay against Chelsea at Highbury on 20 March 1973. The Gunners went through 2–1.

After the highs came the lows, including a 5–0 defeat by Sheffield United and an early League Cup exit after going down 1–0 to Tranmere Rovers at Highbury. In the FA Cup Arsenal went out in the fourth round following a lost replay against Aston Villa.

In the summer of 1974, Arsenal let another good player go; Ray Kennedy was transferred to Liverpool, where he would have a new lease of life as a left-sided midfielder. To replace Kennedy, Arsenal bought Brian Kidd from Manchester United, the left-footed opportunist who had celebrated his 19th birthday by replacing the injured Denis Law in Manchester United's 1968 European Cup final attack against Benfica at Wembley, and scoring. The brave and agile keeper Jimmy Rimmer, who'd arrived, himself, from Old Trafford the previous season, now had the formidable task of succeeding Bob Wilson in the Arsenal goal.

The team made a disastrous beginning to the 1974/75 season, mired in a run of 10 matches without a win; only for sunlight suddenly to shine through the clouds with an emphatic 3–0 victory over West Ham United at Highbury. The season, which saw Arsenal finish a dismal 16th in the

League and exit from the FA Cup in the sixth round, provided some consolation, however, in the dazzling emergence of the young Liam Brady. Spotted by a Welsh scout visiting Dublin at the age of 13, he was invited for a trial in London. Brady later remembered: 'I did well in my trial. All my school holidays from then on I spent over there.' Lodging with a family in Finsbury Park, he recalled being a 'little homesick in the first year, it was very tough.' On his first impressions of Highbury he said, 'You knew you were coming into a top Club, a place with style and swagger.'

Brady made his first team debut at the age of 17 in October 1973 and played 13 League games that season, initially on the left wing. In 1973/74 he would come fully into his own as an inside left in the great Highbury tradition of playmakers that had begun with Alex James.

In the summer of 1975 Charlie George was sold to Derby County for £90,000. Extravagantly gifted, the darling of the North Bank, George was endlessly subject to his unpredictable temperament. He had sworn at Bertie Mee when dropped after a 5–1 defeat at Wolverhampton and had given the Derby crowd a two fingered salute after scoring

a goal for Arsenal at the Baseball Ground, and he had time and again been guilty of violent episodes. Yet in the words of Bob Wilson, 'I don't think we'd have won the Double without Charlie. He was our one free spirit.' Such was the affection that the fans had for George that, when he returned to Highbury to play there for Derby County, a fan came out of the North Bank to present him with a bunch of flowers.

In April 1976 Bertie Mee stood down. It was a season in which the Gunners finished a depressing 17th in the Championship, and there were alarming gaps on the terraces at Highbury, with attendances sometimes even below 20,000. The new incumbent, Terry Neill, was a popular choice, for years an Arsenal player, a Northern Ireland international, more recently the moderately successful manager of their historic rivals, Tottenham Hotspur.

Neill's Arsenal

Neill lost no time in making his presence felt in the transfer market and over the next few seasons made a number of key signings both of players and coaching staff. Brian Kidd had moved on, a new striker was badly needed, and Neill ambitiously and successfully set his sights on one of the most successful in the First Division: Malcolm Macdonald of Newcastle United, the Tyneside's idolised centre forward, a lethally effective goal-scorer, possessed of pace, power and a devastating left foot.

Another of Neill's inspired signings was that of Alan Hudson from Stoke City. As a young inside right with Chelsea, Hudson had seemed one of the great emerging talents of English football. But he broke a leg shortly before the 1970 Cup final, fell out with Chelsea's then manager, Dave Sexton, and went North to Stoke. Neill had no doubt of his abilities.

1976/77 was essentially and perhaps inevitably a transitional season, though the disastrous League positions of the previous two seasons were radically improved; Arsenal finished a respectable eighth. In the FA Cup the team crashed out 4–1 at Middlesbrough in the fifth round.

Frank Stapleton, a former Arsenal apprentice, made his League debut in March 1975, became an ideal partner for Macdonald, and, strongly built, adroit, quick-minded and quick of foot, a powerful force himself after Macdonald had gone. In the close season of 1977, Neill brought off two more

HIGHBURY HEROES

David O'Leary 1975/76–1992/93

The precocious David O'Leary, signed for Arsenal as an apprentice in 1973, and made his first appearance in the League in August 1975. He was among the finest and most versatile of all Arsenal's centre halves. 'To be honest,' he said, 'I didn't want my time at Arsenal to end. But I was thrilled to be able to compete 20 full years of service with them.' During his years as an Arsenal player, he made a record 772 apperances and won winners' medals in the League Championship (1988/89, 1990/91), FA Cup (1978/79, 1993/94) and League Cup (1986/87). He was capped for Ireland 68 times.

important strokes. He persuaded Don Howe to return as coach to Highbury from Leeds. And for a derisory £40,000 he signed one of the finest goalkeepers of that or any other era, Pat Jennings, from his former club Tottenham Hotspur. Arsenal's goalkeeping hero, Bob Wilson, was another of Neill's signings. He recalls. 'I'd begun to realise the need for a specialist [goalkeeping] coach. Wilson asked, "What on earth am I going to do with Pat Jennings?" I said, "Just keep him happy," and Bob did.'

Cup finals lost and won

In the 1977/78 season, the Club moved up to fifth place in the Championship, and went all the way to the final of the FA Cup for the first time since 1972. The opposition was Ipswich, reaching Wembley for the first time.

Arsenal began the match briskly and well, but Ipswich took up the running, Paul Mariner, their centre forward, hit the bar, Pat Jennings, who'd been playing at Wembley since his youth international days, looked strangely ill at ease. At half time, the question was whether Ipswich had missed their chance. Towards the end of the second half Pat Jennings made a glorious right-handed save from the right back George Burley. But, six minutes later, even he could do nothing when Geddis

beat Nelson on the outside and crossed the ball, Young made minimal connection, Osborne banged the loose ball between Jennings and the near post, and the Cup went to Ipswich.

Arsenal were resilient enough to reach the following season's Cup final too, after a remarkable saga that included a gruelling three-match series against Sheffield Wednesday at Leicester City's ground in the third round; a 2–2 draw, a hectic 3–3 draw, finally a 2–0 victory for the Gunners. By contrast, the 1–0 victory over Brian Clough's Nottingham Forest in the fifth round was memorable. The Gunners had to withstand a real battering. But in the end Frank Stapleton just walked Forest's centre half Larry Lloyd beyond the near post, dropped off from a corner, got the yard that he needed, and managed a near-post header.

Following a comfortable 2–0 win in the semi-final at Villa Park against Wolves, the Cup final, against Manchester United, had one of the most extraordinary, dramatic conclusions of any seen at Wembley, involving three goals in the breathless last three minutes.

At half time Arsenal were leading 2–0, courtesy of Brian Talbot (a recent signing from Ipswich) and Stapleton. But on 86 minutes, United suddenly got back in the game with a goal from Gordon McQueen and two minutes later with

another from Sammy McIlroy. But not for long. In the 89th minute Alan Sunderland got on the end of a cross from Graham Rix and the Cup was back at Highbury. Don Howe said, ' It was a story book ending, if an author had written that, nobody would have believed it.'

Success without silverware

The 1979/80 season was one of marvellous moments but without trophies. Arsenal achieved fourth place in the League, and were beaten in two Cup finals; the FA Cup and the European Cup Winners' Cup. It was the season in which the exuberant Johnny Hollins arrived from Queens Park Rangers. It was arguable that the Gunners suffered that season from their success through the huge demands of an overcrowded football season, although nobody could have predicted the four-match semi-final marathon against Liverpool through which Arsenal reached the FA Cup final for the third year in a row. The initial game against Liverpool at Hillsborough ended in a goalless draw. There followed two 1–1 draws at Aston Villa's ground, until at last a goal by Brian Talbot put Liverpool out at Coventry's Highfield Road.

Before the first semi-final against Liverpool, Arsenal had been obliged to play twice in a week, including a torrid semi-final first leg of the European Cup Winners' Cup at Highbury and a Monday fixture away to Spurs. The latter was the match in which the highly promising 17-year-old playmaking left-footer Paul Davis made his debut. Just two days later in Turin, the Gunners had to play the first leg of the semi-final against Juventus.

The home leg against Juventus on 9 April played in front of a crowd of 51,998, which ended 1–1, saw Marco Tardelli, destined to score for Italy in the World Cup final of 1982 in Madrid,

sent off; and the usually urbane and elegant Roberto Bettega guilty of a crippling foul on David O'Leary, that went unpunished. The return visit to Turin provided a memorable win for the Gunners. The only goal was powerfully headed by a newcomer, the young Paul Vaessen, exploiting a cross from Rix. Within two years Vaessen suffered a career-ending knee injury, and this talented player died sadly young.

The FA Cup final at Wembley was an all London affair, the opposition being West Ham. After such a debilitating programme, Arsenal's minds seemed as weary as their legs. West Ham would become the third Second Division team to win the Cup in seven years. Arsenal's right-flank defence looked slow and vulnerable, Brady was dropping too deep, Stapleton and Sunderland up front were inadequately served and largely dominated by the West Ham centre backs, Alvin Martin and Billy Bonds. The only goal came from a rare header by Trevor Brooking.

Only four days later, poor, weary Arsenal had another final to contend with, that of the European Cup Winners' Cup against Valencia in Brussels. It was another disappointing game, which went to penalties after a goalless draw and extra time. Arsenal's two renowned left-footers each missed from the spot, first Liam Brady, then, decisively, poor Graham Rix.

Team changes

1980/81 saw the loss of the irreplaceable Liam Brady to Juventus. At least Arsenal could rely on the inventions of Graham Rix, while the promising youngster, Paul Davis, was clearly coming up on the rails. Davis had been with the Club since he was 13 years old and turned up at Highbury for schoolboys' training. 'It was fantastic,' he recalled recently, 'because I supported them from when I was ten. The stadium is for me my life. Even now. The stadium itself is part of me. I've spent as much time there as any other building.'

Arsenal in the summer of 1980 did acquire, in a curiously convoluted deal, the Crystal Palace and future England left back, Kenny Sansom. But only after they had bought the young Queens Park Rangers centre forward Clive Allen for a million pounds, and passed him on to Palace pre-season without his having played an Arsenal game. In retrospect, perhaps it would have been even better had Arsenal held on to both players, for Clive Allen would go on to score

prolifically for Spurs. Stapleton, in his last season, scored 14 League goals. No one else achieved Double figures. But third place in the League was the best that Arsenal had attained for years, even if there was disappointment in the domestic cups. The Gunners were eliminated by Everton in the FA Cup, defeated by Spurs in the League Cup.

In the 1981/82 season, without the firing power of Stapleton, the Gunners took fifth place in the League, but scored a mere 48 goals. To rub salt in the wound, Stapleton was now playing for Manchester United. The North Bank greeted him with choruses of derision whenever he came back to Highbury with United.

The season also saw the Gunners go out of the FA Cup to the eternal rivals Spurs at White Hart Lane in the third round by a solitary goal. They were also ejected from the League Cup at Anfield where Liverpool beat them 3–0 after a goalless draw at Highbury. In the 1982/83 season, in which the team finished 10th in the League and lost to Manchester United in an FA Cup semi-final, the home crowd at Highbury also had the misfortune to witness a crushing 5–2 defeat by Spartak Moscow in the second leg of the first round of the UEFA Cup. Terry Neill later admitted, 'They murdered us. A bit of a shock to the system. But the good old Arsenal fans recognised a good performance.'

Rising to the occasion
Frank Stapleton in action against Southampton at Highbury on 19 August 1980. He scored the only goal of the match to give the Gunners a 1–0 victory.

Good buys and goodbye

One of Neill's best buys, Tony Woodcock, who signed for the Club in 1982, played in that game and in 34 League matches, scoring 14 goals in season 1982/83. Woodcock had made his name under Brian Clough with his local club, Nottingham Forest. Then he had gone to Cologne, where he had flourished in the Bundesliga. 'It was a question of patience, really,' Neill reflects. 'That deal took four or five months to accomplish. A marvellous player.'

Another new arrival was Charlie Nicholas, bought from Celtic in the summer of 1983 in what would prove to be Neill's last major signing. Several other clubs, not least Manchester United, were interested in the young Scottish international forward, who would prove another of those tantalising mavericks who never quite fulfilled their promise. It was in fact, the resourceful Ken Friar, Arsenal's long-serving director, who clinched the deal in Glasgow, while Arsenal were on

summer tour. Taking a two pence piece from his pocket, Friar put it on the table and said, 'Gentlemen, I think that raises our offer above the others.' So Nicholas came to Highbury.

Neill himself would not be at the Club much longer. His departure had been made inevitable by defeat in November 1983 in a Football League Cup tie at Walsall. Things had been going awry that season, apart from a spanking 6–2 home victory in the League against Aston Villa. An embattled Neill said bitterly of his team, 'They don't seem to know what it is to hunger for goals and glory … But I'll tell you now, we'll finish in the top six again this season. Whether or not I'll be around to see it is another matter.' He wasn't, but they did.

Howe re-makes the team

It seemed the natural thing to promote Don Howe in Neill's place and it was duly done, giving Howe at last the job he must long have coveted. On Boxing Day 1983, Don Howe took

Standing room only
A packed North Bank watches the first game of the 1983/84 season, against Luton Town, 27 August 1983. The Gunners won 2–1 with goals from McDermott and Woodcock.

his Arsenal team to Tottenham Hotspur for the traditional north London derby, and won 4–2. 'We did it for Terry Neill,' Howe told the Press. He took over a team that was essentially in a state of transition. Liam Brady and Frank Stapleton had gone, but in due course, Howe would discover he had a highly promising centre forward on the books in the shape of the tall young Irishman Niall Quinn. He had joined Arsenal at the age of 17, and made his League debut two years later on the same day in 1985 as another 19-year-old with a great future with the Gunners ahead of him, Martin Keown, secured a regular first team place. Another new arrival was the English international centre forward Paul Mariner, who was signed from Ipswich Town and made his debut in February 1984. To replace the wonderfully durable Pat Jennings, Howe signed John Lukic from Leeds United, giving him his League debut in April 1984 against Stoke. Finally, recognising that as manager, he himself could no longer coach day by day, Howe installed John Cartwright as his coach.

At the end of Howe's first period in charge, Arsenal finished a respectable sixth in the League, and were knocked out in the third round of the FA Cup 3–2 at Middlesbrough.

The 1984/85 season saw the arrival of the accomplished right back Viv Anderson from Nottingham Forest. This time Arsenal finished seventh in the League, but having knocked little Hereford United out of the FA Cup in the third round 7–2 at Highbury after a 1–1 draw away, in the next round they fell somewhat embarrassingly away to York City, 1–0, having gone down in the League Cup at Oxford United.

The 1985/86 season would prove Howe's last. Once again the team took an undistinguished seventh place in the League and once again the Gunners needed a replay to knock out lowly Hereford United, this time in the League Cup. The team went on to reach the fifth round, where they lost to Aston Villa. But they crashed out of the FA Cup at Luton in a fifth round second replay, 3–0.

Crucially for Arsenal's board, the supporters were voting with their feet; regular attendances at Highbury went down alarmingly to fewer than 20,000, the lowest since Herbert Chapman's day. The consequence for Howe was inevitable. He recalls, 'That same March, the Arsenal Chairman, Peter Hill-Wood, said to me in a nice way, "I think we're going to have a change." I said, "Fine." '

Stars of the future

Some familiar faces in the 1983 Arsenal Youth team, among them: Tony Adams (back row fourth from left); Martin Hayes (back row third from left); Martin Keown (back row, far right); and David Rocastle (front row, far left).

Graham strolls back

Who next? The board were known to favour Terry Venables, who had been burning so brightly in Catalonia with Barcelona. But Venables was not available. So in May 1986 Arsenal turned to their elegant attacker of the 1970/71 Double-winning team, George Graham, then manager of the south London club Millwall.

Graham, beyond all doubt, hit the ground running. His first season was successful beyond all expectation; fourth place in the Championship, which the Gunners led for a dozen weeks, and victory in the League Cup. It was arguable that the vibrant young team would have done better still had it not been for a profusion of fixtures, including three gruelling League Cup ties against the historic rivals Spurs, the last of which saw Paul Davis seriously injured when fouled by Clive Allen, and forced out of the side for key games.

Like most Arsenal players and managers, Graham was enchanted by the Arsenal Stadium; its marbled walls, its heating. He described his feelings about what he termed '*the* stadium in England': 'To think there was actually a

stadium with underground heating in the famous Marble Halls. When I joined the Club, you noticed there was heating in both dressing rooms and then, those two stands!'

The team takes shape

Martin Hayes, who had signed for the Gunners in 1983/84, found effective form on the left flank. On the other flank was the dashing 19-year-old David Rocastle. Then, most precocious of all, there was Tony Adams, who had made his League debut in November 1983 as a 17-year-old, and began to appear regularly in the first team in season 1986/87. 'I never had any doubts about him,' says Don Howe, 'I told the board, this lad will play for England, because I knew he was a good leader, in a similar mould to Frank McLintock.'

Celebrating a century

How appropriate that when Arsenal's 100th anniversary arrived in December 1986, the Gunners should, against all early expectations, be top of the League; even though the cautious Graham insisted they could not win it. Celebrations took place before the home game against Southampton, just two days after the centenary fell. A mass of red and white balloons were released, a hundred young fans and past heroes such as Ted Drake, Joe Mercer, and George Male appeared on the pitch. The occasion produced a 1–0 victory.

That season Huddersfield Town, Manchester City and Nottingham Forest were beaten on the way to the League Cup semi-finals against Spurs. This proved to be a three-match series: a 1–0 home defeat in February, followed by two demanding games in three days at White Hart Lane, each won 2–1. The team had set a club record of 22 matches unbeaten, coming to an end ultimately in an ill-tempered match against Manchester United at Old Trafford.

There was disappointment at Highbury in the sixth round of the FA Cup when Watford came to Highbury and Arsenal, badly missing Davis's creativity again, went down 1–3. So Arsenal were left with just one trophy to play for, the Littlewoods League Cup, the opposition Liverpool. Ian Rush put Liverpool ahead after 23 minutes. Ominously, Liverpool had never lost a match in which Rush had scored first. To their credit, Arsenal shrugged off the early reverse and proceeded to command the rest of the game. Charlie Nicholas

HIGHBURY HEROES

Tony Adams 1983/84–2001/02

No history of Arsenal would be complete without a tribute to this inspirational captain. Romford-born Adams made his first-team debut in November 1983 at Highbury against Sunderland. As part of the legendary Arsenal back four of the late 1980s and 1990s, his leadership and resolve were key to the Club's success during his period as skipper. He left the Club in 2002, with a European Cup Winners' Cup medal (1993/94), four League Championship winners' medals (1988/89, 1990/91, 1997/98, 2001/02), three FA Cup winners' medals (1992/93, 1997/98, 2001/02) and two League Cup winners' medals (1986/87, 1992/93). He was capped for his country 66 times.

scored what George Graham described as 'a couple of scruffy goals,' but they were enough to win the match. The equaliser was prodded in just on the half hour. Seven minutes from the final whistle, Perry Groves cut devastatingly through a baffled Liverpool defence and found Nicholas, whose somewhat indifferent shot was lethally deflected, to spin tantalisingly past Liverpool goalkeeper Bruce Grobbelaar. The League Cup was Arsenal's.

Before that season ended, Graham had already secured a player who would have a key role in the team's success; Alan Smith, the Leicester City centre forward. Adept at taming and shielding the ball, he was also dangerous in the air. Continuing to exploit his knowledge of the Second Division, gleaned when he was at Millwall, Graham also signed Watford's Kevin Richardson, a right-footed midfielder who could also operate on the left flank, and the Wimbledon left back, Nigel Winterburn. Winterburn though a left-footed player found

himself largely deployed at right back, since Kenny Sansom remained supreme on the left.

The season did not begin well, Liverpool gaining some kind of consolation for what happened at Wembley by winning the opening League match at Highbury 2–1. Winning ways were restored a couple of weeks later, however, with Portsmouth receiving a 6–0 thrashing at Highbury. The team eventually finished sixth in the Championship, and had a strong run in the FA Cup, beating Manchester United at Highbury 2–1 in the fifth round but losing 2–1 to Nottingham Forest, again at home, in the sixth. But the Gunners once again reached the final of the Littlewoods League Cup. Missing David O'Leary's powerful presence, his young deputy Gus Caesar had a memorably traumatic afternoon. Luton Town were the opposition. Arsenal, who had accounted for Everton away and at home in the League Cup semi-final, looked unassailable, but in the event they lost 3–2 through a series of missed chances and defensive errors.

New business at the Clock End

During the 1980s Arsenal Football Club and its Highbury home had already begun to evolve into a focus for much more than on-the-pitch activity, becoming a modern business and a centre of community-based initiatives. Arsenal decided to join a growing, money-spinning trend in English football by building a suite of private boxes at Highbury. Other clubs had increased their stadiums' earning power by setting aside areas for corporate business and wealthy individuals to entertain clients or friends, and it made financial sense for the Gunners to do it too. The board judged that the best place for Highbury's corporate boxes would be at the top of a newly

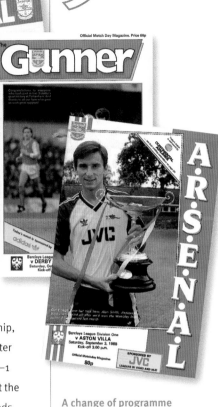

A change of programme
In season 1987/88 the Club experimented with a change of title for their matchday programmes from simply 'Arsenal' to 'The Gunner'. From top, programme covers for 21 February 1987 (v Barnsley in the FA Cup), 24 October 1987 (v Derby County in the League) and 3 September 1988 (v Aston Villa in the League).

Show the colours
An Arsenal rosette from the Littlewoods League Cup final of 1987. The Gunners won the trophy, beating Liverpool 2–1.

The Clock in its a new home

The redeveloped Clock End, opened in 1989, saw the basic terracing on which generations of hardy fans had braved the elements converted to a modern covered stand with 54 boxes for corporate clients.

constructed stand at the Clock End, and the 54 corporate boxes were opened in 1989. They were a commercial success, as Arsenal managed to sell them all on 10-year leases, which paid for the construction work.

The new construction left the lower tier of the Clock End available for non-corporate spectators, and the project also saw the sports hall move to the first floor, providing room for covered parking underneath the building. Stadium manager John Beattie said: 'The work meant we had to move the clock. Of course, the season we moved it we won the League, which maintained a fine Arsenal tradition. We have shifted the clock three times, and every time we have won the title in that season.' The Highbury pitch was also given a make-over in 1989, being completely re-laid. There was a story circulating during Graham's period as manager alleging that he had the pitch narrowed to give his team an advantage. In fact, as Graham himself pointed out, not only did he do nothing of the sort, but he believed that the smaller the pitch, the

greater the advantage to a technically superior team, more capable of operating in the limited space. The Highbury pitch has been a credit to the Club's groundstaff who have won the FA's Groundsman of the Year award nine times, including Highbury's final season 2005/06.

Local links

Highbury has always been more than just a football ground, and Arsenal as a Club has always been about more than trophy-hunting, being keen to put plenty back into the community that sustains it. During the mid-1980s Arsenal's community programme was actively developed into an important agent of social cohesion in north London. Talking in 2006, Freddie Hudson, senior sports development officer for Arsenal's community programme, described the origins of the programme: 'The programme started 21 years ago as a Sports Council initiative at a time when London had just experienced the Brixton Riots. There was a widespread

was revamped in 1988/89 at a cost of £1.5 million, providing a venue for after-school football sessions at Highbury, as well as fitness and aerobics sessions for the public. Within three years of its launch, Arsenal's community scheme was touching and improving the lives of hundreds of people in the locality. Arsenal Football Club, as had been hoped, turned out to be the perfect focus for community action in its area of north London, and the first projects proved to be an outstanding success. When the Sports Council's initial injection of funding for the initiative came to an end, Arsenal continued to support the community schemes and they have continued to expand.

Triumph and tragedy

Back on the pitch, season 1988/89 began for Arsenal with a bang – a 5–1 drubbing handed out to Wimbledon at Plough Lane – and ended with a louder one still, a triumphantly dramatic League game at Liverpool that would breathlessly give them the title. It was a season in which the Highbury pitch became a winter quagmire, in which only 17 players were used in the Championship, and in which two defenders shrewdly bought from Stoke City – Lee Dixon right back and centre half Steve Bould would contribute memorably to the Arsenal defence. Paul Merson, who had risen through Arsenal's apprenticeship scheme, and cost nothing, began to make a real difference with his impressive pace and penetration on the left flank, while the supremely talented Alan Smith scored no fewer than 23 goals in his 36 appearances. It was also the season in which tragedy at Hillsborough would signal massive changes to the way football was watched at Highbury and in football stadiums throughout the country.

November 1988 saw a three-match League Cup series against Liverpool, a 1–1 draw at Anfield, a goalless draw at Highbury, finally a 2–1 defeat at Villa Park. Four days after the first of these games, Arsenal had a notable victory at Nottingham Forest, 4–1, both centre backs, Steve Bould and Tony Adams, scoring. Adams, indeed, was always threatening with his head at set pieces, while he was also capable of long, thrilling runs from his own half of the field. In early January the Gunners were eliminated in the third round of the FA Cup in a limp exhibition at Highbury against West Ham.

feeling that more had to be done to bring disadvantaged inner-city communities together.'

Within three years a whole series of ventures had mushroomed. The first was the pensioners' bowls club, giving elderly people the chance to get together twice a week. But there was also plenty of activity for younger people in the Islington area. One of the aims of the initiative was to encourage 16–24-year-olds with a history of unemployment to get some extra education or training, especially in the field of youth leadership. That fed into a new project where coaches from Arsenal's community scheme went into 12 local primary schools to coach the children in football, hockey, short tennis and quick cricket. The popular hockey coaching led to links with the celebrated Old Loughtonians club in Essex, and a large number of youngsters progressed to play first team hockey in England's national league.

The Arsenal Sports Centre at the Clock End became the centre of the Club's community sports activities after the hall

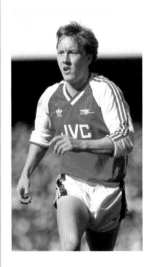

Solid at the back
Lee Dixon and Steve Bould, two of the defenders who made Arsenal such a formidably difficult team to beat. Dixon joined from Stoke City in July 1986. Bould also joined from Stoke, in June 1988, and remained a key player in the Wenger era. Both of these long-serving players were part of the Double-winning team of 1997/98.

In the League, January 1989 saw the Gunners go top of the table after overwhelming Everton at Goodison Park 3–1. In the early months of 1989, Liverpool's phenomenal 28-match unbeaten run since the New Year had made up a leeway of 19 points, while Arsenal had a late-season dip in form with a crushing 3–1 defeat by Nottingham Forest at Highbury, and a 2–2 draw at home to Charlton. As the season approached its climax, the question was, could the Gunners hold off Liverpool's challenge? Club Chairman Peter Hill-Wood was cheerfully optimistic. 'My feeling is that whether we win the League or not, I see no reason why we shouldn't go on to have a great deal of success with this team. I've never been so hopeful of the future.'

However, on 15 April 1989 the entire footballing community was to be shaken to its foundations when Liverpool fans were hideously embroiled in the disaster of Hillsborough. Ninety-six Liverpool supporters, penned back by security fences, were fatally crushed as the crowd surged forward. This calamity led to the Taylor Report, the institution of all-seater stadiums in the top division, and a radical change in the profile of English football.

The remainder of the season continued under the deep shadow of that star-crossed semi-final. Liverpool predictably postponed their matches, one of which was the potentially

May Day celebration
David Rocastle battles for the ball with Norwich City's Dean Coney as Steve Bould (left) looks on. Rocastle scored one of the goals in Arsenal's 5–0 victory over the Canaries on 1 May 1989.

decisive game against Arsenal at Anfield. Arsenal, just as predictably, would have no truck with the Football League's suggestion that they should play their own next game, and did not take the field again for another 16 days. This was the return at Highbury with Norwich City.

Though injury had put the influential winger Brian Marwood out for the remainder of the season, Arsenal simply swept Norwich aside. Both Arsenal full backs, Dixon and Winterburn, now made full use of the opportunities the sweeper system gave them to attack down the flanks. Indeed it was Winterburn who scored the first of Arsenal's five unanswered goals. A formidable volley by Alan Smith, in sparkling form, made it 2–0 just before half time. Thomas, Smith and Rocastle scored in the second half. 'The First Division leaders,' wrote Stuart Jones in *The Times*, 'whose reaction to Hillsborough was so honest and dignified, confirmed that they will show no mercy to opponents or to Merseyside.' Not that it would now be all plain sailing. Middlesbrough were narrowly beaten, away. Then, alas, came a couple of home hiccups. Derby County beat the Gunners 2–1 and four days later, Wimbledon forced an unexpected 2–2 draw at Highbury.

Championship cliffhanger

So the season came to a climax in what Arsenal chairman Peter Hill-Wood has described as 'without question, the most dramatic ending to a domestic League campaign in history'. On 26 May the two Championship contenders Arsenal and Liverpool would meet in the final League game of the season at Anfield. Liverpool, three points ahead, could lose by anything less than two goals, and the title would be theirs. 'I hope we get this sort of pressure every year,' said George Graham. 'This is enjoyable pressure. I don't know whether we will win. I know that we can win. Any team can win one game, particularly with an away record like we've got.'

Against the odds

Statistics were hardly encouraging. The Gunners hadn't won at Anfield for 15 years. In almost 20 years, Liverpool had lost there by a two-goal margin just nine times. Traffic jams that impeded Arsenal supporters driving up from London caused the kick-off to be delayed. The atmosphere was one of intense anticipation. Before the kick-off, Arsenal handed over a £30,000 cheque to the Hillsborough Disaster Fund, then the players distributed bouquets of flowers to the fans.

As the match kicked off, watched by an estimated worldwide TV audience of 600 million, it was clear that Arsenal would not confine themselves to counter-attack. They took a combative grip on the game from the first. Richardson, Thomas and Rocastle took a hold on midfield. Steve Bould

gave the dangerous John Aldridge neither room nor time. Alan Smith excelled. In the first half Arsenal came near to scoring with a header from Bould. Ian Rush, who'd produced Liverpool's only shot of any significance, did not survive the first half, being replaced through injury by little Peter Beardsley. In the second half in the 51st minute, Arsenal scored. A foul by Nicol on the left-hand fringe of the penalty box enabled Nigel Winterburn to send his free kick to the far post and Alan Smith headed the ball neatly into the corner of the net. Liverpool at once besieged the referee David Hutchinson. They pointed out that the linesman had fleetingly raised his flag, either for a foul or because the indirect free kick had swirled in, untouched by Smith, rendering the goal illegal. But it hadn't, and the goal stood.

Now, could Arsenal get that crucial second goal? It proved anything but easy. Sixteen minutes from time, a pass by Kevin Richardson reached Michael Thomas, some 12 yards out, but Bruce Grobbelaar, who'd not been in a losing Liverpool team in 28 games, had no trouble with the shot.

Michael Thomas makes history

As the match entered its 89th minute, Liverpool's Steve McMahon famously signalled to his team mates that they needed to hang on and defend for only one more minute for the Championship and the Double to be theirs. Arsenal had the same amount of time to score the goal that would give them the title. As the match neared the end of the two minutes of stoppage time, John Lukic cleared, Lee Dixon sent a long pass through, calmly collected by the irrepressible Alan Smith, who from some 30 yards out coolly and precisely lobbed a ball for Michael Thomas to dash on to. Steve Nicol came across to challenge, but luck now favoured Arsenal. The ball bounced off Nicol putting Thomas clear. The desperate efforts of Ray Houghton and Nicol to intercept the attack were in vain. So was the attempt of Grobbelaar to rush out to dive and block the ball. Thomas calmly paused for what seemed to everyone watching like an eternity, then flicked the ball over the keeper's body, into the right hand corner of the Liverpool goal. Thomas somersaulted with glee. With only 30 seconds left to play, the Championship was Arsenal's. 'We have laid a foundation of belief at Highbury,' pronounced George Graham. 'If you lose hope or lose belief, you may as well get

out of football. Tonight was the fairy tale, the unpredictable that makes us all love football.'

Scenes of celebration

As the ball hit the back of the net, the Arsenal's travelling supporters at the Anfield End erupted into ecstatic celebrations. The scenes in north London were no less euphoric, with fans, who had been watching the game in pubs and homes in Highbury, spontaneously gathering in the streets to share the moment of glory. Nick Hornby memorably described the scene in his novel *Fever Pitch*: 'I could hear whoops and screams from pubs and shops and houses all around me; and as fans began to congregate at the stadium, some draped in banners, some sitting on top of tooting cars, everyone embracing strangers at every opportunity, and TV cameras arrived to film the party for the late news, and club officials leaned out of the windows to wave at the bouncing crowd, it occurred to me that I was glad I hadn't been up to Anfield and missed out on this joyful almost Latin explosion on my doorstep.' In fact, Highbury was just starting a three-day weekend of celebration, including a triumphant open-top bus parade through Islington, in which the victorious team were applauded by tens of thousands of grateful fans. By common consent, this had been the most memorable climax to a season ever witnessed – and no Arsenal fan of the time will ever forget being part of that famous victory.

It's up for grabs now!
Top: Michael Thomas scores the crucial goal at Anfield that secured the League title for Arsenal on 26 May 1989.
Above: Thomas and his team mate, Martin Hayes, pose with the team's trophies.

Highbury and the Premiership

Arsenal enters the modern era of football and completes the conversion of Highbury into an all-seater stadium. The team builds on the Championship success of 1989, winning the League title again in 1991, the FA Cup in 1993 and the European Cup Winners' Cup in 1994.

CHAPTER

10

By the end of the 1980s major changes in the way British football fans watched their sport had become inevitable, but it took the deaths of 96 supporters at Hillsborough in April 1989 to make them a reality. For decades Britain's football grounds had been deadly, dirty places. At regular intervals over a century disaster had struck inside stadiums, leaving dozens dead, and there had been no effective attempt at addressing the problems through Government legislation. In 1946, 33 fans were killed in a crush at Burnden Park during a quarter-final FA Cup tie between Bolton Wanderers and Stoke City. Glasgow Rangers' home ground, Ibrox Park, was the scene of another disaster in 1971 when 66 fans died as they rushed for the exits after a Rangers–Celtic derby. In May 1985 fire in an antiquated wooden stand at Valley Parade, the home of Bradford City, claimed the lives of 56 supporters. After Hillsborough, Britain's football clubs could no longer ignore their responsibility for the safety of fans at their stadiums. At last football was forced to act decisively to make its grounds fit for human beings to watch a sporting event with a reasonable chance of not being killed.

The Taylor Report heralds a new era

Following the Hillsborough disaster, Lord Justice Taylor was commissioned to prepare a report on safety at the country's football grounds. He came to the subject with an outsider's eye, and was genuinely astonished with the conditions he found. The judge expressed disbelief that so many people 'could die from overcrowding before the very eyes of those controlling the event'. He published his 104-page report in January 1990, and made 76 recommendations. Taylor insisted that fences between the terraces and the pitch had to go: supporters would not be treated like 'prisoners of war' again. He went further, and called for the immediate modernisation of the Victorian relics that passed for places of mass entertainment in the last decade of the 20th century. He wrote: 'The years of patching up grounds, of having periodic disasters and narrowly avoiding many others by muddling through on a wing and a prayer, must be over.'

Even now, Taylor was not convinced football was ready to act. He noted warily that his was the ninth report on safety at football grounds: nothing had been done about the previous eight. But this time there was action. The Government announced that terracing at every First and Second Division ground would become all-seater by August 1994, and at every League ground by 1999.

Arsenal Stadium at the forefront

John Beattie, who took over as stadium manager at Highbury in 1987 and has stepped into the same role at the Emirates Stadium, said Arsenal were already well on their way to complying with the recommendations of the Taylor Report.

'We had never had fences,' John Beattie explained. 'The Club never thought they were safe, and because of that we lost out on staging many FA Cup semi-finals. We were already training and paying our stewards, which wasn't the case at many clubs at the time. And we were already in the process of replacing our public address system. So the Taylor Report came along at a time when we were already making improvements in those areas. We weren't starting from scratch.'

But Arsenal still faced the task of making Highbury all-seater. That meant major works on the North Bank, the Clock End underneath the hospitality boxes and in the enclosure in front of the West Stand. There was much more to do, and the Club directors commissioned a detailed feasibility study for November 1989, for comprehensive redevelopment.

Giant screens at Highbury

As Arsenal re-emerged as one of Britain's footballing powers at the end of the 1980s, the demand to watch their games rocketed. That was true for away games as much as home games, and there was often disappointment when inadequate ticket allocations could not accommodate the team's travelling army of fans.

In 1989/90 the Club acted to ensure as many Gunners as possible could watch the north London derby in October 1989 at White Hart Lane, when Tottenham Hotspur made only a couple of thousand tickets available to Gunners. They erected a giant TV screen on the pitch at Highbury, so fans could watch the match live. About 5,000 Arsenal supporters saw their team lose 2–1 to the old enemy. The experiment was repeated on 19 December the same year, when Arsenal travelled to Glasgow to play in the Zenith Data Systems

All seated
Arsenal fans in the East Stand. After 1989 Highbury like all top-level football stadiums had to become all-seater venues.

Challenge against Rangers. The short-lived competition pitted the English League Champions against the Scottish title-holders. Arsenal won 2–1 in front of 31,118 at Ibrox Park, and the match was beamed back to about 4,000 fans at Highbury. The experiment was popular with Arsenal fans – but not with the Club's groundstaff. Erecting the big screens on the pitch did the playing surface no favours, and the board decided to curtail the experiment. There have, though, been exceptions. When Arsenal were closing in on their first Double under Arsène Wenger, there was a huge clamour to see the away game at Barnsley on 25 April 1998. A victory would leave the Gunners needing just a point to wrap up the title – and seemingly the whole of Islington wanted to be at Oakwell for the big game. Sadly, the south Yorkshire club could offer only a small section of their compact ground to the visitors. The Club resurrected the idea of bringing the match to their supporters via a big screen, and the Jumbotron was dismantled and re-assembled on the pitch. About 16,000 supporters turned up to watch the live feed from Barnsley, and they created a real match-day atmosphere.

Trying new tactics

The 1989/90 season was a curious anticlimax to the euphoria of the winning of the previous season's Championship.

Tactically, the team oscillated all season between the sweeper defence, which they never quite seemed to master, and the familiar 'flat back four'. Before the League season began, they were twice involved at Wembley, first on the thinly attended Makita tournament, then in the packed out Charity Shield, the opposition on each occasion being Liverpool. The Makita tournament was a summer competition involving four European clubs, set up in 1988 by Arsenal, which continued to be played until 1994. Arsenal won it three times, in 1988, 1989 and 1994. The victory against Liverpool in July 1989 was by a scoreline of 1–0. In the Charity Shield two weeks later the scoreline was reversed.

Liverpool, indeed, would have won the Charity Shield by a greater margin were it not for the inspired goalkeeping of John Lukic, whom Arsenal had just tried vainly to replace. Queens Park Rangers had been offered (and had declined) £1.75 million for the reigning England keeper, David Seaman. He would give Arsenal good cause to try again, this time successfully, with his subsequent performances against them in the FA Cup.

League Cup wins and losses

The opening League game of the 1989/90, at Old Trafford, was a dismal beginning; a 4–1 defeat in which the Gunners' rocky sweeper defence gave way to 4-4-2. Yet far from presaging a successful season, United would have a period of such protracted failure in the League that by January, there was even speculation, astonishing as it may now seem, that Alex Ferguson would be replaced as the manager. Arsenal, by contrast, embarked on a season which saw them take a sound enough fourth place in the Championship.

In the League Cup, the Gunners actually had the satisfaction of eliminating Liverpool 1–0 in front of a crowd of over 40,000 at Highbury, only to go down embarrassingly, 3–1 in the fourth round, to humble Oldham. As for the FA Cup, in February 1990 Arsenal were eliminated in the fourth round by Queens Park Rangers under Don Howe. After a 0–0 draw in the home leg, QPR came out of their shell and beat the Gunners 2–0. This was a season blemished in November 1989 by a brawl at the North Bank end, between Arsenal and Norwich City players, which cost Arsenal a £20,000 fine and Norwich one of £50,000.

Smith steps up
Alan Smith follows up a shot from Lee Dixon in a League game against Norwich City on 4 November 1989, which the Gunners won 4–3. The new Clock End Stand is in the background.

Construction underway

In the brief close season of 1990 hectic work took place as part of the stadium redevelopment scheme. Three different contractors were involved. The remodelling of northwest and southwest spectator entrances, together with the building of new toilets, was performed by Hosier and Dickinson. The emergency vehicle pitch access road was the work of Styles and Wood, also responsible for the first-aid centre. John Lelliott Ltd thoroughly refurbished the East Stand club offices, booking hall, boardroom and cocktail lounge, as well as a new Press suite beneath the upper tier.

The changing rooms, whose heated marble floors had so impressed generations of Arsenal footballers, were also rebuilt, but strictly in accordance with their original character. In January 1991, designs were initiated to replace the famous North Bank terrace with what was intended to be the finest stand in Europe.

Seaman steps up

New blood had arrived. Now David Seaman was brought to Highbury, and John Lukic returned to his former club, Leeds United. By the time he joined Arsenal, Seaman was already a goalkeeper of huge authority, outstanding physique, and

an acrobatic flexibility that belied his size. Anders Limpar, a fast and incisive Swedish international outside left, arrived from Cremonese in Italy. And Paul Davis, who had managed just 11 League appearances the previous season, at great cost to the team's capacity to surprise, was now fit enough to make regular appearances for the Club.

The team made a promising beginning. Early in September, Chelsea were despatched 4–1 at Highbury. After a dull first half, in which Chelsea's static defence frustrated an Arsenal team playing 4-4-2, Limpar again found exuberant form. He put the Gunners ahead on 52 minutes, provoked a clear penalty converted by Lee Dixon, rolled the ball to Merson for the third goal, gave the diagonal pass from which Rocastle easily drove in the fourth. Chelsea's late goal was scant consolation for the visitors.

In late October the team was again involved in a damaging fight on the pitch with potentially catastrophic results for the Club. The incident took place during the match against Manchester United at Old Trafford. Two points were deducted following a fight between the players in October. United had one point deducted and both teams were fined £50,000. The points penalty resulting from these unedifying events left Liverpool eight points clear at the top of the League.

David Seaman 1990/91–2002/03

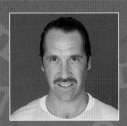

Rotherham-born David Seaman played for Peterborough United, Birmingham City and Queens Park Rangers before signing for the Gunners in 1990. His good-humoured solidity behind the back four provided the bedrock for the attacking team's successes. One of Arsenal's finest goalkeepers, he made 563 appearances for the Club and was capped for England 75 times. With Arsenal, he won the European Cup Winners' Cup (1993/94), the League Championship (1990/91, 1997/98, 2001/02) and the FA Cup (1992/3, 1997/98, 2001/02, 2002/03).

In late November, Manchester United came to Highbury and overwhelmed the Gunners in the League Cup in a shattering 6–2 victory. Yet Arsenal proceeded four days after the rout to thrash Liverpool 3–0 at Highbury. David O'Leary, still arguably Arsenal's most talented defender, had returned to the team and Lee Dixon scored one of the goals.

Adams in court

Just as the team were beginning to clock up a series of impressive results, including a 4–0 victory over Southampton at Highbury, the Club and its supporters had to deal with the loss of their captain, Tony Adams, who was given a gaol sentence of four months for drink driving. George Graham was predictably distressed. 'He is my eyes and ears in the dressing room and my sergeant major on the pitch,' he proclaimed. Arsenal continued to pay Adams his salary while he was in gaol. 'The player has made a mistake," said Ken Friar, the managing director, 'and has been punished for it. As far as the Club are concerned, he will continue to be an Arsenal player and will receive our full support.' In Adams' absence, Arsenal were able to call on Andy Linighan, signed in the summer from Norwich City, who capably held the fort.

FA Cup campaign

In the New Year, it took an exhausting four games to eliminate Leeds United in the fourth round of the FA Cup. There was a goalless draw at Highbury, a 1–1 draw at Leeds, another goalless draw at Highbury and finally a well-deserved 2–1 win for the Gunners at Elland Road. The toll this sequence of games had taken on the team was probably to blame for the Gunners' only League defeat that season – a 2–1 loss against Chelsea at Stamford Bridge on 2 February 1991.

In the quarter-final, the Gunners made surprisingly heavy weather of beating Cambridge United of Division Three, 2–1 at Highbury in front of the season's largest crowd of 42,960 on 9 March 1991. Cambridge counter-attacked vigorously with two rapid wingers. In the 20th minute, a neat glancing header by Kevin Campbell put Arsenal into the lead, but five minutes into the second half, Cambridge stunned Arsenal with an equaliser. Tony Adams, showing typical persistence, followed up Smith's header, to score Arsenal's second goal.

Spurs in the semi-final

Wembley was the venue for the potentially explosive clash between Arsenal and Spurs in the semi-final on 14 April. The choice of Wembley was arrived at out of concern to avoid anything like a repeat of the Hillsborough tragedy of two years before. The demand for tickets was likely to be huge for such a crucial match and a large stadium seemed essential.

While Arsenal, flying high in the League, were keenly focused on the chance of a second Double, they were meeting a Spurs team in deep financial trouble for whom success in the Cup might make the difference between survival and financial catastrophe. The talented Paul Gascoigne was returning to the Spurs team after an operation, and it was he who opened the scoring with a 30-yard free kick in the fifth minute of the game. Spurs' Gary Lineker scored a second goal five minutes later. Alan Smith closed the gap for Arsenal, but another Lineker goal put the match out of reach with a final score of 3–1.

George Graham, who had endorsed the idea of playing at Wembley, thought, 'There was nothing to choose between the sides after the first 20 minutes. That's where the match was won and lost. In fact we probably shaded it from that point onwards, but the damage had been done by then. You can't give a highly motivated team a two-goal start in Cup semi-finals because they're going to fight tooth and nail to protect it. It was a bitterly disappointing experience for my players, but the true test of their character is whether they can bounce back from these things.'

Bouncing back

The team certainly did bounce back from defeat. With a three point lead over Liverpool and a clutch of games at home, the

League was clearly Arsenal's to lose. In the words of Nigel Winterburn, who didn't miss a Championship match, 'We could easily have gone unbeaten in the League all the way to February for nothing. Nobody would have remembered us for coming second in the table and going out in the FA Cup semi-finals. Or at least they wouldn't have remembered us for the right reasons. If we'd blown the last few games, we'd never have lived it down. People would simply have thought we'd bottled it at Wembley and bottled it on the League run in, and we deserved better than that.'

Following a 2–2 draw with Manchester City, Queens Park Rangers were duly beaten 2–0, at Highbury. But at Sunderland, only a glorious late save by Seaman from Owers preserved a goalless draw. Earlier on the same day, the Gunners heard the good news that Liverpool, their only challengers, had gone down 4–2 at Chelsea.

May Celebrations

On the evening of 6 May, Arsenal hosted Manchester United. Once more the Gunners would know the result of their rivals, before they kicked off. When the news came through that Liverpool had gone down 1–0 at Nottingham Forest, they knew that the Championship was Arsenal's. A joyous North Bank saluted the happy team, who booted balls into the crowd in celebration.

Seaman, Dixon and Thomas donned comic hats. Anders Limpar, back again, juggled with a football. Then Manchester United were put to the sword. Alan Smith scored twice in the first half, first from Lee Dixon's right wing cross, then from a pass by Kevin Campbell. When Steve Bruce handled in the United box, it was Smith who put away the penalty for his hat-trick. Bruce himself got the late consolation goal for United in the 3–1 defeat.

In the dressing room, Graham's delighted players chanted, with supreme irony, the familiar adage of, 'Boring, boring Arsenal!' George himself didn't join the subsequent lap of honour, led by Tony Adams after he'd brandished the Championship trophy. 'I didn't think it was important for me to join in,' Graham explained. 'The players are the ones who have done it. I can enjoy all the reflective glory because of their efforts, but they deserve all the credit and limelight. The fans pay their money every week to watch them play football, not to watch me in the dugout. I felt it was appropriate for me to stay in the background this time. 'There was still a final game, at home, to come against Coventry, and Arsenal won it in style; a 6–1 victory with a hat-trick from Anders Limpar.

Arsenal's success was particularly admirable for the fact that it had been achieved with so many young players groomed at Highbury: Adams, Campbell, Hillier, Davis, Merson. But quite the most unusual and inventive player of the team had been Limpar, the Swedish international of Hungarian extraction. Before he came to Highbury, he had been known as a central midfielder, but George Graham had decided to use him profitably on the left wing. With four goals in the last ten minutes, two of them by Limpar, Arsenal were the emphatic winners. So to a new season, which would at last bring them back into Europe.

Quicker than Speed
Lee Dixon sprints away from Leeds United midfielder Gary Speed at Highbury, 27 January 1991. The Gunners drew the fourth round FA Cup game 0–0, but finally won the tie 2–1 in a third replay.

Troubled times

Each of Arsenal's Championship successes under George Graham was followed by a season of anticlimax. To finish fourth in the League in season 1991/92 was no disgrace, but there was initially a rude awakening, outbreaks of indiscipline, controversy over the rebuilding of the North Bank, a lesson from Benfica in the European Cup and disaster in the third round of the FA Cup.

Graham brought no new players to Highbury in the summer of 1991, but in September he paid £2.5 million for the Crystal Palace centre forward, Ian Wright. Though this may originally have radically changed the pattern of play, with Alan Smith uneasy at what he saw as his new role of flicking the ball on for Wright to chase, there was no doubt of Wright's prolific goal-scoring talents. The new striker proceeded to score 24 goals in 30 League games.

Wright, who had won his first England cap seven months earlier, scored Arsenal's goal on his debut in a League Cup match at Leicester City. Then on his League debut, he got a hat-trick at Southampton. Highbury had a new hero. With Wright on form, Gunners might have done better in their second round European Cup games against Lisbon's Benfica, but he'd been signed too late to be qualified.

HIGHBURY HEROES
Ian Wright 1991/92–1997/98

The ebullient Ian Wright started his football-playing career with non-League Greenwich Borough, signing for Crystal Palace and turning full professional only in 1985 at the age of 22. As one of Arsenal's most colourful characters, he won a League Cup winners' medal in 1992/93, a European Cup Winners' Cup medal in 1993/94, FA Cup winners' medals in 1992/93 and 1997/98 and a League Championship medal in 1997/98. He beat the overall record of 178 goals set by Cliff Bastin in the 1930s, finishing his stay at Highbury with a total of 184 goals. He also won 33 England caps.

In and out of Europe

In 1991/92 Arsenal returned to European football in the European Cup for the first time since the ban on English clubs following the Heysel Stadium disaster of 1985. Their first round home tie with Austria Vienna on 18 September was a deceptively easy 6–1 romp. The Gunners' 1–0 defeat in the return leg was academic.

The Portuguese team Benfica were the opposition in the next round. Given Benfica's vast experience in Europe, winners of the European Cup in 1961 and 1962, beaten finalists against Manchester United at Wembley in 1968, the Gunners did well to hold them to a 1–1 draw in the away leg in Lisbon. Functioning on this occasion as marker rather than creator, Paul Davis largely nullified Benfica's Brazilian-born playmaker, Isaias. But being out of European football for so many years was bound to be a great disadvantage for Arsenal, and in the return match, at home at Highbury, they looked almost naïve by comparison with the Portuguese team. This time, there was no subduing Isaias. There was something of a false dawn when of all unlikely scorers Colin Pates, a reserve defender from Chelsea via Charlton, playing only his tenth game in 18 months, put the Gunners ahead. As it was, a spectacular 30-yard volley from Isaias forced the match to extra time in which Benfica eventually ran out winners, with goals by the Russian international Kulkov, and Isaias, again.

Wrecked by Wrexham

By contrast, elimination in the third round of the FA Cup by Fourth Division Wrexham was a massive embarrassment. There was no Ian Wright at Wrexham, because he was suspended. Shortly before half time, disaster seemed distant when Alan Smith, who this season would score 12 goals in 39 League games, shot home. It seemed, even if the Gunners couldn't score again, that this goal would be enough, but after 82 minutes, Wrexham's Mickey Thomas, the 37-year-old former Welsh international winger, scored with a ferocious free kick. Almost immediately, his team-mate Gordon Davies crossed from the right and Steve Watkin hooked the ball past David Seaman for the traumatising winner. George Graham called it 'the lowest point of my career'. Nor would there be any consolation from the League Cup, after a third round 1–0 defeat at Coventry. The Gunners finished fourth in the table.

North Bank reconstructed

Work on the new North Bank had begun in January 1991. In May 1992, the old North Bank saw its last game – a suitably emphatic 5–1 defeat of Southampton. Later that month 75 years of North Bank history disappeared under the wrecking balls, when it was demolished by Norwest Holt Construction. During the construction of the new stand, the capacity at Highbury was reduced to around 29,000 and home games were regularly sold out.

The new two-tier stand, built after overcoming some local opposition to the scheme, included an up-to-date interior that resembled a shopping mall, with spacious facilities for supporters to drink, snack, have a meal and visit the Arsenal museum housed within the stand or the Club shop. The excellent view of the pitch was a radical improvement on the old North Bank terracing.

Facsimile fans

While work was in progress on the North Bank, the front of the stand was famously screened by a vast mural, 75 yards long, 18 yards high, covering an area of over 12,000 square feet on which were painted the faces of a multitude of fans. However, there was one problem, stadium manager John Beattie recalled: 'We were embarrassed because the artist painted a sea of faces, and every single one of them was a white face. We had given the artist photographs of the supporters on the old North Bank to work with. Arsenal's support has been multi-ethnic for many years, but that wasn't reflected in the mural. We had to get the artist back in to change some of the faces.'

On the day the mural was unveiled, a parachutist was scheduled to land on the centre spot as part of the festivities. Sadly, the skydiver missed his mark and drifted into the rubble behind the hoarding. 'We needed to send a search party out to find him,' remembers John Beattie.

Captive audience
Arsenal in action in front of the mural that was erected across the front of the North Bank in 1992 during the reconstruction of Highbury's famous old terrace.

An all-seater stadium

The new all-seater North Bank opened in August 1993, with a capacity reduced to 12,400 from 18,500. The remaining areas of terracing in the rest of the stadium were seated during that season, and the installation of giant 'Jumbotron' video screens provided the finishing touches to the new-look, all-seated, 38,500-capacity Highbury.

'The changes proved pretty popular,' John Beattie said. 'The only complaints we had were about the use of foul language. I don't think there was any more bad language. But in the past, if you had been standing near some idiots on the terrace, you could edge away from them. When you were sat down, you could have the same person sat right behind you for the whole 90 minutes. So there was a cultural change. The experience was slightly different.'

The 1990s also saw other changes around Highbury. There were major renovations to the East Stand, where old sections of terracing were dug out to provide room for better catering facilities and toilets. Whole sections of seats that hadn't been changed since the 1930s were replaced, and when Arsenal returned to Highbury for Champions League games after a brief spell at Wembley, a new camera gantry was built in front of the West Stand upper tier. John Beattie said: 'The TV people said it was one of the best-sited gantries in the country. They liked it.'

Life-long Arsenal fan David Barnett provides a telling perspective on how Highbury changed after it went all-seater. Mr Barnett went to his first game at Highbury in 1952, and was a North Bank regular throughout the 1950s and 1960s. His work took him overseas for the next two decades and he hardly saw a ball kicked at Highbury in all those years. He came back to the new-look ground in the early 1990s, and felt right at home, despite the developments. 'It looked and felt strange to see all the seats where there had been big banks of terracing, but in terms of the atmosphere it was as if I had never been away,' he said. 'The crowd in the 1990s might have looked different – it wasn't a working-class, cloth cap crowd any more. But the spirit was the same. The enthusiasm for the team was as strong as ever. If anything it was more tribal and more passionate. I know there were dire predictions that the ground would be quieter when it was all-seater, but I don't think that was the case at all. As soon as

anything happened of note, the crowd quickly jumped to their feet anyway, so it made no difference. Lots of people spent most of the match standing up ... I still love Highbury. I love it because you are surrounded by people who have joined the Club, and once you choose your club, that's it for the rest of your life ... Highbury has become such an important part of my life, and I'll be sorry to say goodbye to the old place.'

Highbury's changing face

If the rebuilding of the North Bank was, with hindsight, inevitable, the decision to issue bonds for the resulting season tickets was bound to cause more controversy. Critics feared a process of gentrification; a marked change in the social profile of those who watched the games. In the event, this isn't the impression one has when going to games nowadays at Highbury, even if the aggressively masculine character of terraces such as the North Bank has mellowed somewhat, bringing many more women to games.

Farewell to the Championship

The 1991/92 season had seen the end of the old-style League Division One. By 1992/93 the new Premier League, in the foundation of which Arsenal's vice-chairman David Dein had

played a hugely influential part, was in place. Through the new system, the elite clubs would have access to greater resources from television rights and other marketing opportunities, enabling the clubs to commit to greater investment in top players from around the world and to create stadium facilities that would match this prestigious new competition. English football had entered a new era.

In this watershed season the tactics of the team were changing. Signing Ian Wright, who proceeded right away to become the Premiership's top goal-scorer, meant a major strategic readjustment to the explosive style of the Gunners' new striker. In these circumstances, it was natural that certain other players would be disenchanted. Michael Thomas, scorer of that dramatic goal at Anfield in 1989, had been

The new North Bank
Viewed from the east, the reconstructed North Bank was an impressive structure. Its modern styling nevertheless incorporated some features, such as the art-deco style fan lights, that echoed the old East and West Stands.

Familiar landmark
The back of the reconstructed North Bank provided a familiar sight to supporters approaching the stadium from the north. The white façade with red detailing were essential elements of Highbury style.

signally out of form well before George Graham transferred him – ironically – to Liverpool; where he almost at once flourished again. Arsenal would become increasingly reliant on the firepower of Ian Wright who hugely endeared himself to the Highbury fans. Their chorus of, 'Ian Wright, Wright, Wright!' became a constant at Highbury and he continued to reward them with his abundant goals.

In the summer of 1992, George Graham had signed the diminutive, left-footed Danish international midfielder, John Jensen, who had scored a sensational goal from outside the box in the final of the 1992 European Championship in Sweden. Disappointingly, it would be many a moon before he scored at all for the Gunners, so much so that he became familiar with plaintive cries of 'Shoot!' from the Highbury crowd, when he was in possession. Promoted from within the Club, young, energetic Ray Parlour from Essex, who had played half a dozen League games the previous season, now became a regular performer.

It was a strange paradox of a season. In early November 1992, after beating Coventry City 3–0 at Highbury, Arsenal were actually leading the Premiership, top of the table for the first time since May 1991. It wouldn't last; indeed there would be a spell of eight games without a win to follow. Arsenal's fans were noisily resentful of the exclusion from so many matches of Anders Limpar, while the inventive Paul Davis also found himself left out for many weeks. When Arsenal met Chelsea at Highbury on 3 October, the supporters booed when Limpar was brought on only five minutes from the end. Limpar promptly provided the cross for Ian Wright to drive in the winning goal. Limpar did it again when, in the next home

game against Everton, he again came on as substitute, scored an elegant solo goal, and Arsenal won 2–0.

Cup winners twice over

That season, Arsenal would carry off both the League and the FA Cup. On 6 March 1993 the Gunners knocked Ipswich Town out of the FA Cup 4–2. They had previously beaten non-League Yeovil Town on their notorious sloping pitch and Leeds United in an Elland Road replay. This put the Gunners into a semi-final against Spurs, which seemed potentially explosive after an acrimonious League confrontation the previous December at White Hart Lane.

While Arsenal's form in the Premiership oscillated, they had also made progress in the Coca-Cola League Cup, though not without great difficulty in the initial tie with Millwall. The southeast London club were actually 1–0 ahead at Highbury when Kevin Campbell, a late substitute, equalised. At the replay at the Den, Campbell once again had to come to the Gunners' rescue in a 1–1 draw, Arsenal prevailing only after a penalty shoot-out.

Campbell proceeded to score in both ties against Derby County in the next round, gaining a 1–1 draw at the Baseball Ground, and contributing to a 2–1 win at Highbury. Nigel Winterburn scored the only goal at foggy Scarborough in January, where the underdogs pushed Arsenal hard. In the quarter-final at home to Nottingham Forest, Ian Wright scored both goals in a 2–0 win. This pitted him in the semi-finals against his former club, Crystal Palace, scoring from a penalty in a 3–1 win at Selhurst Park in February, and again at Highbury in March, where Palace were beaten 2–0.

From Spurs to Sheffield

On 4 April 1993 Arsenal met Spurs in an FA Cup semi-final, played at Wembley. In the event, Tony Adams was able to answer the taunts of 'donkey' levelled at him in the December derby by the Spurs full back Justin Edinburgh, by scoring the only goal of a mediocre game, when he headed in a free kick by Paul Merson, on the far post.

Arsenal's opponents at Wembley in both the League Cup final and the FA Cup final were Sheffield Wednesday. In the first of these meetings – the Coca-Cola Cup final on 18 April lacking several players, George Graham gambled by bringing

back Paul Davis, barely recovered from a hamstring pull, and using the Northern Ireland defender, Stephen Morrow, beside him in central midfield. For Morrow, it would be a day of triumph and disaster.

Wednesday scored early in the game through the resilient midfielder John Harkes, captain of the USA national team. On 20 minutes, when the ball was headed down to Merson just outside the penalty area following a free kick, he struck it with the outside of his right foot, imparting a diabolical swerve that quite deceived Chris Woods the Sheffield Wednesday goalkeeper, and finished just inside the right hand post. On 68 minutes it was Merson who set up the winner. Racing through on the left and crossing for Morrow, who had never scored for the Gunners before, to drive the ball past Woods. Unfortunately for Morrow, his celebrations were curtailed when, at the final whistle, an exuberant Adams heaved him on to his shoulders, only to drop him, breaking his arm. Adams was so distressed that he had to be coerced by Stewart Houston, then the assistant manager, to climb the steps to receive his medal.

So to the FA Cup final where Wednesday were the opposition again. Arsenal had every excuse if they felt tired. This would be Arsenal's 58th match of the season and their 12th in six weeks. The invaluable Ian Wright would play even though he had a broken toe. Despite clearly being handicapped, he put Arsenal ahead after 21 minutes with a header. But on 68 minutes, David Hirst, the Sheffield Wednesday centre forward, equalised.

So to the replay, the following Thursday, a game blemished by close encounters of the harsh kind. Adams clashed with Hirst and Jensen with Waddle, with no serious consequences. But after 19 minutes, a blow from Mark Wright's elbow left Andy Linighan with a broken nose. No yellow card was shown by the referee Mr Barratt, but Linighan would have his ample revenge. On 33 minutes, a clever pass from Alan Smith, restored to the team, sent Ian Wright away to score what was his fourth goal in an FA Cup final. After another 33 minutes, Chris Waddle's volley was deflected past David Seaman for Wednesday's equaliser. Bright, from a mere ten yards, and Paul Merson missed palpable chances to win the game.

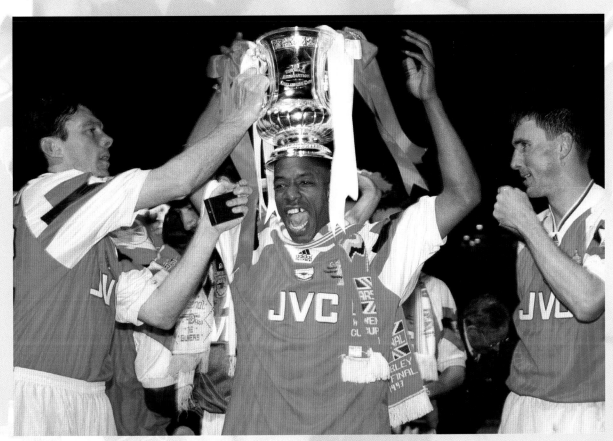

Cup king

Ian Wright is crowned with the FA Cup after Arsenal beat Sheffield Wednesday 2–1 in the FA Cup final replay at Wembley, May 1993.

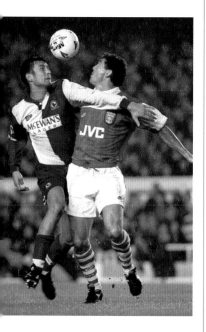

That's mine
Martin Keown tussles with Chris Sutton of Blackburn Rovers at Highbury, 31 August 1994. The Arsenal back-four kept another clean sheet in a 0–0 draw.

So two tired teams played out extra time, and it was close to the end when, with Mr Barratt looking at his watch, Paul Merson took a corner. Tony Adams and Andy Linighan, to George Graham's alarm, trotted upfield to exploit it. Over came the corner, Woods stayed on his line, and Linighan, so often the butt of the Highbury crowd, now became the hero of the moment when he jumped high above Mark Bright, to head the winning goal. Nigel Worthington the Wednesday left back tried to kick the ball clear but succeeded only in booting it into the roof of the net. Arsenal had once again brought back the FA Cup to Highbury.

A fitting goodbye

David O'Leary, the Gunners' long-serving defender, going out in style after a splendid career, had come on in both finals as a substitute for Ian Wright. A fitting celebration of this Highbury hero came in his testimonial match against Manchester United, attended by 22,117 supporters.

O'Leary's departure would leave a gaping hole in the Arsenal defence. With this in mind, in February 1993, Graham had brought Martin Keown back to Highbury from Everton, to play a number of games at centre back. The following season would see him make numerous appearances. His career had begun at Highbury after being discovered as a youngster in his native Oxford, when he was only 12 years old. He had then left for Aston Villa, later signing for Everton.

Wright keeps scoring

1993/94 will be remembered for the Gunners' defiant victory in the final of the European Cup Winners' Cup against Parma in Copenhagen. The Charity Shield curtain-raiser at Wembley against the Premier League Champions, and holder of the European Cup Winners' Cup, Manchester United, was lost only on penalties, with the score at 1–1. The last, decisive, penalty save was made by one goalkeeper from another; Peter Schmeichel from David Seaman. Surprisingly, another penalty was not put away by Ian Wright, who would be hero of another season in which he scored a cornucopia of goals – 23 League goals in 39 games.

That season the team's domestic performance had been frequently criticised, to George Graham's displeasure, for lack of invention in midfield. In the end, Arsenal took a respectable enough fourth place in the Premiership, but finished 21 points adrift of the winners Manchester United.

Following a 2–1 League victory over Newcastle United at Highbury in November, Wright received a generous compliment from Kevin Keegan after he had headed a goal and quite outshone Newcastle's own striker, Andy Cole, once at Highbury but sold by Graham to Bristol City. 'Andy will have to look at what Wright achieved for Arsenal today,' said Keegan. 'He is a really good footballer and it's just a pity he is thirty, and has taken this long to reach the top. But like Beardsley, who is 32, he has the enthusiasm to go on for years.' But in the following match at Highbury, Aston Villa knocked the Gunners out of the League Cup, 1–0, giving them, in the process, a lesson in passing and tactics.

On the road to success

But at least Arsenal had been making steady progress in the European Cup Winners' Cup. Odense of Denmark and Standard Liège of Belgium were eliminated. After a 3–0 victory at home, the 7–0 thrashing of Liège (a scoreline that at the time of writing remains the Gunners' highest in European competition) in the away leg of their tie was one of the highpoints of the season. In the next round a single goal, headed by the adventurous Tony Adams at Highbury, was enough to take them through against Torino, after forcing a goalless draw in Italy. Next, in the semi-finals, came dangerous opponents in Paris Saint-Germain, then unbeaten in their previous 35 first class matches.

Ian Wright, whom Graham had boldly replaced with Kevin Campbell in the away tie against Torino, now led the attack again, hard on the heels of a hat-trick against Ipswich Town. And he scored again in Paris, heading Paul Davis's free kick narrowly inside the far post. PSG equalised, but Arsenal held out, taking back to Highbury the precious away goal. A 1–0 win at home secured the Gunners' place in the final. By then they had lost their hold on the FA Cup, beaten 3–1 at Highbury by Bolton Wanderers in a fourth round replay.

European glory

The European final against Parma in Denmark on 4 May was played without the suspended Ian Wright. Parma had a wealth of attacking talent: the little Sardinian Gianfranco

Zola, who was to become so popular at Chelsea, Tino Asprilla, the eccentric but elusive Colombian, Tomas Brolin, the experienced Swedish international. David Seaman would need all his famous anticipation and agility to keep them out.

An Arsenal team below full strength, wearied by its heavy burden of matches, and less fit, as George Graham admitted, than Parma, stuck gamely to its task. Overall, however, Arsenal's defence – four across the back on this occasion, rather than with a sweeper – contained Parma's attack resourcefully, with Steve Bould having one of his most dominant games. In the absence of Wright, however, Alan Smith rose superbly to the occasion, as decisive a factor as he had been when the Gunners beat Liverpool at Anfield to win the Championship so dramatically. On 19 minutes, Smith scored the goal that would decide the game. That he should have scored the decisive goal, and scored it so well, was wholly appropriate. He was surely the finest player on the field, adding to his usual self sacrifice tremendous qualities of heart, intelligence and commitment. Smith later recalled the moment: ' Lee Dixon threw it in to me. I took a touch and played it back to him and Lee kind of helped it forward, and

from what I remember, it's just gone into their defence and Minotti tried to kick it over his head. And I collected it and chested it down. Probably about three players were covering. I had to take it quickly, I had to take it quite high. I jumped and hit it with my right foot. Bucci, the goalkeeper, dived in front of the ball, and I couldn't see it then. Then he fell and I saw it; it was in the opposite corner, it had hit the inside of the right-hand post and nestled in the other corner. It was an incredible feeling'

Turbulent times

Season 1994/95 would prove challenging for the Gunners, and especially for George Graham, who would leave Highbury before the end of the season. A difficult season, too, for Paul Merson, who revealed that he was addicted, trebly, to cocaine, alcohol and gambling. So, in November, Merson went into rehabilitation and would not play again till the following February; a substantial blow to an attack which had long relied on his talents. Both Arsenal and the Football Association treated him with tolerance; Merson escaped with a two-month ban.

Wonderful Copenhagen
The Arsenal players celebrate after capturing the European Cup Winners' Cup in Copenhagen, beating Italian side Parma 1–0 with an Alan Smith goal on 4 May 1994.

Graham steps over the line

As early as June 1993, an English Sunday newspaper had alluded to strange goings on in the Scandinavian transfer market. It was not, however, until late in 1994 that Henrik Madsen, a Danish television football journalist, accused an unnamed Arsenal official of pocketing £200,000 of the notional £1.1 million the Club paid for John Jensen. The English newspaper had reported that Rune Hauge, a Norwegian agent, was taking huge percentages of transfer fees, fixing them over and above what the selling Scandinavian clubs received, and putting money into an account in Guernsey. It was alleged that Jensen had in fact cost the Club £1.7 million, which meant that there was a £600,000 surplus.

The case of the Norwegian international full back Pal Lydersen was also cited. The player had played very few games for the Gunners since they bought him for £500,000 from the Norwegian club IK Start, which however got only half that fee. The Football Association announced that they would hold their own investigation.

By early December 1994, the Inland Revenue had discovered that Graham had not declared the £285,000 and proceeded accordingly. The matter could no longer be ignored. It was imperative for the Premier League to act,

which they did, setting up an investigating committee before which Rune Hauge testified for five hours. Graham meanwhile insisted that he had returned over £450,000 to Arsenal. In February, the Premier League tribunal published its conclusions. On 21 February 1995 Arsenal dismissed Graham, who complained of a 'kangaroo court'. The Football Association suspended Graham for a year. Arsenal's assistant manager, Stewart Houston, moved up as interim manager.

It was sad that Graham's going should be so ignominious, after so many years and so many triumphs with the Club, both as player and manager. He had successfully revitalised a team in the doldrums, won new honours after long, barren seasons, bought exciting new talent into the team, although by the time of his departure, his regime had been losing the love of its supporters. All managerial careers are finite, and Graham's was no different.

Graham's legacy

Up to this point in the season, League and Cup form had largely been dismal, and the supporters were palpably unhappy. The low point was reached when Millwall came to Highbury on 18 January 1995 in a third round FA Cup replay, deservedly winning 2–0 against a team not only sterile in attack but unusually vulnerable in defence. Just a week earlier, the Gunners had gone down honourably enough 1–0 at Liverpool in a Coca-Cola League Cup quarter-final.

In his final season Graham had bought two new attackers, the big, blond, 19-year-old Welsh international John Hartson from Luton Town, for over £1 million, and Chris Kiwomya, from Ipswich Town. But the midfield was still unproductive even if, on the last day of 1994, John Jensen had at long last scored his first goal for the

Gunners, after exchanging passes with Nigel Winterburn and then curling in a splendid shot in front of the North Bank. Alas, Queens Park Rangers won this Highbury game 3–1.

European success

At least there would be the consolation of another European Cup run, even if it would end, in Paris, in strange anti-climax, and a bizarre winning goal. The arrival of fleet-footed Dutch left winger Glenn Helder much improved the attack, although alas he would be ineligible for the Cup Winners' Cup. His arrival, and the improvement of Paul Merson after an inevitably uneasy return, compensated for the fact that Anders Limpar was now flourishing with Everton. Having accounted in the first two rounds for Omonia Nicosia of Cyprus, beaten home and away, and Brondby of Denmark, After the winter break, Arsenal faced Auxerre, the club managed with shrewd skill by the celebrated Guy Roux, who had raised it from obscurity. The Gunners drew 1–1 in front of a crowd of over 35,500 at Highbury, but came through 1–0 in the away leg in France.

The Saturday before they were due to receive the Italian team Sampdoria at home in the semi-final, the Gunners suffered a run of four successive League defeats, followed by a thumping 5–1 home win over Norwich City. A crowd of over 38,000 for the match against Sampdoria saw a remarkable two goals by central defender Steve Bould. The first arrived when Walter Zenga, Sampdoria's Italian international goalkeeper, blocked a shot from David Hillier and Bould followed up. His second was scored just a couple of minutes later, when he leaped to get his head to the ball from Stefan Schwarz's corner, at the near post.

In the 59th minute, Vladimir Jugovic made it 2–1, but 18 minutes later, Paul Merson's devastating long ball through the middle was pursued by Ian Wright, who lost two defenders before flicking the ball past the advancing Zenga. The visitors, however, were playing the better football and Jugovic scored again, giving his team a solid platform of away goals on which to build in the return in Genoa.

There, there would be goals galore. The first of them went to Sampdoria after 13 minutes. So it stood until the 62nd minute, when Hartson headed in Merson's corner and the ball somewhat fortuitously bounced off the lively Ian Wright

to equalise. So Wright had scored in every round, but he came in for some bruising treatment and eventually had to be substituted.

Sampdoria's attack continued to threaten. Hardly had Wright gone off, when their free kick bounced off the Arsenal wall, to be deflected home by Claudio Bellucci. The same player next minute exploited a run and cross by the tireless right winger, Attilio Lombardo, to make it 3–1; with just six minutes left. There were just three to go when Schwarz struck a 35-yard free kick, which found its way through the defensive wall and past Zenga. Which made the aggregate 5–5 and took the game to extra time and then to penalties.

It was David Seaman who majestically saw Arsenal through. After Lee Dixon had put away the first penalty, Seaman went to his left to save from the formidable left foot of the Yugoslav international Sinisa Mihailovic. Eddie McGoldrick, the busy right winger who had come from Crystal Palace, hoofed over the bar, whereupon Seaman, diving this time to his right, frustrated the other Yugoslav, Vladimir Jugovic. Hartson then scored for Arsenal, Aspero for Sampdoria, and Tony Adams for the Gunners. Sampdoria made it 3–2, leaving Paul Merson with the chance to finish the job. Zenga thwarted him, but the phenomenal Seaman proceeded to save from Lombardo, and Arsenal had prevailed and would go through to the final.

Penalty parried

David Seaman makes a crucial save in the penalty shoot-out that settled Arsenal's Cup Winners' Cup semi-final on 20 April 1995 against Sampdoria in Genoa. The scores were tied 5–5 on aggregate and the Gunners won 3–2 on penalties.

Short stay

Bruce Rioch managed Arsenal from 1995–96 before Arsène Wenger took over. The Gunners finished fifth in the Premiership in Rioch's only full season as boss.

Final disappointment

The European Cup Winners' Cup final, in Paris, would pit them against the Spaniards, Real Zaragoza, and it was the ultimate irony that, this time, Seaman would unhappily concede the decisive goal. This match, too, went to extra time, with the Argentine striker Juan Esnaider putting Zaragoza ahead. John Hartson equalised for the Gunners, and penalties seemed inevitable. Instead, with 25 seconds left, Nayim, the Moroccan-born playmaker, who had spent five years somewhat frustratingly with Spurs, elected to shoot, from the right, at a distance of at least 50 yards. David Seaman was some ten yards out of his goal. Desperately, as the ball came towards him, he attempted to retreat into his goal. He succeeded in touching it, but it floated into the net to win Zaragoza the Cup Winners' Cup.

A year of transition

Stewart Houston stepped aside as interim manager in June 1995 to make way for the Club's new appointment, Bruce Rioch, the former manager of Bolton Wanderers. In his time

he had been a forceful left sided midfielder for Scotland, Derby County and Everton. Although Rioch would not stay long in the job, he would leave the Club with a golden legacy.

Rioch made two costly signings: the Dutch international attacker Dennis Bergkamp, who cost a hefty £7.5 million from Internazionale of Milan, and the England international David Platt, bought for £4.5 million from Sampdoria. They'd had contrasting experiences in Italy. Where Platt, who made his name with a superb volleyed winning goal against Belgium in Bologna in the 1990 World Cup, had flourished with Bari, Juventus and Sampdoria, Bergkamp had had two miserable seasons at Inter, despite having settled in Milan. He was constantly played out of position as an out and out striker, where his ideal role was operating just behind the front line.

Bergkamp brings a touch of class

After a somewhat uneasy start that season for both Club and country, Bergkamp would settle down to display, for many years to come, his dazzling array of talents. In February that season, Paul Merson expressed his colossal admiration for

his newly arrived Dutch team mate. He spoke of coming off the field after training, taking a shower, having lunch, chatting with his team mates, only to find, a good hour later, that Bergkamp was still out on the pitch, practising free kicks. 'It's true,' he commented. 'However hard you work, you can't work as hard as Dennis.'

Platt by contrast proved something of an anti-climax. He succumbed early in the season to cartilage trouble and dropped out to have an operation. Though he made 88 appearances in his three seasons at Highbury they brought him a mere 13 goals.

For Ian Wright, the 1995/96 season was not without its problems. He was, as usual, top scorer with 15 goals out of a modest League total of 49, but in February he actually put in for a transfer; even though he would later change his mind. There was something of a reconciliation in April when he scored twice at Highbury in a 2–1 victory over Leeds, and said afterwards, 'Without doubt, I'd love to finish my days here. My main concern is to be in there and scoring goals. Arsenal is the main thing in my life just now.'

The team climbed seven places in the League, from twelfth to fifth, had a creditable run in the Coca-Cola League Cup, beating Hartlepool, Barnsley, Sheffield Wednesday and

Newcastle United, before losing in the semi-finals to Aston Villa, after drawing home and away, but losing on away goals. By contrast, the Gunners didn't survive beyond the third round of the FA Cup, knocked out at Bramall Lane in a replay against First Division Sheffield United.

Rioch departs

It was a season blemished by injuries to Tony Adams, David Platt, Ray Parlour and Steve Bould. Rioch changed the pattern of play to 3–5–2. Fortunately, Martin Keown, standing in as captain for Adams, was in resilient form, helping the team to concede only seven goals in 13 games. In their last League game of the season, Arsenal rose from the dead to beat Bolton Wanderers 2–1 at Highbury and thus qualify for the following season's UEFA Cup. They were a goal down with eight minutes to go when David Platt, criticised previously for having lain untypically and unprofitably deep, equalised, and Dennis Bergkamp scored the winner. 'That's what I bought them for,' enthused Rioch. However, just five days before the start of the next Premiership season, Arsenal's board announced that, in the words of the chairman Peter Hill-Wood, 'it was in the best interests of the Club that Bruce Rioch should leave'.

In the meantime, it had become known that Arsenal were planning to appoint Arsène Wenger as their new manager. A former player for Strasbourg, and for seven years the successful manager of Monaco in the French League, Wenger was at the time managing the Japanese club Nagoya Grampus Eight, for whom former England striker Gary Lineker had once played. Two days after Rioch's departure, it was announced that Arsenal, on Wenger's advice, had signed two French midfielders, the young Senegal-born Patrick Vieira, who would become a legendary figure at Highbury, and the experienced French international Remi Garde. A new era at Highbury was about to dawn.

We've got Dennis Bergkamp
Bruce Rioch welcomes a significant signing at Highbury, Dennis Bergkamp. Rioch smashed Arsenal's transfer record to bring the great Dutch striker from Internazionale to the Club.

HIGHBURY HEROES

Dennis Bergkamp 1995/96–2005/06

Having started his footballing career at Ajax in 1986/87, Dutchman Bergkamp moved to Internazionale in 1993/94 and signed for Arsenal in 1995. His superlative skills soon saw him virtually deified by the Highbury fans. Dubbed 'The Iceman', his cool and incisive judgement on the pitch would make an immeasurable contribution to Arsenal's successes during his time at Highbury. Having won 79 caps and scoring 37 goals for his country, he left the Club in 2006 with Premier League Championship medals in 1997/98, 2001/02 and 2003/04, and FA Cup winners' medals in 1997/98, 2001/02, 2002/03 and 2004/05.

Arsenal under Wenger

CHAPTER 11

With the arrival of Arsène Wenger, the Arsenal Stadium at Highbury entered its final era, one that would bring superb football and trophies galore to the Club. In this period the stadium's history is inextricable from the matches it staged and the unforgettable moments of football it witnessed.

The stadium's final decade as the home of Arsenal Football Club was also the decade in which the team was managed by one of the Club's most inspirational and successful managers. Arsène Wenger was born in Strasbourg, Alsace, in 1949. Having played for some years as an amateur, he had a handful of games for Strasbourg's first team. He in due course became in 1983 a player-coach of the youth team at Cannes, becoming manager of Nancy and then Monaco. In his first season, Wenger won the French Championship, and stayed at the club for seven distinguished years, twice refusing to take on the management of the French national team. In 1994 he moved to Japan, where he revived the fortunes of the Nagoya Grampus Eight team.

Getting fit for the top

Wenger arrived from Japan at the end of September 1996, beginning his tenure in innovative fashion. Revolutionary training ideas were introduced, not least in diet. 'I lived for two years in Japan,' Wenger said, 'and it was the best diet I ever had … Their diet is basically boiled vegetables, fish and rice. No fat, no sugar.' The players were about to experience a massive lifestyle change. Nigel Winterburn, however, continued to be permitted to eat his traditional meal of poached eggs on toast before a match.

Arsène Wenger

Arsène Wenger salutes the fans at Highbury, where he took over as manager in September 1996. He brought about a revolution in training methods at the Club and guided Arsenal to new heights of achievement.

Training-ground development

Until 1961, Arsenal players did most of their training at Highbury, either running laps around the old cinder track at the side of the pitch, or working out on the shale surface just outside the ground, or even jogging around the streets surrounding the stadium. In 1961 the focus of the players' training moved to University College of London Student Union's sports centre in Hertfordshire.

With Wenger's new emphasis on high levels of fitness, which could be seen as continuing the legacy of the legendary Tom Whittaker, it was natural that he should want the best facilities for training and physiotherapy. This was the impetus behind the planning of the brand-new Arsenal Training Centre, a 143-acre site at London Colney in Hertfordshire, which was eventually completed in October 1999. Wenger and his staff were given a free rein to work with architects to come up with the perfect lay-out for their needs. Gary Lewin, the Club's physiotherapist, shaped the centre's medical facilities. Tony Colbert, Arsenal's fitness coach, was able to design exactly the right gymnasium for the players' requirements. The centre features six changing rooms, a steam-room, swimming pool, treatment rooms, massage baths, a Press briefing building and a restaurant. Arsenal have also done their bit for the environment by planting 45 acres with 25,000 trees.

By 2006 the training ground was the workplace for the first team squad and the first- and second-year Academy players. Youth team matches and reserve team friendlies are also played on the 10 full-sized pitches, tended by groundsman Steve Braddock and his award-winning team. These pitches, two of which have under-soil heating, were marked out to the precise dimensions of the Highbury pitch.

Sean O'Connor, the facilities manager at the training centre, said: 'It's a wonderful training complex, and we're proud of every aspect of it. The pitches, for example. It cost £2m to build them from scratch. Two of them have under-soil heating, and you won't find better playing surfaces anywhere in Europe … The results are there to see, and the word had clearly got around. Visiting national sides have asked to train at London Colney, and we've had Brazil, Argentina and Germany here. The England team have been here to train at least three times.'

Coaching staff

Although the new manager made a point of retaining many of the existing staff, following Wenger's appointment, new faces also appeared. Former player Pat Rice became the assistant manager, and the first team coach would be Boro Primorac, a 41-year-old Bosnian from Mostar, who in his time had won 18 caps as a centre back for Yugoslavia and latterly had worked with Wenger at Nagoya Grampus Eight in Japan. There were the French dieticians Dr Yann Rougier and his deputy Herve Castel, and an osteopath, Philippe Boixel, never afraid to try unorthodox methods. Almost concurrently with the arrival of Arsène Wenger, the celebrated former Gunner Liam Brady returned to Highbury after a 16-year absence, to be in charge of the Club's Academy, or youth scheme.

In touch with the top

In September 1996 a 2–0 win over a nine-man Sunderland team at Highbury had lifted Arsenal into second place, and after Wenger assumed control, no goals were given away in the next three League games, including a 3–0 win at Highbury over Leeds United, now managed by George Graham. Patrick Vieira, the Club's new midfielder, lost little time in picking up the pace to become the propulsive, superbly athletic force in midfield he would continue to be for the next decade. Born in Senegal (a fact regularly celebrated in song by the fans at Highbury: 'He comes from Senegal! He plays for Arsenal!'), he became a huge favourite with the Highbury crowd, and would eventually captain the team. Any doubts about the impact he would make were surely settled very early in the victory against Leeds. Picking up the ball from a throw in, some 40 yards from the Leeds goal, he set out on a mesmerising run, effortlessly eluding the defence, finding himself well placed for a shot at goal, only, unselfishly, to roll the ball to Lee Dixon, whose shot rocketed into the net.

The season provided some memorable highpoints for the Highbury crowd, such as a satisfiying 3–1 victory over Tottenham Hotspur, with goals by Wright, Adams and Bergkamp. And a week later, the Gunners found themselves leading the Premiership with a remarkable 2–1 victory at St James' Park against Newcastle United. Disappointingly, any hope of taking the title was undermined by home defeats in the New Year, within four February days, first by Manchester United then, more traumatically, by modest Wimbledon. Wenger conceded that the Championship was now beyond Arsenal's reach. The Gunners finished an honourable third and the season left no doubt of Wenger's impressive impact.

Highbury attracts the best

In the close season of 1997, Wenger was able to focus on squad changes, using his in-depth knowledge of promising players in Europe to telling effect. In what was seen as a major coup, Wenger had already signed the precocious 17-year-old Nicolas Anelka from Paris Saint Germain for no fee in February 1997. Wenger brought off two further coups in the transfer market. From Monaco, his former club, he signed the powerful left-sided midfielder, Emmanuel Petit. From Ajax came the fleet, elusive winger, Marc Overmars, capable of doing damage on either flank. Wenger also signed the combative midfielder Gilles Grimandi from Monaco. It was the beginning of a transfer policy that would revolutionise the profile of the team, giving it an increasingly cosmopolitan appearance, drawing talent from many nations.

Other signings that season included two young attackers, the Portuguese left-winger Luis Boa Morte from Sporting Lisbon and the Liberian Chris Wreh from Monaco. These arrivals coincided with the departure for Middlesbrough of a

Training for success
Arsenal's purpose-built new training ground at London Colney, Hertfordshire. Arsène Wenger and his staff designed a 21st-century centre with everything they needed to prepare Arsenal's players for success, from top quality pitches to hydrotherapy pools and gymnasium facilities.

ARSENAL FOOTBALL CLUB

Name:

Membership No:

Address:

PEPSI
MEMBE

also gave young supporters the chance to attend a variety of special events organised by the Club, such as Christmas parties in which they could meet the players.

Following the abandonment of an earlier scheme, a fully fledged ticket registration scheme was introduced in 1997/98. This was partly to regulate the allocation of tickets at a time when home games at Highbury were massively oversubscribed. In effect, this limited the sale of tickets to registered members, in all but the least popular games. A side effect of this was that the Club was able to exert some influence over the behaviour of its supporters, in that fans behaving in a violent or racist manner would risk losing their membership and therefore their ability to attend matches in future. Other membership-style schemes included those for pensioners and the disabled. Arsenal allocated special areas of the stadium for visually impaired supporters and for wheelchair-bound fans and their escorts. In 2004 Arsenal converted the ticket registration scheme into a more formal voluntary membership scheme for the Club.

On the cards
Membership and ticket registration cards for the Club. From left to right, Adult Family Enclosure Membership Card 1996/97, Junior Gunners Membership Card 1996/97, Adult Silver Membership Card 2005/06.

player who had done memorable things for Arsenal, Paul Merson. Wenger started the process of remodelling the team in the way that reflected his vision and ambition for Arsenal Football Club.

Highbury registers support

In the later 1990s, football was increasing in popularity as a spectator sport and during the 1990s Arsenal Football Club introduced a number of different forms of Club membership. Membership schemes for young fans and their families had existed in the form of the Junior Gunners and Cannon Club (for 16- to 18- year-olds) since 1984, enabling youngsters to enjoy matches from seats close to the pitch in the Family Enclosure areas in the East and West Stands. Membership

Wright overtakes Bastin

Ian Wright began the season within touching distance of Cliff Bastin's long-standing record of 178 goals scored for Arsenal. To the joy of his team mates and the fans, he finally overhauled the record with a hat-trick against Bolton

Front-row seats
Arsenal take on Chelsea on 8 February 1998 watched by fans in the section of the lower East Stand reserved for disabled supporters. The Gunners won the match 2–0 with both goals from Stephen Hughes.

Wanderers at Highbury on 13 September 1997. This took his total to 180. 'The fans have been fantastic,' said Wright. 'I think they even sucked the goals in for me, today.'

Three days later, alas, in a first leg, first round of the UEFA Cup, without the irreplaceable Dennis Bergkamp and with an untypically subdued Ian Wright, Arsenal went down to the modest PAOK team in Salonika. Bergkamp's

absence was the result of his fear of flying, which would deprive the Club of his talents in a succession of European away games to come. PAOK then came to Highbury for the second leg and forced a 1–1 draw. Bergkamp's spectacular goal was the highlight of a glittering performance.

Leading the League

In the League Arsenal continued to flourish, delighting the Highbury fans with some superb performances, such as their 4–0 demolition of West Ham United. It featured another triumphant display by Dennis Bergkamp, of whom Arsène Wenger said, 'He has this feeling always to know where his position is a threat to the opponent. Sometimes he's in front, sometimes he's between the lines, sometimes he's in midfield.' After this game, the Gunners found themselves top of the League on goal difference.

A thrilling meeting at Highbury on 9 November 1997 against Manchester United saw Arsenal rise impressively to the occasion. Within the first half hour, the Gunners had gone 2–0 ahead. First, Anelka beat Peter Schmeichel in the United

goal; then, with a fierce diagonal drive, Patrick Vieira doubled the score. United revived, bringing the scoreline to 2–2, but David Platt headed the winning goal at 3–2.

Yet it was at that very point when things went alarmingly wrong. League matches were lost and it was not until Christmas with Vieira returning from injury that things began to look happier for the fans at Highbury with a 2–1 home win over Leicester on Boxing Day. But by the turn of the year, Manchester United were a dozen points ahead and Arsenal lying sixth.

Back on track

The New Year, however, brought a change of fortune. Following a win in the League Cup against West Ham at Upton Park, on 10 January 1998, Leeds United were beaten 2–1 at Highbury, with both goals from Overmars. In the Cup, having finally dispatched Port Vale, with whom the Gunners had previously drawn at Highbury, through a penalty shoot-out in the replay, Arsenal dismissed Middlesbrough 2–1 in the fourth round. Late in January the fans at Highbury were treated to a 3–0 win over Southampton, Adams himself heading one of the goals. That victory followed a 2–1 home victory against Chelsea in the first leg of the semi-final of the League Cup. The return at Stamford Bridge would see Chelsea running out 3–1 winners, thus qualifying for the final. In between those two League Cup ties, Chelsea came to Highbury in the League and were beaten 2–0.

The fifth round of the FA Cup threw up another London derby, this time at Highbury against Crystal Palace, with the Gunners held to a frustrating 0–0 draw, before winning the replay at Selhurst Park to go through to the sixth round. This was a home tie against West Ham United. The match was

HIGHBURY HEROES

Patrick Vieira 1996/97–2004/05

Born in Dakar, Senegal, in 1976, Patrick Vieira was for eight seasons the lynchpin of the Arsenal midfield. A youthful captain of Cannes, he moved to AC Milan in 1995/96. He signed for Arsenal in the summer of 1996 and quickly made an impact with his imposing presence and confident distribution of the ball. Taking over from Tony Adams as skipper in 2002, his leadership was an essential element in the unbeaten run of 2003/04. He ended his stay with the Club with the FA Cup-winning penalty of 2005. He left for Juventus with three Championship winners' medals (1997/98, 2001/02, 2003/04), three FA Cup winners' medals (1997/98, 2002/03, 2004/05). As a part of the French team, he gained winners' medals in the 1998 World Cup and Euro 2000.

Just done it!
Ian Wright celebrates beating Cliff Bastin's Arsenal scoring record of 178 goals during the game against Bolton Wanderers at Highbury on 13 September 1997. Wright scored a hat-trick and Parlour grabbed the other in Arsenal's 4–1 win.

goal from the magisterial captain Tony Adams, memorably galloping through to make it 4–0. David Seaman hadn't been obliged to make a single save. Arsène Wenger had won the title in his first full season as manager. Fans in the stadium and all over Highbury went wild as Tony Adams lifted the Premiership trophy. 'This is my greatest ever achievement as a manager,' Wenger said, 'I am surprised but delighted that we have won the title so soon, but this team can get better.'

Double delight

A 1–0 defeat of Wolverhampton Wanderers in the semi-final saw Arsenal pitted against Newcastle United at Wembley. Arsenal were clearly the form team. At Wembley, the Gunners took the lead when Emmanuel Petit chipped a ball forward, there was Overmars, with his devastating acceleration, to tear through the Newcastle defence and shoot between Newcastle's Irish international goalkeeper Shay Given's legs.

Newcastle had their opportunities. In the first half, Seaman saved from the clever Temuri Ketsbaia. And after 63 minutes, a mistake by Keown let the formidable Alan Shearer through only to hit the post. Five minutes later, Parlour found Anelka, who raced away to beat Given for a second goal, this time driven into the corner of the net. It was Arsenal's second Double of the century, and an extraordinary triumph for Wenger. 'The Championship was our main aim,' he said, 'but it would have been terrible to have lost at Wembley when we really wanted the FA Cup.'

drawn but the Gunners eventually won the replay after the match went to extra time and penalties.

As they travelled north to Old Trafford on 14 March, the Gunners were just nine points away from Manchester United. The Gunners won an important victory with a single goal by Marc Overmars. Nicolas Anelka expressed his gifts at last when he headed on a ball to Overmars, who speeded on to shoot between Peter Schmeichel's legs. The race for the title was emphatically open. Arsenal were now firing on all cylinders, beating both Sheffield Wednesday and Bolton 1–0. The Gunners then unleashed a fusillade of goals. At Highbury. Newcastle United were beaten 3–1 and Blackburn Rovers were swept aside 4–1 at home in perhaps Arsenal's best display of the season, with two goals from Ray Parlour.

On 18 April, at Highbury, Wimbledon were crushed 5–0 and Arsenal were top of the League.

Claiming the title

On 3 May Arsenal knew that victory at Highbury over an Everton team desperately battling relegation would give them the title. They won in style. The sun shone literally and metaphorically on the Gunners as they crushed Everton in a match that included a 90th-minute

Farewell to Wrighty

In the close season, Ian Wright moved to West Ham United and, in September, too late to qualify for European Championship matches, there arrived a player who would galvanise the team for many years to come; the 21-year-old Swedish international Fredrik Ljungberg, from Halmstads, a player of versatility, technically adroit and a goal-scorer. Later another signing was the Nigerian striker, Nwankwo Kanu, a true conjurer of the ball. He was bought from Internazionale of Milan, having survived heart surgery.

A second home at Wembley

The 1998/99 season began well with a 3–0 win over Manchester United in the Charity Shield at Wembley. And for

that season Wembley would become the Gunners' second home. Arsenal had elected to play their UEFA Champions League games at Wembley, which seemed a sensible move. The chairman Peter Hill-Wood put it cogently. 'We'd have preferred to play at Highbury,' he said, 'but we couldn't play at Highbury and provide normal service for our supporters. That was the deciding factor. UEFA'S regulations on the size of perimeter board advertising would have meant taking up several rows around the stadium with advertising boards. By the time we'd complied with that, we'd have lost many thousands of seats from our capacity.'

The difference in capacity was enormous. Highbury now could contain little more than 38,000 fans, at a time when Old Trafford was to be enlarged to take 67,000. It was around this time that the possibility of a new stadium for the Club began to be mooted in the Arsenal boardroom. Meanwhile, going to Wembley was a godsend to the thousands who had been unable to get a seat at Highbury; and some Wembley tickets cost a mere £10.

At home and abroad

Arsenal's first European group qualifying game, however, was not at Wembley but in Lens, and was a disappointment, a 1–1

draw. Arsenal subsequently played hosts at Wembley to Panathinaikos of Athens. Panathinaikos were beaten 2–1. Unusually, both the Gunners' goals came from headers by their centre backs, Tony Adams and Martin Keown.

In the League, a 3–0 crushing of Manchester United at Highbury in September provided supporters at Highbury with a memorable display that included goals from Adams, Anelka and Ljungberg. At 'home' at Wembley against powerful Dynamo Kiev, Arsenal were seriously below strength, with Vieira once again suspended and Petit injured. Yet Arsenal actually took the lead with a gloriously worked goal by Dennis Bergkamp. However, the Gunners were held to a draw by a merited late equalizer scored by Sergei Rebrov.

A fortnight later, in Kiev, Petit and Vieira were back, but Arsenal took a radically weakened team to the Ukraine. The score was 3–1 to the Ukrainians and qualification for the next round was in danger. Defeat by Lens at Wembley in the next game, with Parlour expelled, put it beyond reach. When Wenger later decided to send a reserve team to Athens to play Panathinaikos in a match that did not matter, it seemed

Gunned down

Top: Tony Adams soars above Jaap Stam to score the opener against Peter Schmeichel as Arsenal beat Manchester United at Highbury on 20 September 1998. The Gunners won 3–0, with Anelka and Ljungberg also scoring. Above: The matchday programme for the game, featuring Marc Overmars and Dennis Bergkamp on the cover.

Play it again

Marc Overmars leaps over Sheffield United goalkeeper, Alan Kelly, in the replayed fifth round FA Cup tie, 23 February 1999, following the dispute over a goal in the first game. Overmars and Bergkamp scored in the Gunners' 2–1 win in the replay.

a kind of suicide. But in Athens the reserves didn't sink; they triumphantly swam, achieving a 3–1 win. This in contrast to the 5–0 defeat in November of an Arsenal 'second team' by Chelsea at Highbury in the Worthington League Cup.

Kanu's flouts custom

Arsenal's defence of the FA Cup had started in the third round with a 4–2 away victory over Preston North End. Wolverhampton Wanderers were beaten 2–1 in the fourth round at Molineux, with goals by the Dutchmen Bergkamp and Overmars. The fifth round, in which Arsenal played

Sheffield United at Highbury on 13 February, gave rise to a bizarre incident, resolved in the event by a mixture of sportsmanship on the part of Arsène Wenger, and a hasty, well-intentioned but manifestly illegal judgement by the Football Association.

The score in the second half was 1–1. Arsenal were having much the better of the argument, when Gilles Grimandi, filling in at centre back, brought down Lee Morris in the penalty box. The referee Peter Jones refused a spot kick, Morris lay injured in the area, and when the ball reached the other end of the field, the Sheffield United keeper, Alan Kelly, kicked it out of

play to enable his team mate to have treatment. When play restarted Ray Parlour picked the ball up and threw it towards a United player, as had become the chivalrous but strictly unofficial custom. Kanu, who had been on the pitch for only eight minutes as a substitute, knew nothing of this custom. Intercepting the ball, he trundled it down the right wing, watched by stunned United players, pulling it into the goalmouth, where an unopposed Marc Overmars tapped it into the net. There was instant uproar and protests from the United bench. The game resumed with United's kick off, the score remained 2–1 to the Gunners, but when it was over, Arsène Wenger generously offered to replay. His offer was accepted by the Football Association. So, ten days later, the match was replayed, and Arsenal repeated their 2–1 victory.

19 unbeaten

In the meantime, the Gunners had been picking up points galore in the League, embarking, after a defeat at Villa Park on 13 December, on a remarkable 19-match unbeaten run, beginning with a 3–1 home win over Leeds. The 5–0 defeat of Leicester City at Highbury saw a hat-trick for Anelka. Another win 3–0 at home to Sheffield Wednesday provided a showcase for Bergkamp at his best. A satisfying revenge on Wimbledon was achieved with a crushing 5–1 victory at Highbury. Then, with Anelka returning to partner Kanu in attack, there was a devastating 6–1 away win at Middlesbrough.

In the FA Cup sixth round, the Gunners, this time without Patrick Vieira, made hard work of beating Derby County 1–0 at Highbury in March. Kanu got the only goal in the final minute of the game. So for the fourth time that season, Arsenal would meet Manchester United – this time at Villa Park in the semi-final. With Arsenal reduced to 10 men

following the sending off of Nelson Vivas, the result was a 0–0 draw. The replay only three days later on 14 April saw Manchester United win 2–1 in a match packed with drama and controversy: one goal each in ordinary time (from Beckham and Bergkamp), a sending off (United's Roy Keane), a 90th-minute penalty (for the Gunners) saved by Peter Schmeichel, and a spectacular winning goal (from Ryan Giggs) for United.

So all hope and ambition was focused on the League. On 2 May Derby County came to Highbury and were beaten, the only goal being scored by Anelka, who had recently been named Young Player of the Year. Following a satisfying 3–1 victory over Spurs at White Hart Lane, the penultimate League match was at Leeds United, where former Gunner David O'Leary was in charge. The only goal, late in the game, was scored by Jimmy Floyd Hasselbaink for Leeds. The Championship was now out of reach and the Gunners finished runners up a single point behind Manchester United.

Henry signs

Summer 1999 brought a well-earned rest for the players, but Arsène Wenger was busy in the transfer market. The disaffected Anelka was sold to Real Madrid for the astonishing price of £23 million, a £22.5 million profit for Arsenal's coffers. The money was immediately put to good use in the purchase of a player who was to become one of the Club's greatest stars. Wenger bought his former protégé at Monaco, 21-year-old Thierry Henry from Juventus. He had been used at outside right by France in the early stages of the 1998 World Cup. Wenger would successfully move him

Highbury hat-tricks

Fifty players scored a total of 126 hat-tricks at Highbury. The top Highbury hat-trick scorers were:

Jimmy Brain (11)

Thierry Henry (8)

Jack Lambert (7)

Doug Lishman (7)

Ted Drake (6)

Ian Wright (6)

David Herd (5)

David Jack (5)

Ronnie Rooke (5)

to centre forward, resulting in a haul of 17 League goals in his first season, equal to Anelka's tally a year earlier. Henry, with his dazzling footwork, his dynamic pace, his ability to switch exuberantly to the left wing soon made himself decisive and hugely popular presence.

'Wenger has revolutionised the Club and its structures,' Henry would later say. Subsequently declaring, 'I am happy with my life in London and love Arsenal. Most of all, I am happy working with Arsène Wenger. I owe him so much.'

Other signings included Davor Suker, Croatia's veteran centre forward from Real Madrid, Dynamo Kiev's defender Oleg Luzhny and the Brazilian left back Silvinho.

Stuttering start

In 1999/2000 once again, the season began with a win, over Manchester United at Wembley in the Charity Shield. But the visit to Highbury of United in the League was another story. Missing strength in the midfield with Petit injured, the game was lost 2–1, signalling the end of Arsenal's 20-month unbeaten League run at home. Freddie Ljungberg, sent through by Dennis Bergkamp, put the Gunners ahead but two goals by Roy Keane won the game for United. A weary team went down 2–0 at Anfield, but things looked up at Highbury when Aston Villa were soundly beaten 3–1 just three days before the Gunners were due to open their UEFA Champions League campaign in Italy.

European hopes dashed

In Florence, to which Dennis Bergkamp travelled by car, overall the Gunners were the better team in a goalless draw. Next up in Europe were AIK Solna of Stockholm, hosted by the Gunners at Wembley. Bergkamp, in transcendent form, sent Ljungberg through for the opening goal with an inspired pass.

Krister Nordin equalised, but with the end of the 90 minutes in sight, the Gunners scored twice more. It wasn't a bad beginning, and to force a draw at Nou Camp against Barcelona in the third game suggested progress could be made to the next round.

First, Barcelona came to Wembley and won 4–2. Wenger felt the game was determined by the highly dubious goal with which Barça took the lead. It came when the Dutch international, Philip Cocu, blatantly flung himself across Tony Adams' leg, thus securing the unjustified penalty from which Barcelona's formidable Brazilian attacker Rivaldo scored.

It was therefore imperative to beat Fiorentina at Wembley in the next group game, and on the face of it, victory seemed probable. It proved another traumatising evening for the Gunners, beaten by a single thundering goal from Gabriel Batistuta. Eliminated from the Champions League, Arsenal would now compete in Europe in the UEFA Cup, where the home matches would be played at Highbury, ending the Club's experiment with a second home at Wembley.

Champions League challenge
Above: Arsenal put pressure on the goalkeeper as they take on AIK Solna in the Champions League at Wembley, 22 September 1999. Arsenal won 3–1. Left: a ticket for the same game. Playing at Wembley allowed many more home fans to attend matches.

Arsenal's League form was substantially better than their faltering performance in Europe. Three days before the humbling defeat by Barcelona at Wembley, Everton had been brushed aside 4–0 at Highbury, a week after that came the satisfaction of a 3–2 win over Chelsea at Stamford Bridge, notable for the inspired virtuosity of Kanu, who scored an astonishing hat-trick. At home to Middlesbrough in November, Arsenal ran riot. The 5–1 score included a hat-trick from Overmars, in devastating form, and two from Bergkamp.

Leicester City's revenge

In January 2000 the Gunners had surprisingly gone out of the FA Cup in the fourth round against a Leicester City team they had easily beaten 3–0 at Leicester in the League, some five weeks earlier. But Leicester achieved two goalless draws, away and at home, winning at Filbert Street on penalties.

League form continued to be too erratic to maintain a true challenge. Hard on on the heels of a commendable 1–1 draw at Old Trafford against Manchester United, there was an ignominious defeat at, of all places, Bradford City. Victory eight days later on 13 February in the home game against Liverpool was mandatory, but the Gunners lost that too, by a single goal. Patrick Vieira admitted, 'We have to improve, or we could end up with nothing.'

Highbury hosts Europe

Now at Highbury for their European home games, the Gunners were able to achieve a remarkable home victory in the fourth round of the UEFA Cup against Spain's Deportivo La Coruña in March 2000, having eliminated Nantes in the previous round. Both Lee Dixon, with an enterprising header, and Thierry Henry scored before half time. In the second half the game changed dramatically when Deportivo's young attacker, Djalminha, was sent off controversially after a clash with Gilles Grimandi, just after scoring a penalty. The Gunners now ran riot, adding another three goals for a famous victory. Two of the five went to Thierry Henry, but the most remarkable and gloriously idiosyncratic was undoubtedly scored by Kanu, who with sublime impertinence dummied the visiting keeper, Jacques Songo'o, strolling past him to put the ball in the empty net. With a makeshift central defence, the Gunners kept the score down to a 2–1 defeat in La Coruña and thus

moved on into the next round with an aggregate win of 6–3. This provided a comfortable 2–0 home victory against the German side Werder Bremen. The away leg saw a dynamic performance and a hat-trick by Ray Parlour. The Gunners surged into a 2–0 lead. The final score would be 4–2, a 6–2 aggregate. But the game also cost the Gunners the harsh expulsion of Thierry Henry. Henry was thus ruled out of the ensuing first leg of the semi-final versus Lens at Highbury. When Arsenal opened the scoring against Lens after a mere couple of minutes, the kind of ample victory they'd enjoyed over Deportivo in the previous round seemed well in prospect. Petit certainly began the game in style, with a fine through ball, which Bergkamp shot into an empty net. But no more goals were forthcoming and 1–0 was the final score. With Adams and Henry back in the side and Bergkamp travelling, Arsenal completed the double in France with a 2–1 win and so progressed to the final.

Turkish trauma

The final was against the Turkish team Galatasaray in Copenhagen. Arsenal's confidence was boosted by the fact that in the European Cup Galatasaray had been thrashed 5–0 in Istanbul by Chelsea. Yet the Gunners never really hit their stride. In a match marred by violence off the pitch, the team

Deportivo destroyed
Ljungberg and Henry celebrate Arsenal's third in a 5–1 win v Deportivo La Coruña in the UEFA Cup fourth round first leg at Highbury, 2 March 2000. Dixon, Henry (2), Kanu and Bergkamp scored the goals.

missing their clearest chance when Martin Keown, at point blank range, shot over the bar in the second half. Galatasaray became predictably defensive, and the match ended goalless, necessitating the lottery of penalties. A speciality which Arsenal over the seasons had seemingly failed to master. This time, too, they failed at the final hurdle. Davor Suker and Patrick Vieira both struck the woodwork. Ray Parlour duly scored, but it was left to a former Tottenham Hotspur player, the Romanian defender Gheorghe Popescu, to drive the last nail into the Gunners' coffin.

The team ended the season as runners up in the Premiership, but with no first-team trophies. One consolation, however, was the performance of the junior team, coached by Don Howe, who won the FA Youth Cup beating their Coventry City equivalent 5–1 on aggregate.

On the attack

Robert Pires sweeps forward during Arsenal's dramatic 3–2 Champions League win over Shakhtar Donetsk at Highbury, 20 September 2000. Arsenal's goals came from Wiltord and Keown (2).

Rebuilding a winning formula

The summer of 2000 saw Emmanuel Petit and Marc Overmars both leave Highbury for Barcelona. Wenger filled the gaps by signing Robert Pires from Olympique Marseille. A French international he was capable of playing on either wing. From Real Mallorca came Lauren, a Cameroon international right back. Striker Sylvain Wiltord arrived from Bordeaux. And from Corinthians of Sao Paolo, Brazil, Wenger signed Edu, a fluent midfielder, who arrived at Highbury in February 2001.

Highbury makes an impression

Pires later recalled his first impressions of the Arsenal Stadium and the Club: 'I was very, very surprised to see the supporters so close to the pitch. I found this fantastic, because, you know, before coming to Highbury, Thierry Henry, Patrick Vieira and Emmanuel Petit, had told me, Robert, you'll see at Highbury, when you play here, you are going to explode. And it's there every time I go out on the field. It's always a gift. I never thought beforehand of a "quarter" like Highbury. That I would find a stadium in the middle of all those houses, those apartments.

'When I look at Olympique Marseille, it's always the same circus, and the players' daily life is always as difficult! Arsenal is the opposite of that ambience. It's enough to see the relaxed atmosphere which exists at the London Colney training ground. All you see there are people from the Club, it's super-functional. You arrive knowing for sure that you are going to work calmly. That goes with the philosophy of Arsène Wenger ... When their club goes through a bad patch, the fans show their support with a lot of energy. At Highbury, if you are behind at half time, the crowd applauds you the moment play resumes.'

The 2000/01 season could hardly have had a more explosive beginning. At Sunderland, the Gunners were beaten 1–0, Patrick Vieira was contentiously sent off, and Arsène Wenger of all people would be charged with pushing the referee in the tunnel after the game. This was an unfounded charge that would ultimately be dropped.

Liverpool defeated

In the next match, versus Liverpool at Highbury, which Arsenal won 2–0, Vieira was sent off again. Arsenal now had

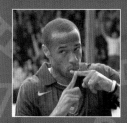

HIGHBURY HEROES
Thierry Henry 1999/00–

Thierry Henry is without doubt one of Arsenal's all-time 'greats'. The Club's most prolific goal-scorer to date was born in Paris in 1977. After playing for Monaco and Juventus, he signed for the Gunners in August 1999. Moved by Arsène Wenger from the wing to the centre forward position, he has time and again delighted fans with his speed, control and goal-scoring instinct. The Gunners' captain at the time of the move to Emirates Stadium, he won League Championship medals in 2001/02 and 2003/04, FA Cup winners' medals in 2001/02, 2003/04 and 2004/05, and was a member of France's 1998 World Cup-winning squad.

once more to do without him, this time for five games. It was, however, an important victory for the Gunners, who had not defeated Liverpool for six years. The adventurous Lauren put Arsenal ahead, Thierry Henry made it 2–0 in the closing minutes. There was still time, before his long suspension, for Vieira to inspire, with his two goals, Arsenal's success in a 5–3 victory over Charlton Athletic at Highbury. But now, in the Premiership, the Gunners would have to do without him.

Champions League at Highbury

In the first phase of the 2000/01 European Champions League, Arsenal won all three September games. Sparta Prague were beaten on their own ground with a dazzling solo goal by Silvinho. Back at Highbury, now hosting Champions League games for the first time, the Gunners made hard work of beating Shakhtar Donetsk from the Ukraine. Without Tony Adams, a weakened defence allowed the Gunners to go embarrassingly behind by two goals within a three-minute spell. Sylvain Wiltord came on as a substitute soon after the second Donetsk goal and cut the lead almost on half time. But it took two goals in the last five minutes from an unexpected saviour, central defender Martin Keown, to give Arsenal the game.

After such an uneven performance, it seemed likely that Lazio, of Rome, would stretch the Gunners at Highbury. In the event, however, Arsenal rose powerfully to the occasion, inspired by Dennis Bergkamp, who set up a goal in each half for Freddie Ljungberg. The return of Tony Adams steadied the defence, 2–0 was the winning margin. Arsenal then went to Rome and gained a 1–1 draw at the Stadio Olimpico, with the Gunners' goal coming from Robert Pires, his first for the Club.

Sparta Prague came to Highbury, and Arsenal, with two goals in the first 11 minutes by Ray Parlour and Lauren, won comfortably 4–2, Lee Dixon getting one of his rare goals. For their last group game, the Gunners travelled to Donetsk. The 3–0 defeat was academic. The Gunners had qualified for the second phase.

Thierry stings United

In the League, despite the protracted absence of Vieira, the Gunners embarked on a 12-match unbeaten run, the centrepiece being the 1–0 victory at Highbury on 1 October 2000 over the favourites for the title, Manchester United; gained through a suitably spectacular goal from Thierry Henry. The French striker flicked the ball up, spun, and hit a fierce, curling volley past the United goalie, fellow French international Fabien Barthez. Thierry Henry urged caution, however: 'We've got an important result against a big team but you can't just base a whole season on beating Manchester United.'

November would prove a month of anti-climax for the Gunners, winning only a single game out of seven, in a period during which Manchester United surged

One nil to the Arsenal
The scoreboard tells the familiar story as Thierry Henry holds off Gary Neville during Arsenal's 1–0 win over Manchester United at Highbury, 1 October 2000. Henry scored the first-half winner.

ahead by eight points. Although the Gunners' form was erratic, there were two thumping 5–0 home wins, both at Highbury, first against Manchester City at the end of October, then against Newcastle United in early December. On Boxing Day against Leicester City at Highbury, just three days after the Gunners had been crushed 4–0 at Anfield against Liverpool, Adams scored a memorable solo goal in the 6–1 win, running half the length of the field to score.

Champions League
at Highbury
Highbury decked out in Champions League colours. Following the experiment with hosting home games in the Champions League at Wembley, from 2000/01 the Gunners returned to Highbury.

Bayern draws at Highbury

In the second group phase of the UEFA Champions League against Spartak in Moscow, Arsenal had been soundly beaten 4–1. But at Highbury against the German champions, Bayern Munich, the team managed a draw, 2–2. They probably should have won it, establishing but losing a 2–0 lead. Once again, the Gunners scored a very early goal, this time in just four minutes from Thierry Henry, another goal coming on 55 minutes from Kanu. But in the very next minute after Kanu's goal, Tarnat got one back for Bayern. Bayern went after the equaliser and got it, ten minutes after their first goal, from the clever German international playmaker, Mehmet Scholl. Mathematically, the Gunners could still qualify for the quarter-final, but the prospect of two games against Lyon and a return game in Munich, suggested it would be an uphill task.

Great wins, great losses

On 9 December Highbury was cheered by a triumphant 5–0 home win over Newcastle United in the League in which Ray Parlour scored another well-deserved hat-trick. But the team was brought back down to earth by a pre-Christmas 4–0 beating at Anfield by Liverpool. David Seaman returned to the team at last on 13 January for a home League game against Chelsea, drawn 1–1. He would also play in every FA Cup tie all the way to the final, beginning with the fourth-round game against his former club, Queens Park Rangers, thrashed 6–0 at Loftus Road, with Wiltord in deadly form.

In an action-packed February 2001, Chelsea returned to Highbury for the fifth round of the FA Cup and were defeated 3–1. The following week, Lyon were the visitors, and Arsenal with a makeshift central defence – Oleg Luzhny and Gilles Grimandi – managed to hold out for a 1–1 draw. Bergkamp scored for Arsenal after 33 minutes, with Lyon's equaliser coming from Edmilson.

However, four days later on 25 February came the disaster of Old Trafford, Arsenal ripped apart in the League, 6–1, by Manchester United. No Adams, again, no Keown, this time Luzhny paired with his fellow East European Igor Stepanovs, who had an afternoon to forget. 'Everything went wrong for us today,' admitted Wenger. Yet there was consolation in the FA Cup and the Champions League, alike. On 8 March Spartak, who had thrashed the Gunners in Moscow, came to Highbury, a much-diminished side. There were eight minutes left when Thierry Henry scored the game's only goal. One nil to the Arsenal and hope survived.

Continuing Cup campaigns

Arsenal breezed through the FA Cup quarter-final against Blackburn Rovers 3–0, despite resting Thierry Henry and

Patrick Vieira. The team could now turn their full attention to the vital return match in Munich against Bayern. It was lost, by a solitary goal, scored after only ten minutes by the elusive Brazilian, Elber. Qualification for the quarter-finals now depended on what happened in Moscow between Spartak and Lyon. When the game in Munich ended, four minutes still remained in Moscow, where the score was 1–1, and a victory for Lyon would put them rather than the Gunners in the next round. 'It was like ninety minutes for me,' confessed Wenger. But the score stayed unchanged and Arsenal were through to meet the formidable opposition of Valencia.

In the semi-final of the FA Cup, the Gunners were up against their traditional north London rivals, Tottenham Hotspur. First, however, there would be something of a dress rehearsal for the semi-final when the clubs met in the League at Highbury. A game sadly overshadowed by the death that very morning, at the pitifully early age of 33, of David 'Rocky' Rocastle, once such an exuberant and popular outside right at Highbury. A one-minute silence was held and impeccably observed before the Spurs game, which Arsenal won 2–0.

Dominant throughout, it was 70 minutes before an all-French move was crowned by Robert Pires cutting in to score from the left. Henry at last got the goal he had been threatening throughout on 87 minutes.

Four days later, Valencia came to Highbury for the first leg of the Champions League quarter-final. With Keown able to partner Adams in central defence, with the promising Ashley Cole, still only 20 years old, at left back, it looked a powerful Arsenal team. The Valencia side included such stars as the Argentinian centre back Ayala and his compatriot Pablo Aimar in attack, supporting the giant Norwegian international centre forward John Carew. A goal behind at half time, the Gunners were looking decidedly second best. After the break, however, with Wiltord taking over from Ljungberg in attack, the Gunners scored two goals within a couple of minutes; Henry got the equaliser, and Parlour the winner.

Semi-final success

The FA Cup semi-final was at Old Trafford. Spurs' hopes rose when their Irish international Gary Doherty put them ahead.

11

Parlour game

Gunners midfielder Ray Parlour takes on Vicente of Valencia in the first leg of the Champions League quarter-final at Highbury, 4 April 2001. Parlour scored Arsenal's second in a 2–1 win. Henry netted the first.

Arsenal were the dominant team, but it wasn't until the 33rd minute that Patrick Vieira broke through to equalise. The Gunners had to wait until the 74th minute for Robert Pires at last to provide them with what turned out to be the winning goal in a match won 2–1. Arsenal had once again battled through to the FA Cup final.

In Valencia those chances missed in the first leg would prove costly. It was mostly a defensive performance by the Gunners, who needed only a draw to qualify for the semi-finals. But on 75 minutes, Carew leaped above Tony Adams, no mean feat, and headed the decisive goal. Arsenal never recovered from this set-back and were out of Europe.

Although Manchester United were beginning to look unassailable in the League, it was still essential to finish high enough in the Premiership to qualify for the following season's Champions League. A comfortable 4–1 home win over Everton brought that target, and the prospect of an eventual second place, closer.

A Cardiff Cup final

The FA Cup final this time would be at Cardiff, the opposition, as in 1971 at Wembley, would be Liverpool. With Liverpool largely content to soak up pressure, Thierry Henry got away after seven minutes, went skilfully round the Liverpool keeper, Sander Westerveld, and shot for goal. There on the line by the post, Liverpool's Swiss centre back, Stephan Henchoz, seemed to block the ball with his arm. The referee appeared unaware of it, the linesman, who could see what happened, clearly decided that the handball was unintentional. So it was not until the 72nd minute that Arsenal took the lead they surely deserved on the balance of play, when Ljungberg scored. But in a devastating five-minute spell, between the 83rd and the 88th minute, the

dynamic little England centre forward, Michael Owen, was simply too quick and elusive for Arsenal defenders. First, when Liverpool's Gary McAllister sent in a testing free kick, Owen drove the ball past David Seaman for the equaliser. Barely five minutes later Owen evaded Dixon and Adams, shooting past David Seaman again to give Liverpool the Cup they couldn't win in 1971.

After the final, there remained, unusually, the anticlimax of a couple of League games. Arsenal needed a single point to consolidate second place and thus qualify for the Champions League. They duly got that point at Newcastle, then lost away to Southampton in the last game of the season. They finished 10 points behind Manchester United.

Campbell turns Gunner

At the end of season 2000/01, Arsène Wenger had announced, 'This team has huge potential, but we need some extra quality to take us that step further. I know who I want and we have enough time to sort it all out.' Time enough, above all, to persuade the dominating England centre half, a free agent under the Bosman ruling, to leave White Hart Lane for Highbury. Sol Campbell was a key acquisition at a time when Tony Adams, the victim of so many injuries, was plainly on his way out of a game he'd served so well; it was clearly imperative that the Gunners' central defence be

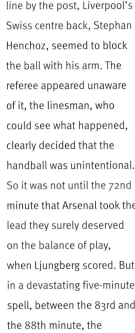

Cardiff bound

Patrick Vieira scores Arsenal's first in the 2001 FA Cup semi-final victory over Spurs at Old Trafford, 8 April 2001. Ljungberg scored the second in the Gunners' 2–1 win to set up a meeting with Liverpool in the final at the Millennium Stadium, Cardiff.

strengthened. Substantially less successful, alas, was the arrival from Everton of the striker Francis Jeffers. The signing of the injury-prone Jeffers was a gamble justified on the basis of a proportion of the fee being dependent on the player's appearances. In fact these amounted to a meagre half dozen in the Premiership that season, with just two goals scored, before returning to Everton for a period on loan in summer 2003. From Glasgow Rangers came the Dutch international left-footed midfielder, Giovanni Van Bronckhorst, while from Ipswich Town came the young goalkeeper, Richard Wright.

The 2001/02 season began with a flourish, a 4–0 win at Middlesbrough. This was followed by the anticlimax of a 2–1 home defeat by Leeds, and indeed consistency would be elusive throughout the season's opening weeks. Four days after the Leeds match, however, Leicester were brushed aside 4–0 at Highbury, a stroll in the roasting sunshine for the Gunners, but a game that saw both Patrick Vieira and Leicester's famously abrasive Dennis Wise sent off.

Staying the course in Europe

The European Cup campaign began badly at Real Mallorca in early September, where the Gunners went down to a 11th minute penalty conceded by Ashley Cole, who was sent off. Nor was the next game against the German team Schalke 04 at Highbury reassuring. In a two-minute first half spell, Arsenal went two up through Ljungberg and Henry. Two minutes from the interval, though, Van Hoogdalem replied for Schalke. Henry's penalty a couple of minutes after the break restored the two goal advantage, but the forceful Belgian international attacker, Mpenza, brought it back to 3–2. Panathinaikos beat the Gunners by the only goal in Greece and at home they made hard work of disposing of the Greek team 2–1, Henry scoring both goals. Ultimately with a 3–1 win against Mallorca at Highbury, and in spite of a defeat away at Schalke, the Gunners qualified for the next group stage.

This next phase of the competition would see both glory and anguish. In November the Gunners lost 2–0 away to Deportivo La Coruña. Yet Arsenal's home form in Europe was more impressive. Juventus were the visitors at Highbury in early December. 3–1 was the margin of the Gunners' memorable win in a performance that Arsène Wenger in his delight described as 'perfect'. There were the electric pace

and insidious free kicks of an inspired Thierry Henry, the opportunism of Freddie Ljungberg, scorer of the first and third Arsenal goals, the dynamism of Patrick Vieira and the sublime dexterity of Dennis Bergkamp. It was an untypical error by the highly regarded Juve and Italy keeper Gianluigi Buffon, failing to save a shot from Ljungberg that gave Arsenal a 21st-minute lead. Henry scored the Gunners' second goal with a 25-yard drive. Best of all, perhaps, was Dennis Bergkamp, who set up Ljungberg's second goal with phenomenal skill. Confronted by a posse of defenders, he calmly kept the ball, taking a total of eleven touches until the final pass to Ljungberg. As the European campaign took a midwinter break, Arsenal were looking and feeling strong.

League form

During the autumn of 2001 the Gunners went eight consecutive matches in the Premiership without defeat, before surprisingly collapsing at home 4–2 to Charlton Athletic in November. The south Londoners had not won at Highbury for 46 years. Thereafter, however, things would radically improve, although a blunder by Richard Wright would cost Arsenal a victory and him his place in the subsequent 1–1 draw against Spurs at White Hart Lane. Oblivious of the abuse from unforgiving Spurs supporters, Sol Campbell had a majestic game.

Reserve goalkeeper Stuart Taylor made his first-team League debut in goal, and had the immediate satisfaction of helping to beat Manchester United at Highbury on 25 November 2001. United, despite being largely under

Defensive pact
Arsenal and England defensive duo Sol Campbell and Ashley Cole discuss tactics during training at London Colney, August 2003.

Updated crest
The Victoria Concordia Crescit crest was updated for the last time for the 2001/02 season.

Barthez beaten

Thierry Henry slots home his second and Arsenal's third goal past fellow Frenchman Fabien Barthez at Highbury in the 3–1 win against Manchester United, 25 November 2001. Ljungberg was also on the scoresheet.

Gunnersaurus on the ball

Arsenal mascot Gunnersaurus Rex leads the Highbury cheers during Arsenal's 1–0 win against Liverpool in the FA Cup fourth round, 27 January 2002. Gunnersaurus made his first appearance before a League game against Coventry in August 1993.

pressure, took the lead on 14 minutes through Paul Scholes. In the 48th minute the Gunners equalised, when Ljungberg clipped over the head of United's gifted but idiosyncratic goalkeeper Fabien Barthez. This seemed to unsettle Barthez, who inexplicably, and to the delight of the Highbury crowd, began to take gratuitous risks. In the last 10 minutes, his fellow French international, Thierry Henry, exploited his folly by beating him twice, bringing the final score to 3–1.

Highbury highs and lows

Winning form followed this encouraging victory until a week before Christmas, against Newcastle United at Highbury. When Robert Pires gave the Gunners the lead on 20 minutes, victory seemed probable. Instead, the Gunners conceded three times in the second half. The sublime perversity of football was shown when Arsenal promptly went up to Anfield and beat Liverpool 2–1 with ten men.

That December saw two more 2–1 home victories against Chelsea and Middlesbrough. 2002 began with a comfortable 4–2 home victory over Watford in the FA Cup. Next Liverpool came to Highbury for the return League fixture, and this time forced a 1–1 draw. But the Gunners soon got their revenge in a heartening home victory over Liverpool in the FA Cup fourth round, Dennis Bergkamp scoring the only goal. David Seaman was at last able to return for the 4–1 home League win over Fulham late in February.

Back in Europe

The Champions League campaign resumed in February, and Arsenal met Bayer Leverkusen twice, deservedly drawing 1–1 in Germany, then at Highbury producing a resounding victory against a team destined to go all the way to the final. At Highbury Dennis Bergkamp influentially returned for what Matt Dickinson in *The Times* described as 'a display of such sweeping beauty that it could be set to music'. Patrick Vieira in majestic form outplayed Leverkusen's fulcrum, Michael Ballack, and paved the way to the Gunners' first goal, strongly tackling the Brazilian international Lucio. The ball went loose to

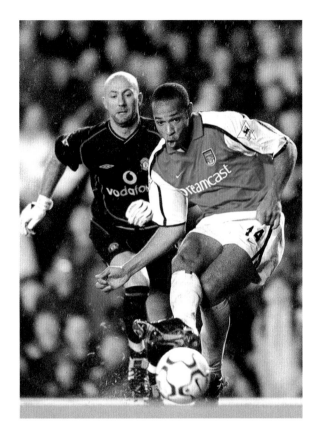

Pires, who raced out of his own half while the German defence retreated, and sent a low shot curling past the Leverkusen keeper Jorg Butt. Two minutes later, Vieira claimed a ball, and launched an attack that ended with Thierry Henry shooting past Butt. A couple of minutes into the second half, Arsenal made it three. Vieira this time was scorer rather than provider, bending to head in at the far post when Henry's free kick was inadvertently touched on by the Bulgarian striker, Dimitar Berbatov. The fourth Arsenal goal was the most spectacular of all, a gem of virtuosity from Bergkamp. On 83 minutes, taking the ball with his back to the goal, he swiftly pivoted, then from 20 yards lobbed the ball over the head of Butt. Leverkusen got a late consolation goal with a fierce shot by Zoltan Sebescen, but the result was a 4–1 victory for the Gunners.

Two weeks later, Deportivo La Coruña came to Highbury; and Arsenal's European dreams were abruptly and emphatically ended with a 2–0 defeat. The result meant that Arsenal would fail to progress. So the European mirage disappeared again, leaving behind the memory of the superb display against Leverkusen at Highbury.

Domestic focus

The Gunners' progress in the League had remained solid. On 2 March at Newcastle, travelling supporters were to be treated to a Bergkamp goal of dazzling technique, when he took a pass from Pires with his back to goal and, with a conjuror's touch, sent the ball spinning past one side of his marker, meeting it on the other side, and driving it home. Arsenal won that League game 2–0.

A week later, Arsenal were back at St James' Park for a sixth round Cup tie, but this time they were held to a 1–1 draw. At Highbury for the replay, Arsenal cruised to 3–0 victory with goals from Pires, Campbell and Bergkamp. The victory, however, was blemished by an injury to Robert Pires that would keep him out for the rest of the season. Arsenal survived this blow to go unbeaten in their final 21 League games of the season.

The FA Cup semi-final against Middlesbrough at Old Trafford was a tense affair won by Arsenal through an own goal in the first half, deflected in off a defender. This set up an all-London final in Cardiff against Chelsea.

In the League, the impressive series of victories continued. There were successive home wins against Spurs, Ipswich and West Ham. The latter represented the game the Gunners had in hand. Winning it would give them a lead of four points over second-place Liverpool with just four Championship games to go. Goalless until half time, in the second half the Gunners gradually found their range and in the 77th minute Ljungberg at last broke the deadlock with a goal, to be followed by a second, from Kanu. When Arsenal proceeded to win at Bolton, with goals by Ljungberg and Wiltord, it meant that they had to win just one of their last two matches to claim the League title. One of those matches was an away meeting with Manchester United.

A glorious farewell

The FA Cup final would be Tony Adams' last game for the Gunners. And his career would go out with a bang at Cardiff rather than a

Wenger waits
Manager Arsène Wenger watches from behind the hoardings in front of the Highbury dugout as Arsenal battle it out with Bayer Leverkusen in the Champions League, 27 February 2002.

Pat trick
Patrick Vieira scores Arsenal's third with a superb diving header against Bayer Leverkusen, 27 February 2002. Arsenal won the Champions League tie at Highbury 4–1, with Pires, Henry and Bergkamp also on target.

whimper, It was a final that took some time to ignite. And when the Gunners did go ahead, in the 70th minute, it was in what might be termed their traditional way; on the counter-attack. At a moment when Chelsea seemed to be calling the tune, Adams found Wiltord, who in turn served Parlour, some 40 yards from goal. Parlour advanced and, 25 yards out, let fly a fulminating shot, which sped past Carlo Cudicini in the Chelsea goal. Ten minutes more, and Freddie Ljungberg snapped up a ball on the left flank, shook off a challenge from Chelsea's formidable centre back, John Terry, and beat Cudicini for the second time with a cleverly swerving shot. The Cup was once again held aloft by a triumphant Adams. It was Arsenal's first trophy for four years, and within as many days they'd have another. With the League programme still to complete, the Gunners travelled to Old Trafford. Arsenal scored after 57 minutes when Fabien Barthez parried a shot from Ljungberg and Wiltord drove past him. Arsenal had gained the Premiership title.

The last League game took place at Highbury against Everton with the title won. The scene was one of jubilation. Wenger fielded a team including several reserves, but it was still good enough to win, 4–3, giving the Gunners 87 points from their 38 matches, without a single defeat away from Highbury, or a single League game in which they failed to score.' Adams finished his playing career as the first player to win a Championship title in three different decades.

Seaman's last season

Season 2002/03 would be the last at Highbury for David Seaman, transferred in the summer of 2003 to Manchester City. Arsène Wenger's transfer coup in July was to sign the resolute Brazilian central midfielder Gilberto Silva, who had just helped his country to win the 2002 World Cup. From Lille came the tall centre back, Pascal Cygan. The curtain-raiser Community (previously the Charity) Shield game against Liverpool in Cardiff saw Gilberto score the winner.

Islington celebrates
Arsenal's jubilant supporters mob the bus carrying the victorious Double-winning team through the streets of Islington, 12 May 2002.

At the start of the season proper, the question was how long would the team's unbeaten away record of 20 matches since the start of the previous season survive. Despite the absence of the two injured flankmen, Pires and Ljungberg, Arsenal maintained a promising start, with Wiltord managing to score half a dozen times in the first six games. But when Arsène Wenger speculated on the possibility of the Gunners going unbeaten through the season, he turned out to be a year ahead of his time.

Borussia Dortmund beaten

Ljungberg was back for Arsenal's opening Champions League game, scoring their second goal at Highbury in a 2–0 win over Borussia Dortmund. Bergkamp, who scored the first goal, was also on dazzling form. This win was followed by a masterly 4–0 win against PSV in Eindhoven, which included the fastest goal ever scored in the Champions League by Gilberto after 22 seconds. This winning form in Europe was continued in France against Auxerre, but it wouldn't last.

After a 24-match unbeaten run, three games were disastrously lost in succession, starting with a defeat at Everton. Just three days later, Arsenal lost at Highbury to Auxerre 2–1. Two more depressing results followed: Arsenal lost 2–1 in Dortmund and then PSV came to Highbury and forced a goalless draw. But Arsenal had done enough to qualify for the next group stage.

Things improved in November with three League wins in a row, the third of them a satisfying 3–0 home victory against Spurs. A buoyant Arsenal went to the Stadio Olimpico in the first match of the second group stage and beat Roma 3–1 with a glorious hat-trick by Henry. But when Arsenal received Valencia in December, they were held to a goalless draw. The tournament then went into its usual winter hibernation.

Early December saw the crucial Premiership meeting at Old Trafford with Manchester United. The Gunners recovered from the 2–0 defeat in that game to embark on a 12-match unbeaten run in the Championship. While in the fifth round of the FA Cup there was sweet revenge over Manchester United at Old Trafford, with goals from Edu and Wiltord supplying the 2–0 victory.

Against Ajax at Highbury, Sylvain Wiltord raised hope after only five minutes by racing on to Bergkamp's pass to shoot powerfully home. But the lead endured only a dozen minutes,

until Nigel De Jong equalised. And so it stayed. A crushing 5–1 win over Manchester City at Maine Road raised hopes of similar success in Amsterdam. But the game produced no goals, and one more European anticlimax was in prospect. After that fine 3–1 win away against Roma, it was legitimate to expect another victory at Highbury, especially when Roma were reduced to ten men by the sending off of Totti. Instead, the Italians held on to draw 1–1. This meant that the Gunners had to avoid defeat in their final group match in Valencia. But this was not to be, and Arsenal went down 2–1, thus ending their European campaign.

Cup consolation

The Gunners had maintained their long unbeaten run against Chelsea with a 2–2 draw at Highbury in the FA Cup quarter-final, followed by a 3–1 win at Stamford Bridge in the replay. This put the Gunners into a semi-final against Sheffield United at Old Trafford, a match in which a collision between the referee Graham Poll and Michael Tonge of United contributed to Arsenal's goal – the only one of the game. The match was also notable for a stupendous save by David Seaman, one of the best of his career. Arsenal had secured their place in the FA Cup final for the third year in succession.

Now Manchester United, who had edged ahead in the Championship, came to Highbury for a match the Gunners had to win. They drew 2–2, despite Thierry Henry scoring

Three of the best
Patrick Vieira, Thierry Henry and Dennis Bergkamp line up in a wall in the Champions League encounter with Borussia Dortmund on 17 September 2002 at Highbury. The Gunners won the match 2–0.

A new identity
Arsenal launched this new Club crest in 2002. Unable to copyright the old crest, which had evolved piecemeal over many decades, the Club felt that the time had come for a completely new look for the new century.

twice. The crucial moment came when Sol Campbell's foul saw him sent off, incurring a four match suspension.

The Gunners fought back with a 2–0 win at Middlesbrough, but with a draw at Bolton, the title slipped away from them. As the season drew to a close, Leeds United, made dangerous by the threat of relegation, came to Highbury and won 3–2. Picking themselves up from this depressing result, the Gunners proceeded to score 10 goals in their last two League games, four away at Sunderland, and significantly, six of them at home to Southampton, due to be their opponents in the FA Cup final.

The Saints succumb

Both Vieira and Campbell were missing for the FA Cup final against Southampton. The Gunners should really have had the game done and dusted in the first half. They could well have scored in a mere 20 seconds, when the Finnish keeper, Antti Niemi, saved a shot from Thierry Henry. On 38 minutes, however, came the only goal of the game. Ray Parlour found Henry, whose skilful pass freed Bergkamp. Ljungberg met his pass with a shot that rebounded from Lundekvam. The ball ran straight to Robert Pires, eight yards out, and in it went. Other chances came and went, but although Southampton belatedly revived, the Gunners held out for a 1–0 win.

'We were so determined to win the game today,' said Seaman, 'after our disappointment in the League, and we knew we would be under pressure till the last minute from Southampton. It may not have been a great final, but we are lifting the trophy, and that's all that matters.' And for Seaman himself it was a fitting farewell to the club he had served with such distinction for so many years.

Unbeatable in the League

Season 2003/04 was the one in which Arsenal, for the first time since Preston North End in season 1888/89, went through a whole Championship season unbeaten. New faces appeared at Highbury, notably the experienced German international keeper Jens Lehmann, and the hugely promising 16-year-old midfielder, Francesco 'Cesc' Fabregas, a precocious talent whisked away from Barcelona. In addition, the Ivory Coast international midfielder, Kolo Toure, was successfully converted into a dominating centre back.

The Gunners made a confident start to the League campaign. Everton were beaten 2–1 at Highbury, Middlesbrough overwhelmed 4–0 at the Riverside Stadium. At home, three days later, Aston Villa succumbed, 2–0. Arsenal would eventually stretch their unbeaten Premiership run to a phenomenal 49 matches.

Pushed by Pompey

Yet the run could have ended early on, for the home match against Portsmouth was breathlessly close. Arsenal went a goal down, but equalised just before half time with a penalty given for a foul on Pires, but bitterly disputed by the Pompey manager Harry Redknapp. The score remained at 1–1 and the Gunners survived unbeaten.

On 17 September Inter Milan came to Highbury to run riot, achieving a 3–0 win against the Gunners. It was the eighth time the Gunners had lost a European game at Highbury. In the wake of this defeat, perhaps it was inevitable that the League match at Old Trafford four days later would be explosive. What provoked the alarming scenes at Old Trafford was clearly the moment when United's Dutch striker Ruud van Nistelrooy went to ground seemingly untouched by the foot of Patrick Vieira, who was none the less sent off. When, in the last throes of the 0–0 draw, van Nistelrooy missed a penalty, he was surrounded by taunting Arsenal players, Martin Keown to the fore, and chaos ensued. The FA's draconian response was a deluge of suspensions and fines for a number of players from both clubs.

Newcastle came to Highbury five days later, giving the Gunners a good run for their money, losing 11 minutes from time 3–2 to a coolly taken penalty by Thierry Henry, who would end a prolific League season with 30 goals. But things

continued to be difficult in Europe. Vieira, Campbell and Ljungberg were all absent for the visit to Moscow to meet Lokomotiv, where the team hacked out a goalless draw. Then the Gunners travelled to Ukraine for their tie against the now-familiar foes Dynamo Kiev, where they gave a lively performance but one not good enough to escape a 2–1 defeat. These games sandwiched significant League victories over Liverpool at Anfield and Chelsea at Highbury, both won 2–1. Leeds were also easily crushed 4–1 at Elland Road. So in the League the Arsenal juggernaut rolled on.

Inter in tatters

As the European campaign continued, Dynamo Kiev were narrowly beaten at Highbury on 5 November 2003, Ashley Cole, diving to head in Sylvain Wiltord's cross in the dying moments of the game. A victory memorably surpassed by an astonishing 5–1 thrashing of Internazionale in the San Siro stadium. There was no Vieira, no Bergkamp, but Kanu made one of his few appearances that season up front, beside an irresistible Thierry Henry. The first half gave little indication of what would so dramatically follow in the second. Thierry Henry put Arsenal ahead, but on 32 minutes the powerful Italian international, Vieri, equalised when his shot deflected off Sol Campbell. When Ljungberg made it 2–1 four minutes

into the second half, the spirit seemed to go out of Inter. Not least in the last five, devastating minutes, when the Gunners scored no fewer than three times. Henry made it 3–1, Edu 4–1, then away on an inspired break went the 20-year-old French substitute, Jeremie Aliadiere, ultimately finding Pires, who drove in the fifth goal. It was the first English team to beat Inter at the San Siro since Birmingham City in season 1960/61. It was Arsenal's largest victory to date in the Champions League, putting them in second place in Group B and in sight of a qualification, which their 2–0 win at home to Lokomotiv Moscow sealed.

In January, there would be three games against Middlesbrough in three competitions. In the two that mattered, League and FA Cup, Arsenal won 4–1 at Highbury on both

occasions. In between these games, a team made up of talented but inexperienced youngsters lost 1–0 at Highbury in the Carling League Cup semi-final and would go on to lose the return at Riverside, 2–1.

José at Highbury

In late January 2004, Wenger made a significant acquisition, the 20-year-old striker José Antonio Reyes from Seville. Fast, skilled and penetrative, Reyes would soon become a favourite of the crowd, who serenaded him – 'José Antonio, José Antonio!'. The first goal he scored, unfortunately, was an own goal at Middlesbrough in the second leg Carling Cup semi-final, but he was soon able to atone in the fifth round of the FA Cup at home to Chelsea on 15 February.

Adrian Mutu put Chelsea in front, but Reyes was rampant. Ten minutes into the second half, he dashed in from the right to beat Cudicini with a handsome 25-yard drive into the top corner, which the young Spaniard followed seven minutes later with another goal. When, late in the game, he was

substituted, he came off the field to huge applause. There was a new hero at Highbury.

Six days later in the League, the Gunners beat Chelsea again by the same score at Stamford Bridge. Winning all five Championship games in February, establishing a new club record of 24 unbeaten matches they won 3–1 at Wolverhampton Wanderers, and were now setting a hot pace at the top of the League, with Henry scoring four out of seven goals in three victorious games.

New stadium plans get the go-ahead

Late in February in the first knock-out stage of the Champions League, the Gunners went to Spain and recorded a memorable 3–2 victory over Celta Vigo; their first ever victory on Spanish soil. Almost on the eve of the match, there had been the encouraging news that the Club had resolved the financing arrangements for the building of a new stadium within sight of Highbury at Ashburton Grove, and that the project to build the Gunners a new home to match their footballing ambitions would proceed. A new era for the Club was about to dawn, but the team was firmly focused on the business of winning matches.

Warming up for the return with Celta Vigo, the Gunners demolished Portsmouth at Fratton Park in the sixth round of the FA Cup. 5–1 was the score and when Vieira, Ljungberg and Henry were substituted in the 70th minute, the Pompey supporters gave them a rare and generous ovation. Celta Vigo came to Highbury and were duly despatched. The scoreline was 2–0; Thierry Henry scored both goals in the first half.

On target

José Antonio Reyes scores the first goal in Arsenal's 2–1 win against Chelsea in the FA Cup fifth round at Highbury, 15 February 2004. Reyes also scored the second.

The quarter-finals of the Champions League set up a London derby versus Chelsea at Stamford Bridge. The Gunners had already beaten Chelsea three times that season by 2–1. Arsenal conceded first, when Lehmann kicked the ball recklessly against Chelsea's Eidur Gudjohnsen, who promptly scored. However, Robert Pires soon levelled and the match ended in a 1–1 draw.

Leading the League

Before the return leg with Chelsea at Highbury, the Gunners had to overcome two meetings with Manchester United in a week. First in the Premiership at Highbury, by which time the Gunners led them by 12 points, then in the semi-final of the FA Cup at Villa Park. Henry gave the Gunners the lead at Highbury in the opening minutes of the second half with a powerful, swerving shot, but Louis Saha scored a late equaliser. It was Arsenal's 30th consecutive Premiership game without defeat. They were less successful at Villa Park, and the Gunners lost their first FA Cup tie in 19 games by a narrow margin of 1–0.

In the return quarter-final match against Chelsea in the Champions League at Highbury, Arsenal called the tune for most of the first half, with Henry flanked by Reyes, but Chelsea defended resiliently. In the final minute of the half, however, Lauren centred, Henry headed the ball back, and Reyes scored from five yards. Now Chelsea pulled off their central midfielder, Scott Parker, and put on the Danish right winger, Jespar Gronkjaer, shifting their balance to attack. This change of tactic was rewarded when on 51 minutes Frank Lampard drove in an equaliser. There were three minutes left when another defender, Wayne Bridge, the left back, overlapped to score the winner from the verge of the penalty box. European success had continued to elude the Gunners.

But the unbeaten run in the League would continue to the end of the season and beyond, ensuring another Premiership title for the Gunners. As the season drew to a triumphant close, Highbury witnessed a 4–2 victory against Liverpool in the League, which included a superb hat-trick from Henry, the remaining goal provided by Pires. More emphatic still was the 5–0 home win against Leeds United, notable for the four goals scored by Thierry Henry; the first time an Arsenal player had achieved this since Ian Wright in 1991 against Everton.

Taking the title at White Hart Lane

Arsenal made sure of the title in their next match at White Hart Lane, even though Spurs came from behind a 2–0 deficit to draw 2–2. Finishing their remaining games unbeaten, including a 2–1 win over Leicester City in the last game of the season at Highbury, Arsène Wenger and his team had demonstrated their quality in the clearest way possible and on this day of celebration, the fans at Highbury were delighted to show their appreciation as the team performed a lap of honour around the stadium.

The achievement of the 'unbeaten season' was one that no subsequent events can take away, but good things come to an end. Notable departures in the summer of 2004 included those of two Highbury stalwarts, Martin Keown and Ray Parlour. New arrivals were the talented young Dutch striker Robin van Persie and the young French midfielder Mathieu Flamini. At the start of season 2004/05 the Gunners continued their unbeaten run with flair and confidence, with a 3–1 Community Shield victory over Manchester United and August wins in the League over Everton, Middlesbrough and Blackburn. September saw the return of European football as the Champions League got under way. The first group game was won at Highbury with difficulty against PSV Eindhoven,

View of the future

The spiral stairway to the upper tier of the North Bank provided a modern echo of the styling of the East and West Stands. From this vantage point, supporters were able to view the progress of the construction of Emirates Stadium at Ashburton Grove.

We won the League

Arsenal fans celebrate winning the Premiership title at White Hart Lane, 25 April 2004. The game with Spurs ended in a 2–2 draw, with Vieira and Pires scoring for the Champions.

1–0, through an own goal by the visiting centre back, the Brazilian Alex. The Gunners also made unexpectedly heavy going of their away match against Rosenborg of Norway, drawing 1–1. Through September and early October, Arsenal recovered their confident form, winning four and drawing one game in the Premiership. On October 16, after the Gunners had run Aston Villa ragged – the 3–1 score a pale reflection of the play – the former Arsenal centre half now Villa's manager David O'Leary had eulogised: 'It's the best team that has been at Highbury for me … They've got a wonderful team to go into a wonderful new stadium. They're big, they're strong, they're quick, they're fit. Everything about them is good to watch.' But it was at this point that things began to go wrong for the Gunners. Just four days after the Aston Villa game came a 2–2 draw in Athens against the Greek team Panathinaikos. Worse was to come.

The fatal fiftieth

The manner in which Arsenal's phenomenal unbeaten run in the Premiership concluded in October 2004 at Old Trafford was bitterly controversial. From the start, an unprotected Reyes, operating on the left, was subjected to consistently

harsh treatment by the United and England right back, Gary Neville. Ruud van Nistelrooy, United's Dutch striker, committed a serious foul on Ashley Cole which would bring him a three match suspension. The crucial, deeply debatable, goal came after 72 minutes when Sol Campbell stretched out a leg, Rooney fell over it, the referee gave a penalty from which van Nistelrooy scored. Arsenal, who by general consent had played the better football, waned in the final minutes, and in the 90th Paul Scholes and Alan Smith set up Rooney to score United's second.

The defeat had a traumatising effect on the Arsenal team. On the eve of this turbulent match, United were 11 points behind Arsenal. November would find them two points ahead. Eventually, the Gunners would finish in second place.

In Europe there was scant consolation when the Greek team Panathinaikos forced a draw at Highbury. The Gunners stayed alive in Europe by hacking out a draw in the penultimate match away against PSV Eindhoven. By contrast, the final group match was handsomely won at home against Rosenborg, 5–1, the highlight for the Highbury fans being a goal from Fabregas, at 17 years old the youngest player to score for Arsenal in European competition.

FA Cup hopefuls

Arsenal made an uneasy beginning to their FA Cup campaign, stretched by Stoke City at Highbury in the third round. Indeed there was a spell when it seemed quite possible that the Gunners would lose their first home Cup tie for eight years. Goals by Reyes and van Persie, however, took Arsenal into the fourth round, in which Wolverhampton Wanderers were despatched 2–0 at Highbury. Yet again the Cup draw paired Arsenal with Sheffield United at Highbury on 19 February 2005. In what was a bad-tempered match, Bergkamp was sent off. Arsenal's ten men took the lead through a Pires goal. Close to the end, however, Philippe Senderos handled, United secured a penalty, and the replay went to Bramall Lane. This proved another tight game, this time without a goal. But in the ensuing penalty shoot-out, the Gunners' Spanish goalkeeper Manuel Almunia saved twice to usher the Gunners through to the sixth round quarter-finals.

Bayern, Bolton and Blackburn

Meanwhile in Europe there was a momentous meeting in the knock-out stages of the Champions League with the German team Bayern Munich. The away leg in Munich produced a depressing 3–1 defeat, which gave the Gunners only a slim chance of survival. Arsenal did retrieve some dignity in the return at Highbury on 9 March, where they won 1–0, but the bar had been set too high. It was yet another European anticlimax. 'We lost to one of the best teams that we have played in the last few years in Bayern,' said Arsène Wenger in the aftermath.

Back at home, the quarter-finals of the FA Cup brought a visit to Bolton, and a goal by Freddie Ljungberg in the third minute, which turned out to be enough to see Arsenal through to a semi-final meeting with Blackburn Rovers, in Cardiff. A series of fine saves by Brad Friedel, Blackburn's goalkeeper, kept the Gunners at bay until the 42nd minute when Robert Pires scored. Then in the last four minutes, the incisive Robin van Persie scored twice, the first after a splendid solo, the second played carefully wide of Friedel from the edge of the box.

Manchester again

The Gunners' opponents in the FA Cup final would be Manchester United, who had already beaten them home and away in the Premiership. The League defeat to United at

Premiership presentation
The pitch at Highbury is prepared for the presentation of the gleaming Premiership trophy after the match against Leicester City at Highbury, 15 May 2004. The Gunners marked the occasion by winning 2–1 with a Henry penalty and a goal from Vieira.

Highbury on 1 February had been a lively, entertaining game. In only the eighth minute, Vieira headed in Henry's corner. Wayne Rooney and Paul Scholes set up Ryan Giggs for a shot that flew in off Ashley Cole. Dennis Bergkamp, in scintillating form, restored the Gunners' lead when he shot between the legs of the keeper Roy Carroll. Again United equalised, this time with a remarkable goal by the Portuguese winger Cristiano Ronaldo, switching the ball from right foot to left to shoot home. Then United took the lead when, rushing out of his goal, Manuel Almunia failed to prevent Giggs from crossing from a tight angle, allowing Ronaldo to find the empty net. John O'Shea overlapped almost casually from left back to make it 4–2.

In the run up to the Cup final, Arsenal had provided themselves with a confidence-building 7–0 thrashing of hapless Everton in the final home game of the season. The game was also the last game played by the team at Highbury wearing their familiar red and white strip. The Gunners had finished the season in second place, securing their place in the next season's UEFA Champions League. It was the eighth season in succession that the team had finished either as champions or runners up.

Arsenal win on penalties

The Cup final at Cardiff was something of a paradox. 'MISSION: Whatever It Takes' read the notice pinned on the

Arsenal's dressing room door. What it took was a quite untypically defensive display, which led in the end to victory on penalties. With Henry missing because of injury, Bergkamp admitted that he found it difficult playing the role of the lone striker. Sol Campbell was again absent from Arsenal's defence, but Philippe Senderos had an outstanding game, all the more important in that the full backs, Lauren and Ashley Cole, were given a torrid time by Wayne Rooney and Cristiano Ronaldo. Jens Lehmann, in his most defiant form, repelled a 20-yard shot from Rooney with his feet. In the second half Rooney shot against a post, and Ljungberg headed van Nistelrooy's point blank header out from beneath the bar. So it would go to extra time. At last the United keeper Roy Carroll had to make a save, soaring to his right to reach a free kick by van Persie, who had come on as an 86th minute sub. Only a notable save by Lehmann prevented Scholes scoring with a point blank shot on the turn.

So it came to penalties. Van Nistelrooy converted the first penalty for United; Lauren responded. Next came the fatal moment for United. Paul Scholes took the kick, but Lehmann, diving low to his right, kept the ball out. Ljungberg, van Persie and Ashley Cole all put away their penalties for Arsenal, Ronaldo, Rooney and Keane scored for United. So it came to Patrick Vieira's potentially decisive kick at 4–4. He duly succeeded, and the FA Cup was back at Highbury.

The future awaits

For the Gunners, the backdrop to the later 1990s and early years of the new millennium was the impending move to a new stadium. As the 1990s wore on and Arsenal's waiting list for season tickets grew and grew, the case for a move from Highbury became stronger by the year. Gunners looked on enviously as Manchester United expanded Old Trafford up to the heavens, taking their capacity over 70,000. Arsenal, meanwhile, were hemmed in by their location, unable to redevelop the ground. It was a physical impossibility to raise the capacity of Highbury over 40,000, and the Club was suffering because of it. The frustration grew because they knew many, many thousands wanted to get in to see games at Highbury. The tipping point came when the waiting list for season tickets equalled the old ground's capacity. It was time for sentiment to give way to hard-nosed business sense.

A new home for a new century

While the leaving of beloved Highbury was bound to be tinged with sadness, the new Emirates Stadium provided a truly exciting prospect. Planned with meticulous care, it would provide the team and the supporters with a home that matched their ambition for the Club in the 21st century.

Prime movers

From top, Club directors Danny Fiszman, Ken Friar and Keith Edelman.

rute economic logic dictated that Arsenal would have to leave their cherished stadium at Highbury, a stadium which, in the 1930s, was so far ahead of its time, with its two splendid art deco stands and its unrivalled facilities. The East and West Stands would be preserved as Grade II listed buildings, in a new development, but the old Arsenal Stadium, the 'home of football', would no longer be the stage on which the drama, suspense, misery and joy of the beautiful game would be played. Just as in Henry Norris's time, Arsenal Football Club found itself in the position of having to make a bold decision to break with its past and move into a new era. But the 2006 stadium move was in many ways less traumatic than that of 1913, the new stadium being only a few hundred metres away from Highbury on Ashburton Grove, and within Arsenal's heartland of support. This had not been the case in 1913.

The background to the move

Just before Arsenal left Highbury, the Club's commercial director, Adrian Ford, said: 'There had been talk within the Club about moving to a new ground as far back as the early 1970s. Believe it or not, at that time there were serious talks with Tottenham about a ground share, and the two parties had even identified a potential site, at Alexandra Palace. In the end the plan was unworkable.

'By the end of the 1990s it was clear Arsenal had to move, or else get left behind. By the 1998/99 season, a new ground was very much under discussion, and the issue started appearing regularly on the agenda at board meeetings. You can date the serious intention to move from Highbury to that season. The will was there to drive the move through, for the good of the Club.

'Highbury is beautiful, but it is an antique. Highbury is great to look at, but in terms of the modern era, it does not fit in. The size of Highbury meant that the scope for driving revenue was always going to be limited. We were hamstrung by physical constraints, so it wasn't possible to expand the existing ground. We had to watch while Manchester United developed their stadium upwards and outwards, and increased their revenue streams as they went. Arsenal were being left far behind. The only way the Club could increase revenue was to move somewhere else. Demand to watch

games was far in excess of supply, so to tap that demand we needed a new home. That was the economic reality.'

The challenge for the Club was to find a site for a stadium big enough to match Arsenal's ambitions. And they were desperately keen to stay close to their Islington roots. 'Our heartland is in Islington, and we didn't want to stray far,' said Ford. 'It was important to stay close to our roots, and our partnership with Islington Council was important too. The Council was sympathetic to the Club's aims, and it was vital to have an understanding local authority to work with through the planning and building process. In the end we were delighted to locate a brownfield site that enabled us to build the stadium we wanted, with the capacity to keep our loyal supporters happy – but not too big, because empty seats are bad for business and atmosphere. We were able to plan a ground we could count on filling most of the time.'

A difficult decision

In August 2005, Arsène Wenger declared, 'The project was vital. It was that or die over the long term at top level. It's as simple as that.'

Danny Fiszman, a senior director, who with the long-serving director Ken Friar had been a main mover in the huge project, admitted, at the same ceremony, 'It has been said we went through some difficult times. Had we known all the difficulties we had to overcome, I doubt we would have gone ahead. We knew we had to move. It was a question of whether we would stay in Islington or relocate to a site near the M25. Looking back, we were probably crazy but we know this stadium will put us on a par with all the strongest clubs who are self sustaining. Over the past few years, we have always punched above our weight. Now we will be able to compete with everyone off the pitch, and that will help us compete on the pitch. Nothing has frustrated me more than to read time after time that the budget of the manager has been affected. It has not, nor will it be.'

Fiszman, who has followed Arsenal from his first visit to Highbury at the age of 12, was undoubtedly right when he declared, 'I believe there have been three major moments in the Club's history: the initial creation of the Club in southeast London in 1886, the move to Highbury in 1913 and now our move to Emirates Stadium.' His credentials as a genuine fan

were substantiated by his admission that 'one episode I will never forget was after we won the Fairs Cup in 1970. I must admit I broke the rules and ran out onto the pitch at the end of the match. Fortunately there were lots of Arsenal fans doing the same, so I didn't get caught. It was a great day.'

The new stadium, Fiszman emphasised, 'will allow an extra 22,000 people to see a live game. I hope it will allow us to keep a reasonable number of seats as affordable as possible so that fans who do not have as much money as others are not left out in the cold. It will also give us the financial strength to be able to compete in the transfer market and to retain a world class team and be competitive with any other normal club in Europe, or in the world, for that matter. In short, it will give our fans a fantastic stadium and a fantastic team to play in that stadium.'

Fiszman is somewhat misleadingly defined as a non-executive director. In fact for four years he has chiefly devoted himself, flanked by Ken Friar and Keith Edelman, Arsenal's managing director, to the planning and building of the £357-million stadium. The three men have presided over the acquisition of the site itself, planning permission, the selling of surplus land, dealings with legal teams and with the Sir

Robert McAlpine construction company. 'The biggest challenge,' Fiszman believes, 'was retaining belief that it would all actually happen. The emotional roller coaster that exists in a major development such as this is tremendous. We had huge highs and huge lows. Some days we were absolutely certain everything was going to happen because it was all going well. Then at other moments there was just too much against us, too many hurdles to overcome. We were

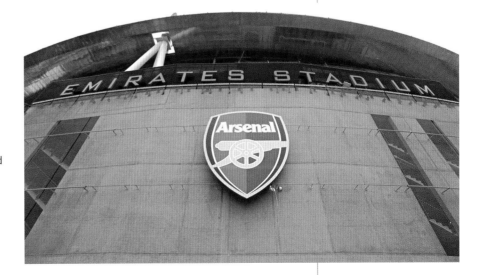

kicked quite a number of times, but I think the spirit of the development team was very much like the spirit of Arsenal football team: we don't give up ... There has also been a huge sacrifice from the massive team of people helping on the project. And a huge sacrifice from the families of those people. All their support has been absolutely invaluable.'

For a long time, he says, he was working 16 hours a day on the project. 'We did it against all the odds, in a time-frame which, in property development terms, was dramatically quick ... When that stadium is up and finished it will be the proudest moment in my entire business career.'

From Ashburton Grove to Emirates

That it will be known as Emirates Stadium rather than the Arsenal Stadium or Ashburton Grove has been a matter of economic reality. The sponsorship deal with Emirates, which lasts until 2021, is expected eventually to be worth £100 million, and will include shirt sponsorship. Keith Edelman is particularly enthusiastic. 'This long term association,' he believes, 'is an excellent opportunity for both of us. It will help Arsenal reach new markets and build on our existing fan base across the world, thanks in no small part to the airline's global route network.'

Glittering future

The glass façades of Emirates Stadium offer stupendous views over London. This computer-generated impression shows the spacious forecourts and the futuristic roof design.

EMIRATES STADIUM

Raising the vast amount of money needed for this ambitious project was a huge challenge even to a successful football club. An initial deal with Nike for sponsorship of the kit provided the Club, in the words of a lawyer prominent in the enterprise, with 'substantial payments in the early years of the deal, so Arsenal could inject more equity into the deal. The banks had to lend less money, so they reduced their risks.' In the early weeks of 2004, Arsenal negotiated bank loans worth £260 million.

The ramifications of the project were enormous. Planning permission had to be gained from Islington Borough Council, a new waste and recycling centre had to be built to replace the old one on which the new pitch was to be laid. Other local authority facilities had to be relocated to properties nearby. Local businesses, understandably reluctant, in some cases, to move, after having long been established there, had to be displaced, which had the potential to lead to court action.

Three new companies had to be formed. Ashburton Properties for the building of the stadium, Highbury Holdings for the redevelopment of the old Arsenal Stadium, Ashburton Trading for other residential developments around the stadium. 'We have a monthly meeting,' said project controller Philip Nash, 'to review potential changes to the stadium build. For example, if we want to change something like the seating quality, we discuss the proposal with AYH (the stadium's construction consultancy) who price the change, and with the contractors Sir Robert McAlpine, to ensure the change will not slow down the construction programme. We then present the proposal changes to the banking group and its technical advisers.' Nash added that, 'We didn't want the banks telling us which players to buy and sell and this was reflected in the final deal structure.'

Wenger's contribution

Arsenal's manager Arsène Wenger is proud to have 'been involved in every aspect of the players' facilities at Emirates Stadium and I am involved in regular update meetings. I have also tried to visit the new stadium site as often as possible during the construction process.' He was, he said, 'looking forward to having a bit more space at the new stadium. At the moment, everything is too tightly packed in at Highbury. By having more space, it can create a brighter atmosphere. We have the advantage of building a new stadium from nothing. So what we have done is to get everybody together who has an important role on matchday. For example Gary Lewin [the Club's physiotherapist] and Vic Akers [the kit manager]. We have all been involved in the development stages because we know what we need on a matchday. At Highbury, over the years, we have gradually added extra required space to the dressing room area, so it means that it doesn't look harmonious. What we want to achieve at Emirates Stadium is to bring all this together, in a bigger space.'

Wenger disclosed that the Club, for so long famous for the heated marble of its Highbury dressing rooms, was looking into a system where the heat will come through from an area of the floor near the bench. The dressing rooms will also include a physiotherapy area and a hydrotherapy spa.

What Wenger wanted to take from Highbury, he said, was 'the closeness between the supporters and the players. They should be almost at touching distance.' This is in marked contrast to all too many modern stadiums. 'Unfortunately,' Wenger continued, 'I don't think it will be able to be quite as close as Highbury, due to the shape, but that's something I want. The soul and spirit of Highbury is not transferable ... but there will be many advantages at Emirates Stadium that supporters will enjoy.'

Partnership with Islington

The vast stadium-building project was greatly facilitated by the positive attitude of Islington Council, whose Deputy Leader, Councillor Bridget Fox, said, 'Because Arsenal Football Club is such a strong part of the community and a source of civic pride in the Borough, the fact they are staying in Islington is a result in itself. It's a big development, and the stadium is obviously at the heart of it, but it's also giving us 2,000 new homes, including 25 per cent affordable housing with key worker homes on top of that. And it's also bringing us a large amount of new commercial space that will create valuable jobs ... There was overwhelming support from the Council ... On the Ashburton Grove site, we had an out of date waste disposal site that needed updating and saw that a potential re-use of that could be a new stadium. So when the site was then considered as an option, it offered the area a fantastic opportunity for regeneration.'

Surprisingly, perhaps, the design and construction of the stadium itself with all its technological innovations was substantially easier than negotiating the maze of planning regulation. Ken Friar explained, 'We had worked with our chosen architects HOK Sport before. They designed the North Bank Stand which was built in the early 1990s. They're one of the leading architects for sports stadia in the world, having created Stadium Australia and, together with Sir Norman Foster, designed the new Wembley Stadium amongst others. They're very much at the forefront of their profession, and that's why we chose them.'

'The facilities in the new stadium,' continued Ken Friar – himself a warm admirer of the old one – 'will be vastly improved from Highbury. We will have far better catering and toilet facilities, merchandise, box office and ticketing points. Arsène Wenger has been involved with the design of the impressive player facilities and dressing rooms, and for the pitch, we've employed one of the top experts in John Hewitt to design and install it. They designed the pitch at Highbury and at our training centre in Hertfordshire. Overall, it's very much going to be a state of the art stadium.'

Philip Nash, the project controller, declared that the new stadium's 'bowl' design 'will give us far more choice in terms of concessions and admissions level, a wider range of entertainments, more toilet facilities and more space to move

High-tech pitch

The pitch is laid at the new stadium. State-of-the-art drainage and heating systems will ensure that the new pitch maintains the high standard set at Highbury.

The North Bridge

Connecting Emirates Stadium with Drayton Park near to Gillespie Park, the North Bridge will provide the most direct pedestrian route to Arsenal underground station.

Emirates innovations

Seating for ordinary supporters will afford great views throughout the stadium. Among the innovations that the new stadium will provide are new electronic ticketing systems that will cut down on touting. Improved access to high-quality catering facilities is also a key element of the stadium plan. Corporate facilities will be second-to-none, including a new Club Level area, providing corporate hospitality at affordable prices. There will be 150 luxurious executive boxes on the middle tier, which will be accessed by separate entrances and fitted with screens and bars.

around in general. Sightlines will be far better, with fewer restricted views and the playing facilities will be excellent, with high-quality changing rooms and warm-up areas. There will also be a wider range of corporate hospitality facilities.'

'We are constantly trying to push the boundaries in every job we do,' said Chris Lee of HOK Sport. 'For Arsenal's new stadium, the Club is very much embracing new technology … On approaching the new stadium, the first thing fans will see is the huge roof floating above the whole stadium with a gently undulating bowl sitting beneath it.'

A tale of two bridges

A massive and imposing feature of the new stadium is the pair of enormous bridges, the North and South Pedestrian bridges, that span the Moorgate to Finsbury Park railway tracks, connecting the stadium to Drayton Park. The North Bridge is situated near the entrance to Gillespie Park, the South Bridge near the entrance to Drayton Park railway station. The North Bridge was installed in May 2004, a massive undertaking. The bridge was divided into two sections, each weighing about 180 tons. The crane employed to move these sections came from Germany, weighed a colossal 600 tons and took three days to assemble.

The South Bridge was by far the larger, weighing more than a thousand tons. Twenty metres wide, it provides a route for the entry of emergency vehicles to the stadium complex. The bridge consists of 18 sections, each ten metres long. Fifteen engineers oversaw the positioning of the bridge from where it was put together in Ashburton Grove, over the railway track to Drayton Park. It was completed with a concrete deck.

As for the daringly futuristic roof, its design was elaborated by Prater Roofing. It is supported by the trusses above, which thus give spectators an unimpeded view of the pitch. The roof itself has two layers, an underside largely constructed of aluminium trays, giving a clean, smooth surface; above, profiled steel decking and ply sheeting have been waterproofed, using a special, Swiss PVC membrane.

Highbury transformed

As part of the stadium-building project, the site of the old stadium will be redeveloped into a housing complex to be known as Highbury Square. The famous East and West Stands

are listed and the frontages will be preserved as part of the new development. In the East Stand, the Marble Halls will be incorporated as the foyer area. The pitch will be transformed into a communal garden. As well as a selection of one-, two- and three-bedroom apartments, there will be a fitness centre and swimming pool. Concierge servicing will be provided and the complex will incorporate an underground car park.

The future awaits

State of the art, you might well say of it all. But then futuristic design has always been something at which Arsenal has excelled. Arsenal supporters and Islingon residents have been able to view the progress of Emirates Stadium project from the ground and from vantage points in the old stadium as the construction has advanced. Arsenal Football Club is without doubt looking forward to its future in the same optimistic mood as when the Gunners played their first match at Highbury in 1913.

Highbury Square
Below: The famed Highbury pitch will become a leafy enclave within the Highbury Square complex. Bottom: The East Stand of the old Arsenal Stadium is seen in this artist's impression preserved as the frontage of the new residential complex of Highbury Square.

The Final Salute

As Arsenal entered its final season at its beloved old home, the Club prepared a programme of celebrations entitled 'The Final Salute'. The Club colours and branding were given a nostalgic make-over and special events were organised for each home game. And there was football to be played ...

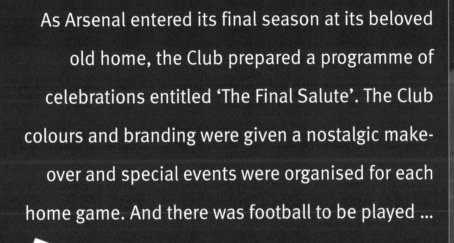

F.A. BARCLAYS PREMIERSHIP

ARSENAL v

WIGAN ATHLETIC

SUNDAY 7TH MAY KICK OFF 3.00PM

FOR MATCH AND TICKET INFORMATION
CONTACT THE BOX OFFICE ON 020 7704 4242

S eason 2005/06 was the last that Arsenal would play at Highbury and the Club was determined to make this final season at Highbury live in the memory of all who follow the Gunners. To this end they came up with a number of initiatives to give the old stadium the send off it deserved. A series of innovative ideas were devised that came under the banner 'The Final Salute'. A new branding and crest were created and used throughout the season on everything from the programme to the Club gates. Key to this was a move away from the Club's traditional bright red of recent decades to a darker shade of 'redcurrant'.

The reason for this surprising move lay in the Club's history. The new colour was that of the first ever strip worn at Highbury back in 1913, when the Gunners opened their Highbury life with a 2–1 win over Leicester Fosse. It seemed somehow appropriate that the Club should acknowledge those pioneering first days at Highbury as players and supporters prepared to say goodbye to the old stadium. The more familiar red and white strip would return at for the first season at Emirates Stadium.

Wenger was enthusiastic about the Club's decision to revert to the original colour of the jerseys worn by Arsenal at the time of the move across the river to Highbury in 1913. 'It will be very emotional,' said Wenger, 'when we move from Highbury to Emirates Stadium, and it is great that the Club is finding ways to celebrate our last season at this fantastic stadium. Personally, I love the fact the team will be wearing a home kit that is inspired by the first one ever worn at Highbury. It's not only a way of encapsulating more than 90 years of memories, but it also takes us right back to when we started at this ground in 1913.'

Theme matchdays

Every home game was allocated a special theme. The themes ranged from Wenger Day and Captains Day, to Junior Gunners' Day and Home Grown Players Day. On each matchday before kick-off there were presentations, interviews and nostalgic footage on the big screens to remind the fans of the stadium's and the Club's history. The visit of West Bromich Albion in April was designated Dennis Bergkamp Day. Thousands of fans wore the Dutch orange in homage to their hero – and he obliged with a stunning goal to seal a 3–1 win. The Junior Gunners donned Edwardian clothing for 1913 Day, while Alan Smith led out former favourites on Players Day (Arsenal v Newcastle United, 14 August 2005) . One of the most emotional days was for the 5–0 win over Aston Villa on 1 April. It was designated David Rocastle Day in honour of the former star who died in 2001. The last Highbury match (against Wigan Athletic) was Goals Day, remembering some of the scoring feats of the Gunners' strikers through the years.

The stadium looks back

Among the special stadium features devised for the final season was an electronic clock to countdown the last season in N5. There was a welcome return (for those old enough to remember it first time around) for the old-style wooden scoreboard. Situated in the southeast corner of the stadium, it hadn't been seen at Highbury since the 1980s. Operated by selected membership holders, at half time every match the scores from other major games were shown.

Even London Underground entered into the spirit of the moment by providing the location for a stunning 52-metre mural in the main walkway of the Arsenal Underground station on the Piccadilly Line on 12 January 2006. The mural was created by primary and secondary school children, local residents, disabled supporters and over-60s from the local area. Each contributed paintings, drawings and photographs depicting 93 glorious years at the old stadium.

'It's wonderful that the Arsenal community has come together to depict Highbury's history and express in this way what the Arsenal Stadium means to them.' commented skipper Thierry Henry.

Programmed salutes

Arsenal's matchday magazine played a major part in the Final Salute celebrations. Every issue had a special 16-page 'Historic Highbury' pullout with reproductions of former programmes, features on past games, Highbury memories from fans and journalists and quirky tales from the stadium's history. 'Hidden Highbury' also examined those areas deep in the stadium which fans do not get the opportunity to see. The final programme of the season also contained an A–Z of Highbury supplement. Publications manager Andy Exley and his team were rewarded with the coveted Premiership Programme of the Year award – and the Historic Highbury section was singled out for special praise. The monthly official *Arsenal Magazine* also joined the countdown with former player, coach and manager Don Howe sharing his Highbury tales in each issue – and comedian Paul Kaye giving his original take on his final season as a West Stand season ticket holder.

Souvenirs for sale

Arsenal compiled a list of over 2,700 historic items from the stadium, which were sold in a special Highbury Auction after the move to Emirates Stadium. The wide range of items up for sale at the auction included the goalposts and nets, corner flags, the centre circle, Arsène Wenger's seat in the dug out, leather chairs and a table from the managing director's office, selected carpets from VIP areas, George Graham's old desk, a red double-decker bus used in the 1989 League Championship trophy parade, all the numbered boot pegs from the Highbury boot room, stadium turnstiles and even 20 red Arsenal wheelie bins! However, not everything at Highbury was sold. Some items, including the famous Herbert Chapman bust and the clock from the Clock End, were taken to Emirates Stadium as part of the Club's heritage.

The final season

In footballing terms, the final season at Highbury also produced some unforgettable moments. The team was once again undergoing a transformation, notably as a result of the departure of Patrick Vieira for Juventus in the summer of 2005. Much would now depend on the Gunners' young midfielder Cesc Fabregas. And as this oddly anomalous

season advanced, Fabregas matured remarkably. There had never been any doubt about his skill, his flair, his awareness, but to what avail were they if he could too easily be brushed aside by bigger opponents? Yet the longer the season went on, the more apparent it became that he was rapidly gaining confidence, strength and effectiveness.

Another of Wenger's recent signings was also to enjoy an unexpected spell in the Highbury limelight, Mathieu Flamini. Arsenal had begun the season with two excellent left backs, but first-choice Ashley Cole was injured for most of the season. Gael Clichy, his talented young French understudy, was hurt when playing for his country versus the England under-21 team. How to fill the breach? With what transpired to be one of his most successful experiments, Wenger unexpectedly gave the role to Flamini; a right-footed midfielder. And he proceeded to fill it with signal brio, sturdy in defence and eager to attack.

Contradictions at home and abroad

Wenger's regime had produced manifold achievements in the Premiership and in the FA Cup, but European competitions had proved an anticlimax. No matter how the Arsenal team was faring domestically, no matter who the ultimate European opponents, the quarter-finals had proved an

Fabulous Fabregas
The Gunners' young midfielder Cesc Fabregas wearing the 'redcurrant' shirt adopted for the final season at Highbury.

Real roasted
Freddie Ljungberg holds off Real Madrid's Sergio Ramos in the home leg of the Champions League quarter-final at Highbury, 8 March 2006. The Gunners held on for a 0–0 draw to progress to the semi-final on a 1–0 aggregate.

insuperable barrier. In the 2005/06 season that pattern was radically transformed. Domestically, the Gunners' results had been a disappointment. Chelsea had hopelessly outstripped them in the League. They had been bundled out of the FA Cup in the fourth round by Bolton Wanderers. Nor had they began their UEFA Champions League adventure with any great panache. The modest Swiss team FC Thun were their first opponents, and were overcome with surprising difficulty. At Highbury in the first leg, only a fine goal in injury time by the indestructible Dennis Bergkamp, gave the Gunners a 2–1 win.

Four successive European games without defeat followed. The away game against Sparta Prague on 18 October 2005 saw Thierry Henry overtake Ian Wright's goal-scoring record for the Club. His second goal in the 2–0 victory was his 186th goal for Arsenal. The Czech side was later summarily despatched 3–0 at Highbury. Then FC Thun were defeated 1–0 away. The last European game of 2005 was a dull goalless draw with Ajax, played at Highbury.

February, however, brought the formidable challenge in the first knock out round against Real Madrid. It was surmounted in splendour. Though often thwarted on their visits to Spain, Arsenal at the Bernabeu simply ran their opponents ragged and became the first English team to defeat Real Madrid at home. In the first half, they should have scored at least three times. The final score of 1–0, through Thierry Henry's cleverly taken goal, was a meagre reward for such dominance. It was a game in which the rapidly improving Eboue played his third consecutive European game in place of the injured Lauren, while Philippe Senderos the young Swiss centre back was in defiant form, taking the place of Sol Campbell. Jens Lehmann had regained his place in goal from the Spaniard Manuel Almunia, and would proceed to find his best form. On the return leg at Highbury in March, in what was a tense and hard-fought game, Real Madrid were held to a goalless draw. Jens Lehmann distinguished himself with a masterful second-half save from Raul.

Vieira returns

The aggregate victory took them through to a quarter-final duel with Juventus on 28 March at Highbury. The young Fabregas was pitted in midfield against his old team mate and Arsenal legend, Patrick Vieira. In that glorious night of football in front of a crowd of 35,472, there was no question that the winner was Fabregas, hands down. Vieira, who was given a warm welcome by the Arsenal fans as he appeared on the pitch, looked much slower and less mobile than in his best Arsenal days, while Fabregas was aflame; eager for the ball, eager to thrust forward. He provided inspired support for the inimitable Thierry Henry, even to strike for goal as he so successful and enterprisingly did, to put the Gunners ahead in the first half. Henry, the supreme technician, would score the second. Juventus that night were well and truly beaten, their panoply of stars overplayed. In the away leg, Arsenal held firm for a goalless draw and so progressed to the semi-final for the first time in the Club's history.

Highbury hosts Europe for the last time

On 19 April 2006 the home leg of the semi-final against Villarreal, a remarkable little Spanish club from a small industrial city, was an appropriately momentous occasion for Highbury's last ever game in Europe. A packed stadium provided an electric atmosphere for this meeting with a team that included international stars, such as the Argentinian

international playmaker Juan Román Riquelme and Diego Forlan, the Uruguayan striker. In the event, Arsenal gave Riquelme very little scope, and Villarreal were all too often reduced to gamesmanship.

Arsenal's winning goal, shortly before half time, was admirably worked out. Henry took a corner at the Clock End. When the ball came back to him from Marcus Senna's header, he ran across the field, waiting for the precise moment to pick out the advancing Alexander Hleb. With the Spanish defence for once in confusion, Hleb crossed from the left and Kolo Toure, who had stayed upfield after the corner, scored. The 1–0 result, which importantly deprived the Spaniards of an away goal, left Arsenal with a distinct advantage for the return match away at Villarreal. With the game goalless, there was a dramatic ending when the Gunners conceded a late penalty. But all was well when Lehmann, in majestic form, duly saved it. The Gunners had reached the Champions League final for the first time in their history. The match would take place in Paris against Barcelona.

The final in Paris on 17 May ended in bitter, but defiant, anticlimax, as the Gunners battled to maintain their challenge with 10 men after Jens Lehmann was sent off in the 18th minute for bringing down Samuel Eto'o just outside the box. Yet amazingly the Gunners actually went ahead with a superb

header by Sol Campbell from a free kick. They defended their lead heroically, and even created further goal-scoring chances, until, in the final minutes, the tiring Gunners conceded two goals. The European dream had once again eluded the team. But it had been a brave and entirely creditable performance.

Fighting for fourth

As Arsenal were vying for the greatest prize in European football, their domestic season was moving towards a tense conclusion. Points dropped early in the season left the Gunners battling for the precious fourth position in the table that would guarantee them a place in the qualifying rounds for the next season's Champions League. The rival for that place was the old enemy Tottenham Hotspur. The 151st and last ever north London derby at Highbury on 22 April produced a 1–1 draw. With the Villarreal return game so close, Wenger had decided to rest key players, above all Thierry Henry. In the event, Spurs dominated the first half, but couldn't turn chances into goals. When they did score in the second half it was controversial. Eboue had crashed into Gilberto and stayed down. Spurs' Michael Carrick hesitated and, instead of kicking the ball out, played on, passing to Edgar Davids, on the left flank, who then crossed to Robbie

Pitch invasion

The Champions League semi-final first leg against Villarreal on 19 April 2006 took a break from the seriousness of the occasion when a squirrel invaded the Highbury pitch during the first half to the amusement of the crowd. He seems to have been a lucky omen as the Gunners won 1–0 with a goal from Kolo Toure.

Final showdown

The teams line up before the start of Arsenal's first Champions League final at the Stade de France on 17 May 2006. Arsenal lost 2–1 to Barcelona, battling bravely for three-quarters of the game with only ten men after goalkeeper Jens Lehmann was sent off early in the first half.

Spurs halted

Thierry Henry wheels away in celebration as he scores the equaliser that secured an all-important draw in the last north London derby at Highbury on 22 April 2006.

Farewell fixture

Wigan Athletic provided the opposition for the final game at Highbury on Sunday, 7 May 2006.

Keane, who scored with ease. Henry was brought on as a substitute and he duly equalised, with a splendid shot hit with the outside of his right foot. This result left Arsenal in the possible plight of having to win the European title to enter the next Champions League, should they fail to gain the increasingly elusive fourth place in the Premiership.

Farewell to Highbury

The very last game at Highbury, played against Wigan Athletic in the bright Sunday sunshine of 7 May 2006, was full of significance. No planning on the part of the Club could have ensured that the Arsenal's final game at their old stadium would be such a critical match for the team, as well as an occasion for celebration of the Club's history. It was essential Arsenal should win the game to have any chance of finishing in the vital fourth position. Tottenham Hotspur, with just a point's advantage, were meanwhile engaged a few miles away in a local derby against West Ham United. A win for Spurs would secure fourth place for them regardless of the result at Highbury.

The spectators on all four sides of the Arsenal Stadium were attired in alternating blocks of red and white – a splendidly vivid

tableau. Before the game began, two huge metal containers, on either side of the tunnel entrance, belched flames like a couple of dragons. The Highbury crowd in the packed stadium were in festive mood, thunderously celebrating their old home with the familiar chants from all four sides of the stadium, 'We're the North Bank/Clock End/West Stand/East Stand at Highbury' for the last time.

In the game itself, Robert Pires gave the Gunners the lead, only for defensive blunders to enable Wigan to score twice and take an alarming lead. Jens Lehmann, so recently the hero against Villarreal, allowed a seemingly straightforward free kick to sail past him, after a first goal was carelessly conceded when another free kick, this time from the left enabled the defender Paul Scharner to flick the ball in from close range. But on 35 minutes, Alexander Hleb combatively won the ball, found Pires, who coolly sent Thierry Henry clean through to equalise. In the second half, Henry scored twice more, including a penalty after which he kissed the Highbury turf. He had claimed his eighth Highbury hat-trick.

Let the celebrations begin!

Throughout the match, news of the score in the Spurs–West Ham game had periodically rippled through the stadium. There were cheers as West Ham went ahead, groans as Spurs equalised and, as both games drew to a close there was the welcome news that the Hammers had scored another and had won the game 2–1, thus securing the Gunners a place in Europe. The Arsenal fans were jubilant, and the away fans were also generous in their applause. Then the celebrations began. First there was a uniformed marching band, but for those with long memories, the highpoint was the appearance of the splendid singing policeman of by-gone days, Constable Alex Morgan, who gave a fine rendition of 'O Sole Mio'.

There followed a parade of past players, introduced from a white dial in the middle of the pitch by Tom Watt, actor, broadcaster and author, and matchday announcer Paul Burrell. Among the first to appear was Alf Fields, who after serving in the forces, returned to Highbury and played six momentous winning games at the start of the season 1947/48 at centre half in the absence of the cricketing Leslie Compton. With the end of his playing days, he stayed on as a valued youth coach.

John Radford was reminded by Tom Watt of the spectacular goal he scored in a 3–0 European win at Highbury against Belguim's Anderlecht. Frank McLintock, skipper of the 1970/71 Double-winning side said he was sad about the demise of Highbury, 'but it's the only thing Arsenal can do.' Michael Thomas, scorer of that dramatic title-winning goal at Liverpool, remembered his awe-stuck reaction to the Marble Halls as a 19-year-old. Malcolm Macdonald commented 'There isn't an empty space to be seen in the ground, and that's the greatest compliment you can pay to us.' And then, to huge delight in the crowd, the prolific Ian Wright stepped up. 'When I came here,' he remembered, 'I couldn't even believe it. I was just pleased to be in the side ... I scored goals for the fans. I'd love to be doing it now.'

Other celebrities with Highbury connections also appeared, including former boxer Sir Henry Cooper. Rock-star and Arsenal supporter Roger Daltrey sang a special song he wrote for the day 'Highbury Highs'. There was an impressive display by the Junior Gunners, representing the myriad trophies won by the Club during its period at Highbury, and the Ladies team was cheered onto the pitch to display their Premier League trophy and FA Women's Cup.

Then, after the first team had done a lap of honour to rapturous applause, it was left to Arsène Wenger to lead the countdown of the official last ten seconds of Highbury as Arsenal's home. At 6:30pm on Sunday, 7 May 2006 the counters hit zero, fireworks fired into the sky, red and silver streamers rained onto the pitch, and an emotional crowd bid farewell to their beloved Highbury.

So the redcurrant shirts, worn at home all season, as they had been when the Gunners arrived in 1913 from Plumstead, would be discarded for a second time. As the bright array of colours in the stands foretold, the red and white jerseys would be back when the team started the next phase of their history at Emirates Stadium.

A colourful farewell
Above: The fans dressed in red and white t-shirts supplied for the occasion provide the backdrop for the farewell ceremony.
Above left: An emotional Thierry Henry kisses goodbye to the Highbury turf after completing a dramatic last-day hat-trick.

The final countdown
Above: The countdown clock at Highbury signals the end of an era.
Right: Red and silver streamers cascade down onto the pitch in the final moments of the farewell celebrations.

Highbury statistics

SEASON-BY-SEASON PLAYING RECORD AT HIGHBURY

	LEAGUE						F A CUP						FA CHARITY SHIELD						FOOTBALL LEAGUE CUP						EUROPE					
	P	W	D	L	F	A	P	W	D	L	F	A	P	W	D	L	F	A	P	W	D	L	F	A	P	W	D	L	F	A
1913/14	19	14	3	2	34	10																								
1914/15	19	15	1	3	52	13	1	1	0	0	3	0																		
1919/20	21	11	5	5	32	21	1	1	0	0	4	2																		
1920/21	21	9	8	4	31	25																								
1921/22	21	10	6	5	27	19	3	1	2	0	4	1																		
1922/23	21	13	4	4	38	16	1	0	0	1	1	4																		
1923/24	21	8	5	8	25	24	1	1	0	0	4	1																		
1924/25	21	12	3	6	33	17	1	0	1	0	2	2																		
1925/26	21	16	2	3	57	19	3	3	0	0	6	1																		
1926/27	21	12	5	4	47	30	3	3	0	0	5	1																		
1927/28	21	10	6	5	49	33	4	4	0	0	14	5																		
1928/29	21	11	6	4	43	25	3	3	0	0	5	1																		
1929/30	21	10	2	9	49	26	2	1	1	0	4	2																		
1930/31	21	14	5	2	67	27	1	0	1	0	2	2																		
1931/32	21	14	5	2	52	16	2	2	0	0	15	3																		
1932/33	21	14	3	4	70	27																								
1933/34	21	15	4	2	45	19	3	2	0	1	9	2																		
1934/35	21	15	4	2	74	17							1	1	0	0	4	0												
1935/36	21	9	9	3	44	22	2	2	0	0	7	1	1	0	0	1	0	1												
1936/37	21	10	10	1	43	20	1	1	0	0	5	0																		
1937/38	21	15	4	2	52	16	2	1	0	1	3	2																		
1938/39	21	14	3	4	34	14							1	1	0	0	2	1												
1946/47	21	9	5	7	43	33	1	0	1	0	1	1																		
1947/48	21	15	3	3	56	15	1	0	0	1	0	1																		
1948/49	21	13	5	3	51	18	1	1	0	0	3	0	1	1	0	0	4	3												
1949/50	21	12	4	5	48	24	4	4	0	0	6	1																		
1950/51	21	11	5	5	47	28	2	1	1	0	3	2																		
1951/52	21	13	7	1	54	30	1	1	0	0	4	0																		
1952/53	21	15	3	3	60	30	3	2	0	1	11	4																		
1953/54	21	8	8	5	42	37	2	1	0	1	6	3	1	1	0	0	3	1												
1954/55	21	12	3	6	44	25	1	1	0	0	1	0																		
1955/56	21	13	4	4	38	22	3	1	1	1	7	6																		
1956/57	21	12	5	4	45	21	3	2	0	1	7	5																		
1957/58	21	10	4	7	48	39																								
1958/59	21	14	3	4	53	29	2	1	1	0	6	2																		
1959/60	21	9	5	7	39	38	1	0	1	0	1	1																		
1960/61	21	12	3	6	44	35																								
1961/62	21	9	6	6	39	31	1	1	0	0	3	0																		
1962/63	21	11	4	6	44	33	3	2	0	1	8	3																		
1963/64	21	10	7	4	56	37	3	2	0	1	4	2													2	0	1	1	3	4
1964/65	21	11	5	5	42	31																								
1965/66	21	8	8	5	36	31																								
1966/67	21	11	6	4	32	20	1	1	0	0	3	0							3	1	1	1	7	4						

	LEAGUE						F A CUP						FA CHARITY SHIELD						FOOTBALL LEAGUE CUP						EUROPE					
	P	W	D	L	F	A	P	W	D	L	F	A	P	W	D	L	F	A	P	W	D	L	F	A	P	W	D	L	F	A
1967/68	21	12	6	3	37	23	2	1	1	0	3	1							4	4	0	0	8	4						
1968/69	21	12	6	3	31	12	2	2	0	0	4	0							4	4	0	0	9	2						
1969/70	21	7	10	4	29	23	1	0	1	0	1	1							2	1	1	0	2	0	6	6	0	0	20	1
1970/71	21	18	3	0	41	6	2	2	0	0	4	2							2	1	0	1	4	2	4	4	0	0	10	1
1971/72	21	15	2	4	36	13	1	0	1	0	0	0							3	2	1	0	5	0	3	2	0	1	7	1
1972/73	21	14	5	2	31	14	3	2	1	0	6	3							3	2	0	1	6	3						
1973/74	21	9	7	5	23	16	2	0	1	1	2	4							1	0	0	1	0	1						
1974/75	21	10	6	5	31	16	4	1	2	1	4	3							1	0	1	0	1	1						
1975/76	21	11	4	6	33	19													1	0	0	1	0	1						
1976/77	21	11	6	4	37	20	1	1	0	0	3	1							4	3	1	0	7	3						
1977/78	21	14	5	2	38	12	2	2	0	0	6	2							5	4	1	0	11	3						
1978/79	21	11	8	2	37	18	3	2	1	0	5	1													3	2	1	0	5	1
1979/80	21	8	10	3	24	12	3	3	0	0	7	1							4	3	1	0	14	2	4	3	1	0	10	3
1980/81	21	13	8	0	36	17													1	1	0	0	3	1						
1981/82	21	13	5	3	27	15													3	2	1	0	3	0	2	2	0	0	3	1
1982/83	21	11	6	4	36	19	5	4	1	0	10	5							5	4	0	1	9	5	1	0	0	1	2	5
1983/84	21	10	5	6	41	29													2	1	0	1	2	2						
1984/85	21	14	5	2	37	14	1	1	0	0	7	2							1	1	0	0	4	0						
1985/86	21	13	5	3	29	15	2	1	1	0	5	1							3	1	1	1	3	3						
1986/87	21	12	5	4	31	12	3	2	0	1	9	4							5	4	0	1	9	2						
1987/88	20	11	4	5	35	16	3	2	0	1	5	3							4	4	0	0	10	1						
1988/89	19	10	6	3	35	19	1	0	0	1	0	1							2	1	1	0	3	0						
1989/90	19	14	3	2	38	11	1	0	1	0	0	0							2	2	0	0	3	0						
1990/91	19	15	4	0	51	10	4	2	2	0	4	2							2	1	0	1	7	6						
1991/92	21	12	7	2	51	22													1	1	0	0	2	0	2	1	0	1	7	4
1992/93	21	8	6	7	25	20	2	1	1	0	4	2							4	3	1	0	7	2						
1993/94	21	10	8	3	25	15	1	0	0	1	1	3							3	0	2	1	2	3	4	3	1	0	6	1
1994/95	21	6	9	6	27	21	1	0	0	1	0	2							3	3	0	0	6	0	5	2	3	0	9	5
1995/96	19	10	7	2	30	16	1	0	1	0	1	1							4	3	1	0	11	3						
1996/97	19	10	5	4	36	18	2	0	1	1	1	2							1	1	0	0	5	2	1	0	0	1	2	3
1997/98	19	15	2	2	43	10	3	0	3	0	1	1							3	3	0	0	7	2	1	0	1	0	1	1
1998/99	19	14	5	0	34	5	3	3	0	0	5	2							1	0	0	1	0	5						
1999/2000	19	14	3	2	42	17	2	1	1	0	3	1							1	1	0	0	2	1	4	4	0	0	11	1
2000/01	19	15	3	1	45	13	2	2	0	0	6	1							1	0	0	1	1	2	7	5	2	0	15	8
2001/02	19	12	4	3	42	25	3	3	0	0	9	2							2	2	0	0	6	0	6	5	0	1	15	8
2002/03	19	15	2	2	47	20	3	2	1	0	9	3							1	0	0	1	2	3	6	1	4	1	5	4
2003/04	19	15	4	0	40	14	2	2	0	0	6	2	*Includes a drawn match won on penalties						3	2*	0	1	6	3	5	3	0	2	6	5
2004/05	19	13	5	1	54	19	3	2	1	0	5	2							1	1	0	0	3	1	4	3	1	0	8	2
2005/06	19	14	3	2	48	13	1	1	0	0	2	1							2	2	0	0	5	1	6	4	2	0	8	1
Total	1689	980	413	296	3372	1692	142	92	32	18	305	123	5	4	0	1	13	6	98	69	14	15	195	74	76	50	17	9	153	60

Total record Played 2010, Won 1195, Drawn 476, Lost 339 Goals for 4038, Goals against 1955

MANAGER'S RECORDS AT HIGHBURY

GEORGE MORRELL (1913–15)

	P	W	D	L	F	A
League	38	29	4	5	86	23
FA Cup	1	1	0	0	3	0
Total	**39**	**30**	**4**	**5**	**89**	**23**

LESLIE KNIGHTON (1919–25)

	P	W	D	L	F	A
League	126	63	31	32	186	122
FA Cup	7	3	3	1	15	10
Total	**133**	**66**	**34**	**33**	**201**	**132**

HERBERT CHAPMAN (1925–34)

	P	W	D	L	F	A
League	179	109	37	33	460	209
FA Cup	18	16	2	0	51	15
Total	**197**	**125**	**39**	**33**	**511**	**224**

GEORGE ALLISON / JOE SHAW

(Caretaker managers Jan–May 1934)

	P	W	D	L	F	A
League	10	7	1	2	19	13
FA Cup	3	2	0	1	9	2
Total	**13**	**9**	**1**	**3**	**28**	**15**

GEORGE ALLISON (1934–47)

	P	W	D	L	F	A
League	126	72	35	19	290	122
FA Cup	6	4	1	1	16	4
FA Charity Shield	3	2	0	1	6	2
Total	**135**	**78**	**36**	**21**	**312**	**128**

TOM WHITTAKER (1947–56)

	P	W	D	L	F	A
League	197	116	43	38	458	239
FA Cup	18	12	2	4	41	17
FA Charity Shield	2	2	0	0	7	4
Total	**217**	**130**	**45**	**42**	**506**	**260**

JACK CRAYSTON (1956–58)

	P	W	D	L	F	A
League	34	18	8	8	75	50
FA Cup	3	2	0	1	7	5
Total	**37**	**20**	**8**	**9**	**82**	**55**

GEORGE SWINDIN (1958–62)

	P	W	D	L	F	A
League	84	44	17	23	175	133
FA Cup	4	2	2	0	10	3
Total	**88**	**46**	**19**	**23**	**185**	**136**

BILLY WRIGHT (1962–66)

	P	W	D	L	F	A
League	84	40	24	20	178	132
FA Cup	6	4	0	2	12	5
Europe	2	0	1	1	3	4
Total	**92**	**44**	**25**	**23**	**193**	**141**

BERTIE MEE (1966–76)

	P	W	D	L	F	A
League	210	119	55	36	324	162
FA Cup	18	9	7	2	27	14
League Cup	24	15	4	5	42	18
Europe	13	12	0	1	37	3
Total	**265**	**155**	**66**	**44**	**430**	**197**

TERRY NEILL (1976–83)

	P	W	D	L	F	A
League	156	85	48	23	249	125
FA Cup	14	12	2	0	31	10
League Cup	24	18	4	2	49	16
Europe	10	7	2	1	20	10
Total	**204**	**122**	**56**	**26**	**349**	**161**

DON HOWE (1983–86)

	P	W	D	L	F	A
League	49	32	13	4	88	40
FA Cup	3	2	1	0	12	3
League Cup	4	2	1	1	7	3
Total	**56**	**36**	**15**	**5**	**107**	**46**

STEVE BURTENSHAW

(Caretaker manager Mar–May 1986)

	P	W	D	L	F	A
League	5	1	2	2	5	6
Total	**5**	**1**	**2**	**2**	**5**	**6**

GEORGE GRAHAM (1986–95)

	P	W	D	L	F	A
League	175	95	50	30	307	141
FA Cup	16	7	4	5	23	17
League Cup	26	19	4	3	49	14
Europe	9	5	3	1	18	7
Total	**226**	**126**	**61**	**39**	**397**	**179**

STEWART HOUSTON

(Caretaker manager Feb 1995–May 1995, Aug–Sep 1996)

	P	W	D	L	F	A
League	9	4	3	2	16	8
Europe	3	1	1	1	6	6
Total	**12**	**5**	**4**	**3**	**22**	**14**

BRUCE RIOCH (1995–96)

	P	W	D	L	F	A
League	19	10	7	2	30	16
FA Cup	1	0	1	0	1	1
League Cup	4	3	1	0	11	3
Total	**24**	**13**	**9**	**2**	**42**	**20**

PAT RICE (Caretaker manager Sept 1996)

	P	W	D	L	F	A
League	2	2	0	0	6	1
Total	**2**	**2**	**0**	**0**	**6**	**1**

ARSENE WENGER (1996–2006)

	P	W	D	L	F	A
League	186	134	35	17	420	150
FA Cup	24	16	7	1	47	17
League Cup	16	12	0	4	37	20
Europe	39	25	10	4	69	30
Total	**265**	**187**	**52**	**26**	**573**	**217**

PLAYERS' APPEARANCES AT HIGHBURY

LEAGUE

454 players made appearances for Arsenal in League matches at Highbury, of which 44 made one appearance only. 152 players appeared as substitutes in a total of 922 substitutes used, 14 players made appearances only as a substitute.

Top Highbury appearances
(+ = substitute appearances)

1	256 + 21	David O'Leary
2	262 + 1	Tony Adams
3	248 + 6	George Armstrong
4	220 + 13	Lee Dixon
5	215 + 4	Nigel Winterburn
6	214	Bob John
7	202	David Seaman
8	199 + 1	Pat Rice
9	197	Eddie Hapgood
10	190 + 3	Peter Storey
11	189 + 2	John Radford
12	178 + 8	Peter Simpson
13	169 + 6	Graham Rix
14	174	Cliff Bastin
15	171	Joe Hulme
16	161 + 9	Paul Davis
17	150 + 19	Paul Merson
18	133 + 35	Dennis Bergkamp
19	167	Jack Kelsey
20	164	Alf Baker

F A CUP

293 players made appearances for Arsenal in FA Cup matches at Highbury, of which 67 made one appearance only. 57 players appeared as substitutes in a total of 90 substitutes used, 13 players made appearances only as a substitute.

Top Highbury appearances
(+ = substitute appearances)

1	25 + 1	David O'Leary
2	22 + 1	Tony Adams
3	21	Bob John
=	21	Nigel Winterburn
=	20 + 1	Lee Dixon
6	20	Pat Rice
7	19	Alf Baker
=	19	David Seaman
=	18 + 1	George Armstrong
=	17 + 2	Patrick Vieira
11	18	Peter Simpson
=	17 + 1	Peter Storey
13	17	Joe Hulme
=	16 + 1	Ray Parlour
=	16 + 1	Dennis Bergkamp
16	15 + 1	Graham Rix
17	15	Jack Butler
=	15	Jimmy Logie
=	15	Tom Parker
=	14 + 1	John Radford

FOOTBALL LEAGUE CUP

202 players made appearances for Arsenal in Football League Cup matches at Highbury, of which 53 made one appearance only. 66 players appeared as substitutes in a total of 94 substitutes used, 18 players made appearances only as a substitute.

Top Highbury appearances
(+ = substitute appearances)

1	35 + 1	David O'Leary
2	28	Tony Adams
3	23 + 4	Paul Davis
4	23 + 2	Graham Rix
5	24	Kenny Sansom
=	24	Nigel Winterburn
7	23	Lee Dixon
8	22	Pat Rice
=	21 + 1	Peter Storey
10	21	George Armstrong
=	20 + 1	Peter Simpson
12	20	Frank McLintock
=	20	John Radford
14	19	David Seaman
=	18 + 1	Paul Merson
16	18	Pat Jennings
=	17 + 1	Alan Smith
18	17	Steve Bould
19	16	George Graham
=	16	John Lukic
=	16	Sammy Nelson
=	15 + 1	David Rocastle

EUROPEAN COMPETITIONS

134 players made appearances for Arsenal in European Competitions matches at Highbury, of which 26 made one appearance only. 63 players appeared as substitutes in a total of 144 substitutes used, 10 players made appearances only as a substitute.

Top Highbury appearances
(+ = substitute appearances)

1	35 + 1	Thierry Henry
2	24 + 11	Dennis Bergkamp
3	31	David Seaman
=	28 + 3	Robert Pires
5	30	Patrick Vieira
6	26 + 3	Freddie Ljungberg
7	22 + 4	Lauren
8	22	Lee Dixon
=	9 + 13	Kanu
10	20 + 1	Ashley Cole
=	14 + 7	Ray Parlour
12	9 + 11	Sylvain Wiltord
13	18	Tony Adams
=	16 + 2	Kolo Toure
15	17	Sol Campbell
=	14 + 3	Martin Keown
17	14 + 2	Gilberto
18	14	Nigel Winterburn
=	12 + 2	George Armstrong
=	12 + 2	Gilles Grimandi

F A CHARITY SHIELD

38 players made appearances in the five FA Charity Shield matches played at Highbury. Wilf Copping and George Male made 3 appearances each, Wally Barnes, Cliff Bastin, Leslie Compton, Jack Crayston, Ted Drake, Eddie Hapgood, Frank Hill, Bryn Jones, Bernard Joy, Jimmy Logie, Joe Mercer, Don Roper, George Swindin all appeared twice.

GOALSCORERS

LEAGUE

Excluding 63 opponents' own goals, 268 players got their names on the score sheet in League matches at Highbury, of whom 51 scored only once.

Top Highbury goalscorers

1	114	Thierry Henry
2	88	Cliff Bastin
=	88	Doug Lishman
4	80	Jimmy Brain
5	74	Ted Drake
6	71	Ian Wright
7	66	Joe Hulme
8	65	John Radford
9	63	David Herd
10	61	Reg Lewis
11	60	David Jack
12	59	Joe Baker
=	59	Jack Lambert
14	54	Paul Merson
15	51	Don Roper
16	49	Cliff Holton
17	48	Ronnie Rooke
=	48	Frank Stapleton
19	47	Alan Smith
20	46	Jimmy Logie
=	46	Dennis Bergkamp

F A CUP

Excluding 7 opponents' own goals, 110 players got their names on the score sheet in FA Cup matches at Highbury, of whom 45 scored only once.

Top Highbury goalscorers

1	14	Cliff Bastin
2	11	Jimmy Brain
3	9	Alan Sunderland
4	8	Joe Hulme
=	8	Reg Lewis
6	7	Dennis Bergkamp
=	7	David Jack
=	7	Jack Lambert
9	6	Jimmy Logie
=	6	Don Roper
11	5	George Armstrong
=	5	Pat Beasley
=	5	David Herd
=	5	John Radford
=	5	Geoff Strong
=	5	Brian Talbot
=	5	Sylvain Wiltord
=	5	Robert Pires
19	4	9 players

FOOTBALL LEAGUE CUP

Excluding 2 opponents' own goals, 72 players got their names on the score sheet in Football League Cup matches at Highbury, of whom 30 scored only once.

Top Highbury goalscorers

1	15	Ian Wright
2	11	Alan Sunderland
3	10	John Radford
=	10	Alan Smith
5	8	Frank Stapleton
6	7	Liam Brady
7	6	Dennis Bergkamp
8	5	George Graham
=	5	Sylvain Wiltord
10	4	Ray Kennedy
=	4	Malcolm Macdonald
=	4	Paul Merson
=	4	Charlie Nicholas
=	4	David Rocastle
15	3	10 players

EUROPEAN COMPETITIONS

Excluding 3 opponents' own goals, 52 players got their names on the score sheet in European Competitions matches at Highbury, of whom 24 scored only once.

Top Highbury goalscorers

1	20	Thierry Henry
2	9	Dennis Bergkamp
3	8	Freddie Ljungberg
=	8	John Radford
=	8	Ian Wright
6	6	George Graham
=	6	Jon Sammels
=	6	Alan Sunderland
9	5	Charlie George
=	5	Ray Kennedy
11	4	Kanu
=	4	Robert Pires
=	4	Alan Smith
=	4	Willie Young
15	3	Robin van Persie
16	2	13 players

F A CHARITY SHIELD

The 13 Arsenal goals in the FA Charity Shield matches at Highbury were scored by the following players: Ted Drake (3), Reg Lewis (2), Doug Lishman (2), Cliff Bastin, Ralph Birkett, Bryn Jones, Tommy Lawton, James Marshall and Ronnie Rooke (1 each).

HAT-TRICKS

50 players scored a total of 126 hat-tricks at Highbury – 116 in the League, 5 in the FA Cup, 4 in the Football League Cup, and 1 in European competitions. Jimmy Brain leads the list with 11, followed by Thierry Henry (8), Jack Lambert and Doug Lishman (7 each), Ted Drake and Ian Wright (6 each), David Herd, David Jack and Ronnie Rooke (5 each).

SEASON-BY-SEASON MATCH RECORD AT HIGHBURY

1913/14
LEAGUE DIVISION TWO
Final position – 3rd

Sep 6 Leicester Fosse 2–1
(Jobey, Devine [pen]) Att: 20,000
Lievesley, Shaw, Fidler, Grant, Sands,
McKinnon, Greenaway, Hardinge, Jobey,
Devine, Winship.

Sep 15 Notts County 3–0
(Stonley 2, Grant) Att: 20,000
Lievesley, Shaw, Sands, Grant, Thomson,
McKinnon, Greenaway, Hardinge, Stonley,
Devine, Winship.

Sep 20 Hull City 0–0
Att: 28,000
Caldwell, Shaw, Fidler, Grant, Sands,
McKinnon, Greenaway, Hardinge, Stonley,
Devine, Burrell.

Oct 4 Bury 0–1
Att: 30,000
Caldwell, Sands, Fidler, Thomson, Jobey,
McKinnon, Greenaway, Hardinge, Graham,
Devine, Burrell.

Oct 18 Lincoln City 3–0
(Flanagan, Stonley 2) Att: 25,000
Lievesley, Shaw, Fidler, Thomson, Jobey,
McKinnon, Lewis, Flanagan, Stonley, Hardinge,
Burrell.

Nov 1 Nottingham Forest 3–2
(Rutherford 2, Flanagan) Att: 30,000
Lievesley, Shaw, Fidler, Thomson, Jobey,
McKinnon, Rutherford, Flanagan, Stonley,
Hardinge, Winship.

Nov 22 Birmingham 1–0
(Flanagan) Att: 25,000
Lievesley, Shaw, Fidler, Jobey, Sands,
McEachrane, Rutherford, Flanagan, Stonley,
Hardinge, Winship.

Dec 6 Leeds City 1–0
(Benson [pen]) Att: 18,000
Lievesley, Shaw, Benson, Jobey, Sands,
Graham, Rutherford, Hardinge, Stonley, Devine,
Lewis.

Dec 20 Glossop North End 2–0
(Stonley, Devine) Att: 14,500
Lievesley, Shaw, Benson, Jobey, Sands,
Graham, Greenaway, Hardinge, Stonley, Devine,
Lewis.

Dec 26 Bradford Park Avenue 2–0
(Hardinge, Flanagan) Att: 30,000
Lievesley, Shaw, Benson, Jobey, Sands, Graham,
Rutherford, Flanagan, Stonley, Hardinge, Lewis.

Jan 3 Wolverhampton Wanderers 3–1
(Rutherford 2, Hardinge) Att: 20,000
Lievesley, Shaw, Benson, Jobey, Sands, Graham,
Rutherford, Flanagan, Stonley, Hardinge, Lewis.

Jan 24 Barnsley 1–0
(Rutherford) Att: 19,000
Lievesley, Shaw, Benson, Jobey, Sands,
McKinnon, Rutherford, Flanagan, Stonley,
Devine, Lewis.

Feb 14 Huddersfield Town 0–1
Att: 25,000
Lievesley, Shaw, Benson, Jobey, Sands,
McKinnon, Rutherford, Groves, Stonley, Devine,
Lewis.

Feb 28 Blackpool 2–1
(Jobey, Slade) Att: 20,000
Lievesley, Shaw, Benson, Jobey, Sands,
McKinnon, Rutherford, Flanagan, Slade,
Hardinge, Lewis.

Mar 14 Fulham 2–0
(Flanagan, Slade) Att: 30,000
Lievesley, Shaw, Benson, Jobey, Sands,
McKinnon, Lewis, Flanagan, Slade, Hardinge,
Winship.

Apr 4 Bristol City 1–1
(Winship) Att: 12,000
Lievesley, Shaw, Benson, Jobey, Sands,
McKinnon, Rutherford, Flanagan, Stonley,
Lewis, Winship.

Apr 13 Stockport County 4–0
(Flanagan 2, Rutherford, Benson) Att: 18,000
Lievesley, Shaw, Benson, Grant, Sands,
Graham, Rutherford, Flanagan, Stonley, Slade,
Lewis.

Apr 18 Clapton Orient 2–2
(Flanagan 2) Att: 35,000
Lievesley, Shaw, Benson, Grant, Sands,
Graham, Rutherford, Flanagan, Stonley, Slade,
Lewis.

Apr 23 Grimsby Town 2–0
(Stonley, Flanagan) Att: 25,000
Lievesley, Shaw, Benson, Grant, Sands,
Graham, Lewis, Flanagan, Stonley, Slade,
Winship.

NOTE: There were no FA Cup matches at
Highbury this season.

1914/15
LEAGUE DIVISION TWO
Final position – 5th

Sep 1 Glossop North End 3–0
(Bradshaw, King 2) Att: 7,000
Lievesley, Shaw, Benson, Grant, Buckley,
Graham, Rutherford, Flanagan, King, Bradshaw,
Lewis.

Sep 12 Fulham 3–0
(King 2, Rutherford) Att: 10,000
Lievesley, Shaw, Benson, Grant, Buckley,
Graham, Rutherford, Flanagan, King, Bradshaw,
Winship.

Sep 26 Hull City 2–1
(Hardinge 2) Att: 20,000
Lievesley, Shaw, Benson, Grant, Buckley,
Graham, Rutherford, Hardinge, King, Bradshaw,
Winship.

Oct 10 Clapton Orient 2–1
(Bradshaw, King) Att: 30,000
Lievesley, Shaw, Benson, Grant, Buckley,
Graham, Rutherford, Hardinge, King, Bradshaw,
Winship.

Oct 17 Blackpool 2–0
(King 2) Att: 17,000
Lievesley, Shaw, Benson, Grant, Buckley,
Graham, Rutherford, Hardinge, King, Bradshaw,
Winship.

Oct 31 Lincoln City 1–1
(Hardinge) Att: 15,000
Lievesley, Shaw, Benson, Grant, Buckley,
Graham, Rutherford, Flanagan, Hardinge,
Bradshaw, Winship.

Nov 14 Grimsby Town 6–0
(Bradshaw, King 3, Benson [pen], McKinnon)
Att: 15,000
Lievesley, Shaw, Benson, Grant, Buckley,
McKinnon, Lewis, Hardinge, King, Bradshaw,
Norman.

Nov 28 Bristol City 3–0
(Hardinge 2, King) Att: 7,000
Lievesley, Shaw, Benson, Grant, Buckley,
McKinnon, Rutherford, Hardinge, King,
Bradshaw, Lewis.

Dec 12 Preston North End 1–2
(Hardinge) Att: 10,000
Lievesley, Shaw, Benson, Grant, Graham,
McKinnon, Rutherford, Hardinge, King,
Bradshaw, Lewis.

Dec 26 Leicester Fosse 6–0
(Lewis 3, McKinnon, King [pen], Flanagan)
Att: 6,000
Lievesley, Shaw, Benson, Grant, Buckley,
McKinnon, Rutherford, Flanagan, King, Blyth,
Lewis.

Jan 2 Wolverhampton Wanderers 5–1
(King 4, Buckley) Att: 9,000
Lievesley, Shaw, Ford , Grant, Buckley,
McKinnon, Groves, Flanagan, King, Bradshaw,
Lewis.

Jan 23 Stockport County 3–1
(Flanagan 2, Bradshaw) Att: 6,000
Lievesley, Shaw, Ford, Grant, Buckley,
McKinnon, Rutherford, Flanagan, King,
Bradshaw, Lewis.

Feb 6 Leeds City 2–0
(Rutherford, Bradshaw) Att: 10,000
Lievesley, Shaw, Ford, Grant, Buckley,
McKinnon, Rutherford, Flanagan, King,
Bradshaw, Lewis.

Feb 27 Derby County 1–2
(King [pen]) Att: 18,000
Lievesley, Sands, Shaw, Graham, Buckley,
McKinnon, Rutherford, Flanagan, King, Blyth,
Winship.

Mar 13 Birmingham 1–0
(Bradshaw) Att: 19,000
Lievesley, Shaw, Benson, Graham Sands,
McKinnon, Greenaway, Flanagan, King,
Bradshaw, Lewis.

Mar 27 Huddersfield Town 0–3
Att: 14,000
Lievesley, Shaw, Benson, Graham, Buckley,
McKinnon, Rutherford, Flanagan, King,
Bradshaw, Lewis.

Apr 5 Barnsley 1–0
(Lewis) Att: 15,000
Lievesley, Shaw, Benson, Graham, Sands,
McKinnon, Greenaway, Flanagan, King, Blyth,
Lewis.

Apr 10 Bury 3–1
(Flanagan 2, Blyth) Att: 12,000
Lievesley, Shaw, Benson, Fletcher, Sands,
Graham, Rutherford, Flanagan, King, Blyth,
Lewis.

Apr 24 Nottingham Forest 7–0
(Benson 2, King 4, Rutherford) Att: 10,000
Lievesley, Sands, Shaw, Graham, Buckley,
Bradshaw, Rutherford, King, Benson, Blyth,
Lewis.

FA CUP

Jan 9 Merthyr Town* 3–0
(King 3 [1 pen]) Att: 9,000
Kempton, Shaw, Ford , Grant, Buckley,
McKinnon, Rutherford, Flanagan, King,
Bradshaw, Lewis.

* Played at Highbury by arrangement

1915 to 1919

During World War I, competitive football was
organised on a regional basis, and for the next
four seasons, Arsenal competed in the London
Combination League.

1919/20
LEAGUE DIVISION ONE
Final position – 10th

Aug 30 Newcastle United 0–1
Att: 40,000
Williamson, Shaw, Bradshaw, Graham, Voysey,
McKinnon, Rutherford, Groves, White, Blyth,
Baker.

Sep 8 Liverpool 1–0
(Rutherford) Att: 20,000
Williamson, Shaw, Bradshaw, Graham, Voysey,
McKinnon, Rutherford, Burgess, White, Blyth,
Groves.

Sep 20 Sunderland 3–2
(White 3) Att: 42,000
Williamson, Shaw, Hutchins, Graham, Buckley,
McKinnon, Rutherford, Burgess, White, Blyth,
Groves.

Oct 4 Blackburn Rovers 0–1
Att: 30,000
Williamson, Shaw, Bradshaw, Graham, Buckley,
McKinnon, Rutherford, Burgess, White, Blyth,
Groves.

Oct 18 Everton 1–1
(Groves) Att: 30,000
Williamson, Shaw, Hutchins, Graham, Buckley,
McKinnon, Rutherford, Groves, White, Blyth,
Toner.

Oct 25 Bradford City 1–2
(Graham [pen]) Att: 35,000
Williamson, Shaw, Hutchins, Graham, Buckley,
McKinnon, Rutherford, White, Pagnam, Blyth,
Toner.

Nov 8 Bolton Wanderers 2–2
(Pagnam, Rutherford) Att: 30,000
Williamson, Shaw, Bradshaw, Groves, Buckley,
McKinnon, Rutherford, White, Pagnam,
Hardinge, Toner.

Nov 22 Notts County 3–1
(Pagnam 2, Toner) Att: 25,000
Williamson, Shaw, Bradshaw, Butler, Buckley,
McKinnon, Rutherford, White, Pagnam,
Hardinge, Toner.

Dec 6 Chelsea 1–1
(White) Att: 50,000
Williamson, Shaw, Bradshaw, Butler, Buckley,
McKinnon, Rutherford, White, Pagnam,
Hardinge, Toner.

Dec 20 Sheffield Wednesday 3–1
(Hardinge, Pagnam, Butler) Att: 30,000
Williamson, Shaw, Bradshaw, Butler, Buckley,
McKinnon, Rutherford, Groves, Pagnam,
Hardinge, Toner.

Dec 26 Derby County 1–0
(Groves) Att: 25,000
Williamson, Shaw, Bradshaw, Baker, Buckley,
McKinnon, Rutherford, Groves, Pagnam,
Hardinge, Lewis.

Jan 3 Manchester City 2–2
(White, Lewis) Att: 32,000
Williamson, Shaw, Bradshaw, Baker, Butler,
McKinnon, Rutherford, Groves, White,
Hardinge, Lewis.

Jan 24 Aston Villa 0–1
Att: 55,000
Dunn, Shaw, Bradshaw, Graham, Butler,
McKinnon, Pagnam, Groves, White, Blyth,
Lewis.

Feb 7 Oldham Athletic 3–2
(Graham [pen], North, Blyth) Att: 32,000
Dunn, Cownley, Bradshaw, Graham, Buckley,
McKinnon, Rutherford, White, North, Blyth,
Toner.

Feb 21 Manchester United 0–3
Att: 25,000
Dunn, Cownley, Bradshaw, Graham, Buckley,
McKinnon, Rutherford, Butler, White, Blyth,
Toner.

Mar 13 Sheffield United 3–0
(Graham, Pagnam 2) Att: 35,000
Dunn, Peart, Bradshaw, Baker, Butler, McKinnon,
Rutherford, Bradshaw, Pagnam, Graham, Blyth.

Mar 27 Middlesbrough 2–1
(Blyth, Groves) Att: 25,000
Dunn, Peart, Hutchins, Baker, Buckley,
McKinnon, Rutherford, Groves, Pagnam,
Graham, Blyth.

Apr 5 West Bromwich Albion 1–0
(Blyth) Att: 40,000
Dunn, Shaw, Hutchins, Baker, Butler, McKinnon,
Rutherford, Groves, Pagnam, Bradshaw, Blyth.

Apr 10 Burnley 2–0
(Bradshaw, Pagnam) Att: 20,000
Dunn, Shaw, Hutchins, Baker, Butler, McKinnon,
Rutherford, Groves, Pagnam, Bradshaw, Blyth.

Apr 24 Preston North End 0–0
Att: 35,000
Williamson, Shaw, Hutchins, Baker, Butler,
McKinnon, Rutherford, Groves, Pagnam, White,
Blyth.

May 1 Bradford Park Avenue 3–0
(Groves, Bradshaw, Pagnam) Att: 30,000
Williamson, Shaw, Hutchins, Baker, Pattison,
McKinnon, Greenaway, Groves, Pagnam,
Bradshaw, Blyth.

FA CUP

Jan 10 Rochdale* 4–2
(Rutherford, Graham, Pagnam, Groves)
Att: 26,596
Williamson, Shaw, Bradshaw, Graham, Butler,
McKinnon, Rutherford, Groves, White, Pagnam,
Lewis.

*Played at Highbury by arrangement

1920/21
LEAGUE DIVISION ONE
Final position – 9th

Aug 30 Manchester United 2–0
(Pagnam, Smith) Att: 25,000
Williamson, Shaw, Hutchins, Baker, Buckley,
McKinnon, Smith, Groves, Pagnam, Bradshaw,
Blyth.

Sep 4 Aston Villa 0–1
Att: 45,000
Williamson, Shaw, Hutchins, Baker, Graham,
McKinnon, Smith, Groves, Pagnam, Bradshaw,
Blyth.

Sep 11 Manchester City 2–1
(Pagnam, Groves) Att: 42,000
Williamson, Shaw, Hutchins, Baker, Graham,
McKinnon, Smith, White, Pagnam, Groves,
Blyth.

Sep 25 Middlesbrough 2–2
(Pagnam, Graham [pen]) Att: 40,000
Williamson, Shaw, Hutchins, Baker, Graham,
McKinnon, Smith, White, Pagnam, Groves,
Blyth.

Oct 9 Bolton Wanderers 0–0
Att: 38,000
Williamson, Shaw, Hutchins, Baker, Graham,
McKinnon, Rutherford, White, Pagnam,
Bradshaw, Blyth.

Oct 30 Derby County 2–0
(Pagnam, White) Att: 45,000
Williamson, Bradshaw, Hutchins, Baker,
Graham, McKinnon, Rutherford, White,
Pagnam, Blyth, Paterson.

Nov 13 **Blackburn Rovers** **2–0**
(White, Pagnam) Att: 40,000
Williamson, Shaw, Hutchins, Baker, Buckley, McKinnon, Smith, White, Pagnam, Blyth, Paterson.

Nov 27 **Huddersfield Town** **2–0**
(Pagnam 2) Att: 35,000
Williamson, Shaw, Hutchins, Baker, Graham, Butler, Smith, White, Pagnam, Blyth, Paterson.

Dec 11 **Chelsea** **1–1**
(Blyth) Att: 50,000
Williamson, Shaw, Hutchins, Baker, Graham, McKinnon, Rutherford, White, Pagnam, Blyth, Paterson.

Dec 27 **Everton** **1–1**
(Pagnam) Att: 40,000
Williamson, Shaw, Hutchins, Baker, Butler, McKinnon, Rutherford, White, Pagnam, Blyth, Paterson.

Jan 1 **Bradford City** **1–2**
(Graham [pen]) Att: 20,000
Williamson, Shaw, Hutchins, Baker, Graham, McKinnon, Rutherford, White, Pagnam, Blyth, Toner.

Jan 22 **Tottenham Hotspur** **3–2**
(Rutherford 2, White) Att: 60,600
Dunn, Bradshaw, Hutchins, Baker, Butler, McKinnon, Rutherford, White, North, Blyth, Paterson.

Jan 29 **Sunderland** **1–2**
(Pagnam) Att: 40,000
Williamson, Bradshaw, Hutchins, Baker, Graham, McKinnon, Rutherford, White, Pagnam, Blyth, Paterson.

Feb 19 **Oldham Athletic** **2–2**
(Rutherford, Walden) Att: 40,000
Williamson, Bradshaw, Hutchins, Baker, Graham, McKinnon, Rutherford, Groves, Walden, Blyth, Paterson.

Mar 19 **Burnley** **1–1**
(Baker [pen]) Att: 45,000
Williamson, Bradshaw, Hutchins, Baker, Pattison, McKinnon, Rutherford, Burgess, White, Blyth, Paterson.

Mar 26 **Sheffield United** **2–6**
(White, Baker) Att: 30,000
Williamson, Bradshaw, Hutchins, Baker, Graham, McKinnon, Rutherford, Groves, White, Blyth, Paterson.

Mar 28 **West Bromwich Albion** **2–1**
(Graham [pen], Blyth) Att: 20,152
Williamson, Shaw, Hutchins, Baker, Graham, Whittaker, Rutherford, McKenzie, North, Blyth, Paterson.

Apr 9 **Bradford Park Avenue** **2–1**
(Toner, Rutherford) Att: 30,000
Dunn, Shaw, Bradshaw, Baker, Graham, McKinnon, Rutherford, McKenzie, North, Blyth, Toner.

Apr 23 **Newcastle United** **1–1**
(Rutherford) Att: 20,000
Dunn, Shaw, Hutchins, Baker, Graham, McKinnon, Rutherford, Blyth, North, Hopkins, Toner.

Apr 25 **Preston North End** **2–1**
(Hopkins, McKinnon) Att: 12,000
Dunn, Bradshaw, Hutchins, Pattison, Graham, McKinnon, Rutherford, Blyth, North, Hopkins, Toner.

May 2 **Liverpool** **0–0**
Att: 17,000
Dunn, Peart, Hutchins, Whittaker, Pattison, McKinnon, Rutherford, Burgess, Blyth, Hopkins, Toner.

NOTE: There were no FA Cup matches at Highbury this season.

1921/22

LEAGUE DIVISION ONE
Final position – 17th

Aug 27 **Sheffield United** **1–2**
(White) Att: 40,000
Williamson, Shaw, Hutchins, Baker, Graham, McKinnon, Rutherford, Blyth, White, North, Voysey.

Sep 5 **Preston North End** **1–0**
(White) Att: 20,000
Williamson, Cownley, Hutchins, Whittaker, Butler, McKinnon, Rutherford, McKenzie, White, North, Hopkins.

Sep 17 **Manchester City** **0–1**
Att: 25,000
Williamson, Cownley, Hutchins, Baker, Butler, McKinnon, Rutherford, McKenzie, White, Graham, Blyth.

Oct 1 **Everton** **1–0**
(White) Att: 35,000
Williamson, Cownley, Hutchins, Whittaker, Butler, McKinnon, Rutherford, White, Baker, Bradshaw, Blyth.

Oct 15 **Sunderland** **1–2**
(Bradshaw) Att: 40,000
Williamson, Cownley, Hutchins, Whittaker, Butler, McKinnon, Rutherford, White, Baker, Bradshaw, Paterson.

Oct 29 **Huddersfield Town** **1–3**
(North) Att: 30,000
Williamson, Shaw, Hutchins, Baker, Butler, McKinnon, Rutherford, Maxwell, North, Blyth, Paterson.

Nov 12 **Birmingham** **5–2**
(Whittaker, Hopkins 2, Baker, North) Att: 30,000
Williamson, Bradshaw, Hutchins, Baker, Butler, Whittaker, Rutherford, Blyth North, Hopkins, Toner.

Dec 10 **Blackburn Rovers** **1–1**
(Hopkins) Att: 35,000
Williamson, Bradshaw, Hutchins, Baker, Butler, Whittaker, Rutherford, Blyth, Henderson, Hopkins, Toner.

Dec 12 **Bolton Wanderers** **1–1**
(Butler) Att: 10,000
Williamson, Bradshaw, Hutchins, Baker, Butler, Whittaker, Rutherford, White, North, Boreham, Toner.

Dec 24 **Oldham Athletic** **0–1**
Att: 20,000
Williamson, Bradshaw, Hutchins, Whittaker, Butler, McKinnon, Rutherford, White, North, Boreham, Toner.

Dec 26 **Cardiff City** **0–0**
Att: 35,000
Williamson, Bradshaw, Hutchins, Whittaker, Graham, McKinnon, Rutherford, White, Butler, Hopkins, Toner.

Jan 14 **Chelsea** **1–0**
(Boreham) Att: 40,000
Williamson, Bradshaw, Hutchins, Baker, Graham, Whittaker, Creegan, Blyth, White, Boreham, Toner.

Jan 21 **Burnley** **0–0**
Att: 23,000
Williamson, Bradshaw, Hutchins, Milne, Graham, Whittaker, Rutherford, Blyth, White, Baker, Toner.

Feb 4 **Newcastle United** **2–1**
(Toner, Boreham) Att: 30,000
Dunn, Bradshaw, Turnbull, Baker, Graham, Whittaker, Rutherford, Blyth, White, Boreham, Toner.

Mar 22 **Liverpool** **1–0**
(Baker) Att: 12,000
Williamson, Bradshaw, Hutchins, Baker, Graham, Whittaker, Creegan, White, Young, Boreham, Toner.

Mar 25 **Aston Villa** **2–0**
(White, Boreham) Att: 40,000
Williamson, Bradshaw, Hutchins, Baker, Graham, Whittaker, Creegan, White, Young, Boreham, Toner.

Apr 1 **Middlesbrough** **2–2**
(Boreham, White) Att: 30,000
Williamson, Bradshaw, Hutchins, Baker, Graham, Whittaker, Creegan, White, Young, Boreham, Blyth.

Apr 5 **Manchester United** **3–1**
(Boreham, White, Butler) Att: 25,000
Williamson, Bradshaw, Hutchins, Baker, Graham, McKinnon, Rutherford, White, Butler, Boreham, Toner.

Apr 18 **West Bromwich Albion** **2–2**
(Graham [pen], White) Att: 23,663
Williamson, Bradshaw, Hutchins, Baker, Graham, Whittaker, Rutherford, White, Young, Boreham, Blyth.

Apr 22 **Tottenham Hotspur** **1–0**
(Graham [pen]) Att: 42,000
Williamson, Bradshaw, Hutchins, Baker, Graham, Whittaker, Rutherford, White, Young, Boreham, Blyth.

May 6 **Bradford City** **1–0**
(Blyth) Att: 32,000
Williamson, Bradshaw, Hutchins, Baker, Graham, Whittaker, Rutherford, Young, Turnbull, Boreham, Blyth.

FA CUP

Jan 7 **Queens Park Rangers** **0–0**
Att: 31,000
Williamson, Turnbull, Hutchins, Milne, Pattison, Whittaker, Hopkins, Baker, White, Bradshaw, Toner.

Feb 18 **Leicester City** **3–0**
(White 2, Rutherford) Att: 39,421
Williamson, Bradshaw, Turnbull, Baker, Graham, Whittaker, Rutherford, Butler, White, Blyth, Toner.

Mar 4 **Preston North End** **1–1**
(White) Att: 37,517
Williamson, Bradshaw, Turnbull, Baker, Graham, Whittaker, Rutherford, Butler, White, Blyth, Toner.

1922/23

LEAGUE DIVISION ONE
Final position – 11th

Aug 28 **Burnley** **1–1**
(Young) Att: 25,000
Williamson, Bradshaw, Turnbull, Baker, Voysey, Whittaker, Rutherford, White, Young, Boreham, Blyth.

Sep 2 **Liverpool** **1–0**
(Hutchins [pen]) Att: 35,000
Williamson, Bradshaw, Hutchins, Baker, Voysey, Whittaker, Rutherford, White, Young, Boreham, Blyth.

Sep 16 **Cardiff City** **2–1**
(Boreham, Young) Att: 40,000
Dunn, Bradshaw, Hutchins, Baker, Voysey, Whittaker, Rutherford, White, Young, Boreham, Paterson.

Sep 30 **Tottenham Hotspur** **0–2**
Att: 55,000
Dunn, Bradshaw, Hutchins, Baker, Voysey, Graham, Rutherford, White, Young, Boreham, Blyth.

Oct 7 **West Bromwich Albion** **3–1**
(White, Voysey, Boreham) Att: 32,500
Dunn, Turnbull, Hutchins, Baker, Voysey, Graham, Rutherford, White, Young, Boreham, Paterson.

Oct 28 **Newcastle United** **1–2**
(Roe) Att: 35,000
Dunn, Bradshaw, Turnbull, Milne, Graham, John, Henderson, Baker, Roe, Boreham, Paterson.

Nov 11 **Everton** **1–2**
(Blyth) Att: 30,000
Dunn, Bradshaw, Turnbull, Milne, Graham, Whittaker, Rutherford, Blyth, Roe, Boreham, Paterson.

Nov 25 **Sunderland** **2–3**
(Turnbull 2) Att: 30,000
Dunn, Bradshaw, Hutchins, Milne, Butler, Whittaker, Rutherford, Voysey, Turnbull, Boreham, Paterson.

Dec 9 **Birmingham** **1–0**
(Graham [pen]) Att: 25,000
Dunn, Mackie, Kennedy, Milne, Graham, John, Rutherford, Voysey, Turnbull, Boreham, Paterson.

Dec 16 **Huddersfield Town** **1–1**
(Rutherford) Att: 25,000
Dunn, Mackie, Kennedy, Milne, Graham, John, Rutherford, Voysey, Turnbull, Boreham, Paterson.

Dec 26 **Bolton Wanderers** **5–0**
(Turnbull 4, Blyth) Att: 35,000
Robson, Mackie, Kennedy, Milne, Butler, John, Baker, Blyth, Turnbull, Boreham, Paterson.

Dec 30 **Stoke City** **3–0**
(Blyth, Boreham, Turnbull) Att: 25,000
Robson, Mackie, Kennedy, Milne, Butler, John, Baker, Blyth, Turnbull, Boreham, Paterson.

Jan 20 **Manchester City** **1–0**
(Turnbull) Att: 25,000
Robson, Mackie, Kennedy, Milne, Graham, John, Baker, Blyth, Turnbull, McKenzie, Paterson.

Feb 10 **Nottingham Forest** **2–0**
(Baker 2) Att: 20,000
Robson, Mackie, Kennedy, Milne, Butler, John, Rutherford, Blyth, Turnbull, Baker, Paterson.

Feb 24 **Chelsea** **3–1**
(Baker, Blyth 2) Att: 35,000
Robson, Mackie, Kennedy, Milne, Butler, John, Rutherford, Blyth, Turnbull, Baker, Paterson.

Mar 10 **Middlesbrough** **3–0**
(Turnbull 3) Att: 25,000
Robson, Mackie, Kennedy, Milne, Butler, John, Rutherford, Blyth, Turnbull, Baker, Paterson.

Mar 17 **Oldham Athletic** **2–0**
(Blyth, Freeman [og]) Att: 30,000
Robson, Mackie, Kennedy, Milne, Butler, Whittaker, Rutherford, Blyth, Turnbull, Baker, Paterson.

Mar 31 **Aston Villa** **2–0**
(Blyth, Baker) Att: 45,000
Robson, Mackie, Kennedy, Milne, Butler, John, Rutherford, Blyth, Turnbull, Baker, Paterson.

Apr 2 **Blackburn Rovers** **1–1**
(McKenzie) Att: 32,000
Robson, Mackie, Kennedy, Milne, Butler, John, Rutherford, Blyth, Turnbull, McKenzie, Paterson.

Apr 14 **Preston North End** **1–1**
(Boreham) Att: 23,000
Robson, Elvey, Baker, Milne, Butler, Young, McKenzie, Blyth, Turnbull, Boreham, Paterson.

Apr 28 **Sheffield United** **2–0**
(Turnbull, Blyth) Att: 25,000
Robson, Mackie, Kennedy, Milne, Butler, John, Clark, Blyth, Turnbull, Boreham, Paterson.

FA CUP

Jan 17 **Liverpool** **1–4**
(Turnbull) Att: 39,000
Robson, Mackie, Kennedy, Milne, Voysey, John, Baker, Townrow, Turnbull, Boreham, Paterson.

1923/24

LEAGUE DIVISION ONE
Final position – 19th

Aug 25 **Newcastle United** **1–4**
(Turnbull) Att: 45,000
Robson, Mackie, Kennedy, Milne, Butler, John, Baker, Woods, Turnbull, Young, Toner.

Sep 10 **West Ham United** **4–1**
(Woods, Graham [pen], Earle 2) Att: 36,000
Robson, Mackie, Kennedy, Milne, Graham, John, Rutherford, Earle, Turnbull, Woods, Haden.

Sep 15 **West Bromwich Albion** **1–0**
(Voysey) Att: 36,004
Robson, Mackie, Kennedy, Milne, Graham, John, Rutherford, Voysey, Turnbull, Boreham, Haden.

Sep 29 **Birmingham** **0–0**
Att: 35,000
Robson, Mackie, Kennedy, Milne, Graham, John, Rutherford, Voysey, Turnbull, Blyth, Haden.

Oct 13 **Manchester City** **1–2**
(Turnbull) Att: 32,000
Robson, Mackie, Kennedy, Milne, Graham, Baker, Rutherford, Woods, Turnbull, Blyth, Paterson.

Oct 27 **Bolton Wanderers** **0–0**
Att: 30,000
Robson, Mackie, Kennedy, Milne, Butler, Blyth, Rutherford, Townrow, Young, Woods, Paterson.

Nov 3 **Middlesbrough** **2–1**
(Townrow, Woods) Att: 25,000
Robson, Mackie, Kennedy, Graham, Butler, Blyth, Paterson, Townrow, Young, Woods, Haden.

Nov 17 **Tottenham Hotspur** **1–1**
(Townrow) Att: 50,000
Robson, Mackie, Whittaker, Graham, Butler, Blyth, Rutherford, Townrow, Turnbull, Woods, Paterson.

Dec 1 **Blackburn Rovers** **2–2**
(Young, McIntyre [og]) Att: 20,000
Robson, Mackie, Whittaker, Milne, Graham, Blyth, Rutherford, Townrow, Young, Woods, Paterson.

Dec 15 **Huddersfield Town** **1–3**
(Young) Att: 25,000
Robson, Mackie, Whittaker, Graham, Butler, Blyth, Rutherford, Earle, Young, Woods, Paterson.

Dec 27 **Notts County** **0–0**
Att: 16,000
Robson, Mackie, Baker, Milne, Graham, Young, Paterson, Blyth, Turnbull, Woods, Haden.

Dec 29 **Chelsea** **1–0**
(Turnbull) Att: 38,000
Robson, Mackie, Baker, Milne, Graham, Young, Paterson, Blyth, Turnbull, Woods, Haden.

Jan 19 **Cardiff City** **1–2**
(Turnbull) Att: 30,000
Robson, Mackie, Baker, Milne, Graham, Young, Paterson, Blyth, Turnbull, Woods, Haden.

Feb 16 **Aston Villa** **0–1**
Att: 35,000
Robson, Baker, Kennedy, Milne, Graham, John, Rutherford, Blyth, Butler, Haden, Paterson.

Feb 25 **Sheffield United** **1–3**
(Milne) Att: 15,000
Robson, Mackie, Kennedy, Milne, Butler, John, Paterson, Blyth, Woods, Baker, Toner.

Mar 1 **Liverpool** **3–1**
(Woods 2, Rutherford) Att: 35,000
Robson, Mackie, Kennedy, Milne, Graham, John, Rutherford, Blyth, Woods, Ramsay, Haden.

Mar 22 **Nottingham Forest** **1–0**
(Neil) Att: 20,000
Robson, Baker, Kennedy, Milne, Butler, Young, Paterson, Neil, Woods, Ramsay, Haden.

Apr 5 **Burnley** **2–0**
(Ramsay, Neil) Att: 30,000
Robson, Baker, Kennedy, Milne, Butler, Young, Paterson, Neil, Woods, Ramsay, Haden.

Apr 12 **Sunderland** **2–0**
(Woods, Haden) Att: 18,000
Robson, Baker, Kennedy, Milne, Butler, Young, Paterson, Neil, Woods, Ramsay, Haden.

Apr 21 **Everton** **0–1**
Att: 25,000
Robson, Mackie, Kennedy, Milne, Butler, John, Rutherford, Neil, Woods, Ramsay, Haden.

May 3 **Preston North End** **1–2**
(Turnbull) Att: 25,000
Robson, Baker, Kennedy, Milne, Butler, Young, Paterson, Neil, Turnbull, Jones (F), Haden.

FA CUP

Jan 12 **Luton Town** **4–1**
(Milne, Blyth, Woods, Turnbull) Att: 37,500
Robson, Mackie, Baker, Milne, Graham, Young, Paterson, Blyth, Turnbull, Woods, Haden.

1924/25

LEAGUE DIVISION ONE

Final position – 20th

Sep 1 **Manchester City** **1–0**
(Neil) Att: 25,000
Robson, Baker, Kennedy, Milne, Butler, John, Rutherford, Neil, Woods, Ramsay, Toner.

Sep 6 **Liverpool** **2–0**
(Woods 2) Att: 45,000
Robson, Baker, Kennedy, Milne, Butler, John, Rutherford, Neil, Woods, Ramsay, Toner.

Sep 20 **Sheffield United** **2–0**
(Rutherford, Butler) Att: 40,000
Robson, Baker, Kennedy, Milne, Butler, John, Rutherford, Neil, Woods, Ramsay, Toner.

Oct 4 **Blackburn Rovers** **1–0**
(Neil) Att: 40,000
Robson, Baker, Kennedy, Milne, Butler, John, Rutherford, Neil, Woods, Ramsay, Toner.

Oct 13 **Bury** **0–1**
Att: 20,000
Robson. Baker, Kennedy, Milne, Butler, John, Rutherford, Neil, Woods, Ramsay, Toner.

Oct 18 **Aston Villa** **1–1**
(Butler) Att: 40,000
Robson, Mackie, Kennedy, Milne, Butler, John, Rutherford, Neil, Turnbull, Ramsay, Toner.

Oct 26 **Tottenham Hotspur** **1–0**
(Brain) Att: 51,000
Robson, Mackie, Kennedy, Milne, Butler, John, Rutherford, Brain, Woods, Ramsay, Toner.

Nov 8 **Notts County** **0–1**
Att: 35,000
Robson, Baker, Kennedy, Milne, Butler, John, Rutherford, Brain, Woods, Ramsay, Toner

Nov 22 **Sunderland** **0–0**
Att: 35,000
Lewis, Baker, Kennedy, Milne, Butler, John, Clark, Neil, Young, Ramsay, Toner.

Dec 6 **Preston North End** **4–0**
(Woods 3, Toner) Att: 30,000
Lewis, Baker, Kennedy, Milne, Butler, John, Rutherford, Brain, Woods, Ramsay, Toner.

Dec 20 **Leeds United** **6–1**
(Woods, Brain 4, Ramsay) Att: 30,000
Lewis, Baker, Kennedy, Milne, Butler, John, Rutherford, Brain, Woods, Ramsay, Toner.

Dec 26 **Birmingham** **0–1**
Att: 40,000
Lewis, Baker, Kennedy, Milne, Butler, Young, Rutherford, Brain, Woods, Ramsay, Toner.

Dec 27 **Nottingham Forest** **2–1**
(Ramsay, Butler) Att: 12,000
Lewis, Baker, Kennedy, Milne, Butler, John, Hoar, Woods, Brain, Ramsay, Toner.

Jan 17 **Newcastle United** **0–2**
Att: 30,000
Lewis, Baker, Kennedy, Milne, Butler, John, Hoar, Woods, Brain, Ramsay, Toner.

Feb 14 **Huddersfield Town** **0–5**
Att: 25,000
Lewis, Baker, Mackie, Young, Blyth, John, Hoar, Brain, Woods, Ramsay, Toner.

Mar 7 **Bolton Wanderers** **1–0**
(Blyth) Att: 35,000
Robson, Mackie, Kennedy, Baker, Butler, John, Hoar, Brain, Cock, Blyth, Haden.

Mar 21 **Everton** **3–1**
(Baker, Woods 2) Att: 20,000
Robson, Mackie, Kennedy, Baker, Butler, John, Hoar, Brain, Woods, Blyth, Haden.

Mar 23 **West Ham United** **1–2**
(Baker) Att: 10,000
Robson, Mackie, Kennedy, Whittaker, Baker, John, Hoar, Brain, Woods, Blyth, Haden.

Apr 4 **Cardiff City** **1–1**
(Brain) Att: 35,000
Robson, Baker, Kennedy, Milne, Butler, John, Hoar, Brain, Woods, Blyth, Haden.

Apr 14 **West Bromwich Albion** **2–0**
(Brain, John) Att: 21,000
Robson, Mackie, Kennedy, Milne, Butler, John, Rutherford, Brain, Young, Blyth, Haden.

Apr 18 **Burnley** **5–0**
(Woods, Brain 3, Haden) Att: 25,000
Robson, Mackie, Kennedy, Milne, Butler, Ramsay, Rutherford, Woods, Brain, Blyth, Haden.

FA CUP

Jan 21 **West Ham United** **2–2**
(Brain 2) Att: 34,160
Lewis, Baker, Kennedy, Milne, Butler, John, Hoar, Brain, Woods, Ramsay, Toner.

1925/26

LEAGUE DIVISION ONE

Final position – 2nd

Aug 29 **Tottenham Hotspur** **0–1**
Att: 53,183
Robson, Mackie, Kennedy, Milne, Butler, John, Hoar, Buchan, Cock, Ramsay, Toner.

Aug 31 **Leicester City** **2–2**
(Neil, Brain) Att: 23,823
Robson, Mackie, Kennedy, Milne, Butler, John, Hoar, Buchan, Brain, Neil, Toner.

Sep 12 **Liverpool** **1–1**
(Buchan) Att: 32,533
Robson, Mackie, Kennedy, Milne, Butler, Blyth, Hoar, Buchan, Brain, Neil, Haden.

Sep 21 **West Ham United** **3–2**
(Buchan 2, Neil) Att: 24,800
Robson, Mackie, Kennedy, Baker, Butler, Blyth, Hoar, Buchan, Brain, Neil, Haden.

Sep 26 **Leeds United** **4–1**
(Brain 2, Buchan, Neil) Att: 32,531
Lewis, Mackie, Kennedy, Baker, Butler, Blyth, Hoar, Buchan, Brain, Neil, Haden.

Oct 10 **Bolton Wanderers** **2–3**
(Buchan, Baker) Att: 41,076
Lewis, Mackie, Kennedy, Baker, Butler, Blyth, Hoar, Buchan, Brain, Neil, Haden.

Oct 17 **Cardiff City** **5–0**
(Brain 3, Neil, Blyth) Att: 38,130
Lewis, Mackie, Kennedy, Baker, Butler, Blyth, Hoar, Buchan, Brain, Neil, Haden.

Oct 31 **Everton** **4–1**
(Brain 3, Hoar) Att: 24,926
Robson, Mackie, John, Baker, Butler, Blyth, Hoar, Buchan, Brain, Neil, Haden.

Nov 14 **Bury** **6–1**
(Brain 3, Buchan 2, Baker) Att: 22,566
Harper, Mackie, John, Baker, Butler, Blyth, JJ Rutherford, Buchan, Brain, Neil, Haden.

Nov 28 **Sunderland** **2–0**
(Buchan, Brain) Att: 44,870
Harper, Mackie, John, Baker, Butler, Blyth, Hoar, Buchan, Brain, Neil, Haden.

Dec 12 **West Bromwich Albion** **1–0**
(Blyth) Att: 34,178
Harper, Mackie, John, Baker, Butler, Blyth, Hoar, Buchan, Brain, Neil, Haden.

Dec 25 **Notts County** **3–0**
(Neil, Buchan, Hoar) Att: 33,398
Harper, Mackie, John, Baker, Butler, Blyth, Hoar, Buchan, Brain, Neil, Haden.

Jan 16 **Manchester United** **3–2**
(Brain 2, Buchan) Att: 25,252
Harper, Mackie, John, Baker, Butler, Blyth, Rutherford (J), Buchan, Brain, Neil, Haden.

Feb 3 **Burnley** **1–2**
(Buchan) Att: 14,800
Harper, Mackie, John, Baker, Butler, Blyth, Lawson, Buchan, Brain, Neil, Haden.

Feb 13 **Newcastle United** **3–0**
(Buchan, Blyth, Paterson) Att: 48,346
Harper, Mackie, John, Baker, Young, Blyth, Hulme, Buchan, Brain, Ramsay, Paterson.

Mar 17 **Sheffield United** **4–0**
(Brain 2, Buchan, Blyth) Att: 15,609
Harper, Mackie, John, Baker, Butler, Blyth, Hulme, Buchan, Brain, Ramsay, Lawson.

Mar 20 **Manchester City** **1–0**
(Blyth) Att: 34,974
Harper, Mackie, John, Baker, Butler, Blyth, Hulme, Buchan, Brain, Ramsay, Rutherford (J).

Apr 3 **Blackburn Rovers** **4–2**
(Baker, Blyth, Lawson, Buchan) Att: 31,031
Lewis, Parker, Mackie, Baker, Butler, Blyth, Lawson, Buchan, Brain, Ramsay, Hulme.

Apr 5 **Aston Villa** **2–0**
(Brain 2) Att: 25,990
Lewis, Parker, Mackie, Baker, Butler, Blyth, Lawson, Buchan, Brain, Ramsay, Hulme.

Apr 17 **Huddersfield Town** **3–1**
(Lawson, Hulme, Parker [pen]) Att: 34,110
Lewis, Parker, John, Young, Butler, Blyth, Lawson, Buchan, Brain, Ramsay, Hulme.

May 1 **Birmingham** **3–0**
(Brain 2, Parker [pen]) Att: 22,240
Lewis, Parker, John, Young, Butler, Blyth, Lawson, Buchan, Brain, Ramsay, Hulme.

FA CUP

Jan 13 **Wolverhampton Wanderers** **1–0**
(Baker) Att: 42,823
Harper, Mackie, John, Baker, Butler, Blyth, Woods, Buchan, Brain, Neil, Haden.

Jan 30 **Blackburn Rovers** **3–1**
(Haden, Brain, Hope [og]) Att: 44,836
Harper, Mackie, John, Baker, Butler, Blyth, Rutherford (J), Buchan, Brain, Neil, Haden.

Feb 24 **Aston Villa** **2–0**
(Paterson, Brain) Att: 71,446
Harper, Mackie, John, Baker, Butler, Blyth, Lawson, Buchan, Brain, Ramsay, Paterson.

1926/27

LEAGUE DIVISION ONE

Final position – 11th

Aug 28 **Derby County** **2–1**
(Parker [pen], Buchan) Att: 32,990
Harper, Parker, John, Baker, Butler, Blyth, Hulme, Buchan, Brain, Ramsay, Haden.

Sep 1 **Bolton Wanderers** **2–1**
(Hulme 2) Att: 23,002
Harper, Parker, John, Baker, Butler, Blyth, Hulme, Buchan, Brain, Ramsay, Haden.

Sep 11 **Leicester City** **2–2**
(Brain, Hulme) Att: 30,800
Harper, Parker, John, Baker, Butler, Blyth, Hulme, Buchan, Brain, Lambert, Lee.

Sep 18 **Liverpool** **2–0**
(Brain, Hoar) Att: 35,497
Harper, Parker, Kennedy, Baker, Butler, John, Hulme, Lambert, Brain, Buchan, Hoar.

Oct 2 **Newcastle United** **2–2**
(Buchan, Parker [pen]) Att: 38,842
Harper, Parker, John, Baker, Butler, Blyth, Hulme, Buchan, Brain, Lambert, Lee.

Oct 16 **West Ham United** **2–2**
(Lambert, Brain) Att: 35,534
Harper, Parker, John, Young, Butler, Blyth, Hulme, Buchan, Brain, Lambert, Haden.

Oct 23 **Sheffield Wednesday** **6–2**
(Brain 4, Haden 2) Att: 27,846
Harper, Parker, John, Young, Butler, Blyth, Hulme, Buchan, Brain, Lambert, Haden.

Nov 6 **Blackburn Rovers** **2–2**
(Brain, Buchan) Att: 29,439
Harper, Parker, John, Seddon, Butler, Blyth, Hulme, Buchan, Brain, Ramsay, Haden.

Nov 20 **Sunderland** **2–3**
(Buchan, Ramsay) Att: 20,087
Harper, Parker, John, Seddon, Butler, Blyth, Hulme, Brain, Buchan, Ramsay, Haden.

Dec 4 **Bury** **1–0**
(Brain) Att: 30,375
Harper, Parker, John, Seddon, Young, Blyth, Hulme, Brain, Buchan, Lambert, Haden.

Dec 18 **Tottenham Hotspur** **2–4**
(Butler, Brain) Att: 49,429
Harper, Parker, John, Seddon, Butler, Blyth, Hulme, Brain, Buchan, Ramsay, Haden.

Dec 28 **Manchester United** **1–0**
(Blyth) Att: 30,111
Lewis, Parker, Cope, Milne, Baker, John, Hulme, Buchan, Brain, Blyth, Hoar.

Jan 1 **Cardiff City** **3–2**
(Brain 3) Att: 30,000
Lewis, Parker, Cope, Milne, Baker, John, Hulme, Buchan, Brain, Blyth, Hoar.

Jan22 **Sheffield United** **1–1**
(Buchan) Att: 16,831
Lewis, Parker, Cope, Milne, Butler, John, Hulme, Buchan, Brain, Blyth, Hoar.

Feb 12 **Leeds United** **1–0**
(Buchan) Att: 25,961
Harper, Parker, Cope, Milne, Baker, Barley, Hulme, Buchan, Brain, Blyth, Hoar.

Feb 26 **Burnley** **6–2**
(Brain 4, Hoar, Buchan) Att: 29,070
Lewis, Parker, Cope, Baker, Seddon, John, Hulme, Buchan, Brain, Blyth, Hoar.

Mar 19 **Everton** **1–2**
(Buchan) Att: 33,788
Harper, Parker, Cope, Baker, Seddon, John, Hulme, Tricker, Buchan, Blyth, Hoar.

Apr 2 **Huddersfield Town** **0–2**
Att: 24,409
Lewis, Parker, Cope, Milne, Butler, John, Haden, Buchan, Brain, Blyth, Hoar.

Apr 15 **Aston Villa** **2–1**
(Brain 2) Att: 38,096
Lewis, Parker, Kennedy, Baker, Seddon, John, Hoar, Buchan, Brain, Blyth, Peel.

Apr 16 **West Bromwich Albion** **4–1**
(Brain, Parker [pen], Buchan 2) Att: 24,506
Lewis, Parker, Kennedy, Blyth, Seddon, John, Haden, Buchan, Brain, Shaw, Peel.

Apr 30 **Birmingham** **3–0**
(Tricker, John, Brain) Att: 22,619
Harper, Parker, Kennedy, Baker, Butler, John, Hulme, Tricker, Brain, Peel, Haden.

FA CUP

Finalists

Feb 2 **Port Vale** **1–0**
(Buchan) Att: 35,781
Lewis, Parker, Cope, Baker, Butler, John, Hulme, Buchan, Brain, Blyth, Hoar.

Feb 19 **Liverpool** **2–0**
(Brain, Buchan) Att 43,000
Harper, Parker, Cope, Baker, Butler, John, Hulme, Buchan, Brain, Blyth, Hoar.

Mar 5 **Wolverhampton Wanderers** **2–1**
(Blyth, Butler) Att: 52,821
Lewis, Parker, John, Baker, Butler, Barley, Hulme, Buchan, Brain, Blyth, Hoar.

1927/28

LEAGUE DIVISION ONE

Final position – 10th

Aug 31 **Burnley** **4–1**
(Brain 2, Buchan, Blyth) Att: 19,910
Lewis, Parker, Cope, Baker, Butler, John, Hulme, Buchan, Brain, Blyth, Hoar.

Sep 3 **Sheffield United** **6–1**
(Blyth, Buchan 2, Hulme, Brain, Parker [pen])
Att: 30,910
Lewis, Parker, Cope, Baker, Butler, John, Hulme, Buchan, Brain, Blyth, Hoar.

Sep 17 **Sunderland** **2–1**
(Baker, Brain) Att: 45,501
Lewis, Parker, Cope, Baker, Butler, John, Hulme, Buchan, Brain, Blyth, Hoar.

Oct 1 **West Ham United** **2–2**
(Brain 2) Att: 34,931
Moody, Parker, Cope, Baker, Butler, John, Hulme, Buchan, Brain, Blyth, Hoar.

Oct 15 **Leicester City** **2–2**
(Brain, Hoar) Att: 36,640
Lewis, Parker, Cope, Baker, Butler, John, Hulme, Buchan, Brain, Blyth, Hoar.

Oct 29 **Bolton Wanderers** **1–2**
(Buchan) Att: 35,787
Lewis, Parker, Cope, Seddon, Butler, John, Hulme, Buchan, Brain, Blyth, Hoar.

Nov 12 **Middlesbrough** **3–1**
(Buchan 2, Hulme) Att: 25,921
Lewis, Parker, Cope, Roberts, Butler, John, Hulme, Tricker, Buchan, Brain, Hoar.

Dec 10 **Newcastle United** **4–1**
(Hoar, Hulme, Brain, Parker [pen]) Att: 42,630
Lewis, Parker, Cope, Baker, Butler, John, Hulme, Buchan, Brain, Blyth, Hoar.

Dec 24 **Everton** **3–2**
(Hulme, Buchan, Blyth) Att: 27,995
Lewis, Parker, Cope, Baker, Butler, John, Hulme, Buchan, Brain, Blyth, Hoar.

Dec 31 **Bury** **3–1**
(Lambert, John, Parker [pen]) Att: 20,742
Lewis, Parker, Cope, Baker, Butler, John, Hoar, Lambert, Brain, Blyth, Peel.

Jan 2 **Tottenham Hotspur** **1–1**
(Hoar) Att: 13,518
Moody, Parker, Hapgood, Baker, Butler, John, Hulme, Buchan, Brain, Blyth, Hoar.

Jan 21 **Aston Villa** **0–3**
Att: 32,505
Lewis, Parker, Cope, Baker, Butler, John, Hulme, Blyth, Brain, Barley, Hoar.

Feb 4 **Derby County** **3–4**
(Brain 3) Att: 21,405
Paterson, Parker, Cope, Baker, Butler, Seddon, Hulme, Buchan, Brain, Blyth, Hoar.

Mar 7 **Liverpool** **6–3**
(Brain 3, Hulme, Buchan, Lambert) Att: 14,037
Lewis, Parker, John, Baker, Butler, Blyth, Hulme, Buchan, Brain, Lambert, Peel.

Mar 17 **Blackburn Rovers** **3–2**
(Hoar, Buchan 2) Att: 33,446
Paterson, Parker, John, Baker, Butler, Blyth, Hulme, Buchan, Brain, Lambert, Hoar.

Mar 28 **Portsmouth** **0–2**
Att: 15,416
Lewis, Parker, Cope, Baker, Butler, Blyth, Hoar, Lambert, Buchan, Thompson, Peel.

Mar 31 **Birmingham** **2–2**
(Buchan 2) Att: 13,990
Lewis, Parker, Cope, Baker, Butler, Blyth, Hoar, Buchan, Brain, Lambert, John.

Apr 6 **Cardiff City** **3–0**
(Brain, Buchan, Hulme) Att: 36,828
Lewis, Parker, John, Baker, Butler, Blyth, Hulme, Buchan, Brain, Lambert, Hoar.

Apr 14 **Huddersfield Town** **0–0**
Att: 38,707
Lewis, Parker, John, Baker, Butler, Blyth, Hulme, Buchan, Brain, Tricker, Hoar.

Apr 28 **Manchester United** **0–1**
Att: 22,452
Lewis, Parker, John, Baker, Butler, Blyth, Hulme, Shaw, Brain, Peel, Hoar.

May 2 **Sheffield Wednesday** **1–1**
(Brain) Att: 15,818
Lewis, Parker, John, Baker, Butler, Blyth, Hulme, Shaw, Brain, Lambert, Peel.

FA CUP

Jan 14 **West Bromwich Albion** **2–0**
(Brain, Hulme) Att: 43,322
Lewis, Parker, Cope, Baker, Butler, John, Hulme, Buchan, Brain, Blyth, Hoar.

Jan 28 **Everton** **4–3**
(Brain, Hulme 2, Buchan) Att: 44,328
Lewis, Parker, Cope, Baker, Butler, John, Hulme, Buchan, Brain, Blyth, Hoar.

Feb 18 **Aston Villa** **4–1**
(Lambert, Brain 2, Hulme) Att: 58,505
Lewis, Parker, Cope, Blyth, Butler, John, Hulme, Buchan, Brain, Lambert, Hoar.

Mar 3 **Stoke City** **4–1**
(Hoar 2, Blyth 2) Att: 41,974
Lewis, Parker, Cope, Baker, Butler, John, Hulme, Buchan, Brain, Blyth, Hoar.

1928/29

LEAGUE DIVISION ONE
Final position – 9th

Aug 29 **Derby County** **1–3**
(Blyth) Att: 20,064
Lewis, Parker, Cope, Baker, Butler, John, Hulme, Blyth, Brain, Thompson, Jones (C).

Sep 1 **Bolton Wanderers** **2–0**
(Brain, Peel) Att: 35,124
Paterson, Parker, Cope, Baker, Butler, John, Hulme, Peel, Brain, Jones, Hoar.

Sep 15 **Birmingham** **0–0**
Att: 30,118
Paterson, Parker, John, Baker, Butler, Blyth, Hulme, Jones, Brain, Lambert, Peel.

Sep 29 **Huddersfield Town** **2–0**
(John, Lambert) Att: 39,938
Lewis, Parker, Cope, Baker, Roberts, John, Hulme, Brain, Lambert, Thompson, Hoar.

Oct 13 **West Ham United** **2–3**
(Jones 2) Att: 43,327
Lewis, Parker, Cope, Baker, Roberts, John, Hulme, Brain, Lambert, Thompson, Jones.

Oct 27 **Liverpool** **4–4**
(Davidson [og], Thompson 2 [2 pens], Brain)
Att: 33,782
Lewis, Parker, Cope, Baker, Roberts, Blyth, Hulme, Jack, Brain, Thompson, Jones.

Nov 10 **Sheffield United** **2–0**
(Hulme, Jack) Att: 28,560
Lewis, Parker, Cope, Blyth, Butler, Barley, Hulme, Jack, Brain, Thompson, Jones.

Nov 24 **Aston Villa** **2–5**
(Jack 2) Att: 30,491
Lewis, Parker, Cope, Blyth, Butler, John, Hulme, Jack, Lambert, Thompson, Jones.

Dec 8 **Manchester United** **3–1**
(Jack 2, Brain) Att: 18, 923
Lewis, Parker, Cope, Blyth, Butler, John, Hulme, Jack, Brain, Peel, Jones.

Dec 22 **Burnley** **3–1**
(Hulme, Peel, Brain) Att: 14,990
Lewis, Parker, Cope, Blyth, Butler, John, Hulme, Jack, Brain, Peel, Jones.

Dec 26 **Sunderland** **1–1**
(Peel) Att: 15,747
Lewis, Parker, Cope, Baker, Butler, Blyth, Hulme, Jack, Brain, Peel, Jones.

Dec 29 **Sheffield Wednesday** **2–2**
(Brain, Hulme) Att: 39,255
Lewis, Parker, Cope, Baker, Butler, Blyth, Hulme, Jack, Brain, Peel, Jones.

Jan 19 **Portsmouth** **4–0**
(Jack 2, Peel, Brain) Att: 32,224
Lewis, Parker, Hapgood, Baker, Butler, John, Hulme, Jack, Brain, Peel, Jones.

Feb 2 **Manchester City** **0–0**
Att: 13,764
Lewis, Parker, Hapgood, Baker, Roberts, John, Hulme, Jack, Brain, Peel, Jones.

Mar 16 **Cardiff City** **2–1**
(Brain, Jack) Att: 28,393
Lewis, Parker, Hapgood, Baker, Roberts, John, Hulme, Brain, Jack, Peel, Jones.

Mar 29 **Blackburn Rovers** **1–0**
(Brain) Att: 39,038
Lewis, Parker, Hapgood, Blyth, Roberts, John, Hulme, Brain, Jack, Peel, Jones.

Mar 30 **Bury** **7–1**
(Jack 4, Parkin 2, Thompson) Att: 22,577
Lewis, Parker, Hapgood, Baker, Roberts, John, Hulme, Parkin, Jack, Thompson, Jones.

Apr 2 **Newcastle United** **1–2**
(Jack) Att: 21,699
Lewis, Parker, Hapgood, Baker, Roberts, John, Hulme, Parkin, Jack, Thompson, Jones.

Apr 13 **Leicester City** **1–1**
(Parker [pen]) Att: 19,139
Paterson, Parker, Hapgood, Baker, Roberts, John, Hulme, Brain, Jack, Peel, Jones.

Apr 22 **Everton** **2–0**
(Jack, Parker [pen]) Att: 11,696
Paterson, Parker, Hapgood, Baker, Butler, John, Hulme, Brain, Jack, Peel, Jones.

Apr 27 **Leeds United** **1–0**
(Peel) Att: 21,465
Paterson, Parker, Hapgood, Baker, Butler, John, Hulme, Brain, Jack, Peel, Jones.

FA CUP

Jan 12 **Stoke City** **2–1**
(Brain, Hulme) Att: 30,762
Lewis, Parker, Cope, Baker, Roberts, Barley, Hulme, Jack, Brain, Peel, Jones.

Jan 26 **Mansfield Town** **2–0**
(Peel, Jack) Att: 44,493
Lewis, Parker, Hapgood, Baker, Butler, Blyth, Hulme, Jack, Brain, Peel, Jones.

Feb 20 **Swindon Town** **1–0**
(Brain) Att: 44,582
Lewis, Parker, Hapgood, Baker, Roberts, John, Hulme, Jack, Brain, Peel, Maycock.

1929/30

LEAGUE DIVISION ONE
Final position – 14th

Aug 31 **Leeds United** **4–0**
(Jack 2, Hulme, Parker [pen]) Att: 41,885
Lewis, Parker, Hapgood, Baker, Roberts, John, Hulme, Brain, Jack, James, Jones.

Sep 11 **Manchester City** **3–2**
(Johnstone, Jack 2) Att: 23,057
Preedy, Parker, Hapgood, Seddon, Roberts, John, Hulme, Jack, Johnstone, Thompson, Jones.

Sep 14 **Burnley** **6–1**
(Hulme, Lambert 2, Jack, James, Waterfield [og]) Att: 38,556
Preedy, Parker, Hapgood, Seddon, Roberts, John, Hulme, Jack, Lambert, James, Jones.

Sep 28 **Bolton Wanderers** **1–2**
(Jones) Att: 42,723
Lewis, Parker, Hapgood, Seddon, Roberts, Baker, Hulme, Jack, Brain, James, Jones.

Oct 12 **Derby County** **1–1**
(Parker [pen]) Att: 42,448
Lewis, Parker, Hapgood, Seddon, Roberts, John, Hulme, Bastin, Jack, James, Jones.

Oct 19 **Grimsby Town** **4–1**
(Lambert 3, Hulme) Att: 43,794
Lewis, Parker, Hapgood, Seddon, Roberts, John, Hulme, Jack, Lambert, James, Jones.

Nov 2 **West Ham United** **0–1**
Att: 44,828
Lewis, Parker, Hapgood, Baker, Roberts, John, Hulme, Brain, Lambert, James, Jones.

Nov 27 **Middlesbrough** **1–2**
(Jack) Att: 28,326
Preedy, Parker, Hapgood, Baker, Roberts, John, Hulme, Jack, Halliday, James, Jones.

Nov 30 **Newcastle United** **0–1**
Att: 40,365
Lewis, Parker, Hapgood, Baker, Roberts, John, Hulme, Jack, Halliday, James, Jones.

Dec 14 **Huddersfield Town** **2–0**
(Jack, Hulme) Att: 34,097
Lewis, Parker, Hapgood, Seddon, Roberts, John, Hulme, Jack, Halliday, James, Jones.

Dec 26 **Portsmouth** **1–2**
(Hulme) Att: 49,433
Lewis, Parker, Hapgood, Haynes, Butler, John, Hulme, Jack, Halliday, James, Bastin.

Jan 4 **Sheffield Wednesday** **2–3**
(Parker, Bastin) Att: 40,766
Lewis, Parker, Hapgood, Baker, Roberts, Haynes, Hulme, James, Jack, Jones, Bastin.

Feb 8 **Everton** **4–0**
(Lambert 3, Williams) Att: 27,302
Lewis, Parker, Hapgood, Baker, Roberts, John, Williams, Jack, Lambert, James, Bastin.

Mar 12 **Manchester United** **4–2**
(Bastin, Williams, Lambert, Hulme) Att: 18,082
Lewis, Parker, John, Baker, Seddon, Jones, Hulme, Bastin, Lambert, James, Williams.

Mar 15 **Birmingham** **1–0**
(James) Att: 32,174
Lewis, Parker, Hapgood, Baker, Seddon, Jones, Hulme, Jack, Lambert, James, Williams.

Mar 29 **Blackburn Rovers** **4–0**
(Williams, Hulme, Lambert 2) Att: 40,459
Lewis, Parker, Hapgood, Haynes, Seddon, John, Hulme, Bastin, Lambert, James, Williams.

Apr 2 **Liverpool** **0–1**
Att: 18,824
Lewis, Parker, Hapgood, Haynes, Seddon, John, Hulme, Bastin, Lambert, Jones, Williams.

Apr 12 **Sheffield United** **8–1**
(Hulme, Johnstone 2, Bastin, Lambert 3, James)
Att: 24,217
Preedy, Parker, Hapgood, Haynes, Seddon, John, Hulme, Johnstone, Lambert, James, Bastin.

Apr 18 **Leicester City** **1–1**
(James) Att: 46,663
Preedy, Parker, Hapgood, Baker, Seddon, John, Hulme, Jack, Lambert, James, Jones.

Apr 28 **Sunderland** **0–1**
Att: 31,250
Preedy, Parker, Hapgood, Baker, Seddon, John, Hulme, Jack, Lambert, James, Bastin.

May 3 **Aston Villa** **2–4**
(Lambert 2) Att: 37,020
Preedy, Parker, Hapgood, Haynes, Seddon, John, Hulme, Jack, Lambert, James, Bastin.

FA CUP
Winners

Jan 11 **Chelsea** **2–0**
(Lambert, Bastin) Att: 55,579
Lewis, Parker, Hapgood, Haynes, Roberts, John, Hulme, Jack, Lambert, Thompson, Bastin.

Jan 25 **Birmingham** **2–2**
(Jack, Bastin) Att: 43,274
Preedy, Parker, Hapgood, Baker, Roberts, John, Hulme, Jack, Lambert, Jones, Bastin.

1930/31

LEAGUE DIVISION ONE
Final position – Champions

Sep 6 **Leeds United** **3–1**
(Lambert 2, Jack) Att: 40,828
Keizer, Parker, Hapgood, Jones, Roberts, John, Hulme, Jack, Lambert, James, Bastin.

Sep 10 **Blackburn Rovers** **3–2**
(Bastin 2, Johnstone) Att: 20,863
Keizer, Parker, Hapgood, Jones, Roberts, John, Hulme, Jack, Lambert, Johnstone, Bastin.

Sep 20 **Leicester City** **4–1**
(Hulme, Lambert 2, Bastin) Att: 37,851
Keizer, Parker, Hapgood, Seddon, Roberts, John, Hulme, Brain, Lambert, James, Bastin.

Oct 4 **Sheffield United** **1–1**
(Lambert) Att: 47,113
Keizer, Parker, Hapgood, Seddon, Roberts, John, Hulme, Brain, Lambert, James, Bastin.

Oct 25 **West Ham United** **1–1**
(Bastin) Att: 51,918
Keizer, Parker, Hapgood, Seddon, Roberts, John, Williams, Brain, Lambert, James, Bastin.

Nov 8 **Aston Villa** **5–2**
(Bastin 2, Lambert, Jack 2) Att: 56,417
Preedy, Parker, Hapgood, Seddon, Roberts, John, Williams, Jack, Lambert, James, Bastin.

Nov 22 **Middlesbrough** **5–3**
(Lambert 3, Bastin 2 [1 pen]) Att: 32,517
Harper, Parker, Hapgood, Seddon, Roberts, John, Williams, Jack, Lambert, James, Bastin.

Dec 20 **Newcastle United** **1–2**
(Jack) Att: 32,212
Harper, Parker, Hapgood, Seddon, Roberts, John, Williams, Jack, Lambert, James, Bastin.

Dec 26 **Manchester City** **3–1**
(Bastin, John, Hulme) Att: 17,624
Harper, Parker, Hapgood, Jones, Roberts, John, Hulme, Jack, Lambert, James, Bastin.

Dec 27 **Blackpool** **7–1**
(Brain 3, Jack 3, Bastin) Att: 35,113
Harper, Parker, John, Jones, Roberts, Male, Hulme, Brain, Jack, James, Bastin.

Jan 17 **Sunderland** **1–3**
(James) Att: 35,975
Harper, Parker, Hapgood, Seddon, Roberts, John, Hulme, Brain, Jack, James, Bastin.

Jan 28 **Grimsby Town** **9–1**
(Jack 4, Lambert 3, Bastin, Hulme) Att: 15,751
Preedy, Parker, Hapgood, Jones, Roberts, John, Hulme, Jack, Lambert, James, Bastin.

Jan 31 **Birmingham** **1–1**
(Lambert) Att: 30,913
Preedy, Parker, Hapgood, Jones, Roberts, John, Hulme, Jack, Lambert, James, Bastin.

Feb 14 **Derby County** **6–3**
(Bastin 3 [1 pen], Hulme, James, Jack)
Att: 34,785
Preedy, Cope, Hapgood, Jones, Roberts, John, Hulme, Brain, Jack, James, Bastin.

Feb 21 **Manchester United** **4–1**
(Hulme, Jack, Brain, Bastin) Att: 41,510
Preedy, Parker, Hapgood, Jones, Roberts, John, Hulme, Brain, Jack, James, Bastin.

Mar 7 **Huddersfield Town** **0–0**
Att: 31,058
Preedy, Parker, Baker, Jones, Roberts, Male, Hulme, Brain, Jack, James, Bastin.

Mar 21 **Sheffield Wednesday** **2–0**
(Jack, Bastin) Att: 47,872
Harper, Parker, Hapgood, Jones, Roberts, John, Jack, Brain, Lambert, James, Bastin.

Apr 4 **Chelsea** **2–1**
(Hulme, Bastin) Att: 53,867
Harper, Parker, Hapgood, Jones, Roberts, John, Hulme, Jack, Lambert, James, Bastin.

Apr 6 **Portsmouth** **1–1**
(James) Att: 40,490
Harper, Parker, Hapgood, Jones, Roberts, John, Hulme, Jack, Lambert, James, Bastin.

Apr 18 **Liverpool** **3–1**
(Jack, Bastin, Lambert) Att: 39,143
Harper, Parker, Hapgood, Jones, Roberts, John, Hulme, Jack, Lambert, James, Bastin.

May 2 **Bolton Wanderers** **5–0**
(Jack 2, Lambert 2, James) Att: 35,406
Harper, Parker, Hapgood, Jones, Roberts, John, Hulme, Jack, Lambert, James, Bastin.

FA CUP

Jan 10 **Aston Villa** **2–2**
(Lambert, Jack) Att: 40,864
Harper, Parker, Hapgood, Seddon, Roberts, John, Hulme, Jack, Lambert, James, Bastin.

1931/32

LEAGUE DIVISION ONE
Final position – 2nd

Aug 29 **West Bromwich Albion** **0–1**
Att: 52,478
Harper, Parker, Hapgood, Jones, Roberts, John, Hulme, Jack, Lambert, James, Bastin.

Sep 9 **Portsmouth** **3–3**
(Lambert 2, Bastin) Att: 25,403
Preedy, Parker, Hapgood, Jones, Roberts, John, Hulme, Jack, Lambert, James, Bastin.

Sep 12 **Sunderland** **2–0**
(Hulme 2) Att: 22,926
Preedy, Parker, Hapgood, Jones, Roberts, John, Hulme, Parkin, Lambert, James, Bastin.

Sep 26 **Everton** 3–2
(Hulme, Jack, Lambert) Att: 47,637
Preedy, Parker, Hapgood, Jones, Roberts, John, Hulme, Jack, Lambert, James, Bastin.

Oct 17 **Bolton Wanderers** 1–1
(Hulme) Att: 42,141
Preedy, Parker, Hapgood, Jones, Roberts, John, Hulme, Jack, Lambert, James, Bastin.

Oct 31 **Aston Villa** 1–1
(Jack) Att: 54,951
Preedy, Parker, Hapgood, Seddon, Roberts, John, Hulme, Jack, Lambert, James, Bastin.

Nov 14 **West Ham United** 4–1
(Hulme, Jack 3) Att: 41,028
Preedy, Parker, Hapgood, Jones, Haynes, Male, Hulme, Jack, Lambert, James, Bastin.

Nov 28 **Liverpool** 6–0
(Jack 2, Lambert 3, Hulme) Att: 29,220
Moss, Parker, Hapgood, Jones, Roberts, John, Hulme, Jack, Lambert, James, Bastin.

Dec 12 **Huddersfield Town** 1–1
(Jack) Att: 39,748
Moss, Parker, Hapgood, Jones, Roberts, John, Hulme, Jack, Lambert, James, Bastin.

Dec 26 **Sheffield United** 0–2
Att: 55,207
Moss, Parker, Cope, Seddon, Roberts, John, Hulme, Jack, Bastin, James, Williams.

Jan 16 **Birmingham** 3–0
(Hulme, Bastin, Booton [og]) Att: 37,843
Moss, Parker, Hapgood, Haynes, Roberts, John, Hulme, Jack, Lambert, James, Bastin.

Jan 30 **Manchester City** 4–0
(Parkin 3, James) Att: 39,834
Moss, Parker, Hapgood, Jones, Roberts, John, Hulme, Jack, Parkin, James, Bastin.

Feb 17 **Grimsby Town** 4–0
(Bastin, Jack, Parkin, James) Att: 20,980
Moss, Parker, Hapgood, Jones, Roberts, John, Hulme, Jack, Parkin, James, Bastin.

Feb 20 **Blackpool** 2–0
(Jack, Parkin) Att: 39,045
Moss, Parker, Hapgood, Jones, Roberts, John, Hulme, Jack, Parkin, James, Bastin.

Mar 5 **Leicester City** 2–1
(Hulme, Bastin [pen]) Att: 53,920
Moss, Parker, Hapgood, Jones, Roberts, John, Hulme, Jack, Coleman, James, Bastin.

Mar19 **Newcastle United** 1–0
(Hulme) Att: 57,516
Moss, Parker, Hapgood, Jones, Roberts, John, Hulme, Coleman, Lambert, James, Bastin.

Mar 25 **Derby County** 2–1
(Lambert 2) Att: 56,435
Moss, Parker, Hapgood, Jones, Roberts, John, Hulme, Jack, Lambert, James, Bastin.

Apr 2 **Chelsea** 1–1
(Lambert) Att: 56,124
Moss, Parker, Hapgood, Jones, Roberts, Male, Hulme, Jack, Lambert, John, Bastin.

Apr 16 **Sheffield Wednesday** 3–1
(Jack, John 2) Att: 25,220
Moss, Parker, Hapgood, Jones, Roberts, Male, Hulme, Jack, Lambert, Bastin, John.

Apr 30 **Middlesbrough** 5–0
(Bastin 2, Lambert 2, Webster [og]) Att: 30,714
Moss, Compton (L), Hapgood, Male, Haynes, John, Hulme, Stockill, Lambert, Jones, Bastin.

May 7 **Blackburn Rovers** 4–0
(Stockill, Lambert 2, Hutton [og]) Att: 23,127
Moss, Compton (L), Hapgood, Male, Haynes, John, Hulme, Stockill, Lambert, Jones, Bastin.

FA CUP
Finalists

Jan 9 **Darwen** 11–1
(Hulme 2, Jack 3, Lambert 2, Bastin 4) Att:37,486
Moss, Parker, Hapgood, Jones, Roberts, John, Hulme, Jack, Lambert, James, Bastin.

Jan 23 **Plymouth Argyle** 4–2
(Lambert 2, Hulme, Roberts [og]) Att: 65,386
Moss, Parker, Hapgood, Jones, Roberts, John, Hulme, Jack, Lambert, James, Bastin.

1932/33

LEAGUE DIVISION ONE
Final position – Champions

Aug 31 **West Bromwich Albion** 1–2
(Stockill) Att: 37,748
Moss, Compton (L), Hapgood, Male, Roberts, John, Hulme, Jack, Stockill, James, Bastin.

Sep 3 **Sunderland** 6–1
(Hulme 3, Coleman, Jack, Bastin) Att: 28,896
Moss, Compton (L), Hapgood, Jones, Haynes, John, Hulme, Jack, Coleman, James, Bastin.

Sep 17 **Bolton Wanderers** 3–2
(Hulme, Coleman, Bastin) Att: 42,395
Moss, Parker, Hapgood, Jones, Haynes, John, Hulme, Jack, Coleman, James, Bastin.

Sep 24 **Everton** 2–1
(Coleman, Jack) Att: 51,182
Moss, Parker, Hapgood, Jones, Roberts, John, Hulme, Jack, Coleman, James, Bastin.

Oct 8 **Derby County** 3–3
(Coleman 2, Hulme) Att: 32,055
Moss, Parker, Hapgood, Jones, Roberts, John, Hulme, Jack, Coleman, James, Bastin.

Oct 29 **Leicester City** 8–2
*(Coleman 2, Jack, Hulme 3, Bastin 2)*Att: 36,714
Moss, Male, Hapgood, Hill, Roberts, John, Hulme, Jack, Coleman, James, Bastin.

Nov 12 **Newcastle United** 1–0
(Hulme) Att: 56,498
Moss, Male, Hapgood, Hill, Roberts, John, Hulme, Jack, Coleman, James, Bastin.

Nov 26 **Middlesbrough** 4–2
(Coleman 2, Hulme, Jack,) Att: 34,640
Moss, Male, Hapgood, Hill, Roberts, John, Hulme, Jack, Coleman, Parkin, Bastin.

Dec 10 **Chelsea** 4–1
(Bastin 2, Hulme, Coleman) Att: 53,206
Moss, Male, Hapgood, Hill, Roberts, John, Hulme, Jack, Coleman, James, Bastin.

Dec 24 **Sheffield United** 9–2
(Bastin 3, Jack, Lambert 5) Att: 41,520
Moss, Male, Hapgood, Hill, Roberts, John, Hulme, Jack, Lambert, James, Bastin.

Dec 26 **Leeds United** 1–2
(Hulme) Att: 55,876
Moss, Male, Hapgood, Hill, Roberts, John, Hulme, Jack, Lambert, James, Bastin.

Dec 31 **Birmingham** 3–0
(James, Jack, Bastin) Att: 37,800
Moss, Male, Hapgood, Hill, Roberts, John, Hulme, Jack, Coleman, James, Bastin.

Jan 21 **Manchester City** 2–1
(Bastin 2) Att: 32,456
Moss, Male, Cope, Hill, Roberts, Sidey, Hulme, Jack, Coleman, James, Bastin.

Feb 11 **Blackpool** 1–1
(Coleman) Att: 35,180
Moss, Male, Cope, Parkin, Roberts, John, Hulme, Jack, Coleman, James, Bastin.

Feb 25 **Blackburn Rovers** 8–0
(Stockill, Coleman 3, Bastin 2, Hulme 2) Att: 27,576
Moss, Male, Hapgood, Jones, Roberts, John, Hulme, Stockill, Coleman, James, Bastin.

Mar 4 **Liverpool** 0–1
Att: 42,868
Moss, Male, Hapgood, Jones, Roberts, John, Hulme, Jack, Coleman, James, Bastin.

Mar 18 **Wolverhampton Wanderers** 1–2
(Bowden) Att: 44,711
Moss, Male, Hapgood, Jones, Roberts, John, Hulme, Bowden, Coleman, James, Bastin.

Apr 1 **Aston Villa** 5–0
(Jack, Lambert 2, Bowden, James) Att: 54,265
Moss, Male, Hapgood, Hill, Roberts, John, Jack, Bowden, Lambert, James, Bastin.

Apr 14 **Sheffield Wednesday** 4–2
(Lambert, Hulme 2, Bastin) Att: 61,945
Moss, Male, Hapgood, Hill, Roberts, John, Hulme, Bowden, Lambert, James, Bastin.

Apr 15 **Portsmouth** 2–0
(Lambert, Bastin) Att: 42,809
Moss, Male, Hapgood, Hill, Roberts, Jones, Hulme, Bowden, Lambert, James, Bastin.

Apr 29 **Huddersfield Town** 2–2
(Bastin 2) Att: 30,779
Moss, Male, Hapgood, Hill, Roberts, Jones, Hulme, Bowden, Lambert, James, Bastin.

NOTE: There were no FA Cup matches at Highbury this season

1933/34

LEAGUE DIVISION ONE
Final position – Champions

Aug 26 **Birmingham** 1–1
(Jack) Att: 44,662
Moss, Male, Hapgood, Hill, Roberts, John, Hulme, Jack, Coleman, James, Bastin.

Sep 6 **West Bromwich Albion** 3–1
(Lambert, Bastin 2 [1pen]) Att: 34,688
Moss, Male, Hapgood, Hill, Roberts, John, Coleman, Jack, Lambert, Bowden, Bastin.

Sep 9 **Manchester City** 1–1
(Coleman) Att: 43,412
Moss, Male, Hapgood, Hill, Roberts, John, Coleman, Jack, Lambert, Bowden, Bastin.

Sep 30 **Middlesbrough** 6–0
(Jack 2, Birkett 2, Bowden, Bastin) Att: 28,293
Moss, Male, Hapgood, Jones, Sidey, John, Birkett, Bowden, Dunne, Jack, Bastin.

Oct 14 **Newcastle United** 3–0
(Birkett, Bowden, Fairhurst [og]) Att: 32,821
Moss, Male, John, Jones, Sidey, Hill, Birkett, Bowden, Dunne, James, Jack.

Oct 21 **Leicester City** 2–0
(Dunne 2) Att: 44,014
Moss, Male, Hapgood, Jones, Sidey, John, Birkett, Bowden, Dunne, James, Bastin.

Nov 4 **Portsmouth** 1–1
(Bastin) Att: 51,765
Moss, Male, Hapgood, Jones, Sidey, John, Hill, Bowden, Dunne, James, Bastin.

Nov 18 **Stoke City** 3–0
(Hulme, Dunne, John) Att: 32,972
Moss, Male, Hapgood, Jones, Sidey, John, Hulme, Coleman, Dunne, Bowden, Bastin.

Dec 2 **Liverpool** 2–1
(Hulme, Dunne) Att: 38,362
Moss, Male, Hapgood, Jones, Sidey, John, Hulme, Coleman, Dunne, James, Bastin.

Dec 16 **Chelsea** 2–1
(Beasley 2) Att: 43,897
Moss, Male, Hapgood, Jones, Roberts, John, Birkett, Bastin, Bowden, James, Beasley.

Dec 26 **Leeds United** 2–0
(Dunne, Bowden) Att: 22,817
Moss, Male, Hapgood, Jones, Roberts, John, Birkett, Bowden, Dunne, Bastin, Beasley.

Jan 6 **Sheffield Wednesday** 1–1
(Dunne) Att: 45,156
Moss, Male, Hapgood, Jones, Roberts, Hill, Coleman, Bowden, Dunne, Bastin, Beasley.

Jan 31 **Tottenham Hotspur** 1–3
(Bastin) Att: 68,828
Moss, Male, Hapgood, Jones, Roberts, John, Birkett, Bowden, Dunne, Bastin, Beasley.

Feb 3 **Everton** 1–2
(Birkett) Att: 24,025
Moss, Male, Hapgood, Hill, Roberts, John, Birkett, Coleman, Dunne, Bastin, Beasley.

Feb 21 **Blackburn Rovers** 2–1
(Beasley, Bastin) Att: 29,886
Moss, Male, Hapgood, Parkin, Roberts, John, Beasley, James, Dunne, Dougall, Bastin.

Mar 10 **Aston Villa** 3–2
(Jack, Roberts, Hulme) Att: 41,169
Wilson, Male, Hapgood, Parkin, Roberts, John, Hulme, Jack, Cox, James, Beasley.

Mar 24 **Wolverhampton Wanderers** 3–2
(James, Bastin, Drake) Att: 41,143
Moss, Male, Hapgood, Jones, Roberts, John, Hulme, Jack, Drake, James, Bastin.

Mar 30 **Derby County** 1–0
(James) Att: 69,070
Wilson, Male, Hapgood, Jones, Roberts, John, Beasley, Bowden, Drake, James, Bastin.

Apr 7 **Huddersfield Town** 3–1
(Beasley, Drake, Bowden) Att: 55,930
Moss, Male, Hapgood, Hill, Roberts, John, Beasley, Bowden, Drake, James, Bastin.

Apr 21 **Sunderland** 2–1
(Drake, Beasley) Att: 37,783
Moss, Male, Hapgood, Parkin, Roberts, Hill, Birkett, Jack, Drake, Bastin, Beasley.

May 5 **Sheffield United** 2–0
(Drake 2) Att: 25,265
Moss, Male, Hapgood, Hill,Roberts, John, Beasley, Jack, Drake, James, Bastin.

FA CUP

Jan 27 **Crystal Palace** 7–0
(Dunne 2, Beasley 2, Birkett, Bastin 2) Att:56,177
Wilson, Male, Hapgood, Jones, Roberts, John, Birkett, Bowden, Dunne, Bastin, Beasley.

Feb 17 **Derby County** 1–0
(Jack) Att: 66,905
Moss, Male, Hapgood, Jones, Roberts, John, Beasley, Jack, Dunne, Dougall, Bastin.

Mar 3 **Aston Villa** 1–2
(Dougall) Att: 67,366
Moss, Male, Hapgood, Jones, Roberts, John, Beasley, Jack, Dunne, Dougall, Bastin.

1934/35

LEAGUE DIVISION ONE
Final position–Champions

Sep 1 **Liverpool** 8–1
(Bowden 3, Drake 3, Crayston, Bastin) Att:54,062
Moss, Male, Hapgood, Crayston, Roberts, Copping, Beasley, Bowden, Drake, James, Bastin.

Sep 5 **Blackburn Rovers** 4–0
(Drake 2, Bowden, Bastin) Att: 39,654
Moss, Male, Hapgood, Crayston, Roberts, Copping, Beasley, Bowden, Drake, James, Bastin.

Sep 15 **West Bromwich Albion** 4–3
(James, Drake, Bastin, Bowden) Att: 40,016
Moss, Male, Hapgood, Crayston, Roberts, Copping, Beasley, Bowden, Drake, James, Bastin.

Sep 29 **Birmingham** 5–1
(Drake 4, Bastin) Att: 47,868
Moss, Male, John, Crayston, Roberts, Copping, Hulme, Marshall, Drake, James, Bastin.

Oct 13 **Manchester City** 3–0
(Bowden 2, Bastin) Att: 68,145
Moss, Male, Hapgood, Crayston, Roberts, Copping, Beasley, Bowden, Drake, James, Bastin.

Oct 20 **Tottenham Hotspur** 5–1
(Beasley, Drake 3, Evans [og]) Att: 70,544
Moss, Male, Hapgood, Crayston, Roberts, John, Beasley, Bowden, Drake, James, Bastin.

Nov 3 **Everton** 2–0
(Bastin 2) Att: 50,350
Moss, Male, Hapgood, Crayston, Roberts, Copping, Beasley, Bowden, Dunne, James, Bastin.

Nov 17 **Aston Villa** 1–2
(Bastin [pen]) Att: 54,226
Moss, Male, Hapgood, Crayston, Roberts, Copping, Hulme, Marshall, Drake, James, Bastin.

Dec 1 **Wolverhampton Wanderers** 7–0
(Drake 4, Birkett 2, Bowden) Att: 39,532
Moss, Male, Hapgood, Crayston, Roberts, Copping, Birkett, Bowden, Drake, James, Bastin.

Dec 15 **Leicester City** 8–0
(Hulme 3, Drake 3, Bastin 2) Att: 23,689
Moss, Male, Hapgood, Crayston, Roberts, Copping, Hulme, Bowden, Drake, James, Bastin.

Dec 25 **Preston North End** 5–3
(Bastin, Hulme 2, Bowden, Hough [og]) Att:40,201
Moss, Compton (L), Hapgood, Crayston, Roberts, Copping, Hulme, Bowden, Drake, James, Bastin.

Dec 29 **Portsmouth** 1–1
(Drake) Att: 36,054
Moss, Male, Hapgood, Hill, Roberts, Copping, Hulme, Bowden, Drake, John, Bastin.

Jan 19 **Leeds United** 3–0
(Bastin, Bowden 2) Att: 37,026
Moss, Male, Hapgood, Crayston, Roberts, Copping, Hulme, Bowden, Drake, Dougall, Bastin.

Feb 2 **Sheffield Wednesday** 4–1
(James 3, Bastin) Att: 57,922
Moss, Male, Hapgood, Crayston, Roberts, Copping, Hulme, Bastin, Drake, James, Beasley.

Feb 20 **Stoke City** 2–0
(Davidson, Hill) Att: 27,067
Moss, Male, Hapgood, Crayston, Sidey, Copping, Birkett, Davidson, Drake, Dougall, Hill.

Mar 9 **Sunderland** 0–0
Att: 73,295
Moss, Male, Hapgood, Crayston, Roberts, Copping, Kirchen, Davidson, Drake, James, Bastin.

Mar 23 **Grimsby Town** 1–1
(Drake) Att: 33,591
Wilson, Male, Hapgood, Crayston, Roberts, Hill, Kirchen, Davidson, Drake, Dougall, Bastin.

Apr 6 **Chelsea** 2–2
(Drake, Compton,L [pen]) Att: 54,020
Wilson, Compton (L), John, Crayston, Roberts, Hill, Kirchen, Davidson, Drake, James, Beasley.

Apr 19 **Middlesbrough** 8–0
(Drake 4, Rogers 2, Bastin, Beasley) Att: 45,719
Wilson, Male, Hapgood, Crayston, Roberts, Hill, Rogers, Bastin, Drake, James, Beasley.

Apr 20 **Huddersfield Town** 1–0
(Beasley) Att: 41,892
Wilson, Male, Hapgood, Crayston, Roberts, Hill, Rogers, Davidson, Drake, Dougall, Beasley.

May 4 **Derby County** 0–1
Att: 36,421
Wilson, Male, Trim, Hill, Roberts, John, Rogers, Davidson, Drake, James, Beasley.

NOTE: There were no FA Cup matches, at Highbury this season.

FA CHARITY SHIELD

Nov 28 **Manchester City** 4–0
(Marshall, Birkett, Bastin, Drake) Att: 10,888
Moss, Male, Hapgood, Hill, Sidey, Copping, Birkett, Marshall, Drake, John, Bastin.

1935/36
LEAGUE DIVISION ONE
Final position – 6th

Aug 31 **Sunderland** 3–1
(Drake 2, Bastin) Att: 66,428
Wilson, Male, Hapgood, Crayston, Roberts, Copping, Milne, Davidson, Drake, James, Bastin.

Sep 11 **Grimsby Town** 6–0
(Milne 3, Beasley, Bowden, Drake) Att: 33,633
Wilson, Male, Compton (L), Crayston, Roberts, Copping, Beasley, Bowden, Drake, Davidson, Milne.

Sep 14 **Sheffield Wednesday** 2–2
(Drake, Milne) Att: 59,492
Wilson, Male, Hapgood, Crayston, Roberts, Copping, Beasley, Bowden, Drake, Davidson, Milne.

Sep 21 **Manchester City** 2–3
(Bastin [pen], James) Att: 61,290
Wilson, Male, Crayston, Roberts, Hill, Milne, Davidson, Drake, James, Bastin.

Oct 5 **Blackburn Rovers** 5–1
(Milne, Bowden 3, Bastin) Att: 45,981
Wilson, Male, Hapgood, Crayston, Roberts, Hill, Milne, Bowden, Drake, James, Bastin.

Oct 26 **Preston North End** 2–1
(Bastin, Drake) Att: 42,126
Wilson, Male, Hapgood, Crayston, Roberts, Copping, Hulme, Bowden, Drake, James, Bastin.

Nov 9 **Derby County** 1–1
(Drake) Att: 54,027
Wilson, Male, Hapgood, Crayston, Roberts, Copping, Hulme, Bowden, Drake, Bastin, Milne.

Nov 23 **Wolverhampton Wanderers** 4–0
(Rogers, Drake 2, Hulme) Att: 39,860
Wilson, Male, Hapgood, Crayston, Roberts, Copping, Hulme, Bowden, Drake, Bastin, Rogers.

Dec 9 **Middlesbrough** 2–0
(Rogers 2) Att: 23,365
Wilson, Male, Hapgood, Crayston, Roberts, Copping, Rogers, Bowden, Drake, Bastin, Beasley.

Dec 26 **Liverpool** 1–2
(Hulme) Att: 57,035
Wilson, Male, Hapgood, Crayston, Sidey, Copping, Hulme, Bastin, Drake, James, Beasley.

Jan 4 **Birmingham** 1–1
(Drake) Att: 44,534
Moss, Male, Hapgood, Crayston, Roberts, Copping, Hulme, Bowden, Drake, Bastin, Beasley.

Feb 1 **Stoke City** 1–0
(Drake) Att: 49,347
Moss, Male, Hapgood, Crayston, Sidey, Copping, Hulme, Bowden, Drake, James, Bastin.

Feb 22 **Portsmouth** 2–3
(Dougall, Compton,L) Att: 21,728
Wilson, Compton (L), Hapgood, Cartwright, Sidey, Copping, Hulme, Davidson, Dunne, Dougall, Beasley.

Mar 7 **Huddersfield Town** 1–1
(Bastin) Att: 43,930
Wilson, Male, Hapgood, Cartwright, Roberts, Copping, Hulme, Bastin, Cox, Dougall, Beasley.

Mar 25 **Everton** 1–1
(Hulme) Att: 18,593
Wilson, Male, Compton (L), Hill, Crayston, Copping, Hulme, Bastin, Cox, Dougall, Rogers.

Apr 1 **Bolton Wanderers** 1–1
(Westcott) Att: 10,485
Wilson, Compton (L), John, Hill, Joy, Copping, Hulme, Rogers, Westcott, James, Beasley.

Apr 4 **Brentford** 1–1
(Dougall) Att: 28,303
Wilson, Compton (L), John, Hill, Joy, Copping, Hulme, Rogers, Dunne, Dougall, Beasley.

Apr 10 **West Bromwich Albion** 4–0
(Crayston, Dunne, Hulme, James) Att: 59,245
Wilson, Male, Hapgood, Crayston, Roberts, Copping, Hulme, Bastin, Dunne, James, Beasley.

Apr 18 **Aston Villa** 1–0
(Drake) Att: 55,431
Wilson, Male, Hapgood, Crayston, Sidey, Copping, Kirchen, Bastin, Drake, James, Beasley.

Apr 27 **Chelsea** 1–1
(Drake) Att: 40,402
Wilson, Male, Hapgood, Crayston, Sidey, Copping, Hulme, Bowden, Drake, Bastin, Beasley.

May 2 **Leeds United** 2–2
(Kirchen, Bastin [pen]) Att: 25,920
Wilson, Male, Hapgood, Crayston, Tuckett, John, Kirchen, Bastin, Bowden, James, Beasley.

FA CUP – Winners

Feb 19 **Newcastle United** 3–0
(Bastin 2 [2pens], Beasley) Att: 62,391
Wilson, Male, Hapgood, Crayston, Roberts, Copping, Hulme, Bastin, Bowden, James, Beasley.

Feb 29 **Barnsley** 4–1
(Beasley 2, Bowden, Bastin [pen])
Att: 60,420
Wilson, Male, Hapgood, Crayston, Roberts, Copping, Hulme, Bastin, Bowden, James, Beasley.

FA CHARITY SHIELD

Oct 23 **Sheffield Wednesday** 0–1
Att: 13,300
Wilson, Male, Hapgood, Hill, Joy, Copping, Milne, Crayston, Dunne, Davidson, Beasley.

1936/37
LEAGUE DIVISION ONE
Final position – 3rd

Aug 29 **Everton** 3–2
(James, Hapgood, Bowden) Att: 50,321
Wilson, Male, Hapgood, Crayston, Roberts, Copping, Hulme, Bowden, Drake, James, Bastin.

Sep 9 **Brentford** 1–1
(Drake) Att: 44,010
Swindin, Male, Hapgood, Crayston, Sidey, Copping, Milne, Bastin, Drake, James, Beasley.

Sep 12 **Sunderland** 4–1
(Crayston, Beasley, Bastin, Roberts) Att: 56,820
Swindin, Male, Hapgood, Crayston, Roberts, Copping, Beasley, Bowden, Drake, James, Bastin.

Sep 26 **Derby County** 2–2
(Drake, Compton, D) Att: 61,390
Swindin, Male, Hapgood, Crayston, Roberts, Copping, Beasley, Bowden, Drake, Bastin, Compton (D).

Oct 10 **Sheffield Wednesday** 1–1
(Drake) Att: 46,421
Swindin, Male, Hapgood, Crayston, Roberts, Copping, Kirchen, Bowden, Drake, Bastin, Compton (D).

Oct 24 **Grimsby Town** 0–0
Att: 51,202
Swindin, Male, Hapgood, Crayston, Roberts, Copping, Kirchen, Davidson, Bowden, James, Bastin.

Nov 7 **Leeds United** 4–1
(Kirchen, Drake, Milne, Davidson) Att: 32,535
Swindin, Male, Hapgood, Bastin, Roberts, Copping, Kirchen, Bowden, Drake, Davidson, Milne.

Nov 21 **Middlesbrough** 5–3
(Milne 2, Drake, Bowden, Bastin) Att: 44,829
Swindin, Male, Hapgood, Bastin, Roberts, Copping, Kirchen, Bowden, Drake, Davidson, Milne.

Dec 5 **Manchester City** 1–3
(Drake) Att: 41,783
Wilson, Male, Compton (L), Hapgood, Crayston, Roberts, Copping, Kirchen, Bowden, Drake, Davidson, Milne.

Dec 19 **Chelsea** 4–1
(Drake , Davidson, Kirchen 2) Att: 49,917
Swindin, Male, Compton (L), Crayston, Roberts, Copping, Kirchen, James, Drake, Davidson, Milne.

Dec 25 **Preston North End** 4–1
(Kirchen, Drake 2, Milne) Att: 42,781
Swindin, Male, Compton (L), Crayston, Roberts, Copping, Kirchen, James, Drake, Davidson, Milne.

Jan 2 **Huddersfield Town** 1–1
(Kirchen) Att: 44,224
Boulton, Male, Compton (L), Crayston, Sidey, Copping, Kirchen, Bastin, Drake, James, Milne.

Jan 23 **Wolverhampton Wanderers** 3–0
(Bastin [pen], Drake, Bowden) Att: 33,896
Boulton, Male, Compton (L), Bastin, Roberts, Copping, Kirchen, Bowden, Drake, Davidson, Milne.

Feb 6 **Manchester United** 1–1
(Davidson) Att: 37,236
Boulton, Male, Compton (L), Bastin, Roberts, Copping, Kirchen, James, Drake, Davidson, Milne.

Feb 24 **Charlton Athletic** 1–1
(Kirchen) Att: 60,568
Boulton, Male, Hapgood, Crayston, Roberts, Copping, Kirchen, Bowden, Drake, Davidson, Bastin.

Mar 10 **Liverpool** 1–0
(Kirchen) Att: 16,145
Boulton, Male, Hapgood, Copping, Roberts, John, Kirchen, Davidson, Bowden, James, Compton (D).

Mar 20 **Birmingham** 1–1
(Bowden) Att: 46,086
Boulton, Male, Hapgood, Crayston, Roberts, John, Kirchen, Bastin, Bowden, Davidson, Compton (D).

Mar 26 **Stoke City** 0–0
Att: 59,495
Boulton, Male, Hapgood, Crayston, Roberts, Copping, Kirchen, Bowden, Drake, James, Compton (D).

Apr 3 **West Bromwich Albion** 2–0
(Davidson, Nelson) Att: 38,773
Boulton, Male, Hapgood, Crayston, Roberts, Copping, Kirchen, Bastin, Bowden, Davidson, Nelson.

Apr 17 **Portsmouth** 4–0
(Compton, D 2, Nelson, Kirchen) Att: 29,098
Boulton, Compton (L), Hapgood, Crayston, Joy, Copping, Nelson, James, Kirchen, Davidson, Compton (D).

May 1 **Bolton Wanderers** 0–0
Att: 22,875
Boulton, Male, Hapgood, Crayston, Sidey, Copping, Nelson, James, Kirchen, Davidson, Bastin.

FA CUP

Jan 30 **Manchester United** 5–0
(Bastin, Kirchen, Davidson, Drake, Brown [og]) Att: 45,637
Boulton, Male, Compton (L), Bastin, Roberts, Copping, Kirchen, James, Drake, Davidson, Milne.

1937/38
LEAGUE DIVISION ONE
Final position – Champions

Sep 1 **Huddersfield Town** 3–1
(Drake, Crayston, Bastin) Att: 32,758
Wilson, Male, Hapgood, Crayston, Roberts, Copping, Hulme, Bowden, Drake, Bastin, Milne.

Sep 4 **Wolverhampton Wanderers** 5–0
(Crayston, Hulme, Bastin [pen], Drake 2) Att: 67,311
Wilson, Male, Hapgood, Crayston, Roberts, Copping, Hulme, Bowden, Drake, Bastin, Milne.

Sep 18 **Sunderland** 4–1
(Milne, Hulme, Drake, Davidson) Att: 65,635
Boulton, Male, Hapgood, Crayston, Roberts, Copping, Hulme, Bastin, Drake, Davidson, Milne.

Oct 2 **Manchester City** 2–1
(Milne, Kirchen) Att: 68,353
Wilson,, Compton (L), Hapgood, Crayston, Roberts, Copping, Kirchen, Bastin, Hunt, Davidson, Milne.

Oct 16 **Portsmouth** 1–1
(Hunt) Att: 45,150
Boulton, Compton (L), Hapgood, Crayston, Roberts, Copping, Kirchen, Bowden, Hunt, Bastin, Milne.

Oct 30 **Middlesbrough** 1–2
(Milne) Att: 39,066
Wilson, Compton (L), Hapgood, Crayston, Roberts, Copping, Hulme, Bastin, Bowden, Davidson, Milne.

Nov 13 **West Bromwich Albion** 1–1
(Compton,L) Att: 34,324
Wilson, Compton (L), Hapgood, Crayston, Joy, Copping, Milne, Biggs, Kirchen, Jones (L), Compton (D).

Nov 27 **Leeds United** 4–1
(Drake 2, Kirchen, Bastin [pen]) Att: 34,350
Boulton, Male, Hapgood, Crayston, Joy, Copping, Kirchen, Hunt, Drake, Jones (L), Bastin.

Dec 11 **Preston North End** 2–0
(Milne, Bastin) Att: 35,679
Boulton, Male, Hapgood, Cartwright, Joy, Copping, Milne, Hunt, Drake, Jones (L), Bastin.

Dec 27 **Blackpool** 2–1
(Bastin, Cartwright) Att: 54,163
Boulton, Male, Hapgood, Cartwright, Joy, Copping, Kirchen, Hunt, Drake, Jones (L), Bastin.

Jan 1 **Everton** 2–1
(Lewis, Hunt) Att: 36,953
Boulton, Male, Hapgood, Cartwright, Sidey, Copping, Kirchen, Hunt, Lewis, Jones (L), Bastin.

Feb 2 **Leicester City** 3–1
(Drake, Bastin, Jones,L) Att: 23,839
Swindin, Male, Hapgood, Crayston, Joy, Copping, Griffiths, Hunt, Drake, Jones (L), Bastin.

Feb 5 **Derby County** 3–0
(Lewis, Crayston 2) Att: 47,263
Swindin, Male, Hapgood, Crayston, Joy, Copping, Griffiths, Hunt, Lewis, Jones (L), Bastin.

Feb 19 **Chelsea** 2–0
(Griffiths, Drake) Att: 49,573
Swindin, Male, Hapgood, Crayston, Joy, Copping, Griffiths, Jones (L), Drake, Carr, Bastin.

Mar 5 **Stoke City** 4–0
(Carr, Griffiths 2, Drake) Att: 35,296
Swindin, Male, Hapgood, Crayston, Joy, Collett, Griffiths, Jones (L), Drake, Carr, Bastin.

Mar 19 **Grimsby Town** 5–1
(Griffiths 2, Bastin 2 [1pen], Jones,L) Att: 40,701
Swindin, Male, Hapgood, Crayston, Sidey, Copping, Griffiths, Jones (L), Carr, Drury, Bastin.

Apr 2 **Charlton Athletic** 2–2
(Carr, Drake) Att: 52,858
Swindin, Male, Hapgood, Collett, Joy, Copping, Drury, Jones (L), Drake, Carr, Bastin.

Apr 15 **Brentford** 0–2
Att: 51,299
Swindin, Male, Hapgood, Cartwright, Joy, Copping, Griffiths, Jones (L), Drake, Drury, Bastin.

Apr 16 **Birmingham** 0–0
Att: 35,161
Swindin, Male, Hapgood, Jones (L), Joy, Copping, Kirchen, Carr, Lewis, Drury, Bastin.

Apr 30 **Liverpool** 1–0
(Carr) Att: 34,703
Swindin, Male, Hapgood, Crayston, Joy, Copping, Drake, Jones (L), Carr, Drury, Bastin.

May 7 **Bolton Wanderers** 5–0
(Kirchen, Carr 2, Bastin 2) Att: 40,500
Swindin, Male, Hapgood, Jones (L), Joy, Copping, Kirchen, Bremner, Carr, Drury, Bastin.

FA CUP

Jan 8 **Bolton Wanderers** 3–1
(Bastin 2, Kirchen) Att: 64,016
Boulton, Male, Hapgood, Crayston, Joy, Copping, Kirchen, Hunt, Drake, Jones (L), Bastin.

Feb 12 **Preston North End** 0–1
Att: 72,121
Swindin, Male, Hapgood, Crayston, Joy, Copping, Kirchen, Hunt, Drake, Jones (L), Bastin.

1938/39
LEAGUE DIVISION ONE
Final position – 5th

Aug 27 **Portsmouth** 2–0
(Rochford [og], Jones,B) Att: 54,940
Swindin, Male, Hapgood, Crayston, Joy, Copping, Kirchen, Jones (L), Drake, Jones (B), Bastin.

Sep 10 **Everton** 1–2
(Jones,B) Att: 64,555
Swindin, Male, Hapgood, Crayston, Joy, Copping, Nelson, Jones (L), Carr, Jones (B), Bastin.

Sep 14 **Derby County** 1–2
(Drake) Att: 25,756
Swindin, Male, Hapgood, Jones (L), Joy, Copping, Nelson, Bremner, Drake, Jones (B), Bastin.

Sep 24 **Aston Villa** 0–0
Att: 66,456
Swindin, Male, Hapgood, Crayston, Joy, Copping, Kirchen, Bremner, Drake, Jones (B), Cumner.

Oct 8 **Grimsby Town** 2–0
(Bremner, Kirchen) Att: 39,174
Swindin, Male, Hapgood, Jones (L), Joy, Copping, Kirchen, Bremner, Drake, Jones (B), Cumner.

Oct 22 **Preston North End** 1–0
(A. Beattie [og]) Att: 40,296
Swindin, Male, Compton (L), Crayston, Joy, Collett, Walsh, Bremner, Drake, Drury, Bastin.

Nov 5 **Leeds United** 2–3
(Drake, Bastin) Att: 39,092
Swindin, Male, Compton (L), Jones (L), Joy, Copping, Walsh, Jones (B), Drake, Drury, Bastin.

Nov 19 **Leicester City** 0–0
Att: 36,407
Swindin, Male, Hapgood, Crayston, Joy, Copping, Kirchen, Jones (B), Drake, Bastin, Cumner.

Dec 3 **Birmingham** 3–1
(Drake, Crayston, Nelson) Att: 33,710
Swindin, Compton (L), Hapgood, Crayston, Joy, Copping, Nelson, Jones (L), Drake, Drury, Bastin.

Dec 17 **Stoke City** 4–1
(Lewis 2, Bastin, Drury) Att: 30,006
Wilson, Compton (L), Hapgood, Crayston, Joy, Copping, Nelson, Jones (L), Lewis, Drury, Bastin.

Dec 31 **Huddersfield Town** 1–0
(Drake) Att: 34,146
Wilson, Male, Hapgood, Crayston, Joy, Copping, Drake, Bremner, Lewis, Drury, Bastin.

Jan 21 **Charlton Athletic** 2–0
(Crayston, Lewis) Att: 39,702
Wilson, Male, Hapgood, Crayston, Joy, Copping, Drake, Drury, Lewis, Jones (B), Kirchen.

Feb 1 **Wolverhampton Wanderers** 0–0
Att: 33,103
Wilson, Male, Hapgood, Crayston, Joy, Collett, Drake, Drury, Lewis, Jones (B), Kirchen.

Feb 4 **Sunderland** 2–0
(Bastin, Lewis) Att: 45,875
Wilson, Male, Hapgood, Pryde, Joy, Collett, Kirchen, Bremner, Lewis, Drury, Bastin.

Feb 18 **Chelsea** 1–0
(Bremner) Att: 54,510
Wilson, Male, Hapgood, Pryde, Joy, Copping, Drake, Bremner, Lewis, Drury, Kirchen.

Mar 4 **Bolton Wanderers** 3–1
(Drake 2, Winter [og]) Att: 29,814
Wilson, Compton (L), Hapgood, Crayston, Joy, Collett, Kirchen, Drury, Drake, Jones (B), Cumner.

Mar 18 **Liverpool** 2–0
(Kirchen, Drake) Att: 31,495
Wilson, Compton (L), Hapgood, Crayston, Joy, Collett, Kirchen, Drury, Drake, Jones (B), Bastin.

Apr 1 **Middlesbrough** 1–2
(Bremner) Att: 34,669
Wilson, Compton (L), Hapgood, Crayston, Joy, Collett, Kirchen, Bremner, Drake, Jones (B), Bastin.

Apr 10 **Blackpool** 2–1
(Compton,L [pen], Drake) Att: 30,760
Swindin, Male, Compton (L), Crayston, Fields, Cartwright, Drake, Jones (B), Lewis, Curtis, Kirchen.

Apr 15 **Manchester United** 2–1
(Drake, Crayston) Att: 25,741
Swindin, Male, Compton (L), Crayston, Joy, Cartwright, Drake, Jones (B), Lewis, Curtis, Kirchen.

May 6 **Brentford** 2–0
(Kirchen, Drake) Att: 30,928
Marks, Compton (L), Hapgood, Crayston, Joy, Jones (L), Kirchen, Farr, Drake, Drury, Nelson.

NOTE: There were no FA Cup matches at Highbury this season.

FA CHARITY SHIELD

Sep 26 **Preston North End** 2–1
(Drake 2) Att: 7,233
Swindin, Male, Compton (L), Crayston, Joy, Copping, Kirchen, Jones (L), Drake, Jones (B), Cumner.

1939 to 1946

Only three fixtures of the 1939/40 season had been completed (two at Highbury – Aug 30 v Blackburn Rovers 1–0, and Sep 2 v Sunderland 5–2) at the outbreak of World War II. Regular football was abandoned immediately and the playing details expunged from the records. Arsenal Stadium was closed to football. Football was organised on a regional basis, and for the whole of this wartime period, Arsenal played their home matches at White Hart Lane.

1946/47

LEAGUE DIVISION ONE
Final position – 13th

Sep 4 **Blackburn Rovers** 1–3
(Lewis) Att: 28,700
Swindin, Scott, Joy, Nelson, Compton (L), Waller, O'Flanagan, McPherson, Lewis, Drury, Hodges.

Sep 7 **Sunderland** 2–2
(Lewis 2) Att: 60,000
Swindin, Scott, Joy, Nelson, Compton (L), Waller,O'Flanagan, McPherson, Lewis, Logie, Smith (A).

Sep 21 **Derby County** 0–1
Att: 60,673
Swindin, Scott, Joy, Bastin, Compton (L), Logie, McPherson, Drury, O'Flanagan, Jones (B), Nelson.

Oct 12 **Brentford** 2–2
(Lewis, Logie) Att: 45,000
Swindin, Joy, Collett, Waller, Compton (L), Jones (B), McPherson, Logie, Lewis, Curtis, O'Flanagan.

Oct 19 **Stoke City** 1–0
(O'Flanagan) Att: 62,000
Swindin, Scott, Joy, Male, Compton (L), Waller, McPherson, Gudmundsson, Lewis, Curtis, O'Flanagan.

Nov 2 **Sheffield United** 2–3
(Logie, Lewis) Att: 45,000
Swindin, Scott, Joy, Male, Compton (L), Waller, McPherson, Logie, Lewis, Jones (B),Smith (A).

Nov 16 **Leeds United** 4–2
(Lewis 2 [1pen], Logie, McPherson) Att: 40,000
Platt, Scott, Wade, Sloan, Compton (L), Collett, McPherson, Logie, Lewis, Curtis, O'Flanagan.

Nov 30 **Bolton Wanderers** 2–2
(Lewis [pen], O'Flanagan) Att: 47,000
Platt, Scott, Barnes, Sloan, Compton (L), Mercer, McPherson, Logie, Lewis, Jones (B), O'Flanagan.

Dec 14 **Charlton Athletic** 1–0
(Rooke) Att: 45,000
Swindin, Male, Barnes, Sloan, Compton (L), Mercer, McPherson, Logie, Rooke, Jones (B), O;Flanagan.

Dec 25 **Portsmouth** 2–1
(Rooke, Logie) Att: 38,000
Swindin, Male, Barnes, Sloan, Compton (L), Mercer, McPherson, Logie, Rooke, Jones (B), O'Flanagan.

Dec 28 **Wolverhampton Wanderers** 1–1
(Rooke) Att: 62,827
Swindin, Scott, Barnes, Sloan, Compton (L), Mercer, McPherson, Logie, Rooke, Jones (B), O'Flanagan.

Jan 18 **Aston Villa** 0–2
Att: 61,000
Swindin, Compton (L), Collett, Sloan, Fields, Waller, McPherson, Lewis, Rooke, Logie, Rudkin.

Feb 1 **Manchester United** 6–2
(Rudkin, Logie, McPherson, Rooke 3) Att: 38,000
Swindin, Male, Barnes, Sloan, Compton (L), Mercer, McPherson, Logie, Rooke, Jones (B), Rudkin.

Feb 8 **Blackpool** 1–1
(Rooke) Att: 36,000
Swindin, Male, Barnes, Sloan, Compton (L), Mercer, McPherson, Logie, Rooke, Curtis, Rudkin.

Mar 1 **Chelsea** 1–2
(Rudkin) Att: 57,000
Swindin, Scott, Barnes, Sloan, Compton (L), Mercer, McPherson, Logie, Rooke, Jones (B), Rudkin.

Mar 15 **Preston North End** 4–1
(Lewis 3, Rooke) Att: 50,000
Swindin, Scott, Barnes, Sloan, Compton (L), Mercer, McPherson, Rooke, Lewis, Jones (B), Calverley.

Apr 4 **Huddersfield Town** 1–2
(Jones,B) Att: 50,000
Swindin, Scott, Barnes, Sloan, Compton (L), Mercer, McPherson, Rooke, Lewis, Jones (B), Calverley.

Apr 12 **Middlesbrough** 4–0
(Rooke 4 [1pen]) Att: 50,000
Swindin, Male, Barnes, Sloan, Compton (L), Mercer, Jones (B), Logie, Lewis, Rooke, Calverley.

Apr 26 **Grimsby Town** 5–3
(Lewis 4, Compton,D) Att: 42,100
Swindin, Scott, Barnes, Sloan, Compton (L), Mercer, McPherson, Logie, Lewis, Rooke, Compton (D).

May 24 **Liverpool** 1–2
(McPherson) Att: 48,000
Swindin, Male, Barnes, Sloan, Fields, Mercer, McPherson, Logie, Lewis, Rooke, Calverley.

May 31 **Everton** 2–1
(Rooke, Lewis) Att: 30,000
Swindin, Scott, Barnes, Sloan, Fields, Mercer, McPherson, Logie, Lewis, Rooke, Calverley.

FA CUP

Jan 15 **Chelsea** 1–1 *
(Rooke) Att: 53,350
Swindin, Male, Barnes, Sloan, Compton (L), Mercer, McPherson, Lewis, Rooke, Logie, Curtis.

*After extra time

1947/48

LEAGUE DIVISION ONE
Final position – Champions

Aug 23 **Sunderland** 3–1
(McPherson, Logie, Rooke) Att: 58,184
Swindin, Scott, Barnes, Macaulay, Fields, Mercer, Roper, Logie, Lewis, Rooke, McPherson.

Sep 3 **Charlton Athletic** 6–0
(Lewis 4, Rooke 2) Att: 54,684
Swindin, Scott, Barnes, Macaulay, Fields, Mercer, Roper, Logie, Lewis, Rooke, McPherson.

Sep 6 **Manchester United** 2–1
(Rooke, Lewis) Att: 64,905
Swindin, Scott, Barnes, Macaulay, Fields, Mercer, Roper, Logie, Lewis, Rooke, McPherson.

Sep 10 **Bolton Wanderers** 2–0
(McPherson, Rooke [pen]) Att: 45,969
Swindin, Scott, Barnes, Macaulay, Fields, Mercer, Roper, Logie, Lewis, Rooke, McPherson.

Sep 20 **Stoke City** 3–0
(Logie, McPherson 2) Att: 61,579
Swindin, Male, Barnes, Macaulay, Compton (L), Mercer, Roper, Logie, Rooke, Jones (B), McPherson.

Oct 4 **Portsmouth** 0–0
Att: 62,461
Swindin, Scott, Barnes, Male, Compton (L), Sloan, Roper, Logie, Lewis, Rooke, McPherson.

Oct 11 **Aston Villa** 1–0
(Rooke) Att: 60,427
Swindin, Scott, Barnes, Macaulay, Compton (L), Mercer, Roper, Logie, Rooke, Jones (B), McPherson.

Oct 25 **Everton** 1–1
(Lewis) Att: 56,647
Swindin, Scott, Barnes, Macaulay, Compton (L), Mercer, Roper, Logie, Lewis, Rooke, McPherson.

Nov 8 **Blackpool** 2–1
(Rooke [pen], Roper) Att: 67,057
Swindin, Scott, Barnes, Macaulay, Compton (L), Mercer, Roper, Lewis, Rooke, Logie, McPherson.

Nov 22 **Huddersfield Town** 2–0
(Logie, Rooke) Att: 47,514
Swindin, Scott, Barnes, Macaulay, Compton (L), Mercer, Roper, Lewis, Rooke, Logie, McPherson.

Dec 6 **Manchester City** 1–1
(Rooke [pen]) Att: 41,274
Swindin, Scott, Barnes, Macaulay, Compton (L), Mercer, Roper, Lewis, Rooke, Logie, McPherson.

Dec 27 **Liverpool** 1–2
(Lewis) Att: 56,650
Swindin, Scott, Wade, Macaulay, Compton (L), Mercer, Roper, Logie, Lewis, Rooke, McPherson.

Jan 3 **Sheffield United** 3–2
(Rooke 2, Lewis) Att: 48,993
Swindin, Male, Scott, Macaulay, Compton (L), Mercer, Roper, Logie, Lewis, Rooke, McPherson.

Jan 31 **Preston North End** 3–0
(Lewis 2, Rooke) Att: 63,162
Swindin, Scott, Barnes, Macaulay, Compton (L), Mercer, Roper, Logie, Rooke, Lewis, McPherson.

Feb 14 **Burnley** 3–0
(Roper, Rooke 2) Att: 62,123
Swindin, Scott, Barnes, Macaulay, Compton (L), Mercer, Roper, Logie, Rooke, Jones (B), Compton (D).

Mar 6 **Wolverhampton Wanderers** 5–2
(Forbes, Logie, Roper, Rooke 2) Att: 57,711
Swindin, Scott, Barnes, Macaulay, Compton (L), Mercer, Roper, Logie, Rooke, Forbes, Compton (D).

Mar 20 **Chelsea** 0–2
Att: 56,596
Swindin, Scott, Barnes, Macaulay, Compton (L), Mercer, Roper, Logie, Rooke, Forbes, Compton (D).

Mar 26 **Middlesbrough** 7–0
(Roper, Compton,D 2, Rooke 3, Robinson [og])
Att: 57,557
Swindin, Scott, Barnes, Macaulay, Compton (L), Mercer, Roper, Logie, Rooke, Forbes, Compton (D).

Apr 3 **Blackburn Rovers** 2–0
(Logie, Rooke) Att: 45,801
Swindin, Scott, Barnes, Macaulay, Compton (L), Mercer, Roper, Logie, Rooke, Forbes, Compton (D).

Apr 17 **Derby County** 1–2
(Roper) Att: 49,677
Swindin, Scott, Barnes, Macaulay, Compton (L), Mercer, Roper, Logie, Rooke, Forbes, Compton (D).

May 1 **Grimsby Town** 8–0
(Rooke 4, Forbes, Compton,D 2, Logie [pen])
Att: 34,644
Swindin, Male, Scott, Macaulay, Smith (L), Mercer, Roper, Logie, Rooke, Forbes, Compton (D).

FA CUP

Jan 10 **Bradford Park Avenue** 0–1
Att: 47,738
Swindin, Male, Scott, Macaulay, Compton (L), Mercer, Roper, Logie, Lewis, Rooke, McPherson.

1948/49

LEAGUE DIVISION ONE
Final position – 5th

Aug 25 **Stoke City** 3–0
(Logie, Forbes, Roper) Att: 43,867
Swindin, Barnes, Smith (L), Macaulay, Compton (L), Mercer, Roper, Logie, Rooke, Forbes, McPherson.

Aug 28 **Manchester United** 0–1
Att: 64,150
Swindin, Barnes, Smith (L), Macaulay, Compton (L), Mercer, Roper, Logie, Rooke, Forbes, McPherson.

Sep 8 **Liverpool** 1–1
(Rooke) Att: 41,571
Swindin, Barnes, Smith (L), Macaulay, Compton (L), Mercer, Roper,Logie, Rooke, Lishman, Vallance.

Sep 11 **Aston Villa** 3–1
(Rooke 2 [2 pens], Roper) Att: 54,144
Swindin, Scott, Barnes, Macaulay, Compton (L), Mercer, Roper, Jones (B), Rooke, Lishman, Compton (D).

Sep 25 **Wolverhampton Wanderers** 3–1
(Lewis 2, Compton,D) Att: 56,869
Swindin, Barnes, Smith (L), Forbes, Compton (L), Mercer, Roper, Macaulay, Lewis, Jones (B), Compton (D).

Oct 9 **Burnley** 3–1
(Lewis 2, Logie) Att: 53,647
Swindin, Barnes, Smith (L), Macaulay, Compton (L), Mercer, Roper, Logie, Lewis, Rooke, Jones (B).

Oct 23 **Everton** 5–0
(Rooke 2, Logie 2, Forbes) Att: 49,048
Swindin, Scott, Smith (L), Macaulay, Compton (L), Mercer, Roper, Logie, Rooke, Forbes, McPherson.

Nov 6 **Birmingham City** 2–0
(Forbes, Lewis) Att: 61,511
Swindin, Scott, Barnes, Macaulay, Compton (L), Mercer, Roper, Logie, Lewis, Forbes, McPherson.

Nov 20 **Newcastle United** 0–1
Att: 68,263
Swindin, Barnes, Smith (L), Macaulay, Compton (L), Mercer, Roper, Logie, Lewis, Forbes, Rooke.

Dec 4 **Manchester City** 1–1
(Rooke) Att: 48,960
Swindin, Barnes, Smith (L), Macaulay, Compton (L), Mercer, Roper, Logie, Rooke, Forbes, McPherson.

Dec18 **Huddersfield Town** 3–0
(Rooke 3) Att: 36,825
Swindin, Barnes, Smith (L), Macaulay, Compton (L), Mercer, Roper, Logie, Rooke, Lewis, McPherson.

Dec 25 **Derby County** 3–3
(Logie, Rooke, McPherson) Att: 40,665
Swindin, Barnes, Smith (L), Macaulay, Compton (L), Mercer, Roper, Logie, Rooke, Lewis, McPherson.

Jan 15 **Sheffield United** 5–3
(Logie 2, Lishman, Rooke, McPherson)
Att: 46,727
Swindin, Barnes, Smith (L), Macaulay, Compton (L), Mercer, Roper, Logie, Rooke, Lishman, McPherson.

Feb 5 **Sunderland** 5–0
(Lewis, Macaulay, McPherson, Lishman, Vallance) Att: 53,742
Platt, Barnes, Smith (L), Macaulay, Compton (L), Mercer, McPherson, Logie, Lewis, Lishman, Vallance.

Feb 26 **Bolton Wanderers** 5–0
(Logie 2, Lewis, Vallance, McPherson)
Att: 50,263
Platt, Barnes, Smith (L), Macaulay, Compton (L), Forbes, McPherson, Logie, Lewis, Lishman, Vallance.

Mar 12 **Preston North End** **0–0**
Att: 54,977
Platt, Scott, Smith (L), Macaulay, Compton (L), Mercer, McPherson, Logie, Lewis, Lishman, Vallance.

Apr 9 **Middlesbrough** **1–1**
(Lishman) Att: 51,540
Platt, Scott, Barnes, Macaulay, Compton (L), Forbes, McPherson, Logie, Lewis, Lishman, Vallance.

Apr 18 **Blackpool** **2–0**
(Lishman 2) Att: 45,047
Swindin, Barnes, Smith (L), Mercer, Compton (L), Forbes, McPherson, Logie, Lewis, Lishman, Compton (D).

Apr 23 **Chelsea** **1–2**
(Compton,D) Att: 54,604
Swindin, Barnes, Smith (L), Macaulay, Compton (L), Forbes, McPherson, Logie, Lewis, Lishman, Compton (D).

May 4 **Portsmouth** **3–2**
(Lishman 2, Logie) Att: 56,973
Swindin, Barnes, Smith (L), Macaulay, Compton (L), Forbes, McPherson, Logie, Roper, Lishman, Vallance.

May 7 **Charlton Athletic** **2–0**
(Roper, Lishman) Att: 47,564
Swindin, Barnes, Smith (L), Mercer, Daniel, Forbes, McPherson, Logie, Roper, Lishman, Vallance.

FA CUP

Jan 8 **Tottenham Hotspur** **3–0**
(McPherson, Roper, Lishman) Att: 47,314
Swindin, Barnes, Smith (L), Macaulay, Compton (L), Mercer, Roper, Logie, Rooke, Lishman, McPherson.

FA CHARITY SHIELD

Oct 6 **Manchester United** **4–3**
(Lewis 2, Rooke, Jones,B) Att: 31,000
Swindin, Barnes, Smith (L), Macaulay, Compton (L), Mercer, Roper, Logie, Lewis, Rooke, Jones (B).

1949/50

LEAGUE DIVISION ONE
Final position – 6th

Aug 20 **Burnley** **0–1**
Att: 47,794
Swindin, Barnes, Smith (L), Mercer, Daniel, Forbes, McPherson, Macaulay, Roper, Lishman, Vallance.

Aug 31 **Chelsea** **2–3**
(Goring 2) Att: 52,901
Swindin, Scott, Barnes, Mercer, Compton (L), Shaw, McPherson, Logie, Goring, Lishman, Roper.

Sep 3 **Liverpool** **1–2**
(Lishman) Att: 51,866
Swindin, Scott, Barnes, Mercer, Compton (L), Forbes, McPherson, Logie, Goring, Lishman, Roper.

Sep 14 **West Bromwich Albion** **4–1**
(Lewis, Goring, Roper, Barnes [pen]) Att: 40,775
Platt, Barnes, Smith (L), Macaulay, Compton (L), Mercer, Cox, Lewis, Goring, Logie, Roper.

Sep 24 **Birmingham City** **4–2**
(Logie, Goring 2, Lewis) Att: 50,850
Platt, Barnes, Smith (L), Macaulay, Compton (L), Mercer, Cox, Lewis, Goring, Logie, Roper.

Oct 8 **Everton** **5–2**
(Roper, Lewis 2, Goring 2) Att: 53,224
Platt, Barnes, Smith (L), Macaulay, Compton (L), Mercer, Cox, Logie, Goring, Lewis, Roper.

Oct 22 **Blackpool** **1–0**
(Lewis) Att: 66,389
Platt, Barnes, Smith (L), Macaulay, Compton (L), Mercer, Cox, Logie, Roper, Lewis, McPherson.

Nov 5 **Fulham** **2–1**
(Barnes [pen], McPherson) Att: 40,593
Platt, Barnes, Smith (L), Macaulay, Compton (L), Mercer, Cox, Logie, Roper, Lewis, McPherson.

Nov 19 **Charlton Athletic** **2–3**
(Logie, Lewis) Att: 57,318
Platt, Barnes, Smith (L), Macaulay, Compton (L), Mercer, Cox, Logie, Roper, Lewis, McPherson.

Dec 3 **Wolverhampton Wanderers** **1–1**
(Roper) Att: 56,227
Platt, Barnes, Smith (L), Forbes, Compton (L), Mercer, Cox, Logie, Roper, Lewis, McPherson.

Dec 24 **Sunderland** **5–0**
(Lewis, Forbes, Goring, Logie, McPherson)
Att: 43,284
Platt, Barnes, Smith (L), Forbes, Compton (L), Mercer, Cox, Logie, Goring, Lewis, McPherson.

Dec 27 **Manchester United** **0–0**
Att: 65,133
Swindin, Scott, Barnes, Macaulay, Compton (L), Forbes, Cox, Logie, Goring, Lewis, McPherson.

Jan 14 **Huddersfield Town** **1–0**
(Lewis) Att: 46,815
Swindin, Scott, Barnes, Forbes, Compton (L), Mercer, Cox, Logie, Goring, Lewis, McPherson.

Jan 21 **Bolton Wanderers** **1–1**
(Lewis) Att: 47,493
Swindin, Scott, Barnes, Macaulay, Compton (L), Forbes, Cox, Logie, Goring, Lewis, Compton (D).

Feb 18 **Derby County** **1–0**
(Logie) Att: 67,445
Swindin, Scott, Barnes, Forbes, Compton (L), Mercer, Roper, Logie, Goring, Lewis, Compton (D).

Mar 8 **Middlesbrough** **1–1**
(Forbes [pen]) Att: 34,464
Swindin, Scott, Smith (L), Macaulay, Compton (L), Forbes, McPherson, Logie, Roper, Lishman, Compton (D).

Mar 29 **Aston Villa** **1–3**
(Lishman) Att: 24,736
Platt, Barnes, Smith (L), Macaulay, Compton (L), Mercer, McPherson, Logie, Cox, Lishman, Compton (D).

Apr 1 **Manchester City** **4–1**
(Goring, Lishman, Lewis 2) Att: 39,420
Swindin, Barnes, Smith (L), Forbes, Compton (L), Shaw, Cox, Lewis, Goring, Lishman, Compton (D).

Apr 10 **Stoke City** **6–0**
(Barnes [pen], Goring 2, Lishman 2, Franklin [og]) Att: 27,226
Platt, Barnes, Smith (L), Macaulay,Compton (L), Shaw, McPherson, Logie, Goring, Lishman, Roper.

Apr 15 **Newcastle United** **4–2**
(Goring 3, Lewis) Att: 51,997
Swindin, Barnes, Smith (L), Macaulay, Compton (L), Mercer, Cox, Logie, Goring,Lewis, Compton (D).

May 3 **Portsmouth** **2–0**
(Goring 2) Att: 63,124
Swindin, Scott, Barnes, Forbes, Compton (L), Mercer, Cox, Logie, Goring, Lewis, Compton (D).

FA CUP
Winners

Jan 7 **Sheffield Wednesday** **1–0**
(Lewis) Att: 54,193
Swindin, Scott, Barnes, Forbes, Compton (L), Mercer, Cox, Logie, Goring, Lewis, McPherson.

Jan 28 **Swansea Town** **2–1**
(Logie, Barnes [pen]) Att: 57,305
Swindin, Scott, Barnes, Forbes, Compton (L), Mercer, Cox, Logie, Goring, Lewis, McPherson.

Feb 11 **Burnley** **2–0**
(Lewis, Compton D) Att: 55,458
Swindin, Scott, Barnes, Forbes, Compton (L), Mercer, Cox, Logie, Goring, Lewis, Compton (D).

Mar 4 **Leeds United** **1–0**
(Lewis) Att: 62,573
Swindin, Scott, Barnes, Forbes, Compton (L), Mercer, Cox, Logie, Roper, Lewis, Compton (D).

1950/51

LEAGUE DIVISION ONE
Final position – 5th

Aug 23 **Chelsea** **0–0**
Att: 61,166
Swindin, Barnes, Smith (L), Forbes, Compton (L), Mercer, Cox, Logie, Goring, Lishman, Roper.

Aug 26 **Tottenham Hotspur** **2–2**
(Roper, Barnes [pen]) Att: 64,638
Swindin, Barnes, Smith (L), Shaw, Compton (L), Mercer, Cox, Logie, Goring, Lishman, Roper.

Sep 2 **Sheffield Wednesday** **3–0**
(Lishman, Logie 2) Att: 45,647
Platt, Scott, Barnes, Shaw, Compton (L), Mercer, Cox, Logie, Goring, Lishman, McPherson.

Sep 6 **Everton** **2–1**
(Cox, Barnes [pen]) Att: 36,576
Platt, Scott, Barnes, Forbes, Compton (L), Mercer, Cox, Logie, Goring, Lishman, McPherson.

Sep 16 **Huddersfield Town** **6–2**
(Lishman, Logie 2, Goring 3) Att: 51,518
Swindin, Barnes, Smith (L), Shaw, Compton (L), Forbes, McPherson, Logie, Goring, Lishman, Roper.

Sep 30 **West Bromwich Albion** **3–0**
(Lishman 2, Logie) Att: 51,928
Swindin, Barnes, Smith (L), Forbes, Compton (L), Mercer, McPherson, Logie, Goring, Lishman, Roper.

Oct 14 **Manchester United** **3–0**
(Lishman, Goring, Cockburn [og]) Att: 66,150
Swindin, Barnes, Smith (L), Forbes, Compton (L), Mercer, McPherson, Logie, Goring, Lishman, Roper.

Oct 28 **Derby County** **3–1**
(Logie, Forbes, Goring) Att: 62,889
Platt, Barnes, Smith (L), Forbes, Compton (L), Mercer, McPherson, Logie, Goring, Lishman, Roper.

Nov 11 **Sunderland** **5–1**
(Lishman 4, Roper) Att: 68,682
Platt, Barnes, Smith (L), Forbes, Compton (L), Mercer, McPherson, Logie, Goring, Lishman, Roper.

Nov 25 **Fulham** **5–1**
(Goring, Forbes, Lishman 3) Att: 41,344
Platt, Barnes, Smith (L), Forbes, Compton (L), Mercer, McPherson, Logie, Goring, Lishman, Roper.

Dec 9 **Blackpool** **4–4**
(Lishman, Forbes, Goring, Barnes [pen])
Att: 57,445
Swindin, Barnes, Smith (L), Forbes, Compton (L), Mercer, McPherson, Logie, Goring, Lishman, Roper.

Dec 16 **Burnley** **0–1**
Att: 32,374
Swindin, Scott, Barnes, Forbes, Compton (L), Mercer, McPherson, Logie, Goring, Lishman, Roper.

Dec 25 **Stoke City** **0–3**
Att: 36,852
Swindin, Scott, Barnes, Shaw, Compton (L), Forbes, McPherson, Logie, Goring, Lishman, Cox.

Jan 13 **Middlesbrough** **3–1**
(Goring, Lewis 2) Att: 63,038
Platt, Barnes, Smith (L), Shaw, Compton (L), Forbes, McPherson, Logie, Goring, Lewis, Roper.

Feb 3 **Newcastle United** **0–0**
Att: 55,073
Platt, Barnes, Smith (L), Forbes, Compton (L), Mercer, McPherson, Logie, Goring, Lewis, Roper.

Feb 24 **Charlton Athletic** **2–5**
(Goring 2) Att: 58,137
Kelsey, Barnes, Smith (L), Shaw, Compton (L), Forbes, McPherson, Logie, Goring, Lewis, Roper.

Mar 10 **Aston Villa** **2–1**
(Lewis 2) Att: 43,747
Platt, Barnes, Smith (L), Shaw, Daniel, Forbes, Milton, Logie, Holton, Lewis, Marden.

Mar 23 **Portsmouth** **0–1**
Att: 52,051
Kelsey, Scott, Smith (L), Mercer, Compton (L), Shaw, Roper, Logie, Goring, Lewis, Marden.

Mar 24 **Wolverhampton Wanderers** **2–1**
(Holton 2 [1pen]) Att: 54,213
Kelsey, Scott, Smith (L), Mercer, Compton (L), Bowen, Roper, Logie, Holton, Forbes, Marden.

Apr 7 **Liverpool** **1–2**
(Holton) Att: 34,664
Swindin, Scott, Smith (L), Mercer, Compton (L), Bowen, Roper, Logie, Holton, Lewis, Marden.

Apr 21 **Bolton Wanderers** **1–1**
(Lishman) Att: 45,040
Swindin, Scott, Barnes, Mercer, Compton (L), Bowen, McPherson, Roper, Holton, Lishman, Marden.

FA CUP

Jan 6 **Carlisle United** **0–0**
Att: 57,932
Platt, Barnes, Smith (L), Forbes, Daniel, Mercer, Cox, Logie, Goring, Lewis, Roper.

Jan 27 **Northampton Town** **3–2**
(Lewis 2, Roper) Att: 72,408
Platt, Barnes, Smith (L), Forbes, Compton (L), Mercer, McPherson, Logie, Goring, Lewis, Roper.

1951/52

LEAGUE DIVISION ONE
Final position – 3rd

Aug 18 **Huddersfield Town** **2–2**
(Marden, Holton) Att: 54,072
Swindin, Scott, Barnes, Forbes, Daniel, Bowen, Roper, Logie, Holton, Lishman, Marden.

Aug 29 **Chelsea** **2–1**
(Holton, Lishman) Att: 48,768
Swindin, Scott, Barnes, Forbes, Daniel, Mercer, Roper, Logie, Holton, Lishman, Marden.

Sep 1 **Sunderland** **3–0**
(Lishman 3) Att: 66,137
Swindin, Barnes, Smith (L), Forbes, Daniel, Mercer, Roper, Logie, Holton, Lishman, Cox.

Sep 5 **Liverpool** **0–0**
Att: 50,483
Swindin, Barnes, Smith (L), Forbes, Daniel, Mercer, Roper, Logie, Holton, Lishman, Cox.

Sep 15 **Derby County** **3–1**
(Holton 2, Lishman) Att: 50,181
Swindin, Barnes, Smith (L), Forbes, Daniel, Mercer, Milton, Logie, Holton, Lishman, Cox.

Sep 29 **Tottenham Hotspur** **1–1**
(Holton) Att: 72,164
Swindin, Barnes, Smith (L), Forbes, Daniel, Mercer, Milton, Logie, Holton, Lishman, Cox.

Oct 13 **Burnley** **1–0**
(Lewis) Att: 48,531
Swindin, Barnes, Smith (L), Forbes, Daniel, Mercer, Logie, Lewis, Holton, Lishman, Roper.

Oct 27 **Fulham** **4–3**
(Lishman 3, Holton) Att: 54,178
Swindin, Barnes, Smith (L), Forbes, Daniel, Mercer, Milton, Logie, Holton, Lishman, Roper.

Nov 10 **West Bromwich Albion** **6–3**
(Lishman 3, Holton 2, Logie) Att: 53,432
Swindin, Barnes, Wade, Forbes, Daniel, Mercer, Milton, Logie, Holton, Lishman, Roper.

Nov 24 **Bolton Wanderers** **4–2**
(Lishman 3, Roper) Att: 53,790
Swindin, Chenhall, Barnes, Forbes, Daniel, Mercer, Milton, Logie, Holton, Lishman, Roper.

Dec 8 **Manchester United** **1–3**
(Logie) Att: 55,451
Swindin, Barnes, Smith (L), Forbes, Daniel, Mercer, Milton, Logie, Holton, Lishman, Roper.

Dec 22 **Wolverhampton Wanderers** **2–2**
(Lewis 2) Att: 45,644
Swindin, Barnes, Smith (L), Forbes, Daniel, Bowen, Milton, Lewis, Goring, Lishman, Roper.

Dec 25 **Portsmouth** **4–1**
(Cox, Logie, Lewis, Goring) Att: 54,241
Swindin, Barnes, Smith (L), Forbes, Daniel, Mercer, Cox, Logie, Lewis, Goring, Marden.

Jan 5 **Aston Villa** **2–1**
(Roper 2) Att: 53,540
Swindin, Barnes, Smith (L), Forbes, Daniel, Mercer, Cox, Logie, Goring, Lishman, Roper.

Jan 26 **Manchester City** **2–2**
(Lishman 2) Att: 54,527
Swindin, Barnes, Smith (L), Forbes, Daniel, Mercer, Cox, Logie, Goring, Lishman, Roper.

Feb16 **Preston North End** **3–3**
(Lewis 2, Roper) Att: 61,849
Swindin, Barnes, Smith (L), Forbes, Daniel, Mercer, Cox, Logie, Lewis, Lishman, Roper.

Mar 13 **Charlton Athletic** **2–1**
(Goring 2) Att: 37,985
Swindin, Barnes, Smith (L), Shaw, Daniel, Mercer, Cox, Goring, Holton, Lishman, Roper.

Mar 22 **Middlesbrough** **3–1**
(Holton, Lishman, Milton) Att: 50,979
Swindin, Barnes, Smith (L), Forbes, Daniel, Mercer, Milton, Logie, Holton, Lishman, Cox.

Apr 14 **Blackpool** **4–1**
(Lishman 2, Barnes [pen], Crosland [og])
Att: 50,445
Swindin, Barnes, Wade, Forbes, Shaw, Mercer, Cox, Logie, Holton, Lishman, Roper.

Apr 16 **Newcastle United** **1–1**
(Milton) Att: 53,203
Swindin, Barnes, Wade, Forbes, Mercer, Bowen, Milton, Logie, Goring, Lishman, Roper.

Apr 19 **Stoke City** **4–1**
(Holton 2, Barnes [pen], Lishman) Att: 47,962
Swindin, Barnes, Wade, Mercer, Compton (L), Bowen, Cox, Forbes, Holton, Lishman, Roper.

FA CUP
Finalists

Feb 2 **Barnsley** **4–0**
(Lewis 3, Lishman) Att: 69,466
Swindin, Barnes, Smith (L), Forbes, Daniel, Mercer, Cox, Logie, Lewis, Lishman, Roper.

1952/53

LEAGUE DIVISION ONE
Final position – Champions

Aug 27 **Manchester United** **2–1**
(Cox, Goring) Att: 58,831
Swindin, Wade, Smith (L), Shaw, Daniel, Mercer, Cox, Oakes, Goring, Lishman, Roper.

Aug 30 **Sunderland** **1–2**
(Lishman) Att: 57,873
Swindin, Chenhall, Wade, Shaw, Daniel, Mercer, Cox, Goring, Holton, Lishman, Roper.

Sep 10 **Portsmouth** **3–1**
(Goring, Milton, Roper) Att:40,743
Swindin, Wade, Smith (L), Forbes, Daniel, Mercer, Milton, Logie, Goring, Shaw, Roper.

Sep 13 **Charlton Athletic** 3–4
(Milton, Goring, Daniel [pen]) Att: 61,102
Swindin, Wade, Smith (L), Forbes, Daniel, Mercer, Milton, Logie, Goring, Shaw, Roper.

Oct 4 **Blackpool** 3–1
(Roper 2, Logie) Att: 66,682
Kelsey, Chenhall, Wade, Shaw, Daniel, Forbes, Milton, Logie, Goring, Lishman, Roper.

Oct 11 **Sheffield Wednesday** 2–2
(Roper, Logie) Att: 55,678
Kelsey, Chenhall, Wade, Shaw, Daniel, Forbes, Milton, Logie, Goring, Lishman, Roper.

Oct 25 **Newcastle United** 3–0
(Lishman, Roper 2) Att: 63,744
Kelsey, Wade, Smith (L), Forbes, Daniel, Mercer, Milton, Logie, Goring, Lishman, Roper.

Nov 8 **Middlesbrough** 2–1
(Milton, Holton) Att: 49,564
Kelsey, Wade, Smith (L), Shaw, Daniel, Forbes, Milton, Logie, Holton, Lishman, Roper.

Nov 22 **Manchester City** 3–1
(Lishman, Logie 2) Att: 39,161
Kelsey, Wade, Smith (L), Forbes, Daniel, Mercer, Milton, Logie, Holton, Lishman, Roper.

Dec 20 **Aston Villa** 3–1
(Lishman, Holton, Roper) Att: 32,064
Kelsey, Wade, Smith (L), Shaw, Daniel, Mercer, Milton, Logie, Holton, Lishman, Roper.

Jan 17 **Wolverhampton Wanderers** 5–3
(Daniel [pen], Lishman 2, Logie, Milton)
Att: 58,983
Kelsey, Wade, Smith (L), Forbes, Daniel, Shaw, Milton, Logie, Holton, Lishman, Roper.

Feb 7 **Tottenham Hotspur** 4–0
(Holton 2, Lishman, Logie) Att: 69,051
Kelsey, Wade, Smith (L), Forbes, Daniel, Mercer, Milton, Logie, Holton, Lishman, Roper.

Feb 18 **Derby County** 6–2
(Daniel 2 (2 pens), Lishman 2, Holton 2)
Att: 32,681
Kelsey, Wade, Smith (L), Forbes, Daniel, Shaw, Milton, Goring, Holton, Lishman, Roper.

Mar 7 **Cardiff City** 0–1
Att: 59,580
Kelsey, Wade, Smith (L), Shaw, Daniel, Mercer, Cox, Logie, Holton, Lishman, Roper.

Mar 19 **Preston North End** 1–1
(Mercer) Att: 33,697
Kelsey, Wade, Smith (L), Forbes, Daniel, Mercer, Milton, Logie, Goring, Lishman, Roper.

Mar 21 **West Bromwich Albion** 2–2
(Holton, Roper) Att: 50,078
Kelsey, Wade, Smith (L), Shaw, Daniel, Forbes, Cox, Logie, Holton, Lishman, Roper.

Apr 4 **Liverpool** 5–3
(Roper 2, Lishman, Goring, Hughes [og])
Att: 39,564
Kelsey, Wade, Smith (L), Shaw, Daniel, Forbes, Milton, Logie, Goring, Lishman, Roper.

Apr 6 **Chelsea** 2–0
(Lishman, Marden) Att: 40,536
Swindin, Wade, Smith (L), Forbes, Daniel, Mercer, Roper, Logie, Goring, Lishman, Marden.

Apr 15 **Bolton Wanderers** 4–1
(Goring, Lishman 2, Marden) Att: 35,006
Swindin, Wade, Chenhall, Forbes, Dodgin, Mercer, Roper, Logie, Goring, Lishman, Marden.

Apr 18 **Stoke City** 3–1
(Lishman 3) Att: 47,376
Swindin, Wade, Chenhall, Forbes, Daniel, Mercer, Roper, Logie, Goring, Lishman, Marden.

May 1 **Burnley** 3–2
(Forbes, Lishman, Logie) Att: 51,586
Swindin, Wade, Smith (L), Forbes, Daniel, Mercer, Roper, Logie, Goring, Lishman, Marden.

FA CUP

Jan 10 **Doncaster Rovers** 4–0
(Lishman, Holton, Logie, Roper) Att: 57,443
Kelsey, Wade, Smith (L), Shaw, Daniel, Forbes, Milton, Logie, Holton, Lishman, Roper.

Jan 31 **Bury** 6–2
(Holton, Roper, Lishman, Logie, Milton, DanielT [og]) Att: 45,071
Kelsey, Wade, Smith (L), Forbes, Daniel, Mercer, Milton, Logie, Holton, Lishman, Roper.

Feb 28 **Blackpool** 1–2
(Logie) Att: 69,158
Kelsey, Wade, Smith (L), Forbes, Daniel, Mercer, Milton, Logie, Holton, Lishman, Roper.

1953/54

LEAGUE DIVISION ONE
Final position – 12th

Aug 22 **Huddersfield Town** 0–0
Att: 54,847
Kelsey, Wade, Evans, Forbes, Dodgin, Mercer, Roper, Logie, Holton, Lishman, Ward.

Sep 1 **Sheffield United** 1–1
(Shaw [og]) Att: 43,077
Kelsey, Wade, Evans, Bowen, Dodgin, Forbes, Roper, Logie, Holton, Lishman, Marden.

Sep 5 **Wolverhampton Wanderers** 2–3
(Roper, Holton) Att: 60,460
Kelsey, Wade, Evans, Forbes, Dodgin, Bowen, Roper, Logie, Holton, Lishman, Marden.

Sep 8 **Chelsea** 1–2
(Holton) Att: 55,086
Swindin, Barnes, Smith (L), Forbes, Dodgin, Bowen, Milton, Logie, Holton, Tilley, Roper.

Sep 19 **Manchester City** 2–2
(Lishman 2) Att: 65,869
Kelsey. Wade, Barnes, Shaw, Dodgin, Bowen, Forbes, Logie, Lawton, Lishman, Roper.

Oct 3 **Preston North End** 3–2
(Roper 2, Barnes [pen]) Att: 61,807
Kelsey, Wade, Barnes, Forbes, Dodgin, Mercer, Milton, Logie, Holton, Lishman, Roper.

Oct 17 **Burnley** 2–5
(Forbes, Roper) Att: 47,373
Kelsey, Wills, Barnes, Forbes, Dodgin, Mercer, Milton, Logie, Lawton, Lishman, Roper.

Oct 31 **Sheffield Wednesday** 4–1
(Holton 2, Logie 2) Att: 52,543
Kelsey, Wills, Barnes, Dickson, Dodgin, Mercer, Roper, Logie, Holton, Lishman, Marden.

Nov 14 **Bolton Wanderers** 4–3
(Holton 3, Lishman) Att: 52,319
Kelsey, Wills, Barnes, Dickson, Dodgin, Forbes, Roper, Logie, Holton, Lishman, Marden.

Nov 28 **Newcastle United** 2–1
(Holton, Forbes) Att: 62,456
Kelsey, Wills, Barnes, Dickson, Dodgin, Forbes, Milton, Logie, Holton, Lishman, Roper.

Dec 12 **West Bromwich Albion** 2–2
(Lishman 2) Att: 55,264
Kelsey, Wills, Smith (L), Dickson, Dodgin, Mercer, Roper, Logie, Holton, Lishman, Marden.

Dec 28 **Blackpool** 1–1
(Roper) Att: 62,900
Kelsey, Wills, Barnes, Dickson, Dodgin, Mercer, Milton, Logie, Holton, Lishman, Roper.

Jan 23 **Sunderland** 1–4
(Holton) Att: 60,218
Kelsey, Wills, Wade, Dickson, Dodgin, Forbes, Milton, Lawton, Holton, Lishman, Roper.

Feb 13 **Cardiff City** 1–1
(Lishman) Att: 45,497
Kelsey, Wills, Barnes, Forbes, Dodgin, Mercer, Walsh, Logie, Lawton, Lishman, Roper.

Feb 27 **Tottenham Hotspur** 0–3
Att: 64,211
Kelsey, Wills, Barnes, Forbes, Dodgin, Mercer, Walsh, Logie, Holton, Lishman, Roper.

Mar 13 **Charlton Athletic** 3–3
(Holton, Lishman, Dickson) Att: 41,256
Kelsey, Wills, Evans, Forbes, Dodgin, Dickson, Walsh, Logie, Holton, Lishman, Milton.

Mar 27 **Manchester United** 3–1
(Logie 2, Holton) Att: 42,735
Kelsey, Wills, Smith (L), Dickson, Dodgin, Forbes, Walsh, Logie, Holton, Goring, Roper.

Apr 6 **Aston Villa** 1–1
(Lawton) Att: 14,519
Kelsey, Wills, Wade, Dickson, Dodgin, Mercer, Milton, Lawton, Holton, Lishman, Roper.

Apr 10 **Liverpool** 3–0
(Tapscott 2, Roper) Att: 33,178
Kelsey, Wills, Wade, Bowen, Dickson, Mercer, Milton, Tapscott, Lawton, Lishman, Roper.

Apr 16 **Portsmouth** 3–0
(Tapscott 2, Roper) Att: 44,948
Kelsey, Wills, Wade, Goring, Dickson, Bowen, Milton, Tapscott, Lawton, Lishman, Roper.

Apr 24 **Middlesbrough** 3–1
(Roper, Lishman, Tapscott) Att: 35,196
Kelsey, Wills, Wade, Goring, Dodgin, Dickson, Milton, Logie, Tapscott, Lishman, Roper.

FA CUP

Jan 9 **Aston Villa** 5–1
(Roper 2, Holton, Logie, Milton) Att: 50,990
Kelsey, Wills, Wade, Dickson, Dodgin, Forbes, Milton, Logie, Holton, Lishman, Roper.

Jan 30 **Norwich City** 1–2
(Logie) Att: 55,767
Kelsey, Wills, Smith (L), Dickson, Dodgin, Forbes, Milton, Logie, Holton, Lishman, Roper.

FA CHARITY SHIELD

Oct 12 **Blackpool** 3–1
(Lishman 2, Lawton) Att: 39,853
Kelsey, Wills, Barnes, Forbes, Dodgin, Mercer, Holton, Logie, Lawton, Lishman, Roper.

1954/55

LEAGUE DIVISION ONE
Final position – 9th

Aug 21 **Newcastle United** 1–3
(Lishman) Att: 65,334
Kelsey, Wills, Wade, Forbes, Dickson, Shaw, Walsh, Logie, Holton, Lishman, Roper.

Aug 31 **Everton** 2–0
(Lishman, Roper) Att: 42,146
Kelsey, Wills, Barnes, Goring, Forbes, Bowen, Tapscott, Logie, Lawton, Lishman, Roper.

Sep 4 **Tottenham Hotspur** 2–0
(Logie, Lishman) Att: 53,977
Kelsey, Wills, Barnes, Goring, Forbes, Bowen,Tapscott, Logie, Lawton, Lishman, Roper.

Sep 11 **Sheffield United** 4–0
(Forbes [pen], Lishman, Tapscott, Roper)
Att: 41,679
Kelsey, Wills, Barnes, Goring, Forbes, Bowen, Tapscott, Logie, Lawton, Lishman, Roper.

Sep 14 **Manchester City** 2–3
(Tapscott, Lishman) Att: 33,898
Kelsey, Wills, Barnes, Goring, Forbes, Bowen, Tapscott, Logie, Holton, Lishman, Roper.

Sep 25 **Burnley** 4–0
(Lawton 2, Lishman, Roper) Att: 46,190
Kelsey, Barnes, Wade, Goring, Dickson, Forbes, Tapscott, Logie, Lawton, Lishman, Roper.

Oct 16 **Portsmouth** 0–1
Att: 44,866
Guthrie, Wills, Wade, Goring, Dodgin, Forbes, Walsh, Logie, Holton, Bloomfield, Roper.

Oct 30 **Sunderland** 1–3
(Roper) Att: 65,424
Kelsey, Barnes, Wade, Goring, Dodgin, Forbes, Milton, Tapscott, Holton, Bloomfield, Roper.

Nov 13 **Huddersfield Town** 3–5
(Milton 2, Lishman) Att: 42,950
Kelsey, Barnes, Wade, Goring, Fotheringham, Forbes, Milton, Tapscott, Roper, Lishman, Marden.

Nov 27 **Wolverhampton Wanderers** 1–1
(Roper) Att: 55,055
Kelsey, Wills, Wade, Goring, Fotheringham, Forbes, Milton, Tapscott, Roper, Lishman, Marden.

Dec 11 **Charlton Athletic** 3–1
(Roper 2, Milton) Att: 39,498
Kelsey, Wills, Wade, Goring, Fotheringham, Bowen, Milton, Tapscott, Roper, Lishman, Marden.

Dec 25 **Chelsea** 1–0
(Lawton) Att: 47,178
Kelsey, Barnes, Evans, Goring, Fotheringham, Bowen, Clapton, Tapscott, Lawton, Lishman, Haverty.

Jan 1 **West Bromwich Albion** 2–2
(Tapscott, Lishman) Att: 40,246
Kelsey, Barnes, Evans, Goring, Fothringham, Bowen, Clapton, Tapscott, Lawton, Lishman, Haverty.

Feb 5 **Preston North End** 2–0
(Tapscott, Roper) Att: 41,228
Kelsey, Barnes, Evans, Goring, Fotheringham, Bowen, Roper, Tapscott, Lawton, Lishman, Holton.

Feb 19 **Leicester City** 1–1
(Roper) Att: 27,384
Kelsey, Barnes, Evans, Goring, Fotheringham, Bowen, Tapscott, Herd, Wilkinson, Lishman, Roper.

Feb 26 **Sheffield Wednesday** 3–2
(Tapscott 3) Att: 26,910
Kelsey, Barnes, Evans, Goring, Fotheringham, Bowen, Clapton, Tapscott, Roper, Bloomfield, Haverty.

Mar 12 **Aston Villa** 2–0
(Tapscott, Roper) Att: 30,136
Kelsey, Barnes, Evans, Goring, Fotheringham, Bowen, Clapton, Tapscott, Roper, Bloomfield, Marden.

Mar 26 **Bolton Wanderers** 3–0
(Lishman 2, Roper) Att: 33,852
Sullivan, Wills, Evans, Goring, Fotheringham, Oakes, Clapton, Tapscott, Roper, Lishman, Bloomfield.

Apr 8 **Cardiff City** 2–0
(Tapscott 2) Att: 39,052
Kelsey, Wills, Evans, Goring, Fotheringham, Oakes, Clapton, Tapscott, Roper, Bloomfield, Swallow.

Apr 9 **Blackpool** 3–0
(Lishman 2, Roper) Att: 60,741
Kelsey, Wills, Evans, Goring, Fotheringham, Oakes, Clapton, Tapscott, Roper, Lishman, Bloomfield.

Apr23 **Manchester United** 2–3
(Lishman 2) Att: 42,754
Kelsey, Wills, Evans, Goring, Fotheringham, Oakes, Clapton, Tapscott, Roper, Lishman, Bloomfield.

FA CUP

Jan 8 **Cardiff City** 1–0
(Lawton) Att: 51,498
Kelsey, Barnes, Evans, Goring, Fotheringham, Bowen, Milton, Tapscott, Lawton, Lishman, Haverty.

1955/56

LEAGUE DIVISION ONE
Final position – 5th

Aug 23 Cardiff City 3–1
(Lawton 3) Att: 31,352
Kelsey, Barnes, Evans, Goring, Fotheringham, Bowen, Clapton, Tapscott, Lawton, Lishman, Bloomfield.

Aug 27 **Chelsea** 1–1
(Lawton) Att: 55,011
Kelsey, Barnes, Evans, Goring, Fotheringham, Bowen, Clapton, Tapscott, Lawton, Lishman, Roper.

Sep 6 **Manchester City** 0–0
Att: 30,864
Kelsey, Barnes, Evans, Goring, Fotheringham, Bowen, Clapton, Tapscott, Lawton, Roper, Bloomfield.

Sep 17 **Portsmouth** 1–3
(Lishman) Att: 48,816
Kelsey, Barnes, Evans, Goring, Fotheringham, Bowen, Clapton, Tapscott, Lawton, Lishman, Roper.

Oct 1 **Aston Villa** 1–0
(Nutt) Att: 43,824
Kelsey, Wills, Evans, Goring, Holton, Bowen, Tiddy, Bloomfield, Roper, Lishman, Nutt.

Oct 15 **Newcastle United** 1–0
(Roper) Att: 46,093
Kelsey, Wills, Evans, Goring, Fotheringham, Holton, Tiddy, Bloomfield, Roper, Lishman, Clapton.

Oct 29 **Charlton Athletic** 2–4
(Lishman, Clapton) Att: 47,038
Kelsey, Wills, Evans, Goring, Fotheringham, Holton, Clapton, Bloomfield, Roper, Lishman, Tiddy.

Nov 12 **Sheffield United** 2–1
(Groves, Roper) Att: 46,647
Kelsey, Wills, Evans, Goring, Fotheringham, Holton, Clapton, Roper, Groves, Lishman, Tiddy.

Nov 26 **Burnley** 0–1
Att: 37,583
Kelsey, Wills, Evans, Goring, Fotheringham, Holton, Clapton, Tapscott, Roper, Lishman, Tiddy.

Dec 10 **West Bromwich Albion** 2–0
(Tapscott, Williams [og]) Att: 33,217
Sullivan, Wills, Evans, Goring, Fotheringham, Holton, Clapton, Tapscott, Groves, Bloomfield, Tiddy.

Dec 17 **Blackpool** 4–1
(Groves, Holton, Tapscott, Bloomfield)
Att: 45,086
Sullivan, Wills, Evans, Goring, Fotheringham, Holton, Clapton, Tapscott, Groves, Bloomfield, Tiddy.

Dec 27 **Wolverhampton Wanderers** 2–2
(Tapscott 2) Att: 61,814
Sullivan, Charlton, Evans, Goring, Fotheringham, Holton, Clapton, Tapscott, Groves, Bloomfield, Tiddy.

Dec 31 **Bolton Wanderers** 3–1
(Tapscott 2, Groves) Att: 42,677
Sullivan, Charlton, Evans, Goring, Fotheringham, Holton, Clapton, Tapscott, Groves, Bloomfield, Tiddy.

Jan 14 **Tottenham Hotspur** 0–1
Att: 59,603
Kelsey, Wills, Evans, Forbes, Fotheringham, Holton, Clapton, Tapscott, Groves, Bloomfield, Nutt.

Feb 4 **Sunderland** 3–1
(Herd 2, Bloomfield) Att: 38,780
Kelsey, Charlton, Evans, Goring, Dodgin, Bowen, Clapton, Herd, Groves, Bloomfield, Tiddy.

Feb 21 **Everton** 3–2
(Tapscott 2, Groves) Att: 16,039
Sullivan, Charlton, Evans, Goring, Dodgin, Bowen, Clapton, Tapscott, Groves, Bloomfield, Tiddy.

Mar 6 **Preston North End** 3–2
(Tapscott 2, Groves) Att: 34,672
Kelsey, Charlton, Evans, Holton, Dodgin, Bowen, Clapton, Tapscott, Groves, Bloomfield, Nutt.

Mar 17 **Manchester United** 1–1
(Holton) Att: 50,758
Kelsey, Charlton, Evans, Goring, Dodgin, Bowen, Clapton, Tapscott, Holton, Bloomfield, Haverty.

Mar 31 **Luton Town** 3–0
(Holton 2, Haverty) Att: 45,968
Kelsey, Charlton, Evans, Goring, Dodgin, Bowen, Clapton, Tapscott, Holton, Bloomfield, Haverty.

Apr 2 **Huddersfield Town** 2–0
(Haverty, Holton) Att: 30,836
Kelsey, Charlton, Evans, Goring, Dodgin, Bowen, Clapton, Tapscott, Holton, Bloomfield, Haverty.

Apr 14 **Birmingham City** 1–0
(Tapscott) Att: 31,733
Kelsey, Charlton, Evans, Goring, Dodgin, Forbes, Clapton, Tapscott, Holton, Bloomfield, Haverty.

FA CUP

Jan 7 **Bedford Town** 2–2
(Tapscott, Groves) Att: 55,178
Sullivan, Charlton, Evans, Goring, Fotheringham, Holton, Clapton, Tapscott, Groves, Bloomfield, Tiddy.

Jan 28 **Aston Villa** 4–1
(Tapscott 2, Groves, Charlton [pen]) Att: 43,052
Kelsey, Charlton, Evans, Goring, Dodgin, Holton, Clapton, Tapscott, Groves, Bloomfield, Tiddy.

Mar 3 **Birmingham City** 1–3
(Charlton) Att: 67,872
Kelsey, Charlton, Evans, Goring, Dodgin, Bowen, Clapton, Tapscott, Groves, Bloomfield, Nutt.

1956/57

LEAGUE DIVISION ONE
Final position – 5th

Aug 18 **Cardiff City** 0–0
Att: 51,069
Kelsey, Charlton, Evans, Goring, Dodgin, Bowen, Clapton, Tapscott, Holton, Bloomfield, Tiddy.

Aug 21 **Burnley** 2–0
(Tiddy, Bloomfield) Att: 38,321
Kelsey, Charlton, Evans, Wills, Dodgin, Goring, Clapton, Tapscott, Holton, Bloomfield, Tiddy.

Sep 1 **West Bromwich Albion** 4–1
(Roper 2, Tiddy, Tapscott) Att: 39,973
Kelsey, Charlton, Evans, Wills, Dodgin, Holton, Clapton, Tapscott, Roper, Bloomfield, Tiddy.

Sep 4 **Preston North End** 1–2
(Bloomfield) Att: 40,470
Kelsey, Charlton, Evans, Wills, Dodgin, Holton, Clapton, Tapscott, Roper, Bloomfield, Tiddy.

Sep 15 **Newcastle United** 0–1
Att: 46,318
Kelsey, Charlton, Evans, Wills, Dodgin, Goring, Clapton, Bloomfield, Tapscott, Swallow, Tiddy.

Sep 29 **Manchester United** 1–2
(Evans [pen]) Att: 62,429
Kelsey, Charlton, Evans, Goring, Dodgin, Bowen, Clapton, Tapscott, Groves, Bloomfield, Tiddy.

Oct 6 **Manchester City** 7–3
(Holton 4, Evans [pen], Bloomfield, Haverty)
Att: 33,651
Kelsey, Charlton, Evans, Goring, Dodgin, Bowen, Clapton, Tapscott, Holton, Bloomfield, Haverty.

Oct 20 **Tottenham Hotspur** 3–1
(Herd 2, Haverty) Att: 60,580
Sullivan, Charlton, Evans, Wills, Dodgin, Holton, Clapton, Tapscott, Herd, Bloomfield, Haverty.

Nov 3 **Aston Villa** 2–1
(Groves 2) Att: 40,045
Kelsey, Charlton, Evans, Wills, Dodgin, Bowen, Groves, Tapscott, Holton, Bloomfield, Haverty.

Nov 17 **Bolton Wanderers** 3–0
(Tapscott 2, Haverty) Att: 33,377
Sullivan, Charlton, Evans, Wills, Dodgin, Bowen, Clapton, Tapscott, Holton, Bloomfield, Haverty.

Dec 1 **Sunderland** 1–1
(Tapscott) Att: 36,442
Sullivan, Charlton, Evans, Goring, Dodgin, Bowen, Clapton, Tapscott, Holton, Bloomfield, Haverty.

Dec22 **Birmingham City** 4–0
(Evans [pen], Holton, Bloomfield, Watts [og])
Att: 28,644
Sullivan, Charlton, Evans, Holton, Dodgin, Bowen, Clapton, Tapscott, Herd, Bloomfield, Haverty.

Dec 26 **Chelsea** 2–0
(Clapton, Tapscott) Att: 22,526
Kelsey, Charlton, Evans, Holton, Dodgin, Bowen, Clapton, Tapscott, Herd, Bloomfield, Haverty.

Jan 12 **Portsmouth** 1–1
(Herd) Att: 48,949
Sullivan, Charlton, Evans, Holton, Dodgin, Bowen, Clapton, Tapscott, Herd, Bloomfield, Haverty.

Feb 2 **Sheffield Wednesday** 6–3
(Herd 3, Tapscott 2, Bloomfield) Att: 40,217
Sullivan, Charlton, Evans, Holton, Dodgin, Bowen, Clapton, Tapscott, Herd, Bloomfield, Haverty.

Feb 23 **Everton** 2–0
(Holton, Tapscott) Att: 30,562
Kelsey, Charlton, Wills, Holton, Dodgin, Bowen, Clapton, Tapscott, Groves, Bloomfield, Haverty.

Mar 9 **Luton Town** 1–3
(Tapscott) Att: 41,288
Kelsey, Charlton, Evans, Holton, Dodgin, Bowen, Clapton, Tapscott, Herd, Bloomfield, Haverty.

Mar 23 **Wolverhampton Wanderers** 0–0
Att: 51,021
Kelsey, Charlton, Evans, Holton, Dodgin, Bowen, Clapton, Tapscott, Herd, Bloomfield, Haverty.

Apr 6 **Leeds United** 1–0
(Herd) Att: 40,388
Kelsey, Charlton, Evans, Holton, Dodgin, Bowen, Clapton, Tapscott, Herd, Bloomfield, Haverty.

Apr 19 **Blackpool** 1–1
(Tapscott) Att: 50,270
Kelsey, Charlton, Evans, Holton, Dodgin, Bowen, Clapton, Tapscott, Herd, Bloomfield, Haverty.

Apr 20 **Charlton Athletic** 3–1
(Tapscott 2, Holton) Att: 26,364
Kelsey, Charlton, Evans, Holton, Dodgin, Bowen, Tiddy, Tapscott, Groves, Bloomfield, Haverty.

FA CUP

Jan 5 **Stoke City** 4–2
(Herd 2, Tapscott, Haverty) Att: 56,173
Sullivan, Charlton, Evans, Holton, Dodgin, Bowen, Clapton, Tapscott, Herd, Bloomfield, Haverty.

Feb 19 **Preston North End** 2–1
(Dodgin, Herd) Att: 61,501
Kelsey, Charlton, Evans, Holton, Dodgin, Bowen, Clapton, Tapscott, Herd, Bloomfield, Haverty.

Mar 5 **West Bromwich Albion** 1–2
(Holton) Att: 58,757
Kelsey, Charlton, Wills, Holton, Dodgin, Bowen, Clapton, Tapscott, Herd, Bloomfield, Groves.

1957/58

LEAGUE DIVISION ONE
Final position – 12th

Aug 27 **West Bromwich Albion** 2–2
(Herd 2) Att: 45,998
Kelsey, Charlton, Evans, Holton, Fotheringham, Bowen, Clapton, Herd, Groves, Bloomfield, Haverty.

Aug 31 **Luton Town** 2–0
(Groves, Holton) Att: 50,111
Kelsey, Charlton, Wills, Holton, Fotheringham, Bowen, Clapton, Herd, Groves, Bloomfield, Haverty.

Sep 10 **Everton** 2–3
(Groves 2) Att: 42,010
Kelsey, Charlton, Evans, Holton, Dodgin, Bowen, Clapton, Herd, Groves, Bloomfield, Haverty.

Sep 14 **Leicester City** 3–1
(Groves 2, Herd) Att: 45,321
Kelsey, Charlton, Evans, Holton, Dodgin, Bowen, Clapton, Herd, Groves, Bloomfield, Haverty.

Sep 28 **Leeds United** 2–1
(Herd 2) Att: 39,347
Sullivan, Wills, Evans, Holton, Dodgin, Bowen, Clapton, Swallow, Herd, Bloomfield, Tiddy.

Oct 2 **Aston Villa** 4–0
(Swallow, Tiddy, Bloomfield, Herd) Att: 18,472
Kelsey, Wills, Evans, Holton, Dodgin, Bowen, Clapton, Swallow, Herd, Bloomfield, Tiddy.

Oct 19 **Birmingham City** 1–3
(Swallow) Att: 39,006
Sullivan, Charlton, Evans, Holton, Dodgin, Goring, Nutt, Swallow, Herd, Bloomfield, Tiddy.

Nov 2 **Manchester City** 2–1
(Tapscott, Bloomfield) Att: 43,664
Kelsey, Charlton, Evans, Holton, Dodgin, Bowen, Clapton, Tapscott, Herd, Bloomfield, Haverty.

Nov 16 **Portsmouth** 3–2
(Herd 2, Clapton) Att: 40,528
Kelsey, Charlton, Evans, Holton, Dodgin, Bowen, Clapton, Groves, Herd, Bloomfield, Haverty.

Nov 30 **Newcastle United** 2–3
(Holton, Clapton) Att: 41,694
Kelsey, Charlton, Evans, Wills, Dodgin, Bowen, Clapton, Herd, Holton, Bloomfield, Tiddy.

Dec 14 **Preston North End** 4–2
(Nutt, Herd, Bloomfield, Dunn [og]) Att: 31,830
Kelsey, Charlton, Evans, Holton, Dodgin, Bowen, Le Roux, Herd, Groves, Bloomfield, Nutt.

Dec 21 **Sunderland** 3–0
(Herd 2, Groves) Att: 28,105
Kelsey, Charlton, Evans, Holton, Dodgin, Bowen, Le Roux, Herd, Groves, Bloomfield, Nutt.

Jan 11 **Blackpool** 2–3
(Herd 2) Att: 38,667
Kelsey, Wills, Evans, Goring, Dodgin, Bowen, Clapton, Tapscott, Herd, Groves, Nutt.

Feb 1 **Manchester United** 4–5
(Bloomfield 2, Herd, Tapscott) Att: 63,578
Kelsey, Charlton, Evans, Ward, Fotheringham, Bowen, Groves, Tapscott, Herd, Bloomfield, Nutt.

Feb 18 **Bolton Wanderers** 1–2
(Bloomfield) Att: 28,420
Kelsey, Charlton, Evans, Ward, Fotheringham, Petts, Groves, Tapscott, Herd, Bloomfield, Nutt.

Feb 22 **Tottenham Hotspur** 4–4
(Clapton, Herd, Nutt, Henry [og]) Att: 59,116
Kelsey, Charlton, Evans, Ward, Fotheringham, Petts, Clapton, Groves, Herd, Bloomfield, Nutt.

Mar 8 **Chelsea** 5–4
(Herd 3, Clapton, Bloomfield) Att: 41,570
Kelsey, Charlton, Wills, Ward, Fotheringham, Petts, Clapton, Groves, Herd, Bloomfield, Nutt.

Mar 22 **Sheffield Wednesday** 1–0
(Herd) Att: 28,074
Kelsey, Charlton, Wills, Ward, Fotheringham, Petts, Clapton, Groves, Herd, Bloomfield, Nutt.

Apr 7 **Wolverhampton Wanderers** 0–2
Att: 51,318
Kelsey, Charlton, Wills, Bowen, Fotheringham, Petts, Clapton, Groves, Herd, Bloomfield, Nutt.

Apr 19 **Burnley** 0–0
Att: 31,440
Kelsey, Wills, Evans, Goring, Fotheringham, Bowen, Tiddy, Groves, Herd, Bloomfield, Nutt.

Apr 21 **Nottingham Forest** 1–1
(Bloomfield) Att: 23,217
Kelsey, Charlton, Wills, Ward, Fotheringham, Petts, Tiddy, Groves, Biggs, Bloomfield, Haverty.

NOTE: There were no FA Cup matches at Highbury this season.

1958/59

LEAGUE DIVISION ONE
Final position – 3rd

Aug 26 **Burnley** 3–0
(Bloomfield, Holton, Docherty) Att: 41,305
Kelsey, Charlton, Evans, Ward, Dodgin, Docherty, Clapton, Groves, Holton, Bloomfield, Nutt.

Aug 30 **Leicester City** 5–1
(Holton 2, Evans, Clapton, Nutt) Att: 35,411
Kelsey, Charlton, Evans, Ward, Dodgin, Docherty, Clapton, Groves, Holton, Bloomfield, Nutt.

Sep 9 **Bolton Wanderers** 6–1
(Herd, Nutt 2, Bloomfield, Clapton, Evans [pen])
Att: 45,255
Kelsey, Wills, Evans, Ward, Dodgin, Docherty, Clapton, Groves, Herd, Bloomfield, Nutt.

Sep13 **Tottenham Hotspur** 3–1
(Nutt, Herd 2) Att: 65,565
Kelsey, Wills, Evans, Ward, Dodgin, Docherty, Clapton, Groves, Herd, Bloomfield, Nutt.

Sep 20 **Manchester City** 4–1
(Herd 2, Evans [pen], Bloomfield) Att: 47,878
Kelsey, Wills, Evans, Ward, Dodgin, Docherty, Clapton, Groves, Herd, Bloomfield, Nutt.

Oct 4 **West Bromwich Albion** 4–3
(Henderson 2, Herd, Barlow [og]) Att: 57,770
Kelsey, Wills, Evans, Ward, Dodgin, Docherty, Clapton, Groves, Herd, Bloomfield, Henderson.

Oct 18 **Wolverhampton Wanderers** 1–1
(Biggs) Att: 49,393
Standen, Wills, Evans, Ward, Dodgin, Petts, Clapton, Groves, Biggs, Bloomfield, Nutt.

Nov 1 **Newcastle United** 3–2
(Groves, Henderson 2) Att: 62,801
Kelsey, Wills, Evans, Ward, Dodgin, Docherty, Clapton, Groves, Herd, Bloomfield, Henderson.

Nov 15 **Nottingham Forest** 3–1
(Herd, Henderson, McKinlay [og]) Att: 49,106
Kelsey, Wills, Evans, Ward, Dodgin, Docherty, Clapton, Groves, Herd, Bloomfield, Henderson.

Nov 29 **Blackpool** 1–4
(Clapton) Att: 54,792
Kelsey, Wills, Evans, Docherty, Dodgin, Petts, Clapton, Barnwell, Biggs, Bloomfield, Haverty.

Dec 13 **Aston Villa** 1–2
(Henderson) Att: 32,170
Kelsey, Wills, Evans, Goring, Dodgin, Docherty, Clapton, Ward, Henderson, Bloomfield, Nutt.

Dec 20 **Preston North End** 1–2
(Henderson) Att: 32,860
Kelsey, Wills, Evans, Ward, Dodgin, Docherty, Clapton, Groves, Barnwell, Bloomfield, Henderson.

Dec 27 **Luton Town** 1–0
(Bloomfield) Att: 56,501
Kelsey, Wills, McCullough, Docherty, Dodgin, Petts, Clapton, Groves, Julians, Bloomfield, Henderson.

Jan 17 **Everton** 3–1
(Groves 2, Bloomfield) Att: 39,474
Standen, Wills, Evans, Ward, Docherty, Bowen, Clapton, Groves, Herd, Bloomfield, Henderson.

Feb 24 **Leeds United** 1–0
(Herd) Att: 30,244
Goy, Wills, Evans, Docherty, Dodgin, Bowen, Herd, Goulden, Goring, Barnwell, Haverty.

Feb 28 **Manchester United** 3–2
(Barnwell 2, Herd) Att: 67,386
Standen, Wills, Evans, Docherty, Dodgin, Bowen, Clapton, Ward, Herd, Barnwell, Haverty.

Mar 14 **Blackburn Rovers** 1–1
(Wills [pen]) Att: 40,155
Standen, Wills, McCullough, Docherty, Dodgin, Bowen, Clapton, Barnwell, Herd, Julians, Haverty.

Mar 28 **West Ham United** 1–2
(Henderson) Att: 52,452
Standen, Evans, McCullough, Ward, Dodgin, Docherty, Clapton, Groves, Henderson, Julians, Nutt.

Apr 11 **Chelsea** 1–1
(Ward) Att: 40,900
Standen, Evans, McCullough, Ward, Dodgin, Bowen, Henderson, Groves, Julians, Barnwell, Haverty.

Apr 25 **Portsmouth** 5–2
(Groves 3, Henderson, Gunter [og]) Att: 24,569
Standen, Wills, McCullough, Docherty, Dodgin, Bowen, Clapton, Groves, Julians, Bloomfield, Henderson.

May 4 **Birmingham City** 2–1
(Clapton, Groves) Att: 26,129
Goy, Wills, Evans, Ward, Docherty, Bowen, Clapton, Barnwell, Groves, Bloomfield, Henderson.

FA CUP

Jan 2 8 **Colchester United** 4–0
(Herd 2, Julians, Evans [pen]) Att: 62,686
Kelsey, Wills, Evans, Ward, Docherty, Bowen, Clapton, Groves, Herd, Julians, Henderson.

Feb 14 **Sheffield United** 2–2
(Evans [pen], Julians) Att: 55,407
Kelsey, Wills, Evans, Ward, Dodgin, Bowen, Clapton, Groves, Herd, Julians, Haverty.

1959/60

LEAGUE DIVISION ONE
Final position – 13th

Aug 22 **Sheffield Wednesday** 0–1
Att: 47,585
Standen, Wills, Evans, Docherty, Charles, Ward, Clapton, Groves, Herd, Bloomfield, Henderson.

Sep 1 **Nottingham Forest** 1–1
(Herd) Att: 41,585
Standen, Wills, McCullough, Charles, Dodgin, Groves, Clapton, Barnwell, Herd, Bloomfield, Haverty.

Sep 5 **Tottenham Hotspur** 1–1
(Barnwell) Att: 61,011
Standen, Wills, McCullough, Charles, Dodgin, Docherty, Clapton, Barnwell, Herd, Bloomfield, Haverty.

Sep 12 **Manchester City** 3–1
(Clapton, Barnwell, Haverty) Att: 38,392
Standen, Wills, McCullough, Charles, Dodgin, Docherty, Clapton, Barnwell, Herd, Bloomfield, Haverty.

Sep 15 **Bolton Wanderers** **2–1**
(Herd, Clapton) Att: 38,795
Standen, Wills, McCullough, Ward, Dodgin, Docherty, Clapton, Barnwell, Herd, Bloomfield, Henderson.

Sep 26 **Blackpool** **2–1**
(Barnwell, Herd) Att: 47,473
Standen, Wills, McCullough, Groves, Dodgin, Docherty, Clapton, Barnwell, Herd, Bloomfield, Haverty.

Oct 17 **Preston North End** **0–3**
Att: 44,073
Standen, Wills, McCullough, Docherty, Dodgin, Groves, Henderson, Bloomfield, Julians, Herd, Haverty.

Oct 31 **Birmingham City** **3–0**
(Herd, Barnwell, Henderson) Att: 34,605
Kelsey, Wills, McCullough, Groves, Dodgin, Petts, Henderson, Barnwell, Herd, Bloomfield, Haverty.

Nov 14 **West Ham United** **1–3**
(Bloomfield) Att: 49,760
Kelsey, Wills, McCullough, Charles, Dodgin, Petts, Clapton, Herd, Groves, Bloomfield, Haverty.

Nov 28 **West Bromwich Albion** **2–4**
(Groves, Bloomfield) Att: 41,157
Kelsey, Wills, McCullough, Barnwell, Dodgin, Petts, Clapton, Henderson, Groves, Bloomfield, Haverty.

Dec 12 **Burnley** **2–4**
(Haverty, Bloomfield) Att: 26,249
Kelsey, Wills, McCullough, Groves, Dodgin, Ward, Clapton, Barnwell, Henderson, Bloomfield, Haverty.

Dec 26 **Luton Town** **0–3**
Att: 31,466
Standen, Magill, Evans, Ward, Dodgin, Petts, Herd, Barnwell, Julians, Bloomfield, Clapton.

Jan 2 **Wolverhampton Wanderers** **4–4**
(Evans, Haverty, Charles, Wills [pen]) Att: 47,854
Standen, Magill, Evans, Barnwell, Dodgin, Wills, Henderson, Herd, Charles, Bloomfield, Haverty.

Feb 6 **Blackburn Rovers** **5–2**
(Charles 3, Haverty, Herd) Att: 35,633
Kelsey, Magill, McCullough, Ward, Docherty, Wills, Henderson, Herd, Charles, Bloomfield, Haverty.

Feb 20 **Everton** **2–1**
(Charles 2) Att: 28,872
Kelsey, Magill, McCullough, Ward, Dodgin, Docherty, Henderson, Barnwell, Charles, Groves, Haverty.

Feb 27 **Newcastle United** **1–0**
(Barnwell) Att: 47,657
Kelsey, Magill, McCullough, Ward, Dodgin, Docherty, Henderson, Barnwell, Charles, Groves, Haverty.

Mar 15 **Leicester City** **1–1**
(Herd) Att: 27,838
Standen, Magill, McCullough, Ward, Dodgin, Docherty, Henderson, Herd, Charles, Groves, Haverty.

Mar 26 **Leeds United** **1–1**
(Herd) Att: 19,735
Kelsey, Magill, McCullough, Charles, Dodgin, Groves, Henderson, Barnwell, Herd, Bloomfield, Haverty.

Apr 9 **Chelsea** **1–4**
(Bloomfield) Att: 40,700
Kelsey, Magill, McCullough, Docherty, Dodgin, Groves, Henderson, Barnwell, Herd, Bloomfield, Haverty.

Apr 15 **Fulham** **2–0**
(Henderson, Herd) Att: 37,873
Kelsey, Wills, McCullough, Groves, Docherty, Everitt, Henderson, Herd, Clapton (DP), Bloomfield, Haverty.

Apr 23 **Manchester United** **5–2**
(Bloomfield 3, Clapton, Ward) Att: 41,057
Kelsey, Wills, McCullough, Ward, Docherty, Everitt, Clapton, Henderson, Groves, Bloomfield, Haverty.

FA CUP

Jan 13 **Rotherham United** **1–1**
(Bloomfield) Att: 57,598
Standen, Magill, Evans, Wills, Docherty, Barnwell, Clapton, Henderson, Herd, Bloomfield, Haverty.

1960/61

LEAGUE DIVISION ONE
Final position – 11th

Aug 23 **Preston North End** **1–0**
(Everitt) Att: 31,612
Kelsey, Wills, McCullough, Ward, Docherty, Everitt, Skirton, Barnwell, Herd, Bloomfield, Henderson.

Aug 27 **Nottingham Forest** **3–0**
(Henderson, Skirton 2) Att: 28,878
Kelsey, Wills, McCullough, Everitt, Snedden, Docherty, Skirton, Barnwell, Herd, Bloomfield, Henderson.

Sep 6 **Birmingham City** **2–0**
(Herd, Kane) Att: 20,285
Kelsey, Wills, McCullough, Ward, Snedden, Docherty, Clapton, Bloomfield, Herd, Kane, Henderson.

Sep 10 **Tottenham Hotspur** **2–3**
(Herd, Ward) Att: 60,088
Kelsey, Wills, McCullough, Ward, Snedden, Docherty, Clapton, Bloomfield, Herd, Kane, Henderson.

Sep 17 **Newcastle United** **5–0**
(Herd 3, Strong, Clapton) Att: 34,885
Kelsey, Wills, McCullough, Ward, Snedden, Groves, Clapton, Herd, Strong, Bloomfield, Henderson.

Oct 1 **West Bromwich Albion** **1–0**
(Herd) Att: 27,176
Kelsey, Wills, McCullough, Docherty, Snedden, Groves, Clapton, Herd, Strong, Bloomfield, Henderson.

Oct 15 **Aston Villa** **2–1**
(Herd, Strong) Att: 34,048
Kelsey, Wills, McCullough, Docherty, Snedden, Groves, Clapton, Barnwell, Strong, Herd, Henderson.

Oct 29 **Manchester United** **2–1**
(Barnwell, Herd) Att: 45,715
Kelsey, Wills, McCullough, Docherty, Snedden, Groves, Strong, Barnwell, Charles, Herd, Henderson.

Nov 12 **Chelsea** **1–4**
(Charles) Att: 38,886
Kelsey, Wills, McCullough, Docherty, Snedden, Groves, Strong, Barnwell, Charles, Herd, Henderson.

Nov 26 **Everton** **3–2**
(Herd 3) Att: 36,709
Kelsey, Wills, McCullough, Docherty, Snedden, Groves, Clapton, Barnwell, Strong, Herd, Henderson.

Dec 10 **Bolton Wanderers** **5–1**
(Barnwell, Strong 2, Eastham 2) Att: 30,818
Kelsey, Wills, McCullough, Docherty, Snedden, Groves, Clapton, Barnwell, Strong, Eastham, Henderson.

Dec 17 **Burnley** **2–5**
(Strong, Herd) Att: 37,209
Kelsey, Wills, McCullough, Docherty, Snedden, Groves, Clapton, Eastham, Strong, Herd, Henderson.

Dec 26 **Sheffield Wednesday** **1–1**
(Eastham) Att: 43,555
Kelsey, Magill, McCullough, Neill, Young, Groves, Skirton, Barnwell, Herd, Eastham, Henderson.

Jan 14 **Manchester City** **5–4**
(Herd 3, Henderson, Clapton) Att: 36,440
Kelsey, Magill, McCullough, Neill, Charles, Groves, Clapton, Eastham, Herd, Henderson, Haverty.

Feb 11 **Cardiff City** **2–3**
(Herd 2) Att: 33,754
McClelland, Wills, McCullough, Charles, Young, Groves, Skirton, Strong, Herd, Eastham, Haverty.

Feb 25 **Leicester City** **1–3**
(Henderson) Att: 31,721
Kelsey, Bacuzzi, McCullough, Neill, Charles, Groves, Skirton, Eastham, Herd, Henderson, Haverty.

Mar 11 **Blackburn Rovers** **0–0**
Att: 34,250
Kelsey, Bacuzzi, McCullough, Ward, Charles, Groves, Henderson, Barnwell, Herd, Eastham, Haverty.

Mar 25 **West Ham United** **0–0**
Att: 27,665
Kelsey, Bacuzzi, McCullough, Charles, Neill, Groves, Henderson, Eastham, Herd, Barnwell, Haverty.

Apr 3 **Fulham** **4–2**
(Henderson 2, Barnwell 2) Att: 20,142
Kelsey, Bacuzzi, McCullough, Petts, Neill, Groves, Clapton, Barnwell, Herd, Henderson, Skirton.

Apr 8 **Blackpool** **1–0**
(Herd) Att: 36,301
Kelsey, Bacuzzi, McCullough, Charles, Neill, Groves, O'Neill, Barnwell, Herd, Henderson, Skirton.

Apr 22 **Wolverhampton Wanderers** **1–5**
(Henderson) Att: 34,429
Kelsey, Bacuzzi, McCullough, Charles, Neill, Barnwell, Strong, Griffiths, Herd, Eastham, Henderson.

NOTE:There were no FA Cup matches at Highbury this season.

1961/62

LEAGUE DIVISION ONE
Final position – 10th

Aug 19 **Burnley** **2–2**
(Charles 2) Att: 42,856
Kelsey, Magill, McCullough, Brown, Snedden, Neill, MacLeod, Eastham, Charles, Henderson, Skirton.

Aug 29 **Leicester City** **4–4**
(MacLeod, Eastham, Skirton, Charles) Att:35,055
McClelland, Magill, McCullough, Brown, Snedden, Neill, MacLeod, Eastham, Charles, Henderson, Skirton.

Sep 9 **Manchester City** **3–0**
(Griffiths, Skirton, Sears [og]) Att: 41,478
Kelsey, Magill, McCullough, Brown, Snedden, Neill, MacLeod, Griffiths, Henderson, Eastham, Skirton.

Sep 23 **Birmingham City** **1–1**
(Skirton) Att: 31,749
Kelsey, Magill, McCullough, Brown, Snedden, Neill, MacLeod, Eastham, Charles, Henderson, Skirton.

Oct 7 **Blackpool** **3–0**
(Charles 2, Ward) Att: 41,166
Kelsey, Bacuzzi, McCullough, Ward, Brown, Groves, Skirton, Eastham, Charles, Henderson, MacLeod.

Oct 21 **Manchester United** **5–1**
(Skirton 2, Eastham, Barnwell, Ward)
Att: 54,099
Kelsey, Bacuzzi, McCullough, Ward, Brown, Groves, MacLeod, Barnwell, Charles, Eastham, Skirton.

Nov 4 **Chelsea** **0–3**
Att: 37,590
Kelsey, Magill, McCullough, Ward, Brown, Groves, MacLeod, Barnwell, Charles, Eastham, Skirton.

Nov14 **Sheffield Wednesday** **1–0**
(Strong) Att: 19,331
McKechnie, Bacuzzi, McCullough, Ward, Brown, Groves, MacLeod, Eastham, Strong, Henderson, Skirton.

Nov 18 **Nottingham Forest** **2–1**
(Strong, MacLeod) Att: 34,217
Kelsey, Bacuzzi, McCullough, Clamp, Brown, Groves, MacLeod, Eastham, Strong, Henderson, Skirton.

Dec 2 **West Ham United** **2–2**
(Strong, Skirton) Att: 47,206
Kelsey, Bacuzzi, McCullough, Clamp, Brown, Groves, MacLeod, Ward, Strong, Eastham, Skirton.

Dec 23 **Tottenham Hotspur** **2–1**
(Charles, Skirton) Att: 63,440
Kelsey, Bacuzzi, McCullough, Clamp, Brown, Snedden, MacLeod, Barnwell, Charles, Eastham, Skirton.

Dec 26 **Fulham** **1–0**
(Charles) Att: 32,969
Kelsey, Bacuzzi, McCullough, Clamp, Brown, Snedden, MacLeod, Barnwell, Charles, Eastham, Skirton.

Jan 13 **Bolton Wanderers** **1–2**
(Charles) Att: 33,351
Kelsey, Bacuzzi, McCullough, Clamp, Brown, Snedden, MacLeod, Griffiths, Charles, Eastham, Skirton.

Feb 3 **West Bromwich Albion** **0–1**
Att: 29,597
Kelsey, Bacuzzi, McCullough, Clamp, Brown, Petts, Skirton, Ward, Charles, Griffiths, MacLeod.

Mar 3 **Blackburn Rovers** **0–0**
Att: 25,744
Kelsey, Bacuzzi, McCullough, Neill, Brown, Petts, Skirton, Strong, Groves, Eastham, Armstrong.

Mar 17 **Cardiff City** **1–1**
(Strong) Att: 25,059
Kelsey, Bacuzzi, McCullough, Clamp, Brown, Groves, Clapton, Barnwell, Strong, Eastham, Skirton.

Mar 31 **Aston Villa** **4–5**
(Skirton 2, Strong 2) Att: 20,107
Kelsey, Bacuzzi, Clarke, Clamp, Brown, Groves, MacLeod, Griffiths, Strong, Barnwell, Skirton.

Apr 14 **Wolverhampton Wanderers** **3–1**
(Skirton,Strong 2) Att: 24,367
Kelsey, Magill, McCullough, Brown, Neill, Clamp, MacLeod, Griffiths, Strong, Barnwell, Skirton.

Apr 23 **Ipswich Town** **0–3**
Att: 44,694
Kelsey, Magill, McCullough, Clamp, Neill, Petts, Clapton, Griffiths, Strong, Eastham, MacLeod.

Apr 28 **Sheffield United** **2–0**
(Barnwell, Eastham) Att: 18,761
Kelsey, Magill, McCullough, Brown, Neill, Petts, Clapton, Griffiths, Barnwell, Eastham, Armstrong.

May 1 **Everton** **2–3**
(Griffiths, Armstrong) Att: 20,034
Kelsey, Magill, McCullough, Brown, Neill, Petts, Clapton, Griffiths, Strong, Eastham, Armstrong.

FA CUP

Jan 6 **Bradford City** **3–0**
(Charles 2, Lawlor [og]) Att: 40,232
Kelsey, Bacuzzi, McCullough, Clamp, Brown, Snedden, MacLeod, Barnwell, Charles, Eastham, Skirton.

1962/63

LEAGUE DIVISION ONE
Final position – 7th

Aug 21 **Birmingham City** **2–0**
(Baker, McCullough) Att: 34,004
McKechnie, Magill, McCullough, Brown, Neill, Snedden, Armstrong, Strong, Baker, Barnwell, Skirton.

Aug 25 **Manchester United** **1–3**
(Clamp) Att: 62,308
McKechnie, Magill, McCullough, Clamp, Brown, Snedden, Armstrong, Eastham, Strong, Barnwell, Skirton.

Sep 4 **Aston Villa** **1–2**
(Skirton) Att: 33,861
McClelland, Bacuzzi, McCullough, Clamp, Brown, Snedden, Armstrong, Barnwell, Baker, Eastham, Skirton.

Sep 8 **Sheffield Wednesday** **1–2**
(Baker) Att: 31,115
McClelland, Magill, McCullough, Brown, Neill, Snedden, Armstrong, Eastham, Baker, Barnwell, Skirton.

Sep 22 **Leicester City** **1–1**
(Baker) Att: 31,291
McKechnie, Magill, McCullough, Brown, Neill, Snedden, MacLeod, Strong, Baker, Barnwell, Skirton.

Oct 13 **West Ham United** **1–1**
(Baker) Att: 49,597
McClelland, Magill, McCullough, Neill, Brown, Snedden, MacLeod, Strong, Baker, Eastham, Skirton.

Oct 27 **Wolverhampton Wanderers** **5–4**
(Baker 3, Eastham 2) Att: 43,002
McClelland, Magill, McCullough, Neill, Brown, Snedden, MacLeod, Strong, Baker, Eastham, Skirton.

Nov 10 **Sheffield United** **1–0**
(Strong) Att: 25,503
McClelland, Magill, McCullough, Snedden, Brown, Groves, MacLeod, Strong, Baker, Eastham, Skirton.

Nov 24 **Ipswich Town** **3–1**
(Baker, Armstrong, Barnwell) Att: 25,056
McClelland, Magill, McCullough, Barnwell, Neill, Snedden, MacLeod, Court, Baker, Eastham, Armstrong.

Dec 8 **Blackpool** **2–0**
(Strong, Martin [og]) Att: 23,767
McClelland, Magill, McCullough, Barnwell, Neill, Snedden, MacLeod, Strong, Baker, Eastham, Armstrong.

Dec 15 **Leyton Orient** **2–0**
(Baker 2) Att: 29,075
McClelland, Magill, McCullough, Barnwell, Neill, Snedden, MacLeod, Strong, Baker, Eastham, Armstrong.

Feb 16 **Bolton Wanderers** **3–2**
(MacLeod, Brown, Armstrong) Att: 25,204
McClelland, Magill, McCullough, Barnwell, Brown, Snedden, MacLeod, Strong, Baker, Eastham, Armstrong.

Feb 23 **Tottenham Hotspur** **2–3**
(Strong, Baker) Att: 59,980
McClelland, Magill, McCullough, Barnwell, Brown, Snedden, MacLeod, Strong, Baker, Eastham, Armstrong.

Mar 9 Liverpool **2–2**
(MacLeod, McCullough) Att: 30,496
McClelland, Magill, McCullough, Barnwell, Brown, Snedden, MacLeod, Strong, Baker, Eastham, Anderson.

Mar 23 Blackburn Rovers **3–1**
(Strong 2, MacLeod) Att: 21,467
McClelland, Magill, McCullough, Barnwell, Brown, Snedden, MacLeod, Strong, Baker, Eastham, Skirton.

Mar 26 Everton **4–3**
(Strong, Baker, MacLeod, Skirton) Att: 38,061
McClelland, Magill, McCullough, Barnwell, Brown, Snedden, MacLeod, Strong, Baker, Eastham, Skirton.

Apr 6 Nottingham Forest **0–0**
Att: 25,134
McClelland, Bacuzzi, McCullough, Barnwell, Brown, Neill, MacLeod, Strong, Baker, Eastham, Skirton.

Apr 12 West Bromwich Albion **3–2**
(Strong 2, Skirton) Att: 28,219
McClelland, Bacuzzi, McCullough, Barnwell, Brown, Neill, MacLeod, Strong, Baker, Eastham, Skirton.

Apr 20 Manchester City **2–3**
(MacLeod, Strong) Att: 20,539
McClelland, Magill, McCullough, Barnwell, Brown, Groves, MacLeod, Strong, Baker, Eastham, Anderson.

May 11 Burnley **2–3**
(Skirton, Baker) Att: 23,256
McClelland, Magill, Clarke, Barnwell, Brown, McCullough, MacLeod, Strong, Baker, Eastham, Skirton.

May 14 Fulham **3–0**
(Baker 3) Att: 17,389
McClelland, Magill, McCullough, Barnwell, Brown, Groves, MacLeod, Strong, Baker, Eastham, Armstrong.

FA CUP

Jan 30 Oxford United **5–1**
(Baker 2, Strong 2, MacLeod) Att: 14,649
McClelland, Magill, McCullough, Barnwell, Brown, Snedden, Court, Strong, Baker, Eastham, MacLeod.

Mar 12 Sheffield Wednesday **2–0**
(MacLeod, Strong) Att: 40,367
McClelland, Magill, McCullough, Barnwell, Brown, Snedden, MacLeod, Strong, Baker, Eastham, Skirton.

Mar 16 Liverpool **1–2**
(MacLeod) Att: 55,245
McClelland, Magill, McCullough, Barnwell, Brown, Snedden, MacLeod, Strong, Baker, Eastham, Skirton.

1963/64

LEAGUE DIVISION ONE

Final position – 8th

Aug 24 Wolverhampton Wanderers **1–3**
(Strong) Att: 50,302
McClelland, Magill, McCullough, Barnwell, Ure, Brown, Skirton, Strong, Baker, Eastham, Armstrong.

Aug 27 West Bromwich Albion **3–2**
(Baker 2, Strong) Att: 31,381
McClelland, Magill, McCullough, Barnwell, Ure, Brown, MacLeod, Strong, Baker, Eastham, Skirton.

Sep 7 Bolton Wanderers **4–3**
(Skirton 2, Baker, Ure) Att: 26,016
McKechnie, Bacuzzi, McCullough, Neill, Brown, Ure, MacLeod, Strong, Baker, Eastham, Skirton.

Sep 10 Aston Villa **3–0**
(Baker 3) Att: 29,189
McKechnie, Magill, McCullough, Brown, Ure, Groves, MacLeod, Strong, Baker, Eastham, Skirton.

Sep 21 Manchester United **2–1**
(Eastham, Baker) Att: 56,776
McKechnie, Magill, McCullough, Brown, Ure, Groves, MacLeod, Strong, Baker, Eastham, Armstrong.

Oct 5 Ipswich Town **6–0**
(Strong 3, Baker 2, MacLeod) Att: 31,803
McKechnie, Magill, McCullough, Brown, Ure, Groves, MacLeod, Strong, Baker, Eastham, Armstrong.

Oct 15 Tottenham Hotspur **4–4**
(Eastham 2, Baker, Strong) Att: 67,986
McKechnie, Magill, McCullough, Brown, Ure, Groves, MacLeod, Strong, Baker, Eastham, Armstrong.

Oct 26 Nottingham Forest **4–2**
(Strong 2, Anderson, McKinlay [og]) Att: 41,124
Wilson, Magill, McCullough, Brown, Ure, Barnwell, MacLeod, Strong, Baker, Eastham, Anderson.

Nov 5 Birmingham City **4–1**
(Baker 3, Strong) Att: 23,499
Wilson, Magill, Clarke, Brown, Neill, Barnwell, MacLeod, Strong, Baker, Eastham, Anderson.

Nov 9 West Ham United **3–3**
(MacLeod, Eastham, Anderson) Att: 52,742
Wilson, Magill, McCullough, Brown, Ure, Barnwell, MacLeod, Strong, Baker, Eastham, Anderson.

Nov 23 Blackpool **5–3**
(Strong 2, Barnwell, Brown, Eastham)
Att: 33,847
Furnell, Clarke, McCullough, Brown, Ure, Barnwell, MacLeod, Strong, Baker, Eastham, Anderson.

Dec 7 Liverpool **1–1**
(Baker) Att: 40,551
Furnell, Magill, McCullough, Barnwell, Ure, Snedden, MacLeod, Strong, Baker, Eastham, Armstrong.

Dec 10 Everton **6–0**
(Baker 2, Eastham 2, Armstrong, Strong)
Att: 33,644
Furnell, Magill, McCullough, Barnwell, Ure, Snedden, MacLeod, Strong, Baker, Eastham, Armstrong.

Dec 21 Leicester City **0–1**
Att: 28,019
Furnell, Magill, McCullough, Brown, Ure, Snedden, MacLeod, Strong, Baker, Eastham, Armstrong.

Jan 18 Fulham **2–2**
(Baker, Strong) Att: 35,895
Furnell, Bacuzzi, McCullough, Barnwell, Ure, Snedden, MacLeod, Strong, Baker, Eastham, Armstrong.

Feb 8 Burnley **3–2**
(Strong, Armstrong, Anderson) Att: 30,863
Furnell, Magill, McCullough, Groves, Ure, Snedden, Armstrong, Strong, Baker, Eastham, Anderson.

Feb 29 Stoke City **1–1**
(Baker) Att: 26,208
McClelland, Bacuzzi, McCullough, Groves, Ure, Snedden, MacLeod, Strong, Baker, Eastham, Armstrong.

Mar 14 Chelsea **2–4**
(Neill, Baker) Att: 25,513
Furnell, Bacuzzi, McCullough, Neill, Ure, Simpson, MacLeod, Strong, Baker, Eastham, Armstrong.

Mar 24 Sheffield Wednesday **1–1**
(Strong) Att: 18,221
Furnell, Magill, McCullough, Neill, Ure, Simpson, Armstrong, Strong, Court, Eastham, Anderson.

Mar 28 Sheffield United **1–3**
(Strong) Att: 21,001
Furnell, Magill, McCullough, Neill, Ure, Simpson, Armstrong, Strong, Court, Eastham, Anderson.

Apr 11 Blackburn Rovers **0–0**
Att: 26,164
Furnell, Magill, Clarke, Neill, Ure, McCullough, Skirton, Strong, Baker, Court, Armstrong.

FA CUP

Jan 4 Wolverhampton Wanderers **2–1**
(Strong, Baker) Att: 40,803
Furnell, Magill, McCullough, Barnwell, Ure, Snedden, MacLeod, Strong, Baker, Eastham, Armstrong.

Jan 29 West Bromwich Albion **2–0**
(Armstrong, Strong) Att: 57,698
Furnell, Magill, McCullough, Groves, Ure, Snedden, Skirton, Strong, Baker, Eastham, Armstrong.

Feb 15 Liverpool **0–1**
Att: 61,295
Furnell, Magill, McCullough, Groves, Ure, Snedden, MacLeod, Strong, Baker, Eastham, Armstrong.

INTER-CITIES FAIRS CUP

Oct 22 Staevnet **2–3**
(Skirton, Barnwell) Att: 13,569
McKechnie, Magill, McCullough, Brown, Ure, Groves, Skirton, Strong, Court, Barnwell, Armstrong.

Nov13 Royal Liège **1–1**
(Anderson) Att: 22,003
Wilson, Magill, McCullough, Brown, Ure, Barnwell, MacLeod, Strong, Baker, Eastham, Anderson.

1964/65

LEAGUE DIVISION ONE

Final position – 13th

Aug 25 Sheffield Wednesday **1–1**
(Simpson) Att: 35,590
Furnell, Howe, McCullough, Snedden, Ure, Simpson, Armstrong, Strong, Baker, Eastham, Anderson.

Aug 29 Aston Villa **3–1**
(Armstrong, MacLeod, Strong) Att: 28,732
Furnell, Howe, Clarke, Simpson, Ure, McCullough, MacLeod, Strong, Baker, Eastham, Armstrong.

Sep 8 Blackburn Rovers **1–1**
(Baker) Att: 29,510
Furnell, Howe, McCullough, Strong, Ferry, Neill, Skirton, Court, Baker, Eastham, Armstrong.

Sep 12 Sunderland **3–1**
(Eastham 2, Strong) Att: 34,291
Furnell, Howe, Clarke, Strong, Ferry, Neill, Skirton, Court, Baker, Eastham, Armstrong.

Sep 26 Chelsea **1–3**
(Court) Att: 54,936
Furnell, Howe, Clarke, Strong, Ferry, Neill, Skirton, Court, Baker, Eastham, Armstrong.

Oct 6 Nottingham Forest **0–3**
Att: 35,041
Furnell, Clarke, McCullough, McLintock, Ferry, Neill, Skirton, Strong, Baker, Eastham, Armstrong.

Oct 17 Burnley **3–2**
(Baker, Simpson, Sammels) Att: 24,962
Burns, Howe, Clarke, McLintock, Ferry, Simpson, Anderson, Sammels, Baker, Eastham, Armstrong.

Oct 31 Everton **3–1**
(Baker 2, Anderson) Att: 33,561
Burns, Howe, McCullough, McLintock, Neill, Court, Anderson, Sammels, Baker, Eastham, Armstrong.

Nov 14 West Ham United **0–3**
Att: 36,026
Burns, Howe, McCullough, McLintock, Neill, Court, Skirton, Radford, Baker, Eastham, Armstrong.

Nov 28 Manchester United **2–3**
(Anderson, Eastham) Att: 59,637
Burns, Howe, McCullough, Snedden, Neill, Court, Anderson, McLintock, Baker, Eastham, Armstrong.

Dec 12 Liverpool **0–0**
Att: 25,171
Burns, Howe, McCullough, McLintock, Neill, Court, Skirton, Sammels, Baker, Eastham, Armstrong.

Dec 26 Stoke City **3–2**
(Baker, Sammels, McLintock) Att: 27,663
Burns, Howe, McCullough, McLintock, Ure, Court, Skirton, Sammels, Baker, Eastham, Armstrong.

Jan 2 Wolverhampton Wanderers **4–1**
(Radford 3, Baker) Att: 25,561
Burns, Howe, Clarke, McLintock, Ure, Court, Skirton, Radford, Baker, Eastham, Armstrong.

Jan 23 Leicester City **4–3**
(Baker 2, Eastham, Armstrong) Att: 31,063
Burns, Howe, Clarke, McLintock, Ure, Court, Skirton, Radford, Baker, Eastham, Armstrong.

Feb 13 Leeds United **1–2**
(Eastham [pen]) Att: 32,132
Burns, Howe, Clarke, Neill, Ure, Court, Anderson, Radford, Baker, Eastham, Armstrong.

Feb 20 Fulham **2–0**
(Radford, Baker) Att: 22,101
Burns, Howe, McCullough, Neill, Ure, Court, Tawse, Radford, Baker, Eastham, Armstrong.

Feb 23 Tottenham Hotspur **3–1**
(Baker 2, Radford) Att: 48,367
Burns, Howe, McCullough, Neill, Ure, Court, Tawse, Radford, Baker, Eastham, Armstrong.

Mar 6 Sheffield United **1–1**
(Ure) Att: 22,001
Burns, Howe, McCullough, Neill, Ure, Court, Armstrong, Radford, Baker, Sammels, Eastham.

Apr 3 West Bromwich Albion **1–1**
(Eastham) Att: 18,797
Furnell, Howe, McCullough, Neill, Ure, McLintock, Skirton, Sammels, Baker, Eastham, Armstrong.

Apr 6 Birmingham City **3–0**
(Baker, Skirton, McLintock) Att: 16,048
Furnell, Howe, McCullough, McLintock, Ure, Court, Sammels, Baldwin, Baker, Eastham, Skirton.

Apr 19 Blackpool **3–1**
(Baker 2, Neill) Att: 17,063
Furnell, Howe, McCullough, Neill, Ure, McLintock, Sammels, Court, Baker, Eastham, Armstrong.

NOTE:There were no FA Cup matches at Highbury this season.

1965/66

LEAGUE DIVISION ONE

Final position – 14th

Aug 21 Stoke City **2–1**
(Baker 2) Att: 30,107
Furnell, Howe, McCullough, McLintock, Ure, Neill, Baldwin, Eastham, Baker, Court, Armstrong.

Sep 4 Chelsea **1–3**
(Baker) Att: 45,456
Furnell, Howe, McCullough, Neill, Ure, McLintock, Sammels, Eastham, Baker, Court, Armstrong.

Sep 14 Nottingham Forest **1–0**
(Eastham) Att: 34,542
Furnell, Howe, McCullough, McLintock, Neill, Court, Armstrong, Radford, Baker, Sammels, Eastham.

Sep 25 Manchester United **4–2**
(Baker, Radford, Armstrong, Eastham)
Att: 56,757
Furnell, Howe, McCullough, McLintock, Neill, Court, Armstrong, Radford, Baker, Sammels, Eastham.

Sep 28 Northampton Town **1–1**
(Radford) Att: 33,240
Furnell, Howe, McCullough, McLintock, Neill, Court, Armstrong, Radford, Baker, Sammels (Skirton), Eastham.

Oct 9 Fulham **2–1**
(Sammels, Baker) Att: 32,318
Furnell, Howe, McCullough, McLintock, Neill, Court, Armstrong, Radford, Baker, Sammels, Eastham.

Oct 23 Blackburn Rovers **2–2**
(McLintock, Baker) Att: 27,703
Burns, Howe, McCullough, McLintock, Neill, Court, Armstrong, Radford, Baker, Sammels, Eastham.

Nov 6 Sheffield United **6–2**
(Baker 2, Skirton 2, Armstrong 2) Att: 28,541
Burns, Howe, Storey, McLintock, Neill, Court, Skirton, Sammels, Baker, Eastham, Armstrong.

Nov 20 West Ham United **3–2**
(Skirton 2, Baker) Att: 35,855
Burns, Howe, Storey, McLintock, Neill, Court, Skirton, Sammels (Walley), Baker, Eastham, Armstrong.

Dec 4 Aston Villa **3–3**
(Skirton 2, Eastham) Att: 25,880
Burns, Howe, Storey, McLintock, Neill, Court, Skirton, Radford, Baker, Eastham, Armstrong.

Dec 28 Sheffield Wednesday **5–2**
(Eastham 2, Skirton, Sammels, Baker)
Att: 21,035
Wilson, Howe, Storey, Neill, Ure, Walley, Skirton, Radford, Baker, Sammels, Eastham.

Jan 8 Liverpool **0–1**
Att: 43,917
Furnell, Howe, Storey, McLintock, Neill, Court, Skirton, Sammels, Baker, Radford, Eastham.

Feb 5 Burnley **1–1**
(Sammels) Att: 28,652
Furnell, Howe, Storey, McLintock, Neill, Court, Skirton, Baldwin, Radford, Sammels (Walley), Armstrong.

Mar 5 Blackpool **0–0**
Att: 21,881
Furnell, Howe (Simpson), Storey, McLintock, Neill, Ure, Skirton, Sammels, Radford, Court, Armstrong.

Mar 8 Tottenham Hotspur **1–1**
(Court) Att: 51,805
Furnell, Storey, McCullough, Neill, Ure, Court, Skirton, Sammels, Radford, Eastham, Armstrong.

Mar 12 Everton **0–1**
Att: 24,821
Furnell, Storey, McCullough, McLintock, Ure, Neill, Neilson, Eastham, Radford, Court, Armstrong.

Mar 26 Newcastle United **1–3**
(Noble [og]) Att: 13,979
Furnell, Storey, Simpson, Court, Neill, Ure, Skirton, Sammels, Radford, Eastham, Armstrong.

Apr 5 West Bromwich Albion **1–1**
(Skirton) Att: 8,738
Furnell, Court, Storey, McLintock, Ure, Neill, Skirton, Radford, Baldwin, Eastham, Armstrong.

Apr 23 **Sunderland** 1–1
(Sammels) Att: 25,699
Furnell, Court, Storey, McLintock, Ure, Walley, Skirton, Sammels, Radford, Eastham, Armstrong.

May 5 **Leeds United** 0–3
Att: 4,554
Furnell, Pack, Storey, McGill, Neill, Court, Armstrong, Baldwin, Ure, Sammels, Eastham.

May 7 **Leicester City** 1–0
(Rodrigues [og]) Att: 16,435
Furnell, Court, Storey, McGill, Ure, Walley, Neilson, Simpson, Radford, Eastham, Armstrong.

NOTE: There were no FA Cup matches at Highbury this season.

1966/67
LEAGUE DIVISION ONE
Final position – 7th

Aug 23 **West Ham United** 2–1
(Radford, Baldwin) Att: 40,614
Furnell, Court, Storey, McLintock, Ure, Neill, Skirton (Simpson), Baldwin, Radford, Sammels, Armstrong.

Aug 27 **Aston Villa** 1–0
(Baldwin) Att: 26,762
Furnell, Court, Storey, McLintock, Ure, Neill, Coakley, Baldwin, Radford, Sammels, Armstrong.

Sep 6 **Sheffield Wednesday** 1–1
(Sammels) Att: 28,898
Furnell, Court, Simpson (McGill), McLintock, Ure, Neill, Coakley, Baldwin, Radford, Sammels, Armstrong.

Sep 17 **Blackpool** 1–1
(Coakley) Att: 28,946
Furnell, Simpson, Storey, McLintock, Ure, Neill, Coakley, Addison, Radford (McGill), Sammels, Armstrong.

Oct 1 **Leicester City** 2–4
(Addison, Graham) Att: 33,945
Furnell, Simpson, Storey, McLintock, Ure, Neill (McGill), Coakley, Addison, Graham, Sammels, Armstrong.

Oct 8 **Newcastle United** 2–0
(Boot, Clark [og]) Att: 24,595
Furnell, Simpson, Storey, Boot, Ure, Woodward, Coakley, McLintock, Graham, Sammels, Armstrong.

Oct 22 **West Bromwich Albion** 2–3
(Armstrong 2) Att: 31,636
Furnell, McNab, Storey, McLintock, Ure, Simpson, Boot, Graham, Radford, Sammels, Armstrong.

Nov 5 **Leeds United** 0–1
Att: 24,227
Furnell, Storey, Walley, McLintock, Neill, Simpson, Sammels (Boot), Radford, Graham, Addison, Armstrong.

Nov 19 **Fulham** 1–0
(McLintock) Att: 25,755
Furnell, McNab, Storey, McLintock, Neill, Ure, Neilson, Addison, Graham, Sammels, Armstrong.

Dec 3 **Burnley** 0–0
Att: 23,220
Furnell, McNab (Simpson), Storey, McLintock, Neill, Ure, Neilson, Radford, Graham, Sammels, Armstrong.

Dec 17 **Sunderland** 2–0
(McLintock, Sammels) Att: 20,482
Furnell, McNab, Storey, McLintock, Ure, Neill, Addison, Radford, Graham, Sammels, Armstrong.

Dec 26 **Southampton** 4–1
(Radford 2, Armstrong 2) Att: 29,527
Furnell, McNab, Storey, McLintock, Simpson, Ure, Neilson, Radford, Graham, Sammels, Armstrong.

Jan 7 **Tottenham Hotspur** 0–2
Att: 49,851
Furnell, McNab, Storey, McLintock, Simpson, Ure, Neilson, Radford, Graham, Sammels, Armstrong.

Jan 14 **Manchester City** 1–0
(McLintock) Att: 22,392
Furnell, Simpson, Storey, McLintock, Neill, Ure, Neilson, Radford, Graham, Sammels, Armstrong.

Feb 4 **Chelsea** 2–1
(Graham, Armstrong) Att: 52,467
Furnell, Simpson, Storey, McLintock, Ure, Neill, Neilson, Addison (McNab), Graham, Sammels, Armstrong.

Mar 3 **Manchester United** 1–1
(Sammels) Att: 63,563
Furnell, McNab, Storey, McLintock (Court), Neill, Simpson, Addison, Radford, Graham, Sammels, Armstrong.

Mar 25 **Sheffield United** 2–0
(Sammels, McLintock) Att: 23,099
Furnell, McNab, Simpson, McLintock, Ure, Neill, Court, Radford, Graham, Sammels, Armstrong.

Mar 28 **Liverpool** 1–1
(Graham) Att: 35,877
Furnell, McNab, Simpson, McLintock, Ure, Neill, Court, Radford, Graham, Sammels, Armstrong.

Apr 22 **Nottingham Forest** 1–1
(Storey) Att: 36,196
Furnell, McNab, Storey, McLintock, Neill, Ure, Simpson, Radford, Graham, Sammels, Armstrong.

Apr 25 **Everton** 3–1
(Sammels, Graham, McLintock) Att: 20,567
Furnell, McNab, Storey, McLintock, Neill, Ure, Simpson, Addison, Graham, Sammels, Armstrong.

May 6 **Stoke City** 3–1
(Radford, McLintock, Allen [og]) Att: 24,611
Furnell, McNab, Storey, McLintock, Neill, Ure, Simpson, Radford, Graham, Sammels, Armstrong.

FA CUP

Feb 22 **Bolton Wanderers** 3–0
(Radford 3) Att: 47,050
Furnell, Simpson, Storey, McLintock, Neill, Ure, Neilson, Radford, Graham, Sammels, Armstrong.

FOOTBALL LEAGUE CUP

Sep 13 **Gillingham** 1–1
(Baldwin) Att: 13,029
Furnell, Howe, Walley, McLintock, Ure, Neill, Coakley, Tyrer, Baldwin, Sammels, Armstrong.

Sep 28 **Gillingham** 5–0
(Baldwin 2, McLintock 2, Coakley) Att: 18,409
Furnell, McGill, Storey, McLintock, Ure, Neill, Coakley, Baldwin, Simpson, Sammels, Armstrong.

Oct 5 **West Ham United** 1–3
(Jenkins) Att: 33,647
Furnell, Simpson, Storey, Boot, Ure, Woodward, Coakley, Jenkins, Walley, Sammels, Armstrong.

1967/68
LEAGUE DIVISION ONE
Final position – 9th

Aug 19 **Stoke City** 2–0
(Graham, Sammels) Att: 27,048
Furnell, Court, Storey, McLintock, Neill, Simpson, Johnston, Radford, Graham, Sammels, Armstrong.

Aug 28 **Liverpool** 2–0
(Sammels, Hateley [og]) Att: 33,420
Furnell, Simpson, Storey, McLintock, Neill, Ure, Addison, Radford (Johnston), Graham, Sammels, Armstrong.

Sep 2 **Coventry City** 1–1
(Graham) Att: 30,404
Furnell, Storey, McNab (Court), McLintock, Neill, Simpson, Johnston, Addison, Graham, Sammels, Armstrong.

Sep 16 **Tottenham Hotspur** 4–0
(Radford, Neill [pen], Graham, Addison) Att: 62,836
Furnell, Storey, Simpson, McLintock, Neill, Ure, Radford, Addison, Graham, Sammels, Armstrong.

Sep 23 **Manchester City** 1–0
(Radford) Att: 41,466
Furnell, Storey, Simpson, McLintock, Neill, Ure, Radford, Addison, Graham, Sammels, Armstrong.

Oct 14 **Sunderland** 2–1
(Radford, Graham) Att: 30,864
Furnell, Storey, McNab, McLintock, Neill, Ure, Radford, Simpson (Addison), Graham, Sammels, Armstrong.

Oct 28 **Fulham** 5–3
(Radford 3, Addison 2) Att: 29,974
Furnell, Storey, McNab, McLintock, Neill, Ure, Radford, Addison, Graham, Sammels, Armstrong.

Nov 11 **Everton** 2–2
(Johnston, Sammels) Att: 36,371
Furnell, Storey, McNab, McLintock, Neill, Simpson, Radford, Johnston, Graham, Sammels, Armstrong.

Nov 25 **West Ham United** 0–0
Att: 42,029
Furnell, Storey, McNab, McLintock, Neill, Simpson, Radford, Johnston, Graham (Jenkins), Sammels, Armstrong.

Dec 23 **Nottingham Forest** 3–0
(Graham 2, Armstrong) Att: 32,512
Furnell, Storey, McNab, McLintock, Neill, Ure, Radford, Johnston, Graham, Simpson, Armstrong.

Dec 30 **Chelsea** 1–1
(Radford) Att: 47,157
Furnell, Storey, McNab, McLintock, Neill, Ure, Radford, Sammels, Graham, Simpson, Armstrong.

Jan 13 **Sheffield United** 1–1
(Graham) Att: 27,447
Furnell, Rice, McNab, Simpson, Neill, Ure, Radford, Johnston, Graham, Sammels, Armstrong.

Feb 10 **Newcastle United** 0–0
Att: 36,996
Furnell, Simpson, Storey, McLintock, Neill, Ure, Radford, Gould, Graham, Sammels, Armstrong.

Feb 24 **Manchester United** 0–2
Att: 46,417
Furnell, McNab, Storey, McLintock, Neill, Simpson, Jenkins, Gould, Graham, Sammels, Armstrong.

Mar 16 **Wolverhampton Wanderers** 0–2
Att: 25,983
Wilson, McNab, Storey, McLintock, Simpson (Davidson), Neill, Radford, Gould, Graham, Sammels, Armstrong.

Apr 13 **Leicester City** 2–1
(Gould, Graham) Att: 19,108
Wilson, Storey, McNab, McLintock, Neill, Simpson, Radford, Court, Graham, Gould, Armstrong.

Apr 15 **Southampton** 0–3
Att: 23,165
Wilson, Storey, McNab, McLintock (Sammels), Neill, Simpson, Radford, Court, Graham, Gould, Armstrong.

Apr 27 **Burnley** 2–0
(Court, Armstrong) Att: 15,278
Wilson, McNab, Storey, Court, Neill, Simpson, Radford, Sammels, Graham, Gould, Armstrong.

Apr 30 **Sheffield Wednesday** 3–2
(Court, Radford, Gould) Att: 11,262
Wilson, McNab, Storey, Court, Neill, Simpson, Radford, Sammels, Graham (Rice), Gould, Armstrong.

May 7 **Leeds United** 4–3
(Gould, McLintock, Johnston, Madeley [og]) Att: 25,043
Wilson, McLintock, Storey, Court, Neill, Simpson, Radford, Johnston, Sammels, Gould, Armstrong.

May 11 **West Bromwich Albion** 2–1
(Gould, McLintock) Att: 24,896
Wilson, McNab, McLintock, Court, Neill, Simpson, Radford, Johnston, Sammels, Gould, Armstrong.

FA CUP

Jan 30 **Shrewsbury Town** 2–0
(Sammels, Jenkins) Att: 41,958
Furnell, Simpson, Storey, McLintock, Neill, Ure, Radford, Jenkins (Court), Graham, Sammels, Armstrong.

Mar 9 **Birmingham City** 1–1
(Radford) Att: 45,515
Furnell, Storey, McNab, McLintock, Simpson, Neill, Radford, Gould, Graham, Sammels, Armstrong.

FOOTBALL LEAGUE CUP
Finalists

Oct 11 **Reading** 1–0
(Simpson) Att: 27,866
Furnell, Storey, McNab, McLintock, Neill, Ure, Radford, Simpson, Graham, Sammels, Armstrong.

Nov 1 **Blackburn Rovers** 2–1
(Graham, Addison) Att: 20,044
Furnell, Storey, McNab, McLintock, Neill, Simpson, Radford (Johnston), Addison, Graham, Sammels, Armstrong.

Dec 5 **Burnley** 2–1
(Radford, Neill) Att: 36,570
Furnell, Storey, Rice, McLintock, Neill, Simpson, Radford, Johnston, Graham, Sammels, Armstrong.

Jan 17 **Huddersfield Town** 3–2
(Graham, Radford, McNab) Att: 39,986
Furnell, Simpson, McNab, McLintock, Neill, Ure, Radford, Johnston, Graham, Sammels, Armstrong.

1968/69
LEAGUE DIVISION ONE
Final position – 4th

Aug 13 **Leicester City** 3–0
(Court, Gould 2) Att: 32,164
Wilson, Storey, McNab, McLintock, Neill, Simpson, Radford, Sammels, Graham (Gould), Court, Jenkins.

Aug 17 **Liverpool** 1–1
(Radford) Att: 43,535
Wilson, Storey, McNab, McLintock, Neill, Simpson, Radford, Sammels, Gould, Court, Jenkins.

Aug 27 **Manchester City** 4–1
(Jenkins 2, Sammels, Radford) Att: 40,746
Wilson, Storey, McNab, McLintock, Neill, Simpson, Radford, Sammels, Gould, Court, Jenkins.

Aug 31 **Queens Park Rangers** 2–1
(McLintock, Neill [pen]) Att: 44,407
Wilson, Storey, McNab, McLintock, Neill, Simpson, Radford, Sammels, Gould, Court, Jenkins.

Sep 14 **Stoke City** 1–0
(Neill) Att: 28,275
Wilson, Storey, McNab, McLintock, Neill, Simpson, Radford (Armstrong), Sammels, Gould, Court, Jenkins.

Sep 28 **Sunderland** 0–0
Att: 35,277
Wilson, Storey, McNab, McLintock, Neill, Simpson, Radford, Sammels, Gould, Court, Jenkins.

Oct 12 **Coventry City** 2–1
(Court, Radford) Att: 35,240
Wilson, Storey, McNab, Ure, Neill, Simpson, Radford, Armstrong, Gould, Court, Jenkins (Graham).

Oct 26 **West Ham United** 0–0
Att: 59,533
Wilson, Storey, McNab, McLintock, Neill, Ure, Robertson, Radford, Graham, Simpson, Armstrong.

Nov 9 **Newcastle United** 0–0
Att: 34,277
Wilson, Storey, McNab, Court, Neill, Ure, Robertson (Gould), Radford, Graham, Sammels, Armstrong.

Nov 23 **Chelsea** 0–1
Att: 45,588
Wilson, Storey, McNab, McLintock, Ure, Simpson, Radford, Court, Sammels, Graham (Gould), Armstrong.

Dec 7 **Everton** 3–1
(Radford, Court, Graham) Att: 40,108
Wilson, Storey, McNab, McLintock, Ure, Simpson, Radford, Court, Sammels (Graham), Gould, Robertson.

Dec 21 **West Bromwich Albion** 2–0
(Gould, Fraser [og]) Att: 30,765
Wilson, Storey, McNab, McLintock, Ure, Simpson, Radford, Robertson, Court, Gould, Graham.

Dec 26 **Manchester United** 3–0
(Armstrong, Court, Radford) Att: 62,300
Wilson, Storey, McNab, McLintock, Ure, Simpson, Radford, Graham, Court, Gould, Armstrong.

Jan 11 **Sheffield Wednesday** 2–0
(Gould, Radford) Att: 39,008
Wilson, Storey, McNab, McLintock, Neill, Simpson, Radford, Sammels, Court, Gould, Armstrong.

Feb 1 **Nottingham Forest** 1–1
(Gould) Att: 35,585
Wilson, Storey, McNab, McLintock, Ure, Simpson, Radford, Sammels, Court (Armstrong), Gould, Robertson.

Feb 15 **Burnley** 2–0
(Gould 2) Att: 27,614
Wilson, Storey, McNab, Graham, Ure, Simpson, Robertson, Sammels, Court, Gould, Armstrong.

Feb 18 **Ipswich Town** 0–2
Att: 23,891
Wilson, Storey, McNab, Graham, Ure, Simpson, Robertson (Johnston), Sammels, Court, Gould, Armstrong.

Mar 24 **Tottenham Hotspur** 1–0
(Sammels) Att: 43,972
Wilson, Storey (Graham), McNab, McLintock, Ure, Simpson, Radford, Sammels, Court, Gould, Armstrong.

Mar 29 **Southampton** 0–0
Att: 28,990
Wilson, Storey, McNab, McLintock, Ure, Simpson, Radford, Sammels, Court, Gould, Armstrong.

Apr 7 **Wolverhampton Wanderers** 3–1
(Robertson, Armstrong, Graham) Att: 31,011
Wilson, Storey, McNab, McLintock, Ure, Graham, Robertson, Sammels, Court, Gould, Armstrong.

Apr 12 **Leeds United** 1–2
(Graham) Att: 44,715
Wilson, Storey, McNab, McLintock, Ure, Graham, Robertson, Sammels, Court, Gould (Radford), Armstrong.

FA CUP

Jan 7 Cardiff City 2–0
(Armstrong, Gould) Att: 52,681
Wilson, Storey, McNab, McLintock, Ure,
Simpson, Radford, Sammels, Court, Gould,
Armstrong.

Jan 25 Charlton Athletic 2–0
(Sammels, Robertson) Att: 55,760
Wilson, Storey, McNab, McLintock, Ure,
Simpson, Radford, Sammels, Court, Gould,
Robertson.

FOOTBALL LEAGUE CUP
Finalists

Sep 4 Sunderland 1–0
(Neill) Att: 28,460
Wilson, Storey, McNab, McLintock, Neill,
Simpson, Radford, Sammels, Gould, Court,
Jenkins.

Oct 15 Liverpool 2–1
(Simpson, Radford) Att: 39,299
Wilson, Storey, McNab, McLintock, Neill, Ure,
Radford, Simpson (Gould), Graham, Court,
Armstrong.

Oct 29 Blackpool 5–1
(Armstrong 2, Radford, Gould, Simpson)
Att: 32,321
Wilson, Storey, McNab, McLintock (Court),
Neill, Ure, Radford, Gould, Graham, Simpson,
Armstrong.

Nov 20 Tottenham Hotspur 1–0
(Radford) Att: 55,237
Wilson, Storey, McNab, McLintock, Ure,
Simpson, Radford, Court, Sammels, Graham
(Gould), Armstrong.

1969/70
LEAGUE DIVISION ONE
Final position – 12th

Aug 9 Everton 0–1
Att: 44,364
Wilson, Rice, McNab, McLintock, Neill,
Simpson, Robertson, George, Gould, Graham,
Radford.

Aug 19 Leeds United 1–1
(Rice) Att: 44,923
Wilson, Rice, McNab, Court, Ure, Simpson,
Robertson, George, Storey, Graham, Radford.

Aug 23 Nottingham Forest 2–1
(McNab, Graham) Att: 30,290
Wilson, Rice, McNab, McLintock, Neill,
Simpson, Robertson, George (Gould), Sammels,
Graham, Radford.

Sep 6 Sheffield Wednesday 0–0
Att: 28,605
Wilson, Rice, McNab, Sammels, Neill, Simpson,
Robertson, Gould, Court (Kelly), Graham,
Armstrong.

Sep 16 Tottenham Hotspur 2–3
(Robertson, Radford) Att: 55,280
Webster, Storey, McNab, McLintock, Neill,
Simpson, Robertson, George, Radford, Graham,
Sammels.

Sep 20 Manchester United 2–2
(Graham, Sammels) Att: 59,489
Webster, Storey, Rice, McLintock, Court,
Simpson, Robertson, Armstrong, Radford,
Graham, Sammels.

Oct 4 Coventry City 0–1
Att: 28,877
Barnett, Storey, McNab, McLintock, Roberts,
Simpson, Robertson, Sammels, Court (George),
Graham, Gould.

Oct 7 West Bromwich Albion 1–1
(Radford) Att: 21,165
Barnett, Storey, McNab, McLintock, Roberts,
Simpson, Robertson, Sammels, Graham, Gould,
Radford.

Oct 25 Ipswich Town 0–0
Att: 22,458
Barnett, Storey, Nelson, McLintock, Neill,
Simpson, Robertson, Sammels, Gould (George),
Graham, Radford.

Nov 8 Derby County 4–0
(George, Sammels 2, Armstrong)
Att: 49,763
Barnett, Storey, McNab, Court, Neill (George),
Simpson, Robertson, Sammels, Radford,
Graham, Armstrong.

Nov 22 Manchester City 1–1
(Neill [pen]) Att: 42,923
Barnett, Storey, McNab, Court, Neill, Simpson,
Robertson, Sammels, Radford, Graham,
Armstrong (George).

Dec 6 Southampton 2–2
(Sammels, Radford) Att: 24,509
Barnett, Storey, Nelson, Court, McLintock,
Simpson, Robertson, Sammels, Radford,
Graham, Armstrong.

Dec 13 Burnley 3–2
(Robertson, Radford, Armstrong) Att: 21,404
Wilson, Storey, McNab, Court, McLintock
(Kelly), Simpson, Robertson, Sammels, Radford,
Graham, Armstrong.

Dec 27 Newcastle United 0–0
Att: 39,637
Wilson, Storey, McNab, George, Neill, Simpson,
Robertson, Sammels, Radford, Kelly, Armstrong.

Jan 17 Chelsea 0–3
Att: 53,793
Wilson, Storey, McNab, McLintock, Roberts,
Simpson, Marinello, Sammels, Radford, Kelly
(George), Kennedy.

Feb 7 Stoke City 0–0
Att: 26,601
Wilson, Storey, McNab, McLintock, Roberts,
Simpson, Marinello, Sammels, Radford, George,
Armstrong.

Feb 28 Sunderland 3–1
(Storey [pen], Kennedy, Kelly) Att: 21,826
Wilson, Storey, McNab, McLintock, Roberts,
Kelly, Marinello, Sammels (Court), Radford,
Kennedy, Graham.

Mar 14 Liverpool 2–1
(Sammels, Radford) Att: 32,295
Wilson, Storey, McNab, Kelly, McLintock,
Simpson, Marinello, Sammels, Radford, George,
Graham.

Mar 28 Wolverhampton Wanderers 2–2
(Graham 2) Att: 32,353
Wilson, Storey, McNab, Kelly, McLintock,
Simpson, Marinello, Sammels, Radford, George,
Graham.

Mar 30 Crystal Palace 2–0
(Radford, George) Att: 34,144
Wilson, Storey, Nelson, Kelly, McLintock,
Simpson, Marinello, Sammels, Radford, George,
Graham.

Apr 4 West Ham United 2–1
(Kelly, Radford) Att: 36,212
Wilson, Storey, McNab, Kelly, McLintock,
Simpson, Marinello, Sammels, Radford, George,
Graham.

FA CUP

Jan 3 Blackpool 1–1
(Radford) Att: 32,210
Wilson, Storey, Nelson, Court, Neill, Simpson,
Robertson, Sammels, Radford, Graham,
Armstrong.

FOOTBALL LEAGUE CUP

Sep 4 Southampton 2–0*
(Graham 2) Att: 26,362
Wilson, Storey, McNab, McLintock, Roberts
(Gould), Simpson, Robertson, George, Court,
Graham, Radford.

*After extra time

Sep 24 Everton 0–0
Att: 36,102
Webster, Storey, McNab, Court, McLintock,
Simpson, Robertson, Sammels, Radford,
Graham, Armstrong.

EUROPEAN FAIRS CUP
Winners

Sep 9 Glentoran 3–0
(Graham 2, Gould) Att: 24,292
Wilson, Storey, McNab (Nelson), McLintock,
Simpson, Graham, Robertson, Court (Kelly),
Gould, Sammels, Armstrong.

Nov 26 Sporting Lisbon 3–0
(Radford, Graham 2) Att: 35,253
Barnett, Storey, McNab, Court, Neill, Simpson,
Robertson, Sammels, Radford, Graham,
Armstrong.

Jan 13 Rouen 1–0
(Sammels) Att: 38,018
Wilson, Storey, Nelson, Court (Graham), Neill,
Simpson, Marinello, Sammels, Radford, George,
Armstrong.

Mar 18 Dinamo Bacau 7–1
(Radford 2, George 2, Sammels 2, Graham)
Att: 35,342
Wilson, Storey, McNab, Kelly, McLintock,
Simpson, Marinello, Sammels, Radford, George,
Graham (Armstrong).

Apr 8 Ajax 3–0
(George 2 [1pen], Sammels) Att: 46,271
Wilson, Storey, McNab, Kelly, McLintock,
Simpson, Marinello (Armstrong), Sammels,
Radford, George, Graham.

Apr 28 Anderlecht 3–0
(Kelly, Radford, Sammels) Att: 51,612
Wilson, Storey, McNab, Kelly, McLintock,
Simpson, Armstrong, Sammels, Radford,
George, Graham.

1970/71
LEAGUE DIVISION ONE
Final position – Champions

Aug 22 Manchester United 4–0
(Radford 3, Graham) Att: 54,117
Wilson, Rice, McNab, Kelly, McLintock,
Roberts, Armstrong, Storey, Radford (Marinello),
Kennedy, Graham.

Aug 25 Huddersfield Town 1–0
(Kennedy) Att: 34,848
Wilson, Rice, McNab, Kelly, McLintock,
Roberts, Armstrong, Storey, Radford (Nelson),
Kennedy, Graham.

Sep 1 Leeds United 0–0
Att: 47,749
Wilson, Rice, McNab, Kelly, McLintock, Roberts,
Armstrong, Storey, Radford, Kennedy, Graham.

Sep 5 Tottenham Hotspur 2–0
(Armstrong 2) Att: 48,713
Wilson, Rice, McNab, Kelly, McLintock
(Nelson), Roberts, Armstrong, Storey, Radford,
Kennedy, Graham.

Sep 19 West Bromwich Albion 6–2
*(Kennedy 2, Graham 2, Armstrong, Cantello
[og])* Att: 33,326
Wilson, Rice, McNab, Kelly, McLintock,
Roberts, Armstrong, Storey, Radford, Kennedy,
Graham.

Oct 3 Nottingham Forest 4–0
(Kennedy 3, Armstrong) Att: 32,053
Wilson, Rice, McNab, Kelly, McLintock, Roberts,
Armstrong, Storey, Radford, Kennedy, Graham.

Oct 17 Everton 4–0
(Kennedy 2, Kelly, Storey [pen]) Att: 50,012
Wilson, Rice, McNab, Kelly, McLintock,
Roberts, Armstrong, Storey, Radford, Kennedy,
Graham.

Oct 31 Derby County 2–0
(Kelly, Radford) Att: 43,013
Wilson, Rice, McNab, Kelly, McLintock, Roberts,
Armstrong, Storey, Radford, Kennedy,
Graham.

Nov 14 Crystal Palace 1–1
(Radford) Att: 34,533
Wilson, Rice, McNab, Kelly, McLintock, Roberts,
Armstrong, Storey, Radford, Kennedy, Graham.

Nov 28 Liverpool 2–0
(Graham, Radford) Att: 45,097
Wilson, Rice, McNab, Kelly (Graham),
McLintock, Simpson, Armstrong, Storey,
Radford, Kennedy, Sammels.

Dec 12 Wolverhampton Wanderers 2–1
(Radford, Graham) Att: 38,816
Wilson, Rice, McNab, Storey, McLintock,
Simpson, Armstrong, Sammels, Radford,
Kennedy, Graham.

Dec 26 Southampton 0–0
Att: 34,169
Wilson, Rice, McNab, Storey, McLintock,
Simpson, Armstrong, Sammels, Radford,
Kennedy, Graham.

Jan 9 West Ham United 2–0
(Graham, Kennedy) Att: 49,007
Wilson, Rice, Nelson, Storey, McLintock,
Simpson, Armstrong, Sammels, Radford,
Kennedy, Graham.

Feb 6 Manchester City 1–0
(Radford) Att: 46,122
Wilson, Rice, McNab, Storey, McLintock,
Simpson, Armstrong, Sammels, Radford,
Kennedy, George.

Feb 20 Ipswich Town 3–2
(George, Radford, McLintock) Att: 39,822
Wilson, Rice, McNab, Storey, McLintock,
Simpson, Armstrong, Sammels, Radford,
Kennedy, George.

Mar 20 Blackpool 1–0
(Storey) Att: 37,372
Wilson, Rice, McNab, Storey, McLintock,
Simpson, Armstrong, Graham, Radford,
Kennedy, George.

Apr 3 Chelsea 2–0
(Kennedy 2) Att: 62,087
Wilson, Rice, McNab, Storey, McLintock,
Simpson, Armstrong (Kelly), Graham, Radford,
Kennedy, George.

Apr 6 Coventry City 1–0
(Kennedy) Att: 37,029
Wilson, Rice, McNab, Storey, McLintock,
Simpson, Armstrong, Graham, Radford,
Kennedy, George.

Apr 17 Newcastle United 1–0
(George) Att: 48,106
Wilson, Rice, McNab, Storey, McLintock,
Simpson, Armstrong, Graham, Radford,
Kennedy, George.

Apr 20 Burnley 1–0
(George [pen]) Att: 47,484
Wilson, Rice, Roberts, Kelly, McLintock,
Simpson, Armstrong, Graham, Radford,
Kennedy, George.

May 1 Stoke City 1–0
(Kelly) Att: 55,011
Wilson, Rice, McNab, Storey (Kelly), McLintock,
Simpson, Armstrong, Graham, Radford,
Kennedy, George.

FA CUP
Winners

Feb 1 Portsmouth 3–2
(George, Simpson, Storey [pen]) Att: 47,865
Wilson, Rice, McNab, Storey, McLintock,
Simpson, Armstrong, Sammels, Radford,
Kennedy, George.

Mar 15 Leicester City 1–0
(George) Att: 57,443
Wilson, Rice, McNab, Storey, McLintock,
Simpson, Armstrong, Graham, Radford,
Kennedy, George.

FOOTBALL LEAGUE CUP

Sep 28 Ipswich Town 4–0
(Kennedy 2, Radford, Roberts) Att: 26,379
Wilson, Rice, McNab, Kelly, McLintock,
Roberts, Armstrong, Storey, Radford, Kennedy,
Graham.

Nov 9 Crystal Palace 0–2
Att: 45,026
Wilson, Rice, McNab, Kelly, McLintock,
Roberts, Armstrong, Storey, Radford, Kennedy,
Graham.

EUROPEAN FAIRS CUP

Sep 23 Lazio 2–0
(Radford, Armstrong) Att: 53,013
Wilson, Rice, McNab, Kelly, McLintock,
Roberts, Armstrong, Storey, Radford, Kennedy,
Graham (Nelson).

Nov 4 Sturm Graz 2–0
(Kennedy, Storey [pen]) Att: 37,677
Wilson, Rice, McNab, Kelly, McLintock, Roberts,
Armstrong, Storey, Radford, Kennedy, Graham.

Dec 2 Beveren Waas 4–0
(Kennedy 2, Sammels, Graham) Att: 33,444
Wilson, Rice, McNab, Sammels, McLintock,
Simpson, Armstrong, Storey, Radford, Kennedy,
Graham.

Mar 9 FC Cologne 2–1
(McLintock, Storey) Att: 40,007
Wilson, Rice, McNab, Storey, McLintock,
Simpson, Armstrong, Sammels (Graham),
Radford, Kennedy, George.

1971/72
LEAGUE DIVISION ONE
Final position – 5th

Aug 14 Chelsea 3–0
(McLintock, Kennedy, Radford) Att: 49,174
Wilson, Rice, McNab, Storey, McLintock,
Simpson, Armstrong, Kelly, Radford, Kennedy,
Graham.

Aug 24 Sheffield United 0–1
Att: 45,395
Wilson, Rice, McNab, Storey, McLintock,
Simpson, Armstrong, Kelly, Radford, Kennedy,
Graham.

Aug 28 Stoke City 0–1
Att: 37,637
Wilson, Rice (Roberts), McNab, Storey,
McLintock, Simpson, Armstrong, Kelly, Radford,
Kennedy, Graham.

Sep 11 Leeds United 2–0
(Graham, Storey [pen]) Att: 51,196
Wilson, Rice, McNab, Storey, McLintock,
Roberts, Armstrong, Simpson, Radford,
Kennedy, Graham.

Sep 25 Leicester City 3–0
(Radford 2, Rice) Att: 40,201
Wilson, Rice, Nelson, Storey (George), Simpson,
Roberts, Armstrong, Kelly, Radford, Kennedy,
Graham.

Oct 9 Newcastle United 4–2
(Graham, Kennedy, Armstrong, Kelly)
Att: 40,509
Wilson, Rice, Nelson, McLintock, Simpson,
George, Armstrong, Kelly, Radford (Davies),
Kennedy, Graham.

Oct 30 Ipswich Town 2–1
(George, Sivell [og]) Att: 39,065
Wilson, Rice, Nelson, Storey, Roberts,
McLintock, Armstrong, George, Radford,
Kennedy, Graham.

Nov 13 **Manchester City** 1–2
(Nelson) Att: 47,443
Wilson, Rice, Nelson, Storey, Roberts, McLintock, Armstrong, George, Radford, Kennedy, Graham.

Nov 27 **Crystal Palace** 2–1
(Kelly, Radford) Att: 32,461
Wilson, Rice, McNab, Storey, Roberts, McLintock, Armstrong, Kelly, Radford, Kennedy, Graham.

Dec 11 **Coventry City** 2–0
(Radford 2) Att: 28,599
Wilson, Rice, McNab, Storey, McLintock, Simpson (Marinello), Armstrong, Kelly, Radford, Kennedy, Graham.

Dec 18 **West Bromwich Albion** 2–0
(Roberts 2) Att: 28,177
Wilson, Rice, McNab, Storey, McLintock, Roberts, Armstrong, Kelly, Radford, Kennedy, Graham.

Jan 1 **Everton** 1–1
(Simpson) Att: 47,031
Wilson, Rice, McNab, Kelly, Roberts, Simpson, Armstrong (George), Ball, Radford, Kennedy, Graham.

Jan 22 **Huddersfield Town** 1–0
(Armstrong) Att: 36,670
Wilson, Rice, Nelson, Kelly, McLintock, Simpson, Armstrong, Ball (George), Radford, Kennedy, Graham.

Feb 12 **Derby County** 2–0
(George 2 [1pen]) Att: 52,055
Wilson, Rice, Nelson, Kelly, McLintock, Simpson, Armstrong, Ball, George, Kennedy, Graham.

Mar 28 **Southampton** 1–0
(Marinello) Att: 27,172
Wilson, Rice, Nelson, Storey, McLintock, Simpson, Armstrong, Ball, George, Kennedy, Marinello.

Apr 1 **Nottingham Forest** 3–0
(Kennedy, George [pen], Graham) Att: 33,895
Wilson, Rice, Nelson, Storey, Roberts, Simpson, Armstrong, Ball, George, Kennedy (Graham), Marinello.

Apr 9 **Wolverhampton Wanderers** 2–1
(Graham 2) Att: 38,189
Wilson, Rice, Nelson, Storey, McLintock, Simpson, Marinello (Armstrong), Ball, George, Kennedy, Graham.

Apr 22 **West Ham United** 2–1
(Ball 2) Att: 45,251
Barnett, Rice, McNab, Storey, McLintock (Batson), Simpson, Armstrong, Ball, Radford, George, Graham.

Apr 25 **Manchester United** 3–0
(Radford, Kennedy, Simpson) Att: 49,125
Barnett, Rice, McNab, Roberts, McLintock, Simpson, Armstrong, Nelson, Radford, Kennedy, Graham (Marinello).

May 8 **Liverpool** 0–0
Att: 39,285
Barnett, Rice (Roberts), Nelson, Storey, McLintock, Simpson, Armstrong, Ball, Radford, Kennedy, Graham.

May 11 **Tottenham Hotspur** 0–2
Att: 42,038
Barnett, Rice, McNab, Nelson, McLintock, Roberts, Armstrong, Simpson (Marinello), Radford, Kennedy, Graham.

FA CUP
Finalists

Feb 29 **Derby County** 0–0*
Att: 63,077
Wilson, Rice, Nelson, Storey, McLintock, Simpson, Armstrong, Ball, George, Kennedy (Radford), Graham.

*After extra time

FOOTBALL LEAGUE CUP

Sep 8 **Barnsley** 1–0
(Kennedy) Att: 27,294
Wilson, Rice, McNab, Storey, McLintock, Roberts, Marinello, Kelly, Radford, Kennedy, Graham.

Oct 6 **Newcastle United** 4–0
(Radford 2, Kennedy, Graham) Att: 34,071
Wilson, Rice, Nelson, McLintock, Simpson, Roberts, Armstrong, Kelly, Radford, Kennedy, Graham.

Oct 26 **Sheffield United** 0–0
Att: 44,061
Barnett, Rice, Nelson, Storey, Roberts, McLintock, Armstrong, George, Radford, Kennedy, Graham.

EUROPEAN CUP

Sep 29 **Stromsgodset Drammen** 4–0
(Kennedy, Radford 2, Armstrong) Att: 27,176
Wilson, Rice, Nelson, Kelly, Simpson, Roberts, Armstrong, George, Radford, Kennedy, Graham.

Nov 3 **Grasshoppers** 3–0
(Kennedy, George, Radford) Att: 31,106
Wilson, Rice, Nelson, Storey, Roberts (Simpson), McLintock (McNab), Armstrong, George, Radford, Kennedy, Graham.

Mar 22 **Ajax** 0–1
Att: 56,145
Wilson, Rice, Nelson (Roberts), Storey, McLintock, Simpson, Armstrong, George, Marinello, Kennedy, Graham.

1972/73
LEAGUE DIVISION ONE
Final position – 2nd

Aug 15 **Wolverhampton Wanderers** 5–2
(Radford 2, Kennedy, Simpson, McNab)
Att: 38,524
Barnett, Rice, McNab, Storey, McLintock, Simpson (Roberts), Armstrong, Ball, Radford, Kennedy, Graham.

Aug 19 **Stoke City** 2–0
(Kennedy 2) Att: 42,146
Barnett, Rice, McNab, Storey, McLintock, Roberts, Armstrong, Ball, Radford, Kennedy, Graham.

Aug 29 **West Ham United** 1–0
(Ball [pen]) Att: 43,802
Barnett, Rice, McNab, Storey, McLintock, Simpson, Armstrong (George), Ball, Radford, Kennedy, Graham.

Sep 2 **Chelsea** 1–1
(Webb [og]) Att: 46,675
Barnett, Rice, McNab, Storey, McLintock, Simpson, Armstrong (George), Ball, Radford, Kennedy, Graham.

Sep 16 **Liverpool** 0–0
Att: 47,597
Barnett, Rice, McNab, Storey, McLintock, Roberts, Marinello, Ball, Radford, Kennedy, Graham.

Sep 26 **Birmingham City** 2–0
(Storey, George) Att: 30,003
Barnett, Rice, McNab, Storey, McLintock, Roberts, Marinello, Ball, Radford, Kennedy, George.

Sep 30 **Southampton** 1–0
(Graham) Att: 34,694
Barnett, Rice, McNab, Storey, McLintock, Roberts, Marinello, Ball, Radford, Kennedy (Graham), George.

Oct 14 **Ipswich Town** 1–0
(Graham) Att: 34,196
Barnett, Rice, McNab, Storey, McLintock, Blockley, Marinello, Ball, Radford, Graham, George.

Oct 28 **Manchester City** 0–0
Att: 45,536
Barnett, Rice, McNab, Storey, McLintock, Blockley, Marinello, Kelly, Radford, George, Graham.

Nov 4 **Coventry City** 0–2
Att: 33,699
Barnett, Rice, McNab, Storey, McLintock, Blockley, Marinello, Ball, Radford, George, Kelly (Graham).

Nov 18 **Everton** 1–0
(Radford) Att: 35,728
Barnett, Rice, McNab, Storey, Simpson, Blockley, Marinello, Ball, Radford, George, Kelly.

Dec 2 **Leeds United** 2–1
(Ball [pen], Radford) Att: 39,108
Wilson, Rice, McNab, Storey, Blockley, Simpson, Armstrong, Ball, Radford, Kennedy, Kelly.

Dec 16 **West Bromwich Albion** 2–1
(Radford, Nisbet [og]) Att: 27,119
Barnett, Rice (George), McNab, Storey, McLintock, Simpson, Armstrong, Ball, Radford, Kennedy, Kelly.

Dec 26 **Norwich City** 2–0
(Radford, Ball) Att: 39,038
Wilson, Nelson (George), McNab, Storey, Blockley, Simpson, Armstrong, Ball, Radford, Kennedy, Kelly.

Jan 6 **Manchester United** 3–1
(Kennedy, Armstrong, Ball) Att: 56,194
Wilson, Rice, McNab, Storey, Blockley, Simpson, Armstrong, Ball, Radford, Kennedy, Kelly.

Jan 27 **Newcastle United** 2–2
(Kennedy, Ball) Att: 37,906
Wilson, Rice, McNab, Storey, Blockley, Simpson, Armstrong (George), Ball, Radford, Kennedy, Kelly.

Feb 17 **Leicester City** 1–0
(Manley [og]) Att: 42,047
Wilson, Rice, McNab, Storey, Blockley (George), McLintock, Armstrong, Ball, Radford, Kennedy, Kelly.

Mar 3 **Sheffield United** 3–2
(George 2, Ball) Att: 33,346
Wilson, Rice, McNab, George, McLintock, Batson (Nelson), Armstrong, Ball, Radford, Kennedy, Kelly.

Mar 26 **Crystal Palace** 1–0
(Ball) Att: 41,879
Wilson, Rice, McNab, Storey, McLintock, Simpson, Armstrong, Ball, George, Kennedy, Kelly.

Mar 31 **Derby County** 0–1
Att: 45,217
Wilson, Rice, McNab, Storey, McLintock (Nelson), Simpson, Armstrong, Ball, George, Kennedy, Kelly.

Apr 14 **Tottenham Hotspur** 1–1
(Storey) Att: 50,863
Wilson, Rice, McNab, Storey, Blockley, Simpson, Armstrong, Ball, Radford, Kennedy, Kelly (George).

FA CUP

Jan 13 **Leicester City** 2–2
(Kennedy, Armstrong) Att: 36,433
Wilson, Rice, McNab, Storey, Blockley, Simpson, Armstrong, Ball, Radford, Kennedy, Kelly.

Feb 3 **Bradford City** 2–0
(Ball, George) Att: 40,407
Wilson, Rice, McNab, Storey, Blockley, Simpson, Armstrong, Ball, George (Marinello), Kennedy, Kelly.

Mar 20 **Chelsea** 2–1
(Ball [pen], Kennedy) Att: 62,746
Wilson, Rice, McNab, Storey, McLintock, Simpson, Armstrong, Ball, George, Kennedy, Kelly.

FOOTBALL LEAGUE CUP

Sep 5 **Everton** 1–0
(Storey) Att: 35,230
Barnett, Rice, McNab, Storey, McLintock, Simpson, Marinello, Ball, Radford, Kennedy, Graham.

Oct 3 **Rotherham United** 5–0
(Radford 2, George, Storey, Marinello)
Att: 25,241
Barnett, Rice, Nelson, Storey, McLintock, Roberts, Marinello, Ball, Radford, Graham, George.

Nov 21 **Norwich City** 0–3
Att: 37,671
Barnett, Rice, McNab, Storey, McLintock, Simpson, Marinello, Ball, Radford, George, Kelly.

1973/74
LEAGUE DIVISION ONE
Final position – 10th

Aug 25 **Manchester United** 3–0
(Kennedy, Radford, Ball) Att: 51,501
Wilson, Rice, McNab, Price, Blockley, Simpson, Armstrong, Ball, Radford (Hornsby), Kennedy, George.

Aug 28 **Leeds United** 1–2
(Blockley) Att: 47,429
Wilson, Rice, McNab, Storey, Blockley, Simpson (Price), Armstrong, Ball, Radford, Kennedy, George.

Sep 8 **Leicester City** 0–2
Att: 28,558
Wilson, Rice, McNab, Storey, Blockley, Simpson, Kelly (Armstrong), Ball, Radford, Kennedy, George.

Sep 11 **Sheffield United** 1–0
(Kennedy) Att: 29,434
Wilson, Rice, McNab, Storey, Blockley Simpson, Armstrong, Ball, Radford, Kennedy, Kelly.

Sep 22 **Stoke City** 2–1
(Radford, Ball) Att: 30,578
Wilson, Rice, McNab, Storey, Blockley, Simpson, Armstrong, Ball, Radford, Kennedy, George (Kelly).

Oct 6 **Birmingham City** 1–0
(Kennedy) Att: 23,915
Wilson, Rice, McNab, Storey, Blockley (Brady), Simpson, Armstrong, Chambers, Radford, Kennedy, Kelly.

Oct 20 **Ipswich Town** 1–1
(Simpson) Att: 28,344
Wilson, Rice, McNab, Storey, Simpson, Kelly, Armstrong, George, Batson, Kennedy, Price.

Nov 3 **Liverpool** 0–2
Att: 39,837
Wilson, Rice, McNab, Storey, Simpson, Powling, Armstrong, George, Radford, Kennedy, Kelly (Batson).

Nov 17 **Chelsea** 0–0
Att: 38,677
Wilson, Rice, McNab, Storey, Simpson, Kelly, Ball, George, Hornsby, Kennedy, Armstrong.

Dec 1 **Coventry City** 2–2
(Hornsby, Nelson) Att: 22,340
Wilson, Rice, McNab, Storey, Simpson, Kelly (Nelson), Ball, George, Hornsby, Kennedy, Armstrong.

Dec 4 **Wolverhampton Wanderers** 2–2
(George, Hornsby) Att: 13,482
Wilson, Rice, McNab, Storey, Simpson, Kelly, Ball, George (Hornsby), Radford, Kennedy, Armstrong.

Dec 22 **Everton** 1–0
(Ball) Att: 19,896
Wilson, Rice, McNab, Storey, Blockley, Simpson, Armstrong, Ball, Hornsby, Kennedy, Kelly.

Jan 1 **Newcastle United** 0–1
Att: 29,258
Wilson, Rice, Nelson, Storey, Blockley, Simpson, Armstrong, Ball, Radford, Kennedy, Kelly.

Jan 12 **Norwich City** 2–0
(Ball 2) Att: 22,084
Wilson, Rice, Storey, Kelly, Simpson, Armstrong, Ball, Radford, Kennedy, Brady.

Feb 2 **Burnley** 1–1
(Ball) Att: 20,789
Wilson, Rice, Storey, Kelly, Blockley, Simpson, Armstrong, Ball, Radford, Kennedy, Brady.

Feb 16 **Tottenham Hotspur** 0–1
Att: 38,804
Wilson, Rice, Nelson, Storey, Simpson, Kelly, Armstrong, Ball, Radford, Kennedy, Brady.

Mar 2 **Southampton** 1–0
(Ball) Att: 19,210
Wilson, Rice, Nelson, Storey, Simpson, Kelly, George, Ball, Radford, Kennedy, Armstrong.

Mar 23 **Manchester City** 2–0
(Radford 2) Att: 25,319
Wilson, Rice, Nelson, Storey, Simpson, Kelly (Brady), George, Ball, Radford, Kennedy, Armstrong.

Apr 6 **West Ham United** 0–0
Att: 37,868
Wilson, Rice, Nelson, Storey, Blockley, Kelly, Armstrong, Ball, Radford, Kennedy, George.

Apr 20 **Derby County** 2–0
(Ball [pen], George) Att: 26,017
Wilson, Rice, Nelson, Storey, Blockley, Kelly, Armstrong, Ball, George (Simpson), Kennedy, Brady.

Apr 30 **Queens Park Rangers** 1–1
(Brady) Att: 40,396
Wilson, Rice, Nelson, Storey, Simpson, Kelly, Armstrong, Ball (Brady), Radford, Kennedy, George.

FA CUP

Jan 26 **Aston Villa** 1–1
(Kennedy) Att: 41,682
Wilson, Rice, McNab, Storey, Blockley, Simpson, Armstrong, Ball, Radford, Kennedy, Kelly.

FOOTBALL LEAGUE CUP

Oct 2 **Tranmere Rovers** 0–1
Att: 20,337
Wilson, Rice, McNab, Storey, Blockley, Simpson, Armstrong, Ball (Chambers), Radford, Kennedy, Kelly.

FA CUP
Third place play-off (1972/73)

Aug 18 **Wolverhampton Wanderers** 1–3
(Hornsby) Att: 21,038
Wilson, Batson, McNab, Price, Blockley, Simpson, Chambers, Ball, Radford, Kennedy, Hornsby.

1974/75
LEAGUE DIVISION ONE
Final position – 16th

Aug 20 **Ipswich Town** 0–1
Att: 31,027
Rimmer, Storey, Nelson, Kelly, Matthews, Armstrong, Hornsby, Radford, Kidd, Brady.

Aug 24 **Manchester City** 4–0
(Kidd 2, Radford 2) Att: 27,143
Rimmer, Rice, Nelson, Kelly, Simpson (Armstrong), Storey, Matthews, George, Radford, Kidd, Brady.

Sep 7 Burnley 0–1
Att: 23,546
Rimmer, Rice (Simpson), Nelson, Storey, Blockley, Matthews, Armstrong, Brady, Radford, George, Kidd.

Sep 21 Luton Town 2–2
(Kidd 2) Att: 21,629
Rimmer, Simpson, Nelson, Storey, Blockley, Matthews, Armstrong, Kelly, Radford, Kidd, Brady.

Oct 12 Queens Park Rangers 2–2
(Kidd, Radford) Att: 29,690
Rimmer, Storey, Simpson, Kelly, Powling, Matthews, Armstrong, Ball, Radford, Kidd, Brady.

Oct 26 West Ham United 3–0
(Radford, Brady, Kidd) Att: 41,004
Rimmer, Storey, McNab, Kelly, Mancini, Simpson, Rice (Armstrong), Ball, Radford, Brady, Kidd.

Nov 2 Wolverhampton Wanderers 0–0
Att: 27,572
Rimmer, Storey, McNab, Kelly, Mancini, Simpson, Rice, Ball, Radford, Brady, Kidd.

Nov 16 Derby County 3–1
(Ball 2 [1 pen], Kidd) Att: 32,286
Rimmer, Rice, McNab, Kelly, Mancini, Simpson, Storey, Ball, Radford, Kidd, Brady.

Nov 30 Middlesbrough 2–0
(Brady, Ball [pen]) Att: 25,283
Rimmer, Rice, McNab, Kelly, Simpson, Powling, George, Ball, Radford, Kidd, Brady.

Dec 14 Leicester City 0–0
Att: 20,849
Rimmer, Rice, McNab, Kelly, Mancini, Simpson, Storey, Ball, Radford, Kidd, Cropley.

Dec 26 Chelsea 1–2
(Ball [pen]) Att: 33,784
Rimmer, Rice, McNab, Kelly, Mancini, Simpson, Storey, Ball, Radford, Kidd, Cropley.

Jan 11 Carlisle United 2–1
(Radford, Cropley) Att: 21,538
Rimmer, Rice, McNab, Kelly, Mancini, Simpson, Armstrong, Ball, Radford, Kidd, Cropley.

Feb 1 Liverpool 2–0
(Ball 2 [1 pen]) Att: 43,028
Rimmer, Rice, McNab, Matthews, Mancini, Simpson, Armstrong, Ball (Ross), Brady, Kidd, Storey.

Mar 1 Everton 0–2
Att: 32,216
Rimmer, Rice, McNab, Storey, Mancini, Simpson, Armstrong, Ball, Radford, Kidd, Brady.

Mar 15 Birmingham City 1–1
(Kidd) Att: 17,845
Rimmer, Rice, Nelson, Storey, Mancini, Simpson, Matthews, Ball, Radford, Kidd, Brady.

Mar 18 Newcastle United 3–0
(Kidd, Ball [pen], Rostron) Att: 16,540
Rimmer, Rice, Nelson, Rostron, Mancini, Simpson, Matthews, Ball, Hornsby, Kidd, Brady.

Mar 29 Stoke City 1–1
(Kelly) Att: 26,852
Rimmer, Rice, McNab, Storey, Kelly, Simpson, Matthews, Ball, Stapleton (Brady), Rostron, Hornsby.

Mar 31 Sheffield United 1–0
(Kidd) Att: 24,338
Rimmer, Rice, Nelson, Storey, Mancini, Simpson, Matthews, Kelly, Hornsby, Kidd, Armstrong.

Apr 8 Coventry City 2–0
(Kidd 2) Att: 17,291
Rimmer, Rice, Nelson, Storey, Mancini, Simpson, Matthews, Kelly, Hornsby, Kidd, Armstrong.

Apr 12 Leeds United 1–2
(Kidd) Att: 36,619
Rimmer, Rice, Nelson (Brady), Storey, Mancini, Simpson, Matthews, Kelly, Hornsby, Kidd, Armstrong.

Apr 26 Tottenham Hotspur 1–0
(Kidd) Att: 43,752
Barnett, Rice, Nelson, Storey, Mancini, Simpson, Ball, Brady, Hornsby, Kidd, Armstrong.

FA CUP

Jan 4 York City 1–1
(Kelly) Att: 27,029
Rimmer, Rice, McNab, Kelly, Mancini, Powling, Storey, Ball, Armstrong, Kidd, Cropley.

Jan 29 Coventry City 3–0
(Armstrong 2, Matthews) Att: 30,867
Rimmer, Rice, McNab, Matthews, Mancini, Simpson, Armstrong, Ball, Radford (Brady), Kidd, Storey.

Feb 15 Leicester City 0–0
Att: 43,841
Rimmer, Rice, McNab, Storey, Mancini, Simpson, Armstrong, Ball, Radford, Kidd, Brady.

Mar 8 West Ham United 0–2
Att: 56,742
Rimmer, Rice, McNab, Storey, Mancini, Simpson, Matthews, Ball, Radford (Armstrong), Kidd, Brady.

FOOTBALL LEAGUE CUP

Sep 10 Leicester City 1–1
(Kidd) Att: 20,788
Rimmer, Kelly, Simpson, Storey, Blockley, Matthews, Armstrong, George, Radford, Kidd, Brady.

1975/76

LEAGUE DIVISION ONE
Final position – 17th

Aug 23 Stoke City 0–1
Att: 28,025
Rimmer, Rice, Nelson, Kelly, Mancini, O'Leary, Armstrong, Cropley, Hornsby, Kidd, Brady.

Aug 26 Norwich City 2–1
(Ball [pen], Kelly) Att: 22,613
Rimmer, Rice, Storey, Kelly, Mancini, O'Leary, Armstrong, Cropley, Ball, Kidd, Brady.

Sep 6 Leicester City 1–1
(Stapleton) Att: 22,005
Rimmer, Rice, Nelson, Kelly, Mancini, O'Leary, Ball, Cropley, Stapleton, Kidd, Brady.

Sep 20 Everton 2–2
(Kidd, Stapleton) Att: 24,864
Rimmer, Rice, Nelson, Kelly, Mancini, O'Leary, Ball, Cropley, Stapleton, Kidd, Brady.

Oct 4 Manchester City 2–3
(Ball, Cropley) Att: 24,928
Rimmer, Rice, Nelson, Kelly (Rostron), Simpson, O'Leary, Ball, Cropley, Stapleton, Kidd, Brady.

Oct 11 Coventry City 5–0
(Cropley 2, Ball, Kidd 2) Att: 19,234
Rimmer, Rice, Nelson, Powling, Simpson, O'Leary, Ball, Cropley (Rostron), Stapleton, Kidd, Brady.

Oct 25 Middlesbrough 2–1
(Stapleton, Cropley) Att: 23,591
Rimmer, Rice, Nelson, Kelly (Powling), O'Leary, Simpson, Ball, Cropley, Stapleton, Kidd, Brady.

Nov 8 Derby County 0–1
Att: 32,012
Rimmer, Rice, Storey, Kelly, O'Leary, Powling, Ball, Cropley, Stapleton, Hornsby, Brady.

Nov 22 Manchester United 3–1
(Ball, Armstrong, Greenhoff [og]) Att: 40,102
Rimmer, Rice, Storey, Nelson, O'Leary, Powling, Ball, Armstrong, Stapleton, Kidd, Brady.

Dec 6 Leeds United 1–2
(Brady) Att: 36,003
Rimmer, Rice, Nelson, Storey, O'Leary, Powling, Armstrong, Ball, Stapleton, Kidd, Brady.

Dec 20 Burnley 1–0
(Radford) Att: 16,459
Rimmer, Rice, Simpson, Kelly, Mancini, Powling, Armstrong, Ball, Radford, Kidd, Brady (Stapleton).

Dec 27 Queens Park Rangers 2–0
(Ball, Kidd) Att: 39,021
Rimmer, Rice, Nelson, Storey, O'Leary, Powling, Armstrong, Ball, Stapleton, Kidd, Brady.

Jan 10 Aston Villa 0–0
Att: 24,501
Rimmer, Rice, Nelson, Powling, O'Leary, Mancini, Armstrong, Ball, Stapleton, Kidd, Brady.

Jan 31 Sheffield United 1–0
(Brady) Att: 14,477
Rimmer, Rice, Nelson (Rostron), Ross, Mancini, Powling, Armstrong, Ball, Stapleton, Kidd, Brady.

Feb 21 Birmingham City 1–0
(Brady) Att: 20,907
Rimmer, Rice, Nelson, Ross, Mancini, Powling, Armstrong, Ball, Radford, Kidd, Brady (Simpson).

Feb 24 Liverpool 1–0
(Radford) Att: 36,127
Rimmer, Rice, Nelson, Ross, Mancini, Powling, Armstrong, Ball, Radford, Kidd, Brady.

Mar 16 Newcastle United 0–0
Att: 18,424
Rimmer, Rice, Nelson, Ross, Mancini, Powling, Armstrong, Ball, Radford, Kidd, Brady.

Mar 20 West Ham United 6–1
(Kidd 3, Ball 2 [1 pen], Armstrong) Att: 34,011
Rimmer, Rice (Stapleton), Nelson, Ross, Mancini, Powling, Armstrong, Ball, Radford, Kidd, Brady.

Apr 3 Tottenham Hotspur 0–2
Att: 42,134
Rimmer, Rice, Nelson, Ross, Mancini, Powling, Armstrong, Ball, Radford, Kidd, Brady.

Apr 13 Wolverhampton Wanderers 2–1
(Brady, Mancini) Att: 19,518
Rimmer, Rice, Nelson, Ross, Mancini, Powling, Armstrong, Ball, Radford, Cropley, Brady.

Apr 17 Ipswich Town 1–2
(Stapleton) Att: 26,973
Rimmer, Rice, Nelson, Ross, O'Leary, Powling, Rostron, Ball, Stapleton, Cropley, Brady.

NOTE: There were no FA Cup matches at Highbury this season.

FOOTBALL LEAGUE CUP

Sep 23 Everton 0–1
Att: 21,813
Rimmer, Rice, Nelson, Kelly, Mancini, O'Leary, Ball, Cropley, Stapleton, Kidd, Rostron.

1976/77

LEAGUE DIVISION ONE
Final position – 8th

Aug 21 Bristol City 0–1
Att: 41,082
Rimmer, Rice, Nelson, Ross, O'Leary, Simpson, Ball, Armstrong, Macdonald, Radford, Cropley (Storey).

Sep 4 Manchester City 0–0
Att: 35,132
Rimmer, Rice, Nelson, Ross, O'Leary, Simpson, Ball, Brady, Macdonald, Stapleton (Cropley), Armstrong.

Sep 18 Everton 3–1
(Brady, Stapleton, Macdonald) Att: 34,076
Rimmer, Rice, Nelson, Ross, Howard, Powling, Ball, Brady, Macdonald, Stapleton, Armstrong.

Oct 2 Queens Park Rangers 3–2
(Rice, Brady, Stapleton) Att: 39,442
Rimmer, Rice, Nelson (Storey), Ross, O'Leary, Howard, Ball, Brady, Macdonald, Stapleton, Armstrong.

Oct 16 Stoke City 2–0
(Rice, Macdonald) Att: 28,507
Rimmer, Rice, Storey, Ross, O'Leary, Howard, Ball, Brady, Macdonald, Stapleton (Radford), Armstrong.

Nov 6 Birmingham City 4–0
(Stapleton, Nelson, Macdonald [pen], Ross)
Att: 23,063
Rimmer, Rice, Nelson, Ross, O'Leary (Storey), Simpson, Matthews, Brady, Macdonald, Stapleton, Armstrong.

Nov 20 Liverpool 1–1
(Armstrong) Att: 45,016
Rimmer, Rice, Nelson, Ross, O'Leary, Simpson, Ball, Brady, Macdonald, Stapleton, Armstrong.

Dec 4 Newcastle United 5–3
(Macdonald 3, Ross, Stapleton) Att: 34,053
Rimmer, Rice (Matthews), Nelson, Ross, O'Leary, Howard, Ball, Brady, Macdonald, Stapleton, Armstrong.

Dec 18 Manchester United 3–1
(Macdonald 2, Brady) Att: 39,572
Rimmer, Rice, Powling, Ross, O'Leary, Simpson, Storey, Brady, Macdonald, Stapleton (Rostron), Armstrong.

Jan 3 Leeds United 1–1
(Macdonald) Att: 44,090
Rimmer, Rice, Powling, Ross, O'Leary, Simpson, Hudson, Brady, Macdonald, Stapleton, Armstrong.

Jan 15 Norwich City 1–0
(Rice) Att: 30,537
Rimmer, Rice, Nelson, Ross, O'Leary, Simpson, Hudson, Brady, Macdonald, Stapleton, Armstrong.

Feb 5 Sunderland 0–0
Att: 30,925
Rimmer, Rice, Nelson, Ross, O'Leary, Simpson, Hudson, Brady, Macdonald, Stapleton, Rostron.

Feb 19 West Ham United 2–3
(Brady, Stapleton) Att: 38,221
Rimmer, Rice, Nelson, Ross, Powling, Simpson, Hudson, Brady, Macdonald, Stapleton, Armstrong.

Mar 5 Ipswich Town 1–4
(Macdonald [pen]) Att: 34,688
Rimmer, Rice, Young, Ross, Howard, Powling, Brady, Matthews (Nelson), Macdonald, Stapleton, Armstrong.

Mar 8 West Bromwich Albion 1–2
(Macdonald) Att: 19,517
Rimmer, Rice, Nelson, Price, Young, Howard, Brady, Powling, Macdonald, Stapleton, Armstrong.

Apr 2 Leicester City 3–0
(Rix, O'Leary 2) Att: 23,013
Rimmer, Rice, Nelson, Powling (Matthews), O'Leary, Young, Rix, Price, Macdonald, Stapleton, Armstrong.

Apr 11 Tottenham Hotspur 1–0
(Macdonald) Att: 47,296
Rimmer, Rice, Matthews, Price, O'Leary, Young, Rix (Brady), Hudson, Macdonald, Stapleton, Armstrong.

Apr 23 Coventry City 2–0
(Stapleton, Macdonald) Att: 22,790
Rimmer, Rice, Matthews, Ross (Rix), O'Leary, Young, Brady, Hudson, Macdonald, Stapleton, Armstrong.

Apr 25 Aston Villa 3–0
(Macdonald, Armstrong, Nelson) Att: 23,961
Rimmer, Rice, Nelson, Matthews, O'Leary, Young, Brady (Roston), Hudson, Macdonald, Stapleton, Armstrong.

May 3 Derby County 0–0
Att: 26,659
Rimmer, Rice, Nelson, Matthews, O'Leary, Young (Rix), Brady, Hudson, Macdonald, Stapleton, Armstrong.

May 7 Middlesbrough 1–1
(Stapleton) Att: 23,911
Rimmer, Rice, Nelson, Matthews (Price), O'Leary, Young, Brady, Rix, Macdonald, Stapleton, Armstrong.

FA CUP

Jan 29 Coventry City 3–1
(Macdonald 2, Stapleton) Att: 41,078
Rimmer, Rice, Nelson, Ross, O'Leary, Simpson, Hudson, Brady, Macdonald (Storey), Stapleton, Rostron.

FOOTBALL LEAGUE CUP

Aug 31 Carlisle United 3–2
(Ross 2, Macdonald) Att: 21,550
Rimmer, Rice, Nelson, Ross, O'Leary, Simpson, Ball, Brady, Macdonald, Stapleton, Armstrong.

Sep 28 Blackpool 0–0 *
Att: 27,165
Rimmer, Rice, Nelson (Storey), Ross, O'Leary, Howard, Ball, Brady, Macdonald, Stapleton, Armstrong.

*After extra time

Oct 5 Blackpool 2–0
(Stapleton, O'Leary) Att: 26,791
Rimmer, Rice, Storey, Matthews, O'Leary, Howard, Ball, Brady, Macdonald, Stapleton, Armstrong.

Oct 26 Chelsea 2–1
(Ross, Stapleton) Att: 52,305
Rimmer, Rice, Nelson, Ross, Simpson, Howard, Ball, Brady, Macdonald, Stapleton, Armstrong.

1977/78

LEAGUE DIVISION ONE
Final position – 5th

Aug 23 Everton 1–0
(Powling) Att: 32,954
Jennings, Rice, Nelson, Powling, Young, O'Leary, Brady, Ross, Macdonald, Stapleton, Rix.

Sep 3 Nottingham Forest 3–0
(Stapleton 2, Brady [pen]) Att: 40,810
Jennings, Rice, Nelson, Powling, O'Leary, Young, Brady, Ross, Macdonald, Stapleton, Rix.

Sep 17 Leicester City 2–1
(Stapleton, Macdonald) Att: 27,371
Jennings, Rice, Nelson, Price, O'Leary, Young, Brady, Ross, Macdonald, Stapleton, Rix.

Oct 1 West Ham United 3–0
(Stapleton, Rice, Brady [pen]) Att: 41,245
Jennings, Rice, Nelson, Price, O'Leary, Simpson, Brady, Ross, Macdonald, Stapleton, Rix.

Oct 4 Liverpool 0–0
Att: 47,110
Jennings, Rice, Nelson, Price, O'Leary, Simpson, Brady, Ross (Matthews), Macdonald, Stapleton, Rix.

Oct 15 Queens Park Rangers 1–0
(Macdonald) Att: 36,172
Jennings, Rice, Nelson, Price, O'Leary, Young, Brady, Hudson, Macdonald, Stapleton, Rix.

Oct 29 Birmingham City 1–1
(Rice) Att: 31,355
Jennings, Rice, Nelson, Price (Heeley), O'Leary, Simpson, Brady, Ross, Macdonald, Stapleton, Rix.

Nov 12 Coventry City 1–1
(Coop [og]) Att: 31,563
Jennings, Rice, Nelson, Price, O'Leary, Young, Brady, Sunderland, Macdonald, Stapleton, Rix.

Nov 26 **Derby County** **1–3**
(Nelson) Att: 31,989
Jennings, Rice, Nelson, Price, O'Leary, Young, Brady, Sunderland, Macdonald, Stapleton, Rix.

Dec 10 **Leeds United** **1–1**
(Young) Att: 40,162
Jennings, Rice, Nelson, Price, O'Leary, Young, Brady, Sunderland, Macdonald, Stapleton, Rix.

Dec 26 **Chelsea** **3–0**
(Price, Rix, O'Leary) Att: 46,074
Jennings, Rice, Nelson, Price, O'Leary, Young, Brady, Sunderland, Macdonald, Stapleton (Simpson), Rix.

Jan 2 **Ipswich Town** **1–0**
(Price) Att: 43,705
Jennings, Rice, Nelson, Price, O'Leary, Young, Brady, Sunderland, Macdonald, Heeley (Simpson), Rix.

Jan 14 **Wolverhampton Wanderers** **3–1**
(Brady, Macdonald, Stapleton) Att: 34,784
Jennings, Rice, Nelson, Price, O'Leary, Young, Brady, Sunderland, Macdonald, Stapleton, Rix.

Feb 4 **Aston Villa** **0–1**
Att: 30,127
Jennings, Rice, Nelson, Price, O'Leary, Young, Brady, Sunderland, Macdonald, Hudson, Rix.

Feb 28 **Norwich City** **0–0**
Att: 23,506
Jennings, Rice, Nelson, Price, O'Leary, Young, Brady, Sunderland, Macdonald (Heeley), Stapleton, Hudson.

Mar 4 **Manchester City** **3–0**
(Sunderland, Young, Price) Att: 34,003
Jennings, Rice, Nelson, Price (Walford), O'Leary, Young, Brady, Sunderland, Hudson, Stapleton, Heeley.

Mar 18 **Bristol City** **4–1**
(Stapleton 2, Sunderland, Price) Att: 28,463
Jennings, Rice, Nelson, Price, O'Leary, Young, Brady, Sunderland (Rix), Macdonald, Stapleton, Hudson.

Mar 25 **West Bromwich Albion** **4–0**
(Macdonald 3, Young) Att: 36,763
Jennings, Rice, Nelson, Price, O'Leary, Young, Brady, Sunderland (Rix), Macdonald, Stapleton, Hudson.

Apr 1 **Manchester United** **3–1**
(Macdonald 2, Brady) Att: 40,739
Jennings, Rice, Nelson, Price, O'Leary, Young, Brady, Rix, Macdonald, Stapleton, Hudson.

Apr 15 **Newcastle United** **2–1**
(Brady, Price) Att: 33,353
Jennings, Rice, Nelson, Price, O'Leary, Walford, Brady, Rix, Macdonald, Stapleton, Hudson.

Apr 29 **Middlesbrough** **1–0**
(Stapleton) Att: 32,138
Jennings, Devine, Nelson, Price, O'Leary, Young, Sunderland, Rix, Macdonald, Stapleton, Hudson.

FA CUP
Finalists

Jan 28 **Wolverhampton Wanderers** **2–1**
(Sunderland, Macdonald) Att: 49,373
Jennings, Rice, Nelson, Price, O'Leary, Young, Brady, Sunderland, Macdonald, Hudson, Rix.

Feb 18 **Walsall** **4–1**
(Stapleton 2, Macdonald, Sunderland)
Att: 43,789
Jennings, Rice, Nelson, Price, O'Leary, Young, Brady, Sunderland, Macdonald, Stapleton, Rix.

FOOTBALL LEAGUE CUP

Aug 30 **Manchester United** **3–2**
(Macdonald 2, Brady) Att: 36,171
Jennings, Rice, Nelson, Powling, O'Leary, Young, Brady, Ross, Macdonald, Stapleton, Rix.

Oct 25 **Southampton** **2–0**
(Brady [pen], Stapleton) Att: 40,749
Jennings, Rice, Nelson, Price, Young, Simpson, Brady, Hudson, Macdonald, Stapleton, Rix.

Nov 29 **Hull City** **5–1**
(Matthews 2, Macdonald, Stapleton, Brady)
Att: 25,922
Jennings, Rice, Nelson, Price, O'Leary (Simpson), Young, Brady, Matthews, Macdonald, Stapleton, Rix.

Jan 24 **Manchester City** **1–0**
(Brady [pen]) Att: 57,960
Jennings, Rice, Nelson, Price, O'Leary, Young, Brady, Matthews (Hudson), Macdonald, Stapleton, Rix.

Feb 14 **Liverpool** **0–0**
Att: 49,561
Jennings, Rice, Nelson, Price, O'Leary, Young, Brady, Hudson, Macdonald, Stapleton, Rix.

1978/79
LEAGUE DIVISION ONE
Final position – 7th

Aug 19 **Leeds United** **2–2**
(Brady 2 [1 pen]) Att: 42,057
Jennings, Devine, Nelson, Price (Kosmina), O'Leary, Young, Brady, Sunderland, Macdonald, Stapleton, Harvey.

Sep 2 Queens Park Rangers **5–1**
(Rix 2, Brady, Stapleton 2) Att: 33,883
Jennings, Rice, Nelson, Price, O'Leary, Young, Brady, Sunderland, Walford, Stapleton, Rix.

Sep 16 **Bolton Wanderers** **1–0**
(Stapleton) Att: 31,120
Jennings, Rice, Nelson, Price, Walford, Young, Brady, Sunderland, Stapleton, Heeley, Rix.

Sep 23 **Manchester United** **1–1**
(Price) Att: 45,393
Jennings, Rice, Nelson, Price, O'Leary, Young, Brady, Sunderland, Stapleton, Walford (Heeley), Rix.

Oct 7 **Aston Villa** **1–1**
(Sunderland) Att: 34,537
Jennings, Rice, Nelson, Price, O'Leary, Young, Brady, Sunderland, Stapleton, Walford, Rix.

Oct 21 **Southampton** **1–0**
(Brady) Att: 33,074
Jennings, Rice, Nelson, Stead, Gatting, Young, Brady, Heeley, Stapleton, Walford, Rix.

Nov 4 **Ipswich Town** **4–1**
(Stapleton 3, Nelson) Att: 35,269
Jennings, Rice, Nelson, Price, O'Leary, Young, Brady, Sunderland, Stapleton, Gatting, Rix.

Nov 18 **Everton** **2–2**
(Brady 2 [1pen]) Att: 39,801
Jennings, Rice, Nelson, Price, O'Leary, Young, Brady, Sunderland, Stapleton, Gatting, Rix.

Dec 2 **Liverpool** **1–0**
(Price) Att: 51,902
Jennings, Rice, Nelson, Price, O'Leary, Young, Brady, Sunderland, Stapleton, Gatting, Rix.

Dec 16 **Derby County** **2–0**
(Price, Stapleton) Att: 26,943
Jennings, Rice, Walford, Price, O'Leary, Young, Brady, Sunderland, Stapleton, Gatting, Rix.

Dec 26 **West Bromwich Albion** **1–2**
(Brady [pen]) Att: 40,055
Jennings, Rice, Walford, Price, O'Leary, Young, Brady, Sunderland, Stapleton, Gatting, Rix.

Dec 30 **Birmingham City** **3–1**
(Stapleton, Rice, Sunderland) Att: 27,877
Jennings, Rice, Walford, Price, O'Leary, Young, Brady, Sunderland, Stapleton, Gatting, Rix.

Jan 13 **Nottingham Forest** **2–1**
(Price, Stapleton) Att: 52,158
Jennings, Walford, Nelson, Talbot, O'Leary, Young, Brady, Sunderland, Stapleton, Price, Rix.

Feb 10 **Middlesbrough** **0–0**
Att: 28,371
Jennings, Rice, Nelson, Talbot, O'Leary, Young, Brady, Sunderland, Stapleton, Price, Rix.

Feb 24 **Wolverhampton Wanderers** **0–1**
Att: 32,215
Jennings, Rice, Gatting, Talbot, O'Leary, Walford, Brady, Sunderland, Stapleton, Price, Rix.

Mar 10 **Bristol City** **2–0**
(Rix, Stapleton) Att: 24,288
Jennings, Rice, Nelson, Talbot, O'Leary, Walford, Brady, Heeley (McDermott), Stapleton, Price, Rix.

Mar 24 **Manchester City** **1–1**
(Sunderland) Att: 35,014
Jennings, Rice, Nelson, Talbot, O'Leary, Young (McDermott), Heeley, Sunderland, Stapleton, Price, Rix.

Apr 3 **Coventry City** **1–1**
(Nelson) Att: 30,091
Jennings, Rice, Nelson, Talbot, O'Leary, Young, Gatting, Sunderland, Stapleton, Heeley (Walford), Rix.

Apr 10 **Tottenham Hotspur** **1–0**
(Stapleton) Att: 53,896
Jennings, Rice, Walford, Talbot, O'Leary, Young, Brady, Sunderland, Stapleton, Price, Rix.

Apr 16 **Chelsea** **5–2**
(Stapleton 2, O'Leary, Sunderland, Price)
Att: 37,232
Jennings, Rice, Nelson, Talbot, O'Leary, Walford, Brady, Sunderland, Stapleton, Price, Rix.

Apr 28 **Norwich City** **1–1**
(Walford) Att: 28,885
Jennings, Devine, Nelson, Talbot, Gatting, Walford, Brady, Sunderland, Stapleton, Price, Rix.

FA CUP
Winners

Jan 9 **Sheffield Wednesday** **1–1***
(Brady) Att: 37,987
Jennings, Rice, Nelson, Price, O'Leary, Young, Brady, Sunderland, Stapleton, Gatting, Rix.

*After extra time

Jan 27 **Notts County** **2–0**
(Young, Talbot) Att: 39,195
Jennings, Rice, Nelson, Talbot, O'Leary, Young, Brady, Sunderland, Stapleton, Price, Rix.

Mar 21 **Southampton** **2–0**
(Sunderland 2) Att: 44,820
Jennings, Rice, Nelson, Talbot, O'Leary, Young, Brady (Walford), Sunderland, Stapleton, Price, Rix.

NOTE:There were no Football League Cup matches at Highbury this season

UEFA CUP

Sep 13 **Lokomotiv Leipzig** **3–0**
(Stapleton 2, Sunderland) Att: 34,183
Jennings, Rice, Nelson, Price, Walford, Young, Brady (Gatting), Sunderland, Stapleton, Harvey (Heeley), Rix.

Nov 1 **Hajduk Split** **1–0**
(Young) Att: 41,612
Jennings, Rice, Nelson, Price, O'Leary, Young, Brady, Gatting, Stapleton, Heeley (Kosmina/Vaessen), Rix.

Dec 6 **Red Star Belgrade** **1–1**
(Sunderland) Att: 41,452
Jennings, Rice, Nelson, Price, O'Leary, Young, Heeley (Kosmina), Sunderland, Stapleton, Gatting, Rix (Macdonald).

1979/80
LEAGUE DIVISION ONE
Final position – 4th

Aug 21 **Ipswich Town** **0–2**
Att: 33,255
Jennings, Rice, Nelson, Talbot, O'Leary, Young, Brady, Sunderland, Stapleton, Price (Hollins), Rix.

Aug 25 **Manchester United** **0–0**
Att: 44,380
Jennings, Rice, Nelson, Talbot, O'Leary, Young, Gatting (Walford), Sunderland, Stapleton, Hollins, Rix.

Sep 15 **Middlesbrough** **2–0**
(Sunderland, Stapleton) Att: 30,341
Jennings, Rice, Nelson, Talbot, O'Leary, Young, Brady, Sunderland, Stapleton, Hollins, Rix.

Sep 29 **Wolverhampton Wanderers** **2–3**
(Stapleton, Hollins) Att: 41,844
Jennings, Rice, Nelson, Talbot (Price), Walford, Young, Brady, Sunderland, Stapleton, Hollins, Rix.

Oct 6 **Manchester City** **0–0**
Att: 34,688
Jennings, Rice, Nelson, Talbot, O'Leary, Young, Brady, Sunderland, Stapleton, Hollins, Rix.

Oct 20 **Stoke City** **0–0**
Att: 31,591
Jennings, Rice, Nelson, Talbot, O'Leary, Young, Brady, Sunderland, Stapleton, Hollins, Rix.

Nov 3 **Brighton & Hove Albion** **3–0**
(Rix, Brady [pen], Sunderland) Att: 34,400
Jennings, Devine, Nelson, Talbot, O'Leary, Young, Brady, Sunderland (Gatting), Stapleton, Hollins, Rix.

Nov 17 **Everton** **2–0**
(Stapleton 2) Att: 33,450
Jennings, Devine, Nelson, Talbot, O'Leary, Young, Brady (Gatting), Vaessen, Stapleton, Price, Rix.

Nov 24 **Liverpool** **0–0**
Att: 55,546
Jennings, Devine, Nelson, Talbot, O'Leary, Young, Gatting, Sunderland, Stapleton, Price, Rix.

Dec 8 **Coventry City** **3–1**
(Stapleton, Sunderland, O'Leary) Att: 27,563
Jennings, Devine, Nelson (Gatting), Talbot, O'Leary, Walford, Brady, Sunderland, Stapleton, Hollins, Rix.

Dec 21 **Norwich City** **1–1**
(Stapleton) Att: 18,869
Jennings, Devine, Nelson (McDermott), Talbot, O'Leary, Walford, Brady, Sunderland, Stapleton, Hollins, Rix.

Dec 26 **Tottenham Hotspur** **1–0**
(Sunderland) Att: 44,560
Jennings, Devine, Rice, Talbot, O'Leary, Young, Brady, Sunderland, Stapleton, Hollins, Rix.

Jan 12 **Leeds United** **0–1**
Att: 35,945
Jennings, Rice, Nelson, Talbot, Walford, Young, Brady, Sunderland, Stapleton, Hollins, Rix.

Jan 19 **Derby County** **2–0**
(Brady [pen], Young) Att: 22,091
Jennings, Rice, Nelson, Talbot, Walford, Young, Brady, Sunderland, Stapleton, Price, Rix.

Feb 9 **Aston Villa** **3–1**
(Sunderland 2, Rix) Att: 33,816
Jennings, Rice, Nelson, Talbot, O'Leary, Young, Brady, Sunderland, Stapleton, Price, Rix.

Feb 23 **Bolton Wanderers** **2–0**
(Young, Stapleton) Att: 24, 383
Jennings, Rice (Vaessen), Nelson, Talbot, O'Leary, Young, Brady, Sunderland, Stapleton, Price, Rix.

Mar 11 **Bristol City** **0–0**
Att: 21,559
Jennings, Devine, Nelson, Talbot, O'Leary, Young, Brady, Vaessen, Stapleton, Price, Rix.

Mar 22 **Crystal Palace** **1–1**
(Brady) Att: 37,606
Jennings, Devine, Nelson, Talbot, O'Leary, Young, Brady, Sunderland, Stapleton, Price, Rix.

Apr 5 **Southampton** **1–1**
(Sunderland) Att: 34,593
Jennings, Devine, Walford, Talbot, O'Leary, Young, Brady, Sunderland, Stapleton, Price (Vaessen), Rix.

Apr 26 **West Bromwich Albion** **1–1**
(Stapleton) Att: 30,027
Barron, Rice, Devine, Talbot, Walford, Young (Gatting), Brady, Sunderland, Stapleton, Hollins, Vaessen.

May 5 **Nottingham Forest** **0–0**
Att: 34,632
Jennings, Devine, Nelson, Talbot, O'Leary, Young, Brady, Vaessen, Stapleton (Hollins), Price, Rix.

FA CUP
Finalists

Jan 8 **Cardiff City** **2–1**
(Sunderland 2) Att: 36,155
Jennings, Rice, Nelson, Talbot, Walford, Young, Gatting, Sunderland, Stapleton, Hollins, Rix.

Jan 26 **Brighton & Hove Albion** **2–0**
(Nelson, Talbot) Att: 43,202
Jennings, Rice, Nelson, Talbot, O'Leary, Young, Brady, Sunderland, Stapleton, Price, Rix.

Feb 19 **Bolton Wanderers** **3–0**
(Sunderland 2, Stapleton) Att: 40,614
Jennings, Rice, Nelson, Talbot, O'Leary, Young, Brady, Sunderland, Stapleton, Price, Rix.

FOOTBALL LEAGUE CUP

Sep 4 **Leeds United** **7–0**
(Sunderland 3, Brady 2 [2 pens], Stapleton, Nelson) Att: 35,133
Jennings, Rice, Nelson, Talbot, O'Leary, Young, Brady, Sunderland, Stapleton, Hollins, Rix.

Sep 25 **Southampton** **2–1**
(Stapleton, Brady) Att: 37,348
Jennings, Rice, Nelson, Talbot, Walford, Young, Brady, Sunderland, Stapleton, Hollins, Rix.

Nov 13 **Brighton & Hove Albion** **4–0**
(Stapleton 2, Vaessen 2) Att: 30,351
Jennings, Devine, Nelson, Talbot, O'Leary, Young, Brady, Vaessen, Stapleton, Price, Rix.

Dec 4 **Swindon Town** **1–1**
(Sunderland [pen]) Att: 38,024
Jennings, Devine, Nelson, Talbot, O'Leary, Walford, Gatting, Sunderland, Stapleton, Price (Hollins), Rix.

EUROPEAN CUP WINNERS' CUP
Finalists

Sep 19 **Fenerbahce** **2–0**
(Sunderland, Young) Att: 34,973
Jennings, Rice, Nelson, Talbot, O'Leary, Young, Brady, Sunderland, Stapleton, Hollins, Rix.

Oct 24 **Magdeburg** **2–1**
(Young, Sunderland) Att: 34,575
Jennings, Rice, Nelson, Talbot, O'Leary, Young, Brady, Sunderland, Stapleton, Hollins, Rix.

Mar 5 **IFK Gothenburg** **5–1**
(Sunderland 2, Price, Brady, Young) Att: 36,323
Jennings, Devine, Nelson, Talbot, O'Leary, Young, Brady (Hollins), Sunderland (McDermott), Stapleton, Price, Rix.

Apr 9 **Juventus** **1–1**
(Bettega [og]) Att: 51,998
Jennings, Devine (Vaessen), Walford, Talbot, O'Leary (Rice), Young, Brady, Sunderland, Stapleton, Price, Rix.

1980/81

LEAGUE DIVISION ONE

Final position – 3rd

Aug 19 Southampton 1–1
(Stapleton) Att: 43,050
Jennings, Devine, Sansom, Talbot (McDermott), O'Leary, Young, Hollins,Vaessen, Stapleton, Price, Rix.

Aug 30 Tottenham Hotspur 2–0
(Price, Stapleton) Att: 54,045
Jennings, Devine, Sansom, Talbot, O'Leary, Young, Hollins, Sunderland, Stapleton, Price, Rix.

Sep 13 Stoke City 2–0
(Hollins, Sansom) Att: 27,183
Jennings, Devine, Sansom, Talbot, O'Leary, Young, Hollins, Sunderland, Stapleton, Price, Rix.

Sep 27 Nottingham Forest 1–0
(Rix) Att: 37,582
Wood, Devine, Sansom, Talbot, O'Leary, Young, Hollins, Sunderland, Stapleton, Gatting, Rix.

Oct 4 Leicester City 1–0
(Stapleton) Att: 28,490
Wood, Devine, Sansom, Talbot, Walford, Young, Hollins, Sunderland, Stapleton, Gatting, Rix.

Oct 18 Sunderland 2–2
(Gatting, Young) Att: 32,135
Wood, Devine, Sansom, Talbot (McDermott), Walford, Young, Hollins, Sunderland, Stapleton, Gatting, Rix.

Oct 21 Norwich City 3–1
(Talbot, McDermott, Sansom) Att: 21,839
Wood, Devine, Sansom, Talbot, Walford, Young, Hollins (McDermott), Sunderland, Stapleton, Gatting, Rix.

Nov 1 Brighton & Hove Albion 2–0
(Rix, McDermott) Att: 28,569
Wood, Devine, Sansom, Talbot, Walford, Young, Hollins, Sunderland, Stapleton, McDermott, Rix.

Nov 15 West Bromwich Albion 2–2
(Sunderland, Batson [og]) Att: 25,858
Jennings, Devine, Sansom, Talbot, O'Leary, Young, Hollins, Sunderland, Stapleton, Gatting, Rix.

Nov 22 Everton 2–1
(McDermott, Stapleton) Att: 30,911
Jennings, Devine, Sansom (Gatting), Talbot, O'Leary, Walford, Hollins, Sunderland, Stapleton, McDermott, Rix.

Dec 6 Wolverhampton Wanderers 1–1
(Stapleton) Att: 26,050
Jennings, Devine, Sansom, Talbot, Walford, Young, Hollins (Vaessen), McDermott, Stapleton, Gatting, Rix.

Dec 20 Manchester United 2–1
(Rix, Vaessen) Att: 33,730
Jennings, Devine, Sansom, Talbot, Walford, Young, Vaessen, McDermott, Stapleton, Gatting, Rix.

Dec 27 Ipswich Town 1–1
(Sunderland) Att: 42,818
Jennings, Devine, Sansom, Talbot, Walford, Young, Hollins, Sunderland, Stapleton, Gatting, Rix.

Jan 31 Coventry City 2–2
(Talbot, Stapleton) Att: 24,876
Jennings, Hollins, Sansom, Talbot, Walford, Young, McDermott, Sunderland, Stapleton, Gatting, Rix.

Feb 24 Manchester City 2–0
(Talbot, Sunderland) Att: 24,790
Jennings, Devine, Sansom, Talbot, O'Leary, Young, Hollins, Sunderland, Stapleton, Gatting, Rix.

Feb 28 Middlesbrough 2–2
(Stapleton, Hollins [pen]) Att: 24,504
Jennings, Devine, Sansom, Talbot, O'Leary, Walford, Hollins, Sunderland (McDermott), Stapleton, Gatting, Rix.

Mar 28 Liverpool 1–0
(Sunderland) Att: 47,058
Jennings, Devine, Sansom, Talbot, O'Leary, Young, Hollins (Davis), Sunderland, Stapleton, Nicholas (P), Rix.

Mar 31 Birmingham City 2–1
(Stapleton, O'Leary) Att: 17,431
Jennings, Devine (McDermott), Sansom, Talbot, O'Leary, Young, Davis, Sunderland, Stapleton, Nicholas (P), Rix.

Apr 11 Leeds United 0–0
Att: 29,339
Jennings, Devine, Sansom, Talbot, O'Leary, Young, Hollins (McDermott), Sunderland, Stapleton, Nicholas (P), Davis.

Apr 20 Crystal Palace 3–2
(Talbot, Davis, Young) Att: 24,346
Jennings, Devine, Sansom, Talbot, O'Leary, Young, Hollins, Sunderland (McDermott), Stapleton, Nicholas (P), Davis.

May 2 Aston Villa 2–0
(Young, McDermott) Att: 57,472
Jennings, Hollins, Sansom, Talbot (Nelson), O'Leary, Young, McDermott, Sunderland, Stapleton, Nicholas (P), Davis.

NOTE: There were no FA Cup matches at Highbury this season.

FOOTBALL LEAGUE CUP

Sep 2 Swansea City 3–1
(Hollins [pen], Sunderland, Walford) Att: 26,399
Jennings, Devine, Sansom, Talbot, Walford, Young, Hollins, Sunderland, Stapleton, Price, Rix.

1981/82

LEAGUE DIVISION ONE

Final position – 5th

Aug 29 Stoke City 0–1
Att: 28,012
Jennings, Devine (Vaessen), Sansom, Talbot, O'Leary, Young, Davis, Sunderland, McDermott, Nicholas (P), Rix.

Sep 12 Sunderland 1–1
(Sunderland) Att: 26,527
Jennings, Hollins, Sansom, Talbot, O'Leary, Young, Davis, Sunderland, McDermott, Nicholas (P), Rix.

Sep 22 Birmingham City 1–0
(Talbot) Att: 19,588
Jennings, Devine, Sansom, Talbot, O'Leary, Young, Davis, Sunderland, McDermott, Hollins, Rix.

Sep 26 Manchester United 0–0
Att: 39,797
Jennings, Devine, Sansom, Talbot, O'Leary, Young, Hollins, Sunderland, Hawley, Nicholas (P), Davis.

Oct 17 Manchester City 1–0
(Meade) Att: 25,466
Jennings, Hollins, Sansom, Talbot, O'Leary, Whyte, McDermott, Sunderland, Meade, Nicholas (P), Rix.

Oct 31 Coventry City 1–0
(Thomas [og]) Att: 23,102
Jennings, Hollins, Sansom, Talbot, O'Leary, Whyte, McDermott, Vaessen, Hawley, Nicholas (P), Rix.

Nov 28 Everton 1–0
(McDermott) Att: 25,860
Jennings, Devine (McDermott), Sansom, Talbot, O'Leary, Whyte, Hollins, Sunderland, Davis, Nicholas (P), Rix.

Jan 26 Brighton & Hove Albion 0–0
Att: 17,922
Wood, Robson, Sansom, Talbot, Hollins, Whyte, McDermott, Sunderland, Davis (Meade), Nicholas (P), Rix.

Jan 30 Leeds United 1–0
(Vaessen) Att: 22,408
Wood, Hollins, Sansom, Talbot, O'Leary, Whyte, Vaessen, Sunderland, Davis, Nicholas (P), Rix.

Feb 2 Wolverhampton Wanderers 2–1
(Rix, Vaessen) Att: 15,163
Wood, Hollins, Sansom, Talbot, O'Leary, Whyte, Vaessen, Sunderland (Hawley), Davis, Nicholas (P), Rix.

Feb 13 Notts County 1–0
(Meade) Att: 18,229
Wood, Hollins, Sansom, Talbot, O'Leary, Whyte, Vaessen, Sunderland, Davis, Nicholas (P), (Meade), Rix.

Feb 16 Middlesbrough 1–0
(Rix) Att: 13,738
Wood, Hollins, Sansom, Talbot, O'Leary, Whyte, Vaessen, Sunderland, Davis, Nicholas (P) (Meade), Rix.

Feb 27 Swansea City 0–2
Att: 29,724
Wood, Hollins, Sansom, Talbot, O'Leary, Whyte, Vaessen (Meade), Sunderland, Davis, Nicholas (P), Rix.

Mar 13 Ipswich Town 1–0
(Robson) Att: 25,977
Wood, Hollins, Sansom, Talbot, O'Leary, Whyte, Gorman, Sunderland Davis, Robson, Rix.

Mar 16 West Bromwich Albion 2–2
(Meade, Sunderland) Att: 15,799
Wood, Hollins, Sansom, Talbot, O'Leary, Whyte, Gorman (Meade), Sunderland, Davis, Robson, Rix.

Mar 27 Aston Villa 4–3
(Sunderland, Rix 2, Meade) Att: 24,756
Wood, Hollins, Sansom, Talbot, O'Leary, Whyte, Meade, Sunderland, Davis, Robson, Rix.

Apr 12 Tottenham Hotspur 1–3
(Hawley) Att: 48,897
Wood, Hollins, Sansom, Talbot, O'Leary, Whyte, Meade, Hawley, Nicholas (P), Robson (McDermott), Rix.

Apr 17 Nottingham Forest 2–0
(Talbot, Rix) Att: 21,986
Wood, Hollins, Sansom, Talbot, O'Leary, Whyte, Meade, Hawley, Davis, Robson, Rix.

May 1 West Ham United 2–0
(Rix, Sunderland) Att: 34,977
Wood, Hollins, Sansom, Talbot, O'Leary, Whyte, Hawley, Sunderland, Davis, Robson, Rix.

May 11 Liverpool 1–1
(Sunderland) Att: 30,932
Wood, Hollins, Sansom, Talbot, O'Leary, Whyte, Nicholas (P), Sunderland, Hawley (Meade), Robson, Rix.

May 15 Southampton 4–1
(Davis 2, Robson, Hawley) Att: 28,534
Wood, Hollins, Sansom, Talbot, O'Leary, Whyte, Davis, Sunderland, Hawley, Robson, Rix.

NOTE: There were no FA Cup matches at Highbury this season

FOOTBALL LEAGUE CUP

Oct 27 Sheffield United 2–0*
(Young, Sunderland) Att: 22,301
Jennings, Hollins, Sansom, Talbot, O'Leary, Young, McDermott, Sunderland, Meade (Vaessen), Nicholas (P), Rix.

*After extra time

Nov 10 Norwich City 1–0
(Nicholas,P) Att: 19,899
Jennings, Hollins, Sansom, Talbot, O'Leary, Whyte, McDermott, Sunderland (Meade), Davis, Nicholas (P), Rix.

Dec 1 Liverpool 0–0
Att: 37,917
Jennings, Hollins, Sansom, Talbot, O'Leary, Whyte, McDermott (Hankin), Sunderland, Davis, Nicholas (P), Rix.

UEFA CUP

Sep 30 Panathinaikos 1–0
(Talbot) Att: 23,514
Jennings, Devine, Sansom, Talbot, O'Leary (Whyte), Young, Hollins, Sunderland, McDermott, Nicholas (P), Rix.

Nov 3 KFC Winterslag 2–1
(Hollins, Rix) Att: 22,930
Jennings, Hollins, Sansom, Talbot, O'Leary, Whyte, McDermott, Vaessen (Davis), Meade, Nicholas (P), Rix.

1982/83

LEAGUE DIVISION ONE

Final position – 10th

Aug 31 Norwich City 1–1
(Woodcock) Att: 22,652
Wood, Hollins, Sansom (Devine), Talbot, Davis, Whyte, Robson, Sunderland, Chapman, Woodcock, Rix.

Sep 4 Liverpool 0–2
Att: 36,429
Wood, Hollins, Devine, Talbot, O'Leary, Whyte, Robson, Davis, Chapman, Woodcock, Rix.

Sep 18 Notts County 2–0
(Rix, Hollins [pen]) Att: 20,556
Wood, Hollins, Sansom, Talbot, O'Leary, Whyte, Davis, Robson, Chapman, Woodcock, Rix.

Oct 2 West Ham United 2–3
(Talbot, Davis) Att: 30,484
Wood, Hollins, Sansom, Talbot, O'Leary, Whyte, Davis, Sunderland, Chapman, Woodcock, Rix.

Oct 16 West Bromwich Albion 2–0
(Sunderland, Woodcock) Att: 21,666
Wood, Devine, Sansom, Talbot, O'Leary, Whyte, Davis, Sunderland, Robson, Woodcock, Rix.

Oct 30 Birmingham City 0–0
Att: 20,699
Wood, O'Shea, Sansom, Talbot, O'Leary, Whyte, Davis, Sunderland, Robson, Woodcock (Chapman), Rix.

Nov 13 Everton 1–1
(McDermott) Att: 23,067
Jennings, O'Shea, Sansom, Talbot, O'Leary (McDermott), Whyte, Davis, Chapman, Robson, Woodcock, Rix.

Nov 27 Watford 2–4
(Robson, Talbot) Att: 34,287
Wood, O'Shea, Sansom, Talbot, O'Leary, Whyte, Davis, Sunderland, Robson, Woodcock, Rix.

Dec 7 Aston Villa 2–1
(Whyte, Woodcock) Att: 17,384
Wood, Hollins, Sansom, Talbot, O'Leary, Whyte, Davis, Sunderland, Robson, Woodcock, Rix.

Dec 27 Tottenham Hotspur 2–0
(Sunderland, Woodcock) Att: 51,497
Jennings, Hollins, Sansom, Talbot, O'Leary, Robson, Davis, Sunderland, Nicholas (P), Woodcock, Rix.

Jan 1 Swansea City 2–1
(Sunderland, Woodcock) Att: 25,237
Jennings, Hollins, Sansom, Talbot, O'Leary, Robson, Davis, Sunderland (Chapman), Petrovic, Woodcock, Rix.

Jan 15 Stoke City 3–0
(Rix, Petrovic, Hollins [pen]) Att: 19,428
Jennings, Hollins, Sansom, Whyte, O'Leary (Talbot), Nicholas (P), Davis, Sunderland, Petrovic, Woodcock, Rix.

Feb 5 Brighton & Hove Albion 3–1
(Meade 2, Rix) Att: 17,972
Jennings, Hollins, Sansom, Robson, O'Leary, Nicholas (P), Talbot, Meade, Petrovic, Davis, Rix.

Mar 5 Nottingham Forest 0–0
Att: 21,698
Jennings, Hollins, Sansom, Robson, Whyte, Nicholas (P), Talbot, Davis, Sunderland (Meade), Woodcock, Rix.

Mar 19 Luton Town 4–1
(Woodcock 3, Davis) Att: 23,987
Jennings, O'Leary (Meade), Sansom, Robson, Whyte, Nicholas (P), Talbot, Davis, Sunderland, Woodcock, Rix.

Mar 22 Ipswich Town 2–2
(Rix, Whyte) Att: 17,639
Wood, Hollins, Sansom, Devine, Whyte, Nicholas (P), Talbot, Davis, Sunderland, Woodcock, Rix.

Apr 2 Southampton 0–0
Att: 24,911
Wood, Kay, Sansom, Whyte, O'Leary, Nicholas (P), Talbot, Davis, Sunderland, Woodcock, Rix.

Apr 9 Coventry City 2–1
(Rix, Woodcock) Att: 19,152
Wood, Robson, Sansom, Whyte, Kay, Nicholas,P (Chapman), Talbot, Davis, Petrovic, Woodcock, Rix.

Apr 23 Manchester City 3–0
(Talbot 3) Att: 16,810
Jennings, Kay, Sansom, Whyte, O'Leary, Nicholas (P), Talbot, Davis, McDermott, Woodcock (Hawley), Hill.

May 2 Manchester United 3–0
(O'Leary, Talbot 2) Att: 23,602
Jennings, Devine, Sansom, Whyte, O'Leary, Nicholas (P), Talbot, Davis, McDermott, Hawley (Petrovic), Hill.

May 7 Sunderland 0–1
Att: 18,053
Jennings, Devine (Hawley), Sansom, Whyte, O'Leary, Nicholas (P), Talbot, Davis, Petrovic, McDermott, Hill.

FA CUP

Jan 8 Bolton Wanderers 2–1
(Davis, Rix) Att: 22,576
Jennings, Hollins, Sansom, Talbot, O'Leary, Robson, Davis, Sunderland, Nicholas (P), Woodcock, Rix.

Jan 29 Leeds United 1–1
(Sunderland) Att: 33,930
Jennings, Hollins, Sansom, Robson, O'Leary, Nicholas (P), Talbot, Sunderland, Petrovic, Woodcock, Rix.

Feb 9 Leeds United 2–1
(Woodcock, Rix) Att: 26,802
Jennings, Hollins, Sansom, Robson, O'Leary, Nicholas (P), Talbot, Meade, Petrovic, Woodcock, Rix.

Feb 28 Middlesbrough 3–2
(Talbot, Woodcock, Davis) Att: 28,689
Jennings, Hollins, Sansom, Robson, Whyte, Nicholas (P), Talbot, Davis, Sunderland, Woodcock, Rix.

Mar 12 Aston Villa 2–0
(Woodcock, Petrovic) Att: 41,774
Jennings, Hollins, Sansom, Robson, Whyte, Nicholas (P), Petrovic, Davis, Sunderland, Woodcock, Rix.

FOOTBALL LEAGUE (MILK) CUP

Oct 5 **Cardiff City** **2–1**
(Hollins, Davis) Att: 15,115
Wood, Hollins, Sansom, Talbot, O'Leary, Whyte, Davis, Sunderland, Robson, Woodcock, Rix.

Nov 23 **Everton** **3–0**
(Sunderland 3) Att: 19,547
Wood, O'Shea, Sansom, Talbot, O'Leary, Whyte, Davis, Sunderland, Robson, Woodcock (Chapman), Rix.

Nov 30 **Huddersfield Town** **1–0**
(Sunderland [pen]) Att: 17,742
Wood, O'Shea, Sansom, Talbot, O'Leary, Whyte, Davis, Sunderland, Robson, Woodcock, Rix.

Jan 18 **Sheffield Wednesday** **1–0**
(Woodcock) Att: 30,937
Jennings, Hollins, Sansom, Nicholas (P), O'Leary, Robson, Davis, Sunderland, Petrovic, Woodcock, Rix.

Feb 15 **Manchester United** **2–4**
(Woodcock, Nicholas,P) Att: 43,136
Jennings, Hollins, Sansom, Robson, O'Leary (Davis), Nicholas (P), Talbot, Meade, Petrovic, Woodcock, Rix.

UEFA CUP

Sep 29 **Spartak Moscow** **2–5**
(Chapman, Dasaev [og]) Att: 28,445
Wood, Hollins (Sunderland), Sansom, Talbot, O'Leary, Whyte, Davis (McDermott), Robson, Chapman, Woodcock, Rix.

1983/84

LEAGUE DIVISION ONE

Final position – 6th

Aug 27 **Luton Town** **2–1**
(Woodcock, McDermott) Att: 39,348
Jennings, Robson, Sansom, Talbot, O'Leary, Hill, McDermott, Davis, Woodcock, Nicholas (C), Rix.

Sep 6 **Manchester United** **2–3**
(Woodcock, Talbot) Att: 42,704
Jennings, Robson, Sansom, Talbot, O'Leary, Hill, McDermott (Sunderland), Davis, Woodcock, Nicholas (C), Rix.

Sep 10 **Liverpool** **0–2**
Att: 41,896
Jennings, Robson, Sansom, Talbot, O'Leary, Hill, Sunderland, Davis, Woodcock, Nicholas (C), Rix.

Sep 24 **Norwich City** **3–0**
(Chapman, Sunderland 2) Att: 24,438
Jennings, Robson, Sansom, Whyte, O'Leary, Hill, Sunderland, Davis, Chapman, Nicholas (C), (McDermott), Rix.

Oct 15 **Coventry City** **0–1**
Att: 20,290
Jennings, Robson, Sansom, Whyte (McDermott), O'Leary, Hill, Sunderland, Davis, Chapman, Nicholas (C), Rix.

Oct 22 **Nottingham Forest** **4–1**
(Sunderland, Woodcock 2, Hill) Att: 22,870
Jennings, Robson, Sansom, Whyte, O'Leary, Hill, Sunderland, Davis, Woodcock, Nicholas,C (McDermott), Rix.

Nov 5 **Sunderland** **1–2**
(Woodcock) Att: 26,064
Jennings, Robson, Sansom, Whyte, Adams, Hill, Sunderland (McDermott), Talbot, Woodcock, Nicholas (C), Rix.

Nov 19 **Everton** **2–1**
(Sunderland, Robson) Att: 24,330
Jennings, Robson, Sansom, Whyte, O'Leary, Hill, Sunderland (Meade), Gorman, McDermott, Nicholas (C), Rix.

Dec 3 **West Bromwich Albion** **0–1**
Att: 22,271
Jennings, Robson, Sansom (Meade), Caton, Adams, Hill, Madden, Davis, Woodcock, Nicholas (C), Allinson.

Dec 17 **Watford** **3–1**
(Meade 3) Att: 25,104
Jennings, Hill, Sansom, Cork, Whyte, Caton, Meade, Davis, Woodcock, Nicholas (C), Allinson.

Dec 27 **Birmingham City** **1–1**
(Nicholas [pen]) Att: 25,642
Jennings, Hill, Sansom, Cork, Whyte, Caton (McDermott), Meade, Davis, Woodcock, Nicholas (C), Allinson.

Dec 31 **Southampton** **2–2**
(Cork, Nicholas [pen]) Att: 27,596
Jennings, Hill, Sansom, Cork, O'Leary, Caton, Meade, Davis, Woodcock, Nicholas (C), Allinson.

Jan 21 **Notts County** **1–1**
(Nicholas) Att: 20,110
Jennings, Kay, Sansom, Talbot, Adams (McDermott), Caton, Meade, Davis, Woodcock, Nicholas (C), Rix.

Feb 4 **Queens Park Rangers** **0–2**
Att: 31,014
Jennings, Kay, Sansom, Talbot, O'Leary, Caton, Meade (Cork), Davis, Woodcock, Nicholas (C), Rix.

Feb 18 **Aston Villa** **1–1**
(Rix) Att: 26,640
Jennings, Hill, Sansom, Talbot, O'Leary, Caton, Davis, Nicholas (C), Mariner, Woodcock, Rix.

Mar 10 **Ipswich Town** **4–1**
(Mariner 2, Talbot, Woodcock) Att: 24,000
Jennings, Hill, Sansom, Talbot, O'Leary, Caton, Davis, Nicholas (C), Mariner, Woodcock, Rix (Allinson).

Mar 24 **Wolverhampton Wanderers** **4–1**
(Robson, Woodcock, Nicholas [pen], Rix)
Att: 18,612
Jennings, Hill, Sansom, Talbot, O'Leary, Caton, Robson, Nicholas (C), Mariner, Woodcock, Rix.

Apr 7 **Stoke City** **3–1**
(Nicholas, Mariner, Woodcock) Att: 21,211
Lukic, Hill, Sparrow, Talbot, O'Leary, Caton, Robson, Nicholas,C (Meade), Mariner, Woodcock, Rix.

Apr 21 **Tottenham Hotspur** **3–2**
(Robson, Nicholas, Woodcock) Att: 48,831
Lukic, Hill, Sansom, Talbot, O'Leary, Caton, Robson, Nicholas (C), Mariner, Woodcock, Rix (Davis).

Apr 28 **Leicester City** **2–1**
(Woodcock, Davis) Att: 24,143
Jennings, Hill, Sansom, Talbot (Davis), O'Leary, Caton, Robson, Nicholas (C), Mariner, Woodcock, Rix.

May 7 **West Ham United** **3–3**
(Talbot, Woodcock, Mariner) Att: 33,347
Jennings, Hill, Sansom, Talbot, O'Leary, Caton, Robson, Nicholas (C), Mariner, Woodcock, Rix (Davis).

NOTE: There were no FA Cup matches at Highbury this season.

FOOTBALL LEAGUE (MILK) CUP

Oct 25 **Plymouth Argyle** **1–0**
(Sunderland) Att: 22,640
Jennings, Robson, Sansom, Whyte, O'Leary, Hill, Sunderland, Davis, Woodcock, Nicholas (C), Rix.

Nov29 **Walsall** **1–2**
(Robson) Att: 22,406
Jennings, Robson, Sansom, Whyte, O'Leary, Hill, Sunderland, Davis, Woodcock, Nicholas (C), Allinson.

1984/85

LEAGUE DIVISION ONE

Final position – 7th

Aug 25 **Chelsea** **1–1**
(Mariner) Att: 45,329
Jennings, Anderson, Sansom, Talbot, O'Leary, Caton, Robson, Davis, Mariner, Woodcock, Allinson.

Sep 4 **Newcastle United** **2–0**
(Talbot, Anderson) Att: 37,078
Jennings, Anderson, Sansom, Talbot, O'Leary, Caton, Robson, Davis, Mariner, Woodcock, Nicholas.

Sep 8 **Liverpool** **3–1**
(Talbot 2, Woodcock) Att: 50,006
Jennings, Anderson, Sansom, Talbot, O'Leary, Caton, Robson, Davis, Mariner, Woodcock, Nicholas.

Sep 22 **Stoke City** **4–0**
(Woodcock 2 [1 pen], Mariner, Sansom)
Att: 26,758
Jennings, Anderson, Sansom, Talbot, O'Leary, Caton, Robson, Rix, Mariner, Woodcock, Nicholas.

Oct 6 **Everton** **1–0**
(Nicholas [pen]) Att: 37,049
Jennings, Anderson, Sansom, Talbot, O'Leary, Caton, Robson, Rix, Mariner, Woodcock, Nicholas.

Oct 20 **Sunderland** **3–2**
(Caton, Allinson, Talbot) Att:36,944
Jennings, Anderson, Sansom, Talbot, O'Leary, Caton, Robson, Rix, Allinson, Woodcock (Davis), Nicholas.

Nov 10 **Aston Villa** **1–1**
(Mariner) Att: 33,193
Jennings, Anderson, Sansom, Talbot, O'Leary, Caton (Allinson), Robson, Davis, Mariner, Woodcock, Nicholas.

Nov 17 **Queens Park Rangers** **1–0**
(Woodcock) Att: 34,953
Jennings, Anderson, Sansom, Talbot, O'Leary, Adams, Robson, Davis, Allinson, Woodcock, Nicholas.

Dec 1 **Luton Town** **3–1**
(Allinson, Woodcock, Anderson) Att: 26,366
Lukic, Anderson, Sansom, Talbot, Adams, Caton, Robson, Davis, Mariner, Woodcock, Allinson.

Dec 15 **West Bromwich Albion** **4–0**
(Allinson 2, Talbot, Davis [pen]) Att: 23,728
Lukic, Anderson, Sansom, Talbot, Adams, Caton, Robson, Davis, Mariner, Woodcock, Allinson.

Dec 22 **Watford** **1–1**
(Allinson) Att: 31,302
Lukic, O'Leary, Hill, Talbot, Adams, Caton, Robson, Nicholas, Mariner, Woodcock, Allinson.

Jan 1 **Tottenham Hotspur** **1–2**
(Woodcock) Att: 48,714
Lukic, Anderson, Caton, Talbot, O'Leary, Adams, Robson, Allinson, Mariner, Woodcock, Nicholas (Williams).

Feb 2 **Coventry City** **2–1**
(Meade, Allinson) Att: 21,791
Lukic, Anderson, Sansom, Talbot, O'Leary, Caton (Nicholas), Robson, Williams, Mariner, Meade, Allinson.

Feb 23 **Manchester United** **0–1**
Att: 48,612
Lukic, Anderson, Sansom, Williams, O'Leary, Caton, Robson, Davis (Talbot), Mariner, Woodcock, Nicholas.

Mar 2 **West Ham United** **2–1**
(Mariner, Robson) Att: 25,818
Lukic, Anderson, Sansom, Williams, O'Leary, Caton, Robson, Davis, Mariner, Woodcock, Nicholas.

Mar 16 **Leicester City** **2–0**
(Williams, Meade) Att: 20,663
Lukic, Anderson, Sansom, Williams, Adams, Caton, Robson, Davis, Mariner, Meade, Nicholas (Talbot).

Mar 19 **Ipswich Town** **1–1**
(Meade) Att: 18,365
Lukic, Anderson, Sansom, Williams, Adams, Caton, Robson, Davis (Talbot), Mariner, Meade, Nicholas.

Apr 6 **Norwich City** **2–0**
(Nicholas, Robson) Att: 19,597
Lukic, Anderson, Sansom, Williams, O'Leary, Caton, Robson, Rix, Mariner (Allinson), Talbot, Nicholas.

Apr 13 **Nottingham Forest** **1–1**
(Allinson) Att: 24,152
Lukic, Anderson, Sansom, Williams, O'Leary, Caton, Robson, Rix, Allinson, Talbot, Nicholas.

Apr 27 **Sheffield Wednesday** **1–0**
(Mariner) Att: 23,803
Lukic, Anderson, Sansom, Williams, O'Leary, Caton, Robson (Allinson), Rix, Mariner, Talbot, Nicholas.

May 6 **Southampton** **1–0**
(Rix) Att: 21,214
Lukic, Anderson, Sansom, Talbot, Adams, Davis, Robson, Rix, Mariner, Allinson, Nicholas.

FA CUP

Jan 22 **Hereford United** **7–2**
(Mariner 2, Talbot 2, Nicholas, Anderson, Woodcock) Att: 26,023
Lukic, Anderson, Sansom, Talbot, O'Leary, Caton, Robson, Williams, Mariner, Woodcock, Nicholas.

FOOTBALL LEAGUE (MILK) CUP

Sep 25 **Bristol Rovers** **4–0**
(Woodcock, Anderson, Nicholas 2) Att: 23,871
Jennings, Anderson, Sansom, Talbot, O'Leary, Caton, Robson, Rix, Mariner, Woodcock, Nicholas.

1985/86

LEAGUE DIVISION ONE

Final position – 7th

Aug 20 **Southampton** **3–2**
(Caton, Robson, Woodcock) Att: 21,895
Lukic, Anderson, Sansom, Williams, O'Leary, Caton, Robson, Allinson, Nicholas, Woodcock, Rix.

Aug 24 **Manchester United** **1–2**
(Allinson [pen]) Att: 37,145
Lukic, Anderson, Sansom, Williams (Davis), O'Leary, Caton, Robson, Allinson, Nicholas, Woodcock, Rix.

Aug 31 **Leicester City** **1–0**
(Woodcock) Att: 18,207
Lukic, Anderson, Sansom, Davis, Mariner, Caton, Robson, Allinson, Nicholas, Woodcock, Rix.

Sep 14 **Sheffield Wednesday** **1–0**
(Allinson [pen]) Att: 23,108
Lukic, Anderson, Sansom, Davis, O'Leary, Caton, Robson, Allinson, Nicholas, Woodcock, Rix.

Sep 28 **Newcastle United** **0–0**
Att: 24,104
Lukic, Anderson, Sansom, Davis, O'Leary, Caton, Rocastle, Allinson (Whyte), Nicholas, Woodcock, Rix.

Oct 5 **Aston Villa** **3–2**
(Woodcock, Anderson, Whyte) Att: 18,881
Lukic, Anderson, Sansom, Davis, O'Leary, Caton, Whyte, Allinson, Nicholas, Woodcock, Rix.

Oct 19 **Ipswich Town** **1–0**
(Davis) Att: 19,523
Lukic, Anderson, Sansom, Davis, O'Leary, Caton, Whyte, Allinson, Nicholas (Rocastle), Woodcock, Rix.

Nov 2 **Manchester City** **1–0**
(Davis) Att: 22,264
Lukic, Anderson, Sansom, Davis, O'Leary, Caton, Williams, Allinson (Whyte), Nicholas, Woodcock, Rix.

Nov 16 **Oxford United** **2–1**
(Davis, Woodcock) Att: 19,632
Lukic, Anderson, Sansom, Davis, O'Leary, Caton, Williams, Robson, Nicholas, Woodcock (Allinson), Hayes.

Nov 30 **Birmingham City** **0–0**
Att: 16,673
Lukic, Anderson, Sansom, Davis, O'Leary, Caton, Williams (Allinson), Robson, Nicholas, Woodcock, Hayes.

Dec 14 **Liverpool** **2–0**
(Nicholas, Quinn) Att: 35,048
Lukic, Anderson, Sansom, Davis, O'Leary, Keown, Allinson, Robson, Nicholas, Quinn, Rix.

Dec 28 **Queens Park Rangers** **3–1**
(Rix, Nicholas, Woodcock) Att: 25,770
Lukic, Caesar, Sansom, Davis, O'Leary, Keown, Allinson, Robson (Woodcock), Nicholas, Quinn, Rix.

Jan 1 **Tottenham Hotspur** **0–0**
Att: 45,109
Lukic, Anderson, Sansom, Davis, O'Leary, Keown, Allinson, Rocastle, Nicholas, Quinn (Woodcock), Rix.

Feb 1 **Luton Town** **2–1**
(Allinson [pen], Rix) Att: 22,473
Lukic, Anderson, Sansom, Rocastle, O'Leary, Keown, Allinson, Mariner, Nicholas, Quinn, Rix.

Mar 15 **West Ham United** **1–0**
(Woodcock) Att: 31,240
Lukic, Anderson, Sansom, Williams, O'Leary, Keown, Hayes, Rocastle, Nicholas, Woodcock, Rix.

Mar 22 **Coventry City** **3–0**
(Woodcock, Hayes, McInally [og]) Att: 17,189
Lukic, Adams, Sansom, Williams, O'Leary, Keown, Hayes, Rocastle, Nicholas, Woodcock, Rix.

Mar 31 **Watford** **0–2**
Att: 19,599
Lukic, Anderson, Sansom, Williams, O'Leary, Keown, Hayes (Robson), Rocastle, Nicholas, Mariner, Rix.

Apr 8 **Nottingham Forest** **1–1**
(Allinson [pen]) Att: 15,098
Lukic, Anderson, Sansom, Allinson, Adams, Keown, Robson, Rocastle (Mariner), Nicholas, Quinn, Rix.

Apr 12 **Everton** **0–1**
Att: 28,251
Lukic, Anderson, Sansom, Allinson, Adams, Keown, Robson, Davis, Nicholas, Quinn, Rix.

Apr 26 **West Bromwich Albion** **2–2**
(Robson, Allinson [pen]) Att: 14,843
Lukic, Anderson, Sansom, Hayes, O'Leary, Adams, Robson, Davis, Allinson, Woodcock (Quinn), Rix.

Apr 29 **Chelsea** **2–0**
(Anderson, Nicholas) Att: 24,025
Lukic, Anderson, Sansom, Keown, O'Leary, Adams, Robson, Davis, Nicholas, Woodcock, Rix (Quinn).

FA CUP

Jan 25 **Rotherham United** **5–1**
(Allinson 2 [1 pen], Robson, Nicholas, Rix)
Att: 28,490
Lukic, Anderson, Sansom, Rocastle, O'Leary, Keown, Allinson, Robson (Woodcock), Nicholas, Quinn, Rix.

Mar 3 **Luton Town** 0–0*
Att: 26,547
Lukic, Anderson, Sansom, Williams,
Keown, Allinson, Rocastle, Nicholas, Mariner,
Rix.

*After extra time

FOOTBALL LEAGUE (MILK) CUP

Oct 8 **Hereford United** 2–1*
(Anderson, Nicholas) Att: 15,789
Lukic, Anderson, Sansom, Davis (Rocastle),
O'Leary, Caton, Whyte, Allinson, Nicholas,
Woodcock, Rix.

*After extra time

Nov 19 **Southampton** 0–0
Att: 18,244
Lukic, Anderson, Sansom, Davis, O'Leary, Caton,
Williams, Robson, Nicholas, Woodcock, Hayes
(Allinson).

Feb 4 **Aston Villa** 1–2
(Mariner) Att: 33,091
Lukic, Anderson, Sansom, Rocastle, O'Leary,
Caton, Allinson (Woodcock), Mariner, Nicholas,
Quinn, Rix.

1986/87
LEAGUE DIVISION ONE
Final position – 4th

Aug 23 **Manchester United** 1–0
(Nicholas) Att: 41,382
Lukic, Anderson, Sansom, Robson, O'Leary,
Adams, Rocastle (Hayes), Davis, Quinn,
Nicholas, Rix.

Sep 2 **Sheffield Wednesday** 2–0
(Adams, Quinn) Att: 20,101
Lukic, Anderson, Sansom, Robson, O'Leary,
Adams, Rocastle (Hayes), Davis, Quinn,
Nicholas, Rix.

Sep 6 **Tottenham Hotspur** 0–0
Att: 44,707
Lukic, Anderson, Sansom, Robson, O'Leary,
Adams, Rocastle (Hayes), Davis, Quinn,
Nicholas, Rix.

Sep 20 **Oxford United** 0–0
Att: 20,676
Lukic, Anderson, Sansom, Williams, O'Leary,
Adams, Rocastle, Davis, Quinn, Nicholas, Rix
(Groves).

Oct 11 **Watford** 3–1
(Groves, Hayes [pen], Quinn) Att: 24,076
Lukic, Anderson, Sansom, Williams, O'Leary
(Allinson), Adams, Rocastle, Davis, Quinn,
Groves, Hayes.

Oct 25 **Chelsea** 3–1
(Rocastle, Hayes 2 [1 pen]) Att: 32,990
Lukic, Anderson, Sansom, Williams, O'Leary,
Adams, Rocastle, Davis, Quinn (Allinson),
Groves, Hayes.

Nov 8 **West Ham United** 0–0
Att: 36,084
Lukic, Anderson, Sansom, Williams, O'Leary,
Adams, Rocastle, Davis, Quinn, Groves, Hayes.

Nov 22 **Manchester City** 3–0
(Quinn, Anderson, Adams) Att: 29,009
Lukic, Anderson, Sansom, Williams, O'Leary,
Adams, Rocastle, Davis, Quinn (Merson),
Allinson, Hayes.

Dec 6 **Queens Park Rangers** 3–1
(Hayes 2, Quinn) Att: 34,049
Lukic, Anderson, Sansom, Williams, O'Leary,
Adams, Rocastle, Davis, Quinn, Groves
(Nicholas), Hayes.

Dec 20 **Luton Town** 3–0
(Quinn, Adams, Hayes) Att: 28,217
Lukic, Anderson, Sansom, Williams, O'Leary,
Adams, Rocastle, Davis, Quinn, Groves
(Nicholas), Hayes.

Dec 27 **Southampton** 1–0
(Quinn) Att: 38,138
Lukic, Anderson, Sansom, Williams, O'Leary,
Adams, Rocastle, Davis, Quinn, Nicholas, Hayes
(Allinson).

Jan 1 **Wimbledon** 3–1
(Nicholas 2, Hayes [pen]) Att: 36,144
Lukic, Anderson, Sansom, Williams, O'Leary,
Adams, Rocastle (Allinson), Davis, Quinn,
Nicholas, Hayes.

Jan 18 **Coventry City** 0–0
Att: 17,561
Lukic, Anderson, Sansom, Williams, O'Leary,
Adams, Rocastle, Davis, Quinn, Nicholas, Hayes
(Rix).

Mar 10 **Liverpool** 0–1
Att: 47,777
Lukic, Anderson, Sansom, Thomas, O'Leary,
Adams, Rocastle, Groves, Quinn, Allinson,
Hayes (Caesar).

Mar 17 **Nottingham Forest** 0–0
Att: 18,352
Lukic, Anderson, Sansom, Williams, Caesar,
Adams, Rocastle, Groves (Allinson), Quinn,
Nicholas, Thomas.

Mar 28 **Everton** 0–1
Att: 36,218
Lukic, Anderson, Sansom, Williams, O'Leary,
Adams, Rocastle, Davis, Quinn, Nicholas, Hayes
(Groves).

Apr 11 **Charlton Athletic** 2–1
(Davis, Hayes) Att: 26,111
Lukic, Anderson, Sansom, Williams, O'Leary,
Adams, Rocastle, Davis, Quinn (Groves),
Nicholas, Hayes.

Apr 14 **Newcastle United** 0–1
Att: 17,353
Lukic, Anderson, Thomas, Williams, O'Leary,
Adams, Rocastle (Rix), Davis, Groves, Nicholas,
Hayes.

Apr 20 **Leicester City** 4–1
(Davis, Hayes 2 [1 pen], Nicholas) Att: 18,767
Wilmot, Anderson, Sansom, Williams, O'Leary
(Caesar), Adams, Hayes, Davis, Merson,
Nicholas, Rix.

May 2 **Aston Villa** 2–1
(Hayes 2 [1 pen]) Att: 18,463
Wilmot, Anderson, Thomas, Williams, O'Leary,
Adams, Rocastle, Davis, Quinn (Groves),
Nicholas, Hayes.

May 9 **Norwich City** 1–2
(Merson) Att: 24,001
Wilmot, Anderson (Groves), Thomas, Williams,
O'Leary, Adams, Hayes, Davis, Merson,
Nicholas, Rix.

FA CUP

Jan 31 **Plymouth Argyle** 6–1
(Nicholas, Davis, Quinn, Rocastle, Anderson 2)
Att: 39,029
Lukic, Anderson, Sansom, Williams, O'Leary,
Adams, Rocastle, Davis, Quinn, Nicholas, Hayes
(Groves/Caesar).

Feb 21 **Barnsley** 2–0
(Hayes [pen], Nicholas) Att: 28,302
Lukic, Anderson, Sansom, Allinson (Nicholas),
O'Leary, Adams, Rocastle, Davis, Quinn
(Thomas), Groves, Hayes.

Mar 14 **Watford** 1–3
(Allinson) Att: 43,276
Lukic, Anderson, Sansom, Williams, O'Leary,
Adams, Rocastle, Groves, Quinn, Allinson
(Nicholas), Hayes (Thomas).

FOOTBALL LEAGUE (LITTLEWOODS) CUP
Winners

Sep 23 **Huddersfield Town** 2–0
(Davis, Quinn) Att: 15,194
Lukic, Anderson, Sansom, Williams, O'Leary,
Adams, Rocastle, Davis, Quinn (Groves),
Nicholas, Rix.

Oct 28 **Manchester City** 3–1
(Rocastle, Hayes [pen], Davis) Att: 21,604
Lukic, Anderson, Sansom, Williams, O'Leary,
Adams, Rocastle, Davis, Quinn (Allinson),
Groves, Hayes.

Nov 18 **Charlton Athletic** 2–0
(Quinn, Curbishley [og]) Att: 28,301
Lukic, Anderson, Sansom, Williams, O'Leary,
Adams, Rocastle, Davis, Quinn, Groves
(Allinson), Hayes.

Jan 21 **Nottingham Forest** 2–0
(Nicholas, Hayes) Att: 38,617
Lukic, Anderson, Sansom, Williams, O'Leary,
Adams, Rocastle, Davis, Quinn (Rix), Nicholas,
Hayes.

Feb 8 **Tottenham Hotspur** 0–1
Att: 41,306
Lukic, Caesar (Thomas), Sansom, Williams,
O'Leary, Adams, Groves, Davis, Quinn, Nicholas
(Rix), Hayes.

1987/88
LEAGUE DIVISION ONE
Final position – 6th

Aug 15 **Liverpool** 1–2
(Davis) Att: 54,703
Lukic, Thomas, Sansom, Williams, O'Leary,
Adams, Rocastle (Groves), Davis, Smith,
Nicholas, Hayes.

Aug 29 **Portsmouth** 6–0
(Smith 3, Rocastle, Davis, Adams) Att: 30,865
Lukic, Thomas, Sansom, Williams, O'Leary,
Adams, Rocastle, Davis, Smith, Groves
(Merson), Rix (Richardson).

Sep 19 **Wimbledon** 3–0
(Thomas [pen], Smith, Rocastle) Att: 27,752
Lukic, Thomas, Sansom, Williams (Richardson),
O'Leary, Adams, Rocastle, Davis, Smith, Groves
(Merson), Rix.

Sep 26 **West Ham United** 1–0
(Sansom) Att: 40,127
Lukic, Thomas, Sansom, Williams, O'Leary,
Adams, Rocastle (Hayes), Davis, Smith,
Groves, Rix.

Oct 10 **Oxford United** 2–0
(Davis, Williams) Att: 25,244
Lukic, Thomas, Sansom, Williams, O'Leary,
Adams, Rocastle (Hayes), Davis, Smith (Caesar),
Groves, Richardson.

Oct 24 **Derby County** 2–1
(Richardson, Thomas [pen]) Att: 32,374
Lukic, Thomas, Sansom, Williams, O'Leary,
Adams, Rocastle. Davis, Smith, Groves
(Merson), Richardson.

Nov 3 **Chelsea** 3–1
(Richardson 2, Wegerlie [og]) Att: 40,230
Lukic, Thomas, Sansom, Williams, O'Leary,
Adams, Rocastle, Davis, Smith, Groves,
Richardson.

Nov 21 **Southampton** 0–1
Att: 32,477
Lukic, Thomas, Sansom, Williams, O'Leary,
Adams, Rocastle, Davis, Smith, Groves (Quinn /
Winterburn), Richardson.

Dec 5 **Sheffield Wednesday** 3–1
(Richardson, Groves, Merson) Att: 23,670
Lukic, Thomas, Sansom, Williams, O'Leary,
Adams, Rocastle, Davis (Merson), Smith,
Groves, Richardson.

Dec 19 **Everton** 1–1
(Rocastle) Att: 34,857
Lukic, Thomas, Sansom, Williams, O'Leary,
Adams, Rocastle, Davis, Smith, Groves,
Richardson (Merson).

Dec 26 **Nottingham Forest** 0–2
Att: 31,211
Lukic, Thomas, Sansom, Williams, O'Leary
(Caesar), Adams, Rocastle, Merson (Smith),
Quinn, Groves, Richardson.

Jan 2 **Queens Park Rangers** 0–0
Att: 28,271
Lukic, Winterburn, Sansom, Williams, Caesar,
Adams, Rocastle, Hayes, Smith, Merson
(Groves), Richardson.

Jan 24 **Manchester United** 1–2
(Quinn) Att: 29,392
Lukic, Thomas, Winterburn, Williams, O'Leary,
Adams, Rix (Groves), Smith, Quinn,
Richardson.

Feb 13 **Luton Town** 2–1
(Thomas, Rocastle) Att: 22,615
Lukic, Dixon, Winterburn, Thomas, O'Leary,
Adams (Caesar), Rocastle, Hayes, Smith,
Groves, Richardson.

Feb 27 **Charlton Athletic** 4–0
(Merson 2, Smith, Thomas) Att: 25,394
Lukic, Winterburn, Sansom, Thomas, Caesar,
Adams, Rocastle, Hayes, Smith, Merson
(Quinn), Richardson (Davis).

Mar 6 **Tottenham Hotspur** 2–1
(Smith, Groves) Att: 37,143
Lukic, Winterburn, Sansom, Thomas, Caesar,
Adams, Rocastle, Hayes, Smith, Groves,
Richardson.

Mar 19 **Newcastle United** 1–1
(Groves) Att: 25,889
Lukic, Dixon, Winterburn, Thomas, Caesar,
Adams, Rocastle, Davis, Smith (Quinn), Groves,
Hayes.

Apr 4 **Norwich City** 2–0
(Smith, Groves) Att: 19,341
Lukic, Winterburn, Sansom, Williams, Caesar,
Adams, Rocastle, Davis, Smith, Groves, Hayes.

Apr 15 **Watford** 0–1
Att: 19,541
Lukic, Winterburn, Sansom, Thomas, Caesar,
Adams, Rocastle, Davis, Smith, Merson,
Richardson (Hayes).

May 2 **Coventry City** 1–1
(Marwood [pen]) Att: 16,963
Lukic, Dixon, Sansom, Thomas, Caesar, Adams,
Rocastle, Richardson (Groves), Smith, Merson
(Hayes), Marwood.

FA CUP

Jan 9 **Millwall** 2–0
(Hayes, Rocastle) Att: 42,083
Lukic, Winterburn, Sansom, Williams, O'Leary,
Adams, Rocastle, Hayes, Smith, Merson
(Groves), Richardson.

Feb 20 **Manchester United** 2–1
(Smith, Duxbury [og]) Att: 54,161
Lukic, Winterburn, Sansom, Thomas, O'Leary
(Rix), Adams, Rocastle, Hayes, Smith, Groves,
Richardson.

Mar 12 **Nottingham Forest** 1–2
(Rocastle) Att: 50,157
Lukic, Winterburn, Sansom, Thomas, O'Leary
(Davis), Adams, Rocastle, Hayes (Quinn), Smith,
Groves, Richardson.

FOOTBALL LEAGUE (LITTLEWOODS) CUP
Finalists

Oct 6 **Doncaster Rovers** 1–0
(Rocastle) Att: 18,321
Lukic, Thomas, Sansom, Williams, Caesar,
Adams, Rocastle, Davis, Smith, Groves, Hayes.

Oct 27 **AFC Bournemouth** 3–0
(Thomas [pen], Smith, Richardson) Att: 26,050
Lukic, Thomas, Sansom, Williams, O'Leary,
Adams, Rocastle, Davis, Smith, Groves
(Merson), Richardson.

Nov 17 **Stoke City** 3–0
(O'Leary,Richardson, Rocastle) Att: 30,058
Lukic, Thomas, Sansom, Williams, O'Leary,
Adams, Rocastle, Davis, Smith, Groves (Hayes),
Richardson.

Feb 24 **Everton** 3–1
(Thomas, Rocastle, Smith) Att: 51,148
Lukic, Winterburn, Sansom, Thomas, O'Leary
(Davis), Adams, Rocastle, Hayes, Smith, Groves,
Richardson.

1988/89
LEAGUE DIVISION ONE
Final position – Champions

Sep 3 **Aston Villa** 2–3
(Marwood, Smith) Att: 37,417
Lukic, Dixon, Winterburn, Thomas, O'Leary,
Adams, Rocastle (Groves), Davis, Smith,
Merson, Marwood.

Sep 17 **Southampton** 2–2
(Marwood [pen], Smith) Att:31,384
Lukic, Dixon, Winterburn, Thomas, O'Leary,
Adams, Rocastle, Davis (Richardson), Smith,
Merson (Hayes), Marwood.

Oct 22 **Queens Park Rangers** 2–1
(Adams, Smith) Att: 33,202
Lukic, Dixon, Winterburn, Thomas, Bould,
Adams, Rocastle, Richardson, Smith, Merson
(Groves), Marwood.

Oct 29 **Coventry City** 2–0
(Thomas, Adams) Att: 31,273
Lukic, Dixon, Winterburn, Thomas, Bould,
Adams, Rocastle (Hayes), Richardson, Smith,
Merson (Groves), Marwood.

Nov 19 **Middlesbrough** 3–0
(Merson 2, Rocastle) Att: 32,294
Lukic, Dixon, Winterburn, Thomas, Bould,
Adams, Rocastle, Richardson, Smith, Merson,
Marwood (Hayes).

Dec 4 **Liverpool** 1–1
(Smith) Att: 31,863
Lukic, Dixon, Winterburn, Thomas, Bould,
Adams, Rocastle, Richardson, Smith, Merson,
Marwood (Hayes).

Dec 17 **Manchester United** 2–1
(Thomas, Merson) Att: 37,422
Lukic, Dixon, Winterburn, Thomas, Bould,
Adams, Rocastle, Richardson, Smith, Merson,
Marwood.

Jan 2 **Tottenham Hotspur** 2–0
(Merson, Thomas) Att: 45,129
Lukic, O'Leary, Winterburn, Thomas, Bould,
Adams, Rocastle, Richardson (Davis), Smith,
Merson, Marwood (Groves).

Jan 21 **Sheffield Wednesday** 1–1
(Merson) Att: 33,490
Lukic, Dixon, Winterburn, Davis, O'Leary, Caesar
(Thomas), Rocastle (Groves), Richardson, Smith,
Merson, Marwood.

Feb 4 **West Ham United** 2–1
(Groves, Smith) Att : 40,139
Lukic, Dixon, Winterburn, Thomas, O'Leary
(Bould), Adams, Rocastle, Richardson, Smith,
Merson (Hayes), Marwood.

Feb 25 **Luton Town** 2–0
(Groves, Smith) Att: 31,012
Lukic, Bould, Winterburn, Thomas, O'Leary,
Adams, Rocastle (Merson), Richardson, Smith,
Groves, Marwood.

Feb 28 **Millwall** 0–0
Att: 37,524
Lukic, Bould, Winterburn, Thomas, O'Leary,
Adams, Rocastle (Merson), Richardson (Dixon),
Smith, Groves, Marwood.

Mar 11 Nottingham Forest **1–3**
(Smith) Att: 39,639
Lukic, Bould (Dixon), Winterburn, Thomas, O'Leary, Adams, Rocastle, Richardson, Smith, Groves (Merson), Marwood.

Mar 21 Charlton Athletic **2–2**
(Rocastle, Davis) Att: 30,259
Lukic, Dixon, Winterburn, Davis, O'Leary, Adams, Rocastle, Richardson (Thomas), Smith, Merson (Groves), Marwood.

Apr 8 Everton **2–0**
(Dixon, Quinn) Att: 37,608
Lukic, Dixon, Winterburn, Thomas, O'Leary, Adams, Rocastle, Richardson, Quinn, Bould, Marwood (Merson).

Apr 15 Newcastle United **1–0**
(Marwood) Att: 38,023
Lukic, Dixon, Winterburn, Thomas, O'Leary (Merson), Adams, Rocastle (Groves), Richardson, Quinn, Bould, Marwood.

May 1 Norwich City **5–0**
(Winterburn, Smith 2, Rocastle, Thomas) Att: 28,449
Lukic, Dixon, Winterburn, Thomas, O'Leary, Adams, Rocastle, Richardson, Smith (Quinn), Bould, Merson (Hayes).

May 13 Derby County **1–2**
(Smith) Att: 41,008
Lukic, Dixon, Winterburn, Thomas, O'Leary, Adams, Rocastle, Richardson, Smith, Bould (Hayes), Merson (Groves).

May 17 Wimbledon **2–2**
(Winterburn, Merson) Att: 39,132
Lukic, Dixon, Winterburn, Thomas, O'Leary, Adams, Rocastle, Richardson, Smith, Hayes (Groves), Merson (Bould).

FA CUP

Jan 11 West Ham United **0–1**
Att: 44,124
Lukic, Dixon, Winterburn, Thomas, O'Leary, Adams, Rocastle (Davis), Richardson, Smith, Merson, Marwood (Groves).

FOOTBALL LEAGUE (LITTLEWOODS) CUP

Oct 12 Hull City **3–0**
(Merson, Smith 2) Att: 17,885
Lukic, Dixon, Winterburn, Thomas, Bould, Adams, Rocastle, Davis (Richardson), Smith, Merson (Hayes), Marwood.

Nov 9 Liverpool **0–0***
Att: 54,029
Lukic, Dixon, Winterburn, Thomas, Bould, Adams, Rocastle, Richardson, Smith, Merson (Hayes), Marwood.

*After extra time

1989/90

LEAGUE DIVISION ONE
Final position – 4th

Aug 22 Coventry City **2–0**
(Marwood, Thomas) Att: 33,886
Lukic, Dixon, Winterburn, Thomas, O'Leary, Adams, Rocastle (Groves), Richardson, Smith, Merson, Marwood.

Aug 26 Wimbledon **0–0**
Att: 32,279
Lukic, Dixon, Winterburn, Thomas, O'Leary, Adams, Rocastle, Richardson, Smith, Merson (Groves), Marwood.

Sep 9 Sheffield Wednesday **5–0**
(Merson, Adams, Thomas, Marwood, Smith) Att: 30,058
Lukic, Dixon, Winterburn, Thomas, O'Leary, Adams, Rocastle, Richardson, Smith, Merson, Marwood.

Sep 23 Charlton Athletic **1–0**
(Marwood [pen]) Att: 34,583
Lukic, Dixon, Winterburn, Thomas, O'Leary, Adams, Rocastle (Groves), Richardson, Smith, Merson, Marwood.

Oct 14 Manchester City **4–0**
(Groves 2, Thomas, Merson) Att: 40,414
Lukic, Dixon, Winterburn, Thomas, O'Leary, Adams, Rocastle, Richardson (Jonsson), Smith, Groves, Marwood (Merson).

Oct 28 Derby County **1–1**
(Smith) Att: 33,189
Lukic, Dixon, Winterburn (Jonsson), Thomas, O'Leary, Adams, Rocastle, Richardson, Smith, Quinn (Campbell), Merson.

Nov 4 Norwich City **4–3**
(Dixon 2 (1pen), O'Leary, Quinn) Att: 35,338
Lukic, Dixon, Winterburn, Thomas, O'Leary, Adams, Rocastle, Richardson, Smith, Quinn, Merson (Groves).

Nov 18 Queens Park Rangers **3–0**
(Smith, Dixon [pen], Jonsson) Att: 38,236
Lukic, Dixon, Winterburn, Thomas, O'Leary, Adams, Rocastle (Groves), Richardson, Smith, Quinn, Marwood (Jonsson).

Dec 3 Manchester United **1–0**
(Groves) Att: 34,484
Lukic, Dixon, Winterburn, Thomas, O'Leary, Adams, Rocastle, Richardson, Smith, Groves, Marwood (Merson).

Dec16 Luton Town **3–2**
(Smith, Merson, Marwood) Att: 28,761
Lukic, Dixon, Winterburn, Thomas, O'Leary, Adams, Rocastle, Richardson, Smith (Merson), Groves (Jonsson), Marwood.

Jan 1 Crystal Palace **4–1**
(Smith 2, Dixon, Adams) Att: 38,711
Lukic, Dixon, Winterburn (Davis), Thomas, O'Leary, Adams, Groves, Richardson, Smith (Rocastle), Bould, Merson.

Jan 20 Tottenham Hotspur **1–0**
(Adams) Att: 46,132
Lukic, Dixon, Davis, Thomas, O'Leary, Adams, Rocastle, Richardson, Smith, Bould, Groves.

Mar 7 Nottingham Forest **3–0**
(Groves, Adams, Campbell) Att: 31,879
Lukic, Dixon, Winterburn, Thomas, Bould, Adams, Rocastle, Richardson, Smith, Merson (Campbell), Groves (O'Leary).

Mar 17 Chelsea **0–1**
Att: 33,805
Lukic, Dixon, Winterburn, Thomas, Bould, Adams, Rocastle (Hayes), Richardson, Smith, Campbell (O'Leary), Groves.

Mar 31 Everton **1–0**
(Smith) Att: 35,223
Lukic, Dixon, Winterburn, Thomas, Bould, Adams, Hayes, Richardson (O'Leary), Smith, Campbell (Ampadu), Groves.

Apr 11 Aston Villa **0–1**
Att: 30,060
Lukic, Dixon, Winterburn, Thomas, Bould, Adams, Hayes (Merson), O'Leary, Smith, Campbell, Groves.

Apr 18 Liverpool **1–1**
(Merson) Att: 33,395
Lukic, Dixon, Winterburn, Thomas, Bould (Pates), Adams, Davis, O'Leary, Smith, Merson, Groves (Campbell).

Apr 28 Millwall **2–0**
(Davis, Merson) Att: 25,607
Lukic, Dixon, Winterburn, Thomas (Richardson), Bould, Adams, Rocastle, Davis, Smith, Merson, Marwood (Campbell).

May 2 Southampton **2–1**
(Dixon [pen], Rocastle) Att: 23,732
Lukic, Dixon, Winterburn, Thomas, Bould, Adams, Richardson (Rocastle), Davis, Smith, Merson, Marwood (Groves).

FA CUP

Jan 27 Queens Park Rangers **0–0**
Att: 43,483
Lukic, Dixon, Winterburn, Davis (Thomas), O'Leary, Adams, Rocastle, Richardson, Smith, Bould (Merson), Groves.

FOOTBALL LEAGUE (LITTLEWOODS) CUP

Sep 19 Plymouth Argyle **2–0**
(Smith, Brimacombe [og]) Att: 26,865
Lukic, Dixon, Winterburn, Thomas, O'Leary, Adams, Rocastle, Richardson, Smith, Merson (Groves), Marwood.

Oct 25 Liverpool **1–0**
(Smith) Att: 40,814
Lukic, Dixon, Winterburn, Thomas, O'Leary, Adams, Rocastle, Richardson, Quinn, Merson, Hayes (Smith).

1990/91

LEAGUE DIVISION ONE
Final position – Champions

Aug 29 Luton Town **2–1**
(Merson, Thomas) Att: 32,723
Seaman, Dixon, Winterburn, Thomas, Bould, Adams, Rocastle, Davis, Smith, Merson, Limpar (Groves).

Sep 1 Tottenham Hotspur **0–0**
Att: 40,009
Seaman, Dixon, Winterburn, Thomas, Bould, Adams, Rocastle, Davis, Smith, Merson (Groves), Limpar.

Sep 15 Chelsea **4–1**
(Limpar, Dixon [pen], Merson, Rocastle) Att: 40,475
Seaman, Dixon, Winterburn, Thomas, Bould (Linighan), Adams, Rocastle, Davis, Groves (Campbell), Merson, Limpar.

Oct 6 Norwich City **2–0**
(Davis 2) Att: 36,737
Seaman, Dixon, Winterburn, Jonsson, Bould, Adams, Rocastle, Davis, Smith, Merson (Groves), Limpar (Hillier).

Oct 27 Sunderland **1–0**
(Dixon [pen]) Att: 38,485
Seaman, Dixon, Winterburn, Thomas, Bould, Adams, Rocastle (Groves), Davis, Smith, Merson, Limpar.

Nov 17 Southampton **4–0**
(Smith 2, Merson, Limpar) Att: 36,229
Seaman, Dixon (O'Leary), Winterburn, Thomas, Bould, Adams, Groves (Campbell), Davis, Smith, Merson, Limpar.

Dec 2 Liverpool **3–0**
(Merson, Dixon [pen], Smith) Att: 40,419
Seaman, Dixon, Winterburn, Thomas, Bould, Adams, O'Leary, Davis, Smith, Merson, Limpar.

Dec 15 Wimbledon **2–2**
(Merson, Adams) Att: 30,164
Seaman, Dixon, Winterburn (O'Leary), Thomas, Bould, Adams, Groves, Davis, Smith, Merson, Limpar.

Dec 26 Derby County **3–0**
(Smith 2, Merson) Att: 25,538
Seaman, Dixon, Winterburn, Thomas, Bould, Linighan, Rocastle (Campbell), Davis, Smith, Merson, Limpar (O'Leary).

Dec 29 Sheffield United **4–1**
(Dixon [pen], Smith 2, Thomas) Att: 37,810
Seaman, Dixon, Winterburn (O'Leary), Thomas, Bould, Linighan, Groves (Cole), Davis, Smith, Merson, Limpar.

Jan 19 Everton **1–0**
(Merson) Att: 35,349
Seaman, Dixon, Winterburn, Thomas, Bould (Hillier), Groves, O'Leary, Davis, Smith, Merson, Limpar (Campbell).

Feb 23 Crystal Palace **4–0**
(O'Leary, Merson, Smith, Campbell) Att: 42,162
Seaman, Dixon, Winterburn, Thomas, Bould, Linighan (Pates), O'Leary, Davis, Smith, Merson (Rocastle), Campbell.

Mar 17 Leeds United **2–0**
(Campbell 2) Att: 26,218
Seaman, Dixon, Winterburn, Thomas, Bould, Adams, O'Leary, Hillier, Smith, Merson, Campbell.

Mar 20 Nottingham Forest **1–1**
(Campbell) Att: 34,152
Seaman, Dixon, Winterburn, Thomas, Bould, Adams, O'Leary, Davis (Groves), Smith, Merson (Limpar), Campbell.

Apr 3 Aston Villa **5–0**
(Campbell 2, Smith 2, Davis) Att: 41,868
Seaman, Dixon, Winterburn, Hillier (Thomas), Bould, Adams, Campbell, Davis, Smith, Merson (Groves), Limpar.

Apr 17 Manchester City **2–2**
(Campbell, Merson) Att: 38,412
Seaman, Dixon (O'Leary), Winterburn, Thomas, Bould, Adams, Campbell, Davis, Smith, Merson (Limpar), Groves.

Apr 23 Queens Park Rangers **2–0**
(Dixon [pen], Merson) Att: 42,393
Seaman, Dixon, Winterburn, Hillier, Bould, Adams, Campbell, Davis, Smith, Merson (O'Leary), Limpar (Groves).

May 6 Manchester United **3–1**
(Smith 3 [1pen]) Att: 40,229
Seaman, Dixon, Winterburn, Hillier (Thomas), Bould, Adams, Campbell, Davis, Smith, Merson, Limpar (O'Leary).

May 11 Coventry City **6–1**
(Limpar 3, Smith, Groves, Peake [og]) Att: 41,039
Seaman, Dixon, Winterburn, Hillier, Bould, Adams, Campbell (Groves), Davis, Smith, Merson (Linighan), Limpar.

FA CUP

Jan 5 Sunderland **2–1**
(Smith, Limpar) Att: 35,128
Seaman, Dixon, Winterburn, Thomas, Bould, Linighan, Groves, Davis, Smith, Merson, Limpar (O'Leary).

Jan 27 Leeds United **0–0**
Att: 30,905
Seaman, Dixon, Winterburn, Thomas, Bould, Groves, O'Leary (Hillier), Davis, Smith, Merson, Limpar (Campbell).

Feb 13 Leeds United **0–0***
Att: 30,433
Seaman, Dixon, Winterburn, Thomas, Bould, Groves (Campbell), O'Leary, Davis, Smith, Merson, Limpar (Linighan).

*After extra time

Mar 9 Cambridge United **2–1**
(Campbell, Adams) Att: 42,960
Seaman, Dixon, Winterburn, Thomas, Bould, Adams, O'Leary, Hillier (Davis), Smith, Merson, Campbell.

FOOTBALL LEAGUE (RUMBELOWS) CUP

Oct 9 Chester City **5–0**
(Groves 2, Adams, Smith, Merson) Att: 22,890
Seaman, Dixon, Winterburn, Hillier, Bould (O'Leary), Adams, Rocastle (Campbell), Davis, Smith, Merson, Groves.

Nov 28 Manchester United **2–6**
(Smith 2) Att: 40,884
Seaman, Dixon, Winterburn, Thomas, Bould, Adams, Groves, Davis, Smith, Merson, Limpar (Campbell).

1991/92

LEAGUE DIVISION ONE
Final position – 4th

Aug 17 Queens Park Rangers **1–1**
(Merson) Att: 38,099
Seaman, Dixon, Winterburn, Hillier, O'Leary (Rocastle), Adams, Campbell (Groves), Davis, Smith, Merson, Limpar.

Aug 27 Luton Town **2–0**
(Smith, Merson) Att: 25,898
Seaman, Dixon, Winterburn, Thomas, Linighan, Adams, Rocastle, Davis, Smith, Merson, Limpar.

Aug 31 Manchester City **2–1**
(Smith, Limpar) Att: 35,009
Seaman, Dixon, Winterburn, Thomas, Linighan, Adams, Rocastle (Campbell), Davis, Smith, Merson, Limpar (Pates).

Sep 7 Coventry City **1–2**
(Adams) Att: 28,142
Seaman, Dixon, Winterburn, Campbell, Linighan, Adams, Rocastle, Davis (Thomas), Smith, Merson, Limpar (O'Leary).

Sep 21 Sheffield United **5–2**
(Smith, Dixon [pen], Rocastle, Campbell, Groves) Att: 30,244
Seaman, Dixon, Winterburn (O'Leary), Campbell, Linighan, Adams, Rocastle, Davis, Smith, Merson, Groves (Thomas).

Oct 5 Chelsea **3–2**
(Dixon [pen], Wright, Campbell) Att: 42,074
Seaman, Dixon, Winterburn, Thomas, Linighan, Pates, Rocastle, Wright (O'Leary), Smith, Campbell, Limpar (Merson).

Oct 26 Notts County **2–0**
(Smith, Wright) Att: 30,011
Seaman, Dixon, Winterburn, Davis, Pates, Adams, Rocastle, Wright, Smith, Merson, Campbell (Limpar).

Nov 2 West Ham United **0–1**
Att: 33,359
Seaman, Dixon, Winterburn, Thomas (Groves), Pates, Linighan, Rocastle, Wright, Smith, Merson, Limpar.

Dec 1 Tottenham Hotspur **2–0**
(Wright, Campbell) Att: 38,892
Seaman, Dixon, Winterburn, Hillier, Bould, Linighan, Rocastle (O'Leary), Wright (Limpar), Smith, Merson, Campbell.

Dec 21 Everton **4–2**
(Wright 4) Att: 29,684
Seaman, Dixon, Winterburn, Hillier, Bould, Adams, Rocastle (O'Leary), Wright, Smith, Merson (Campbell), Limpar.

Jan 1 Wimbledon **1–1**
(Merson) Att: 26,839
Seaman, Dixon, Winterburn, Hillier, Linighan, Adams, Rocastle, Wright (Campbell), Smith, Merson, Carter.

Jan 11 Aston Villa **0–0**
Att: 31,413
Seaman, Dixon, Winterburn, Hillier, O'Leary, Adams, Rocastle, Campbell, Smith, Merson (Groves), Carter.

Feb 1 Manchester United **1–1**
(Rocastle) Att: 41,703
Seaman, Dixon, Winterburn, Hillier, Bould, Adams, Rocastle (Pates), Wright, Smith, Merson, Carter (Limpar).

Feb 11 Norwich City **1–1**
(Merson) Att: 22,352
Seaman, Dixon, Winterburn (Parlour), Hillier, Bould, Adams, Pates, Wright, Smith, Merson, Limpar (Campbell).

Feb 15 Sheffield Wednesday **7–1**
(Campbell 2, Limpar 2, Smith, Merson, Wright) Att: 26,805
Seaman, Dixon, Winterburn, Hillier, Bould, Adams, Rocastle, Wright, Smith (Campbell), Merson, Limpar.

Mar 10 Oldham Athletic 2–1
(Wright, Merson) Att: 22,096
Seaman, Dixon, Winterburn, Hillier, Bould, Adams, Rocastle, Wright, Smith, Merson, Limpar (O'Leary).

Mar 22 Leeds United 1–1
(Merson) Att: 27,844
Seaman, Dixon, Winterburn, Hillier (Parlour), Bould, Adams, Rocastle (Limpar), Wright, O'Leary, Merson, Campbell.

Mar 31 Nottingham Forest 3–3
(Dixon [pen], Merson, Adams) Att: 27,036
Seaman, Dixon, Winterburn, Hillier, Bould, Adams, Rocastle (Lydersen), Wright (Smith), Campbell, Merson, Limpar.

Apr 11 Crystal Palace 4–1
(Merson 3, Campbell) Att: 36,016
Seaman, Lydersen, Winterburn (Morrow), Hillier, Bould, Adams, Rocastle, Wright, Campbell, Merson, Limpar (Smith).

Apr 20 Liverpool 4–0
(Hillier, Wright 2, Limpar) Att: 38,517
Seaman, Lydersen (O'Leary), Winterburn, Hillier, Bould, Adams, Rocastle, Wright, Campbell, Merson, Limpar.

May 2 Southampton 5–1
(Wright 3 [1 pen], Campbell, Smith) Att: 37,702
Seaman, Dixon, Winterburn, Hillier, Bould, Adams, Rocastle, Wright, Campbell, Merson (Parlour), Limpar (Smith).

NOTE: There were no FA Cup matches at Highbury this season.

FOOTBALL LEAGUE (RUMBELOWS) CUP

Oct 8 Leicester City 2–0
(Wright, Merson) Att: 28,580
Seaman, Dixon, Winterburn, Thomas, Pates, Adams, Rocastle, Wright (Groves), Smith, Merson, Campbell.

EUROPEAN CUP

Sep 18 FK Austria 6–1
(Smith 4, Linighan, Limpar) Att: 24,124
Seaman, Dixon, Winterburn, Campbell, Linighan, Adams, Rocastle, Davis, Smith, Merson, Limpar (Groves).

Nov 6 Benfica 1–3*
(Pates) Att: 35,815
Seaman, Dixon, Winterburn, Davis, Pates (Bould), Adams, Rocastle, Campbell, Smith, Merson, Limpar (Groves).

*After extra time

1992/93

PREMIER LEAGUE
Final position – 10th

Aug 15 Norwich City 2–4
(Bould, Campbell) Att: 24,030
Seaman, Dixon, Winterburn, Hillier, Bould, Adams, Jensen, Smith, Campbell, Merson (Wright), Limpar.

Aug 26 Oldham Athletic 2–0
(Winterburn, Wright) Att: 20,796
Seaman, Dixon, Winterburn, Hillier, Bould, Adams, Parlour, Wright (Smith), Campbell, Merson (Pates), Morrow.

Aug 29 Sheffield Wednesday 2–1
(Parlour, Merson) Att: 23,389
Seaman, Dixon, Winterburn, Hillier, Bould, Adams, Jensen, Wright, Campbell,Merson (Smith), Parlour.

Sep 12 Blackburn Rovers 0–1
Att: 28,643
Seaman, Dixon, Winterburn, Selley, Bould, Adams, Jensen (Morrow), Wright, Smith, Merson, Parlour (Campbell).

Sep 28 Manchester City 1–0
(Wright) Att: 21,504
Seaman, Dixon, Winterburn, Hillier, Bould, Adams, Jensen, Wright, Smith (Limpar), Merson, Campbell.

Oct 3 Chelsea 2–1
(Merson, Wright) Att: 27,780
Seaman, Dixon, Winterburn, Hillier, Bould, Adams, Jensen, Wright, Smith, Merson (Limpar), Campbell.

Oct 24 Everton 2–0
(Wright, Limpar) Att: 28,052
Seaman, Dixon (Pates), Winterburn, Hillier, Bould, Adams, Jensen, Wright (Limpar), Smith, Merson, Campbell.

Nov 7 Coventry City 3–0
(Smith, Wright, Campbell) Att: 27,693
Seaman, Dixon, Morrow, Hillier, Bould, Adams, Jensen, Wright, Smith, Merson, Campbell (Limpar).

Nov 28 Manchester United 0–1
Att: 29,739
Seaman, Dixon, Morrow, Hillier, Bould, Adams, Jensen (Parlour), Wright, Campbell, Merson, Limpar (Flatts).

Dec 19 Middlesbrough 1–1
(Wright) Att: 23,197
Seaman, Lydersen, Winterburn, Hillier, Linighan, Adams, Flatts, Wright, Smith, Merson (Jensen), Parlour (Campbell).

Dec 26 Ipswich Town 0–0
Att: 26,198
Seaman, Lydersen, Winterburn, Hillier, Bould, Linighan, Jensen (O'Leary), Wright, Smith, Campbell (Limpar), Flatts.

Jan 9 Sheffield United 1–1
(Hillier) Att: 23,818
Seaman, Dixon, Winterburn, Hillier, Linighan, Adams, Jensen, Wright, Smith, Merson (O'Leary), Limpar.

Jan 31 Liverpool 0–1
Att: 27,580
Seaman, Dixon, Winterburn, Hillier (O'Leary / Heaney), Linighan, Adams, Carter, Campbell, Smith, Merson, Parlour.

Feb 10 Wimbledon 0–1
Att: 18,253
Seaman, Keown, Winterburn, Hillier, Linighan, Adams, Selley, Wright, Smith (Morrow), Merson (Carter), Campbell.

Feb 24 Leeds United 0–0
Att: 21,061
Seaman, Keown, Winterburn, Hillier, Linighan, Adams, Selley, Wright, Smith, Merson, Limpar (Campbell)

Mar 20 Southampton 4–3
(Linighan, Merson, Carter 2) Att: 24,149
Seaman, Keown, Winterburn, Davis (Hillier), Linighan, Adams, Carter, Morrow, Campbell, Merson, Limpar (Dickov).

Apr 12 Aston Villa 0–1
Att: 27,125
Seaman, Dixon, Winterburn, Selley, Keown, Adams, Morrow, Wright (Linighan), Smith, Merson, Campbell (Parlour).

Apr 21 Nottingham Forest 1–1
(Wright) Att: 19,024
Seaman, Dixon, Winterburn (Adams), Selley, Linighan, Keown, Jensen, Wright, Smith, Parlour (Campbell), Carter.

May 4 Queens Park Rangers 0–0
Att: 18,817
Miller, Dixon, Keown, Davis, Linighan, Adams, Jensen, Campbell, Smith, Merson (Carter), Heaney.

May 8 Crystal Palace 3–0
(Wright, Dickov, Campbell) Att: 25,225
Seaman, Dixon, Winterburn, Davis, Linighan, Adams, Carter (Dickov), Wright (O'Leary), Campbell,Merson, Parlour.

May 11 Tottenham Hotspur 1–3
(Dickov) Att: 26,393
Miller, Lydersen (McGowan), Keown, Marshall, O'Leary, Bould, Flatts (Carter), Selley, Smith, Dickov, Heaney.

FA CUP
Winners

Jan 25 Leeds United 2–2
(Parlour, Merson) Att: 26,516
Seaman, Dixon, Winterburn, Hillier, Linighan, Adams, Jensen (Carter), Campbell, Smith, Merson, Parlour.

Feb 13 Nottingham Forest 2–0
(Wright 2) Att: 27, 591
Seaman, Dixon, Winterburn, Hillier, Linighan, Adams, Jensen, Wright (Morrow), Selley, Merson, Limpar (Campbell).

FOOTBALL LEAGUE (COCA-COLA) CUP
Winners

Sep 22 Millwall 1–1
(Campbell) Att: 20,940
Seaman, Dixon, Winterburn, Hillier, Bould, Adams, Parlour, Wright, Smith, Merson, Limpar (Campbell).

Dec 1 Derby County 2–1
(Wright, Campbell) Att: 24,587
Seaman, Dixon, Morrow, Hillier, Bould, Adams, Parlour, Wright, Campbell, Merson, Flatts.

Jan 12 Nottingham Forest 2–0
(Wright 2) Att: 25,600
Seaman, Dixon, Winterburn, Hillier, Linighan, Adams, Jensen, Wright, Smith, Merson, Limpar (Campbell).

Mar 10 Crystal Palace 2–0
(Linighan, Wright) Att: 28,584
Seaman, Dixon, Winterburn (Hillier), Davis, Linighan, Adams, Carter, Wright, Smith (Campbell), Merson, Morrow.

1993/94

PREMIER LEAGUE
Final position – 4th

Aug 14 Coventry City 0–3
Att: 26,397
Seaman, Dixon, Winterburn, Davis, Linighan, Adams, Jensen (Keown), Wright, Campbell, Merson (McGoldrick), Limpar.

Aug 24 Leeds United 2–1
(Merson, Newsome [og]) Att: 29,042
Seaman, Keown, Winterburn, Davis (Hillier), Linighan, Selley, Merson, Wright, Campbell, McGoldrick, Parlour.

Aug 28 Everton 2–0
(Wright 2) Att: 29,063
Seaman, Keown, Winterburn, Hillier (Merson), Linighan, Adams, Jensen, Wright, Campbell, McGoldrick, Parlour.

Sep 11 Ipswich Town 4–0
(Wright, Campbell 3) Att: 28,563
Seaman, Keown, Winterburn, Davis, Linighan, Adams, Jensen (Hillier), Wright, Campbell, Merson (Limpar), McGoldrick.

Sep 25 Southampton 1–0
(Merson) Att: 26,902
Seaman, Keown, Winterburn, Davis (Hillier), Linighan, Adams, Jensen, Wright, Campbell, Merson, McGoldrick.

Oct 16 Manchester City 0–0
Att: 29,567
Seaman, Dixon, Winterburn, Davis, Linighan, Adams, Heaney (Campbell), Wright, Smith, Parlour, McGoldrick.

Oct 30 Norwich City 0–0
Att: 30,516
Seaman, Dixon, Winterburn (Keown), Davis, Bould, Adams, Jensen, Wright, Smith (Campbell), Merson, Limpar.

Nov 6 Aston Villa 1–2
(Wright) Att: 31,773
Seaman, Dixon, Winterburn, Selley, Keown, Adams, Jensen, Wright, Campbell, Merson, Limpar.

Nov 27 Newcastle United 2–1
(Wright, Smith) Att: 36,091
Seaman, Dixon, Winterburn, Morrow, Keown, Bould, Jensen, Wright, Smith, Merson, McGoldrick.

Dec 6 Tottenham Hotspur 1–1
(Wright) Att: 35,669
Seaman, Dixon, Keown, Selley, Bould, Adams, Jensen, Wright, Smith (Campbell), Merson, Limpar.

Dec 12 Sheffield Wednesday 1–0
(Wright) Att: 22,026
Miller, Dixon, Morrow, Selley, Keown (Bould), Adams, Jensen, Wright, Smith, Merson (Campbell), Limpar.

Dec 29 Sheffield United 3–0
(Campbell 2, Wright) Att: 27,035
Seaman, Dixon, Winterburn, Parlour (Merson), Bould, Adams, Jensen, Wright (Keown), Campbell, Hillier, McGoldrick.

Jan 3 Queens Park Rangers 0–0
Att: 34,935
Seaman, Dixon, Winterburn, Parlour, Bould, Adams, Jensen (Keown), Wright, Campbell, Hillier, McGoldrick.

Jan 22 Oldham Athletic 1–1
(Wright [pen]) Att: 26,524
Seaman, Dixon, Winterburn, Parlour, Bould, Adams, Jensen (Keown), Wright, Campbell, Hillier, McGoldrick (Merson).

Feb 26 Blackburn Rovers 1–0
(Merson) Att: 35,030
Seaman, Dixon, Winterburn, Davis, Bould, Adams, Jensen, Campbell, Smith, Merson, Parlour.

Mar 22 Manchester United 2–2
(Merson, Pallister [og]) Att: 36,203
Seaman, Dixon, Winterburn, Davis (Campbell), Bould, Adams, Jensen, Wright, Smith, Merson, Selley.

Mar 26 Liverpool 1–0
(Merson) Att: 35,556
Seaman, Dixon, Keown, Parlour, Bould, Linighan, Jensen (Morrow), Wright (Smith), Campbell, Merson, Selley.

Apr 2 Swindon Town 1–1
(Smith) Att: 31,634
Seaman, Dixon, Keown, Davis, Adams, Linighan, Jensen (McGoldrick), Wright, Smith, Merson (Campbell), Parlour.

Apr 16 Chelsea 1–0
(Wright) Att: 34,314
Seaman, Dixon, Morrow, Hillier (Smith), Keown, Adams, Selley, Wright, Campbell, Parlour, McGoldrick.

Apr 19 Wimbledon 1–1
(Bould) Att: 21,292
Seaman, Dixon, Keown, Davis (Flatts), Bould, Adams, Campbell, Wright, Smith, Parlour, Selley.

Apr 30 West Ham United 0–2
Att: 33,701
Miller, McGoldrick (Morrow), Winterburn, Davis, Bould, Linighan, Parlour, Wright, Campbell, Merson (Dickov), Selley.

FA CUP

Feb 9 Bolton Wanderers 1–3*
(Smith) Att: 33,863
Seaman, Dixon, Winterburn, Hillier (Keown), Bould, Adams, Campbell, Wright (McGoldrick), Smith, Merson, Parlour.

*After extra time

FOOTBALL LEAGUE (COCA-COLA) CUP

Oct 5 Huddersfield Town 1–1
(Smith) Att: 18,789
Seaman, Dixon, Winterburn, Parlour, Linighan, Bould, Jensen (Selley), Smith, Campbell, Limpar, McGoldrick (Heaney).

Oct 26 Norwich City 1–1
(Wright) Att: 24,539
Seaman, Dixon, Winterburn, Parlour, Linighan, Adams, Jensen, Wright, Smith, Merson (Campbell), McGoldrick (Davis).

Nov 30 Aston Villa 0–1
Att: 26,453
Seaman, Dixon (Campbell), Winterburn, Morrow, Keown, Bould, Jensen (Davis), Wright, Smith, Merson, McGoldrick.

EUROPEAN CUP WINNERS' CUP
Winners

Sep 29 Odense 1–1
(Campbell) Att: 25,689
Seaman, Dixon, Winterburn, Davis, Keown, Adams, Jensen, Wright (Smith), Campbell, Merson, McGoldrick.

Oct 20 Standard Liege 3–0
(Wright 2, Merson) Att: 25,258
Seaman, Dixon, Winterburn, Davis, Keown (Linighan), Adams, Jensen, Wright (Campbell), Smith, Merson, McGoldrick.

Mar 15 Torino 1–0
(Adams) Att: 34,678
Seaman, Dixon, Winterburn, Davis, Bould, Adams, Jensen (Keown), Wright, Smith, Merson, Hillier (Selley).

Apr 12 Paris St–Germain 1–0
(Campbell) Att: 34,212
Seaman, Dixon, Winterburn (Keown), Davis (Hillier), Bould, Adams, Jensen, Wright, Smith, Campbell, Selley.

1994/95

PREMIER LEAGUE
Final position – 12th

Aug 20 Manchester City 3–0
(Campbell, Wright, Curle [og]) Att: 38,368
Seaman, Dixon, Winterburn, Jensen, Bould, Adams (Keown), Campbell, Wright, Smith, Merson (Dickov), Schwarz.

Aug 31 Blackburn Rovers 0–0
Att: 37,629
Seaman, Dixon, Winterburn, Jensen, Keown, Adams (Linighan), Campbell, Wright, Smith, Merson (Dickov), Schwarz.

Sep 18 Newcastle United 2–3
(Adams, Wright) Att: 36,819
Seaman, Dixon, Winterburn, Jensen (Selley), Keown, Adams, Parlour (Campbell), Wright, Smith, Merson, Schwarz.

Oct 1 Crystal Palace 1–2
(Wright) Att: 34,136
Seaman, Dixon, Winterburn, Davis (Campbell), Linighan, Adams, Selley, Wright, Smith, Merson, Schwarz.

Oct 15 Chelsea 3–1
(Wright 2, Campbell) Att: 38,234
Seaman, Dixon, Winterburn, Jensen (Selley), Bould, Adams (Keown), Parlour, Wright, Smith, Campbell, Schwarz.

Oct 23 Coventry City 2–1
(Wright 2) Att: 31,725
Seaman, Dixon, Winterburn, Selley, Bould, Keown, Campbell, Wright (McGoldrick), Smith, Schwarz, Parlour.

Nov 6 Sheffield Wednesday 0–0
Att: 33,705
Seaman, Keown, Winterburn, Selley, Bould, Adams, Parlour, Dickov, Smith (Campbell), Schwarz, McGoldrick.

Nov 26 **Manchester United** 0–0
Att: 38,301
Seaman, Dixon, Winterburn, Jensen (Keown), Bould, Adams, Morrow, Wright, Smith, McGoldrick, Carter (Dickov).

Dec 17 **Leeds United** 1–3
(Linighan) Att: 38,098
Bartram, Dixon, Winterburn, Morrow, Bould, Keown, Jensen (Linighan), Campbell, Smith (Flatts), Parlour, Schwarz.

Dec 26 **Aston Villa** 0–0
Att: 34,452
Bartram, Dixon, Winterburn, Morrow, Bould, Keown, Hughes (Flatts), Dickov, Campbell, Parlour, Schwarz.

Dec 31 **Queens Park Rangers** 1–3
(Jensen) Att: 32,393
Bartram, Dixon, Winterburn, Jensen, Bould, Keown, Campbell, Wright, Smith (Clarke), Parlour, Schwarz.

Jan 14 **Everton** 1–1
(Wright) Att: 34,743
Seaman, Dixon, Winterburn, Jensen (Morrow), Keown, Linighan, Hillier, Wright, Hartson, Parlour (Kiwomya), Schwarz.

Jan 24 **Southampton** 1–1
(Hartson) Att: 27,213
Seaman, Dixon, Morrow, Keown (Hillier), Bould, Linighan, Jensen, Wright, Hartson, Parlour (Kiwomya), Schwarz.

Feb 11 **Leicester City** 1–1
(Merson) Att: 31,373
Seaman, Dixon, Winterburn, Jensen (Parlour), Linighan, Adams, McGoldrick, Selley (Keown), Hartson, Merson, Kiwomya.

Feb 21 **Nottingham Forest** 1–0
(Kiwomya) Att: 35,441
Seaman, Dixon, Winterburn, Jensen, Bould, Linighan, McGoldrick, Merson, Kiwomya, Schwarz, Helder.

Mar 5 **West Ham United** 0–1
Att: 36,295
Bartram, Dixon, Winterburn, Jensen (Morrow), Bould, Linighan, Parlour, Wright, Helder (Kiwomya), Merson, Schwarz.

Apr 1 **Norwich City** 5–1
(Hartson 2, Dixon, Merson, Newman [og])
Att: 36,942
Bartram, Dixon, Winterburn, Morrow (Keown), Bould, Adams, Hillier, Wright, Hartson (Kiwomya), Merson, Helder.

Apr 12 **Liverpool** 0–1
Att: 38,036
Seaman, Keown, Winterburn, Schwarz, Bould, Adams, Hillier, Wright, McGoldrick, Merson (Parlour), Helder (Hartson).

Apr 15 **Ipswich Town** 4–1
(Merson, Wright 3) Att: 36,818
Seaman, Dixon, Winterburn (Parlour), Schwarz, Bould, Adams, Keown, Wright (Kiwomya), Hartson, Merson, Helder.

Apr 29 **Tottenham Hotspur** 1–1
(Wright [pen]) Att: 38,377
Seaman, Dixon, Winterburn, Schwarz, Bould, Adams, Keown, Wright, Hartson, Merson, Helder (Parlour).

May 4 **Wimbledon** 0–0
Att: 32,822
Seaman, Dixon, Winterburn, Jensen, Linighan, Adams, Parlour, Wright, Hartson (Kiwomya), Merson, Helder.

FA CUP

Jan 18 **Millwall** 0–2
Att: 32,319
Seaman, Dixon, Winterburn, Jensen (Flatts), Keown (Adams), Linighan, Hillier, Wright, Campbell, Parlour, Morrow.

FOOTBALL LEAGUE (COCA-COLA) CUP

Oct 5 **Hartlepool United** 2–0
(Campbell, Dickov) Att: 20,520
Seaman, Dixon, Winterburn, Davis, Bould, Keown, Parlour, Dickov, Campbell, Hillier, McGoldrick.

Nov 9 **Oldham Athletic** 2–0
(Dickov 2) Att: 22,746
Seaman, Keown, Winterburn, Selley (Jensen), Bould, Adams, Parlour, Dickov, Campbell, McGoldrick, Schwarz.

Nov 30 **Sheffield Wednesday** 2–0
(Morrow, Wright) Att: 27,390
Seaman (Bartram), Dixon, Winterburn, Morrow (Keown), Bould, Adams, Campbell, Wright, Smith, McGoldrick (Dickov), Schwarz.

EUROPEAN CUP WINNERS' CUP
Finalists

Sep 29 **Omonia Nicosia** 3–0
(Wright 2, Schwarz) Att: 24,265
Seaman, Dixon, Winterburn, Schwarz, Linighan, Adams, Jensen (Hillier), Wright, Smith, Merson (Campbell), Parlour.

Nov 3 **Brondby** 2–2
(Wright [pen], Selley) Att: 32,290
Seaman, Dixon (Bould), Winterburn, Selley, Keown, Adams, Jensen, Wright (Campbell), Smith, Merson, Parlour.

Mar 2 **Auxerre** 1–1
(Wright [pen]) Att: 35,508
Seaman, Dixon, Winterburn, Schwarz, Bould, Adams, Jensen, Wright, Kiwomya (Parlour), Merson, McGoldrick (Hartson).

Apr 6 **Sampdoria** 3–2
(Bould 2, Wright) Att: 38,089
Seaman, Dixon, Winterburn, Schwarz, Bould, Adams, Hillier, Wright (Kiwomya), Hartson, Merson (Morrow), Parlour.

EUROPEAN SUPER CUP

Feb 1 **AC Milan** 0–0
Att: 38,041
Seaman, Dixon, Winterburn, Schwarz, Bould, Adams, Jensen (Hillier), Wright, Hartson, Selley, Campbell (Merson).

1995/96

PREMIER LEAGUE
Final position – 5th

Aug 20 **Middlesbrough** 1–1
(Wright) Att: 37,308
Seaman, Dixon, Winterburn, Keown, Bould, Adams, Platt, Wright, Merson, Bergkamp, Parlour (Helder).

Aug 29 **Nottingham Forest** 1–1
(Platt) Att: 38,248
Seaman, Dixon, Winterburn, Keown, Bould, Adams, Platt, Wright, Merson, Bergkamp, Parlour (Helder).

Sep 16 **West Ham United** 1–0
(Wright [pen]) Att: 38,065
Seaman, Dixon, Winterburn, Jensen, Bould, Adams, Parlour, Wright, Merson, Bergkamp, Helder.

Sep 23 **Southampton** 4–2
(Bergkamp 2, Adams, Wright) Att: 38,136
Seaman, Dixon, Winterburn, Keown, Bould, Adams, Parlour, Wright, Merson, Bergkamp, Helder.

Oct 21 **Aston Villa** 2–0
(Merson, Wright) Att: 38,271
Seaman, Dixon, Winterburn, Keown, Bould, Adams, Parlour, Wright, Merson, Bergkamp, Helder.

Nov 4 **Manchester United** 1–0
(Bergkamp) Att: 38,317
Seaman, Dixon, Winterburn, Keown, Bould, Adams, Platt, Wright (Hartson), Merson, Bergkamp, Helder.

Nov 21 **Sheffield Wednesday** 4–2
(Bergkamp, Winterburn, Dickov, Hartson)
Att: 34,556
Seaman, Dixon, Winterburn, Keown, Bould, Adams, Platt, Hartson, Merson, Bergkamp, Helder (Dickov).

Nov 26 **Blackburn Rovers** 0–0
Att: 37,695
Seaman, Dixon, Winterburn, Keown (Helder), Bould, Adams, Platt, Hartson (Dickov), Merson, Bergkamp, Hillier.

Dec 16 **Chelsea** 1–1
(Dixon) Att: 38,295
Seaman, Dixon, Winterburn, Keown, Bould, Adams, Platt, Wright, Merson, Hartson, Jensen (Helder).

Dec 26 **Queens Park Rangers** 3–0
(Wright, Merson 2) Att: 38,259
Seaman, Dixon, Winterburn, Jensen, Keown, Adams, Platt, Wright, Merson, Dickov, Clarke.

Dec 30 **Wimbledon** 1–3
(Wright) Att: 37,640
Seaman, Dixon, Winterburn, Jensen (Dickov), Keown, Linighan, Platt, Wright, Merson, Bergkamp, Clarke (Parlour).

Jan 20 **Everton** 1–2
(Wright) Att: 38,275
Seaman, Dixon, Winterburn, Jensen, Linighan, Marshall, Clarke (Dickov), Wright, Merson, Bergkamp, Helder.

Feb 3 **Coventry City** 1–1
(Bergkamp) Att: 35,623
Seaman, Dixon, Winterburn, Jensen (Hughes), Linighan, Marshall, Clarke, Wright, Merson, Bergkamp, Helder.

Mar 5 **Manchester City** 3–1
(Hartson 2, Dixon) Att: 34,519
Seaman, Dixon, Winterburn, Rose, Linighan, Keown, Platt, Hartson, Merson, Bergkamp, Parlour.

Mar 23 **Newcastle United** 2–0
(Marshall, Wright) Att: 38,271
Seaman, Dixon, Winterburn (Helder), Marshall, Linighan, Keown, Platt, Wright (Parlour), Merson, Bergkamp, Hartson.

Apr 6 **Leeds United** 2–1
(Wright 2) Att: 37,619
Seaman, Dixon, Winterburn, Marshall, Linighan, Keown, Platt, Wright, Merson, Bergkamp, Hartson.

Apr 15 **Tottenham Hotspur** 0–0
Att: 38,273
Seaman, Dixon, Winterburn, Marshall, Linighan, Keown, Platt, Wright, Merson (Helder), Bergkamp, Parlour.

May 1 **Liverpool** 0–0
Att: 38,323
Seaman, Dixon, Winterburn, Marshall, Linighan, Keown, Platt, Hartson, Merson, Bergkamp, Parlour.

May 5 **Bolton Wanderers** 2–1
(Platt, Bergkamp) Att: 38,104
Seaman, Dixon, Winterburn, Marshall (Shaw), Linighan, Keown, Platt, Wright (Hartson), Merson, Bergkamp, Parlour.

FA CUP

Jan 6 **Sheffield United** 1–1
(Wright) Att: 33,453
Seaman, Dixon, Winterburn, Jensen, Keown, Adams, Clarke, Wright, Merson, Hartson, Helder.

FOOTBALL LEAGUE (COCA-COLA) CUP

Oct 3 **Hartlepool United** 5–0
(Bergkamp 2, Wright 3) Att: 27,194
Seaman, Dixon, Winterburn, Keown, Bould, Adams, Parlour Wright, Merson (Helder), Bergkamp (Hartson), Jensen.

Nov 29 **Sheffield Wednesday** 2–1
(Wright [pen], Hartson) Att: 35,361
Seaman, Dixon, Winterburn, Jensen, Bould, Adams, Platt, Wright, Merson, Bergkamp (Helder), Hartson.

Jan 10 **Newcastle United** 2–0
(Wright 2) Att: 37,857
Seaman, Dixon, Winterburn, Keown, Bould (Jensen), Adams, Platt, Wright, Merson, Bergkamp, Helder.

Feb 14 **Aston Villa** 2–2
(Bergkamp 2) Att: 37,562
Seaman, Dixon, Winterburn, Jensen, Linighan, Keown, Hillier, Wright, Merson, Bergkamp, Helder (Parlour).

1996/97

PREMIER LEAGUE
Final position – 3rd

Aug 17 **West Ham United** 2–0
(Hartson, Bergkamp [pen]) Att: 38,056
Seaman, Dixon, Winterburn, Keown, Bould, Linighan, Parlour, Morrow, Merson, Bergkamp (Wright), Hartson (Dickov).

Sep 4 **Chelsea** 3–3
(Merson, Keown, Wright) Att: 38,132
Lukic, Dixon, Winterburn, Keown, Bould (Wright), Linighan, Parlour, Morrow (Platt), Merson, Bergkamp, Hartson.

Sep 16 **Sheffield Wednesday** 4–1
(Platt, Wright 3 [1 pen]) Att: 33,461
Seaman, Dixon, Winterburn, Keown, Bould, Linighan, Platt, Wright, Merson, Parlour (Vieira), Hartson.

Sep 28 **Sunderland** 2–0
(Hartson, Parlour) Att: 38,016
Seaman, Dixon, Winterburn (Shaw), Keown, Bould, Adams, Platt, Wright, Merson, Vieira (Parlour), Hartson.

Oct 19 **Coventry City** 0–0
Att: 38,140
Seaman, Dixon, Winterburn, Keown, Bould, Adams, Platt, Wright, Merson, Vieira, Hartson (Bergkamp).

Oct 26 **Leeds United** 3–0
(Dixon, Bergkamp, Wright) Att: 38,076
Seaman, Dixon, Winterburn (Morrow), Keown, Bould, Adams, Platt, Wright (Garde), Merson, Bergkamp, Vieira.

Nov 24 **Tottenham Hotspur** 3–1
(Wright [pen], Adams, Bergkamp) Att: 38,264
Lukic, Dixon, Winterburn, Keown, Bould, Adams, Platt (Hartson), Wright, Merson, Bergkamp (Parlour), Vieira.

Dec 4 **Southampton** 3–1
(Merson, Wright [pen], Shaw) Att: 38,033
Lukic, Dixon, Winterburn, Keown, Bould, Adams, Platt (Parlour), Wright, Merson, Hartson (Shaw), Vieira.

Dec 7 **Derby County** 2–2
(Adams, Vieira) Att: 38,018
Lukic, Dixon, Winterburn, Linighan (Shaw), Bould, Adams, Platt, Wright, Merson, Hartson, Vieira.

Dec 28 **Aston Villa** 2–2
(Wright, Merson) Att: 38,130
Lukic, Parlour, Winterburn, Keown, Bould, Adams, Garde (Morrow), Wright, Merson, Bergkamp, Vieira.

Jan 1 **Middlesbrough** 2–0
(Bergkamp, Wright) Att: 37,573
Lukic, Parlour, Winterburn, Keown, Bould, Adams, Garde (Morrow), Wright, Merson (Shaw), Bergkamp (Hartson), Vieira.

Jan 19 **Everton** 3–1
(Bergkamp, Vieira, Merson) Att: 38,095
Seaman, Dixon, Winterburn, Keown, Bould, Adams, Platt (Hughes), Wright (Dixon), Merson, Bergkamp, Vieira.

Feb 19 **Manchester United** 1–2
(Bergkamp) Att: 38,172
Lukic, Dixon, Winterburn, Keown, Bould, Adams (Hughes), Parlour, Wright, Merson, Bergkamp, Vieira.

Feb 23 **Wimbledon** 0–1
Att: 37,854
Lukic, Dixon, Winterburn, Garde (Shaw), Bould (Morrow), Marshall, Parlour (Hughes), Wright, Merson, Bergkamp, Vieira.

Mar 8 **Nottingham Forest** 2–0
(Bergkamp 2 [1 pen]) Att: 38,206
Lukic, Dixon, Winterburn, Keown, Marshall, Adams, Platt, Hughes (Morrow), Merson, Bergkamp, Vieira.

Mar 24 **Liverpool** 1–2
(Wright) Att: 38,068
Seaman, Dixon (Garde), Winterburn, Keown, Marshall (Parlour), Adams, Platt, Wright, Hughes (Shaw), Bergkamp, Vieira.

Apr 12 **Leicester City** 2–0
(Adams, Platt) Att: 38,044
Seaman, Dixon, Winterburn, Keown, Bould, Adams, Platt, Wright, Hughes (Parlour), Bergkamp, Vieira.

Apr 19 **Blackburn Rovers** 1–1
(Platt) Att: 38,086
Seaman, Dixon, Winterburn, Keown, Bould, Adams, Platt, Wright, Hughes (Parlour), Bergkamp, Vieira.

May 3 **Newcastle United** 0–1
Att: 38,179
Seaman, Dixon, Winterburn, Keown, Bould, Adams (Parlour), Platt (Anelka), Wright, Merson, Bergkamp, Vieira.

FA CUP

Jan 4 **Sunderland** 1–1
(Hartson) Att: 37,793
Lukic, Parlour, Winterburn, Keown, Bould, Adams, Morrow (Shaw), Hartson, Merson, Bergkamp, Vieira.

Feb 4 **Leeds United** 0–1
Att: 38,115
Seaman, Dixon, Morrow, Keown, Bould, Adams, Parlour, Wright, Merson, Hughes (Hartson), Vieira.

FOOTBALL LEAGUE (COCA-COLA) CUP

Nov 13 **Stoke City** 5–2
(Wright 2 [1 pen], Platt, Bergkamp, Merson)
Att: 33,962
Seaman, Dixon, Winterburn, Keown, Bould, Adams, Platt, Wright, Merson, Bergkamp (Hartson), Vieira (Morrow).

UEFA CUP

Sep 10 **Borussia Monchengladbach** 2–3
(Merson, Wright) Att: 36,894
Seaman, Dixon, Winterburn, Keown, Linighan, Parlour (Bould), Platt, Wright, Merson, Bergkamp (Helder), Hartson.

1997/98

PREMIER LEAGUE

Final position–Champions

Aug 11 **Coventry City** **2–0**
(Wright 2) Att: 37,324
Seaman, Garde, Winterburn, Grimandi, Marshall, Petit (Platt), Parlour, Vieira, Wright, Bergkamp, Overmars (Hughes).

Aug 30 **Tottenham Hotspur** **0–0**
Att: 38,102
Seaman, Dixon, Winterburn, Grimandi, Bould, Petit (Platt), Parlour (Anelka), Vieira, Wright, Bergkamp, Overmars.

Sep 13 **Bolton Wanderers** **4–1**
(Wright 3, Parlour) Att: 38,138
Seaman, Dixon, Winterburn, Grimandi, Bould, Petit, Parlour (Platt), Vieira, Wright (Anelka), Bergkamp, Overmars (Boa Morte).

Sep 24 **West Ham United** **4–0**
(Bergkamp, Overmars 2, Wright [pen])
Att: 38,012
Seaman, Dixon (Grimandi), Winterburn (Platt), Bould, Adams, Petit, Parlour, Vieira, Wright (Anelka), Bergkamp, Overmars.

Oct 4 **Barnsley** **5–0**
(Bergkamp 2, Parlour, Platt, Wright) Att: 38,049
Seaman, Dixon, Winterburn, Bould, Adams, Petit, Parlour (Platt), Vieira, Wright (Boa Morte), Bergkamp, Overmars (Anelka).

Oct 26 **Aston Villa** **0–0**
Att: 38,061
Seaman, Dixon, Winterburn, Bould, Adams, Petit, Parlour (Platt), Vieira, Wright, Bergkamp, Boa Morte (Anelka).

Nov 9 **Manchester United** **3–2**
(Anelka, Vieira, Platt) Att: 38,205
Seaman, Dixon, Winterburn, Grimandi, Adams, Platt, Parlour, Vieira (Bould), Wright, Anelka (Wreh), Overmars.

Nov 30 **Liverpool** **0–1**
Att: 38,094
Seaman, Dixon, Winterburn, Keown, Adams, Petit (Grimandi), Platt, Hughes (Wreh), Wright, Bergkamp, Overmars.

Dec 13 **Blackburn Rovers** **1–3**
(Overmars) Att: 38,147
Seaman, Dixon, Winterburn, Keown, Adams, Petit, Parlour (Vieira), Platt (Boa Morte), Wright, Bergkamp, Overmars.

Dec 26 **Leicester City** **2–1**
(Platt, Walsh [og]) Att: 38,023
Seaman, Dixon, Winterburn, Keown, Bould, Vieira, Parlour, Platt (Hughes), Wright (Anelka), Bergkamp, Overmars.

Jan 10 **Leeds United** **2–1**
(Overmars 2) Att: 38,018
Seaman, Dixon, Winterburn, Keown, Bould, Petit, Parlour, Vieira, Wright, Bergkamp, Overmars.

Jan 31 **Southampton** **3–0**
(Bergkamp, Adams, Anelka) Att: 38,056
Manninger, Grimandi, Winterburn, Bould, Adams, Petit, Parlour, Hughes (Platt), Anelka (Wreh), Bergkamp, Overmars.

Feb 8 **Chelsea** **2–0**
(Hughes 2) Att: 38,083
Manninger, Grimandi (Dixon), Winterburn, Bould, Adams, Petit, Parlour, Hughes, Anelka (Wright), Bergkamp, Overmars (Platt).

Feb 21 **Crystal Palace** **1–0**
(Grimandi) Att: 38,094
Manninger, Dixon, Upson, Keown, Grimandi, Vieira, Vernazza (McGowan), Platt, Anelka, Hughes, Boa Morte.

Mar 28 **Sheffield Wednesday** **1–0**
(Bergkamp) Att: 38,087
Seaman, Dixon (Garde), Winterburn, Keown, Adams, Vieira, Parlour (Grimandi), Hughes, Wreh (Anelka), Bergkamp, Overmars.

Apr 11 **Newcastle United** **3–1**
(Anelka 2, Vieira) Att: 38,102
Seaman, Garde, Winterburn, Bould, Adams, Petit, Parlour, Vieira, Wreh (Platt), Anelka (Boa Morte), Overmars (Hughes).

Apr 18 **Wimbledon** **5–0**
(Adams, Overmars, Bergkamp, Petit, Wreh)
Att: 38,024
Seaman, Garde (Dixon), Winterburn, Upson, Adams, Petit, Parlour, Vieira (Platt), Anelka (Wreh), Bergkamp, Overmars.

Apr 29 **Derby County** **1–0**
(Petit) Att: 38,121
Seaman, Dixon, Winterburn, Keown, Adams, Petit, Parlour, Vieira, Anelka (Platt), Bergkamp (Wreh), Overmars.

May 3 **Everton** **4–0**
(Overmars 2, Adams, Bilic [og]) Att: 38,269
Seaman, Dixon, Winterburn, Keown, Adams, Petit (Platt), Parlour, Vieira, Wreh (Bould), Anelka (Wright), Overmars.

FA CUP

Winners

Jan 3 **Port Vale** **0–0**
Att: 37,471
Seaman, Grimandi, Winterburn, Keown, Bould, Petit (Hughes), Parlour (Boa Morte), Vieira, Anelka (Wreh), Bergkamp, Overmars.

Feb 15 **Crystal Palace** **0–0**
Att: 37,164
Manninger, Dixon, Winterburn, Grimandi, Bould (Vieira), Petit, Parlour, Hughes (Platt), Anelka (Wreh), Bergkamp, Overmars.

Mar 8 **West Ham United** **1–1**
(Bergkamp [pen]) Att: 38,077
Manninger, Dixon, Winterburn, Keown, Adams, Petit, Parlour, Vieira, Anelka (Wreh), Bergkamp, Overmars.

FOOTBALL LEAGUE (COCA-COLA) CUP

Oct 14 **Birmingham City** **4–1***
(Boa Morte 2, Platt [pen], Mendez) Att: 27,097
Manninger, Dixon (Crowe), Upson, Grimandi, Marshall, Hughes, Vernazza, Platt, Wreh, Mendez, Boa Morte (Muntasser).

*After extra time

Nov 18 **Coventry City** **1–0***
(Bergkamp) Att: 30,199
Manninger, Dixon, Upson, Keown, Bould, Hughes, Parlour, Platt, Anelka (Wreh), Bergkamp, Mendez (Marshall).

*After extra time

Jan 28 **Chelsea** **2–1**
(Overmars, Hughes) Att: 38,114
Manninger, Grimandi (Platt), Winterburn, Bould, Adams, Petit, Parlour, Hughes, Anelka, Bergkamp, Overmars.

UEFA CUP

Sep 30 **PAOK Salonika** **1–1**
(Bergkamp) Att: 37,982
Seaman, Dixon, Winterburn, Bould, Adams, Petit, Parlour (Anelka), Vieira, Wright, Bergkamp, Overmars (Platt).

1998/99

PREMIER LEAGUE

Final position – 2nd

Aug 17 **Nottingham Forest** **2–1**
(Petit, Overmars) Att: 38,064
Seaman, Dixon, Winterburn, Keown, Adams, Parlour, Vieira, Petit, Overmars, Anelka, Bergkamp.

Aug 29 **Charlton Athletic** **0–0**
Att: 38,014
Seaman, Dixon (Vivas), Winterburn, Keown, Adams, Parlour, Vieira (Hughes), Petit, Overmars, Anelka (Wreh), Bergkamp.

Sep 20 **Manchester United** **3–0**
(Adams, Anelka, Ljungberg) Att: 38,142
Seaman, Dixon, Winterburn, Keown, Adams, Parlour, Vieira, Hughes, Overmars, Anelka (Ljungberg), Bergkamp.

Oct 4 **Newcastle United** **3–0**
(Bergkamp 2 [1 pen], Anelka) Att: 38,102
Seaman, Dixon, Winterburn, Keown (Bould), Adams, Ljungberg (Mendez), Vieira, Petit (Hughes), Overmars, Anelka, Bergkamp.

Oct 17 **Southampton** **1–1**
(Anelka) Att: 38,027
Seaman, Dixon, Winterburn, Keown, Adams, Parlour (Wreh), Vieira, Hughes, Overmars, Anelka, Bergkamp.

Nov 8 **Everton** **1–0**
(Anelka) Att: 38,088
Seaman, Dixon, Winterburn, Keown, Grimandi, Parlour, Vieira, Petit, Overmars, Anelka, Ljungberg.

Nov 14 **Tottenham Hotspur** **0–0**
Att: 38,278
Seaman, Dixon, Winterburn, Keown, Adams, Parlour, Vieira, Petit, Overmars, Anelka (Boa Morte), Ljungberg (Wreh).

Nov 29 **Middlesbrough** **1–1**
(Anelka) Att: 38,075
Seaman, Dixon, Winterburn (Vivas), Keown, Bould, Parlour, Garde, Ljungberg (Caballero), Overmars, Anelka, Wreh (Boa Morte).

Dec 20 **Leeds United** **3–1**
(Bergkamp, Vieira, Petit) Att: 38,025
Manninger, Dixon, Vivas, Keown, Bould, Ljungberg (Grimandi), Vieira, Petit, Overmars (Wreh), Anelka, Bergkamp.

Dec 26 **West Ham United** **1–0**
(Overmars) Att: 38,098
Manninger, Dixon, Vivas, Keown, Bould, Parlour, Vieira, Petit, Overmars, Anelka (Wreh / Grimandi), Bergkamp.

Jan 9 **Liverpool** **0–0**
Att: 38,107
Manninger, Dixon, Grondin, Keown, Bould (Upson), Parlour, Vieira, Petit, Overmars (Garde), Anelka (Wreh), Boa Morte.

Jan 31 **Chelsea** **1–0**
(Bergkamp) Att: 38,121
Seaman, Dixon, Winterburn, Keown, Adams, Parlour, Garde, Petit, Overmars (Diawara), Anelka (Vivas), Bergkamp (Upson).

Feb 20 **Leicester City** **5–0**
(Anelka 3, Parlour 2) Att: 38,069
Seaman, Dixon, Vivas, Grimandi, Adams, Parlour, Vieira (Hughes), Garde, Overmars (Diawara), Anelka (Kanu), Bergkamp.

Mar 9 **Sheffield Wednesday** **3–0**
(Bergkamp 2, Kanu) Att: 37,792
Seaman, Dixon, Vivas, Keown, Adams, Parlour (Petit), Vieira, Ljungberg (Diawara), Overmars, Anelka (Kanu), Bergkamp.

Mar 20 **Coventry City** **2–0**
(Parlour, Overmars) Att: 38,073
Seaman, Dixon (Ljungberg), Winterburn, Keown, Adams, Parlour, Vieira, Petit, Overmars (Diawara), Anelka (Kanu), Bergkamp.

Apr 6 **Blackburn Rovers** **1–0**
(Bergkamp) Att: 37,762
Seaman, Dixon, Winterburn, Keown, Adams, Parlour, Vieira, Vivas, Overmars (Bould), Diawara (Kanu), Bergkamp.

Apr 19 **Wimbledon** **5–1**
(Parlour, Vieira, Bergkamp, Kanu, Thatcher [og])
Att: 37,982
Seaman, Vivas, Winterburn, Keown (Bould), Adams, Parlour, Vieira, Petit, Overmars, Kanu, Bergkamp (Diawara).

May 2 **Derby County** **1–0**
(Anelka) Att: 37,323
Seaman, Dixon, Winterburn, Bould, Adams, Parlour, Vieira, Petit, Overmars (Hughes), Anelka (Diawara), Kanu (Bergkamp).

May 16 **Aston Villa** **1–0**
(Kanu) Att: 38,308
Seaman, Dixon, Vivas (Ljungberg),Keown, Adams, Parlour, Vieira, Petit, Overmars (Diawara), Anelka (Kanu), Bergkamp.

FA CUP

Feb 13 **Sheffield United** **2–1**
(Vieira, Overmars) Att: 38,020
Result Void, match replayed.
Seaman, Vivas, Winterburn, Grimandi, Bould, Parlour, Vieira, Garde (Hughes), Overmars, Diawara (Kanu), Bergkamp.

Feb 23 **Sheffield United** **2–1**
(Overmars, Bergkamp) Att: 37,161
Seaman, Vivas, Winterburn, Bould, Adams, Parlour, Vieira, Hughes, Overmars (Garde), Anelka (Kanu), Bergkamp (Diawara).

Mar 6 **Derby County** **1–0**
(Kanu) Att: 38,046
Seaman, Dixon, Winterburn, Keown, Adams, Parlour, Hughes (Vivas), Ljungberg (Kanu), Overmars (Diawara), Anelka, Bergkamp.

FOOTBALL LEAGUE (WORTHINGTON) CUP

Nov 11 **Chelsea** **0–5**
Att: 37,562
Manninger, Vivas, Grondin, Upson, Grimandi, Ljungberg, Garde (Mendez), Hughes, Boa Morte, Wreh, Bergkamp (Caballero).

UEFA CHAMPIONS LEAGUE

Arsenal's home matches were played at Wembley Stadium this season.

1999/2000

PREMIER LEAGUE

Final position – 2nd

Aug 7 **Leicester City** **2–1**
(Bergkamp, Sinclair [og]) Att: 38,026
Manninger, Dixon, Keown, Grimandi, Winterburn, Parlour (Overmars), Vieira, Petit, Ljungberg (Henry), Kanu, Bergkamp (Silvinho).

Aug 22 **Manchester United** **1–2**
(Ljungberg) Att: 38,147
Manninger, Dixon, Keown, Upson, Silvinho, Parlour, Vieira, Ljungberg, Henry (Suker), Kanu (Overmars), Bergkamp.

Aug 25 **Bradford City** **2–0**
(Vieira, Kanu [pen]) Att: 38,073
Manninger, Vivas, Keown, Grimandi, Silvinho, Parlour, Vieira, Ljungberg, Henry (Overmars), Kanu (Upson), Bergkamp (Suker).

Sep 11 **Aston Villa** **3–1**
(Suker 2, Kanu) Att: 38,093
Manninger, Dixon, Keown, Adams, Winterburn, Parlour, Vieira, Grimandi, Overmars (Henry), Suker (Silvinho), Bergkamp (Kanu).

Sep 25 **Watford** **1–0**
(Kanu) Att: 38,127
Manninger, Luzhny, Keown, Adams, Silvinho, Parlour, Vieira, Ljungberg (Suker), Overmars, Kanu (Vivas), Henry (Bergkamp).

Oct 16 **Everton** **4–1**
(Dixon, Suker 2, Kanu) Att: 38,042
Seaman, Dixon, Keown, Adams, Winterburn, Parlour (Ljungberg), Vieira, Grimandi, Overmars (Silvinho), Suker, Bergkamp (Kanu)

Oct 30 **Newcastle United** **0–0**
Att: 38,106
Seaman, Luzhny, Keown (Upson), Adams, Winterburn, Ljungberg, Vieira, Grimandi, Silvinho (Overmars), Henry (Bergkamp), Suker

Nov 20 **Middlesbrough** **5–1**
(Overmars 3, Bergkamp 2) Att: 38,082
Seaman, Dixon (Vivas), Grimandi (Upson), Adams, Winterburn, Ljungberg, Parlour, Petit, Overmars, Kanu, Bergkamp (Suker).

Nov 28 **Derby County** **2–1**
(Henry 2) Att: 37,964
Manninger, Luzhny, Upson, Adams, Winterburn, Parlour, Grimandi, Petit, Overmars (Malz), Henry (Suker), Bergkamp (Kanu).

Dec 18 **Wimbledon** **1–1**
(Henry) Att: 38,052
Manninger, Dixon, Luzhny, Grimandi, Winterburn (Suker), Silvinho, Ljungberg, Petit, Overmars, Henry, Kanu.

Dec 28 **Leeds United** **2–0**
(Ljungberg, Henry) Att: 38,096
Seaman, Luzhny, Grimandi, Adams, Silvinho, Ljungberg, Vieira, Petit (Winterburn), Overmars, Henry (Suker), Kanu.

Jan 15 **Sunderland** **4–1**
(Henry 2, Suker 2) Att: 38,039
Seaman, Dixon, Keown, Luzhny, Silvinho, Parlour, Vieira, Petit, Ljungberg (Malz), Henry (Barrett), Suker.

Feb 13 **Liverpool** **0–1**
Att: 38,098
Seaman, Dixon, Keown, Grimandi, Silvinho, Parlour, Vieira, Petit (Overmars), Ljungberg (Luzhny), Henry, Bergkamp (Suker).

Feb 26 **Southampton** **3–1**
(Ljungberg 2, Bergkamp) Att: 38,044
Seaman, Dixon, Keown, Adams, Silvinho, Parlour, Vieira, Petit, Ljungberg, Kanu, Bergkamp (Overmars).

Mar 19 **Tottenham Hotspur** **2–1**
(Henry [pen], Armstrong [og]) Att:38,131
Manninger, Dixon, Luzhny, Adams, Silvinho, Parlour, Vieira, Grimandi, Overmars (Ljungberg), Henry (Winterburn), Kanu.

Mar 26 **Coventry City** **3–0**
(Henry, Grimandi, Kanu) Att: 38,027
Seaman, Dixon, Luzhny, Grimandi, Winterburn, Parlour, Vieira, Petit, Overmars (Suker), Henry (Ljungberg), Bergkamp (Kanu).

May 2 **West Ham United** **2–1**
(Overmars, Petit) Att: 38,093
Seaman, Dixon (Petit), Luzhny, Adams, Silvinho, Parlour, Vieira, Grimandi, Overmars, Kanu, Bergkamp.

May 6 **Chelsea** **2–1**
(Henry 2) Att: 38,119
Seaman, Dixon, Grimandi, Adams, Silvinho, Parlour, Vieira, Petit (Luzhny), Overmars (Winterburn), Henry, Bergkamp (Kanu).

May 9 **Sheffield Wednesday** **3–3**
(Dixon, Silvinho, Henry) Att: 37,271
Seaman, Dixon, Keown, Luzhny, Winterburn (Silvinho), Parlour (Bergkamp), Vieira, Grimandi, Overmars, Henry, Kanu.

FA CUP

Dec 13 **Blackpool** **3–1**
(Grimandi, Adams, Overmars) Att: 34,143
Manninger, Dixon, Adams, Luzhny, Silvinho, Ljungberg (Hughes), Grimandi, Petit, Overmars, Suker (Kanu), Henry.

Jan 9 **Leicester City** 0–0
Att: 35,710
Seaman, Dixon, Keown, Grimandi, Silvinho, Ljungberg, Vieira, Petit, Malz (Kanu), Suker, Henry.

FOOTBALL LEAGUE (WORTHINGTON) CUP

Oct 12 **Preston North End** 2–1
(Kanu, Malz) Att: 15,239
Seaman, Luzhny, Grimandi, Upson, Winterburn, Parlour, Vernazza (Overmars), Malz, Silvinho, Kanu (Wreh), Henry.

UEFA CHAMPIONS LEAGUE

Arsenal's home matches were played at Wembley Stadium this season.

UEFA CUP
Finalists

Nov 25 **FC Nantes** 3–0
(Overmars [pen], Winterburn, Bergkamp)
Att: 36,118
Seaman, Vivas, Grimandi, Adams, Winterburn, Ljungberg (Henry), Vieira, Petit (Parlour), Overmars, Kanu (Suker), Bergkamp.

Mar 2 **Deportivo La Coruña** 5–1
(Dixon, Henry 2, Kanu, Bergkamp) Att: 37,837
Seaman, Dixon, Luzhny, Keown, Silvinho, Ljungberg, Grimandi, Petit, Overmars (Kanu), Henry (Suker), Bergkamp (Parlour).

Mar 16 **Werder Bremen** 2–0
(Henry, Ljungberg) Att: 38,009
Seaman,Dixon, Luzhny, Adams, Silvinho, Ljungberg, Vieira, Grimandi, Parlour (Overmars), Henry (Suker), Bergkamp (Kanu).

Apr 6 **RC Lens** 1–0
(Bergkamp) Att: 38,102
Seaman, Dixon, Grimandi, Keown, Silvinho, Parlour, Vieira, Petit, Overmars (Ljungberg), Kanu, Bergkamp (Suker).

2000/01

PREMIER LEAGUE
Final position – 2nd

Aug 21 **Liverpool** 2–0
(Lauren, Henry) Att: 38,014
Seaman, Luzhny, Keown, Adams, Silvinho, Lauren, Grimandi, Vieira, Pires, Henry, Bergkamp (Kanu).

Aug 26 **Charlton Athletic** 5–3
(Vieira 2, Henry 2, Silvinho) Att: 38,025
Seaman, Dixon, Keown, Adams, Silvinho, Lauren (Bergkamp), Grimandi, Vieira, Pires, Henry, Kanu.

Sep 16 **Coventry City** 2–1
(Wiltord, Vernazza) Att: 37,794
Seaman, Luzhny, Keown, Adams, Silvinho, Parlour (Vernazza), Grimandi, Ljungberg, Pires, Bergkamp (Kanu), Wiltord (Henry).

Oct 1 **Manchester United** 1–0
(Henry) Att: 38,146
Seaman, Luzhny, Keown, Adams, Silvinho, Parlour, Grimandi, Ljungberg, Bergkamp (Wiltord), Henry, Kanu (Vivas).

Oct 14 **Aston Villa** 1–0
(Henry) Att: 38,042
Seaman, Dixon, Grimandi, Adams, Silvinho, Lauren, Parlour, Vieira, Bergkamp (Luzhny), Henry (Wiltord), Pires (Kanu).

Oct 28 **Manchester City** 5–0
(Cole, Bergkamp, Wiltord, Henry 2) Att: 38,049
Lukic, Luzhny (Dixon), Keown, Adams, Cole, Parlour (Wiltord), Grimandi, Vieira, Bergkamp,Henry, Pires (Ljungberg).

Nov 11 **Derby County** 0–0
Att: 37,679
Lukic, Luzhny, Keown, Grimandi (Dixon), Silvinho, Ljungberg (Kanu), Parlour, Vieira, Bergkamp, Henry, Wiltord.

Dec 2 **Southampton** 1–0
(Lundekvam [og]) Att: 38,036
Manninger, Luzhny, Keown, Adams, Silvinho (Dixon), Ljungberg, Grimandi, Vieira, Bergkamp, Wiltord (Henry), Pires (Kanu).

Dec 9 **Newcastle United** 5–0
(Henry, Parlour 3, Kanu) Att: 38,052
Manninger, Dixon, Keown, Adams, Vivas, Ljungberg (Luzhny), Grimandi (Lauren), Parlour, Pires, Henry, Kanu (Bergkamp).

Dec 26 **Leicester City** 6–1
(Henry 3, Vieira, Ljungberg, Adams) Att: 38,007
Manninger, Dixon, Stepanovs, Adams, Silvinho, Parlour, Grimandi (Vivas), Vieira, Pires (Cole), Henry, Kanu (Ljungberg).

Dec 30 **Sunderland** 2–2
(Vieira, Dixon) Att: 38,026
Manninger, Dixon, Stepanovs, Adams, Silvinho, Ljungberg, Grimandi, Vieira, Pires, Henry (Danilevicius), Kanu (Parlour).

Jan 13 **Chelsea** 1–1
(Pires) Att: 38,071
Seaman, Dixon, Stepanovs, Keown, Silvinho, Ljungberg (Vivas), Parlour, Vieira, Pires, Henry, Wiltord.

Jan 30 **Bradford City** 2–0
(Parlour, Lauren) Att: 37,318
Seaman, Dixon, Stepanovs, Adams, Cole, Lauren (Grimandi), Parlour, Vieira,Pires, Henry, Bergkamp (Kanu).

Feb 10 **Ipswich Town** 1–0
(Henry) Att: 38,011
Seaman, Dixon, Stepanovs, Adams, Cole, Lauren (Henry), Parlour, Grimandi, Pires, Wiltord (Ljungberg), Bergkamp.

Mar 3 **West Ham United** 3–0
(Wiltord 3) Att: 38,071
Seaman, Dixon, Grimandi, Adams, Cole (Vivas), Ljungberg, Lauren, Vieira, Pires (Edu), Wiltord (Henry), Bergkamp.

Mar 31 **Tottenham Hotspur** 2–0
(Pires, Henry) Att: 38,121
Seaman, Dixon (Luzhny), Keown, Adams, Cole, Lauren (Kanu), Parlour, Vieira, Pires, Henry, Wiltord.

Apr 14 **Middlesbrough** 0–3
Att: 37,879
Seaman, Dixon, Keown, Adams, Silvinho, Ljungberg (Parlour), Edu (Wiltord), Vieira, Pires, Henry, Kanu.

Apr 21 **Everton** 4–1
(Ljungberg, Grimandi, Wiltord, Henry)
Att: 38,029
Seaman, Dixon, Keown, Adams, Cole, Ljungberg, Grimandi (Vivas), Vieira, Pires (Silvinho), Henry, Wiltord.

May 5 **Leeds United** 2–1
(Ljungberg, Wiltord) Att: 38,142
Seaman, Dixon, Keown, Adams, Cole, Ljungberg, Grimandi, Vieira, Pires, Henry, Wiltord (Parlour).

FA CUP
Finalists

Feb 18 **Chelsea** 3–1
(Henry [pen], Wiltord 2) Att: 38,096
Seaman, Dixon, Stepanovs, Luzhny, Cole, Lauren, Vieira, Ljungberg, Pires (Wiltord), Henry, Bergkamp (Vivas).

Mar 10 **Blackburn Rovers** 3–0
(Wiltord, Adams, Pires) Att: 36,604
Seaman, Dixon, Luzhny, Adams, Cole, Lauren, Grimandi, Ljungberg (Silvinho), Pires (Vieira), Bergkamp (Henry), Wiltord.

FOOTBALL LEAGUE (WORTHINGTON) CUP

Nov 1 **Ipswich Town** 1–2
(Stepanovs) Att: 26,105
Taylor, Weston (Canoville), Stepanovs, Upson, Cole, Vivas, Pennant (Mendez), Vernazza, Barrett, Wiltord, Volz (Wreh).

UEFA CHAMPIONS LEAGUE

Sep 20 **Shakhtar Donetsk** 3–2
(Wiltord, Keown 2) Att: 34,922
Seaman, Dixon, Keown, Luzhny, Silvinho, Ljungberg (Bergkamp), Vieira, Grimandi, Pires (Wiltord), Henry, Kanu.

Sep 27 **Lazio** 2–0
(Ljungberg 2) Att: 34,521
Seaman, Luzhny, Keown, Adams, Silvinho, Ljungberg, Vieira, Parlour, Bergkamp (Vivas), Henry (Wiltord), Kanu.

Oct 25 **Sparta Prague** 4–2
(Parlour, Lauren, Dixon, Kanu) Att: 34,479
Seaman, Dixon, Vivas, Luzhny, Silvinho (Cole), Lauren, Vieira, Parlour, Pires (Bergkamp), Henry (Wiltord), Kanu.

Dec 5 **Bayern Munich** 2–2
(Henry, Kanu) Att: 35,318
Manninger, Luzhny (Lauren), Keown, Adams, Cole, Ljungberg, Vieira, Grimandi, Pires (Wiltord), Henry, Kanu.

Feb 21 **Olympique Lyonnais** 1–1
(Bergkamp) Att: 34,303
Seaman, Dixon, Grimandi, Luzhny, Cole, Ljungberg, Vieira, Parlour, Pires (Lauren), Henry (Kanu), Bergkamp (Wiltord).

Mar 6 **Spartak Moscow** 1–0
(Henry) Att: 35,196
Seaman, Dixon, Grimandi, Adams, Cole, Ljungberg, Vieira, Lauren, Pires (Wiltord), Henry (Vivas), Bergkamp (Kanu).

Apr 4 **Valencia** 2–1
(Henry, Parlour) Att: 35,104
Seaman, Dixon, Keown, Adams, Cole, Ljungberg (Wiltord), Vieira, Parlour, Pires, Henry, Kanu (Lauren).

2001/02

PREMIER LEAGUE
Final position – Champions

Aug 21 **Leeds United** 1–2
(Wiltord) Att: 38,062
Seaman, Lauren, Campbell, Adams, Cole, Parlour (Bergkamp), Pires, Vieira, Ljungberg (Jeffers), Henry, Wiltord (van Bronckhorst)

Aug 25 **Leicester City** 4–0
(Ljungberg, Wiltord, Henry, Kanu) Att: 37,909
Seaman, Lauren, Campbell, Adams, Cole, van Bronckhorst, Pires, Vieira, Ljungberg (Grimandi), Bergkamp (Kanu), Wiltord (Henry)

Sep 22 **Bolton Wanderers** 1–1
(Jeffers) Att: 38,014
Seaman, Luzhny, Grimandi (Upson), Adams, Cole, Parlour (Pires), van Bronckhorst (Jeffers), Vieira, Bergkamp, Henry, Wiltord.

Oct 20 **Blackburn Rovers** 3–3
(Pires, Bergkamp, Henry) Att: 38,108
Wright, Lauren, Keown, Upson, van Bronckhorst, Parlour (Kanu), Pires (Wiltord), Vieira, Grimandi, Henry, Bergkamp.

Nov 4 **Charlton Athletic** 2–4
(Henry 2 [1 pen]) Att: 38,010
Wright, Lauren, Keown, Grimandi, Cole (Wiltord), van Bronckhorst, Pires, Vieira, Ljungberg, Henry, Bergkamp.

Nov 25 **Manchester United** 3–1
(Ljungberg, Henry 2) Att: 38,174
Taylor, Lauren, Campbell, Upson, Cole, Parlour, Pires (Grimandi), Vieira, Ljungberg, Henry, Kanu (Bergkamp).

Dec 9 **Aston Villa** 3–2
(Wiltord, Henry 2) Att: 38,074
Taylor, Lauren, Campbell, Upson (Keown), Cole, Parlour, Pires, Vieira, Ljungberg (Wiltord), Henry, Bergkamp (Kanu).

Dec 18 **Newcastle United** 1–3
(Pires) Att: 38,012
Taylor, Lauren, Campbell, Keown, Cole, Parlour, Pires, Vieira, Kanu (van Bronckhorst), Henry, Wiltord (Bergkamp).

Dec 26 **Chelsea** 2–1
(Campbell, Wiltord) Att: 38,079
Taylor, Lauren, Campbell, Keown, Cole, Parlour (van Bronckhorst), Pires, Vieira, Ljungberg (Wiltord), Henry, Kanu (Bergkamp).

Dec 29 **Middlesbrough** 2–1
(Pires, Cole) Att: 37,948
Taylor, Luzhny, Campbell, Keown, Cole, van Bronckhorst, Pires, Vieira, Ljungberg (Wiltord), Henry (Grimandi), Kanu (Bergkamp).

Jan 13 **Liverpool** 1–1
(Ljungberg) Att: 38,132
Taylor, Luzhny (Dixon), Campbell, Keown, Upson, Grimandi, Pires (Wiltord), Vieira, Ljungberg, Henry, Kanu (Bergkamp).

Feb 2 **Southampton** 1–1
(Wiltord) Att: 38,024
Wright, Luzhny, Campbell, Upson, Cole (Grimandi), Parlour, Pires, Vieira (van Bronckhorst), Wiltord, Henry, Bergkamp (Edu).

Feb 23 **Fulham** 4–1
(Lauren, Vieira, Henry 2) Att: 38,029
Seaman, Luzhny, Campbell, Stepanovs, van Bronckhorst (Dixon), Parlour, Pires (Grimandi), Vieira, Lauren, Henry (Aliadiere), Wiltord

Mar 5 **Derby County** 1–0
(Pires) Att: 37,878
Seaman, Lauren, Campbell, Stepanovs, Luzhny (Dixon), Parlour, Pires, Vieira, Wiltord (Edu), Henry, Bergkamp.

Mar 30 **Sunderland** 3–0
(Vieira, Bergkamp, Wiltord) Att: 38,047
Seaman, Luzhny, Campbell, Adams, Cole, Edu, Ljungberg (Kanu), Vieira, Wiltord (Grimandi), Henry, Bergkamp (Jeffers).

Apr 6 **Tottenham Hotspur** 2–1
(Ljungberg, Lauren [pen]) Att: 38,186
Seaman, Lauren, Campbell, Adams, Luzhny, Edu (Kanu), Ljungberg, Vieira, Wiltord (Dixon), Henry, Bergkamp (Parlour).

Apr 21 **Ipswich Town** 2–0
(Ljungberg 2) Att: 38,058
Seaman, Lauren, Keown, Adams, Cole, Edu (Kanu), Ljungberg, Vieira, Parlour, Henry, Bergkamp (Grimandi).

Apr 24 **West Ham United** 2–0
(Ljungberg, Kanu) Att: 38,038
Seaman, Lauren, Keown, Adams, Cole, Edu (Kanu), Ljungberg (Dixon), Vieira, Parlour, Henry, Bergkamp (Grimandi).

May 11 **Everton** 4–3
(Bergkamp, Henry 2, Jeffers) Att: 38,254
Wright (Taylor), Dixon, Luzhny, Stepanovs, Cole, Edu, Grimandi, Parlour (Jeffers), Wiltord (Vieira), Henry, Bergkamp.

FA CUP
Winners

Jan 27 **Liverpool** 1–0
(Bergkamp) Att: 38,092
Wright, Luzhny, Campbell, Keown, Cole, van Bronckhorst (Grimandi), Pires (Parlour), Vieira, Wiltord (Upson), Henry, Bergkamp.

Feb 16 **Gillingham** 5–2
(Wiltord 2, Kanu, Adams, Parlour) Att: 38,003
Wright, Dixon, Campbell, Adams, Juan, Edu (Pires), Parlour, Vieira, Wiltord, Jeffers (Henry), Kanu (Grimandi).

Mar 23 **Newcastle United** 3–0
(Pires, Bergkamp, Campbell) Att: 38,073
Wright, Luzhny, Campbell, Adams, Cole, Edu (Jeffers), Pires (Grimandi), Vieira, Ljungberg, Wiltord (Dixon), Bergkamp.

FOOTBALL LEAGUE (WORTHINGTON) CUP

Nov 5 **Manchester United** 4–0
(Wiltord 3 [1 pen], Kanu [pen]) Att: 30,693
Wright, Luzhny, Tavlaridis, Stepanovs, van Bronckhorst (Halls), Parlour, Grimandi (Itonga), Edu, Pennant (Ricketts), Kanu, Wiltord.

Nov 27 **Grimsby Town** 2–0
(Edu, Wiltord) Att: 16,917
Taylor, Tavlaridis, Keown, Stepanovs, Juan, Inamoto (Halls), van Bronckhorst (Svard), Edu, Pennant (Aliadiere), Bergkamp, Wiltord

UEFA CHAMPIONS LEAGUE

Sep 19 **Schalke 04** 3–2
(Ljungberg, Henry 2 [1 pen]) Att: 35,361
Seaman, Lauren, Grimandi, Keown, van Bronckhorst, Parlour, Pires (Inamoto), Vieira, Ljungberg, Henry (Upson), Wiltord (Bergkamp).

Oct 16 **Panathinaikos** 2–1
(Henry 2 [1 pen]) Att: 35,432
Wright, Lauren, Campbell, Upson, Cole, van Bronckhorst, Pires (Parlour), Vieira, Ljungberg, Henry (Grimandi), Wiltord (Bergkamp)

Oct 24 **Real Mallorca** 3–1
(Pires, Bergkamp, Henry) Att: 34,764
Wright, Lauren, Campbell, Keown, van Bronckhorst, Grimandi (Parlour), Pires,Vieira, Ljungberg (Kanu), Henry, Bergkamp (Wiltord)

Dec 4 **Juventus** 3–1
(Ljungberg 2, Henry) Att: 35,421
Taylor, Lauren, Campbell, Upson, Cole (Keown), Parlour, Pires, Vieira, Ljungberg, Henry (Grimandi), Kanu (Bergkamp).

Feb 27 **Bayer Leverkusen** 4–1
(Pires, Henry, Vieira, Bergkamp) Att: 35,019
Seaman, Dixon, Campbell, Stepanovs, Lauren (Inamoto), Grimandi (Edu), Pires, Vieira, Wiltord (Pennant), Henry, Bergkamp.

Mar 12 **Deportivo La Coruña** 0–2
Att: 35,392
Seaman, Lauren, Campbell, Stepanovs, Luzhny, Grimandi (Ljungberg), Pires, Vieira, Wiltord (Kanu), Henry, Bergkamp.

2002/03

PREMIER LEAGUE
Final position – 2nd

Aug 18 **Birmingham City** 2–0
(Henry, Wiltord) Att: 38,018
Seaman, Lauren, Campbell, Keown, Cole, Parlour, Edu (Toure), Vieira,Wiltord (Aliadiere), Henry, Bergkamp (Gilberto).

Aug 27 **West Bromwich Albion** 5–2
(Cole, Lauren, Wiltord 2, Aliadiere) Att: 37,920
Seaman, Lauren, Campbell, Keown, Cole, Gilberto, Edu, Vieira (Toure), Wiltord (Aliadiere), Henry, Kanu (Parlour).

Sep 10 **Manchester City** 2–1
(Wiltord, Henry) Att: 37,878
Seaman, Luzhny, Campbell, Keown, Cole, Gilberto, Edu (Toure), Vieira, Wiltord, Henry, Bergkamp.

Sep 21 **Bolton Wanderers** 2–1
(Henry, Kanu) Att: 37,974
Seaman, Lauren (Toure), Campbell, Keown, Cole, Gilberto, Ljungberg (Bergkamp), Parlour, Wiltord (Jeffers), Henry, Kanu.

Oct 6 **Sunderland** 3–1
(Kanu 2, Vieira) Att: 37,902
Seaman, Lauren, Campbell, Cygan, Cole, Gilberto, Ljungberg (Toure), Vieira, Wiltord (Edu), Henry (Jeffers), Kanu.

Oct 26 **Blackburn Rovers** 1–2
(Edu) Att: 38,064
Seaman, Lauren, Campbell, Cygan, Cole (Toure), Gilberto, Ljungberg, Edu (Pires), Wiltord, Henry, Kanu (Bergkamp).

Nov 9 **Newcastle United** 1–0
(Wiltord) Att: 38,121
Seaman, Luzhny, Campbell, Cygan, Cole, Gilberto, Ljungberg, Vieira, Wiltord (Edu), Henry, Bergkamp (Pires).

Nov 16 **Tottenham Hotspur** 3–0
(Henry, Ljungberg, Wiltord) Att: 38,152
Shaaban, Luzhny, Campbell, Cygan, Cole, Gilberto, Ljungberg, Vieira (van Bronckhorst), Wiltord, Henry (Jeffers), Bergkamp (Pires)

Nov 30 **Aston Villa** 3–1
(Pires, Henry 2 [1 pen]) Att: 38,090
Shaaban, Luzhny, Campbell, Cygan, van Bronckhorst, Gilberto, Pires (Ljungberg), Vieira, Toure (Keown), Henry, Bergkamp (Wiltord)

Dec 21 **Middlesbrough** 2–0
(Campbell, Pires) Att: 38,003
Seaman, Lauren, Campbell, Keown, Cole, Gilberto, Pires, van Bronckhorst, Ljungberg, Henry, Wiltord.

Dec 29 **Liverpool** 1–1
(Henry [pen]) Att: 38,074
Seaman, Lauren, Campbell, Keown, Cole, Gilberto, Pires (van Bronckhorst), Vieira, Wiltord (Jeffers), Henry, Kanu (Bergkamp).

Jan 1 **Chelsea** 3–2
(van Bronckhorst, Henry, Desailly [og])
Att: 38,096
Seaman, Luzhny, Campbell, Keown, Cole, Gilberto, Pires (van Bronckhorst), Vieira, Wiltord (Lauren), Henry, Bergkamp (Toure).

Jan 19 **West Ham United** 3–1
(Henry 3 [1 pen]) Att: 38,053
Seaman, Lauren, Campbell, Keown, van Bronckhorst, Gilberto, Pires, Edu (Parlour), Wiltord (Luzhny), Henry, Bergkamp (Jeffers).

Feb 1 **Fulham** 2–1
(Pires 2) Att: 38,050
Seaman, Lauren (Toure), Campbell, Keown, Cole, Gilberto (van Bronckhorst), Pires, Vieira, Wiltord (Jeffers), Henry, Bergkamp.

Mar 2 **Charlton Athletic** 2–0
(Jeffers, Pires) Att: 38,015
Seaman, Toure, Campbell, Keown, van Bronckhorst, Parlour, Pires (Gilberto), Edu, Ljungberg (Wiltord), Henry, Jeffers.

Mar 23 **Everton** 2–1
(Cygan, Vieira) Att: 38,042
Taylor, Lauren, Campbell, Cygan, van Bronckhorst, Gilberto, Pires (Parlour), Vieira, Ljungberg, Henry, Bergkamp (Toure).

Apr16 **Manchester United** 2–2
(Henry 2) Att: 38,164
Taylor, Lauren, Campbell, Keown, Cole, Gilberto, Pires (Kanu), Vieira (Edu), Ljungberg, Henry, Bergkamp (Wiltord).

May 4 **Leeds United** 2–3
(Henry, Bergkamp) Att: 38,127
Seaman, Toure (Kanu), Luzhny, Keown, Cole, Gilberto, Pires (van Bronckhorst), Parlour, Wiltord (Pennant), Henry, Bergkamp.

May 7 **Southampton** 6–1
(Pires 3, Pennant 3) Att: 38,052
Taylor, Toure, Luzhny (Tavlaridis), Stepanovs, Garry, Parlour, Pires (Bergkamp), van Bronckhorst, Pennant (Hoyte), Henry, Kanu.

FA CUP
Winners

Jan 4 **Oxford United** 2–0
(Bergkamp, McNiven [og]) Att: 35,432
Seaman, Luzhny, Upson, Keown, van Bronckhorst, Svard (Gilberto), Toure (Bentley), Edu, Pires, Jeffers, Bergkamp (Wiltord).

Jan 25 **Farnborough Town*** 5–1
(Campbell, Jeffers 2, Bergkamp, Lauren)
Att: 35,108
Taylor, Lauren, Campbell, Cygan, van Bronckhorst, Parlour, Toure (Wiltord), Vieira, Pires (Bergkamp), Jeffers, Kanu (Edu).

*Played at Highbury by arrangement

Mar 8 **Chelsea** 2–2
(Jeffers, Henry) Att: 38,104
Seaman, Lauren, Campbell, Keown, van Bronckhorst, Parlour, Edu, Vieira, Ljungberg (Wiltord), Jeffers (Pires), Henry (Toure).

FOOTBALL LEAGUE (WORTHINGTON) CUP

Nov 6 **Sunderland** 2–3
(Pires, Jeffers) Att: 19,059
Taylor, Luzhny, Tavlaridis, Stepanovs, Toure, Svard (Garry), van Bronckhorst, Pires, Pennant (Volz), Jeffers, Kanu.

UEFA CHAMPIONS LEAGUE

Sep 17 **Borussia Dortmund** 2–0
(Bergkamp, Ljungberg) Att: 34,907
Seaman, Luzhny (Lauren), Campbell, Keown, Cole, Ljungberg (Cygan), Gilberto, Vieira, Wiltord (Toure), Henry, Bergkamp.

Oct 22 **AJ Auxerre** 1–2
(Kanu) Att: 35,206
Seaman, Lauren (Toure), Campbell, Cygan, Cole, Ljungberg, Gilberto (Pires), Vieira, Wiltord, Henry, Kanu.

Nov 12 **PSV Eindhoven** 0–0
Att: 35,274
Shaaban, Luzhny, Stepanovs, Cygan, Toure, van Bronckhorst, Edu, Vieira (Gilberto), Pires, Henry (Bergkamp), Jeffers (Wiltord).

Dec 10 **Valencia** 0–0
Att: 34,793
Seaman, Lauren, Campbell, Cygan, Cole, Ljungberg (Wiltord), Gilberto, Vieira (Parlour), Pires (Kanu), Henry, Bergkamp.

Feb 18 **Ajax** 1–1
(Wiltord) Att: 35,427
Seaman (Taylor), Lauren, Campbell, Cygan, Cole, Wiltord, Gilberto (Jeffers), Vieira, Pires, Henry, Bergkamp (Kanu).

Mar 11 **AS Roma** 1–1
(Vieira) Att: 35,472
Seaman, Lauren (Kanu), Keown, Cygan, van Bronckhorst, Wiltord (Ljungberg), Gilberto, Vieira, Pires, Henry, Bergkamp (Jeffers).

2003/04
PREMIER LEAGUE
Final position – Champions

Aug 16 **Everton** 2–1
(Henry [pen], Pires) Att: 38,014
Lehmann, Lauren, Campbell, Toure, Cole, Ljungberg, Gilberto, Vieira, Pires (Parlour), Henry, Wiltord (Keown).

Aug 27 **Aston Villa** 2–0
(Campbell, Henry) Att: 38,010
Lehmann, Lauren, Campbell, Toure, Cole, Ljungberg (Parlour), Gilberto, Vieira, Pires, Henry, Wiltord (Bergkamp).

Sep 13 **Portsmouth** 1–1
(Henry [pen]) Att: 38,052
Lehmann, Lauren, Campbell, Toure, Cole, Parlour, Edu (Ljungberg), Vieira, Pires, Henry, Bergkamp (Wiltord).

Sep 26 **Newcastle United** 3–2
(Henry 2 [1 pen], Gilberto) Att: 38,112
Lehmann, Lauren, Keown, Toure, Cole (Cygan), Parlour (Pires), Gilberto, Vieira (Edu), Ljungberg, Henry, Wiltord.

Oct 18 **Chelsea** 2–1
(Edu, Henry) Att: 38,172
Lehmann, Lauren, Campbell, Toure, Cole, Parlour (Kanu), Gilberto, Edu, Pires (Cygan), Henry, Wiltord (Bergkamp).

Nov 8 **Tottenham Hotspur** 2–1
(Pires, Ljungberg) Att: 38,101
Lehmann, Lauren (Cygan), Campbell, Toure, Cole, Ljungberg, Gilberto (Bergkamp), Parlour, Pires, Henry, Kanu (Edu).

Nov 30 **Fulham** 0–0
Att: 38,063
Lehmann, Toure, Campbell, Cygan, Cole, Ljungberg (Aliadiere), Gilberto (Kanu), Edu, Pires, Henry, Bergkamp.

Dec 14 **Blackburn Rovers** 1–0
(Bergkamp) Att: 37,677
Lehmann, Toure, Campbell, Cygan, Cole, Ljungberg (Edu), Gilberto, Vieira, Pires, Henry, Bergkamp (Parlour).

Dec 26 **Wolverhampton Wanderers** 3–0
(Henry 2, Craddock [og]) Att: 38,003
Lehmann, Toure, Campbell, Cygan, Clichy, Ljungberg (Edu), Parlour, Vieira, Pires (Aliadiere), Henry, Bergkamp.

Jan 10 **Middlesbrough** 4–1
(Henry [pen], Pires, Ljungberg, Queudrue [og])
Att: 38,117
Lehmann, Lauren, Campbell, Cygan, Cole, Ljungberg (Parlour), Gilberto, Vieira, Pires (Edu), Henry, Aliadiere (Kanu).

Feb 1 **Manchester City** 2–1
(Henry, Tarnat [og]) Att: 38,103
Lehmann, Lauren, Campbell, Toure, Cole, Ljungberg (Edu), Gilberto, Parlour, Pires (Cygan), Henry, Bergkamp (Reyes).

Feb 10 **Southampton** 2–0
(Henry 2) Att: 38,007
Lehmann, Lauren, Campbell, Toure, Cole, Parlour, Gilberto, Vieira, Pires, Henry, Reyes (Clichy).

Feb 28 **Charlton Athletic** 2–1
(Pires, Henry) Att: 38,137
Lehmann, Lauren, Campbell, Toure, Cole, Ljungberg (Gilberto), Edu, Vieira, Pires (Cygan), Henry, Bergkamp (Reyes).

Mar 20 **Bolton Wanderers** 2–1
(Pires, Bergkamp) Att: 38,053
Lehmann, Lauren, Campbell, Toure, Cole, Edu, Gilberto (Ljungberg), Vieira, Pires (Cygan), Henry, Bergkamp.

Mar 28 **Manchester United** 1–1
(Henry) Att: 38,184
Lehmann, Lauren, Campbell, Toure, Clichy, Ljungberg (Cygan), Edu, Vieira, Pires (Bergkamp), Henry, Reyes (Gilberto).

Apr 9 **Liverpool** 4–2
(Henry 3, Pires) Att: 38,119
Lehmann, Lauren, Campbell, Toure, Cole, Ljungberg (Keown), Gilberto, Vieira, Pires (Edu), Henry, Bergkamp.

Apr 16 **Leeds United** 5–0
(Pires, Henry 4 [1 pen]) Att: 38,094
Lehmann, Lauren, Campbell, Toure, Clichy, Wiltord, Gilberto (Edu), Vieira, Pires (Parlour), Henry, Bergkamp (Reyes).

May 1 **Birmingham City** 0–0
Att: 38,061
Lehmann, Lauren, Campbell, Toure, Cole, Ljungberg (Pires), Gilberto, Vieira, Reyes (Aliadiere), Henry, Bergkamp (Keown).

May 15 **Leicester City** 2–1
(Henry [pen], Vieira) Att: 38,419
Lehmann, Lauren, Campbell, Toure, Cole, Ljungberg (Keown), Gilberto, Vieira, Pires (Edu), Henry, Bergkamp (Reyes).

FA CUP

Jan 24 **Middlesbrough** 4–1
(Bergkamp, Ljungberg 2, Bentley) Att: 37,256
Lehmann, Lauren, Campbell, Toure, Cole, Ljungberg, Parlour, Vieira (Clichy), Edu, Pires, Bergkamp (Bentley).

Feb 15 **Chelsea** 2–1
(Reyes 2) Att: 38,136
Lehmann, Lauren, Campbell, Toure, Cole, Parlour (Edu), Gilberto, Vieira, Pires, Reyes (Clichy), Bergkamp.

FOOTBALL LEAGUE (CARLING) CUP

Oct 28 **Rotherham United** 1–1*
(won 9–8 on penalties)
(Aliadiere) Att: 27,451
Stack, Hoyte (Spicer), Tavlaridis, Cygan, Clichy, Fabregas (Owusu–Abeyie), Edu, Thomas (Smith), Wiltord, Kanu, Aliadiere.

*After extra time

Dec 2 **Wolverhampton Wanderers** 5–1
(Aliadiere 2, Kanu, Wiltord, Fabregas)
Att: 28,161
Stack, Hoyte (Skulason), Tavlaridis, Simek, Clichy, Fabregas, Vieira, Bentley (Smith), Wiltord, Kanu, Aliadiere (Papadopulos).

Jan 20 **Middlesbrough** 0–1
Att: 31,070
Stack, Toure, Keown, Cygan, Clichy, Gilberto, Edu, Bentley (Smith), Parlour, Kanu, Owusu–Abeyie (Thomas).

UEFA CHAMPIONS LEAGUE

Sep 17 **Inter Milan** 0–3
Att: 34,393
Lehmann, Lauren, Campbell, Toure, Cole, Ljungberg, Gilberto (Kanu), Vieira, Pires (Bergkamp), Henry, Wiltord (Parlour).

Nov 5 **Dynamo Kiev** 1–0
(Cole) Att: 34,419
Lehmann, Lauren, Campbell, Toure, Cole, Ljungberg (Wiltord), Gilberto, Parlour (Kanu), Pires, Henry, Bergkamp (Edu).

Dec 10 **Lokomotiv Moscow** 2–0
(Pires, Ljungberg) Att: 35,343
Lehmann, Toure, Campbell, Cygan, Cole, Ljungberg, Gilberto, Vieira, Pires, Henry, Bergkamp (Kanu).

Mar 10 **Celta Vigo** 2–0
(Henry 2) Att: 35,402
Lehmann, Lauren, Campbell, Toure, Cole, Ljungberg, Edu (Gilberto), Vieira, Pires (Reyes), Henry, Bergkamp (Kanu).

Apr 6 **Chelsea** 1–2
(Reyes) Att: 35,486
Lehmann, Lauren, Campbell, Toure, Cole, Ljungberg, Edu, Vieira, Pires, Henry (Bergkamp), Reyes.

2004/05
PREMIER LEAGUE
Final position – 2nd

Aug 22 **Middlesbrough** 5–3
(Henry 2, Bergkamp, Pires, Reyes) Att: 37,415
Lehmann, Lauren, Toure, Cygan, Cole, Ljungberg (Pires), Gilberto, Fabregas, Reyes (Flamini), Bergkamp, Henry.

Aug 25 **Blackburn Rovers** 3–0
(Henry, Fabregas, Reyes) Att: 37,496
Lehmann, Lauren, Toure, Cygan, Cole, Pennant (Ljungberg), Gilberto, Fabregas (Flamini), Pires, Bergkamp (Reyes), Henry.

Sep 18 **Bolton Wanderers** 2–2
(Henry, Pires) Att: 37,010
Lehmann, Lauren, Toure, Cygan, Cole, Ljungberg, Gilberto (Edu), Vieira, Pires (Clichy), Reyes (Bergkamp), Henry.

Oct 2 **Charlton Athletic** 4–0
(Ljungberg, Henry 2, Reyes) Att: 38,103
Lehmann, Lauren, Toure, Campbell, Clichy, Ljungberg (Pennant), Fabregas (Flamini), Vieira, Reyes, Bergkamp, Henry (van Persie)

Oct 16 **Aston Villa** 3–1
(Pires 2 [1 pen], Henry) Att: 38,137
Lehmann, Lauren, Toure, Campbell, Cole, Pires (van Persie), Fabregas, Vieira (Flamini), Reyes (Pennant), Bergkamp, Henry.

Oct 30 **Southampton** 2–2
(Henry, van Persie) Att: 38,141
Lehmann, Lauren, Toure, Cygan, Cole, Ljungberg (van Persie), Edu (Fabregas), Vieira, Reyes (Pires), Bergkamp, Henry.

Nov 20 **West Bromwich Albion** 1–1
(Pires) Att: 38,109
Lehmann, Lauren, Toure, Cygan, Cole, Ljungberg, Fabregas (Reyes), Vieira, Pires, Bergkamp (van Persie), Henry.

Dec 4 **Birmingham City** 3–0
(Pires, Henry 2) Att: 38,064
Almunia, Lauren, Toure, Campbell, Cole, Ljungberg, Fabregas (Flamini), Vieira, Pires, Reyes (Clichy), Henry.

Dec 12 **Chelsea** 2–2
(Henry 2) Att: 38,153
Almunia, Lauren, Toure, Campbell, Cole, Pires, Fabregas, Flamini, Reyes (Clichy), Bergkamp (van Persie), Henry.

Dec 26 **Fulham** 2–0
(Henry, Pires) Att: 38,047
Almunia, Lauren, Toure, Campbell, Clichy, Ljungberg (Flamini), Fabregas, Vieira, Pires, Bergkamp (van Persie), Henry.

Jan 4 **Manchester City** 1–1
(Ljungberg) Att: 38,086
Almunia, Hoyte, Toure, Senderos, Cole, Ljungberg, Fabregas (Pennant), Vieira, Pires, van Persie, Henry.

Jan 23 **Newcastle United** 1–0
(Bergkamp) Att: 38,137
Almunia, Lauren, Toure, Campbell, Cole, Pires, Flamini, Vieira, Reyes (Fabregas), Bergkamp, Henry.

Feb 1 **Manchester United** 2–4
(Vieira, Bergkamp) Att: 38,164
Almunia, Lauren (Fabregas), Cygan, Campbell (Hoyte), Cole, Ljungberg, Flamini (Reyes), Vieira, Pires, Bergkamp, Henry.

Feb 14 **Crystal Palace** 5–1
(Bergkamp, Reyes, Henry 2, Vieira) Att: 38,056
Lehmann, Lauren, Toure, Cygan, Clichy, Pires (Fabregas), Edu (Flamini), Vieira, Reyes, Bergkamp (van Persie), Henry.

Mar 5 **Portsmouth** 3–0
(Henry 3) Att: 38,079
Lehmann, Toure, Senderos, Cygan (Lauren), Clichy, Fabregas (Ljungberg), Flamini, Vieira, Cole, Owusu–Abeyie (van Persie), Henry

Apr 2 **Norwich City** 4–1
(Henry 3, Ljungberg) Att: 38,066
Lehmann, Lauren, Toure, Cygan, Cole, Ljungberg, Flamini (Fabregas), Gilberto, Pires (Clichy), Reyes (van Persie), Henry.

Apr 25 **Tottenham Hotspur** 1–0
(Reyes) Att: 38,147
Lehmann, Lauren, Toure, Senderos, Cole, Fabregas (Edu), Gilberto, Vieira, Pires, van Persie (Bergkamp), Reyes (Aliadiere).

May 8 **Liverpool** 3–1
(Pires, Reyes, Fabregas) Att: 38,119
Lehmann, Lauren, Toure, Senderos, Cole, Fabregas, Gilberto, Vieira, Pires (Edu), van Persie (Bergkamp), Reyes (Aliadiere).

May 11 **Everton** 7–0
(van Persie, Pires 2, Vieira, Edu [pen], Bergkamp, Flamini) Att: 38,073
Lehmann, Lauren, Campbell, Senderos, Cole, Pires (Fabregas), Edu, Vieira (Flamini), Reyes, van Persie (Henry), Bergkamp.

FA CUP
Winners

Jan 9 **Stoke City** 2–1
(Reyes, van Persie) Att: 36,579
Lehmann, Eboue (Hoyte), Toure, Senderos, Clichy, Pennant, Fabregas, Vieira, Pires, Reyes, van Persie

Jan 29 **Wolverhampton Wanderers** 2–0
(Vieira [pen], Ljungberg) Att: 37,153
Lehmann, Eboue, Cygan, Campbell, Clichy, Ljungberg (Owusu–Abeyie), Flamini, Vieira, Reyes (Pires), van Persie (Fabregas), Henry.

Feb 19 **Sheffield United** 1–1
(Pires) Att: 36,891
Almunia, Eboue, Toure, Senderos, Clichy, Ljungberg, Flamini, Fabregas, Reyes (Cygan), van Persie (Pires), Bergkamp.

FOOTBALL LEAGUE (CARLING) CUP

Nov 9 **Everton** 3–1
(Owusu–Abeyie, Lupoli 2) Att: 27,791
Almunia, Hoyte, Senderos, Djourou, Pennant, Karbassiyoon, Edu (Larsson), Flamini, Smith (Owusu–Abeyie), Lupoli (Cregg), van Persie

UEFA CHAMPIONS LEAGUE

Sep 14 **PSV Eindhoven** 1–0
(Alex [og]) Att: 34,068
Lehmann, Lauren, Toure, Cygan, Cole, Pires, Gilberto, Vieira, Reyes (Edu), Bergkamp, Henry.

Nov 2 **Panathinaikos** 1–1
(Henry [pen]) Att: 35,137
Lehmann, Lauren, Toure, Cygan, Cole, Ljungberg (van Persie), Fabregas, Vieira, Pires, Bergkamp (Reyes), Henry.

Dec 7 **Rosenborg** 5–1
(Reyes, Henry, Fabregas, Pires [pen], van Persie) Att: 35,421
Almunia, Hoyte, Toure, Campbell, Cole (van Persie), Pires (Owusu–Abeyie), Fabregas, Flamini, Reyes, Bergkamp (Clichy), Henry.

Mar 9 **Bayern Munich** 1–0
(Henry) Att: 35,463
Lehmann, Lauren, Toure, Senderos, Cole, Ljungberg (van Persie), Flamini (Fabregas), Vieira, Reyes (Pires), Bergkamp, Henry.

2005/06

PREMIER LEAGUE
Final position – 4th

Aug 14 **Newcastle United** 2–0
(Henry [pen], van Persie) Att: 38,072
Lehmann, Lauren, Cole, Senderos, Toure, Ljungberg (Hleb), Gilberto, Pires (Flamini), Bergkamp (van Persie), Henry.

Aug 24 **Fulham** 4–1
(Cygan 2, Henry 2) Att: 37,867
Lehmann, Lauren, Cole, Cygan, Toure, Hleb (Clichy), Fabregas, Gilberto, Reyes (Flamini), Bergkamp, Henry.

Sep 19 **Everton** 2–0
(Campbell 2) Att: 38,121
Lehmann, Lauren, Cole, Campbell, Toure, Ljungberg, Fabregas, Gilberto, Pires (Hleb), van Persie (Bergkamp), Reyes (Song).

Oct 2 **Birmingham City** 1–0
(Clemence [og]) Att: 37,891
Lehmann, Lauren, Cole, Campbell, Toure, Hleb(Bergkamp), Fabregas, Gilberto, Pires (van Persie), Ljungberg (Flamini), Reyes.

Oct 22 **Manchester City** 1–0
(Pires [pen]) Att: 38,189
Lehmann, Lauren, Clichy, Cygan, Toure, Fabregas, Flamini, Gilberto, Pires, Bergkamp, Henry.

Nov 5 **Sunderland** 3–1
(van Persie, Henry 2) Att: 38,210
Lehmann, Lauren, Clichy, Campbell, Toure, Pires, Fabregas, Gilberto, Reyes (Eboue), van Persie (Bergkamp), Henry.

Nov 26 **Blackburn Rovers** 3–0
(Fabregas, Henry, van Persie) Att: 38,192
Lehmann, Lauren, Cygan, Campbell, Toure, Pires (Flamini), Fabregas, Gilberto, Reyes (Ljungberg), Bergkamp(van Persie), Henry

Dec 18 **Chelsea** 0–2
Att: 38,347
Lehmann, Toure, Lauren, Campbell, Senderos, Ljungberg (Bergkamp), Fabregas, Flamini, Hleb (Pires), van Persie (Owusu–Abeyie), Henry

Dec 28 **Portsmouth** 4–0
(Bergkamp, Reyes, Henry 2 [1 pen]) Att: 38,223
Lehmann, Lauren, Cygan, Campbell, Toure, Pires, Flamini, Gilberto (Fabregas), Reyes (Eboue), Bergkamp, Henry.

Jan 3 **Manchester United** 0–0
Att: 38,313
Lehmann, Lauren, Cygan, Campbell, Toure, Pires, Fabregas (Flamini), Gilberto, Hleb (Bergkamp), Reyes (Eboue), Henry.

Jan 14 **Middlesbrough** 7–0
(Henry 3, Senderos, Pires, Gilberto, Hleb) Att: 38,186
Lehmann, Lauren, Cygan (Cole), Djourou, Senderos, Ljungberg, Fabregas, Gilberto (Flamini), Pires (Hleb), Reyes, Henry.

Feb 1 **West Ham United** 2–3
(Henry, Pires) Att: 38,216
Lehmann, Gilbert (Flamini), Senderos, Campbell (Larsson), Djourou, Ljungberg, Diaby (Bergkamp), Gilberto, Pires, van Persie, Henry

Feb 11 **Bolton Wanderers** 1–1
(Gilberto) Att: 38,193
Lehmann, Flamini, Larsson(Bergkamp), Djourou, Senderos, Fabregas, Diaby(Ljungberg), Gilberto, Reyes(Pires), Adebayor, Henry

Mar 12 **Liverpool** 2–1
(Henry 2) Att: 38,221
Lehmann, Eboue, Flamini, Senderos, Toure, Ljungberg (Pires), Fabregas, Gilberto, Hleb, Adebayor (Bergkamp), Henry

Mar 18 **Charlton Athletic** 3–0
(Pires, Adebayor, Hleb) Att: 38,223
Lehmann, Eboue, Flamini, Senderos, Toure, Hleb (Bergkamp), Fabregas (Song), Gilberto, Pires, Adebayor (van Persie), Henry.

Apr 1 **Aston Villa** 5–0
(Adebayor, Henry 2, van Persie, Diaby) Att: 38,183
Lehmann, Eboue (Djourou), Flamini, Senderos, Toure, Pires, Fabregas (Diaby), Gilberto, Reyes, Adebayor, Henry (van Persie).

Apr 15 **West Bromwich Albion** 3–1
(Hleb, Pires, Bergkamp) Att: 38,167
Lehmann, Eboue, Flamini, Senderos, Toure, Hleb (Pires), Diaby, Gilberto, Reyes, van Persie (Bergkamp), Henry (Adebayor).

Apr 22 **Tottenham Hotspur** 1–1
(Henry) Att: 38,326
Lehmann, Djourou, Flamini, Senderos (Eboue), Toure, Pires, Diaby (Fabregas), Gilberto, Reyes, Adebayor, van Persie (Henry).

May 7 **Wigan Athletic** 4–2
(Pires, Henry 3 [1 pen]) Att: 38,359
Lehmann, Eboue, Cole, Campbell, Toure, Hleb (van Persie), Fabregas, Gilberto, Pires (Ljungberg), Reyes (Bergkamp), Henry.

FA CUP

Jan 7 **Cardiff City** 2–1
(Pires 2) Att: 36,552
Almunia, Gilbert, Senderos, Djourou, Lauren, Pires, Flamini, Gilberto, Reyes (Owusu–Abeyie), van Persie (Larsson), Bergkamp.

FOOTBALL LEAGUE (CARLING) CUP

Nov 29 **Reading** 3–0
(Reyes, van Persie, Lupoli) Att: 36,137
Almunia, Eboue, Djourou, Senderos, Gilbert, Muamba, Flamini, Larsson, Owusu–Abeyie (Bendtner), van Persie (Lupoli), Reyes (Cygan).

Jan 24 **Wigan Athletic** 2–1*
(Henry, van Persie) Att: 34,692
Almunia, Gilbert, Campbell, Senderos, Lauren, Gilberto, Diaby (Flamini), Hleb (Pires), Reyes, Bergkamp, Henry (van Persie).

*After extra time

UEFA CHAMPIONS LEAGUE
Finalists

Sept 14 **FC Thun** 2–1
(Gilberto, Bergkamp) Att: 34,498
Almunia, Lauren, Campbell, Toure, Cole, Ljungberg (Hleb), Fabregas (Bergkamp), Gilberto, Pires, van Persie, Reyes (Owusu–Abeyie)

Nov 2 **Sparta Prague** 3–0
(Henry, van Persie 2) Att: 35,115
Almunia, Lauren, Toure, Clichy, Pires (Fabregas), Flamini, Gilberto, Reyes (Eboue), Bergkamp, Henry (van Persie).

Dec 7 **Ajax** 0–0
Att: 35,376
Almunia, Eboue, Senderos, Toure, Lauren (Gilbert), Hleb (Fabregas), Flamini, Larsson, Owusu–Abeyie, Reyes (van Persie), Henry.

Mar 8 **Real Madrid** 0–0
Att: 35,487
Lehmann, Eboue, Senderos, Toure, Flamini, Ljungberg, Fabregas, Gilberto, Hleb (Bergkamp), Reyes (Pires), Henry.

Mar 28 **Juventus** 2–0
(Fabregas, Henry) Att: 35,472
Lehmann, Eboue, Senderos, Toure, Flamini, Pires, Fabregas, Gilberto, Hleb, Reyes (van Persie), Henry.

Apr 19 **Villarreal** 1–0
(Toure) Att: 35,438
Lehmann, Eboue, Senderos, Toure, Flamini, Ljungberg (van Persie), Fabregas, Gilberto, Hleb (Bergkamp), Pires, Henry

Index

Numbers in *italics* refer to captions and boxed biographies.

Bibliography

Arsenal Brian Glanville (Convoy, 1952)
Association Football And The Men Who Made It William Pickford And Alfred Gibson (Caxton, 1906)
Billy Wright Norman Giller (Robson Books, 2002)
Cliff Bastin Remembers Cliff Bastin (Etterick Press, 1950)
Fever Pitch Nick Hornby (Gollancz, 1992)
Football Ambassador Eddie Hapgood (Sporting Handbooks, 1945)
Football Grounds Of England And Wales Simon Inglis (Harper Collins Willow, 1986)
Gunners On The Target Geoffrey Mowbray (Paul Stanley, 1961)
The Official Illustrated History Of Arsenal Phil Soar And Martin Tyler (Hamlyn, 2004)
Over The Bar Jack Kelsey (Pelham Books, 1958)
Tom Whittaker's Arsenal Story Tom Whittaker (Sporting Handbooks, 1956)
Wenger: The Making of a Legend Jasper Rees (Short Books, 2004)

Acknowledgements

The Publishers would like to express their gratitude to everyone who has helped create this History: Joe Cohen, Iain Cook, Stuart MacFarlane and David Price at Arsenal; Alex Murphy and Matthew Brown for their additional text; Fred Ollier for his invaluable help with fact-checking; Lynn Bresler for proof-reading and compiling the index; Tom Callingham and Tom Harris for additional picture research; and special thanks to Cathy Meeus and Hugh Schermuly whose hard work and enthusiasm for such a monumental project brought the whole thing together.

Edited and designed by **Schermuly Design Co**
Project Editor: **Cathy Meeus**
Art Director: **Hugh Schermuly**
Designer: **Steve Woosnam-Savage**

Executive Editor: **Trevor Davies**
Senior Editor: **Jessica Cowie**
Creative Director: **Tracy Killick**
Executive Art Editor: **Darren Southern**
Picture Research: **Sophie Delpech**
Senior Production Controller: **Martin Croshaw**

Picture acknowledgements

All images have been supplied by Arsenal Football Club plc/Stuart McFarlane, apart from the following:

ActionPlus Sports Images 156 top left, 174 top.
Colorsport 30, 44 top left, 138 bottom right, 143 bottom, 150 top, 152-153, 156 top centre, 157 bottom left, 160, 165, 170, 180 bottom, 184, 187, 188, 191, 192 top, 195 centre right, 195 bottom, 197, 214 centre right, 217 top, 218 top.
Empics 101 bottom, 103, 121 bottom, 129 centre right, 138 top right, 139 bottom right, 139 bottom left, 147, 148, 154, 215 bottom right, 219 top, 220 bottom, 221 left; /Barratts 99 bottom left.
Getty Images 5 centre, 5 centre right top, 16 top left, 26-27 bottom, 28 centre right, 28 bottom left, 29 bottom right, 29 bottom centre, 34-35 bottom, 38 bottom, 39 bottom right, 39 bottom left, 40-41, 42 centre left, 42 top right, 42 bottom right, 46, 47, 48, 48-49 background, 49 top right, 52 bottom left, 60,63, 64 bottom right, 64 top left, 65, 66-67, 71 top, 76 centre left, 77 bottom right, 79 top, 86, 86-87 background, 88 top, 92, 93 top, 97, 105 bottom, 106, 107 bottom right, 114 bottom right, 122 top right, 122 bottom left, 122 top left, 122 centre right, 122 bottom right, 123 bottom right, 125 bottom, 126 bottom, 126 top, 131, 132, 133 top, 133 bottom, 134, 135 bottom right, 135 top, 136-137 background, 137 bottom, 138 centre left, 138-139 top, 150 bottom, 153 bottom, 155 top right, 155 centre right and background, 163, 175 top; /H. Allen 58; /Nicolas Asfouri 176 centre left, 198; /E. Bacon 43 bottom left, 51, 117; /Reg Birkett 98 top right, 120; /Shaun Botterill 171, 177 bottom right, 186 top, 194 bottom; /Clive Brunskill 172 top; /Phil Cole 200; /Davis 72-73 background, 73; /H. F. Davis 5 top centre right, 42 top left, 42 bottom left, 49 top centre, 50 top right, 55 bottom right, 72, 72-73 background, 73, 77 bottom left, 90 top; /E. Dean 87 top; /Adrian Dennis 177 centre left, 189 bottom, 204, 220 top; /George Douglas 98 top left, 119; /J. Gaiger 52 top left, 59 centre right, 59 bottom right; /John Gichigi 176 centre right, 185 bottom; /J. A. Hampton 5 top right, 52 top right, 53 bottom right, 57, 70 top, 70 bottom, 74, 76 bottom left, 78, 101 top left; /Hayters 142 top; /A. Hudson 76-77 top, 79 bottom, 89; /Arthur Jones 5 centre right, 138 bottom left, 141 bottom, 144; /Ross Kinnaird 183 top; /Mike Lawn 138 top left, 140, 146; /Christopher Lee 193; /Miller 61; /Dennis Oulds 115, 128 bottom right; /Gary M. Prior 173; /Ben Radford 153 top, 176 top right, 182 top, 192 bottom, 199 bottom; /David Rogers 174 bottom; /Reg Speller 94; /Harry Todd 123 bottom left, 129 bottom centre; /William Vanderson 96, 104 bottom, 107 top; /Chris Ware 110 bottom; /Ted West 127 top; /Wesley 128 top.
London Metropolitan Archive 28 top right, 28 bottom right, 32, 33 bottom.
Popperfoto 43 bottom right, 45, 50 bottom left, 52 centre, 56, 102 bottom.
TopFoto 44 bottom, 100, 116 bottom, 118, 122 centre left, 125 top, 130 top, 130 bottom, 172 bottom.